ACCLAIM FOR Jorge G. Castañeda's

Compañero

"Brilliant . . . rich in narrative detail."
—*The Christian Science Monitor*

"Brilliant research . . . [reveals] the last myth of 20th-century revolution."
—*Washington Post Book Review*

"Analyzes Guevara and his legacy with the clarity and insight that have earned [Castañeda] his place as one of Mexico's most distinguished political scientists."
—*The New York Times Book Review*

"Astute . . . a gripping tale of a man bent on martyrdom."
—*The Boston Globe*

"Carefully documented and critical . . . [and it] reads like a thriller."
—*Wall Street Journal*

"[Castañeda's] powerful intellect aims at uncovering the roots and development of Che's thinking."
—*The New York Times*

Also by Jorge G. Castañeda

———

Utopia Unarmed

Limits to Friendship
(with Robert Pastor)

The Mexican Shock

Jorge G. Castañeda
Compañero

Jorge G. Castañeda was born and raised in Mexico City. He received his B.A. from Princeton University and his Ph.D. from the University of Paris. He has been a professor of political science at the National Autonomous University of Mexico since 1978. He has also been a senior associate of the Carnegie Institute for International Peace in Washington, D.C., and a visiting professor at Princeton University and the University of California at Berkeley. In 1997 he began a long-term, half-time appointment as Professor of Political Science and Latin American Studies at New York University. He is a regular columnist for the *Los Angeles Times*, *Newsweek International*, and the Mexican weekly *Proceso*.

Compañero

The Life and Death

Compañero

of *Che Guevara*

Jorge G. Castañeda

Translated from the Spanish by Marina Castañeda

Vintage Books
A Division of Random House, Inc.
New York

FIRST VINTAGE BOOKS EDITION, NOVEMBER 1998

Copyright © 1997 by Jorge G. Castañeda

All rights reserved under International and Pan-American Copyright
Conventions. Published in the United States by Vintage Books,
a division of Random House, Inc., New York, and simultaneously in
Canada by Random House of Canada Limited, Toronto.
Originally published in hardcover in the United States
by Alfred A. Knopf, Inc., New York, in 1997.

Library of Congress Cataloging–in–Publication Data
Castañeda, Jorge G., 1953–
Compañero : the life and death of Che Guevara / Jorge G. Castañeda;
translated from the Spanish by Marina Castañeda.
p.   cm.
Includes bibliographical references and index.
ISBN 0-679-75940-9
1. Guevara, Ernesto, 1928–1967.
2. Guerrillas—Latin America—Biography. I. Title.
[F2849.22.G85C282   1998]
980' .03'092—dc 21
[B]   98-26441
CIP

Author photograph © Yissel Ibarra
Book design by Cassandra J. Pappas

Random House Web address: www.randomhouse.com

Printed in the United States of America
10

For Jorge Andrés

who was born in another time
and will live a better life

Contents

16 pages of photographs will be found following page 268

Acknowledgments

This book owes a great deal to many people, but most of all to Miriam Morales, who read it, reread it, and put up with it (and me) endlessly. To her my thanks, as well as to Maria Caldelari, Georgina Lagos, Cassio Luiselli, Joel Ortega, Alan Riding, and my friend and editor at Knopf, Ash Green, who all read the manuscript in its entirety and are responsible for any improvements it may have undergone.

I am also particularly grateful to the Kenneth and Harle Montgomery Endowment at Dartmouth College, where I carried out part of the research for the book; Marisa Navarro, Barbara Gerstner, Lou Anne Cain, and Luis Villar at the Dartmouth College library were extremely generous with their support, time, and patience. I also wish to thank Marisela Aguilar, Lisa Antillón, Carlos Enrique Díaz, Aleph Henestrosa, Silvia Kroyer, Marcelo Monges, Marina Palta, Christian Roa, Tamara Rozental, and John Wilson at the Lyndon Baines Johnson Presidential Library at the University of Texas in Austin, for their invaluable help in researching the material for the book.

Many friends in many places provided precious help in obtaining access to interviews, archives, or documents: Gerardo Bracho, Zarina Martínez-Boerresen, Arturo Trejo, and Abelardo Treviño in Moscow, Juan José Bremer and Adriana Valadés in Germany, Miguel Díaz Reynoso in Havana, Jorge Rocío in Mexico, Sergio Antelo and Carlos Soria in Bolivia, Alex Anderson and Dudley Ankerson in England, Rogelio García Lupo and

Acknowledgments

Felisa Pinto in Argentina, Leandro Katz in New York, Jules Gérard-Libois in Brussels, Anne-Marie Mergier in France, and Carlos Franqui in Puerto Rico. I am particularly indebted to Kate Doyle and Peter Kornbluh at the National Security Archive in Washington, D.C., for their constant support in obtaining documents from the U.S. government. I must also acknowledge and be thankful for Jennifer Bernstein's infinite patience and help at Knopf in getting the manuscript into shape.

Finally, a special word of thanks to Homero Campa, Régis Debray, Chichina Ferreyra, Enrique Hett, James Lemoyne, Dolores Moyano, Jesús Parra, Susana Pravaz-Balán, Andrés Rozental, and Paco Ignacio Taibo II. Each in their way made a very special contribution to this book. I am deeply indebted to them. And lastly, my warmest appreciation to Marina Castañeda, who not only did a splendid job of translating and editing from the Spanish, but did so at breakneck speed and, moreover, under extreme, often irrational, and always irritating pressure from her brother the author, or the author her brother.

J.G.C.

Prologue

They uncovered his face, now clear and serene, and bared the chest wracked by forty years of asthma and months of hunger in the wilds of the Bolivian southeast. Then they laid him out in the laundry room at the hospital of Nuestra Señora de Malta, raising his head so all could look upon the fallen prey. As they placed him on the concrete slab, they undid the ropes used to tie his hands during the helicopter trip from La Higuera, and asked the nurse to wash him, comb his hair, and trim the sparse beard. By the time journalists and curious townspeople began to file past, the metamorphosis was complete: the dejected, angry, and disheveled man of the day before was now the Christ of Vallegrande, reflecting in his limpid, open eyes the tender calm of an accepted sacrifice. The Bolivian army had made its only field error after capturing its greatest war trophy. It had transformed the resigned and cornered revolutionary, the defeated fugitive from the Yuro ravine, face shadowed by fury and frustration, into the magical image of life beyond death. His executioners had bestowed a human face upon the myth that would circle the world.

Whoever examines these photographs will wonder how the despondent Guevara at the little school of La Higuera was transfigured into the beatific icon of Vallegrande, captured for posterity by the masterful lens of Freddy Alborta. The secret is simple, as General Gary Prado Salmón, Che's captor and the most lucid and professional of his pursuers, explains:

They washed, dressed and arranged him following instructions from the forensic physician. . . . We had to prove his identity and show the world that we had defeated . . . Che. There was no question of displaying him the way other guerrillas were always exhibited, as corpses on the ground but with expressions that always had an enormous impact on me . . . their faces all twisted. That was one of the things that made me put the handkerchief on Che's jaw, precisely so it wouldn't be deformed. But what everyone wanted, instinctively, was to show that this was Che; to be able to say, "Here he is, we won": this was the feeling among the armed forces of Bolivia. There should be no doubt as to his identity, because if we had exhibited him as he was, all dirty, tattered, and uncombed, there would have been a doubt.[1]

What his hunters did not foresee was that this logic would apply not only to them but also to those who would mourn him in the years to come. The emblematic impact of Ernesto Guevara is inconceivable without its dimension of sacrifice: a man who has everything—power, glory, family, and comfort—renounces it for an idea, and does so without anger or reservation. His undeniable willingness to die is not to be found in Che's speeches or writings, nor in the eulogies delivered by Fidel Castro, not even in the posthumous exaltation of his martyrdom, but rather in his mortuary gaze. It is as if the dead Guevara looks upon his killers and forgives them; and upon the world, proclaiming that he who dies for an idea is beyond suffering.

The other Guevara, whose rage and dejection were not reflected in his death mask, would hardly have become an emblem of heroism and sacrifice. The vanquished Che, with dirty hair, tattered clothes, and feet wrapped in Bolivian *abarcas,* a stranger to friends and enemies alike, would never have aroused the sympathy and admiration awakened by the martyr of Vallegrande.* No wonder, then, that the three extant photographs of Che just after his capture did not circulate until twenty years after his execution. Neither Felix Rodríguez, the CIA operative who took one of them, nor General Arnaldo Saucedo Parada, who snapped the others, made them public until then. Again, the reason was perverse. Though it was acknowledged a few days after the Yuro ambush that Che did not die in combat, it was still best to conceal the ultimate proof of his summary execution: the pictures of Che alive after his capture. The dead Che was compelling without being accusatory, and generated an inexhaustible myth. The pictures of Che alive would have aroused pity in the best of cases, but raised doubts as to his identity; they pointed to a murder unacknowledged though known to all. The Christlike image prevailed; the other, ravaged and somber, vanished.

*"He had a full beard. And his hair was long, very long, like this. His hair was very dirty. We changed his clothes because they were very dirty. We put a pajama on him. A hospital pajama, they put on him." Susana Oviedo, interview with the author, Vallegrande, October 27, 1994.

Ernesto Guevara came to inhabit the social utopias and dreams of an entire generation through an almost mystical affinity with his era. Another person in the gentle yet angry sixties would have left but a slight trace. Che himself, in a time less idealistic and turbulent, would have passed unnoticed. Guevara has survived as a figure worthy of interest and remembrance largely because of the generation he inspired. His relevance does not stem from his works or ideas but from his almost perfect identification with an historical period. Premature death negating life's promise became a leit-motif of the era, starting with James Dean in the mid-fifties, Lenny Bruce in the mid-sixties, and then the icons of the decade: Jimi Hendrix, Janis Joplin, and Jim Morrison, but also Malcolm X, Martin Luther King, and the Kennedys. But no one symbolized it as clearly as Che Guevara. Myriad consonances helped create that crucial identification between myth and context. Another life would never have captured the spirit of its time; another historical moment would never have found itself reflected as it did in him.

As with the decade that saw him live and die, a guiding principle in the life of Ernesto Guevara was the exaltation of will, bordering on willfulness or, as some might say, omnipotence. In his stark and enigmatic letter of farewell to his parents, he refers to it in no uncertain terms: "A willpower that I have polished with an artist's care will carry my weak legs and tired lungs."[2] From his youthful rugby days in Córdoba to his execution in the jungles of Bolivia, he always started off from the premise that it was enough to want or will something for it to happen. There was no obstacle too great for willpower. Che's loves and travels, his political vision and his military and economic leadership were permeated by an indomitable will which would permit extraordinary feats and achieve outstanding victories. It would also engender recurrent, and ultimately fatal, mistakes.

The origins of that almost narcissistic willfulness are many: his own determination, his lifelong struggle with asthma, and his mother's unending vigilance, full of adoration and guilt. But beyond the question of origins, there is the effect. Few figures have attained the self-confidence of Ernesto Guevara which allowed him to undertake the most inconceivable follies and conduct the most lucid and merciless bouts of self-analysis. If anyone ever believed that wanting the world was enough to have it, and have it now, that man was Che Guevara. If there was ever a time when millions thought the same thing, it was the sixties.

Another thread unifying his life and the times he embodied lay in his eternal refusal of ambivalence, a trait shared by too many in the generation he personified. To a large extent, the sixties were based upon a wholesale rejection of life's contradictions. The era was writ in black and white. Many members of the first postwar cohort simply excluded from their souls the very principle of contradictory feelings, of conflicting desires, of mutually incompatible political goals. Who better than Che to incarnate that generation's inability to live at cross-purposes?

Che Guevara's legendary willpower was shattered by time, geopolitics, and the intractable complexities of social struggle. The fervent idealism and generational arrogance of 1968, from Berkeley to Beijing and Prague to Mexico City, led to undeniable cultural changes whose scope we are only beginning to understand. But there was no return to Eden, no storming of the Winter Palace. The political shifts stemming from those heady days of student protest and intellectual ferment, unequaled in the postwar era, led to significant though highly localized victories: the end of the Vietnam war, the departure of General de Gaulle in France, a hint of liberalization in Mexico at the beginning of Luis Echeverría's presidential term, exemplary and long-lived social conquests in Italy—not much to show for all the struggle. Still, 1968 left us a lasting legacy. And so did the one man who most closely embodied its deeper meaning.

Relevance cannot be separated from context. Che's ideas, his life and opus, even his example, belong to the past. As such, they will never be current again. Of course, history is far from over: the idea of social revolution might one day reappear. But the window of opportunity is closing. Che's aspirations died at the close of the millennium, within the prolonged agony of nineteenth-century socialism. The fleeting references to Guevara within a few internal debates in Cuba do not signify a rehabilitation, or even an adaptation of his ideas to contemporary history. The main theoretical and political doctrines associated with Che—the armed struggle, the *foco* guerrilla movement, the creation of a new man and the primacy of moral incentives, the struggle for militant international solidarity—are virtually meaningless today. The Cuban Revolution—his greatest triumph and truest success—is now disintegrating, and lingers on thanks only to a wholesale rejection of Guevara's ideological heritage.

Nostalgia endures, though. Subcomandante Marcos, the media-friendly leader of the Zapatista uprising in Chiapas, often invokes (graphically or verbally) the example and images of Che Guevara—especially those recalling betrayal and defeat. In response to a devastating offensive by the Mexican armed forces on February 9, 1995, Marcos brandished two icons: Emiliano Zapata at Chinameca, and Che at Vado del Yeso and the Yuro ravine.* Che also lives on in the media. His ongoing appeal harks back to

---

*Zapata was ambushed and assassinated at the Hacienda de Chinameca in 1919. The rear guard of Che's guerrilla column in Bolivia was annihilated in Vado del Yeso; Che himself was taken prisoner at la Quebrada del Yuro, on the outskirts of a town called La Higuera. The communiqué from Marcos appeared in *La Jornada* (Mexico City), February 25, 1995.

that final call for a modern utopia. It reflects that last convergence of our era's great and generous ideals—equality, solidarity, individual and collective liberation—with actual men and women who tried to make them reality. The values of Che Guevara are still relevant, together with those of his generation. The hopes and dreams of the sixties still resonate at the close of a century bereft of utopias, lacking in a collective project, and torn by the conflicts inherent in our monolithic ideological uniformity.

Che's fifteen minutes of fame have survived him. More than anyone else, he continues to shed light and meaning upon a moment of time whose memory endures, albeit faintly. His life, like the sixties, should be played in fast-forward; that is how it was lived. The story should be read like that of the sixties: high-strung, eventful, and fleeting. In his childhood, youth, maturity, and death can be found the keys to deciphering the mystic encounter of a man and his world.

Compañero

Chapter 1

---

*Childhood, Youth, and Asthma
in Argentina*

Argentina before the Great Depression was not a bad country to be born and raised in—especially if, like the first son of Ernesto Guevara Lynch and Celia de la Serna y Llosa, one belonged to a blue-blooded aristocracy. Ernesto Guevara de la Serna was born on June 14, 1928, in Rosario—the third largest city in a country of 12.5 million inhabitants. On his father's side, the Guevara Lynch family had lived in Argentina for twelve generations: more than enough to fulfill the requirements of nobility in a land of immigrants, most washed up only recently on the shores of "God's country South." On his mother's side, there was also a long and distinguished lineage, as well as extensive property, which in Argentina meant money.

From his father Ernesto inherited Irish and Spanish blood. His great-grandfather, Patrick Lynch, had fled from England to Spain, and eventually to Argentina, assuming the governorship of Río de la Plata in the second half of the eighteenth century. He even had Mexican-American parentage: Che's paternal grandmother, Ana Lynch, was born in California in 1868. Roberto Guevara, Che's paternal grandfather, was also originally from the United States, though only by chance: his parents had joined in the California Gold Rush of 1848, returning to the land of their birth a few years later.

Not only by birth were the Guevaras of old Argentine stock. The Guevara Lynch branch of the family was so closely identified with the history of the local aristocracy that Gaspar Lynch was one of the nineteenth-century founders of the Argentine Rural Society—a genuine board of directors for the country's landowning oligarchy. If Enrique Lynch was one of that oligarchy's mainstays toward the end of the nineteenth century, Ana Lynch, the only grandmother Che ever knew, was a liberal and iconoclast. She became a significant figure in his youth; his decision to study medicine rather than engineering was partly due to her illness and death.

On his mother's side, Guevara's landed roots went back to General José de la Serna e Hinojosa, the last Spanish viceroy of Peru, whose troops were defeated by Sucre in the historic battle of Ayacucho in 1820, when South America's independence was finally secured.* A daughter of Juan Martín de la Serna y Edelmira Llosa, Celia was not yet twenty-one when she married the young former architecture student in 1927. Her parents had died years earlier: Don Juan shortly after her birth, according to one of his granddaughters, by throwing himself overboard at sea on discovering he had syphilis[1]; and Edelmira soon afterward. Celia was raised by her older sister, Carmen de la Serna, who in 1928 married the Communist poet Cayetano Córdova Itúrburu. They were both card-carrying members of the Argentine Communist Party; the couple's affiliation lasted fourteen years.[2]

Celia's family "had lots of money," as her husband would admit unblushingly. Her father had inherited "a great fortune . . . and several ranches. A cultivated man, very intelligent, he was active in the ranks of the Radical Party," participating in the "revolution of 1890."[3] Though the family fortune was divided among seven children, it was initially large enough for all of them. The Guevara de la Serna family would live from Celia's rents and inheritance, much more than from the failed business ventures repeatedly launched by the head of the household. If Celia received, on her mother's side, a classical Catholic education at the School of the Sacred Heart, the freethinking, radical, leftist beliefs of her sister would make her into a singular figure: a socialist, anticlerical feminist.† She held endless meetings in her own home during the many struggles led by Argentine women during

---

*Marx and Engels mention General de la Serna in an article entitled, precisely, "Ayacucho." See I. Lavretsky, *Ernesto Che Guevara* (Moscow: Progress Publishers, 1976), p. 13. Lavretsky's true name was Josef Grigulevich; he was a well-known Soviet historian and veteran KGB agent whose career extended from the Spanish Civil War to the Sandinista revolution.

† "Our upbringing was totally anticlerical. Our mother, even more so. She was strongly anticlerical." Roberto Guevara de la Serna, quoted in Claudia Korol, *El Che y los argentinos* (Buenos Aires: Editorial Dialéctica, 1988), p. 32.

the twenties and thirties,* maintaining, both before and after her marriage, an identity of her own until her death in 1965.

This exceptional woman was the most important affective and intellectual figure in the life of her eldest son, at least until he met Fidel Castro in Mexico in 1955. Nobody—not his father, his wives, or children—would play as crucial a role for Che as did Celia, his mother. A woman who lived for twenty years under the threat and stigma of cancer; a militant who spent weeks in jail shortly before her death for being the mother of her son; a mother who raised five children virtually on her own—she had a profound influence on Che Guevara. Only Castro would have a similar impact on him, later, during a brief interlude in both their lives. Few things illustrate the glory and tragedy of Guevara's saga as aptly as his aching lament when in the Congo, that perpetual heart of darkness, he learned of his mother's death:

> Personally, however, [Machado Ventura] brought me the saddest news of the war: in a telephone conversation with Buenos Aires he was told my mother was very ill, in a tone which made me suppose it was but a preparatory announcement. . . . I had to spend a month in this sad uncertainty, awaiting the results of something I could guess at but still hoping there was a mistake, until I received confirmation of my mother's death. She had wanted to see me shortly before my departure, perhaps feeling ill, but this was not possible as my trip was already far advanced. She did not receive the letter of farewell I left for my parents in Havana; it was to be delivered only in October, after my departure had been made public.†

Unable to say good-bye, Che was also denied the chance to grieve in the full measure of his sorrow. The African revolution, merciless tropical dis-

---

*In 1926 Argentine women won a first series of civil rights, including that of contracts without their husbands' consent, and child custody for widows. There was a vigorous women's movement, if not a feminist one, in Argentina during the twenties. It was mainly of intellectual and socialist origins, and Celia de la Serna and her sister Carmen were doubtless in contact with it. The movement was identified to some extent with writers like Victoria Ocampo and Alfonsina Storni, as well as the struggle for women's suffrage, which would only be attained in 1948 through the influence of Evita Perón. See *Women, Culture and Politics in Latin America* (Berkeley: University of California Press, 1990), chapters 5–8.

† Ernesto Che Guevara, "Pasajes de la guerra revolucionaria (el Congo)," unpublished manuscript, Havana, p. 17. This text, based on Che's Congo campaign journals, remains unpublished although it has been extensively quoted, particularly in Paco Ignacio Taibo II, Felix Guerra, and Froilán Rodríguez, *El año que estuvimos en ninguna parte* (Mexico City: Planeta, 1994). In Chapter 9 of the present book, I will quote extensively from Che's original, complete manuscript, made available to me in Havana by generous Guevaristas. Its authenticity was corroborated on comparing the copy thus obtained to that held by several of Che's aides, including Jesús Parra, a former secretary of Che's, who allowed me to compare the manuscript with his own in Havana.

eases, and unending tribal conflicts prevented it. Celia died in Buenos Aires, expelled from the hospital of her choice and torn from her deathbed for having given birth to Che thirty-seven years earlier. He mourned her in the hills of Africa, driven from the successive countries he had adopted as his own. He himself would perish barely two years later: two deaths too closely related.

The Argentina that saw the birth of Ernesto (soon to be nicknamed Teté) was still in 1928 a dynamic country in full swing, blessed by an economic and even political prosperity which would soon fade. During the twenties it resembled the British domains populated by "white settlers," rather than the rest of Latin America. On the eve of World War I, its principal sociodemographic indicators made it more like Australia, Canada, or New Zealand than Colombia, Peru, Venezuela, or Mexico.* The country had already received three times more direct foreign investment than Mexico or Brazil. The amount of railroad track per thousand inhabitants was three to ten times higher than that of its hemispheric neighbors.[4] In 1913, the southern nation's per capita income was the thirteenth-largest in the world and slightly higher than that of France. The European conflagration and headlong growth of the twenties would not alter this ranking. Argentina's weak points—its meager industrialization, excessive foreign debt, highly vulnerable export sector—would soon quash the modernizing pretensions of its local elites. But at the time of his birth, Che Guevara's country still exuded a buoyant and legitimate self-confidence. It aspired to become part of the First World *avant la lettre,* and was unconcerned by the ominous economic and social signs already looming on the horizon.

The introduction in 1912 of secret, universal suffrage (for male Argentine citizens) led to the electoral victory, four years later, of the Radical Civic Union and its legendary champion, Hipólito Yrigoyen. He was reelected for a second time a few months after Che's birth in 1928, following the uninspired interregnum of Marcelo T. de Alvear. Socially minded, democratizing, Yrigoyenism continued to challenge and constrain the old oligarchical, ranching Argentina of the Rural Society. But it did not fulfill the huge expectations it had aroused in the country's emerging middle sectors and the new working class of Buenos Aires, an eclectic and unstable mixture of immigrants and second-generation Argentines from the interior.† Pres-

---

*For instance, Argentina's infant mortality rate at the time was 121 per thousand, Colombia's 177, Mexico's 228, and Chile's 261, while Australia's stood at 72. The proportion of inhabitants living in large cities was 31 percent, while in Brazil it was 10.7 percent and in Peru 5 percent. Victor Bulmer-Thomas, *Economic History of Latin America* (New York: Cambridge University Press, 1994), p. 86.

† Che's father was not among the disappointed; he cast his first vote, in 1918, for the Argentine Socialist Party.

sure from the right, the disillusionment of the middle classes, and the effects of the Depression put an end to this democratic interval: in 1930 the military took power—the first coup in this century to overthrow a democratically elected Latin American government. In place of the almost blind, ancient Yrigoyen, the armed forces imposed the first in a long series of military rulers and fraudulent elections.

Ernesto was born in Rosario by accident. After their marriage in Buenos Aires a year earlier, his parents had left for Puerto Caraguatay in the Upper Paraná, in the territory of Misiones. There, Ernesto's father planned to cultivate some 200 hectares sown with maté, or Argentine tea leaves, the "green gold" so abundant in that part of the country.* When Celia was seven months pregnant they traveled to Rosario, the closest town, both for her to give birth and to study the possibility of buying a maté mill. The farming project and maté plantation soon collapsed, as would happen with all of Guevara Lynch's business ventures. But the other project prospered: Ernesto was born in Rosario, one month premature.

Soon after Che's birth, the family left the Misiones area, Guevara Lynch becoming a partner in a struggling shipbuilding firm in San Isidro, near Buenos Aires. This is where Ernesto's first asthma attack took place, on May 2, 1930, just weeks before his second birthday. According to Guevara Lynch, his wife (an excellent swimmer) often took the child to the Nautical Club at San Isidro, on the banks of the River Plate. The father leaves little doubt as to his wife's responsibility:

> On a cold morning in the month of May, with a strong wind, my wife went swimming in the river with our son Ernesto. I arrived at the club to look for them and take them to lunch, and found the little boy shivering in his wet bathing suit. Celia was inexperienced and did not realize that the change in weather at that time of year could be dangerous.†

In fact, the infant suffered his first pulmonary crisis—from pneumonia—

---

*Ernesto Guevara Lynch himself, for neither the first nor the last time, provides contradictory explanations on the origin of the funds which allowed him to purchase the land in Puerto Caraguatay. In his book *Mi hijo el Che* (Madrid: Editorial Planeta, 1981), he says he had received an inheritance from his father, and planned using it to buy land in Misiones. This version is reiterated by an official Cuban source, the *Atlas histórico, biográfico y militar de Ernesto Guevara*, vol. 1, published in Havana in 1990 (p. 25). But in a long interview with Josef Grigulevich included in the latter's book (Lavretsky, *Guevara*, p. 14), Che's father states: "Celia inherited a maté plantation in Misiones."

† Guevara Lynch, p. 139. In another version, Guevara changed the roles but not the blame: "On May 2, 1930, Celia and I went swimming at the pool with Teté. The weather turned cold and windy, and suddenly Teté began to cough. We took him to the doctor, who diagnosed asthma. Perhaps he already had a cold, or perhaps he inherited the illness, since Celia had been asthmatic as a child." Lavretsky, *Guevara*, p. 15.

forty days after birth, from which "he almost died," according to his aunt Ercilia Guevara Lynch.[5] This early illness casts some doubt on the father's explanation; an earlier history of lung ailment preceded the cold. In any case, through June 1933 Ernestito's asthma attacks were an almost daily occurrence. They caused terrible anxiety for both parents, but especially Celia, who besides tending to the child was overburdened by guilt. To that, instilled by her husband over the river incident, she piled on hereditary factors, which at the time were only suspected, though they are now known to be the single most significant cause of asthma. Celia herself had suffered from this respiratory ailment as a child; the probabilities of one of her offspring contracting the disease were nearly one in three, and everything indicates that that is what occurred with Che. The early episodes of pneumonia and colds were only triggers for a high-risk candidate; they did not provoke Che's asthma.

The three years between the first appearance of the illness and its stabilization seem to have left a profound mark on parents and child alike; accounts by relatives, friends, and the parents themselves are deeply moving.* It was doubtless during this time that Celia built with her son a relationship infused with obsessiveness, guilt, and adoration. This bond soon translated into a home-based education, which would instill in Che Guevara a lifelong love of books and an insatiable intellectual curiosity.

The family wandered throughout Argentina for five years, seeking a site that would help, or at least not aggravate, the boy's condition. They finally found it in Alta Gracia, a summer resort town 40 kilometers from the city of Córdoba, at the foot of the Sierra Chica and almost 600 meters above sea level. A neat, clean, well-laid-out town of white middle-class Argentines, it catered to vacationers and the infirm, not unlike the mountain or hot-springs health spas of Western and Central Europe. The thin, dry air, which attracted tourists and tuberculosis patients, attenuated Teté's asthma attacks—though it did not eliminate or even space them to any significant degree. The illness gradually became more manageable, thanks to the better climate, medical care, the child's personality, and his mother's exceptional devotion.

Ernesto Guevara was raised, then, on this magic mountain at the foot of the Córdoba Sierra. His father built houses in the small town, while his mother devoted herself to raising and educating Ernesto, his two sisters, Celia and Ana María, and a brother, Roberto, born in those years; another

---

*Whatever defects Guevara Lynch may have had as a father, Che's mother attests to his devotion in caring for the child: "At age 4 Ernesto could no longer tolerate the capital's climate. Guevara Lynch became accustomed to sleeping seated on the bed of his eldest son, so that the latter, reclining on his chest, could better bear the asthma." Celia de la Serna, quoted in *Granma* (Havana), October 16, 1967, p. 8.

brother, Juan Martín, would arrive in 1943. The Guevara home was an oasis of security in a country that was fast leaving its golden years behind. Like the rest of the world, Argentina was entering the hardships of the Depression and its unexpected political consequences. The Crash of 1929 not only ruined the maté hopes of Che's father, it also shattered in a few short years the myth of a peaceful and prosperous Argentina. The 1930 coup ushered in a long period of political instability. A collapse in prices and in international demand for the country's major exports brought about an unending economic slowdown, interrupted only by a brief boom in raw materials during the immediate postwar period. But the crisis also led to social mobilization, ideological polarization, and cultural changes affecting even Alta Gracia and the sheltered, enlightened elites of Córdoba.

Because its main exports—beef and wheat—were less vulnerable to European demand, Argentina was initially less affected by falling international prices than were other Latin American nations. Still, Argentina's export revenues fell by almost 50 percent between 1929 and 1932, a plunge ultimately as devastating and laden with consequence as it was for other countries in the region. It had a twofold effect on Argentine society. First, there was a steep rise in agricultural unemployment, as myriad foreclosures hit the pampas. Second, import restrictions due to a lack of hard currency and foreign credit promoted the development of domestic manufactures, in both consumer and some capital sectors. This in turn caused an accelerated growth in the Argentine working class. By 1947, 1.4 million immigrants from rural areas had relocated to Buenos Aires, and half a million workers found jobs in industry, doubling the ranks of labor in barely a decade. These migrants would become the famous *cabecitas negras* (literally, "dark heads"). A new working class was emerging, darker-skinned and less immigrant-based, and located more in domestic industry than in processing goods for export. The gap between the middle-class, educated, and traditional sectors on the one hand, and the new industrial class on the other, would be reflected ten years later in the distance between a Socialist, intellectual, and petit-bourgeois left and a populist, irreverent Peronism.

But other concerns were more important for Ernesto during those years. The habits of his personal and family life were becoming more clearly defined. The first was his parents' continual roving, now limited to the perimeter of Alta Gracia. According to Che's younger brother, after living six months in the Grutas Hotel in Alta Gracia, they drifted from Villa Chichita in 1933 to Villa Nydia, then to the Fuentes chalet in 1937, the Forte chalet, the Ripamonte and Doce chalets between that year and 1940, and, in 1940–41, back to Villa Nydia. Each time the lease ran out—a frequent occurrence—the family had to move.[6] It would be far-fetched to attribute the roaming spirit of Che Guevara to this endless wandering by his family.

But the constant comings and goings of his childhood years could not help but become a sort of second nature. From city to city until the age of five, and house to house until he turned fifteen: the Guevaras' norm was movement. It also served to spice an otherwise monotonous existence, and to rekindle the illusion of starting anew and overcoming the family tensions—affective and financial—which were hardly lacking in the growing household of Ernesto and Celia.

It was during this period that the relationship between Celia and Teté became central to both their lives. It extended far beyond the intensity and closeness of Ernestito's link with his father, or that of the other children with their mother. Che's illness largely explains this: there is nothing like a mother's anguish and guilt to create in her a boundless devotion to her child. The symbiosis between Celia and her son, which would nourish their correspondence, their emotional bond, and their very lives for more than thirty years, began during that placid time in Córdoba when Ernesto learned, on his mother's lap, to read and write, to see her and, above all, be seen by her. Celia's gaze distinguished and "constituted" him to such an extent that those who knew Ernesto in his youth were astonished by the physical contrast between him and his siblings. It was notorious long before the eldest son became famous, inevitably casting a shadow over the other members of the family. Why was there such a difference? One may assume that it derived largely from Ernesto's relationship with his mother; the other children probably received a simpler kind of maternal affection.[7]

Another distinctive sign became apparent in this prelude to adolescence: a certain definition, and confirmation, of the head of the household's role in the family. Guevara Lynch was simultaneously a *bon vivant,* a marvelous friend to his children, a mediocre provider, and a distant father. He did devote hours to his son, swimming, playing golf, and talking with him. But he remained aloof and remote the rest of the time, often indifferent to the needs of his child and family. While the mother served as teacher, household organizer, and nurse, Guevara Lynch was sporadically building houses in partnership with his brother and lingering at the Sierras Hotel, a haven of rest and relaxation for the wealthy society of Alta Gracia.*

---

*Certainly, when they first arrived in Alta Gracia, the Guevara de la Serna couple went out together. Although the testimony of witnesses like Rosario González, a servant in charge of the children from 1933 to 1938, should be taken with a grain of salt, it points to a trend which would intensify in time: "Ernesto's parents went out a lot, they were late-nighters, and would go to the Sierras Hotel for dinner every night at about seven. They would return at dawn, at four, at five. . . . Every day, that was very common for them. They would leave at seven, eight o'clock, they'd leave and not return for dinner. The children had dinner alone." Rosario González, interview with the author, Alta Gracia, February 17, 1995.

His illness continued to afflict Ernestito, preventing him from having a "normal" primary education. Celia took up the slack:

> I taught my son his first letters, but Ernesto was unable to go to school because of his asthma. He only attended the second and third grades on a regular basis; the fifth and sixth grades, he attended as much as possible. His siblings copied the schoolwork and he studied at home.[8]

Ernesto's father played a central role, however, in transmitting to the asthmatic child a voracious love of sports and exercise, and the conviction that through willpower alone he could overcome the limitations and hardships imposed by his illness.* Both Ernesto's father and mother were athletic; they loved nature and the countryside, and instilled that inclination in their son. Since any enjoyment of exercise or the outdoors implied enormous effort for him, Ernesto developed uncommon willpower from his earliest years. It was Che's parents who discovered the only possible remedy for what became a chronic affliction. They quickly concluded that the only reasonable solution for their son's bronchial asthma was to continue medicating him and to strengthen him through tonics and swimming, climbing hills, and horseback riding.[9]

Ernesto's fierce determination to overcome his physical shortcomings was thus a major factor in the development of his personality from early years. Another was his easy contact with a broad range of people. The children's circle was varied and gregarious; they were in constant touch with friends from different social classes, including caddies from the Alta Gracia golf club, serving boys from hotels, the children of construction workers from the sites run by Ernesto's father, and poor families from the emerging slums near the family's rented villas. Some of Che's little friends were middle-class, others of low income; some were white like him and his siblings, others, dark-skinned *morochos* like Rosendo Zacarías, who sold candy in the streets of Alta Gracia. Half a century later, Zacarías still remembers (perhaps aided by the mythical idea that "Che was a perfect child, without any defect"[10]) how they all played together without distinctions or hierarchy, and how easily Ernesto related to people from different social and cultural milieux.

---

*Once again, there are many interpretations of the precise responsibility of Che's parents during this phase. According to his brother Roberto, even in this area the central role was taken by his mother: "He was a very sick boy. . . . But his character and willpower allowed him to overcome and vanquish it. My mother had a great influence in this sense." Roberto Guevara de la Serna, quoted in Adys Cupull and Froilán González, *Ernestito: Vivo y presente: Iconografía testimoniada de la infancia y la juventud de Ernesto Che Guevara, 1928–1953* (Havana: Editora Política, 1989), p. 82.

The asthmatic boy also spent long hours in bed, developing an intense love of books and literature. He devoured the children's classics of the time: the adventure novels of Dumas *père,* Robert Louis Stevenson, Jack London, Jules Verne, and Emilio Salgari. But he also explored Cervantes and Anatole France, Pablo Neruda and Horacio Quiroga, and the Spanish poets Machado and García Lorca. Both his parents transmitted to him their passion for reading during this period of home education: Ernesto Guevara Lynch his penchant for adventure novels, and Celia for poetry and the French language.

At school, Ernesto was a good student but nothing more, one of his teachers recalls; as intelligent as his younger sisters, but not as hardworking. Perhaps the greatest impact of the two schools he attended in Alta Gracia had to do with the fact of receiving a public education during the waning years of an oligarchical Argentina.

According to his teacher Elba Rossi Oviedo Zelaya, Ernesto had two different family links to education: one through Celia, ever present and attentive to her son's instruction, and the other, much more lax, through his father. In the words of Che's teacher,

> I only knew the mother. She was really very democratic, a lady who didn't mind picking up any child and taking him home, and helping the school; she had a lovely temperament. . . . She came every day and to all the parents meetings, with all her kids in the little car and then other kids joining in. The father was a very distinguished man who spent a lot of time at the Sierras Hotel because he came from a distinguished family. I might have seen him once by chance; he didn't speak with the teachers. I only knew he went a lot to the Sierras because at that time the Sierras was the best hotel in Alta Gracia. With her I talked many times, about school and other things. I never met him at the school, though I might have seen him on some occasion; someone might have said, that's Sr. Guevara.[11]

The fact that Ernesto attended public school was typical, yet highly significant. Although Argentine society was still relatively homogeneous, its growing diversity was already coming into conflict with the standardizing pressures of public, lay, compulsory education. When his asthma kept Ernesto at home, his mother actually received notices from the truant officer, inquiring as to the reasons for his absence; the compulsory character of primary education was not just a matter of principle but a strictly enforced reality. The two schools Che attended in Alta Gracia received pupils from the destitute homes on the city outskirts, poor infants from *el campo,* or else urban *morochos*—either way, children from modest families, for whom this was the first generation going to school. The enormous difference between Argentina and the rest of Latin America in those years (with the exception of Uruguay and possibly Chile), lay precisely in the existence of public education. Established before universal suffrage, it was, together with military conscription, the equalizing institution *par excellence*. The immense gap between the adult Che and many of his companions from Cuba and the rest of Latin America, in his relations with different classes, races, ethnic groups, and educational levels, stemmed from this early experience of equality. Che's experience was not at all typical in a continent whose elites rarely encounter people different from themselves.

However, to strive for equality is not the same as achieving it. The brutal emergence in the thirties of new working classes—including second-generation immigrants and laborers from the old agricultural sector of *gauchos* and cattle ranches—did not spare any level of Argentine society. Ernesto's schools were attended by poor children of Italian, Spanish, and rural origins; thanks to his teachers and the exceptional cultural heritage he received from Celia, Che was blessed with unique and obvious opportunities for confronting the contours of equality. But these schools also bestowed upon him, paradoxically, the distinction of being a precocious *primus inter pares.* The culture and (relative) prosperity of his parents, as well as the self-confidence generated by a stable if not peaceful home, provided Ernesto with the privilege of standing out from a very young age. He was a ringleader at school and among his friends. The early vocation for leadership that many of Che's admirers have traced back to his childhood may indeed have stemmed from innate talents—but it also involved his privileged social position.*

Last but not least, these languid years in Alta Gracia also saw Ernesto's incipient politicization. The Spanish Civil War had a major impact on him, as it did on millions of young people and adults throughout the world. His interest in the triumphs and tragedies of Madrid, Teruel, and Guernica did not center on the conflict's ideological, international, or even political aspects. Rather, as befitted a boy between the ages of eight and eleven, he was inspired by its military and heroic aspects. In 1937, he hung a map of

*"I remember that the children followed him around a lot in the schoolyard; he would climb up a big tree that was there, and all the kids stood around him as if he were the leader, and when he ran the others would follow behind him; it was clear that he was the boss. Perhaps it was the family, because it was a different sort of family; the kid knew how to speak better and all that. You could tell there was a difference. Because they came from Buenos Aires, that made them seem superior. Those kids had another atmosphere at home; they never lacked any school materials, whereas the poorer children often needed more things, or didn't have any coloring pencils or anything to paint with. These never lacked anything, they were in another category; well, not that one could tell their category because they were snobbish, not at all. But they spoke better, they did things better, their homework, everything. They didn't skip the homework like other kids; often at home they don't get any help, and so they come back to school without the homework." Elba Rossi Oviedo Zelaya, interview with the author, Alta Gracia, February 17, 1995.

Spain on the wall of his room, using it to follow the movements of the Republican and Francoist forces. He also built a miniature battlefield in the garden, complete with trenches and mountains.[12]

In 1937, Ernesto's uncle, the poet Cayetano Córdova Itúrburu, left for Spain. A journalist and committed member of Argentina's Communist Party, Córdova was hired as a foreign correspondent. Aunt Carmen and the two children went to live at the Guevara home in Alta Gracia during his absence. So all the dispatches, notes, and articles that Córdova Itúrburu sent from the front passed through the villa in Alta Gracia. The arrival of news from overseas was a major event. The poet-turned-reporter occasionally sent Spanish books and magazines. This continual stream of detailed information flowed straight into the imagination of the boy, where it would remain.

Another important factor in Che's growing politicization was the subsequent arrival in Córdoba and then Alta Gracia of several refugee families fleeing from Spain. The one closest to the Guevaras was that of the physician Juan González Aguilar, who had previously dispatched his wife and children to Buenos Aires and then Alta Gracia. Paco, Juan, and Pepe, the three sons of the González Aguilar family, enrolled at the same school in Córdoba that Che began attending while still living in Alta Gracia. For a year, they often traveled together the thirty-five kilometers to school. As the Republican front collapsed, González Aguilar fled to Argentina, joining his family in Alta Gracia.

The friendship between the two families would last for decades. The stories told by the González Aguilars and other refugees like General Jurado and the composer Manuel de Falla would help inspire in Ernesto a deep sympathy toward the Republican cause. The Spanish Civil War—perhaps the last civil conflict until the Cuban Revolution to be broadly, almost unanimously, perceived as a battle between good and evil—was the decisive political event in Che's childhood and adolescence. Nothing else in those years would mark him as profoundly as the Loyalist struggle and defeat: not the French Popular Front or Mexico's oil expropriation, not Roosevelt's New Deal or the Argentine coup of 1943, nor even the rise of Perón on October 17, 1945, would have such an impact on the young Guevara.

Ernesto's parents also transmitted their own political views to him. After the Republican defeat in Spain, the father of the eleven-year-old boy founded a local section of Acción Argentina and enrolled him in its youth section. A typical antifascist organization, Acción Argentina did a bit of everything during those years. It organized meetings, collected funds for the Allies, opposed Nazi penetration in Argentina, uncovered cases of infiltration by former crew members of the German battleship *Graf Spee* (sunk in Montevideo Bay in 1940), and disseminated information about Allied advances during the war. As Guevara Lynch recalls, "every time an event was organized by Acción Argentina or we had a serious investigation to do, Ernesto went with me."[13]

The Spanish war coincided with the emergence in Argentina of a nationalistic, Catholic, and virtually fascist right. The nation's intellectuals—especially those with radical, socialist, or communist sympathies and aristocratic, Italian, or Spanish roots—rallied against it, denouncing all forms of xenophobia and conservatism. They were particularly opposed to the views expressed by writers like Leopoldo Lugones, or publications like *Crisol* (Crucible), *La Bandera Argentina* (The Argentine Flag), and *La Voz Nacionalista* (The Nationalist Voice), as well as to their political expression among mid-level army officers. Argentine nationalism during the thirties embraced anti-Semitism, racism and eugenics, fascism, and Nazism. It quite naturally sided with Franco when the Spanish Civil War broke out in 1936. Xenophobia was especially dear to it, given the emergence of a new working class from the interior made up of "blacks" or "redskins."* That this nationalism also had its "social" and "anti-imperialist" aspects, its "developmentalist" components, did not prevent the traditional Argentine left from regarding it with dread—and justifiably so.

The final outcome of these trends confounded all expectations. The advent of Perón in 1945 would leave the nationalists unsatisfied, and the left disoriented and bereft of popular support. The growth of that conservative, Catholic nationalism provides an at least partial, and tentative, answer to the riddle of Argentina's left and Che's attitude toward the chief political event of his youth: Perón's rise to power. As we shall see, Ernesto followed in his parents' footsteps. To the extent that he cared at all, his youthful anti-Peronism was as visceral as his family's, as wholehearted as that of his fellow university students, and as unrealistic as that of the left in general. Che would complete the circle only twenty years later, when he became friends with Perón's representatives in Havana, especially John William Cooke.[†] He even served as Perón's contact with Algerian president Ahmed Ben Bella, requesting his help to arrange a meeting between Perón and Gamal Abdel Nasser.[14]

*Lugones, insisting that Argentina was a white nation, advocated an end to all nonwhite immigration. In his article "Splendor and Decadence of the White Race," Alejandro Bunge wrote that "all the vigor of the race . . . the patriotism of superior men and the abnegation of the Christian spirit must devote themselves from now on to restoring the concept of the blessing of children and large families, especially among the more fortunate classes." Quoted in David Rock, *La Argentina autoritaria* (Buenos Aires: Ariel, 1993), p. 117.

[†] The friendship between Che and Cooke began when the latter arrived in Cuba in 1960, and Che received him at Havana airport. Ernesto Goldar, "John William Cooke: De Perón al Che Guevara," in *Todo es historia* (Buenos Aires), vol. 25, no. 228, June 1991, p. 26.

On the eve of the Guevaras' departure for Córdoba in 1943, the patterns of Che's family life were set. The house was always open. There was an endless procession of children, visitors, friends, and travelers, all within a great disorder governed only by two rules: hospitality for guests and freedom for the children. Bicycles and tricycles circulated indoors, meals were served at all times, and there were scores of guests. Money was always short. The couple's financial problems, the father's chronic absenteeism, and the mother's indifference to household matters doubtless helped perpetuate the chaos. The children's enormous freedom had as its counterpart a certain lack of structure. When the Guevaras' marriage began to show strains, the disorder became even more apparent.

In 1942, a year before moving to the city, Ernesto's parents enrolled him at the Colegio Nacional Deán Funes of Córdoba, an excellent public secondary school belonging to the Ministry of Education. It was not precisely intended for poor students, but was less exclusive than the Colegio Montserrat; the latter was the institution usually attended by Córdoban members of the regional elite—to which Ernesto belonged as a matter of course—while those from the emerging middle classes tended to enroll at Deán Funes. The parents' choice was a fortunate one. Ernesto spent five years among young people of different social and professional origins.

One should not, however, exaggerate their diversity. In the forties, Córdoba was still a fairly homogeneous, white, bureaucratic center within a prosperous agricultural province. The social differences that did exist were increasingly concealed by geographical segregation. Things were changing, however. The population skyrocketed, surging from 250,000 inhabitants in 1930 to 386,000 in 1947. Lower-income residents, recently arrived from the countryside and working in the services sector, began settling in the city's outskirts. In some areas, slums appeared directly alongside "fashionable" neighborhoods. With the arrival of the automobile industry in the late forties, industrialization was just around the corner.

A new phase had begun for Ernesto, in school and in his eternal struggle against asthma. He began to compete in team sports, especially rugby. Both rough and cerebral, it was the favorite sport of Anglophile Argentina. Many of the matches took place at Córdoba's Lawn Tennis Club, where Ernesto also swam and played tennis or golf. There and then the secondary-school student became friends with two brothers, Tomás and Alberto Granado, the former his own age, the latter six years older. Tomás was the closest friend of his adolescent years; Alberto, of his youth, travels, and first forays into the world. They attended the same high school, suffered through their first loves side by side, and witnessed together the political ferment that shook Argentina beginning on October 17, 1945, when Perón, borne by a tidal wave of both *cabecitas negras* and Catholic, conservative, and authoritarian elites, erupted into the life of his country.

Rugby had two implications for the young asthma patient, already marked by the disease's classically deformed chest. First of all, it entailed an exceptional challenge. It was already known then (and even more so now) that strenuous exercise is the single most frequent trigger for asthma attacks.* Overcoming the crises and controlling them through willpower, an inhaler, and even epinephrine injections, soon became a routine that Guevara would endure until the end of his life.

Secondly, rugby assigns players different roles and functions, some more strenuous than others. The position of half-scrum held for Ernesto the great advantage of being more static and strategic, less mobile and tactical.† It benefited him in two ways, offering him an opportunity to develop his skills as a leader and strategist, and allowing him to play without running from one end of the field to the other throughout a match, thus preventing him from tiring too early. But he was not entirely spared; the attacks came on during the game sometimes, driving him off the field and to the bleachers, where he would inject himself with adrenaline right through his clothes, perhaps in some cases to call attention to himself.[15] The challenge was enormous, but manageable under certain conditions—a combination which would persist throughout Guevara's life, as did the asthma. For Ernesto's ailment was not totally typical: unlike many cases of childhood asthma, it did not disappear with age.

Psychoanalytic views on the origins of asthma are in general no longer viewed favorably by physicians‡; the widely accepted etiology is hereditary. Interpretations based upon a patient's anxiety, his incapacity to externalize it and to cope with the ambivalence triggering that anxiety, are perhaps better suited to explain the disorder's lasting nature in cases like Che's than its origin. They are particularly suggestive given his obvious difficulty in facing

---

*"Exercise is the most common trigger of asthma. Eighty percent of people with asthma get some degree of chest tightness, cough, or wheeze when they exercise." Thomas F. Plant, *Children with Asthma* (New York: Pedipress, 1985), p. 56.

† "The half-scrum is the link between attackers and defenders. . . . He is the man who initiates the attack . . . and the most likely to become a leader on the field, because he must constantly give orders to the forward players. . . . His function does not require speed, but skill with the ball. . . . He was required to fill a static function (in which he did not run the risk of becoming breathless)." Hugo Gambini, *El Che Guevara* (Buenos Aires: Paidós, 1968), p. 48.

‡ "Asthma is caused by a complex set of physiological reactions which are not yet completely understood. We can say for sure, however, that asthma is not due to a defective mother-child relationship or to any other psychological problem, as has been suggested in the past." Plant, *Asthma*, p. 62.

and accepting conflicting emotions or desires—whether in his family, at school, in love, or, years later, in politics. In this view, asthma was Ernesto's response to a primary, recurring anxiety which caused him to suffocate. This anxiety was in turn exacerbated by his frequent exposure to ambivalence, intolerable to him precisely because of the anxiety it generated. The only possible cure was to avoid ambivalence—through distance, travel, and death.

There are several known triggers for asthmatic episodes: viral infections, exercise, dust or other allergies, and climate changes. Attacks can also be brought on by emotional catalysts: a sense of imminent or expected danger, or highly conflictive situations with no apparent way out, and for which any alternative entails an exorbitant cost. The known connection between the dilation of contracted bronchia and a surge of adrenaline implies that situations devoid of ambivalence—such as combat, for instance—produce an endogenous discharge of adrenaline and thus can deter asthmatic attacks. Conversely, other situations—for example, those requiring long deliberations and tortuous decisions—can actually provoke them, precisely owing to the absence of endogenous discharges of adrenaline.* If this interpretation is correct, it may explain Che's subsequent incapacity to accept the simultaneous presence of opposites: his parents' problems and equivocal estrangement, the intrinsic contradictions of Peronism, the ambiguities of his relationship with Chichina Ferreyra, and later, the need to reconcile the pragmatic imperatives of the Cuban Revolution's survival with his own formidable social and humanistic values.†

What with his asthma and problems at home, Ernesto was, as his report cards indicate, only an average student, with occasional high marks in the humanities. Thus, in 1945, in his fourth year of middle school, he received excellent grades in literature and philosophy; barely passing marks in mathematics, history, and chemistry; and truly disastrous ones in music and physics.[16] His complete tone-deafness became legendary: he simply could not distinguish among rhythms or melodies, never learning to dance or play any musical instrument. As Alberto Granado would recount years later,

> We had agreed that I would give him a kick every time there was a dance he could do; the only dance he had learned was the tango, which is the only

*The list of triggers, as well as the hereditary etiology of asthma and its relationship to endogenous adrenaline discharges, all stem from a highly useful and interesting conversation between the author and Dr. Roberto Krechmer, one of Mexico's leading experts on children's asthma, in Mexico City, December 20, 1995.

† I owe the outlines of this interpretation to Susana Pravaz-Balán, who, in the course of a conversation in New Brunswick, New Jersey, on December 1, 1995, transmitted to me with more knowledge and perspicacity than these lines suggest, a series of ideas about asthma, Che, and ambivalence.

thing you can dance if you don't have any ear. The day of his birthday he made a fantastic speech, which proved to me that the boy was not crazy, that there was something to him. He was dancing with an Indian girl, a nurse from the leper colony in the Amazon region. Suddenly the band played "Delicado," a *baión* that was very much in fashion, a favorite of the girlfriend he had left in Córdoba. When I gave him a little kick to remind him, he started dancing the tango. He was the only one doing it. I couldn't stop laughing; when he realized what was happening he got terribly angry.[17]

Che's English was also appalling: he achieved an average of 3 out of 10 in his fourth year.[18] In contrast, his French, learned at home with Celia, eventually became cultivated and fluent to some extent. And his general level of culture and education was higher than that of his peers, according to his classmates. He bought and read the books of all the winners of the Nobel Prize for Literature, and held intensive discussions with his history and literature professors. As his friends recall, he was much more knowledgeable than they in many subjects they didn't even approach.[19] His barely adequate performance in school* was perhaps due to his many extracurricular activities: sports, chess (always a favorite pastime, in which he acquired a certain mastery), his first job with the provincial highway department (initially in Córdoba and then, after he completed high school, at Villa María, halfway between Córdoba and Rosario). All in all, as his father said, "he was a wizard in his use of time."[20]

An anecdote from this period reveals Ernesto's stubborn and generous efforts to bridge the gap separating him from the poorer sectors of Córdoba society, and to oppose blatant cases of oppression and injustice. The Guevaras' street, Calle Chile, bordered on one of the city's poorest neighborhoods. There, as in all Latin America, marginalized and dispossessed immigrants from the countryside lived in houses made of cardboard and zinc. This was also the territory of a Dantesque personage known as the Man of the Dogs: a legless cripple who hauled himself along on a little cart pulled by a brace of dogs, upon which he vented all his rage at his hapless fate. Every morning as he dragged himself out of the hole in the ground that was his home, he would whip the dogs as they struggled to pull him onto the pavement. The dogs' whimpers always preceded his appearance—a major event in the neighborhood. One day, the local children started taunting the Man of the Dogs and throwing stones at him. Ernesto and his friends witnessed this spectacle and tried to stop it, Ernesto pleading with the children.

*There is a certain continuity in his preferences at school. In a primary-school report card dated 1938, his best results were in history, followed by civic and moral instruction, while he did poorly in drawing, crafts, and music, with average grades in arithmetic and geometry. Korol, *El Che*, p. 35.

But instead of thanking him the Man of the Dogs mocked him, his icy stare filled with an ageless, irreparable class hatred. In the words of Dolores Moyano Martín, a friend of young Ernesto's and Chichina's cousin, who tells the story, the tramp illustrated an important distinction: his enemies were not the poor children throwing stones at him but the rich children trying to defend him*—a lesson that Ernesto would learn only in part.

His parents were drawing further and further apart, and the disorder and money problems already present in Alta Gracia became more acute in Córdoba. These years witnessed the romance—more or less public in the small world of a mid-sized provincial town—between Ernesto Guevara Lynch and Raquel Hevia, a Cuban of exceptional beauty widely known in the city as a seductive, cheerful woman.† This was neither the first nor the last of the elder Ernesto's affairs; as Carmen Córdova, Che's cousin, recalls, "Everyone knew he was a ladies' man; Celia knew."[21] Raquel's mother, an actress of some talent, had moved to Córdoba with her daughter for health reasons. The daughter's liaison with Ernesto senior began during the war.[22] Despite the widely publicized nature of the affair ("it was a scandal in Córdoba"[23]), Ernesto senior once brought Raquel home for a visit, which can hardly have pleased Che and his mother. The entire relationship marked Che so strongly that when his girlfriend "Chichina" Ferreyra happened to recall the woman's name a few years later, he snapped, "Never mention that name in my presence."‡

The Guevaras' marital difficulties were becoming more serious and now affected five children, three of them nearly adult. As described by Betty Feigín, a contemporary of Guevara's and the wife of Gustavo Roca, a lawyer from Córdoba who became a friend of Che's later in life,

> Family life was complicated. I remember when Juan Martín, the smallest of Ernesto's brothers, was born and I went to see him. I remember the house where they lived, [in] such disorder. It gave an impression of poverty, neglect. Celia was a very intelligent woman, very attractive as a person, one could speak with her very easily, but one did not feel that things were going well. And then there were those things the kids talked about, that Ernesto was separated. There were many periods of great marital disagreement,

---

*Dolores Moyano Martín, "A Memoir of the Young Guevara: The Making of a Revolutionary," in *The New York Times Magazine,* August 18, 1968, p. 51. According to Moyano Martín, the story was told her by Jorge Ferrer, a boyhood friend of Guevara's.

† "Raquel Hevia was delightful. She was extremely attractive and Ernesto was enchanted by her." Betty Feigín, interview with the author, Córdoba, February 18, 1995.

‡ María del Carmen ("Chichina") Ferreyra, interview with the author, Córdoba, February 18, 1995. Dolores Moyano Martín confirms that Chichina told her about Ernesto's reaction years earlier. Dolores Moyano Martín, interview with the author, Washington, D.C., February 26, 1996.

with financial problems as well. They even lived poorly: all right from a sociocultural point of view, but with very serious economic limitations.*

Dolores Moyano Martín has her own theory about the Guevaras' home life during this time. In her loneliness, the adored and adoring mother may well have yielded to the temptation of casting her eldest son in a father's role, as she tried to raise the younger children in an atmosphere of chaos, financial hardship, and marital tension. The couple's estrangement and first separation—temporary, ambiguous, incomplete—did not actually occur until 1947 in Buenos Aires, though some place it earlier, in Córdoba.† The entire situation left a mark on Carmen Córdova, Che's young cousin: "It was as if Ernesto [senior] just left, because he decided to leave, but then he would return. It was not a full break for the couple, or as if the marriage had ended."[24] In any case, the process that led to these tensions—and worse ones—was already well underway. In 1943 the couple's final child, Juan Martín, was born in Córdoba. His relationship with Ernesto would be a crucial part of Che's adolescence and youth and, of course, of the life of the younger Guevara:

> I was a sort of brother-son; Ernesto was both my father and my brother. He would take me out for walks, carry me on his shoulders, play with me, and I saw him as my father.[25]

In regard to other domestic responsibilities—and obviously not just household chores—Celia was perhaps beginning to place unconscious but compelling demands on her oldest and favorite son. According to a cousin

---

*Feigín, interview. Che's father alludes to these "marital disagreements" in the following way: "The world press . . . threw itself into the fray with lies and inventions. Some 'commentators' have even asserted that my wife and I sat down to meals in our home with revolvers at our waists in order to settle any discussion with gunfire. But they have said nothing about how directly complementary we were to each other in everything concerning the struggle for political and social ideals." Guevara Lynch, *Mi hijo,* p. 105.

†Thus, in *The Black Beret: The Life and Meaning of Che Guevara* (New York: Ballantine, 1969), p. 27, Martin Resnick asserts: "In 1945, while Ernesto was still in high school, the Guevaras finally separated. Señor Guevara moved into a separate residence, but saw his wife and children daily." In contrast, Daniel James writes in *Che Guevara: A Biography* (New York: Stein and Day, 1969) that the separation took place when the family moved to Buenos Aires in 1947. Martin Ebon agrees, in *Che: The Making of a Legend* (New York: Basic Books, 1969), p. 15: the separation occurred in Buenos Aires in 1947. Lastly, Carlos María Gutiérrez, the best-informed of Che's abortive biographers—though his manuscript has never been published in its entirety—states that the separation occurred in 1950 (Luis Bruschstein and Carlos María Gutiérrez, *Los Hombres: Che Guevara, Página 12* (Buenos Aires, n.d.), p. 1. Needless to say, neither Che's father nor any official or unofficial source in Cuba mentions the couple's conflicts and distances. Apparently they wish to preserve the immaculateness, at all imaginable levels, of Ernesto Guevara's childhood—even his most tender years.

of Che's, he would always hand to his mother part of the wages he obtained from the many odd jobs he held during those years; "I had the impression he sort of replaced his father."[26] These demands were probably never verbalized or made explicit: the communication between mother and son had plenty of room for insinuation and double entendres. Perhaps in response, Che gradually drew away: not in his love for his family but in his physical presence. This might help explain the beginning of his travels and his perpetual movement.* It also partly clarifies his initial inclination to study engineering in Córdoba, though his parents and siblings had already left for Buenos Aires. The moment of his final leavetaking from them had not yet arrived, however. For several reasons, Ernesto changed his mind. He followed his family to the capital to study, but soon took off, overtaken by his aversion for immobility. As it turned out, he never really put down roots in Buenos Aires.

His encounter with María del Carmen ("Chichina") Ferreyra also dates from his time in high school, though the relationship would not really blossom until later, when Guevara was already studying medicine at the University of Buenos Aires. But Che's friends during that period were already converging with Chichina's: many of her cousins from the Roca and Moyano families were also close to the Guevaras, Granados, and other acquaintances. Convergence but not assimilation: Che was beginning to stand out from his friends. He dressed differently (in a careless, almost slovenly way), had contrasting tastes, and was by now far more cultivated. There also began to appear in some hidden niche of his psyche a glimmer of politicization, though still on a purely emotional level. It consisted in a certain sympathy and generosity toward those less fortunate than himself, and a willingness to fight by whatever means—but without knowing very well why or to what end. One of the most repeated anecdotes in Che's biography, which appears in almost every account, is that told by Alberto Granado concerning his own detention in Córdoba in 1943 for having attended a student antimilitary demonstration.[27] When Ernesto went to visit him at the police station, Granado suggested that he and other friends organize demonstrations with the secondary-school students. Che answered: "Dem-

---

*In a personal communication, Jorge Ferrer disagrees emphatically with the interpretation expressed to the author by Dolores Moyano Martín. "In none of our conversations did Ernesto ever mention or say anything about feeling pressured by Celia in any sense, or overwhelmed by the family's financial straits. Knowing Celia, I am convinced that she would never, under any circumstance, have burdened any of her children with her problems, much less with financial problems." It is worth recalling that the years mentioned by Moyano correspond to the Córdoba period, while Ferrer was closer to Che in Buenos Aires. Furthermore, she refers more to unconscious, less literal impulses. Ferrer seeks an explicitness that might never have existed, but whose absence does not invalidate Moyano Martín's more sophisticated analysis.

onstrate in order to have the shit beaten out of us? No way. I won't march if I'm not carrying a piece [a gun]." More than a portent of Che's revolutionary vocation, or even of any violent proclivities in him at age sixteen, the incident suggests an indeterminate combativeness and a certain idea of power relations: don't fight if you can't win. He would, repeatedly.

This incipient political awareness was marked by the influence of his parents, the intellectual atmosphere of Córdoba at the time, and Che's scant familiarity with politics. No one recalls any special interest in politics on his part, or his holding any clear stance*—though he already showed some signs of anti-Americanism, not untypical of "learned" Córdoba intellectuals at the time.† Che also had definite anti-Peronist feelings, but they derived more from the antiauthoritarian cycle of the war in Spain, the struggle against Nazism in Europe, and opposition to the rise of Perón by the traditional middle-class and intellectual left. Yet Ernesto seems to have been largely indifferent to the most important sociopolitical event of his lifetime thus far: the demonstrations of October 17, 1945, when the working class of Buenos Aires took to the streets to rescue Perón from his island prison, carrying him (physically and metaphorically) to the presidency of Argentina.

Ernesto completed his high school studies toward the end of 1946. He spent the summer working with the roads department of the province of Córdoba. Many factors induced him to study engineering in Córdoba, among them the fact that his family had already left for Buenos Aires, settling down in the house of Guevara Lynch's mother on Arenales Street. But in 1947 she fell ill, and Ernesto moved to the capital to help care for her. When Ana Lynch died, Ernesto made a far-reaching decision. He enrolled at the Faculty of Medicine of Buenos Aires, and went to stay with his parents on Araoz Street, which, however, was no longer quite the family home. As Roberto Guevara euphemistically expresses it, "Ernesto often went to a studio my old man had on Paraguay Street, number 2034, apartment A on the first floor."[28] Or, as one of their cousins—closer to Roberto than to Che by age and vocation—recalls: "Toward the end of Ernesto's years in Buenos Aires, their parents were practically separated; Ernesto's father rarely slept at home. While the rest of the family lived in Araoz Street, he had his archi-

---

*We know, thanks to the reproduction of several pages from his philosophy notebooks or "Philosophical Dictionary," that he began reading Marx and Engels in 1945, at age seventeen—at least the *Anti-Dühring,* the *Communist Manifesto,* and *The Civil War in France.* However, his annotations reveal that his reading was more philosophically oriented than political, though it doubtless also had a political dimension.

† Thus, the barman at the Sierras Hotel, which Ernesto senior and then his son and friends used to frequent, remembers that he never asked for Coca-Cola. If offered any, he would reject it vehemently and "become very upset." The precision of the barman's memory, however, leaves something to be desired. Francisco Fernández, interview with the author, Alta Gracia, February 17, 1995.

tect's office in Paraguay Street, where he stayed most of the time."[29] Ernesto lived in the house on Araoz Street until he left Argentina in 1953. Che thus arrived in Buenos Aires barely a year after Perón's enthronement; he would depart from his native country forever a year after Evita Perón died on February 26, 1952, as Peronism entered its prolonged twilight.

Chapter 2

Years of Love and Indifference in Buenos Aires: Medical School, Perón, and Chichina

T he Buenos Aires period was both formative in itself and a prelude to what awaited Che as a young man. It encompassed Che's first loves, travels, and the making of his failed profession, as well as a further glimmer of political awakening. And it took place in an exceptional context: the profound transformation of Argentina began in 1946, with the inauguration of Juan Domingo Perón as president of the Republic.

Three explanations are frequently given for Ernesto Guevara's decision to enroll at the Faculty of Medicine at the University of Buenos Aires. The first was the death of his grandmother Ana Lynch. Because her passing coincided with Ernesto's decision to become a physician, when he was already registered at the School of Engineering, this interpretation has many advocates.*

*The first is Ernesto's father, who directly associates Che's decision to study medicine with the death of his grandmother: "I remember what he said to me: 'Old man, I am changing professions. I will not continue with engineering and will devote myself to medicine.'" Ernesto Guevara Lynch, *Mi hijo el Che* (Madrid: Editorial Planeta, 1981), pp. 226, 247. Che's sister Celia also shares this opinion: "He saw that he could do nothing for her, because she was dying, and so he thought he should study medicine. . . . That is why he switched from engineering to medicine." Celia Guevara de la Serna, quoted in Adys Cupull and Froilán González, *Ernestito: Vivo y presente: Iconografía testimoniada de la infancia y*

25

Ernesto, grieving at the loss of his only living grandmother, with whom he had had a close and loving relationship, reacted like the impulsive and willful youth he had now become. To prevent others from dying of the same illness, he decided to seek a cure for what killed her (a stroke, according to Che's sister).* And the only way to do this was to study medicine.

The second explanation is Celia Guevara de la Serna's breast cancer.[†] According to the information made available to the author by Roberto Guevara, Che's younger brother, and by Roberto Nicholson, a cousin of the surgeon who operated on Celia, she underwent surgery the first time on September 12, 1945.[‡] A large portion of one breast was resected; it had been invaded by a malignant and "highly invasive" tumor. The operation was a success, and for the moment was devoid of any further consequences. The surgery took place, then, two years *before* Che's choice of medicine as a career, and was undoubtedly a decisive consideration. In October 1949 Che's mother complained of discomfort near the scars of the previous operation; in early 1950 she was operated on again; this time her entire breast

la juventud de Ernesto Che Guevara, 1928–1953 (Havana: Editora Política, 1989), p. 111. Other biographers who emphasize this connection include J. C. Cernadas Lamadrid and Ricardo Halac, who state: "The Guevara family had barely arrived in Buenos Aires when grandmother Lynch fell ill. Ernesto . . . was with her every day until her death. This experience seems to have been decisive: soon afterward, he decided to stay in the capital and begin studying medicine." J. C. Cernadas Lamadrid and Ricardo Halac, *Yo fui testigo: El "Che" Guevara* (Buenos Aires: Editorial Perfil, 1986), p. 20. Two Argentine admirers, Esteban Morales and Fabián Ríos, in their "Comandante Che Guevara" (*Cuadernos de América Latina,* October 1, 1968, p. 5), also attribute his switch to medicine to "a particular event: the death of the paternal grandmother."

*Celia Guevara de la Serna, interview in *Granma* (Havana), October 16, 1967. The father also gives the cause of death as a stroke, and not the cancer that several biographers have mentioned. Guevara Lynch, *Mi hijo,* p. 247.

† Advocates of this thesis include Andrew Sinclair: "His grandmother's death from cancer and his mother's struggle against the same disease influenced Che to become a doctor. He wanted to try to find a cure for this disease." Andrew Sinclair, *Che Guevara* (New York: Viking Press, 1970), p. 3. Several other biographers, whose works were published before Guevara Lynch's book *Mi hijo el Che,* mention the mother's illness as a factor in his decision to study medicine. Cf. Marvin Resnick, *The Black Beret: The Life and Meaning of Che Guevara* (New York: Ballantine Books, 1969); Daniel James, *Che Guevara: A Biography* (New York: Stein and Day, 1969); Martin Ebon, *Che: The Making of a Legend* (New York: Universe Books, 1969). A German biographer whose text contains numerous mistakes and several outright fantasies (see footnote, page 41) but also several interesting truths, links the mother's illness with Che's efforts to find a cure for cancer in a small home laboratory, using guinea pigs—but not with his decision to study medicine: "When his mother had to undergo an operation due to a cancerous lump in her breast, he set up an amateur laboratory and began doing experiments on guinea pigs, in the fond hope of unlocking the secret of this disease." Frederik Hetmann, *Yo tengo siete vidas* (Madrid: Lóguez Ediciones, 1977), p. 23.

‡ These facts were provided to the author by Roberto Guevara in the course of a conversation on August 22, 1996, in Buenos Aires. At his suggestion, several physicians directly involved in Celia's surgery were consulted. The researcher who helped the author on this matter was able to corroborate some of the facts with Che's surviving sister, Celia Guevara.

and her reproductive organs were removed: a highly aggressive, terribly traumatic procedure. Celia took much longer to recover from this surgery; she would die of cancer seventeen years later, possibly as a sequel to the initial tumor. One can guess the shattering impact on a boy so attached to his mother to learn that she had cancer, even if physicians described her condition as curable.* If Ernesto studied medicine to prevent others from dying like his grandmother, it is even more likely that he would do so to "avert" a relapse in his mother's health.†

In addition to the repression of information about Che's parents' estrangement, the official silence on Celia's sickness is the first of myriad attempts by the Cuban government and its partisans to rewrite the story of the hero's life. None of the official Cuban sources even mentions Celia's illness, much less its effects on her son's life, studies, or personality.‡ It would appear that revolutionary heroes cannot have embarrassing or painful episodes in their biographies. Perhaps one day it will become clear why Stalinism, in either its polar or its tropical version, acknowledges the existence only of villains or saints. It seems to have no room for ordinary human beings who go on to become extraordinary figures owing to the confluence of their talents and their historical context.

Lastly, there is the thesis that Ernesto studied medicine basically in quest of relief for his own respiratory ailment. Aside from the weight of the testimony supporting this interpretation, it is intrinsically convincing.** Che's

---

* "My wife Celia was treated with radiotherapy to eradicate a malignant tumor. One day she told me she had detected a lump in her breast. . . . The doctors decided to operate immediately. . . . Ernesto . . . was already in the second year [of medicine] . . . [and] when he found out that his mother was being taken into the operating room and that the results were uncertain, he lost his calm. Ernesto followed his mother's treatment step by step." Guevara Lynch, *Mi hijo,* p. 247.

† Jorge Ferrer, a close friend of Ernesto's during those years, disputes this explanation. He states in a written communication that "When Celia's tumor was detected, Ernesto was already in his second year of medicine." Jorge Ferrer, letter to the author, March 11, 1996. The confusion may arise from the likelihood that Celia's illness was largely kept a secret. Dolores Moyano Martín, for instance, believed that her repeated retreats to her bedroom were due to depression, not cancer. Dolores Moyano Martín, interview with the author, Washington, D.C., February 26, 1996.

‡ The mother's illness is not mentioned in any of the Cuban works devoted to this subject: neither the *Atlas biográfico;* nor Adys Cupull and Froilán González in their two works *Un hombre bravo* (Havana: Editorial Capitán San Luis, 1994) and *Ernestito;* nor Haroldo Martínez U. and Hugo Martínez U. in their *Che: Antecedentes biográficos del Comandante Ernesto Che Guevara* (Santiago, 1968: this is a Chilean work based on Cuban sources); nor a more recent work published with the support of Cuban sources, Jean Cormier with Alberto Granado and Hilda Guevara, *Che Guevara* (Paris: Editions du Rocher, 1995).

** The great popularizer of Che's works in the United States, John Gerassi, mentions this explanation: "But Che decided to become an allergist, in part because he wanted to understand and cure his own allergy." John Gerassi, Introduction, in *Venceremos! The Speeches and Writings of Che Guevara* (New York: Clarion Books, 1968), p. 6. This is also

medical specialization was precisely in allergies, as was his research, under Dr. Salvador Pisani at the Faculty of Medicine.* Even during the couple of years he spent in Mexico before embarking on the expedition to Cuba, Che's scant medical research focused on problems in allergology and dermatology.†

Thus, the young Che probably registered at the Faculty of Medicine for a wide variety of reasons, but all of them had to do with external circumstances rather than with any inherent interest. Ernesto chose medicine as a means to an end—to help people, to help his mother, to help himself—not because of any innate passion or early vocation. One should certainly not seek any ideological motivation. As Che would acknowledge years later:

> When I started out to be a doctor, when I began to study medicine, most of the ideas I now have as a revolutionary were absent from the storehouse of my ideals. I wanted to succeed, like everybody; I dreamed of being a famous researcher . . . but at that time it was a personal victory.[1]

His rapid disenchantment with medicine was not unrelated to this tangle of external, indirect, and somewhat confusing reasons.‡ In contrast with the official story circulated years later—and consecrated by Che himself in an account dating from his time in the Sierra Maestra—he lost interest in medicine long before his first exposure to enemy fire.** In this version, the still

the opinion of one of Che's closest college friends, Carlos ("Calica") Ferrer, with whom he would undertake his final departure from Argentina, in 1953: "I think that what most drove Che to study medicine was his own asthma." Carlos Ferrer, telephone interview with the author, Buenos Aires, August 23, 1996. And his friend and classmate Jorge Ferrer offers further corroboration: "Ernesto focused his interest and efforts on allergic diseases . . . working and doing research on asthma." Jorge Ferrer, written communication to the author, March 11, 1996.

*Che's only research project published in those years, written in collaboration with Dr. Pisani, "Sensibilización de cobayos a pólenes por inyección de extracto de naranjo" (Sensitization to Pollen in Guinea Pigs via Injections of Orange Extract), appeared in the journal *Allergy*. Cited in Guevara Lynch, *Mi hijo*, p. 253.

† See, for instance, his only medical publication outside of Argentina, which appeared in the *Revista Interamericana de Alergología* (Mexico City), vol. 2, no. 4, May 1955. It is a study of the dietary origins of certain allergic reactions. Cf. Marta Rojas, "Ernesto, Médico en México," in *Testimonios sobre el Che* (Havana: Editorial Pablo de la Torriente, 1990), p. 111.

‡ The nature of higher education in Argentina may also have played a role. As Jorge Ferrer points out, "Ernesto was fed up with the encyclopedic and often even irrational teaching of medicine in Buenos Aires." Jorge Ferrer, communication to the author.

**This text was "originally" immortalized in the deplorable film *Che* starring Omar Sharif and Jack Palance, but it is still quoted by researchers of all sorts: "This was perhaps the first time I had to face in practical terms the dilemma of my dedication to medicine or my duty as a revolutionary soldier. I had before me a bag full of medicines and a box of bullets; they were too heavy to carry both. I took the box of bullets, leaving the bag. . . ." Ernesto Che Guevara, "Pasajes de la guerra revolucionaria," in *Escritos y discursos*, vol. 2, (Havana: Editorial de Ciencias Sociales, 1977), p. 11.

beardless guerrilla fighter made his choice between medicine and revolution during the first combat after the *Granma*'s landing in Alegría de Pío. Forced to decide between carrying a box of munitions and a first-aid kit, he opted for the munitions. But already in 1952, after four years of medical studies but before completing his degree, he was writing to his girlfriend, Chichina Ferreyra, that he had no intention of being "trapped in the ridiculous medical profession."* And his friends recall that as a medical student, he did not really achieve good grades. He liked some subjects better than others, and he studied more for them, but rarely worked hard on any courses except research, "which he had a feeling for."[2]

Indeed, Che would never be a practicing physician in the way one is, for instance, a courtroom lawyer. Almost from the beginning of his university studies, he leaned toward clinical research. In Mexico, the only country in which he even sporadically practiced his profession, he also focused on allergies. His grades in the different areas of study reflect this inclination: the few "with distinction" marks he received (in four out of thirty subjects), along with eight "good" marks and eighteen "passing" ones,[3] and his failing grades, acknowledged without much shame to Chichina, in neurology and surgical technique.[4] As a fellow student would later comment, "I don't think he attended regularly; rather, he presented many free subjects" (that is, he did not attend classes but instead passed exams at the end of each term).†

Certainly, Guevara reflected upon various aspects of the medical profession, ranging from the treatment of stigmatized patients—lepers in Argentina and then Peru—to socialized medicine. Alberto Granado relates a visit to the San Francisco del Chañar leper colony, during which Che repeatedly insisted on the need for a more humane approach to patients, and especially "on the importance for the lepers' psyches of the friendly way in which we treated them."[5] Granado also describes how, shortly before they left on their trip through South America, they went to the fashionable beach resort at Miramar. A heated discussion arose among the friends of Chichina Ferreyra, Ernesto, and Granado regarding the measures adopted by the British

---

*Letter from Ernesto Guevara de la Serna to Chichina Ferreyra, February 11, 1952, dated from Bariloche. The letters from Che that she did not burn in an attack of amorous rage were given to her cousin, Dolores Moyano Martín, in 1968, to be used but not quoted, in her previously cited *New York Times Magazine* article ("A Memoir of the Young Guevara: The Making of a Revolutionary," August 18, 1968). Moyano Martín subsequently made them available to me, and Chichina Ferreyra authorized their use and citation. They are typed (transcribed by Chichina from almost illegible originals) with her annotated explanations, and are as yet unpublished. I will quote from them extensively.

† Ricardo Campos, quoted in Claudia Korol, *El Che y los argentinos* (Buenos Aires: Ediciones Dialéctica, 1988), p. 70. Or in the words of Che's cousin, Fernando Córdova Itúrburu, "He went to the university just to pass his courses. He did so just barely." Fernando Córdova Itúrburu, interview with the author, Buenos Aires, August 23, 1996.

Labour government of Clement Attlee, particularly the socialization of medicine. The arrogant and abrasive young Ernesto took the floor for almost an hour, defending the abolition of commercial medicine and arguing against inequality in the distribution of doctors between cities and countryside, and the isolation of rural practitioners. Needless to say, he shocked most of his interlocutors.[6]

During these university years in Buenos Aires, Ernesto's life and personality continued to be as multifaceted as ever. Whereas his studies had previously been combined with sports, reading, and his illness, now he spread his time even more thinly. He added new pastimes, girlfriends, and trips, a more diligent study of philosophy, and his job. He hitchhiked constantly back to Córdoba—a seventy-two-hour trek—to visit his *novia* (fiancée) and friends. He also continued to play rugby at the Atalaya Rugby Club of San Isidro and, if we believe his acquaintances, a great deal of golf. He began working as an employee in the supplies section of the city government, where he continued to take notes for a projected philosophical dictionary or notebook he had begun earlier. Finally, he was at least somewhat involved in the turbulent political events which shook Argentina during that period.

Perhaps the first time Che's path crossed that of Perón was when he turned eighteen, in 1946, and had to register for compulsory military service. His asthma should have been enough to exempt him from the draft; in any case, rather than spending two years in the army, both for academic and ideological reasons the young man was quite happy to be deferred until he concluded his studies.

The army was the Peronist stronghold *par excellence*. The workers had not yet achieved their great conquests, nor had the spectacular—though corporativist—strengthening of the labor movement yet occurred, as it would in the golden age of Peronism. For a young man from an anti-Peronist family, as well as for an intellectually alert university student, the very idea of military service was anathema. Perhaps the best way to approach the crucial topic of Che Guevara's "a-Peronism" (as it might be called) during his youth, and the convoluted debate over his anti- or pro-Peronism, is to quote the strange account that Perón himself provided, twenty-five years later, about Ernesto's failure to fulfill his military service:

> They say that Che was among those who opposed us. This is not true. Che was a man close to our positions. His story is quite simple: he had broken the military-service law. If he fell into the hands of the police, he would be pressed into service for four years in the Navy or two years in the Army. When they were about to catch him, we ourselves tipped him off. He bought a motorcycle and went to Chile. Che was a revolutionary, like us. The one who was not with us was the mother. The mother was the one responsible

for everything that happened to the poor guy. Che did not leave the country because we were after him.*

The general was obviously not the only person who has attempted to attribute a posthumous Peronism to Che Guevara in his youth; so have his father and several Cuban compilers of anecdotes and chronologies. All these efforts, however, come up against the same inescapable obstacle. There are no traces of any position or even interest on Che's part regarding political and social events in his country at that time.[†]

In fact, Che was neither pro- nor anti-Peronist. Rather, the entire subject seemed to be a matter of indifference to him. In the letters which survived Chichina's enraged burning of most of their correspondence, there are few references to Perón, and comments on current events are notoriously absent. Che mentions him once, saying only, "A narrow margin of victory is not convincing to me; in this I am like Perón."[‡] Another time, shortly after the romance between the two aristocratic offspring began, he mentions to her, in reference to a canceled trip together to Paris, that he "prefers Peronists to monks."[7] The general's biographers would probably dispute the first statement: there is no evidence that Perón moved only when he was certain of the outcome, or that his margins of victory were as broad as was assumed by the demanding, but apparently frustrated, suitor.

Che's parents were viscerally anti-Peronist. Ernesto himself, like most students, was strongly opposed to the ideological, academic, and authoritarian stances of the new regime. Even before the advent of Perón, the students had adopted a class-oriented slogan: "Yes to books, no to *alpargatas* [rope-soled shoes worn by the lower classes]!" For many members of the intelligentsia, the victory of the general with oily hair on February 12, 1946,

*Quoted in Tomás Eloy Martínez, *Las Memorias del General* (Buenos Aires: Editorial Planeta, 1996), p 53. Martínez makes the following statement by Perón: "In a questionnaire which I sent Perón in 1970, I asked him to clarify this point. How could he, as President of the Republic and as a General, have protected a deserter from military service? It seemed odd to me and I pointed it out in my letter. Perón did not answer the question. Using ink, he crossed out from the *Memorias* draft the reference to Che. The account survived on tape, however, and his words were transcribed from there." Needless to say, Perón's statement has neither head nor tail: the dates do not coincide, and the sequence of events is completely distorted.

[†] In recent times, interviews and testimony have appeared in Argentina to the effect that the young Ernesto attended the founding moment of Peronism, the monster demonstration of October 17, 1945, that propelled the general to power. Roberto Guevara has categorically stated to a researcher assisting the author that his brother was in Córdoba that day, a day not easy to forget for an anti-Peronist family like Che's.

[‡] Ernesto Guevara de la Serna, letter to Chichina Ferreyra, December 5, 1951. Ernesto refers to his possible reaction to "our first copulation," which has evidently not been consummated, and his wish that Chichina's commitment were greater. The narrowness of his victory refers to Chichina's unwillingness to carry their relationship further.

recalled the rise of Hitler or Mussolini. The entire Argentine left united to support Perón's principal opponent, the Democratic Union candidate José P. Tamborini. The latter also received support from the United States Embassy and a large part of the Argentine oligarchy.

The university, especially, became a stronghold for anti-Peronism, mainly due to the regime's growing authoritarianism and anti-intellectualism. The left was devastated by Peronism: never again would the Socialist and Communist parties regain the working-class base—small, but real—that they had consolidated before and during the Depression. Certainly, the emergence of working and previously marginalized masses was not the only factor that alienated intellectuals and the traditional middle class. The main reason was that they identified their opposition to rightist nationalism with the struggle against Franco, the Nazis, fascism, and local authoritarianism.

Conversely, Peronism inspired great sympathy among workers and large parts of the industrial business sector owing to its promotion of social demands on the one hand, and its economic nationalism on the other. This led to a severe polarization of public opinion. The regime had the strong support of nationalists, encouraged by the expropriation of the British-owned railroads, and of Evita Perón's *descamisados* ("shirtless ones"), organized in the General Confederation of Workers. Thanks to reforms that were both symbolic and substantive—minimum wage, pensions system, women's suffrage, social security, paid holidays—the government was highly popular with workers. Thus its strength and the lasting, often implausible memories it left in millions of Argentines.

As long as the postwar export boom continued to generate revenue, most social demands could be satisfied without lashing out at all power groups at once. The virtual schism between the country's intelligentsia and the industrial working class, between the left and its supposed mass base, between the middle class and the neediest sectors of society, would govern the fate of Argentina for the next half-century. The surprising thing about Ernesto Guevara's passage through this period is not his presumed anti-Peronism. Everything impelled him in that direction. Nor would historians be disconcerted if he had reacted against his family, opting for Peronism simply out of rebelliousness, or because of his empathy for the poor. This would have coincided with his character and growing sensitivity. What is striking is his apparent lack of interest, either for or against Peronism, in the most exciting events of his country's modern history.*

---

*Though many biographers have noted this, only a recent one (with little sympathy for Che) has emphasized it: "I am surprised and disconcerted by the political indifference of somebody like Che Guevara at a time like that. It is an incongruous detail in a life marked by congruity." Roberto Luque Escalona, *El mejor de todos: biografía no autorizada del Che Guevara* (Miami: Ediciones Universales, 1994), p. 54.

As a critical biographer has aptly stated:

> An exhaustive search of all the assorted records of groups active at that time has not turned up Guevara's name as a member of any student organization, nor of the official center [i.e., the Medical Students Center, which hewed to official guidelines from the time of its infiltration by the military regime during the thirties].[8]

In dozens of letters to his parents beginning with his first trip in early 1952 and until 1955, when he expresses his reaction to the fall of Perón; in the diary covering his travels through South America; and in accounts collected by Cuban or Argentine researchers from friends, family, and fellow university students, there is no comment of any sort regarding these moments in history.[9] There are no negative or positive views either concerning current events—the Peronist reforms, women's suffrage, the rise of Evita, the general's reelection, the death of Evita—or more abstract political processes. Only several years later, in a letter sent his mother from Mexico in 1955, does he ask for information: "Send me all the news you can, as we are completely misinformed here since newspapers cover only Perón's problems with the clergy and we know nothing about the real situation."[10]

As his sister Ana María said, in relation to Peronism: "He did not take sides one way or the other. He sort of stayed on the sidelines."[11] His membership in the University Federation of Buenos Aires (FUBA) was more administrative than political. Che was not a student activist: "Ernesto's political participation was circumstantial; he was not a militant, though he shared the FUBA's ideology."[12] And the same applies to his exchanges with friends, girlfriends, and others. Politics in general, and Peronism in particular, were simply not topics of conversation for him: "At least with me, he never talked politics."[13]

This attitude is completely at odds with the image often provided of Che Guevara's youth, stemming from an effort to "salvage" him for Peronism. The rescue operation has relied mainly on a letter Che wrote from Mexico in 1955, when a military coup toppled Perón and sent him into exile for almost twenty years. Che's father himself indulges in this rewriting of history, claiming that his son was no anti-Peronist militant. When he was a boy, the father argues, he adopted the stance as a game, but when he was twenty-six and had acquired greater political maturity, Guevara Lynch claims that his son did not hesitate to support the Peronist working masses against the "military" coup.[14]

Indeed, by the time Che was in Mexico, ten years after the rise of Perón and long after Perón's moments of greatest strength and popularity, his moderate distaste for the regime had evolved into a more politicized rejection of the coup d'état that ended the supposed idyll of the *descamisados*. In a 1955 letter to Tita Infante, a friend from the Faculty of Medicine, Guevara outlines his contradictory reflections on the fall of Perón:

> With all due respect to Arbenz [the reformist president of Guatemala, recently overthrown in a CIA-sponsored coup], who was totally different from Perón from an ideological viewpoint, the fall of the Argentine government is following in the footsteps of Guatemala in a strangely faithful way, and you will see how the complete handing over of the country, and [making a] political and diplomatic break with the popular democracies, will be a sad but familiar corollary.[15]

A convoluted and contradictory commentary, to say the least. It posits both a parallelism between Perón and Arbenz and an ideological and personal contrast. As became clear in later years, the Guatemalan phase of Che's political and ideological thinking was the beginning of his anti-imperialism (which would be permanent), and of his "pure" Communist phase (which would last until his first travels through Eastern Europe and the Soviet Union in the early sixties). The importance Che attributes to this "break" with the "popular democracies" already points to the direction his growing politicization would take.

This brief comment on the overthrow of Perón reveals neither a marked interest in nor a particularly profound analysis of events. There are few significant similarities between the military *pronunciamientos* that respectively toppled Arbenz and Perón. The latter's nationalist period had already come to an end. And if the Guatemalan masses did not defend the Arbenz government because nobody gave them the weapons to do so (a view questioned by some, but ultimately adopted by Che), the Argentine people did not even try to fight for a regime that had already abandoned them. Finally, Che's allusion to a "strange" parallelism between both covertly organized coups, based upon a supposed United States involvement, poses several problems. Though Washington's participation in the overthrow of Arbenz has been amply documented, the same cannot be said of Argentina's "Liberating Revolution" of 1955.

In the previously quoted letter to Celia, Ernesto does indeed take a clearer position with regard to the recently toppled regime. He reiterates several arguments from the letter to Tita, though more forcefully—perhaps because he is addressing his mother. He mentions to her, with some indignation, that he followed "the fate of the Peronist government with some anxiety, naturally,"[16] and that "the fall of Perón embittered me profoundly, not for his sake but because of its meaning for all of Latin America."[17] He writes pointedly to his mother, an impassioned anti-Peronist, "you must be glad . . . you'll be able to say whatever you please, with the absolute impunity granted you as a member of the ruling class."[18] In contrast, he confesses almost timidly to his aunt Beatriz, "I don't really know what will happen, but I was *somewhat* affected by the fall of Perón."[19]

Che's later comments about Perón and his misadventures cannot anachronistically be projected into the past. Furthermore, they are not particularly clear opinions; and they have strong emotional overtones. They certainly do not contradict the indisputable fact that the young university student was politically indifferent during Perón's stellar years in power.

We can only speculate as to Guevara's "a-Peronism" during his youth. Obviously, his bond with his parents—especially Celia, whose animosity toward the populist regime was far more pronounced than that of her husband—played a crucial role. It is possible that his reluctance or incapacity to coexist with conflicting emotions or viewpoints was also critical in Che's aloofness from university politics.

For a youth whose social awareness was growing exponentially, to side with the white, oligarchical Catholic elites against the uprisings of the disadvantaged *morocho* multitudes would have been an aberration. To find himself on the same side of the barricades as his ranch-owning cousins and uncles, as "people like you who are hoping for the dawn of a new day" (as he reproached his mother at the height of the *pronunciamiento*),[20] would have been a terrible blow to his ego, his cult of eccentricity, and his passion for social justice. Someone like Che—intent on knowing his country in all its vastness, in daily contact with the poverty and marginalization evident in public health and medicine, at once affronted and fascinated by the opulence and rank aristocracy of Chichina's family and friends—could not help but see the obvious: "the social revolution that was Peronism."[21] In the words of the fiercely anti-Peronist historian Tulio Halperín Donghi, "Under the aegis of the Peronist regime, relations among social groups were suddenly redefined and to see this, it sufficed merely to walk the streets or take the tram."[22] Che was, precisely, a person who walked the streets and took the tram.

But breaking with Celia and the entire family in the midst of a highly polarized situation was equally unacceptable. Even more so when his mother was laboring under an uncertain prognosis, estranged from Guevara Lynch, and burdened by the financial hardship of raising four children, without any great inclination for the task. A quarrel with her was inconceivable for Che. But any hint of sympathy for Peronism would have implied a break: his mother's passionate opinions, and the conflicts smoldering within society, allowed for no compromise solutions. The only way to reconcile Che's love for his mother with his social and political sensibilities was to take refuge in his studies* and, increasingly, to travel. The only exit was flight, whether in unexpected, banal, or heroic ways, now and for the rest of his life.

The recurrent trips he began at such an early age were largely motivated by his insatiable curiosity about and fascination with anything that was different, strange, alien, and mysterious. The webs of contradictions that enveloped him also contributed—chiefly, his mother's uncertain health and his parents' on-again, off-again marriage. The father spent nights more frequently at his study on Paraguay Street, but would return often, sometimes daily, to the family home at Araoz for lunch with the children. Only later did he meet his second wife, Ana María Erra, a teacher who performed secretarial tasks for the architect. During this period in Buenos Aires, Che could easily have referred to the ambiguity and irresolution of his parents' bond in the same way he would describe his relationship with Fidel Castro fifteen years later: "neither marriage nor divorce." A brief text of his that remained unpublished until 1992, "Anguish," reflects the young man's state of mind in those difficult years. It was part of one of his first travel journals, written as he steamed through the Caribbean; the habit of writing them would accompany him to his death:

> But this time the sea is my salvation as the hours and days go by; anguish bites me, takes me by the throat, by the chest, strikes my stomach, grips my gut. I no longer like the dawn, I don't want to know where the wind blows from, nor the height of the waves; my nerves rattle, my sight clouds over, my disposition sours.[23]

His friends of the opposite sex grasped his uneasiness and ill-defined yearning for a different life. In the words of Tita Infante, "Ernesto knew that he would find there [at the university] very little of what he sought."[24] Or, as Chichina expressed it:

> I think he saw me as a person who was going to be a burden in his life. As if I were a obstacle to the life he wanted, the adventurer's life. He saw himself as trapped, in a way, and probably wanted to free himself from it all. To be free, to leave, and I must have been an obstacle at that moment. I don't know where he wanted to go. He wanted to travel, explore the world, look around.[25]

*An acquaintance of that time, Ricardo Campos, describes him as follows: "He would spend twelve or fourteen hours studying in the library, alone. One would see him only at moments . . . he would disappear for long periods and then reappear." Korol, *El Che,* p. 72.

The same impulses and passions as with his parents and Perón config-
ured his relationships with women. Five years passed between his youth and
early adulthood, culminating in his relationship with Chichina Ferreyra, his
only known lasting love relationship before his Guatemala meeting with
Hilda Gadea, whom he would marry in Mexico. There were plenty of brief
romances, however. According to his brother, "he always had a girlfriend
around. He was as strong as any of us, but he probably lived his amorous
adventures more intensely,"[26] and his cousin Fernando Córdova recalls how
the doctor-to-be could not keep his hands off the women around him at the
time: "he was after the whole world."[27] He was good-looking, sure of himself, and, according to his friends, fairly forward with women. He was "fun,
the most fun of the group."[28] There were possibly a few passions between
1947 and 1950; the one supposedly with Carmen Córdova de la Serna, *la
Negrita,* a first cousin on his mother's side, who had fallen in love with
Ernesto during their childhood in Córdoba, never went anywhere, though
the affection was mutual.* There may also have been a relationship with a
fellow student who was in any case a close friend, Tita Infante, a constant
correspondent of Che's until the sixties. She died some time after Che's execution in Bolivia.

According to Guevara's younger sister, Tita Infante was "very much in
love with him,"[29] though she did not know "the degree of intimacy in their
relationship."[30] Neither Che's father nor Tita Infante's brother ever dared to
say publicly that the bond between them was anything other than friendly,
but this may be due to the same kind of puritanical discretion that also surrounded the separation between Che's parents. What is known is that Tita
Infante was a member of the Communist Youth and a fellow student of
Che's at the Faculty of Medicine. They addressed each other with the formal "usted," at least in their letters. It is also clear from surviving descriptions and photographs that she had a strong, if homely, personality. She was
a couple of years older than Che, and when they met in 1948, politics clearly
played a central role in their relationship, in contrast to Che's other liaisons
at the time.

The published correspondence between them contains almost no affectionate words or phrases. Che's epistolary tone, over and beyond the use
of "usted," contrasts strongly with that of his letters to Chichina Ferreyra.
In addition, the fact that Che repeatedly asks Tita to do things for him
suggests a bond that, while tender and trustful, has a practical tinge to

---

*"Fernando Barral told Che after several years in Cuba: Did you know I was in love
with your cousin? And Che replied, I was too." Carmen Córdova de la Serna, interview
with the author, Buenos Aires, August 21, 1996.

it.* Everything indicates that their connection never went beyond a platonic friendship. Those of Che's friends who still recall his way of relating the delights and torments of his love affair with Chichina do not remember him ever speaking of Tita Infante in the same terms. Che's correspondence with his faraway friend represents an invaluable record of the young expatriate's political journey, but it cannot be read as love letters, revealing the passions or growing pains of a young man whose inner torments are just beginning to take shape.

Conversely, the importance of Ernesto Guevara's relationship with María del Carmen Ferreyra is justified not only by the many references to it but also by the fact that his liaison with Chichina is the only one of Che's love affairs on which his own writings are available today. Ernesto and Chichina had met previously, but their romance did not blossom until a night in early October 1950 in Córdoba, at the wedding of Carmen Aguilar.[31] In Chichina's words, she was "completely enraptured"[32]:

> I saw him in that house, he was coming down the stairs and I was thunderstruck. He had an impact on me, a tremendous impact, this man was coming down the stairs and then we started talking and we spent the whole night talking about books.[33]

For Ernesto it was also love at first sight, if we are to judge by the letter he wrote Chichina a few days later from Buenos Aires. She was then, and remains now, a remarkably attractive and captivating woman: several years younger than he, a teenager really, thin and fair, who very nearly lost control of her aristocratic passion in her encounters with the unkempt but irresistible student. The letter begins with a verse both hesitant and obvious in its intent: "For those green eyes, whose paradoxical light announces to me the danger of losing myself in them."[34] There was indeed danger, but also light and rapture. According to Chichina, Guevara wrote her several times in Malagueño during the ensuing months. Then, "early in the following year, he arrived and proposed that we be *novios* [a relationship more formal than

---

*For instance: "I would very much like to have news of you from the city. . . . And now Tita here comes the homework section: I am including the address of a Peruvian doctor . . . he is interested in Pío del Río Ortega's classification of the nervous system. I think your friend made a change in it, and I would like you to obtain it; if this is not possible, do the following: call 719925, which is the house number of my great friend Jorge Ferrer, and tell him to look for this classification at home. . . . If this doesn't work out, for any reason, you can call my brother Roberto at 722700 and ask him to send the book as soon as possible. . . . Well Tita, of course I am leaving unsaid many of the things I would have liked to talk about with you." Ernesto Guevara de la Serna, letter to Tita Infante, Lima, May 6, 1952, quoted in Adys Cupull and Froilán González, *Cálida presencia: Cartas de Ernesto Guevara de la Serna a Tita Infante* (Santiago de Cuba: Editorial Oriente, 1995), pp. 27–28.

going steady, but less so than an engagement]," which Chichina tremblingly accepted and which led to the "first fleeting kiss."[35] From then on, through 1951, Ernesto's pilgrimages to Malagueño became more frequent—not as regular as Chichina would have liked, but with a growing involvement on Che's part. The courtship was interrupted for a short time due to Ernesto's stint as a nurse in the Argentine merchant marine; he had originally meant to travel to Europe ("because Europe attracts me enormously").[36]

By the end of that year, the long-distance suitor was forced to acknowledge that he was deeply in love with Chichina, but that love was countered by his thirst for travel and freedom. He would soon take off for the first of his trips abroad, across Latin America with his friend Alberto Granado. It is not entirely clear from the correspondence or Chichina's memories whether Ernesto left because the relationship did not fulfill his expectations, or if he merely presented the fait accompli of his departure as a consequence of problems in the relationship, while actually undertaking his "voyage with no return"[37] for very different, unrelated reasons. Separating the two motives is difficult, not least because Che's letter of farewell begins with a protest over Chichina's flirtation with somebody else.

On the one hand Che admits to his girlfriend,

> I know how I love you and how much I love you, but I cannot sacrifice my inner freedom for you; it means sacrificing myself, and I am the most important thing in the world, as I have already told you.[38]

Obviously, the young man already had an elevated conception of himself and the destiny he was embarking on; and he saw his girlfriend as an obstacle on his path. But his grievance was abstract: the separation was due to Che's own personality, not to the relationship itself. To some extent, we are faced with a *Le Cid,* Corneille-type dilemma, slightly presumptuous and naively romantic. When fate and love come into conflict, the former must always win; for love will fade if it rests upon indignity or abdication. Rodrigo would not be worthy of Ximena's love if he did not first avenge her father's affront to his father's honor.

On the other hand, Ernesto immediately proceeded to beleaguer the object of his desire with a radically different set of demands, now passionate and uninhibited, from which the idea of his own destiny has completely disappeared. Indeed, he passed shamelessly from one register to the other:

> Furthermore, a conquest based on my continual presence would eliminate a large part of my attraction to you. You would be the prey captured after a struggle. . . . Our first copulation would be a triumphal procession in honor of the victor, but there would always be the phantom of our union in and of itself, because it was the right or the "exotic" thing to do.[39]

The wide gap separating Che from Chichina might help solve the mystery. The light-mindedness of Chichina's circle, however cultivated it may have been, was legendary, while Ernesto's seriousness and devotion to reading and study were increasing with each month. The gaping difference was obviously part of their attraction; the girl's family was, by Córdoba standards, fabulously wealthy, while Che's déclassé status and his economic straits were common knowledge in the community. Nothing in the young Guevara's dress, habits, strut, or friendships could account for the bond between the two young people, unless it was the passionate allure exerted by Chichina's radical contrasts with Che's own self-image. Chichina's love for him would prove short-lived. Little in her later life would rival that early infatuation. In contrast, Che's attachment was only the beginning of a long journey, from Malagueño to La Higuera: he would always be drawn to the strange and the different.

Chichina's description of her boyfriend's constant provocations reinforces the view that theirs was an attraction of opposites. Che repeatedly alienated his *novia*'s family and friends, deliberately and even maliciously. Obviously, he did not dress in a sloppy, distasteful way merely to provoke others or call attention to himself. But, lacking the resources* to compete with the elegance of Chichina's other suitors or her friends and cousins, he also made a virtue of necessity and proudly wore clothes that would shame or even enrage his refined and gracious companion. In her words,

> It was not out of malice, but there were things that irritated me. I remember one time in Miramar, I was very irritated when we went to the casino. I don't know how they arranged it, but Granado was very well dressed, and Ernesto was more or less dressed, I think. In the beginning it didn't bother me, but this time it did. A friend, or I myself, lent him a dress jacket, and then I think there was an admission fee, and he did something so as not to pay, to get the three of us in without paying, and that led to us being insulted. Then we went to various places where he didn't get along with people, and when groups of people don't get along it's terrible. Our group in Miramar was not very chic or sophisticated, they were normal, ordinary people from the Buenos Aires bourgeoisie, and he hated that kind of people.[40]

Che's messy, slovenly appearance would prove permanent. The man whose personal charm, smile, and gestures captivated millions never cared about the way he dressed. His unpressed clothing, untied shoes, and un-

---

*Dolores Moyano Martín describes how the family's financial straits had worsened: the little Juan Martín slept in a box instead of a cradle, and on one occasion Ana María Guevara refused to come down to Moyano Martín's birthday party because she did not have any "presentable" shoes. Dolores Moyano Martín, interview with the author, Washington, D.C., February 26, 1996.

combed hair were a trademark from his early youth, and would be notorious until his death. Later, of course, they became a mere habit; but in the elegant circles frequented by Chichina and himself, they implied a certain defiance. Moreover, his provocations were not limited to his clothes. José González Aguilar recalls a scene characteristic not because of the topic at hand (Winston Churchill's attitude toward socialized medicine shortly after his return to power in 1950) but because of Che's attitude. In the course of an argument with Che during dinner at Malagueño, Chichina's father, Don Horacio Ferreyra, stood up from the table exclaiming, "I cannot tolerate this any longer!" Ernesto sat silently in his seat. Even his friend was outraged: "I looked at Ernesto thinking that we were the ones who should leave, but he simply grinned like a naughty child and started eating a lemon with deliberate little bites, peel and all."[41]

Che's eccentricity was destructive in other ways. The chasm separating him from Chichina, which so fascinated him, also doomed him to withdraw and eventually flee. To maintain and develop the relationship Che would have had to reconcile opposites, negotiate the families' hostility, and smooth over many rough edges.* The courtship would founder on the shoals of Che's travels; much the same would occur with his two marriages.

In early 1949, Guevara had already traveled through the northern part of his country on a sort of motorized bicycle that he himself had designed and built. His itinerary included the San Francisco de Chañar leper colony, where he had what was probably his first encounter with extreme suffering. He passed through Santiago del Estero, Tucumán, and Salta, where his glimpse of the bountiful, exuberant tropics fascinated him—as the exotic always would, throughout his life. The trip also allowed him to break with orthodox forms of tourism. He developed what we would now call the backpacker's approach to travel:

> I do not cultivate the same tastes as tourists . . . the Altar of the Fatherland, the cathedral . . . the gem of a pulpit and the miraculous little virgin . . . the Hall of the Revolution. . . . This is no way to learn about a people, its manner of living or interpretation of life; that is a luxurious cover-up; its soul is reflected in the hospital-bound sick, the prison inmates, the anxious pedestrian one talks with, watching the Rio Grande's turbulent flow at one's feet.[42]

*According to some accounts, Ernesto proposed either marriage or cohabitation, and in any case a trip together. Thus, Frederik Hetmann in *Yo tengo siete vidas,* pp. 24–26, constructs a fairly elaborate set of hypotheses, supposedly based upon letters exchanged by Ernesto and Chichina. In a communication to the author dated June 6, 1995, in Malagueño, Chichina denies both the existence of such letters and any proposals of marriage or cohabitation, as well as a series of allusions to her father made by Hetmann. Hetmann's source for the letters—the Uruguayan daily *El Diario* dated September 12, 1969—does not contain any such letters or references.

He returned to Buenos Aires at the end of the summer holidays to continue his medical studies, but became restless again by the end of the year.
He undertook a new voyage, this time for work. With the hyperbole he
would never relinquish, he noted in his travel journal how he was changing:
"I realize now that something in me has flowered some time ago: a hatred of
civilization."[43] Beginning in December 1950, he enrolled as a nurse for the
Ministry of Public Health in Argentina's merchant marine. His trips on
cargo ships and oil tankers would take him to Brazil, Trinidad, and Venezuela, and more often to Comodoro Rivadavia and southern Argentina. He
did not enjoy it very much: in a letter to his mother he complained that too
much time was spent on board, while there was not enough to visit the ports
of call.* But these voyages opened new horizons for him, confirming his
taste for everything new and foreign, as well as his boredom with the familiar. As he wrote to his aunt Beatriz, first from Porto Alegre and then
Trinidad:

> From this land of fair and passionate women I send you a loving, compas-
> sionate hug to Buenos Aires, which seems more and more boring to me. . . .
> After overcoming a thousand hardships, combating typhoons, fires, sirens
> with their melodious songs (here they are brown sirens), I am taking away
> as a souvenir of this marvelous island . . . a heart saturated with "beauties."[44]

Chichina had already had time to lament these repeated departures,
added to Che's unavoidable absences due to his studies in Buenos Aires. Just
weeks after they formally became *novios,* Ernesto announced to his beloved
that "My trip is a fact and I will probably leave in the first days of the
month, so we will see each other again when I return." As was to be
expected, Chichina did not take to the idea of her new fiancé's leaving at the
first opportunity: "You can imagine how sad I was after this."[45]

The faraway gleam of other realities was irresistible for Che. He adored
Chichina because he was a misfit in her milieu, and because she clashed
with his fantasies. But he was also fascinated by the tropics with their
mulatto and black exoticism, so starkly different from his white, middle-
class Buenos Aires. He was slowly becoming immersed in the vicissitudes of
human suffering, in contrast to his life of ease as an aristocratic university
student. Once again, he would take flight.

Though he hurt Chichina by casually insinuating that his trip through
Latin America with Granado would be one "with no return," at the same
time he promised to come back. His letters and the travel journal he kept

---

*"It was a comfortable trip, but he wasn't convinced; only four hours to unload oil on
an island, with fifteen days going and fifteen days coming." Quoted in Celia Serna de Guevara, interview with Julia Constenla, published in *Bohemia* (Havana), August 28, 1961.

from the beach resort of Miramar, where he said good-bye to Chichina, to Venezuela, suggest that distance, in his mind at least, did not cancel his bond with her. Just as he thought he would return to finish his studies, he imagined a future life with Chichina—with some skepticism and reservations, but without entirely rejecting the possibility. He named the puppy he gave her when he left Miramar Comeback (in English), indicating clearly enough under what flag he would sail in the months ahead. His return was not impossible, after all.*

As would happen so frequently in the years to come, his own thoughts about his destiny and future clashed with the wishes and decisions of others. Chichina finally broke off their formal relationship as *novios;* and, in a sense, his link with his country of origin was also sundered. Just one month after his departure from Miramar, Chichina made a heart-wrenching decision—under pressure from her mother, but her own nonetheless: "I had to write Ernestito a letter, practically forced by my mother. I remember shutting myself into the library at Chacabuco and crying my eyes out as I wrote it."[46] In the letter, she ended their relationship. Ernesto received her announcement, on the faraway lakes of Bariloche, as a wound to the heart: "I read and reread the incredible letter. Just like that, all the dreams of my return, linked to those eyes that saw me leave Miramar, were crumbling without any apparent reason . . . it was useless to insist."[47] Forty-five years later, Alberto Granado confided to Chichina that he had never seen Che so upset and consternated as when he received the fateful letter.[48] In his reply (the next-to-the-last letter he would ever write her), he verbalized a "reason" which he doubtless already knew, at least unconsciously. The pilgrim Ernesto Guevara described that unique moment in their lives as

the present in which we both live: one fluctuating between a superficial admiration and deeper links binding her to other worlds, the other caught between an affection which he believes profound and a thirst for adventure, for new knowledge, which invalidates that love.[49]

Thus did Che embark upon his long cycle of separations and farewells. From now on, his life would be a series of emotional, geographic, and political fractures. They explain his perpetual flight, first manifested on the beach at Miramar and then in the classrooms of Buenos Aires. Our man not only flees contradiction; his is a role in search of a tragedy.

---

*Chichina herself recalls that "when Ernesto left our relationship as *novios* was still solid, and I found it quite natural that he should leave." Chichina Ferreyra, letter to the author, March 7, 1996.

Chapter 3

First Blood:
Navigating Is Necessary,
Living Is Not

C he Guevara began his first trip abroad in early January 1952: five countries in almost eight months in the company of his friend from Córdoba, Alberto Granado—an extended spring break, in a way. He discovered a continent still unknown to him, the exoticism he craved, and a certain maturity, all in one sweep. This trip would represent something more than an initiation rite, and something less than a definitive break with his country, family, and profession. The journey was a sort of advance preview: the main feature would screen only a year later, after he kept his promise to Celia, his mother, to return and finish his studies before taking off again.

He departed from Córdoba, stopping briefly at Miramar at the peak of the summer high season to take his leave from Chichina. The week at the beach was idyllic, if we believe the lovelorn traveler's journal, the first of many he would write:

> It was all a continual honeymoon with that slightly bitter taste of an impending departure, stretching out day after day until reaching eight days.

Every day I like or love my other half even more. Our leavetaking was long, as it lasted two days and was close to ideal.*

Che's initial intention was to carry out the entire trip on a Norton motor-cycle baptized *La poderosa II* (the Powerful One II), a feat similar—though more ambitious—to the one he had accomplished in the northern provinces of Argentina. The itinerary involved crossing over into Chile through the southern part of the Andes, via the lakes region and San Carlos Bariloche, then Temuco and finally Santiago. Things did not go quite as planned. From the first approach to the mountain range, the Norton showed unmistakable signs of fatigue and a reluctance to push forward. After repeated mishaps and repairs, it had to be hauled onto a truck in the southern Chilean village of Los Angeles, and was finally abandoned in Santiago. So the trip on motorbike, immortalized in the *Motorcycle Diary,* did not really happen. Only a small part of the journey was done on the Norton.†

Thanks to the journal Che kept throughout his odyssey and the countless descriptions published by Granado, there is a wealth of accounts, memories, and notes from the two young explorers. Their adventures, ranging from Che's alcohol-induced attempt to seduce the wife of a Chilean mechanic in Lautaro, to the argonauts' brave defense against bandits, "tigers," and assorted evildoers roaming the Andean heights, tell a story of initiation and commencement, of awakening and freedom. The tales of adventure and tribulation that fill the pages of their diaries contain a central element of the later Guevara myth: the fulfillment of fantasy. The two young men did virtually everything they set out to do. They visited the ruins of Machu Picchu and the leper colonies of Peru. They watched the sun set on the banks of Lake Titicaca, rafted down the Amazon, crossed the Atacama desert at night, gazed upon the eternal snows of the Peruvian highlands. They talked with Communist miners in Chuquicamata and with ageless and

*Ernesto Guevara Lynch, *Mi hijo el Che* (Madrid: Ediciones Planeta, 1981), p. 280. Che's father quotes verbatim from his son's diary, reconstructed from notebooks found in the family home. Years later, Che's widow, Aleida March, transcribed the diaries and published them as *Notas de viaje.* For some reason, the passage quoted here (about that week in Miramar) does not appear in the version published by Aleida March. Either Che himself did not include it in his rewritten journal, or else his widow decided to discard it. Chichina recalls that José Aguilar, who lived for many years in Cuba after having known Che as a child, told her how annoyed Aleida was over Ernesto's comments in his diary regarding his Argentine sweetheart. Chichina Ferreyra, letter to the author, August 22, 1996.

† The motorcycle's breakdown was actually a blessing in disguise, as Alberto Granado noted: "There is no doubt that the trip would not have been as useful and beneficial as it was, as a personal experience, if the motorcycle had held out. . . . This gave us a chance to become familiar with the people. We worked, took on jobs to make money and continue traveling. Thus we hauled merchandise, carried sacks, worked as sailors, cops and doctors, busboys." Alberto Granado, interview with Aldo Medrón del Valle, *Granma* (Havana), October 16, 1967, p. 7.

enigmatic Indians on buses crawling along the Andean crests. Such a trip was the stuff of dreams for the youth of Che's world: the postwar, middle-class, college-educated Americas. It was a world of distances and adventure, and nearly half a century later it hasn't changed that much. It is no coincidence that Che's most popular works, thirty years after his death, are the two journals describing his travels in South America and Bolivia.[1] Somewhere in the psyche of the sixties and the nineties, Guevara's saga became a road book, or road movie: Jack Kerouac in the Amazon, Easy Rider on the Andes.

Che's text was transcribed from his notes "more than a year" after the actual experience.[2] He would follow this pattern until Bolivia, writing everything twice: a first draft during the actual event being described, and then a later revision. He would do the same in the Sierra Maestra, with "Pasajes de la guerra revolucionaria," and in the Congo, where he drafted a journal, still lost, which served as the basis for another text. Thus the anecdotes and reflections recorded by Che on his trip are neither spontaneous notes nor accurate memories. As documents, they are priceless. As sources, they must be scrutinized to correct for the stylistic care of an author fascinated by writing, the descriptive reelaborations of a potentially great narrator, and the shifts of emphasis onto other events or memories as they reappear. They are useful, but only if one does not lose their thread.

To judge by these accounts, Che's politicization had grown by leaps and bounds, but it fell far short of that of an aspiring revolutionary. The essential quality of Che's first political awakening in Buenos Aires persisted: he still had a moral (one might say youthful) vision of politics. His sensitivity to poverty, injustice, and arbitrariness weighed far more than culture or abstract knowledge. His approach remained naive and incomplete: indignation and common sense made up for serious deficiencies in analysis. The wrenching description he gives of an old asthmatic woman he met in a Valparaíso tavern says as much about him as it does about Latin America's ancestral plight:

> There, in those last moments of people whose furthest horizon has always been tomorrow, is where we can capture the profound tragedy in the life of the proletariat around the world; there is in those dying eyes a humble begging for forgiveness and also, very often, a desperate appeal for consolation which is lost in the void, just as their bodies will soon be lost in the magnitude of the mystery surrounding us. How long this order of things, based on an absurd sense of caste, will endure is not something I can answer, but it is time for the government to spend less time propagating its bounties as a regime and more money, much more money, on works that are socially useful.[3]

Che clearly wishes to help others (usually patients) and concurrently sketches a broader vision of "the order of things." He is appalled by the poverty and desperation stemming from the inequality and helplessness of the poor, but has reached a level of sophistication where he establishes a causal link between the deplorable destiny of "the proletariat around the world" and an "absurd sense of caste"—that is, the economic, social, and political status quo. Yet the remedy he proposes is still quite limited. It is a typically middle-class lamentation, within the most simplistic common-sense approach. Governments must stop spending on their own exaltation (like Perón), and pay more attention to the poor. Little is said of why governments act as they do, or what can be done beyond the ritual incantation that they should stop acting as they habitually do. Che's appeal is moral, not really political, arising from an individual, ethical stance against the way things are. With time, his political acumen would become more focused and complex, as befits a leader. But it would never entirely lose that original innocence, springing from the young medical student's encounter with pain and suffering, and strangely but also lastingly, from a certain distance, a deliberately assumed marginal position.

Che's lucid self-analysis helped to center his judgment; it always would, except at moments of feverish or asthmatic delirium in the Congo or Bolivia. The poor, the proletarians, and Communists might be brothers— but they were essentially foreign to him. There was no possible assimilation between him and the workers, the Indians of the high plateaus, the blacks of Caracas. They were, and always would be, different; and in this difference lay both their attraction for him and the limits to his identification with them. This is clear in Che's description of a Communist couple the travelers encountered in Chuquicamata, the world's largest open-cut copper mine and a bastion of the Communist Party in Chile. Guevara evokes the cold of the night and the warmth he feels in their company:

> The couple, freezing in the desert night, nestling together, were a living representation of the proletariat anywhere in the world. . . . That was one of the coldest times I've ever lived, but also the closest to this strange (to me) human species. . . . Leaving aside the danger that the "communist worm" might represent, or not, to the healthy life of a group, it had flourished here simply out of a natural desire for something better, as a protest against unceasing hunger, translated into love for that strange doctrine whose essence they might never understand, but whose translation into the words "bread for the poor" was within their reach; indeed, filled their existence.[4]

Che was disturbed by the chasm between the mine foremen—"the masters, the blond and efficient, insolent administrators . . . the Yankee masters"—and the miners. He related it to the political battle which even then

was raging around the nationalization of Chile's copper.* The approxima-
tion to politics shows a perspicacious interest in Chilean issues, but, again,
also that certain distance; the entire matter is still fundamentally alien to
him. Guevara's text, then, is not a journalistic report or even a series of
political reflections, but rather a travel journal. His summary of the struggle over Chile's copper mines reflects this attitude:

> An economic and political battle is going on in this country between those
> who support nationalizing the mines, including leftist and nationalist
> groups, and those who, parting from the ideal of free enterprise, think it
> better to have a mine that is well-managed (even if it is in foreign hands),
> rather than subject to a dubious administration by the State. . . . Whatever
> the result of the battle, it would be wise not to forget the lesson taught by
> the miners' cemeteries, which contain only a few of the enormous quantities
> of people devoured by cave-ins, silica and the infernal mountain climate.[5]

The emphasis on people and an apparent indifference to the outcome of
the political battle pervade the otherwise rigorous presentation of the issue,
which in turn reflects most of the descriptions of Che's travels through
Chile. His approach to social and political processes remains clinical: "The
general state of sanitation in Chile leaves much to be desired," Guevara
notes, though he immediately admits, "I learned later that it was much better than in other countries I've come to know."[6] The bathrooms are dirty,
sanitary awareness is limited; people also have "the habit of throwing used
toilet paper outside, on the ground or in boxes, instead of in the latrine."[7]
Che peers out at life as a medical student, not necessarily thinking things
through politically or socially. The sanitary difference between Argentina
and the rest of Latin America in fact does not derive from a lower "social
state of the Chilean people," but from a more general and substantive gap
between his country and others. The problem is that most Latin American
nations, unlike Argentina, do not have sewage networks; thus the ecologi-
cally sound, though unsanitary, practices he describes. Che shows greater
lucidity in evaluating the central political dilemma of a country like Chile.
Though it has exceptionally abundant resources, it must "get its uncomfortable Yankee friend off its back; and that task is, for the moment at least,

---

*Che's recent biographer, French journalist Jean Cormier, doubtless under the influence
of Alberto Granado, attaches great importance to this visit to the mine. He virtually makes
it into a key moment of Che Guevara's political awakening: "It is in Chuquicamata,
between the 13th and 16th of March, 1952, that Ernesto Guevara starts to become
Che . . . after Chuquicamata, he is in a state of revolutionary incubation." Jean Cormier,
Che Guevara (Paris: Editions du Rocher, 1995), pp. 37, 50. Perhaps, but nothing in Che's
own words reflects this transmutation, either then or even a bit later.

herculean, given the amount of dollars they have invested and the ease with which they can exert effective economic pressure the moment their interests are threatened."[8] Salvador Allende would feel the effectiveness of that pressure and the sensitivity of those interests twenty years later.

There are few strictly political passages in this early work. Che is surprised by the admiration his Chilean and Peruvian interlocutors have for Perón and his wife,* and expresses some penetrating though abstract thoughts on the "fair" city of Lima (as opposed to the country's *mestizo* heritage).[†] It is on the margins of politics, in his encounter and fascination with the indigenous world of Latin America, that one may appreciate the real impact of the trip on Ernesto Guevara. Except for his nautical junkets to the Caribbean and Brazil, Guevara's ethnic and social horizons had never extended beyond the white middle-class urban centers of Córdoba and Buenos Aires. These were among the most prosperous cities of Latin America. For their inhabitants, the idea of an indigenous population belonged more to epic poems and history books than to daily life. Even a person with the exceptional social awareness of Ernesto, familiar with poverty and marginalization, knew nothing of the great indigenous tragedy of Latin America and that bewitching combination of resignation and mystery that permeates the region's Indian landscape. Guevara was spellbound by the richness of the ancient Indian cultures, and upset by the poverty in the living and labor conditions of contemporary native communities. If some of his comments and reactions seem "politically incorrect," they should be evaluated as part of Che's introduction to hallucinatory exoticism and to its seduction.

Perhaps the most interesting text in this phase of the young writer's life is an essay on Machu Picchu, which was published in Panama in December 1953. The travelers had already covered most of their itinerary: Chile, Lake Titicaca, the winding paths at fifteen thousand feet above sea level between Cuzco and the border. They had already had their first encounter with "that race of the defeated, who watch us pass along the village streets. Their expressions are tame, almost fearful and completely indifferent to the external world."[9] They had taken the train from Cuzco to the ruins, with its "third class reserved for Indians," and noted "the Indians' slightly animal conception of modesty and hygiene, which makes them relieve themselves

*"According to them [we were a couple of demigods] coming from Argentina, the wonderful country of Perón and his wife, Evita, where the poor have the same things the rich do and the rich are not exploited." Ernesto Che Guevara, *Mi primer gran viaje: de la Argentina a Venezuela en motocicleta* (Buenos Aires: Seix Barral, 1994), p. 107.

† "Lima is the perfect representative of a Peru which has not yet surpassed the feudal condition of a colony: it still awaits the blood of a truly liberating revolution." Ibid., p. 167.

on the roadside, the women wiping themselves with their skirts and casually walking on."[10] Che had already personally experienced the paradoxes of discrimination. Caught in a rainstorm between Juliaca and Puno, "their two white majesties" were invited into the cab of a truck to the exclusion of several Indian women, old people, and children. Despite their embarrassed protests, the two Argentines completed the journey sheltered from the storm, while the natives were exposed to the elements.[11]

From his arrival in Peru, Che was captivated by the architectural and cultural syncretism of colonial architecture, though the term was probably unknown to him. He lamented the sad fate of the *mestizo*—trapped in "the bitterness of his double existence."[12] He sensed the terrible, magical symbiosis between syncretism and mestization, on the one hand, and the fact of conquest on the other; as Paul Valéry would say, the one is nothing without the other. He developed a Vasconcelos-style *mestizo* pride, leading him to evoke a fictional homogeneousness: "For my race the spirit shall speak," proclaimed Mexico's writer and first postrevolutionary minister of education. As Che lyrically and incorrectly stated in one of his first "public" addresses, on thanking the inhabitants of an Amazonian village for his birthday party, "we constitute a single *mestizo* race with remarkable ethnographic similarities from Mexico to the Straits of Magellan."[13]

Guevara was entranced by the mystery of the hidden city of Machu Picchu, and celebrated its discovery by explorer Hiram Bingham. He also expressed his sadness at the consequences of the find: "All the ruins were completely stripped of anything that fell into the researchers' hands."[14] He easily distinguished between buildings of different quality, commenting on the "magnificent temples" of the religious area, the "extraordinary artistic value" of the nobles' residential areas, and "the lack of care in polishing the stone" characteristic of ordinary homes. Che noted that the site had survived thanks to its topographical location and defendability. He summarized the extraordinary circumstances of Machu Picchu—its civilization, its survival on the margins of the Spanish conquest of the New World, and its location:

> We find ourselves here before a pure expression of the most powerful indigenous civilization of America, untouched by any contact with the victorious armies and full of evocative treasures amidst its dead walls, or in the marvelous landscape surrounding it and giving it a frame that will drive any dreamer to ecstasy.[15]

The spell cast by archaeology and exploration allowed Che to understand phenomena that later enthusiasts would put to good use decades later, among them Steven Spielberg, who unknowingly owes a great deal to Guevara. Thirty years before the irruption of Indiana Jones onto movie screens and into children's imaginations around the world, Guevara discovered the U.S. filmmaker's secret in the fantasies of Hiram Bingham: "Machu Picchu was to Bingham the crowning of all his purest dreams as an adult child—which is what most enthusiasts of these sciences are."[16] Che grasped that the attraction of archaeology for Bingham, Harrison Ford, and himself derived from their own special status as "adult children." Spielberg would later translate into film this perception that children love nothing better than to see grown-ups acting like them.

A last passage from this noteworthy chronicle also deserves mention. It is the first article that Guevara ever published under his name, and reflects both his objectivity and his passionate feelings toward the United States. His anti-Americanism was growing week by week. His comment about the "Yankee tourists' " incapacity to perceive the "subtleties that only a Latin American spirit can appreciate" is highly revealing. But common sense prevented him from taking his hostility to the extreme. He did not allow it to distort his vision of the inescapable facts inherent in any scientific investigation. Writing about the undeniable tragedy of Machu Picchu's archaeological plunder, he remarked:

> Bingham is not guilty, objectively speaking, nor are the Americans guilty, and a government unable to finance an expedition like that led by the discoverer of Machu Picchu is not guilty either. Is no one guilty then? Let us accept that. But where can one admire or study the treasures of the indigenous city? The answer is obvious: in the museums of the United States.[17]

From the Andean highlands the explorers roamed on to Lima and then the Peruvian Amazon. Their stay in the old capital of the viceroys made but a faint impression on the "antitourists," except for Che's brief romance with Zoraida Boluarte, a social worker at the leper colony run by the Communist physician Hugo Pesci.[18] Boluarte obtained lodging for the travelers at the nun-administered colony, and invited them to her house for dinner almost daily. The correspondence between Zoraida and Ernesto would extend through 1955. Ernesto's inscription to her on a photograph taken months later reveals his attachment to her, and his view of his own wanderings: "To Zoraida with the intention that she will always be ready to receive a couple of vagabonds floating in from anywhere and going anywhere else, always adrift with neither past nor future, and in the hope that she will never lose her compulsion to feed idlers."[19] The letters between them always use the formal "usted" already underlined in the correspondence with Tita Infante, and the tone does not suggest a very intimate relationship. But both during that trip and following Ernesto's return to Lima at the end of 1953, there may have been some romantic involvement.*

The two rovers then traveled up the Ucayali River to the leper colony of San Pablo, in the heart of the region where the Amazon begins its long, languid trip to the sea. Now deep in the humid and pestilent jungle, Ernesto suffered asthma attacks so withering he recounted them in unsparing detail. The tale is even more poignant when one realizes that they took place in rapid succession, a series of violent episodes in the river port of Iquitos, where the young man had to "spend the days in bed" and inject himself with adrenaline up to four times a day.[20] If, in general, Che devoted little space to these bouts with asthma, Granado's more mundane account reflects an almost daily series of attacks. Virtually every two pages he describes how his companion falls prey to respiratory crises, obliging the travelers to seek water and fire so as to sterilize the syringes and inject him with adrenaline or whatever was available.[21] Che's courage and tenacity during these episodes were equaled only by their frequency. Forced to bear the exhaustion and desperation they inflicted on him and the eternal difficulty of obtaining medicines, Che asked himself the question that would haunt him for the next fifteen years, and which he would always answer in the same way, except perhaps on the eve of his death, which would finally bring relief:

> The immense vault my eyes could see in the star-filled sky twinkled joyously, as if replying affirmatively to the question rising from my lungs: is this worth it?[22]

The fortnight spent at the leper colony helped reestablish Guevara's health, if only in contrast to the plight around him. Che was both repulsed and fascinated by the terrifying features of the centuries-old illness and stigma: "One of the most interesting spectacles we have seen thus far: an accordion player who had no fingers on his right hand, replacing them with some sticks tied to his wrist; the singer was blind and almost all of them had monstrous faces due to the nervous form of the disease. . . . A spectacle from a horror movie."[23]

The two friends then rafted down the Amazon toward Colombia, entering at the sleepy, sultry village of Leticia. Their two weeks in Colombia passed without any major adventures except for a small run-in with the Bogota police, who mistreated them when Ernesto thoughtlessly pulled a knife out of his pocket to draw a map on the ground. He was not sorry to

---

*According to a Cuban researcher, Zoraida "does not like to speak of Ernesto's passage through her home because she believes it was a very insignificant and fortuitous event in the life of Comandante Guevara." Marta Rojas, *Granma* (Havana), June 9, 1988.

leave for Venezuela, regretting the repressive nature of the local dictatorship and the omnipresence of the police. Too bad about the "suffocating climate," he pined, but "if the Colombians want to put up with it, that's their privilege; we're getting out as soon as possible."[24]

Caracas seems to have been a stopover lacking in any great attraction. Still, Che's continuing encounters with worlds, societies, races, and cultures totally alien to him until then kept producing strong reactions, as reflected in his comments on the population of African origin in Venezuela. This is not necessarily his first contact with "the blacks": during his naval trips to Trinidad and Porto Alegre, in southern Brazil, he had probably met descendants of the slaves kidnapped off the western coast of Africa centuries earlier. The impact of "otherness" is obvious, but his reaction—which might seem racist today, in a different cultural context—is surprising:

> The blacks, the same magnificent examples of the African race who have maintained their racial purity thanks to their scant affection for bathing, have seen their territory invaded by a new type of slave: the Portuguese. . . . Contempt and poverty unite them in their daily struggle, but their different ways of facing life set them completely apart: the indolent and dreamy black spends his few cents on any frivolity or amusement, while the European has a tradition of hard work and thrift.[25]

The voyagers were delayed in Caracas while obtaining a visa for the United States. Though Granado decided to stay on in Venezuela, an Argentine friend offered Ernesto the chance to fly back to his country in a plane carrying racehorses. But there was a small problem: he would have to go via Miami, and incur a month-long stopover. An Argentine journalist with United Press offered his good offices to obtain the visa from the United States Embassy, while bragging over dinner about his close ties to the U.S. mission. The journalist proceeded to sing the praises of the northern colossus, and lamented the way Latin Americans—and especially Argentine *criollos*—had wasted their opportunity: unable to accept their defeat of 1806, they had lost their chance to become part of the United States. The patriotic and increasingly anti-American young tourists, offended in their newfound Latin American identity, immediately rose to the occasion. Granado retorted indignantly that they might just as well have been undernourished, illiterate Indians and subjects of the British Crown. Guevara exclaimed, "Well, I'd rather be an illiterate Indian than an American millionaire."[26] The protest was both sincere and symptomatic: the greatness and the tragedy of his life may have lain in Che's belief that all Latin Americans agreed with him, while in reality most probably shared the simplistic views of the United Press journalist, and would have preferred to be American millionaires than illiterate Indians.

Che's stay in Miami gave rise to scant comment in his diary. Except for a week in New York in 1964 attending the United Nations General Assembly, it would be his only exposure to life in the United States. Only the memories of Jimmy Roca, Chichina's cousin, remain; she had given Che his address and fifteen dollars to buy her a bathing suit. According to Roca, with whom Che spent those weeks, "During that time we shared the limitations of the student life I was living. We passed the time drinking beer and eating French fries; we didn't have enough for anything else."[27] As Che confessed to his friend Tita Infante when he returned to Buenos Aires, "Those were the hardest and most bitter days of my life."[28] There were many reasons— financial, ideological, personal—for this lament.

Che's South American trip was a personal and political epiphany for him. But his own evaluation of the nature and magnitude of the change in his character and world view should not be taken at face value. Undoubtedly, Che believed that "the person who wrote these notes died when he set foot on Argentine soil once again; he who is organizing and polishing them, *myself*, is not me."[29] And it was doubtless during the trip that he decided to continue traveling, returning to Buenos Aires only to finish his studies and fulfill his promise to his mother. He planned to reunite with Granado in Venezuela as soon as he graduated, and work at the leper colony where his friend already had a job. While waiting in Miami for Chichina's cousin's plane to be repaired, Che reflected intensely upon his future. It did not lie in Argentina. Eight months and an eternity after having left, he returned to Buenos Aires on August 31, 1952, with his mind fully set on leaving again as soon as possible.

Several biographies and accounts of Che's youth have constructed a legend ascribing his politicization and militancy to the South American trip. This does not quite coincide with Che's own notes, however. His powerful attraction to things and people different or novel is undeniable, but it goes no further than that. The young wayfarer's reactions to the indigenous population and culture of Latin America are still poor in political content and knowledge, as befits a twenty-five-year-old medical student without any political education or experience; he still misses many things. Just as he is formulating his thoughts and doubts about the Peruvian Indians' apathy and misfortune, for example, revolution breaks out in Bolivia. The first rebellion of indigenous peasants in Latin America since the Zapatista uprising in Mexico, half a century before, is not mentioned in Che's travel journal.[30]

His reflections on himself, his goals, his likes and dislikes throughout the trip are more perceptive and meaningful than his political and cultural analyses. He has decided to leave his country, family, career, and ex-girlfriend, but he has not yet found his destiny, nor does he even know where to look for it. The making of the hero and his myth has not yet begun. When Che pledges on his return to Buenos Aires that "I will be with the people; I will dip my weapons in blood and, crazed with fury, I will cut the throats of my defeated enemies. I can already feel my dilated nostrils savoring the acrid smell of gunpowder and blood, of death to the enemy,"[31] he is simply ranting and raving. He has not yet heard "the animal howl of the victorious proletariat"[32] or met the people, events, and passions that will transform him. Two central ingredients which will lead to his metamorphosis and glory are still missing: Fidel Castro and the advent of rebellion and revolution.

Che's homecoming was facilitated by his certainty that he would soon be leaving again. His parents and siblings received him with all the love and enthusiasm merited by this return of the prodigal son. But they soon realized that something had changed in the manner and bearing of the young man. The boyish face and thin frame were still there, but his expression showed his age. Ernesto moved into the house of his aunt Beatriz to study hard and pass the mountain of leftover courses still lacking for his degree. Aside from his impatience to set out once more, another incentive was driving him. Peronism, now in its declining years, had become more personalized and authoritarian. Beginning in 1954, university students would have to study *justicialismo* (the official name of Peronist doctrine) and receive "political education" in order to graduate. The a-Peronist Che had no intention of doing so. Furthermore, he experienced new problems with his military service (which might explain Perón's incomprehensible comments quoted in the previous chapter). He knew that his deferment would run out upon graduation; he would have to appear once again before the conscription board. This time he took no chances. According to Granado, "he showered in freezing water before being examined by the medical commission, triggering an asthma attack, thanks to which he was declared unfit for military service."[33] As his mother would say years later:

> If Comandante Che Guevara had had to spend a year doing the shopping for a first lieutenant's wife or polishing the cartridge belt that his superior would never use . . . it would have been a shameful absurdity. But he was declared unfit. There is justice after all.[34]

Ernesto devoted himself to his studies, working fourteen hours a day, and presented his exams in four series: one subject in October, three in November, and ten in December. On July 12, 1953, he received his M.D.

from the Faculty of Medicine at the University of Buenos Aires. Less than a month later, and barely a year after his return home, he boarded a train at the Retiro station with his childhood friend Carlos "Calica" Ferrer. The first stop would be Bolivia, on his way back to Venezuela.

Not much is known about the ten months of Ernesto Guevara's last stay in Buenos Aires. In October he spoke with Chichina,[35] and he saw her in November or December in Buenos Aires after learning that she was in town. The meeting seems to have brought no regrets or consequences; Chichina's attitude was "cold and distant."[36] They last saw each other in Malagueño in early 1953. Some of the old passion was still there, as Chichina describes it: "More than once, we gazed at each other for a long time."[37]

During those months, Che worked as an allergist at the laboratory of Dr. Salvador Pisani. His talent and dedication were such that the professor asked him to stay on as a researcher, even offering to pay him (a rare privilege, according to his colleagues).[38] He brought as much intensity to his laboratory work as to his studies at home or the library. At the same time, according to his friends, "he was already speaking [with] great passion of Yankee imperialism and Latin American subjection, and the need for liberation."[39] He wrote few letters and hardly saw his childhood and university friends during this period; most of his spare time was spent composing his travel journal, transforming it into the text that would later be published. As José Aguilar recalls, describing a long walk with his friend on the eve of his departure, he was already very interested in politics, but his intention when he left for Venezuela was still "to work as a doctor."[40]

Why did Che leave his country shortly after his twenty-fifth birthday, never really to return? There is no single reason, but rather a series of factors: some attracting, others repulsing him; some were momentary and only skin-deep, others long-term and profoundly psychological. He himself says, "The only thing I did was to flee from all the things that were bothering me."[41]

Another explanation is provided by Isaías Nougués, whose father received Ernesto and Calica Ferrer in La Paz:

He said his departure from Argentina was due to the Peronist dictatorship, which disgusted him, and that he preferred to leave than live with it. However, his companion Ferrer thought the true motive was his situation at home, where the strong—and unpleasant—character of his mother diluted and frustrated the personality of his father."*

*Letter from Isaías Nougués to the author, Buenos Aires, March 29, 1996. On questioning, Carlos Ferrer did not deny this factor, but attached less importance to it: "I suppose it did affect him, particularly since the parents' relationship had worsened in recent times, but somehow I don't think it was important." Carlos Ferrer, phone interview with the author, Buenos Aires/Gualeguachu, August 25, 1996.

For Jorge Ferrer, Calica's brother, the main reason for Che's new and definitive semi-exile was not any need to escape, but rather his desire to explore the world, understand the problems and realities of Latin America, and continue discovering the mysteries and enchantments of foreign cultures.[42] Then there was his promise to Granado to work together in the leper colony. Further, Che's fascination with the unknown continued to draw him afar, together with the constantly conflicting sentiments awakened by his life in the capital: his parents' stop-and-go marriage and endless bickering; the political, existential, and family quandary that Peronism represented for him; his interest and distance vis-à-vis his profession; and his boredom with the lingering, placid monotony of Buenos Aires in mid-1953.

Leaving his family was painful for all, but especially for his mother. According to her daughter-in-law,

> When he left, I remember that his mother Celia was sitting in an armchair; she took my hand and said to me, "Minucha, I am losing him forever, I will never see my son Ernesto again." Then we went to the train station, Celia was there, I remember that when the train pulled out Celia ran, ran, ran along the platform, next to the train."[43]

Che was leaving behind an Argentina up-ended by seven years of Peronist rule and an entire decade under the general's influence. There had been great changes in the country: a growing sense of dignity among workers, the rise of an industrial bourgeoisie, a new international preeminence—no longer based upon polo players or the tangos of Gardel, but upon its (ultimately unsuccessful) attempt to find an intermediate position in the bipolarity of the Cold War. But things were drifting in a new direction. After Evita's death, Perón's alignment with sectors that had previously opposed his views and policies—foreign capital, the ranching oligarchy, the United States—bought him more time, but certainly not the sympathy of his old enemies. And it undermined his grassroots backing.

This new focus of the government also impelled it toward greater rigidity and desperation. The personality cult of Perón and his dead wife became more exacerbated. The regime tried to retain the support it had originally gained by making real, though now pallid, changes through mere propaganda. After the Korean War, the economy no longer generated the resources needed to bankroll the social generosity of the Argentine state. The society Che left behind in 1953 was as disheartened as he by the lack of options: there was nothing to be done, either against Perón (because of what he had accomplished) or with him (because of what he had become).

The first stopover for Ernesto Guevara and Calica Ferrer was Bolivia. It was not chosen as a result of any inherent interest or social or political considerations, but simply because it was the cheapest way to reach Venezuela by rail. After an eternity in a train packed with "people of very humble condition . . . laborers from northern Argentina or Bolivia who were going home after earning a few pesos in Buenos Aires" and a violent asthma attack during the ascent up the mountain range,[44] the new pair of travelers finally arrived in La Paz on July 11, 1953. The Nationalist Revolutionary Movement (MNR) led by Víctor Paz Estenssoro had taken power just a year earlier, and the country was still in the midst of an effervescent period of reform.

They spent five weeks in Bolivia. Biographies and analyses of Che's life would later focus on this visit in great detail, as still another formative moment, particularly from a political standpoint. This is how Calica Ferrer saw the time spent in Bolivia with Che. Having known Ernesto since Alta Gracia, having seen him often in Buenos Aires after his trip with Granado, Ferrer believes today that his friend's political coming of age occurred in Bolivia, together with the development of a powerful anti-American anger. The latter stemmed especially from a visit they undertook to a mine in the mountains outside La Paz, where they witnessed the abuses committed by U.S. supervisors against the local workers.[45] However, Che's stay in Bolivia can hardly have contained all the meetings, analyses, and events that have been mentioned ever since.* There are huge numbers of people with Che anecdotes from Bolivia. Even the president in 1996, Gonzalo Sánchez de Losada, remembers meeting him at a social gathering in Cochabamba. And Mario Monje, former leader of the Bolivian Communist Party, describes how Che visited the tin mines during his stay:

> Che Guevara gets a job in a mine called Bolsa Negra, near La Paz, a rather cold place. Of course the miners' group is small, but to be its leader one had to spend time there, and it was best to work inside the mine, not as a doctor. He is a doctor, his link is only circumstantial. That is how, I would say, he arrives in Bolivia—like a kind of orchid seed, looking for a place to settle.[46]

Che was rapidly and somewhat naively captivated by the Bolivian revolution, though he was irritated soon enough by its obvious shortcomings. In his letters, he initially emphasized its positive aspects: the revolutionary government's creation of armed militias, the agrarian reform, the nationalization of the tin and antimony mines. Thus, on July 24—barely ten days

---

*Thus a Peruvian biographer describes how Che "drafted press releases at the presidential information office, and it is said he even stood guard at the Quemado Palace." Carlos J. Villar Borda, *Che Guevara: Su vida y su muerte* (Lima: Editorial Gráfica Pacific Press, 1968), p. 66. And a Cuban who met Che in Guatemala recalls how "Dr. Guevara then met Juan Lechín, the legendary tin mine union leader." Mario Mencia, "Así empezó la historia del guerrillero heróico," *Revista de la Biblioteca Nacional José Martí* (Havana), May–August 1987, p. 48.

after his arrival in the capital city—he wrote to his father that the country "is living a particularly interesting moment" and that he had seen "incredible marches of people armed with Mausers and noisemakers."[47] In a letter to Tita Infante dated in Lima in early September, he noted:

> Bolivia is a country which has given a really important example to America. . . . Here revolutions are not done as they are in Buenos Aires . . . the government is supported by the armed people so there is no possibility of its being overthrown by an armed movement from abroad; it can only succumb to its own internal struggles.[48]

Che's disenchantment with the MNR's revolution stemmed mainly from one incident. In the now consecrated version, the two travelers seek a meeting with Ñuflo Chaflés, the minister of *campesino* affairs. In his waiting room there are throngs of Indian *campesinos*. They have come for the land promised by the regime's agrarian reform. As they wait to be received, a ministry employee passes among them, spraying them with insecticide. Ernesto and Calica are understandably horrified at the humiliation inflicted on the authors of the revolution. As Ernesto writes,

> I wonder what the future of this revolution will be. The people in power fumigate the Indians with DDT to rid them temporarily of the fleas they carry, but do not resolve the essential problem of the insects' proliferation.[49]

In Ferrer's later account, he merely notes more impersonally that "when the *coyas* [Indians] go into town to present a request to the authorities, the government employees quite openly disinfect them with DDT."[50] Ricardo Rojo, a young lawyer and political refugee from Argentina who had become friends with Che in La Paz and accompanied him to the minister's office, provides the most complete account of Che Guevara's misadventure with the Bolivian fleas. His book narrates the incident in a more complete and abstract manner. The two Argentines witness the Indians' fumigation and then complain to the minister about this degrading practice. The official answers that it is indeed unfortunate, but necessary. Indians are not familiar with soap and it will take years for the new educational policy to change their habits. The focus of the story is Che's emblematic reaction:

> This revolution will fail unless it succeeds in breaking through the Indians' spiritual isolation, touching them to the core, shaking them to their very bones, giving them back their stature as human beings. Otherwise, what good is it?[51]

An iconoclastic comment indeed, but one that does not necessarily imply a political position. Guevara's stance is still fundamentally ethical, devoid of political depth. He is appalled by these successive signs of the Indians' humiliation; he is upset at the hardship visited upon cultures, ethnic groups, and individuals that he admires more and more. He cannot separate the *coyas* waiting outside the government offices in La Paz, with their millenarian patience, from the splendor of the ruins at Tiahuanaco, at the top of the world. His sense of justice is outraged at the contempt and arrogance implicit in society's attitude toward the supposed beneficiaries of the 1952 revolution: "So-called decent, cultivated people are amazed at the course of events and curse the importance given the Indians and *cholos. . . .*"[52]

Che's moral musings are doubtless welcome and indispensable in understanding a continent torn by inequality. To give the eternally oppressed a fraction of the pride and respect they have lacked for centuries is one of the highest goals and potential accomplishments of any political undertaking in Latin America—and especially of any revolution worthy of the name. Guevara does not yet see this idea in strictly political terms. His intuitive, momentary reaction is still inscribed within a context of relative confusion concerning the MNR's merits and defects. But he is beginning to develop a different political approach. In this sense, his passage through Bolivia was much more than just ground time.

Ernesto Guevara did not work in the tin or antimony mines of Bolivia, though he visited the mining basins of Oruro and Cataví.* Nor did he see all the valleys and peaks of the country which would bury him fourteen years later, though he did explore the semitropical region of Los Yungas. He did talk at great length with the thinkers and politicians involved in the vast reform movement led by Paz Estenssoro. He devoted long hours to conversation, discussion, and learning in the bars and cafés of Avenida 16 de Julio and the Sucre Palace Hotel. This was his first genuine experience of the complex and contradictory world of politics, whether traditional or revolutionary. His insightful intuitions concerning indigenous and social problems led to serious disagreements with many of his interlocutors. Because of them, and his emotional reaction to the ignominy he witnessed every day in the city streets and countryside, he grew increasingly skeptical and intransigent. This eventually blinded him to the limited, but real, successes of the 1952 revolution.

This blind spot, this reservation—doubtless justified, but still extreme due to his scant political training—would be stored in Guevara's widening political memory. Thirteen years later he would retrieve it, only to have it

---

*"I almost went to work in a mine but was not willing to stay more than a month and I was offered three as a minimum, so I decided against it." Ernesto Guevara de la Serna, letter to Celia de la Serna de Guevara, August 22, 1953, quoted in Ernesto Guevara Lynch, *Aquí va un soldado de América* (Buenos Aires: Editorial Sudamericana/Planeta, 1987), p. 19.

wreak havoc on his perception of the historical moment in Bolivia. It would lead him to underestimate the miners' combativeness and to disregard the *campesinos'* appreciation of an agrarian reform which, however thwarted, distributed land to thousands of rural dwellers:

> It was a picturesque but hardly virile demonstration. The weary pace and lack of enthusiasm among all of them drained it of vital energy; the determined faces of the miners were missing. . . .[53]

The same distortion led him to misjudge the scope of the negotiations between the new regime in La Paz represented by Paz, Juan Lechín, and Hernán Siles Suazo on the one hand, and U.S. envoy Milton Eisenhower on the other, when the brother of Normandy's hero visited Bolivia in mid-July 1953. The agreement they reached, just as Che was passing through Bolivia, was successful against all odds. It avoided a confrontation with the United States, while preserving a significant proportion of the regime's conquests and reforms. It bestowed self-confidence on Bolivia's army and political class as well as a willingness to ask for external help, in a combination rare among the ruling classes of Latin America. Fourteen years later, Che Guevara would confront—and die at the hands of—the army's blend of nationalism—limited but deeply rooted—and its close ties with the U.S. armed forces, suffering the consequences of his perceptive, but finally erroneous, reading of Bolivian history.

Neither Che nor his friends of the time left any available record of their views on the agreement between the revolutionary regime and the Eisenhower administration. As in the case of Lázaro Cárdenas in Mexico in 1938—and in contrast to Cuba in 1959–60 and then Chile in 1970–73—the MNR revolution was able to wrest from the U.S. government a reluctant but resigned acceptance of its agrarian reform and expropriation of mostly locally owned natural resources. Obviously, there was a price: other aspects of the reform process were sacrificed, nationalized companies had to be compensated, and the regime was forced to submit to a rigid ideological alliance with a foreign country. Whatever the final assessment, it is surprising that one of the most idiosyncratic features of the 1952 revolution in Bolivia should not have evoked any reaction in young Ernesto. Either his political curiosity was still immature, or else he was prey to a more profound underestimation of the importance of external influence in a revolutionary process like that of Bolivia. A change in his thinking—or maturity—would soon appear. Guatemala would be the next stop on Guevara's journey.

There was no reason to dawdle in Bolivia, no matter how interesting the political panorama. Che and Calica left in mid-August and, upon the former's insistence, retraced his earlier steps with Alberto Granado. The newly graduated physician returned to Cuzco, Machu Picchu, and then Lima to meet again with Zoraida Boluarte and Dr. Pesci. There they were joined by Ricardo Rojo and, after a couple of weeks in the Peruvian capital, left for Guayaquil, a tropical and infernal hothouse if there ever was one. Marooned in the banana port for almost three weeks, along with other friends from Argentina, Guevara suffered constant, wrenching distress, both financially and healthwise. Finally, the ragged and destitute vagabonds secured free passage to Panama on a White Fleet ship of the United Fruit Company. By then Che had learned that if the altitude of high plateaus was physically harmful to him, the heat and damp of the tropics were devastating.

In the stifling, sweltering heat of Guayaquil, Ricardo Rojo and the others led Che to make a decision that would prove pivotal. He abandoned his plans to meet with Granado in Venezuela and opted instead to travel to Guatemala with his companions.* The call of the exotic and new reasserted its priority. In Guatemala, an unfamiliar, indigenous country, Guevara sought and found a reform process similar to that in Bolivia—but perhaps more radical and, in any case, fresher and more defiant toward the United States. The trip to Guatemala proved arduous, though. Ernesto's asthma, the ramblers' lack of funds, and the constant changes in their group—Calica Ferrer stayed in Quito, later heading for Venezuela—made the journey longer and more difficult. It took them two full months to reach Guatemala City after a series of more or less planned stops, mainly in San José, Costa Rica, and Panama, where Che was published for the first time.† He toured the canal and noted the contrast, greater then than now, between Panamanian neighborhoods and the Canal Zone. The latter was tidy, clean, and prosperous, Anglo-Saxon and white—a classic colonial enclave in a supposedly free country. During those months, Guevara also saw the immense plantations of the United Fruit Company in Costa Rica, which evoked from him a caustic comment, almost caricatural in its rhetoric:

I had the opportunity of traveling through the domains of United Fruit, confirming once again the terrible nature of these capitalist octopuses. I have sworn before a picture of our old, much lamented comrade Stalin [who had died nine months earlier] that I will not rest until I see these capitalist octopuses annihilated.[54]

In San José, Guevara had his first and perhaps last politically neutral

---

*He did not break his promise to Granado; the idea, according to Calica Ferrer, "was for Che to go to Guatemala and he to Venezuela, where he would contact Granado; they would all three travel somewhere else together." Carlos Ferrer, interview.

† The previously quoted essay on Machu Picchu was published then.

encounter with the newly born social democracy of Latin America. He met several times with Rómulo Betancourt, who would later be president of Venezuela precisely when Ernesto Guevara, by then a Cuban minister, was conspiring with Venezuelan guerrilla forces. He also encountered his first Latin American Communist leader, Manuel Mora Valverde. The contrast between his accounts of the two meetings points unmistakably to the direction Che was to follow:

> We met with Manuel Mora Valverde. He is a quiet man, very serene. He gave us a splendid explanation of current politics in Costa Rica. Our meeting with Rómulo Betancourt did not resemble the history lesson taught us by Mora. Betancourt gave us the impression of a politician with a few solid social ideas in his head and the rest wavering and easily shifting whichever way the wind blows.[55]

He had a spat with Betancourt, suggestive of his emerging political inclinations and the path he would travel for the next nine years, until his experience with the U.S.S.R. finally disabused him. While discussing the presence of the United States throughout Latin America, Ernesto asked the Venezuelan outright, "In case of war between the United States and the U.S.S.R., whose side would you take?" Betancourt replied he would support Washington—enough for Guevara to brand him a traitor on the spot.[56]

Che also recognized both the potential and the limitations of the government of José Figueres, who since 1948 had tried to build an extensive, anti-Communist welfare state in Costa Rica. But his brief stay in San José mainly served another crucial purpose. It was there that he had his first contact with Cubans, meeting two exiled survivors of the so-called Moncada assault that took place in the eastern city of Santiago on July 26, 1953. Calixto García and Severino Rossel were the first to tell him the incredible story of Fidel Castro's attempt to overthrow the regime of Fulgencio Batista by storming the military garrison of Cuba's second largest city. Guevara was initially skeptical.[57] But gradually the Cubans' natural charm, the greatness and tragedy of their epic, and their contrast with the moderation of Costa Rican politics persuaded him. The friendship begun in San José was reinforced in Guatemala, where he met other Moncada veterans. Among them was Ñico López, who arrived in the Guatemalan capital at around the same time as Ernesto, bringing more and fresher news from the island.

Che arrived in Guatemala on New Year's Eve, 1953. He would remain there until he obtained safe conduct to Mexico from the Argentine Embassy, where he had requested asylum after the June 1954 coup against the regime of Colonel Jacobo Arbenz. Guatemala was then a country of three million inhabitants, mostly poor, marginalized Indians. The largest and most populous Central American nation, it had—and still has—a typ-

ical plantation economy based on coffee, bananas, and cotton, with atro-
cious social conditions. Almost all its indicators placed it in the third place
from the bottom of the Latin American scale in 1950, followed only by
Haiti and Bolivia. In that year, Guatemala had the worst (with the exception of Bolivia) rates of urban and rural unemployment and underemploy-
ment in all of Latin America.[58] Even in 1960, the life expectancy of its
population at birth was the lowest in the region.[59]

Before Guatemala the Argentine's journey had been important, but only
in an emotional and cultural sense. Now Ernesto Che Guevara would experience his true political rite of passage during those troubled months when
the futile attempt of a decent Guatemalan officer to improve the dreadful
state of his fellow citizens shattered against the inescapable polarity of the
Cold War and the intransigence of the banana companies. Doubtless, Guevara had arrived with an already heavy ideological load in his worn knapsack, but he would leave Guatemala with entire trunks full of ideas,
affinities, hatreds, and judgments.

He stayed in Guatemala for eight and a half months—a short time
chronologically, but forever in ideological terms. His days were filled with
various occupations: politics, as he followed closely the outcome of the
Guatemalan drama; his unceasing, unsuccessful search for a job as a doctor,
nurse, or anything related to his profession; his perennial struggle against
illness; and the beginning of his relationship with the Peruvian Hilda
Gadea, who would later become his first wife. He planned to stay in
Guatemala for a longer stretch, two years if possible, before heading for
Mexico, Europe, and China.* He intended to make a living in his profession, but was soon frustrated by a contradiction common to most of Latin
America. On the one hand, there were not enough doctors, and too many
diseases; on the other, the barriers placed before a foreign physician were
insurmountable. The best he could obtain was a small salary at a laboratory
in the Ministry of Sanitation, after a period of selling encyclopedias.

At first his complaints about his failure to find a job were full of humor:
"I went to see the minister of public health and asked him for a post, but I
demanded a clear-cut response, either yes or no. . . . The minister did not
disappoint me. He gave me a clear-cut response: no."[60] Soon his good-
natured lamentations gave way to bitter frustration: "The sonofabitch who

---

*"My plan for the next few years: stay at least six months in Guatemala, unless I get a
well-paid job that would allow me to stay for two years . . . then go work in another country for one year . . . Venezuela, Mexico, Cuba, the United States . . . after a short visit,
Haiti and Santo Domingo, Western Europe, probably with mother." Ernesto Guevara de la
Serna, letter to Beatriz Guevara Lynch, February 12, 1954, quoted in Guevara Lynch, *Aquí
va,* p. 38.

was supposed to hire me made me wait for a month, only to have me informed that he couldn't."[61] Che confronted many obstacles in his attempt to work as a doctor. One of them, according to a recurring anecdote, was the fact that he was not a card-carrying member of the Communist Party (officially called the Guatemalan Labor Party, or PGT by its initials in Spanish). However, in his correspondence Ernesto placed greater emphasis on the "reactionary" medical profession. In any case, his motivations were increasingly financial, and Ernesto was quickly losing whatever interest he still had in medicine as such. Politics and archaeology were rapidly taking its place as his favorite fields of endeavor.

Che repeatedly complained about not being able to visit Petén and Tikal; he only traveled to the villages of the Guatemalan highlands near Lake Atitlán.* He had to renounce his dream of exploring the Mayan culture of the jungle for several reasons: his interminable political discussions, the ravaging effect of Guatemala City's climate on his illness, and his increasing intimacy with Hilda Gadea. Only a couple of years later, during a sort of honeymoon with Hilda, was he able to visit the archaeological sites of Palenque and the Yucatán Peninsula, in southern Mexico. Moreover, Guatemala's political and conspiratorial ferment certainly merited long hours of intense debate with revolutionaries and curious observers from many places: Rojo and the Argentines, the recently arrived Cubans, leftist or undefined academic figures from the United States (Harold White of Utah or Robert Alexander of New Jersey), and quasi-Communist Central American sociologists like Edelberto Torres and his daughter Myrna.

He met Myrna, and many other friends in Guatemala and later in Mexico, thanks to Hilda Gadea. Hilda was a decisive figure in his life, but their ties remained devoid of intensity; the bond was more fraternal and ideological than romantic or erotic. Che's illness and his fascination with the alien nature of her Indian features and background help explain the initial attraction. Fixed up on a blind date with Ernesto by friends, she found him in the midst of one of his asthmatic episodes, broke, bedridden, cold, and hungry. He asked for help; she gave it. Finding him in these desperate straits, Hilda immediately vouched for his rent in a pension, obtained medicines and books for him, and in a few short days reorganized his life. Aside from her generosity and support, she possessed other charms: she had marked Indian traits, and was three and a half years older than Che. Their short-lived mar-

---

*Hugo Gambini maintains that Che did fulfill his dream of visiting Petén, but does not provide any source or information to support his statement. Hugo Gambini, *El Che Guevara* (Buenos Aires: Editorial Paidós, 1968), p. 91.

riage would produce one daughter who, when asked years later in Havana for a token or memento of her father's attraction to her mother, answered with one word full of sadness and pride: "Myself."[62]

Che first mentioned Hilda in a letter to his mother dated April 1954. He spoke of her in an affectionate tone, reflecting the tenor of their relationship: "She has a heart of platinum, to say the least. I feel her support in all the actions of my daily life (beginning with the rent)."[63] The two stormers of winter palaces forged a link based upon their ideological affinities and her medical, financial, and spiritual support for the undocumented Argentine. Like many Peruvians, Hilda had strong Chinese and indigenous traces in her genetic configuration. According to several friends and photographs, she was rather short and plump.*

Obviously, Ernesto's enchantment with the experienced APRA militant[†] was not based upon any orthodox ideal of beauty. It had more to do with her archetypical Indian traits and the way in which she took charge of many facets of Che's life, including his asthma, his employment concerns, his ideological development. She also helped him to broaden his circle of friends. The couple would marry a year later in Mexico, where their daughter was born. By then, the course of the relationship would be clear in terms of its intensity, meaning, and future. Hilda was different enough from Che to seduce him. But she was too different from Chichina, almost her polar opposite, to awaken in him the passion he had felt in Malagueño.

Hilda recalls that Ernesto declared his love and proposed marriage to her at a party. She suggested they wait, more for political than for emotional reasons.[64] Much of Ernesto's life in Guatemala revolved around her: she took care of him, introduced him to friends, lent him books, and talked endlessly with him about psychoanalysis, the Soviet Union, the Bolivian revolution, and, of course, daily events in the country. The relative importance in their relationship of love, his attraction to difference, camaraderie, and ideological affinity is difficult to establish. What is certain is that Hilda had a powerful influence on the young revolutionary, and that his long-

---

*The terms used by some to describe her raise a number of questions. According to Rojo, Hilda was "a young woman of exotic traits." Ricardo Rojo, *Mi amigo el Che* (Buenos Aires: Editorial Legasa, 1985; first edition, 1968), p. 67. In whose eyes was she "exotic"? And in what way? Other adjectives, mentioned even in highly favorable biographies, are just as vague and unfortunate in Spanish. According to Hugo Gambini, among a group of APRA militants living in the same pension as Che "there was a stocky girl with almond eyes, but ugly, quite ugly. . . ." Gambini, *El Che,* p. 89.

† Peru's APRA (People's Revolutionary American Alliance) was founded in 1924 by Víctor Raúl Haya de la Torre. It was a classic Latin American nationalist-popular movement, whose members shared an unbounded devotion for their leader and a broad scope of ideological positions ranging from a virulent anti-Communist nationalism to a Latin American version of Marxism-Leninism, which was especially popular among its student members. Hilda Gadea clearly belonged to this latter school of thought.

lasting respect and affection derived in large part from his feeling of indebtedness.

Everything, including Hilda's own memoirs, suggests that the romance was platonic for a long time. It was consummated only in mid-May, a year later, in Cuernavaca, Mexico, when the couple spent a weekend in Malcolm Lowry's adopted hometown.* They had already decided to marry, but had been unable to do so because of the Mexican authorities' bureaucratic and immigration requirements.[65] In Hilda's account, it was Che who made the decision. He insisted on marriage, while she accepted his demands in fulfillment of earlier promises. Indeed, the tone in her book points to a certain reluctance on her part. More mature than he, she sensed that the relationship would be difficult if not impossible in the long term, and that Ernesto would not withstand the rigors and obligations of a "bourgeois" marriage.

The wedding took place on August 18, 1955, in the colonial town of Tepotzotlán, barely a few days after she discovered she was pregnant. The causal connection is suggested by Hilda herself. She attributes to Ernesto the following statement, when he learned of her pregnancy: "Now we must hurry and have a legal ceremony and inform our parents."[66] One of Che's biographers states that they were "forced" to marry.[67] Oleg Daroussenkov, a Soviet official who eventually forged a close friendship with Guevara, recalls a conversation with him in Murmansk in the early sixties. After downing a few vodkas to offset the Arctic cold, Che confessed that he had wed because Hilda was expecting a child[68]; he had had too many tequilas one night and made a foolish attempt at chivalry.

Regardless of the version one subscribes to, Che's encounter with Hilda derives its meaning from later consequences in Mexico, from her intellectual and political impact on Guevara's evolution, and from the fraternal affection they shared in Guatemala, Mexico, and then Cuba (though under different circumstances). Its significance does not stem from any great emotional intensity inherent in the rapport.

Che's stay in the Mayan nation was not a period of passionate sentiments, but of political awakening. Indeed, Guatemala marked a crucial time in Che's life and in the history of the entire region, inaugurating the Cold War in Latin America. It became a stereotypical example of flagrant, heavy-handed aggression by a hegemonic power, in the vernacular of the time. The caricature of a banana republic, Guatemala had, for perhaps the only moment in its history, an honest, well-intentioned regime, though it was also weak, divided, and mediocre.

---

*"We had set aside a weekend to go to Cuernavaca . . . so we decided to be united in fact. . . . And we were." Hilda Gadea, *Che Guevara, Años decisivos* (Mexico City: Aguilar, 1972), p. 116.

The whole episode began in 1950 when, for only the second time since its independence a century and a half earlier, Guatemala held democratic presidential elections. The winner was Jacobo Arbenz Guzmán, who took office on March 15, 1951. Upon assuming the presidency, Arbenz promoted a series of social and economic reforms in a country where 2 percent of the population held 70 percent of the land. The new government launched an ambitious public-works program, including a port on the Atlantic coast, a highway to the coast, and a hydroelectric plant. These projects interfered with monopolies owned by the United Fruit Company, which also controlled most of the land and politicians in the country. On June 27, 1952, Arbenz signed into law an agrarian reform which included the expropriation of uncultivated *latifundia* (large landed estates), with compensation on the basis of their declared value. Quite logically, this did not please the banana company. The decree also established an income tax—for the first time in the nation's history—and consolidated a series of workers' rights, including collective bargaining, the right to strike, and a minimum wage.

Washington launched a policy of harassment against the Arbenz regime, for both economic reasons—the interests of United Fruit—and ideological ones—the increasingly active participation in government and the reform process of the Communist Guatemalan Labor Party (PGT). Despite its small size, the PGT wielded a disproportionate influence, thanks to the competence and dedication of its cadres. In addition, Arbenz had begun to draw closer to the Socialist bloc. So, in 1954, Washington launched an explicit campaign to overthrow the government, if possible with inter-American support. Thus an Organization of American States conference was convened in Caracas in March 1954, at which the U.S. delegation, led by Secretary of State John Foster Dulles, openly demanded a condemnation of the Arbenz government. The motion was supported by every regime in Latin America save those of Mexico and Argentina, which led Che to revise some of his previous opinions about Perón.* The combination of external pressures, disenchantment within the ranks of Arbenz supporters, dissension within the army, and the president's indecisiveness climaxed in a coup in June 1954. A column commanded by Colonel Carlos Castillo Armas, directed and financed by the Central Intelligence Agency, entered Guatemala from Honduras. Using a sophisticated propaganda campaign, it forced Arbenz to resign even though the military balance of power was not conclusively unfavorable to him.†

---

*A year later, Ernesto would write to his father: "Argentina is the oasis of America, we must support Perón as much as possible. . . ." Ernesto Guevara de la Serna, letter to Ernesto Guevara Lynch, quoted in Guevara Lynch, *Aquí va,* p. 89.

† The CIA's role in the coup led by Castillo Armas has been widely documented in recent years. The most important books in this respect are Stephen Schlesinger and Stephen

Guatemala's impact on the life of Che Guevara can be measured along two vectors: his analysis of events and his actual participation in them. Ernesto was initially enthusiastic about the reform process launched by Arbenz. He wrote, "There is no country in all America as democratic" as Guatemala.[69] He also perceived the intrinsic weaknesses in the process ("there are arbitrary abuses of power and thefts") and the contradictions in the military's policy ("the newspapers run by United Fruit are such that if I were Arbenz, I'd shut them down in five minutes"). He soon understood the dilemmas faced by the regime. On the one hand, it needed the PGT's support to implement urgently needed reforms, beginning with land distribution*; on the other, it had to protect itself from U.S. attacks, all based on a supposed Communist and Soviet conspiracy in Guatemala. Che realized that the PGT was at once the staunchest and most dangerous of all Arbenz's allies, due to the effects it was generating abroad. At first he considered that the risks to the regime were very real, but only in the medium term ("I believe the most difficult moment for Guatemala will be in three years, when it has to elect a new president"[70]—this, three months before the overthrow of Arbenz). He did detect the seriousness of the threat looming over the beleaguered government, though in April 1954 he still misjudged the reasons for it:

> The fruit company is howling with rage, and of course Dulles and Co. want to intervene in Guatemala for the terrible crime it has committed in buying arms wherever it can, as the United States hasn't sold a single cartridge in a long time.[71]

In his letters to Buenos Aires, Che revealed great lucidity as to the nature of the imminent aggression, but overestimated the forces available to deter it. On June 20—just a week before Arbenz's resignation and on the very day of the pseudo-invasion from Honduras led by Castillo Armas—Che wrote to his mother that "the danger is not in the total number of troops currently entering [Guatemalan] territory, as it is quite small, nor in the airplanes which are only bombing civilian homes and machine-gunning a few people;

Kinzer, *Bitter Fruit* (New York: Doubleday, 1982), and Piero Gleijeses, *The United States and the Guatemalan Revolution* (Princeton, N.J.: Princeton University Press, 1989). The CIA's Center for the Study of Intelligence has promised to declassify all of its files on Guatemala in 1954; at this writing it had not yet done so.

*"[The Communists] are the only political group asking the government to fulfill a program in which personal interests don't count (though there might be a demagogue or two among their leaders)." Ernesto Guevara de la Serna, letter to Tita Infante, March 1954, quoted in Adys Cupull and Froilán González, *Cálida presencia: Cartas de Ernesto Guevara de la Serna a Tita Infante* (Santiago de Cuba: Editorial Oriente, 1995), p. 53.

the danger lies in how the *gringos* are running their stooges at the United Nations."[72] Which was true, as our apprentice field strategist perceived.

At the same time, however, he assured his mother that "Colonel Arbenz is very brave, without a doubt, and is willing to die at his post if necessary. . . . If things reach the extreme of having to fight the modern planes and troops sent by the fruit company or the United States, people will fight."[73] He could not have been more mistaken. A week later, Arbenz would be forced to resign by the combined pressures of the United States, the "invading" column approaching the capital, and the demands of his colleagues in the army. Though historians and witnesses are still arguing over what might have happened if the PGT's worker and *campesino* militias had been given arms and Arbenz had led the struggle from the countryside, the fact is that "the people" did not really defend "their" government. Che grasped this perfectly two weeks later, when he wrote to his mother that "Arbenz did not know how to rise to the occasion . . . treason continues to be the vocation of the army, and once again we see confirmed that saying which dictates the elimination of the army as the true beginning of democracy (if the saying does not exist, I have now invented it)."[74]

Finally, Guevara bitterly concluded that "We are like the Spanish Republic, betrayed from within and without, but we did not fall with the same dignity."[75] Ricardo Rojo relates that Che mistrusted the nationalist and reformist potential of the regime; in Guevara's view, the government should have formed people's militias to defend the capital, thus preventing the debacle.[76] According to Hilda Gadea, in an article Che wrote entitled "I Saw the Fall of Jacobo Arbenz," which was lost when he left Guatemala, he argued that the regime would have survived if the people had been armed.[77] Gadea states:

> He was certain that if the people were told the truth and given arms, the revolution could be saved. Even if the capital had fallen, the struggle could have continued in the countryside; in Guatemala there are suitable mountainous areas.*

Perhaps Che still believed, in this youthful, radical, and still relatively innocent stage, that one could have everything: first, an army promoting reform, and then a military institution which would suddenly become revolutionary and give up its monopoly on weapons, handing rifles to workers and farmers.† He was obviously inspired in this by the example of Bolivia's

---

*Gadea, *Años decisivos,* p. 74. It is a bit difficult to see how Che could have known, *at that time,* which mountainous areas were "suitable" and which were not.

† According to Hilda Gadea's memoir, a year later her husband criticized José Manuel Fortuny, secretary-general of the Communist Party, for not having fought. In his memoirs,

popular militias, which had very much impressed him just a few months earlier.

Guevara rightly attributed Arbenz's defeat to disunity among the country's progressive forces, as well as their lack of leadership and decisiveness, and the duplicity of the armed forces before the U.S. onslaught. In fact, the real cause for the failure of the Guatemalan revolution was to be found in the United States, both in Che's mind and in reality. The great lesson for the young Argentine revolutionary concerned Washington's presumed *a priori* and ruthless opposition to any attempt at social and economic reform in Latin America. One must be prepared to fight U.S. interference, rather than try to avoid or neutralize it. The other moral of the story, in Che's view, was that Arbenz had erred in giving his enemies too much freedom, especially in the press.*

Che would have needed far vaster political experience, a more solid knowledge of history, and doubtless greater maturity to assimilate the hard lessons of Guatemala with greater discernment. He still knew next to nothing about the three largest countries of Latin America. He had never set foot in Mexico; in his passage through Brazil he had mainly focused on the beauty of the *mulattas,* and his experience of Argentina had been largely apolitical or disdainful. The two countries he knew best were the poorest and least developed on the mainland of the Americas: Bolivia and Guatemala. The rest of America was summed up for him in Machu Picchu and Chuquicamata, the indigenous cultures and the United Fruit Company in Central America. His knowledge of the region's armies was limited to Arbenz and border troops posted in the Andes and the tropics.

The very real confrontation between the fruit company and the banana republic becomes a caricature when extrapolated to the rest of the hemisphere, with its complex and multifarious history. The specificity of Guatemala was diluted in Che's emotional, sometimes brilliant approach: undeniable particulars became questionable generalizations. As long as this transposition involved similar situations—as in the case of Cuba—it produced valid conclusions. But when it was extended to quite dissimilar situations, it led to sweeping truisms and fatal mistakes.

In Guatemala, Ernesto Guevara was still searching. His attitude toward

---

Fortuny does not mention this meeting, which one might consider worth remembering. Marco Antonio Flores, *Fortuny: Un comunista guatemalteco, Memorias* (Guatemala: Universidad de San Carlos de Guatemala, 1994).

*According to a Guatemalan leader who established a long and close friendship with Guevara at the Argentine Embassy during that year, Che stated: "Too much freedom was given, there was even freedom for the conspirators and agents of imperialism to destroy that democracy." Rolando Morán, unpublished interview with Francis Pisani, provided to the author by Pisani, Mexico, November 18, 1985.

his parents ("I think you should know that even if I am dying I won't ask you for any *guita* [money]"[78]), his comments after the coup on June 26 ("I'm a bit ashamed to admit that I enjoyed myself immensely those days. That magical sense of invulnerability . . . made me smack my lips with glee when I saw people running like crazy when they saw the planes. . . . It was all a lot of fun, what with the shooting, bombs, speeches and other distractions to break the monotony I was living in"[79]), and the explanation given by his mother ("He asks to be allowed to help in the defense. He is told that there will be no defense. He offers to organize it. But who is he? What experience does he have, after all?"[80]), all point to an increasing politicization. He is still rebelling against his parents, though less than before; and his political persona is becoming more clearly defined.

At age twenty-six, Che Guevara was an ardent defender and admirer of the Soviet Union. He intended to give his son (if he had one) a Russian name, Vladimir, in honor of the fatherland of socialism.[81] His wife Hilda also reports: "Guevara displayed great sympathy for the achievements of the Soviet Revolution; I had some reservations."[82] The young man had an obvious inclination for Communism, for both the Guatemalan party* and the general concept, and had decided to join the ranks of the Party (with a capital P) somewhere in the world.†

Once the number of asylum seekers and hangers-on in the Argentine Embassy swelled, a Communist contingent was organized. Led by Víctor Manuel Gutiérrez, the second most important leader of the PGT, it was soon separated from its companions and locked into the Embassy garage. Che was recruited along with the others, according to Rolando Morán, a Guatemalan guerrilla leader who became friends with him at that time, and logically so: his closest affinity at the Embassy was with the Communists.[83] Guevara was a person of insatiable political curiosity, yet persistently lacking in any militant spirit; he held leftist political views, yet had little knowledge of Marxism.‡ He had witnessed a tragic defeat which could have been

---

*"I have adopted a firm position alongside the Guatemalan government and, within it, the Communist PGT. I have also made contact with intellectuals of that tendency who edit a magazine here, and am working as a doctor in the labor unions." Ernesto Guevara de la Serna, letter to Beatriz Guevara Lynch, February 12, 1954, quoted in Guevara Lynch, *Aquí va,* p. 38.

† "After the fall . . . the Communists were the only ones who still kept their faith and camaraderie, and are the only group who continued their work. . . . Sooner or later I will join the Party." And he adds, in an outburst of candor and enthusiasm, "The only thing keeping me is that I want so much to travel in Europe." Ernesto Guevara de la Serna, letter to Celia de la Serna de Guevara, November 1954, quoted in Guevara Lynch, *Aquí va,* p. 80.

‡ "To be absolutely honest . . . Ernesto and I, though very much influenced by the ideology of Marxism-Leninism, still had in our political thinking the populist ideas so much in fashion at the time." Alfonso Bauer Paiz, interview with Aldo Isidrón del Valle, quoted

expected and avoided; he would extrapolate its lessons in the terms in which he lived and suffered them. His convictions about the need for the armed struggle, the implacable hostility of the United States and the impossibility of any negotiation with Washington, his affinity for Communist parties and the Soviet Union, and the imperative need to forestall one's enemies before they could take advantage of existing liberties all formed a collection of beliefs that would be further consolidated during his early years in Mexico. They would accompany him to the Sierra Maestra and throughout his first period in Havana, tempered only gradually by his exceptional intelligence and realism, and by the ravaging lessons of experience.

During the debacle, Che did not help defend the regime, arms in hand. He had no way to do so. Accounts of his frantic attempts to organize a militia in Guatemala City are simply false.* In several interviews attributed to her after Che's death, Hilda Gadea asserts that he did participate in anti-aircraft defense groups and in transporting weapons from one side of the city to the other,[84] but in her book she describes only his frustrated intentions. In an interview in the Sierra Maestra, Che was indulging in poetic license when he stated, "I tried to organize a group of young men like myself to confront the adventurers of United Fruit. In Guatemala, it was necessary that we fight and almost nobody fought. It was urgent that we resist but almost nobody wanted to do so."[85] The official Cuban biographers (or "chronologists," as they sometimes call themselves) took up this idea of Che transporting weapons and his "attempt" to organize young men for combat, but without providing any sources or proof.[86] The most Che himself ever says in his letters—and he surely would have mentioned it to one of his many correspondents if he had done anything else—is that he enrolled at an emergency medical ward and "registered with the youth brigades to receive military instruction and do whatever. I don't think this will come to anything."[87] This was a week before the coup which toppled Arbenz.

A few days after the president's resignation, Ernesto requested asylum at the Argentine Embassy, after a friend who worked there warned him that he was in danger. Though the actual risk was relative,[†] there are indications

---

in *Testimonios sobre el Che* (Havana: Editorial Pablo de la Torrente, 1990), p. 80. Bauer Paiz was a close friend of Che's during his stay in Guatemala.

*For instance, the following story taken from "research carried out by a team of officers from the History Section of the Political Directorate of the Revolutionary Armed Forces of Cuba": "The coup by the traitor Carlos Castillo de Armas [sic] took place the same day that Che, enlisted in the Guatemalan army, was going to be sent to the front." Center for Military History Studies, *De Tuxpan a La Plata* (Havana: Editorial Orbe, 1981), p. 10.

† "Che stayed until the end and then left. There was nothing against him in reality, no arrest warrant or anything. He was able to leave Guatemala legally." Morán, interview with Francis Pisani.

that his activities had been detected. David Atlee Phillips, the CIA station chief in Guatemala during those days in June, recalls in his memoirs:

> A company analyst gave me a sheet of paper a few days after the coup. It contained biographical information about an Argentinian doctor, age 25, who had requested asylum at the Mexican Embassy [sic]. . . . "I suppose we had better open a file," I said. Though his name meant little to me at the time, the file on Ernesto Guevara . . . would one day be one of the thickest in the CIA.*

His status at the Embassy was more that of a guest than a political refugee, which allowed him to enter and exit quite frequently.[†] He spent approximately a month there, along with many other Argentines, but also radical youths from other countries and Guatemala itself. These included the future founder and leader of the Guatemalan Army of the Poor (EGP), Rolando Morán; Tula Alvarenga, already the companion of the secretary-general of El Salvador's Communist Party, Salvador Cayetano Carpio (later the legendary Marcial of the Frente Farabundo Martí de Liberación Nacional, or FMLN). Che refused to return home in an airplane sent by Perón to repatriate the Argentine exiles. Instead, he decided to travel to Mexico as soon as the danger subsided. In the meantime, he helped his colleagues sheltered at the Embassy, and established friendships that would last for years. He particularly treasured the sympathy and camaraderie he had built with the Cuban exiles and the admiration they inspired in him:

> When I heard the Cubans make their grandiloquent statements with absolute serenity I felt tiny. I can make a speech ten times more objective and without commonplaces, I can read it better and I can convince a public that I am telling the truth, but I don't convince myself and the Cubans do. Ñico would leave his soul in the microphone and thanks to that could fill even skeptics like me with enthusiasm.[88]

Ñico López, his first real friend from Cuba, had participated in the assault on the Bayamo barracks, aimed at preventing reinforcements from reaching Santiago de Cuba and the Moncada headquarters in the 1953 uprising. He not only told Che the details of the operation, but also

*David Atlee Phillips, *The Night Watch* (New York: Atheneum, 1977), p. 54. It is difficult to establish whether Phillips fabricated this memory years later as proof of his prescience—or whether he actually opened a file on Che in Guatemala. The file is not included in the CIA's declassified archives; according to a member of the agency's Historical Advisory Board who requested information about it, there is no trace of it.

[†] "Che was not really an asylum-seeker, because he was an Argentine who was, we might say, under the protection of his embassy." Morán, interview with Francis Pisani.

described the virtues of its leader, Fidel Castro. Che first met Ñico, Mario Dalmau, and Darío López in cafés and social meetings during the intense months leading up to the fall of Arbenz and then at the Argentine Embassy. There, he provided them some medical care, read his texts on Guatemala, and put them in contact with his family in Buenos Aires when they left on the Constellation sent by Perón. The Cubans recalled three of Che's traits in particular: his solidarity with them, whenever he could help; his eternal financial difficulties; and his conversation and writings (now lost), in which he expounded his anti-imperialist views and arguments for the armed defense of the capital.[89] In his luggage he carried one last souvenir of Guatemala: the nickname "Che," bestowed upon him by his Cuban friends because of his Argentine nationality and his countrymen's habit of endlessly repeating this expression.

Finally, when things quieted down at the end of August, he left the diplomatic mission, mainly to see Hilda, who was still in Guatemala and had been briefly detained. They made plans to meet soon in Mexico. While awaiting his visa, Che left for Atitlán with his sleeping bag, spending a few days hiking and contemplating one of the most beautiful lakesites in the world; there really was nothing else to do. By mid-September he arrived in Mexico City, the world capital of corruption, as he wrote his aunt Beatriz.[90]

The first months in Mexico, in late 1954, were not easy. Guevara had no money, work, or friends. He carried only the address of several of his father's acquaintances; one of them, a screenwriter named Ulises Petit de Murat, received him warmly. He bought a camera and, together with a friend he had met on the train from Guatemala, started to make his living taking pictures of U.S. tourists on the streets of Mexico City. He also got a poorly paid job as an allergy researcher at the General Hospital under Dr. Mario Salazar Mallén, but admitted, "I am doing nothing new."* He also mentioned that he had begun to put his life in order: "I cook for myself, and bathe every day, [but] do my laundry rarely and badly." He intended to spend about six months in Mexico before leaving for the United States, Europe, and then the Socialist countries of Eastern Europe and the Soviet Union. He thought of applying for a scholarship to do postgraduate studies in some European university, based upon his scientific publications and his experience as a researcher under Dr. Pisani in Buenos Aires.

---

*Nothing except drafting the outline of an ambitious book to be titled "The Physician in Latin America," the writing of which he began during his spare time in Guatemala. It was planned to include fourteen chapters, including a short history of medicine in Latin America as well various reflections on the economic, social, and political context of medicine in the region. See María del Carmen Ariet, quoted in Claudia Korol, *El Che y los argentinos* (Buenos Aires: Ediciones Dialéctica, 1988), p. 101.

His first impressions of Mexico were far from pleasant:

> Mexico is entirely given over to the Yankees. . . . The press says nothing at all. . . . The economic situation is terrible, prices are going up at an alarming rate, and the disintegration is such that all the labor leaders have been bought off and sign unfair contracts with the Yankee companies, in return for suppressing strikes. . . . There is no independent industry, much less any free trade.[91]

In March 1955, an Argentine news agency hired him as a photographer to cover the Pan-American Games. In his free time, he wrote scientific research papers on allergies and attended a congress in Veracruz. Thanks to these activities, he finally got a grant from the General Hospital, which made life easier. He went on exotic expeditions that were madness for an asthma sufferer, such as climbing the Popocatépetl and the Pico de Orizaba:

> I took the Popo by assault, but despite much heroism, I was unable to reach the top. I was ready to die for it, but my Cuban climbing companion scared me because two of his toes froze. . . . We spent six hours fighting the snow that buried us to our waist, and with our feet totally drenched since we lacked the proper equipment. The guide got lost in the fog skirting a crevass, and we were all exhausted from the soft and unending snow. The Cubans won't climb again, but as for me, as soon as I have some money, I will challenge the Popo again, and the Orizaba in September.[92]

He also explored the outskirts of Mexico City, but in those months he did not undertake any of the journeys that would normally have attracted him, as they do so many other foreigners. His dispiritedness was such that he ignored the dazzling beauties of a country that has bewitched so many travelers, dwelling only on its defects—indisputable, but trivial for a person as sophisticated as he now was.

In November 1954, Che had started seeing Hilda again. Thanks to her, he began making contact with militants and politicians from other countries, including Laura de Albizu Campos, the wife of the Puerto Rican nationalist jailed by the U.S. government. Che's courtship of Hilda was complex and ambivalent, as already noted: his affection and loyalty for the Peruvian exile were balanced by a certain aloofness. Hilda was not part of his plans; she did not appear in his projected travels, adventures, or occupations. Ernesto Guevara was at that time essentially a tramp, a wandering photographer, an underpaid medical researcher, a permanent exile, and an insignificant husband—a weekend adventurer.[93]

Then one day he ran into Ñico López at the hospital. The Cuban was now a refugee in Mexico, after a long journey in exile, and had come to the hospital for treatment. In the midst of this languid, drifting though expectant existence came the chance encounter that would make the difference between epic and simple tedium. Fortune alone does not explain it: there also had to be a willingness to seize the opportunity. In June, Ñico Lopez introduced the wandering Argentine doctor to Raúl Castro, a Cuban student leader recently released from a Havana jail. A few days later, Raúl's brother arrived in Mexico, and Raúl took Che to speak with him. And so, in the summer of 1955, Ernesto Guevara met Fidel Castro and discovered the path that would lead him to glory and death.

Chapter 4

Under Fire with Fidel

F idel Castro arrived in Mexico City by bus on July 8, 1955, via Vera-cruz, Havana, and the jail on Isla de Pinos in Cuba. He carried a single suit, no money, and a head full of harebrained ideas that would catapult him into history in three brief years. He had spent twenty-two months in prison for masterminding the assault on the Moncada army barracks in Santiago on July 26, 1953; his release resulted from a foolhardy amnesty decreed by dictator Fulgencio Batista. He immediately headed for Mexico, with a single goal in mind: to launch an insurrection against the Batista regime.

A former university student leader and young politician belonging to the traditional, corrupt Partido Ortodoxo, Castro came of age in an enchanting and cursed country of barely six million inhabitants, ravaged by half a century of late, troubled, and incompletely achieved independence. On March 10, 1952, Batista led a classic coup d'état on the eve of the scheduled presidential elections. Facing a dismal showing of his own, the former sergeant cut short the only period of democratic rule the country had ever known. The elections were suspended, and the constitutional government, in office since 1940, was ousted. Despite huge demonstrations and protests, just three years later the regime felt strong enough to pardon its principal opponents—a fatal mistake.

A virtual semicolony of the United States, the largest island of the Antilles had benefited greatly from the U.S. boom of the fifties. The price of sugar—the only Caribbean crop since time immemorial—had been stable over the entire decade, allowing for modest but sustained per capita growth. The Cuban sugar harvest, stagnant between 1925 and 1940, had begun to grow again—a significant factor, given that half of Cuba's arable land was given over to cane. The sugar sector represented 50 percent of Cuba's agricultural production, a third of its industrial output, and 80 percent of its exports. It employed 23 percent of the labor force and generated 28 percent of GDP.[1] Almost half the sugar produced was exported to the United States. The single crop amounted, in fact, to a single destiny.

Tourists from the U.S. East Coast made Cuba their playground. Hotel construction boomed; countless cabarets, summer villas, and brothels sprouted across the island's beaches and coves. A middle class devoted to the service and pleasure of tourists grew apace. The fun capital of the Caribbean enjoyed a rush of consumption and prosperity that was misleadingly identified with the rest of the country. U.S. nationals, who had owned most of the sugar mills until the fifties, continued to dominate everything else: the economy, politics, and above all the collective psychology of Cubans—to the joy and fortune of some, the misfortune and humiliation of others.

Rates for per capita income, literacy, urbanization, and overall standard of living were among the highest in Latin America. They concealed, however, an abysmal inequality between the capital and a few eastern cities and the rest of the country, between city and countryside, and, especially, between whites and blacks. Cuba's exact ranking within Latin America would be hotly debated for years to come, but in 1950, its per capita income was surpassed only by that of Argentina and Uruguay—logically—as well as Venezuela and Colombia.[2] Life expectancy reached almost sixty years in 1960—the highest in the hemisphere after the two republics bordering the River Plate.[3] Figures for doctors and hospital beds per inhabitant were among the best in the region, and the principal causes of death among adults were those typical of rich countries: malignant tumors and cardiovascular disorders. Educational levels were also high, placing Cuba fourth in Latin America toward the end of the decade, after Argentina, Uruguay, and Costa Rica.[4]

However, income distribution was among the most inequitable in the Americas, due to sugar monocultivation and the resulting unemployment during nine months of each year. In the late fifties, the share of national income going to the poorest 20 percent of the population was only 2.1 percent of the total—that is, a third of the equivalent in Argentina, and less than in Peru, Mexico, or Brazil.[5] Almost all social and economic indicators registered huge discrepancies between town and country, between whites and blacks, and especially between Havana and the rest of the nation. With

26 percent of the country's population, the capital province garnered 64 percent of national income in 1958. Thus, on the eve of the Castro conspiracy hatched in Mexico City, Cuba had a relatively broad middle class (about a third of the population) which was rather prosperous by Latin American standards. But it was also a terribly unequal country, deeply divided in terms of race, geography, and class.

Understandably, then, Cuban politics were somewhat byzantine. Like the Cubans themselves, they were violent and passionate, intricate and personalized. The Moncada assault was exceptional because of the cruel reprisals exacted by Batista's new dictatorship, but it was not an uncommon occurrence. Nobody was surprised that a group of agitators should attempt to overthrow the government in a spectacular *coup de main*. Nor was it unusual that Fidel Castro's struggle should initially focus on restoring the constitutional order of 1940, as became clear during the epic defense he presented at his own trial. Certainly, by the time of the coup, the constitutional regime installed in 1940 had few supporters in Cuba. However, within a generalized climate of corruption, violence, and disorder, the 1940 constitution was a symbol of hope for broad sectors of the population.

But the distinctive feature of Cuban culture and politics was without a doubt the interminable birth pangs of the republic. Since the 1898 Spanish-American War and the Platt Amendment of 1902 granting the United States the right to intervene in Cuba's internal affairs whenever public order was threatened, the island had experienced a sort of national purgatory. It had emerged from the hell of colonial rule without reaching the presumed paradise of independence. Cuba's aspiration to become independent was frustrated. The United States won the war, and Cuba lost its bid for emancipation. In 1902 the survivors of the long struggle (its main heroes José Martí and Antonio Maceo were already dead, and Máximo Gómez was exhausted and isolated) were forced to choose between nominal independence under the terms of the Platt Amendment or a *de jure* colonial status. Cuba's national sovereignty was thus severely curtailed at birth. The resulting trauma would last over half a century, and its sequels would extend to the end of the millennium. It is no wonder that the Cuban people should maintain to this day an obdurate—and often disconcerting—brand of nationalism.

Political life in Cuba between the Platt Amendment and its abrogation in 1934 reflected the original sin at the heart of the republic. From the end of Spanish rule until 1933, politics on the island were characterized by electoral fraud, corruption, and constant meddling by the United States to restore order, protect its interests, and mediate among the different factions of the Cuban elite. Widespread discontent among the people, the *criollo* ruling classes, and lower-ranking army officers finally reached a head in 1933.

An inevitable uprising, led by Antonio Guiteras, ended this tragic phase of Cuba's independent history. But the reformist coalition that emerged from the revolution proved short-lived. It barely had time to rescind the Platt Amendment before being overthrown by the so-called "sergeants' rebellion" headed by Fulgencio Batista. The mulatto sergeant was the power behind the throne until 1940, when he was elected president under a new constitution.

The advent of the military shifted the basic boundaries of political life in Cuba. The repeal of the Platt Amendment and consolidation of the economy's domestic sector were accompanied by the emergence of a powerful labor force and Communist Party. Through the Workers' Confederation of Cuba (CTC), the organized working class played a distinctive role in the coalitions supporting Batista and Ramón Grau San Martín, who succeeded him as president in 1944.* Though it never won more than 7 percent of the vote, mainly concentrated in Havana, the Communist Party (called the Popular Socialist Party, or PSP, after 1944) had a prominent place on the island. Its influence extended far beyond its numbers, thanks to the honesty and dedication of its cadres and militants and its sway over the labor unions.

The Communists were also active in the Congress and within the governments of Batista and Grau. Their leader, Juan Marinello, was named minister without portfolio in February 1942; shortly afterward a thirty-one-year-old economist from the party, Carlos Rafael Rodríguez, joined the cabinet.† The PSP and working-class sectors under its aegis were thus key actors in Cuban politics until their expulsion from the labor unions in 1947, at the beginning of the Cold War. When they reappeared in 1958, just before the fall of Batista, and especially after the triumph of the Cuban Revolution, they were not springing from a void. Their reemergence derived from a long tradition and a significant, if not always glorious, history.

Corruption, gangsterism, and social unrest marked the successive four-year administrations of Batista, Grau, and Carlos Prío Socarrás, culminating in the coup of 1952. Cuba's political parties and Congress were suspended; the posts of president and vice-president were abolished. A new constitutional code was enacted, which included the automatic repeal of individual rights and freedoms under certain conditions. Nobody stood up for the outgoing regime of Prío Socarrás, standard-bearer of the Auténtico Party and enemy of its Ortodoxo competitor. The two traditional parties

---

*Thus the rate of labor union affiliation on the eve of the revolution: in 1958, approximately a million workers belonged to one union or another. Hugh Thomas, *Cuba: la lucha por la libertad, 1909–1958,* vol. 2 (Mexico City: Grijalbo, 1974), p. 1512.

† The survival skills and diplomacy of Rodríguez would put Talleyrand to shame. Half a century later (until the early 1990s, when his health failed), he still held high government office, possibly the third most important within Cuba's revolutionary hierarchy.

had long since worn out their welcome with the citizenry. Their endless rivalry and internal divisions, garrulous but often groundless or irrelevant, had helped disillusion the population. Batista's 1952 coup lacked popular support—but so did the status quo.

Very soon, mid-level officers, old-time politicians, and young university students joined the struggle against the dictatorship, following different paths and with varying hopes of success. One of them, Fidel Castro, an Ortodoxo lawyer of Galician origin known for his fiery speech-making and muscular tactics from his student days, ran for Congress in 1952. When the elections were canceled, Castro promptly proceeded to organize over 150 angry opponents to the regime, in a desperate attempt to overthrow it by force of arms. They failed, were violently repressed and thrown in jail, but assumed a privileged place in Cuba's popular imagination and among the middle classes of Havana and Santiago. The Moncada assault consecrated Fidel Castro as a central figure in Cuba's turbulent politics. Once in Mexico, through his incipient 26th of July Movement (named after the date of the Moncada assault), he became the champion of the most principled and intransigent faction in the opposition, rejecting any compromise with Batista, marking a break from both the traditional parties and the Popular Socialist Party (PSP).*

In a country where corruption and institutional collapse had been endemic since independence, where personal loyalties counted far more than party affiliation, an acute hunger for honest, bold, and radical leadership prevailed. In an unformed nation, where U.S. intervention was an inescapable and congenital fact of life, there was enormous potential for a personality who could capture the people's need to heal their wounded self-respect. Only some theoretical details, and a bit of luck, were missing. Fidel Castro's meeting with Che Guevara would supply the former with both; it would provide the latter with the deep conviction that "it is worth dying on a foreign beach for such a noble ideal."6

Neither Fidel's nor Che's biographers are precise as to the exact date of their first meeting, usually placed in July, August, or September 1955. What is certain is that Raúl Castro met Che thanks to Ñico López, the Cuban

---

*The PSP publicly repudiated the attack on the barracks: "We condemn the *putsch* methods, typical of bourgeois factions, used in the Santiago raid. . . . The heroism displayed by the participants in this action is false and sterile, guided as it is by mistaken bourgeois thinking. . . . All the country knows who organized, inspired and led the action against the barracks and knows that the Communists had nothing to do with it." *Daily Worker* (New York), August 5 and 10, 1953. Quoted in Thomas, p. 1090.

exile friend from his Guatemalan days. Raúl was already an experienced militant in the international Communist movement, espousing Communist "ideas" (in the words of Hilda Gadea[7]), and attending the Vienna Youth Festival of 1951. During his return to Cuba by boat, he encountered a figure central to this story: Nikolai Leonov, then a young Soviet diplomat on his way to Mexico to study Spanish. Leonov would later work as a translator to the Soviet leadership and would be one of the first links between Moscow and the Cuban Revolution, before retiring as a KGB general in the eighties.

In his funeral oration for Che on October 18, 1967, Fidel Castro placed their first meeting in July or August 1955.[8] It seems somewhat unlikely that they would have met so soon after the Cuban's arrival, though in a speech in Chile in 1971 Castro mentions that he met Che "a few days after his arrival in Mexico."[9] Hilda Gadea states in her memoirs that Che recounted meeting Fidel "in early July,"[10] but the Cuban armed forces' semiofficial account asserts that the friendship began in September.[11] Neither Che's biographies nor the more recent ones of Fidel Castro give any additional information, though several of them point out that Che and Fidel were together at the small group of exiles commemorating July 26.[12]

The exact date is important only if the consecrated description of an instantaneous mutual fascination is seen as exaggerated. Why wouldn't the two young men have met or even exchanged a few words before the subsequently famous all-night conversation at the home of María Antonia that led to a decade of unflagging loyalty and respect? In any case, their alliance would add conceptual structure to Castro's brilliant political intuition, and give meaning to Che's life. Che recalled that evening shortly afterward:

> I met him during one of those cold Mexican nights, and remember that our first discussion was about world politics. After a few hours—by dawn—I had already embarked on the future expedition. Actually, after the experience I had had walking through all Latin America and the finishing touch in Guatemala, it wasn't hard to talk me into joining any revolution against a tyrant, but Fidel impressed me as an extraordinary man. He faced and resolved the most impossible things. . . . I shared in his optimism. There was a lot to do, to fight for, to plan. We had to stop crying and start fighting.[13]

In his travel journal, written on the spur of the moment, Guevara noted: "It is a political event to have met Fidel Castro, the Cuban revolutionary, a young man who is intelligent, very sure of himself and remarkably bold; I think there was a mutual liking."[14] This comment, more spontaneous and immediate than the previous one, confirms the impact Castro had on the Argentine, and the admiration he awakened in him. It also reveals that

Che detected Castro's outstanding traits, both good and bad, from the outset.

For his part, Fidel Castro kept a precise memory of the evening when they became friends and colleagues: "In one night he became a member of the future *Granma* expedition."[15] Castro also noted (in a confession all the more interesting because he made it ten years later) that Che's "revolutionary development was more advanced than mine, ideologically speaking. From a theoretical point of view he had a better background, he was more advanced as a revolutionary."[16] One of Fidel's girlfriends, who was also a friend of Che and his wife, corroborated Castro's retrospective opinion:

> Fidel's passion for Cuba and Guevara's revolutionary ideas ignited each other like wildfire, in an intense flare of light. One was impulsive, the other thoughtful; one emotional and optimistic, the other cold and skeptical. One was attached only to Cuba; the other, linked to a framework of social and economic concepts. Without Ernesto Guevara, Fidel Castro might never have become a Communist. Without Fidel Castro, Ernesto Guevara might never have been more than a Marxist theoretician, an idealistic intellectual.[17]

In fact, Che was not quite a well-rounded theoretician. Despite his reading of Marx and Lenin in Mexico,* he had only an unstructured, autodidactic background in Marxist theory, and a mere smattering of history, philosophy, and economics. His political experience in Guatemala and his approach to events resembled that of a passionate and perceptive spectator—but a distant one, nonetheless. The explanation presented by Castro's biographers (or those who knew the two men at that time) is indeed tempting: it posits a friendship based upon matching talents and personalities. But the intellectual or theoretical eminence attributed to Che by Fidel and others must be qualified. In 1955, Che was a sporadic reader of Marxist texts, a man interested in world events within a broad humanistic culture. He came from a family of readers, had had excellent schooling and an adequate university education, and was immensely curious about everything. But, as he himself confessed a year later,

> Before, I more or less devoted myself to medicine and spent my free time studying Saint Karl [Marx] in an informal manner. This new phase in my

---

*His wife mentions other works, instead: *Insurgent Mexico*, by John Reed, and, in preparation for the Cuban expedition, Keynes, Smith, and Ricardo, as well as several Soviet novels. See Hilda Gadea, *Che Guevara: Años decisivos* (Mexico City: Aguilar, 1972), pp. 110, 147, 148. But Juan Ortega Arenas, a friend of Che's in Mexico and one of his main suppliers of books, recalls that he mainly asked for Marxist literature. Juan Ortega Arenas, interview with the author, Mexico City, May 23, 1996.

life requires a change in priorities: now Saint Karl comes first, he is the axis.[18]

Ernesto Guevara was not yet a man of letters, or of endless theoretical speculation. That much is suggested by an exchange attributed to the two men by one of Che's biographers, concerning the 26th of July Movement's program. "FIDEL: So hey, aren't you interested in all of this? GUEVARA: Yes, yes, I'm interested. . . . But I really don't know. First I would create a good army and after winning the war, we'd have to see. . . ."* More than a theorist or thinker, Che at this time was seeking an exit from a dependent existence in Mexico and the unpleasant prospect of a premature return to Argentina. He projected conceptual serenity, a humanistic culture, and a historical and international framework capable of embracing a political program. Castro, in contrast, was eminently a man of action. He may have been dazzled by Che's sophistication and cosmopolitan approach, one that Castro would always admire but never quite achieve, but he did not then, or later, fall under Che's spell. The trust and respect Fidel developed for him, for these reasons as well as the Argentine's natural charm, were but a starting point. A couple of years later, the *líder máximo* would pay a great deal of attention to Che, due to his bravery and dedication to the cause—but not to any political and theoretical expertise.

Che's reaction to the overthrow of Perón in September 1955—already touched on in Chapter 3—reflected the by now well-known stance of the newly recruited revolutionary. His comments to his family in Buenos Aires were acidly ironical, but not particularly lucid or penetrating. His emphasis on Washington's supposed interference was logical and understandable but, by all accounts, totally off the mark.[†] Guevara had just arrived from Guatemala, and his anti-U.S. views were typical of that highly polarized period in the Cold War.[‡] But they had little basis in the reality of Argentina.

---

*Hugo Gambini, *El Che Guevara* (Buenos Aires: Editorial Paidós, 1968), p. 105. Castro corroborates the tenor of this exchange in his interview with Lee Lockwood: "But in those days [in Mexico] we did not discuss these matters [revolutionary theory]. What we discussed was the struggle against Batista, the plan to disembark in Cuba, initiating guerrilla warfare. . . . It was Che's fighting spirit, as a man of action, that led him to join me in my struggle." Fidel Castro, quoted in Lee Lockwood, *Castro's Cuba, Cuba's Fidel* (New York: Macmillan, 1967), pp. 143–144.

† If anything, Perón had just made his peace with Washington: and no historian even mentions a U.S. role in his overthrow in 1955. On the contrary, in his search for foreign capital, Perón from 1953 sought a rapprochement with Washington. This rapprochement took place in the context of the failure to create a "Gran Argentina." Marvin Doldnert, *Democracy, Militarism and Nationalism in Argentina 1930–1966* (Austin: University of Texas Press, 1972), pp. 122, 123.

‡ According to Hilda Gadea, Guevara even blamed the FBI for a robbery at their Mexico City apartment, without any basis or later corroboration in the archives or other accounts. See Gadea, *Años decisivos,* p. 130.

His defense of the Communist Party and the importance he gave it—for instance, in an account to his mother of a lecture-debate he attended in November 1955—were characteristic of the time, but hardly relevant to his country's political situation. In the final analysis, Ernesto Guevara was a brilliant and well-intentioned "fellow traveler" in the international Communist movement, as were millions of other young people throughout the world during those heady, innocent years of the Stockholm Appeal, the Peace Movement of Louis Aragon and Joliot-Curie, of Pablo Neruda and Jorge Amado, Palmiro Togliatti and Maurice Thorez, Mao and Ho Chi Minh, and the Vietminh victory at Dien Bien Phu. The Soviet Communist Party's Twentieth Congress and its denunciation of Stalinism had not yet taken place; nor had the 1956 invasion of Hungary.* It was perfectly normal for a highly politicized and sensitive young man to believe in the infinite evils of imperialism and the countless virtues of the Socialist fatherland, and to see Communist activists as the harbingers of world revolution.[†] None of this, however, made Che a Marxist theoretician. It would take him another five years to attain this (self-taught) distinction.

Ernesto Guevara's life changed after his meeting with Fidel Castro. He married in August, as already noted. In November, while Castro was away on a visit to the United States, he celebrated his honeymoon with Hilda Gadea in southeastern Mexico (at Castro's insistence, according to her). There he finally came around to exploring Palenque, Uxmal, and Chichen-

---

*Carlos Franqui describes how, the first time he met Che in Mexico in 1956, the Argentine was reading Stalin's *Foundations of Leninism*. When Franqui asked him whether he had read Khrushchev's report to the Twentieth Congress, Che replied that it was nothing but imperialist propaganda. Carlos Franqui, interview with the author, San Juan, August 19, 1996. A hostile biographer has a similar anecdote: "In October 1956, when the Soviet army intervened to crush the nationalist Hungarian revolt, Che Guevara had vigorous discussions with one of his companions in which he defended that intervention." Roberto Luque Escalona, *Yo el Mejor de Todos: Una biografía no autorizada del Che Guevara* (Miami: Ediciones Universal, 1994), p. 71. Luis Simón, a university student who spent some time with Che in the Sierra in 1958, states that, on the contrary, Che criticized the Soviet invasion of Hungary, but he also said he had been a Trotskyist in Argentina, which was not true. Luis Simón, "Mis relaciones con el Che," *Revista Cuadernos* (Paris), May 1961. In a cable from the U.S. Embassy in Havana to the Department of State dated July 31, 1959, a correspondent for *Time* magazine quotes an account given him by Andrew St. George, another correspondent and possibly a U.S. intelligence informant. According to St. George, in the Sierra Che defended before him the Soviet intervention in Hungary and stated that "the Budapest insurrection was a fascist conspiracy against the people." Braddock/AmEmbassy Havana to Dept. of State, July 31, 1959 (Confidential), U.S. Department Files, vol. 8, dispatch 163.

[†] In a poem written upon the death of a patient at the General Hospital in Mexico City, Che plays upon all the strings of that era's leftist sentimentalism: "pay heed, proletarian grandmother, believe in the man who is coming, believe in the future you will never see. . . . Above all, you will have a scarlet vengeance, I swear it to all the extent of my ideals, your grandchildren will see the dawn, die in peace, old fighter." Ernesto Che Guevara, untitled poem, quoted in Gadea, *Años decisivos*, p. 232.

Itzá, whose Mayan ruins cannot but have dazzled him, though he wrote nothing about them in his letters home. The only remark to his mother, in slightly derogatory terms, referred to his "little trip to the Mayan region."[19] At the end of his voyage he wrote a fair-to-middling poem entitled "Palenque" which, aside from its obligatory anti-American swipe ("the insolent offense of the *gringo* tourist's stupid 'oh!' is a slap in your face"), its invocation of the mourned Incas ("long dead"), and a sagacious observation about the eternal youth of King Pakal's city, deserves no further mention.[20] Was this curious omission a sign of his ongoing Mexican depression, or of his concentration on the struggle ahead? Either way, the skillful, affectionate descriptions he devoted to the rest of Latin America are missing in the case of Mexico—a country that has enthralled far less sophisticated travelers than Che, and that should have fascinated him much more than the other stops in his Latin American wanderings. Either these pages were never written, or else they lie buried in the Cuban archives.

Training for the armed struggle in Cuba soon began. At first it was rudimentary and rather frivolous, consisting of walks along Avenida Insurgentes in Mexico City, rowing on the lake in Chapultepec Park, diet and exercise under the supervision of a Mexican wrestler, Arsacio Venegas. Then it turned serious, extending to a camp outside of Mexico City in Santa Rosa, a ranch near the town of Chalco. As Fidel Castro related during his first return to Mexico City in 1988, Che would try to scale the Popocatépetl every weekend, without ever making it to the top.* Once his association with the Cubans was underway, Che probably kept trying more as a training exercise than, as previously, as an individual challenge.†

It is clear, however, that Che did not really decide to join the Cuban revolutionary group on the night he met Fidel Castro. There are too many letters to his parents and other correspondents between July 1955 and early 1956 describing new, far-fetched plans for trips, scholarships, and life projects. In September he announced his intention to die fighting in the Caribbean—but also to continue traveling "as long as necessary to complete my education and give myself the pleasures I have allotted myself in

---

*Carlos Fazio, "Castro relata su primer encuentro con el Che en México," *Proceso*, December 12, 1988. Dr. León Bessudo, a Mexican alpinist, contradicts Castro and asserts that Guevara did plant a flag in the crater of Popocatépetl on October 12, 1955. David Bessudo, quoted in *Testimonios sobre el Che* (Havana: Editorial Pablo de la Torriente, 1990), p. 121.

† Che's father recounts that his failed expeditions to the volcano, even before he met Castro, were part of his guerrilla training. In reference to a letter from Che dated July 20, 1955, in which he mentions his "assaults" on the Popocatépetl, his father states: "Che was already in training with the Cubans to liberate Cuba." However, this is contradicted by Castro himself. See Ernesto Guevara Lynch, *Aquí va un soldado de América* (Buenos Aires: Sudamericana/Planeta, 1987), p. 106.

my life project."[21] As late as March 1, 1956, he mentioned to Tita Infante that he was still trying to obtain a scholarship to study in France.[22]

His entrancement with the project of revolution was tempered by the lucidity he had already displayed on several occasions. He had several good reasons for keeping his distance: his proverbial, sound Argentine skepticism and cynicism; his down-to-earth appraisal of the chances for a heterogeneous, inconsistent, and powerless group of Cubans adrift in Mexico City to overthrow a U.S.-supported military dictatorship enjoying an economic miniboom; and, finally, his own tendency always to seek *another* option. Che must also have reflected on the possibility that a foreigner in the expedition could be a political liability for Fidel, and indeed, several problems related to his nationality did spring up. The most important was the generalized discontent that Castro provoked when he named Che head of personnel at the Chalco training camp in April 1956. At least one other foreigner who wished to embark with the group in December 1956 was turned down by Fidel precisely because of his nationality.* Che himself, a couple of years later, would recall his initial reservations: "My almost immediate impression, when I attended the first classes, was about the possibilities of victory: I considered it very doubtful when I enlisted as a rebel commander."[23]

A handful of factors determined his commitment between July–August 1955, when he first signed up for the adventure, and the end of 1956, when the *Granma* actually sailed from the Mexican port of Tuxpan. His growing affinity with Cuban leaders traveling to Mexico to talk and forge alliances with Castro must have influenced the still skeptical Guevara. They included Frank País, the young urban leader of the 26th of July Movement; José Antonio Echevarría, head of the Revolutionary Student Movement, and later, the Communist leader Flavio Bravo, as well as (according to the English historian Hugh Thomas) Joaquín Ordoqui, Lázaro Peña, and Blas Roca, also of the PSP.[24] Che got to know most of them during their visits (though not País, whom he would meet only in the Sierra Maestra), and soon grasped that the outcome of the imminent Cuban Revolution did not rest only on the broad shoulders of Fidel Castro and his band of daredevil conspirators. It hinged upon a vast network of opponents to the regime, including labor and student activists, Communists, and even a few business leaders.

---

*According to Castro, the four foreigners—Che, the Mexican Guillén Zelaya, the Italian Gino Doné, and the Dominican Ramón Mejías del Castillo—were quite enough. Che's Guatemalan friend Julio Cáceres ("el Patojo") was turned away by Castro "not due to any negative attribute of his own, but because we did not wish to make of our Army a mosaic of nationalities." See Ernesto Che Guevara, "El Patojo," in "Pasajes de la guerra revolucionaria," *Escritos y discursos*, vol. 2 (Havana: Editorial de Ciencias Sociales, 1977), p. 292.

Che's growing affection and admiration for Fidel Castro also played an important role. Castro's loyalty and solidarity with his men, his increasing trust in Che—giving him ever greater and more complex responsibilities, like renting the ranch for the training camp as well as naming him head of personnel—also helped dissipate the Argentine's doubts, bolstering his decision to join the expedition. And a decisive element was Fidel's behavior when the Cubans were apprehended by the Mexican police on June 24, 1956.

At the urging of Batista's intelligence services, and thanks to a betrayal within the ranks as well as the infinite corruption of most of the Mexican security apparatus, the authorities finally arrested Fidel Castro in Mexico City. After contemplating resistance, he decided—with the same daunting political instinct that has kept him in power for almost forty years—to surrender, avoid confrontation, and then secure his release through a combination of bribes, rhetoric, and the help of Mexican supporters. Fernando Gutiérrez Barrios, then a young official at the Federal Security Directorate and a pillar of the Mexican government's security and intelligence services for more than a quarter century, remembers his first conversation with Fidel Castro: "We found weapons in your Packard and some documents. What's going on?" Castro remained silent for a few hours, but the police quickly discovered documents, a diagram of the highway exits, and the location of the Santa Rosa ranch in Chalco. Gutiérrez Barrios immediately dispatched his subordinates to the scene; they called back not long after: "Sir, there's a little store near the Hacienda of Santa Rosa they say has been rented; that's where they are training. The people at the little store say they are Cubans, because of their way of speaking and habits." The security official hauled in Fidel for a friendly conversation, confronting him with the evidence and enjoining him to stop wasting time and avoid a firefight that would be neither in their individual interests nor in that of their respective nations. Fidel agreed; Gutiérrez Barrios suggested they travel together to Chalco, where Fidel could order his men to surrender peacefully. They did, and Castro and Gutiérrez Barrios have remained close friends ever since.[25]

Fidel gave in, negotiating with the Mexican authorities the surrender of the other revolutionaries at the Chalco camp, and began to discuss the terms for their freedom. He soon had them all back on the street, except for himself, Calixto García, and Che. Finally only García and the Argentine remained in jail, both in an immigration and political situation more delicate than that of their companions. Che recorded his feelings in his diary:

> Fidel did a few things which we could almost say compromised his revolutionary attitude, for the sake of friendship. I remember that I specifically presented my case to him: I was a foreigner, in Mexico illegally, with a

series of charges against me. I told him the revolution should not in any way be impeded on my account and that he could leave me, that I understood the situation and would try to fight from wherever I was sent, and that he should only try to have me sent to a neighboring country and not Argentina. I also remember Fidel's response: "I will not abandon you." And that's how it was, because valuable time and money had to be diverted to get us out of the Mexican jail. Those personal attitudes of Fidel, with the people he appreciates, are the key to that fanaticism he awakens in others. . . .*

The arrest of the tiny revolutionary army has a privileged status in this Mexican phase of Che and the Cubans. Though Guevara and Cuban historians referred several times to the possible role of U.S. intelligence services in the arrests and subsequent interrogations, everything points to a strictly Mexican-Cuban operation.† And a rather lenient one at that, except for the ill treatment given a few of the prisoners. Castro would later denounce it, in his devastating comments on the actions and practices of the Mexican police. Regarding the detention of three companions, including a Mexican, he notes:

For over six days they were not given any food or water. In the freezing temperatures of early morning, they were tied hand and foot, completely naked, and lowered into tanks of icy water. They were submerged and then, on the point of asphyxiation, were pulled out by their hair for a few seconds before being immersed again. They repeated this operation many times, they took them out of the water and beat them into unconsciousness. A masked man, with a Cuban accent, was the one who interrogated them.‡

*Ernesto Che Guevara, "Pasajes," p. 6. It is difficult to establish whether a poem Che dedicated to Fidel (which is proof that even splendid narrators are not necessarily good poets) was written just before or after Fidel's act of solidarity with his Argentine friend. In any case, both the poem and the proof of Fidel's loyalty took place within a few days of each other.

† According to Gutiérrez Barrios: "No, I don't feel that the Americans exerted any pressure at all. Fidel was traveling to Miami to meet with the leaders, even with Prío who supported him to some extent, thanks to the Auténtico Party, and he also went to New York and had meetings with groups of Cubans, which means that the United States had nothing against him, aside from which the Batista government was collapsing on its own. The Americans were never present, and I do know that, because I was in control, especially at the Ministry of the Interior." Fernando Gutiérrez Barrios, interview with the author, Mexico City, July 28, 1995.

‡ Fidel Castro, Prison of Miguel Schultz, Mexico City, July 9, 1956. Notes for the manuscript of Carlos Franqui, *Diario de la revolución cubana,* Carlos Franqui Archive, Firestone Library, Princeton University, Princeton, N.J., C0644, box 2, file 2. The vast majority of his notes for the *Diario de la revolución cubana* were donated by Franqui—the spokesman for the movement till the victory of the revolution and then the publisher of its main newspaper—to the Firestone Library at Princeton University, and were quoted verbatim in the published book. This was not, however, the case for this text by Fidel Castro—

This was Che Guevara's first contact with prison, police forces, and repression. Until the eve of his execution at La Higuera, it was the only time he would ever spend in jail. His prison stay proved crucial for Che. Not only did it demonstrate the solidarity of Castro and the other Cubans, it also provided him with a firsthand experience of jail and the direct, personal aggressiveness of law enforcement authorities. Immediately before, as well as during his arrest and interrogation, Che had the chance to state repeatedly his identification with the hard-line, Communist, pro-Soviet faction of the revolutionary movement.

Since December 1955, Che had been studying Russian at the Mexican-Soviet Institute of Cultural Relations in Mexico City. His pro-Soviet leanings were already clear, but this additional step deserves emphasis. All Mexicans and foreign exiles living in Mexico at that time knew that the various Soviet missions in the capital—the Embassy, Intourist, Tass and *Pravda*, the cultural and language institutes—were carefully watched by the Mexican authorities and their U.S. "partners," as would be evidenced a few years later by the investigation of Lee Harvey Oswald's activities in Mexico. It is highly unlikely that Che would have attended classes at the Institute solely to read Pushkin and Lermontov *dans le texte*. His desire, unconscious or not, was to assert in a public and provocative way his respect and attachment to the Soviet Union. In this he certainly succeeded. One of the first U.S. intelligence reports mentioning Che Guevara emphasizes his visits to the cultural institute. When Mexican authorities and the Batista propaganda machine made a distinction between him and the other detainees, precisely because of his constant visits to the Soviet missions, Che was either paying a perfectly predictable price or achieving exactly what he wished: to be seen, much to his honor, as a Communist and defender of the Soviet Union, though not a card-carrying Party member.*

A similar thread runs through his meetings with Nikolai Leonov. As the former KGB official stated both in his memoirs and in an interview with the

---

perhaps because of his comments on Mexico. Previous and later passages by Castro are to be found on p. 141 of Carlos Franqui, *Diario de la revolución cubana* (Barcelona: R. Torres, 1976). From now on, when I quote from Franqui I will refer to the Princeton archive only when the notes do not appear in his book; in all other cases, I will refer to the R. Torres edition of the book.

*In what is probably the first reference to Che Guevara in an official U.S. document, the "Argentinian Communist" is accused of being a protégé of Vicente Lombardo Toledano, the Mexican labor leader, intellectual, and politician. The document asserts that Che belonged to the latter's People's Party, and found employment in Mexico thanks to him. Everything indicates that this was not the case: Che was not a member of the People's Party, was not a friend of Vicente Lombardo Toledano, and did not find employment thanks to him. Foreign Broadcast Information Service (FBIS), Daily Report, July 25, 1956, no. 145, p. 5. Quoted in "Possibility of Communist Connections," Department of State, National Archives, lot 60 D 513, MER 1137, box 7–8.

author in Moscow, his whole affair with the Cubans began with the friendship he struck up by accident with Raúl Castro in 1951. Leonov was on his way to study Spanish and work at the Soviet Embassy in Mexico. Four years later, he happened to meet Raúl in the streets of Mexico City, where they renewed their friendship. The Cuban explained the ostensible reasons for his stay in Mexico, as did Leonov. Neither one was exactly forthright, but they obviously hit it off. During one of their many get-togethers at the home of María Antonia, hostess and guardian angel of Fidel and his followers in Mexico, Che suddenly appeared. In the words of Leonov,

> Che looked very well, radiant with happiness because here was a representative of the other world, of the Socialist camp, and we began discussing everything. I approached Raúl for the same reason on the boat, and talked with Che upon the same basis, our conversation taking place in a location where we were equals. He asked me about the Soviet Union because in that year, 1956, a great many things had happened. He was basically well informed, though concrete matters, the Central Committee meetings, did not interest Che. He knew a lot about the Soviet Union, how the society was structured, how the economy functioned, that is, he had a basic understanding of what was then the Soviet Union. At that time everybody had the same vision, the same admiration. He was an admirer of [the Soviet Union].[26]

They talked for a long time. Guevara expressed his interest in Soviet literature and asked if he could visit Leonov at the old house in Tacubaya where the Soviets were quartered, and borrow some books that would help him understand the Soviet people. Leonov handed him the plain business card he carried, identifying him as an attaché at the Embassy, and forthrightly replied, Why not, what books would he be interested in? Che indicated three titles: Ostrovsky's *Thus Is Steel Tempered,* Polevoi's *A True Man,* and *The Defense of Stalingrad.* One day Che simply showed up; as Leonov recalls now, he had the books "ready for him. He was in a great hurry, he surely had more important things to do, and when I invited him to come in for a while and talk he said he had to go."[27]

When Guevara was taken into custody a few weeks later, the Mexican authorities raised an outcry upon finding the Russian diplomat's card in his wallet, immediately accusing Che of being an agent of international communism. Actually, according to Leonov, they had met only a couple of times; and if he himself was quickly dispatched home by an angry ambassador as punishment for the ensuing uproar, this was only a mark of his superior's excessive prudence.

It is absurd to suspect that, thanks to Leonov's delicate footwork, Che was recruited by the U.S.S.R. during those months. However, his account is either specious or simplistic. Che must have been aware that any contact with Soviet personnel at the height of the Cold War, in an arena as important as Mexico (comparable to Vienna or Berlin in those years), was likely to be detected by U.S. and/or Mexican intelligence. He must have known, in one way or another, that the mere fact of having in his possession the card of a Soviet diplomat—while secretly training for guerrilla warfare thirty kilometers from Mexico City—could only be seen as a provocation. It practically guaranteed that he would be accused of links with Moscow, if arrested—which could happen any day. Furthermore, even if Leonov did not originally intend to recruit the Argentine, his conversations with him and growing knowledge of the Cuban group's plans almost demanded that he approach Guevara. He was after all more ideologically committed, more accessible and talented, than most of the other revolutionaries-in-training. One might speculate that if Leonov did not recruit Che, it was not out of indifference; and if Che was not recruited, it was not out of a lack of willingness.

There is also Che's insistence on his Marxist-Leninist orientation during his interrogation at the Ministry of the Interior. Of course he had to admit it, but he went further. He debated with the authorities, defending various Marxist theses and arguing incessantly with Antonio Villalda, the public prosecutor. According to Gutiérrez Barrios,

At that time we proceeded to Miguel Schultz [an immigration services bureau] and took statements from all of them. The only one who confessed to his ideology was Che. When he was questioned by the public prosecutor he stated that his ideology was Marxist-Leninist, quite clearly. The others didn't, because none of them had those characteristics. Fidel Castro was a follower of Martí. But Che made a statement about the situation, expressing the depth of his ideology and beliefs. The public prosecutor was someone I had categorized as our expert on communism, as we called it without any further qualification, and that specialist in communism was the man who questioned Che. Che had already confessed he was a Marxist-Leninist, and this lawyer proposed to discuss that philosophy, but his expertise was very limited compared to Che's profound knowledge. When they entered into a discussion and I saw that, on top of everything, our lawyer was making a fool of himself, I called him over and said, "Counselor, he already told you he's a Marxist-Leninist, just go directly to his offenses and nothing more." Because Che was being very arrogant, with all the weight of his knowledge, and he was winning the entire discussion, in an ideological debate that was completely irrelevant.[28]

Che not only made no effort to conceal his ideological or political inclinations—as all the other detainees were doing—but also took pride in them, actually seeking to convert his captors.* One can hardly imagine the Castros or any of the other Cuban leaders boasting about their political or ideological convictions and holding a heated debate with their jailers. Che was bursting with his new Communist, Soviet, revolutionary faith: far from hiding it, he flaunted it. As long as his impact on the political thinking of the 26th of July Movement remained limited, his militant pride was of little consequence. But as his political influence grew, his ideological vanity would acquire considerable historical importance.

Guevara's burgeoning enthusiasm for the Cuban venture was further strengthened by his physical and military training under the direction of Alberto Bayo, a former officer in the Spanish Republican army. Toward the end of April 1956, Castro obtained the money to purchase the Santa Rosa ranch near Chalco, in the state of Mexico, fifty miles east of Mexico City. By then he had persuaded Bayo to drill the recruits. Che received training in physical exercise and stamina, tactics, and target practice. As the group's head of personnel, Che seems not to have experienced any major difficulties, and it must have been highly gratifying to him to find that, despite his asthma and the altitude, he was able to keep up with his companions and obtain the best grades in the group. In his notes, Bayo wrote of his favorite pupil: "He attended about 20 regular practice sessions, shooting about 650 cartridges. Excellent discipline, excellent leadership qualities, excellent physical stamina. Some disciplinary blunders due to small errors in interpreting orders and slight smiles."[29] Of course, by nighttime Che "looked tired from the marches . . . which left him in pieces."[30] However, Bayo recalls that:

> Guevara was ranked first in the class. He had the highest grade, ten, in everything. When Fidel saw the grades he asked me, why is Guevara always number one? Doubtless because he's the best. That's what I think, I said. I have the same opinion of him, Castro replied.[†]

---

*There is another fact which supports this analysis. In his Sierra Maestra interview with Jorge Masetti, Che said, with regard to his role in Guatemala: "I never held a post in the Arbenz government." Ernesto Che Guevara, interview with Jorge Masetti, reprinted in *Granma* (Havana), Oct. 16, 1967. However, his statement to the public prosecutor in Mexico asserts that "he arrived in this capital approximately a year and a half ago, from Guatemala, which he left at the fall of the Jacobo Arbenz government, of which he was a sympathizer and in whose administration he had served." See Adys Cupull and Froilán González, *Un hombre bravo* (Havana: Editorial Capitán San Luis, 1994), p. 384.

† Alberto Bayo, *Mi aporte a la revolución cubana* (Havana: Imprenta Ejército Rebelde, 1960). In his memoirs, published in 1960 with a preface by Che, Bayo recalls his own appraisal of Che's political affiliation, which is different from the official Cuban description and from the one proposed here: "He had no sympathy for Perón, the dictator who had thrown him in jail [sic]; he called him a Communist and I deduced on a hundred occasions that Guevara, like myself, was not a Communist and had never been one." Ibid., p. 77.

Ever since his rugby-playing days in Córdoba and Buenos Aires, Guevara had tried to prove to himself that his asthma was not an obstacle to any of the physical activities he enjoyed. To a large extent he succeeded. His guerrilla exercises in Mexico constituted the hardest test he had ever set himself, and he passed it with honors. Che could no longer doubt his capacity to overcome the adverse effects of his ailment. It would have been senseless, after such a victory, to pull back for other reasons. Whatever doubts he might still have had disappeared during practice at Santa Rosa. His decision was sealed.

Last and probably least among the factors worth mentioning was the state of Guevara's marriage. The views of Castro's most recent biographer are doubtless extreme: Che did not enroll in the *Granma* expedition in order to leave his wife.[31] But there is no doubt that he considered the relationship a failure, even if Hilda did not. Since the birth of their daughter, Ernesto had had serious misgivings. As he wrote to his friend Tita Infante in Buenos Aires,

> [Little Hilda] has given me a double joy. First of all, her arrival put an end to a disastrous conjugal situation and secondly, I am now completely sure that I will be able to leave, despite everything. My incapacity to live with her mother is greater than my affection for her. For a moment I thought that a combination of the little girl's charm and consideration for her mother (who is in many ways a great woman, who loves me in an almost pathological way) might turn me into a boring family man. Now I know this will not be the case, and that I will pursue my bohemian life until who knows when.*

Once again, Che decided to flee the reality he could not live with. He could no longer tolerate married life, but adored the little girl. Unable to go or to stay, he avoided a clear-cut, explicit separation. What with his training, his fifty-seven days in jail, and increasingly clandestine life, Che was increasingly absent from home—but dared not take any drastic action. When Hilda left for Peru and Che for Cuba, the situation became even more equivocal. Matters were so unresolved that Hilda still believed, when she arrived in Havana after the Revolution, that the marriage could be saved.†

---

*Ernesto Guevara de la Serna, letter to Tita Infante, March 1, 1965, quoted in Adys Cupull and Froilán González, *Cálida presencia* (Havana: Editorial Oriente, 1995), p. 80. The same letter quoted in Guevara Lynch, *Aquí va*, p. 129, does not include this passage. As already noted, Che's father shared the Cubans' compulsion to strip their heroes of any trauma, dilemma, or contradiction.

† Hilda Gadea's account in her memoirs is elliptical but revealing: "When I arrived in Havana . . . Ernesto told me he had another woman . . . and with great pain on my part . . . we decided to divorce. . . . When he saw my pain, he said: 'It would have been better to die in combat.' " Gadea, *Años decisivos*, pp. 201–202. Che's father presented a fictive

Che, in contrast, considered it over as early as October 1956—as he said to others, though not to her, or to his mother. Celia remained unaware of her son's separation until she joined him in Havana after the triumph of the revolution:

> My marriage is almost completely destroyed and will break down completely next month, when my wife goes to Peru. . . . There is a certain bitter taste in this split, as she was a loyal companion and her revolutionary conduct was beyond reproach . . . but our spiritual discord was very great.[32]

Faced with this tangle of mixed feelings, it did not seem a bad idea for Che to break things off tacitly and embark on the Cuban expedition. Obviously, Guevara did not choose the path of revolution only to leave his wife. At the same time, it would be equally misleading not to include it in the reasons for the collapse of his marriage. Che was not a man driven by emotional impulses; yet the great dividing lines in his life were accompanied by moments of emotional distress or romantic disillusion. The essential point was always, however, his quest for a destiny. Purely political and strictly personal concerns were secondary in Che's life.

Neither Che and Fidel, nor their companions in Mexico during those years, assign a major role to Guevara in the strategic debates within the 26th of July Movement. Of course, he was in charge of the future guerrillas' political and ideological training; he imparted instruction at the Santa Rosa ranch, to the Cuban detainees at the immigration services bureau on Miguel Schultz Street, and at the various other places that sheltered Castro and his men before they sailed from Tuxpan. But beyond his teaching—separate from the strategic and tactical discussions within the movement, or between it and other Cuban groups—Guevara's views did not play a prominent part. According to one of his Mexican friends, his silence was due to both conviction and convenience. As a foreigner, he had great respect for the Cubans and did not feel he should intervene in any immediate or important way: "I cannot tell them anything about their own land." His stance was also a matter of convenience: his opinions might have led to disagreements and jeopardized his chief goal, which was to participate in the invasion of Cuba.[33]

Another possible reason for Che's reserve was the frankly reformist nature of the 26th of July Movement (M-26-7), at least in its public manifestations. As has been broadly documented, the political, ideological, social, and economic theses of Fidel Castro and his companions (whether

---

view of the relationship. Speaking in 1957—months after the couple's physical and emotional separation—he wrote: "I had my daughter-in-law Hilda Gadea and our granddaughter Hildita come to stay. They traveled to Buenos Aires to join us. . . ." Ernesto Guevara Lynch, *Mi hijo el Che* (Barcelona: Planeta, 1981), p. 23.

in the Cuban or Mexican jails, in the Sierra Madre, or even during their first months in power) were anything but Marxist or revolutionary in any classical sense. Castro's defense summation at his trial of October 1953, "History will absolve me"; the pamphlet he wrote under the same title, secretly published in April 1954; the Manifesto Number One of the M-26-7 issued in Mexico City, after Fidel's arrival; and his letter of resignation to the Ortodoxo Party on March 19, 1956, are all moderate in their substance and orthodox in their thinking. Theodore Draper, one of the most conservative critics of Castro, even sees in them a growing moderation and "constitutionalism."[34] The sincerity of these texts is a different matter, as it relates to the biography of Fidel Castro and the debates over the nature of the Cuban Revolution. The issue here is Che's position vis-à-vis the Cuban group's program, and his hypothetical willingness to enter into an alleged falsehood or deception.

As it was initially designed, Fidel Castro's program called for five broad reforms: the reestablishment of the 1940 constitution; an agrarian reform that would grant land to peasants with less than 150 acres; a profit-sharing scheme in the sugar mills; a limited reform of the sugar industry; and the confiscation of lands obtained through fraud. It also promised an educational reform consisting mainly of pay raises for teachers, the nationalization of public services and the telephone system, and a housing reform.[35] In itself, this platform was no more radical than those espoused by classical Latin American populists like Perón, Cárdenas, Vargas, or Batista himself in 1940. Yet nothing in Cuba was really comparable to the rest of Latin America. As one of the most recent analyses of its history makes clear,

> In the Cuban context of the fifties, the 26th of July Movement was not a reformist movement. . . . The substance of the reforms it posited was the core of similar reforms in other Latin American countries. But not in Cuba. . . . The Fidelistas called for change in a society where economic and social failings had considerably weakened the possibilities of reform, and used radical means to take power.[36]

Still, even after his resignation from the Ortodoxo Party, Castro continued to receive generous donations from figures like former president Carlos Prío Socarrás; the head of Líneas Aéreas Cubanas, López Vilaboy; and several Cuban expatriates in the United States. The revolutionary nature of the enterprise would thus reside either in the means used, or in the hope (based upon Castro's personality and Che's trust in him) that the struggle would take a more radical turn once victorious. Everything suggests that Guevara was fighting for an ideal of his own, and to be with Fidel, rather than for the Movement's actual program or even the eventual transformation of Cuban society. This was not the first time Ernesto Guevara would emphasize the struggle's method over its content. His decision in Mexico had little to do with any abstract conceptualization; it was based more upon political calculation and a certain emotional state. If Che had entered into prolonged discussions with the Cubans about their platform, he probably would not have agreed with them. Nor, perhaps, would he have convinced himself of the project's viability and its inherent greatness.

The departure for Cuba was preceded by a long series of personal complications and political, logistical, and military setbacks: just days before D-day, the Mexican police confiscated twenty rifles and 50,000 rounds of ammunition from the Cubans in the capital. Finally the *Granma* sailed from Tuxpan, Veracruz, at dawn on November 25, heading for the eastern coast of Cuba. The boat, a recreational yacht purchased from a U.S. resident of Mexico City, had cost $15,000 and was woefully inappropriate for its task. It was small and unstable, and had too short a range. But Fidel was in a hurry—not so much due to the pressures exerted by the Mexican authorities,* or the dangers posed by Batista's agents in Mexico,† but because of his own oft-repeated pledge: "In 1956 we will be free or we will be martyrs." Thus, there was no alternative for the group but to cast themselves upon the Gulf of Mexico before year's end, even if they were not ready for the crossing.

On the night of November 25, the *Granma* glided through the estuary of the Tuxpan River with lights dimmed and motors muffled. Che was leaving Mexico forever, without ever having lived in or loved the country. His stay of over two years was made meaningful by its ending, not by his initially monotonous life in the city. In Mexico, toward the end of his stay, he experienced some of the most meaningful moments of his twenty-eight years: there he had met Castro and joined the Cuban Revolution. But, the country itself had little to do with these events; they could just as well have happened anywhere.

Che enlisted in the expedition as its medical officer. Given the rank of lieutenant, he was in charge of medical supplies and tending to possible casualties among the eighty-two men. He was able to carry out his duties only with great difficulty. He was soon floored by a merciless asthma attack

*Gutiérrez Barrios asserts that the Mexican government did not pressure the Cubans into leaving, and that he helped Castro avoid problems in Tuxpan by calling the men he had there back to Mexico City. Gutiérrez Barrios, interview with the author.

† The official Cuban account attributes their hasty departure to the desertion and subsequent betrayal of two members of the Abasolo camp, in the state of Tamaulipas, on November 21. Without questioning this fact, one can confidently state that many other factors were also involved—including the beginnings of an uprising in Cuba itself. See Centro para el estudio de la historia militar, *De Tuxpan a La Plata* (Havana: Editorial Orbe, 1981), p. 70.

on the high seas, aggravated by the lack of epinephrine or an inhaler. The other members of the crew became seasick almost as soon as they lifted anchor. The ship's doctor was unable to help them, discovering to his dismay that the anti-seasickness pills had been left behind, along with prudence and sound planning. The boat should not have taken on more than twenty passengers; aside from eighty-two men, it carried food and water, arms and ammunition: two antitank guns, thirty-five rifles with telescopic sights, fifty-five Mexican rifles, three Thompson submachine guns, and forty light machine pistols.

The scheme had been closely coordinated with Cuba. The 26th of July Movement on the island, led by Frank País, was ready to launch a popular uprising in Santiago on November 30. It fulfilled its task, though part of the responsibility for its action was mistakenly attributed to others.* The *Granma* was supposed to have moored at Niquero, in the Oriente province, on the same day. Instead, it landed seventy-two hours later on December 2, at Los Cayuelos near Colorados Beach, far from Niquero and in the middle of a nightmarish mangrove swamp. The plans laid in Mexico met with one obstacle after another: the slowness of the boat due to its defective motors and overloading; the bad weather, more or less typical for the season; and navigational errors. Nor did the landing itself go according to schedule. Because of the inhospitable terrain, the rebels had to abandon part of their supplies, struggle through a mangrove swamp for hours on end, and break up into several isolated groups. In addition, because the boat made landfall after the scheduled date, Batista's regime was alerted and ready to counterattack.† Disaster seemed inevitable; indeed, it was not long in coming.

During the hours and days after going ashore, the *Granma*'s crew was dispersed throughout the swamp, where many of its members were rapidly spotted and picked off by government forces. Che Guevara's own baptism of fire took place in the cane fields of the Niquero plantation owned by the Lobo family, one of the wealthiest on the island. The first combat of the revolution broke out on December 5 in Alegría de Pío. Che was caught in a burst of machine-gun fire, receiving a flesh wound in the neck which, though slight, was gory and frightening. It was Che's first brush with death;

---

* A confidential report dated January 4, 1957, addressed to Roy Rubottom, assistant secretary of state for American Republic Affairs, states that "there is proof that the Popular Socialist Party participated in the terrorist activities in Cuba during the last month." Murphy to Rubottom, January 4, 1957, Department of State, National Archives, lot 60 D 513, MER 1137, box 7–8.

† "We ran around at a muddy place, only to get into the worst swamp I have ever seen. . . . we had to leave almost all our supplies in that accursed mangrove swamp . . . to get through that hell." Raúl Castro, "Diario de la guerrilla cubana," quoted in Che Guevara and Raúl Castro, *La conquista de la esperanza* (Mexico City: Ediciones Joaquín Mortíz, 1995), p. 75.

he would later evoke Jack London's classic lines on dying of cold in the Great North as the first thought that came to him. But the more appropriate passage defining his state of mind and his sense of destiny and a preordained death lies in the verses of the Spanish poet León Felipe found in his knapsack a decade later, after his capture in Bolivia:

> Christ: I love you, not because you came down from a star, but because you showed me the light. You taught me man is God, a poor God in sin like You, and he on Your left on the Golgotha, the evil thief, is God too.

The skirmish ended with the revolutionaries' disorderly flight. Some of them, including Ñico López, Che's first Cuban friend, fell beneath the gunfire and shells deployed by Batista's army and navy. Others were captured. The rest were split into small, isolated, and demoralized groups. Che, by now in terrible physical shape, began the march toward the Sierra Maestra, Cuba's highest mountain range, with four companions, joined by three others the next day. Traveling without water and almost no food, with rudimentary arms and very little ammunition, they headed for the mountains hoping to meet with the others—if they were still alive—and evade a new offensive by the army. Che's companions included Ramiro Valdéz, Camilo Cienfuegos, and Juan Almeida, all destined to play key roles in the coming months and years. Sixteen harrowing days later, beset by hunger, thirst, fatigue, and dejection, they arrived at the farm of a peasant named Mongo Pérez, near the foot of the eastern mountain range. There they regrouped with the other survivors, including, among others, Fidel and Raúl Castro. They had previously left their arms at a peasant's home along the way, where they were almost immediately confiscated in an army raid. Fidel Castro was furious: one must never abandon one's arms, and "to leave them was a crime and a stupidity."[37]

Two things kept the *Granma* revolutionaries alive: the remarkable willpower and self-confidence of Fidel Castro, who declared their survival a triumph and promised certain victory to the tiny band of exhausted guerrillas; and the help of the local peasants. Both factors allowed the rebels to make contact with the movement's urban groups (especially that of Celia Sánchez in the neighboring city of Manzanillo) and to reassemble under cover of the Sierra Maestra. There, Fidel Castro's formidable sense of opportunity led to a successful assault on a military position in La Plata, a village near the coast, in mid-January—barely three weeks after the survivors' rendezvous.

The attack was momentous for a number of reasons. First of all, it announced to the rest of Cuba, and especially the movement's supporters, that the group was still operative and capable of inflicting casualties on the army. Secondly, it lifted their own morale, showing that with calm, determination, and daring they could succeed in reversing the December defeat and achieving victory. Finally, it demonstrated to local peasants that the rebels were a force to be reckoned with, able to wage war on the enemy while protecting supporters and punishing traitors. In fact, it was during the combat of La Plata that the 26th of July Movement carried out its first execution. Chicho Osorio, an army informer, fell into the guerrillas' trap when he led them to the small military barracks and was shot as soon as the gunfire began.

The Sierra Maestra and the eastern part of Cuba, where Che and his companions would spend most of the next year and a half, was a poor, sparsely populated, and almost exclusively rural region. It belonged to a handful of landowners; agriculture was limited to sugar cane and coffee; and social indicators lagged behind even the most destitute areas elsewhere on the island. The peasants—white, black, and mulatto in equal proportions—led a precarious, hard, and violent existence. They had nothing to lose and a lot to gain through a radical change in their living conditions. The guerrillas, as they themselves acknowledged, had never come into close contact with such an impoverished peasant population, much less lived among them. It was an emotional encounter. The solidarity, simplicity, and nobility of the Sierra's *guajiros* were for many of them a true revelation. In the words of Raúl Castro, "It is admirable to see how these peasants of the Sierra go out of their way to tend to us and take care of us. All the nobility and generosity of Cuba are concentrated here."[38] For two years, Che's knowledge of Cuba would be restricted to this area. Of course he would meet many other Cubans, from the city or other classes, who came to the Sierra for various reasons—but only briefly and sporadically. As "Pombo" (Harry Villegas), one of his closest aides from the Sierra Maestra all the way through to Bolivia, would remark later, Che himself would come to consider himself a native of the Sierra Maestra, not only because he came to love it, but because it was the only region of Cuba he knew at all.[39] Given his predilection for otherness, his special affection for the peasants was logical, as would be his subsequent and mistaken overestimation of the *campesinos'* role in the struggle.*

The first few months in the Sierra were bittersweet for Ernesto Guevara, encompassing a wide and quite diverse range of experiences. During his second combat, at a place aptly named Hell's Ravine, he killed his first enemy.

---

*Julio Zeñon Acosta was one of the first peasants to join the uprising, and the first whom Che taught to read and write. When he died, Che wrote in his diary: "The man was tireless. He knew the area well, and was always ready to help a companion in trouble or a companion from the city who wasn't yet strong enough to fend for himself. He was the one who brought water from the faraway spring, who could build a fire quickly, and find the kindling needed to make a fire on a rainy day." Ernesto Che Guevara, quoted in Che Guevara and Raúl Castro, *La conquista,* p. 310.

He met Frank País, who arrived in mid-February to coordinate the delivery of arms and reestablish contact between the Revolution's urban and mountain groups. Che was also able to send a short note to his family in Buenos Aires, assuring them that he was still alive despite press reports to the contrary.* He requested books from the city, on algebra, Cuban history, and geography, as well as French texts to teach Raúl Castro the language.†

During those months Che carried out the first execution of a traitor among the guerrilla ranks, Eutimio Guerra.‡ He suffered a violent attack of malaria in early February, when the small band of rebels was subject to systematic raids by the army and air force. Toward the end of that month, he was felled by another asthma attack. The crises were becoming more frequent and intense, and the lack of epinephrine or even an inhaler prevented him from keeping up with the others:

> The asthma was so strong it didn't let me advance. . . . I made it, but with such an asthma attack that every single step was difficult. . . . I had to make a decision, because it was impossible for me to go on . . . [without] at least buying medicines.[40]

Finally, he was able to obtain medication. This, along with some rest and his indomitable willpower, allowed him to catch up with the thin column (of only eighteen men) by mid-March 1957. These were the worst days of the war for him. Within a short time he suffered military setbacks, asthma attacks, and a shortage of medicines. Fortunately, only three weeks passed between his bout with malaria and his arrival at the house of Epifanío Díaz, where he met up with Fidel and the others. He extracted contradictory lessons from the distressing experience. He learned that even under the worst conditions, he could overcome the effects of his illness and keep going. But he did not quite recognize that this was possible only under exceptional circumstances. His recovery occurred because he found somewhere to rest and a family to take care of him; because his companions lent a hand and he ultimately secured the necessary epinephrine or adrena-

---

*"Dear folks: I am perfectly well. I have spent only two and still have five. I am still working on the same thing. News is sporadic and will continue to be but have faith that God is an Argentine. A big hug for all, Teté." Quoted in *Revista de la Casa de las Américas*, no. 168, May–June 1988, p. 6.

† As Raúl Castro noted, "All the books had been requested . . . by the many-faceted Che." Raúl Castro, "Diario," p. 157.

‡ In his recent biography of Guevara, Paco Ignacio Taibo II claims that Che carried out the sentence himself, quoting an unpublished interview of Universo Sanchez by Luis Adrian Betancourt. Paco Ignacio Taibo II, *Ernesto Guevara también conocido como el Che* (Mexico City: Planeta, 1996), pp. 163 and 780. In his biography, Jon Lee Anderson quotes Che's Sierra Maestra diary to the same effect. See Anderson, *Che Guevara* (New York: Grove Press, 1997), p. 237.

line in the city of Manzanillo; and lastly because his enemy, though near, did not concentrate its forces on tracking him down. These fortunate conditions would not necessarily be repeated. In the end, Che probably failed to assimilate a crucial point. His temporary incapacity did not affect the campaign, because it was led by someone else: Fidel Castro. But the same disability, whether temporary or lasting, slight or serious, would have had devastating consequences had Che himself led the column, movement, or struggle.

The guerrillas' prospects began to improve in late February and March. That was when Fidel Castro granted his famous interview to Herbert Matthews of the *New York Times,* proving to the world that he was still alive and providing a vivid, if exaggerated, description of the Rebel Army's forces.* The first reinforcements from the cities began arriving in March, under the command of Jorge Sotús. This occasion prompted one of the few quarrels between Che and Fidel in those years. Guevara was commissioned by him to receive the aspiring guerrillas from the urban wing of the 26th of July Movement. But Sotús "stated that he had orders to transfer the troops to Fidel and that he could not transfer them to anybody else, that he was still in command. At that time I still had my foreigner's complex and did not want to take things too far, though one could see some discontent . . . among the troops."[41] The matter was finally resolved, but in a meeting ten days later when Castro reached the camp, he "criticized . . . my attitude for not imposing the authority he had conferred on me, and leaving it in the hands of the recently arrived Sotús, against whom there was no bad feeling, but whose attitude, in Fidel's view, should not have been permitted."[42]

Che's status remained undefined. He was already more than a medical officer, and his relationship with Fidel placed him in an exceptional position. But he was still a foreigner, and there was no formal recognition of the tasks he was performing. In addition, his views were often disregarded.[†] A first sign of Che's changing fortunes occurred in mid-May of 1957 when, upon the arrival of an arms shipment, Castro assigned to Guevara one of the four heavy machine guns. "I was being initiated as a direct combatant,

---

*Following the interview, and in a classic example of historical blindness, the U.S. ambassador in Havana, Arthur Gardner, commented confidentially: "The controversy over whether Fidel Castro is alive or dead has no real importance." Arthur Gardner to Roy Rubottom, February 28, 1957, Department of State, National Archives, box 2, College Park, Maryland.

† Che's honesty contrasts with that of his epigones. In a recent biography, Jean Cormier attributes to Guevara the Cubans' hugely effective tactic of returning prisoners to the enemy. But Che himself states in his diary: "Against the opinion of the more drastic ones, including myself, the prisoners were questioned and held overnight and then released." Che Guevara and Raúl Castro, *La conquista,* p. 254. Cormier's assertion appears in Jean Cormier, *Che Guevara* (Paris: Editions du Rocher, 1995), p. 131.

which I had already been on an occasional basis even though my fixed position was medical officer. A new phase was beginning for me in the Sierra."[43]
At the same time, during those weeks he worked as a visiting doctor among
the small villages in the area. In modern urban terms, his inexperience and
shortcomings as a physician were undeniable.* But in huts and hamlets that
had never seen a doctor before, his arrival was a major event.

Che was beginning to take or propose initiatives outside his formal brief.
At the end of May, he suggested to Fidel Castro that they ambush one of
the many army trucks patrolling the zone. Fidel rejected the notion, arguing
that an assault upon a nearby barracks on the coast would be more prof-
itable. As Guevara himself expressed it, "his thirst for combat" was running
away with him. He neglected the political and psychological aspects of military action, while for Castro they were of paramount importance. But the
main point is not the military or political merits of each man's position, but
the fact that they were discussing such issues at all—as peers, if not equals.
Furthermore, it reveals that they could resolve their differences quickly and
effectively, without any lasting ill effects. So it would be for several years.

Ironically, one of those who most benefited from Castro's decision to
attack the military barracks was Guevara himself. The battle of Uvero on
May 28, 1957, marked the Rebel Army's coming of age. In it, Che attained
a military rank in accordance with his talent, bravery, and responsibility. As
Pombo recalled many years later, "He was a man who liked to take the lead
in combat, to set an example; he would never say, go and fight, but rather,
follow me into combat."[44] Though assigned a precise and limited task in the
assault, in Castro's words, "Che asked for three or four men and in a matter
of moments started out to launch an attack from that direction."[45] He stood
out not only in battle, but in tending to the wounded among both his men
and the enemy's. He was unable to save six of his companions though, and
the army suffered total losses of fourteen lives, fourteen prisoners, and nineteen wounded. The combat pitted eighty guerrilla fighters against fifty-
three soldiers—the largest battle in the war thus far.

During the month of June, Guevara stayed with the wounded, separated
from the rebels' main column. Lacking medication once again for his
asthma, he was almost as incapacitated as his patients—and just as demoralized, despite the victory at Uvero. The small detachment recorded both
desertions and new arrivals at a dizzying rate. After two weeks, contact was
reestablished with the main column. Che's first experience of independent
command had gone smoothly, if not spectacularly. The guerrillas' situation

---

*A former combatant of the Sierra recalls that Che's hygienic practices were far from
perfect: "He didn't even wash his hands." Francisco Rodríguez, quoted in Martin Resnick,
The Black Beret: The Life and Meaning of Che Guevara (New York: Ballantine Books,
1969), p. 88.

was stabilizing; they now controlled an area which the enemy could not penetrate, at least for the moment. There was thus a certain freedom to "talk during the night," consolidating relations with the peasants and receiving political visitors in a context of relative calm.

Thanks to his bravery and tenacity, Che was promoted to *comandante* on July 21, 1957. In his words, "the dose of vanity that we all have inside made me feel the proudest man on earth."[46] The Rebel Army's second column was placed under his command. It consisted of three platoons of twenty-five men, relatively well equipped and possessing some autonomy of action and movement. Though Fidel gave the orders, in weekly or fortnightly dispatches carried by messenger, Che had a substantial measure of independence. Guevara led several battles, of varying importance, during the following months: at El Bueycito in July, El Hombrito at the end of August, Pino del Agua in early September. Some skirmishes turned out in the rebels' favor, others did not. In some cases, the Fidelista combatants received praise from their commander, while in others his evaluation was more critical. Concerning his first experience in leading a battle, Che wrote to Fidel: "My inauguration as a *comandante* was a success from the point of view of victory, and a failure in terms of organization."[47] In December 1957, after one year in the Sierra, Che was wounded in the foot during a battle in the Altos de Conrado. Castro scolded him: "I seriously suggest that you be careful. I order you not to take on any combat role. Take charge of directing people well, which is the indispensable task at this time."*

During the second half of 1957, Che's position as column commander was firmly established. For the first time, he began to participate actively in the discussions, debates, and disputes within the 26th of July Movement. His diaries and letters expound positions often similar to those of Fidel Castro, but at times he takes more frank or radical stances. He begins to record his thoughts on delicate matters which would accompany the Cuban Revolution like a dark and sad shadow through the rest of the century. Soon after the *Granma* landing, the execution of traitors, informers, or particularly cruel enemy officers was instituted as standing guerrilla practice; that is how Raúl Castro presents it in his diary, right after the execution of the informer Chicho Osorio.† Soon after the battle of El Hombrito, when there was a pause in the war which, among other things, allowed him to set-

---

*Fidel Castro, letter to Ernesto Guevara, quoted in Carlos Franqui, *Diario,* p. 385. Che replies, "I am sorry to have disregarded your advice, but our people's morale was very low . . . and I considered my presence necessary in the line of fire." Ernesto Guevara, letter to Fidel Castro, December 1957, quoted in *Granma* (Havana), October 16, 1967, p. 15.

† "Chicho's fate had been sealed a long time before, like that of any company leader who fell into our hands, and the punishment was summary death by shooting, the only way to deal with these turncoats." Raúl Castro, "Diario," p. 201.

tle down, build a bread oven, and launch a newspaper, *El Cubano Libre*, Che wondered whether capital punishment was fully justified.

His analysis centers on a peasant named Arístido, a bandit who had joined the guerrillas for no particular reason, and who boasted of his intention to desert as soon as the rebel forces moved on. Guevara ordered him shot "after a very summary investigation,"[48] and then entered into a tortuous process of self-doubt: "We asked ourselves whether he was really guilty enough to deserve death, and whether we couldn't have saved his life for the period of revolutionary construction."[49] The brand-new *comandante* resolved the immediate dilemma with analytical and discursive panache. The execution, he explained, took place because the situation demanded it: the guerrilla army was both too weak to afford any other punishment, and strong enough to punish betrayal. Another troubling case involved a young man named Echevarría, whose brother had sailed with the *Granma* and who rapidly turned to banditry and pillage in the areas under revolutionary control. Che hesitated once again—but only in his mind:

> Echevarría could have been a hero of the Revolution . . . but he was unlucky enough to commit crimes during that period and had to pay the price for his wrongdoing. . . . He served as an example, in truth tragic but also valuable, so that people would understand our need to make of the Revolution a pure event and not contaminate it with the vandalism Batista's men had accustomed us to.[50]

Finally, Che analyzed another case, which then and today seems cruel and unnecessary: that of symbolic executions. These involved fake shootings, where the victims had no idea that the wall they were being marched to was a purely ceremonial one. Guevara rightly commented that this might seem a "barbaric" exercise, whose justification lay once again in the lack of any real options. On the one hand, they did not deserve to die; on the other, there were no alternative forms of punishment.

Seemingly flawless, this reasoning is neither fair nor acceptable. Granted, the other leaders of the Cuban Revolution did not even pose the questions raised by Che's inquiring mind. Yet merely analyzing the facts is not enough. Che's reasoning was swift and peremptory. This tactical, simplistic, and bureaucratic logic would preclude any deeper reflection in other, graver circumstances. Not too far in the future—in early 1959—he held in his hands the fate of hundreds of men sentenced to death at La Cabaña, and he authorized with his signature one of the most unsavory episodes of the Revolution. The contradictory nature of Guevara's thinking had become set by now. He would take note of the problem's complexity, ponder it, and proceed to find a response that would allow him to go forward—without, however, really resolving the dilemma.

Che's growing participation in the political debate within the 26th of July Movement focused more on the larger issues: the direction of the struggle, policies for alliance, and the ideology of the leadership. Two key figures arrived in the Sierra in July 1957: Raúl Chibas, brother of Eddy Chibas, the old Ortodoxo leader and protagonist of the first live radio suicide in history, and Felipe Pazos. An economist, Pazos was a former director of the central bank and a prototypical development economist—progressive, but not revolutionary. Along with Regino Boti, a similar-minded economist, he had drafted the "Economic Theses of the Revolutionary 26th of July Movement," published in Mexico in 1956. His intention—like Fidel Castro's, when he received the two men in his mountain hideout—was simple. Their common goal was to forge and consolidate an alliance between the guerrillas of the Sierra and the reformist politicians of the *llano,* or plains (the urban cadres, chiefly), including urban leaders like Frank País (who would die a few weeks later) and the heirs of José Antonio Echevarría (who had perished in a failed attempt on Batista at the National Palace on March 13, 1957) within the Revolutionary Student Directorate. Chibas and Pazos did not belong to any of these branches of the anti-Batista coalition, but were important figures of the moderate opposition who could perhaps be coaxed into more radical positions, enabling Castro to put his stamp of approval on a written agreement dated July 12. Che expressed serious doubts about it, but finally accepted its necessity. In his own notes on the visit by Chibas and Pazos and their "caveman mentality,"[51] Guevara revealed his intense dislike for them, and his adamant opposition to their reformist stances.

Che also expressed his reservations and objections to the written agreement as such, especially the chapter on agrarian reform. He noted sarcastically, "it was a policy that would have been acceptable to the [conservative] *Diario de la Marina.*" To top it all off, it established "prior compensation for previous owners."[52] The text included a series of promises: a pledge to hold free elections after the fall of the government, the return to a constitutional regime, and the establishment of a Revolutionary Civic Front consisting of representatives from all sectors of the opposition. Guevara ultimately understood that the alliance with Pazos and Chibas, like others, was necessary for the guerrillas to continue receiving arms and resources and avoid isolation. He also acknowledged that Castro's undertaking required certain ruses and silences. He viewed the agreements as temporary, to last only as long as the revolutionary process permitted. They contained a measure of deceit—not toward the cosignatories, who were no strangers to Cuban politics, but toward certain sectors of public opinion. The latter could easily believe that the program of the 26th of July was limited to the text of the manifesto, published on July 28 in *Bohemia,* the magazine with the largest circulation in Cuba.

The document was neither more cautious nor less extreme than any of the 26th of July's previous declarations. What led Che to express his reservations was his new status within the guerrilla camp. He was no longer a foreign physician who could be expelled at any time, but a *comandante* who had won his star in combat and who now participated fully in the Revolution's substantive debates. Perhaps the main difference between Che and Fidel and other revolutionaries lay in the well-defined and transparent goals the doctor-cum-guerrilla fighter had set for the struggle. He pursued a far more radical revolution. To attribute Fidel's presumed gradual shift from democrat to hard-line Marxist-Leninist to the Argentine Communist's influence is absurd, but Castro's tactics did include a less clearly defined strategic orientation than Che's abstract ideology. Che in turn was less concerned with immediate realities and more firmly anchored to a sum of ideas. The letters between Che and René Ramos Latour ("Daniel") at the end of 1958 laid bare these differences.

Ramos Latour was Frank País's closest collaborator within the urban front of Santiago. After País's death he succeeded him as the clandestine leader of the 26th of July Movement in the cities. He traveled to the Sierra for the first time in 1957 and returned in May 1958, dying in combat in July of that year. At the end of 1957, he began exchanging letters with Che that underlined the serious divisions within the movement regarding what would be called the Miami Pact. Taking advantage of the agreement they had signed with Castro in July, Felipe Pazos and Raúl Chibas, along with other moderate opposition figures including former president Carlos Prío Socarrás, sought to push matters even further in October. They called for U.S. mediation in the civil war, a declaration of "independence" by the urban and civilian opposition vis-à-vis the military and rural sectors, and the designation of an interim president—none other than Pazos himself. The new pact was signed in October, and the first reports of it appeared in the U.S. press a month later. Weeks after the signing, Castro and the guerrilla command repudiated the Miami Pact, though it had been signed by their representatives.

Writing to "Daniel" on December 14, 1957, Che begins by laying out a number of minor technical and logistical disputes. He and Ramos Latour had already had their disagreements, especially regarding Che's apparent compulsion to accept all sorts of combatants in his column, and to foster relations between "the Sierra" and "the plains" regardless of the national leadership. Guevara was continually going over the heads of municipal leaders, accepting recruits, support, or information from sectors independent of Ramos Latour.[53] As Carlos Franqui recalls, "Che had unleashed a virtual war on the 'plains' 26th of July, and one of the ways he waged this war was by using people who had a bone to pick with the organization, instead of using the movement's personnel."[54]

In this letter, which he himself would later describe as "rather idiotic,"[55] Guevara reveals the intensity of his own ideological beliefs and sets the terms of the debate between "the plains" and "the Sierra"—between the reformists of the cities and the revolutionaries of the mountains, the liberal nationalists and the emerging Marxist-Leninists. He terms the Miami Pact "unspeakable," asserting that "in Miami [they] proffered their ass in the most despicable act of buggery that Cuban history is likely to recall."[56] He then states that Ramos Latour refused to reach a compromise solution, and launches into a ferocious diatribe which is also a confession:

> Because of my ideological training I am one of those who believe that the solution to this world's problems is to be found behind the so-called Iron Curtain. . . . I always viewed Fidel as a genuine leader of the bourgeois left, though his character is enriched by personal qualities of extraordinary brilliance which raise him far above his class. It is in that spirit that I joined the struggle; honestly without any hope of going beyond the country's liberation, ready to leave when the conditions of the struggle would shift toward the right (toward what you represent). . . . What I never imagined was Fidel's radical shift in his positions regarding the Miami Manifesto. I thought impossible what I later learned; to wit, that the wishes of he who is the genuine leader and sole motor of the Movement should thus be distorted. I am ashamed of what I thought at the time.[57]

Che reiterates his right to establish relations with whomever he pleases and to receive support (arms, money, supplies) from anybody—including alleged bandits from the plains. He is writing "for the record" (by now the idea of a personal destiny seems firmly established).* Though in his view the differences between them are probably unbridgeable, they must be set aside for the sake of unity. He recognizes that Ramos Latour might break relations with him, but "the people cannot be defeated."

One may only speculate as to the real course of events. According to several historical accounts, Castro sent one of his closest collaborators, Lester Rodríguez, to Miami in order to negotiate and sign a Pact of Unity. When the agreement was reached, several of Fidel's companions must have been indignant—beginning with Che. Already disappointed or angry at the Manifesto of July 12, perhaps they considered that the Miami conclave, the people involved, and the decision to proclaim the candidacy of Felipe Pazos for

---

*"My historical name cannot be linked to that crime [i.e., the Miami Pact]. . . . I am doing this to have one day a record testifying to my integrity." Ernesto Guevara, letter to René Ramos Latour, December 14, 1957, quoted in Franqui, *Diario,* p. 362.

the post-Batista era constituted a series of concessions dangerously close to treason. They may have angrily reproached Castro for his apparent consent which, given the poor communications between Miami, the Sierra, and the plains, the *caudillo* almost certainly never extended.* After a cryptic silence of several weeks, Castro repudiated the agreement and realigned himself with his left wing, now headed by Guevara.[†] Che must have expressed in a note or message, if not in person, his disapproval or outright rejection of the Miami Pact.[‡] Perhaps Che never believed that Fidel signed the ill-fated document, but by now he knew his friend and boss well: he never shared anything with anybody. One can easily imagine the Argentine radical's discomfort with Castro's public statements against expropriations and communism, with Fidel's custom of baptizing every peasant child born in the Sierra, and with the conservative decrees he issued in the mountains. From there to concluding that Pazos's stay in the Sierra close to Fidel had contaminated him required no more than a small step.** Thus, Che's claim to "Daniel" that Fidel was originally a "bourgeois leftist" (meaning, not a true revolutionary). In a letter to the commander-in-chief immediately after the event, Che summarizes his views:

> You know that I had not the slightest confidence in the people from the national leadership, either as leaders or as revolutionaries. Nor did I believe that they would go to the extreme of betraying you so openly. . . . I think your attitude of silence is not the most advisable at this time. A betrayal of this magnitude clearly indicates the different paths that have been taken. I believe a written document can have the necessary effectiveness and later, if things get complicated, with Celia's help you could remove the entire national leadership.[58]

The document suggested by Che had in fact been drafted the day before, on December 14. The removal proposed by him would take place on May 3 of the following year. When he discovered that Castro either had not actually signed the Miami Pact or had rescinded his signature, Che expressed his joy in a new letter to Fidel:

---

*This is the opinion of Carlos Franqui, who lived these events intensely: "There was no consultation with the leadership in the plains or with Fidel. There was a basis for a pact, so that if Pazos had a deal without these controversial points, matters would have been different. But Fidel never signed." Carlos Franqui, interview.

[†] According to Franqui, those who opposed the Miami Pact from the beginning were Raúl Castro and Che, Evelio Martínez, Julio Martínez, and Franqui himself, as well as "Daniel," who was in hiding. See Franqui, *Diario,* p. 371.

[‡] Tad Szulc emphasizes that, "for some strange reason, Che Guevara initially thought that Castro had authorized the Miami Pact." Tad Szulc, *Fidel: A Critical Portrait* (New York: Avon, 1987; first edition, 1986), p. 469.

**This is Franqui's tentative point of view. Franqui, *Diario,* p. 371.

... I told you that you will always have the merit of having proven the possibility of an armed struggle supported by the people in America. Now you are on the even greater path of becoming one of two or three in America who will have taken power through a multitudinous armed struggle.[59]

To Ramos Latour he confesses his guilt, like the apostle Peter, for having doubted his leader. The "mistakes" that Che will refer to in his letter of farewell to Fidel in 1965 may be precisely these.* His remorse stems from Castro's change of course, as he quickly returned to the revolutionary fold and reasserted his affinity with his Argentine friend and ally.

René Ramos Latour did not suffer Che's onslaught in silence. He responded immediately, and his letter reveals the yawning schisms within the 26th of July Movement that would come to a head in 1959, after the triumph of the Revolution. Latour rejected Che's imputations, explaining repeatedly that he did not feel they applied to him at all. Even if the cities do not offer the opportunities for the type of heroism prevailing in the Sierra, he wrote pointedly, those who raise funds, buy arms and supplies, and distribute them to the mountains are every bit as brave and revolutionary. Most important, wrote "Daniel," salvation is not to be found behind the Iron Curtain. While he categorically refused to be classified as a "rightist," he also marked his distance from Che Guevara:

> In contrast, those who have your ideological training believe that the solution to our ills lies in liberating ourselves from a noxious Yankee domination, by means of a no less noxious Soviet domination.[†]

Ramos Latour does not hesitate to criticize Che's leanings in terms of alliances: "I am a worker, but not one of those who militate in the Communist Party and worry loftily about the problems of Hungary or Egypt, which they cannot solve, yet are incapable of leaving their jobs to join the revolutionary process."[60] Finally, regarding the Miami Pact for Unity, he

---

*"My only mistake of some gravity was not to have trusted you more from the first moments in the Sierra Maestra, and not to have understood soon enough your qualities as a leader and revolutionary." Ernesto Che Guevara, letter to Fidel Castro, January 6, 1958, quoted in Ernesto Che Guevara, *Escritos y discursos,* vol. 9 (Havana: Editorial de Ciencias Sociales, 1977), p. 394.

† "Daniel" 's letter, dated December 18, 1957, was published in Franqui, *Diario,* pp. 365–369. Though the exchange does not appear in any of the editions of Che's correspondence, nor in the various biographies and histories of the Cuban Revolution already cited, there is no reason to doubt its authenticity. One may consult the original notes for Franqui's book in the Franqui Archives at Princeton University. They all agree with the published text. The Cubans have never responded to Franqui's assertions, either to support or deny them. Che's own reference to his "rather idiotic" letter to "Daniel" confirms the existence of the letter, if not its content.

retorts that he never approved of Fidel's association with former president Prío Socarrás. He reminds Che that he always rejected the Florida agreement as long as it did not clearly establish the leadership of the opposition forces on the island; the proposed "unity" should indeed be shattered. But he sets one condition: that there be a clear definition of "where we are going and what we seek to accomplish."[61]

It was during this period that Che deservedly gained his reputation as the guerrillas' "Communist" or radical. But he also became known for his sense of organization. He led his column with decisiveness and ingenuity. More than other commanders, he was able to consolidate his territorial gains, establishing schools, clinics, ovens, small workshops, hospitals, and imposing an iron discipline. He attended to the peasants and instructed the guerrillas in his free time. He had launched *El Cubano Libre* and, shortly afterward, *Radio Rebelde*. He began to receive foreign journalists, and turned his increasingly permanent camps into models of cleanliness, efficiency, and generosity. Legends proliferated, among troops and peasants alike. In the narrative and oral histories of the war, his military deeds became famous along with the meticulous organization of his camps and campaigns.

He also became known for his egalitarian and honest dealings with his troops, which so impressed one of the youngest recruits in his immediate escort. As Joel Iglesias recalls it,[62] they once came to a hut at the foot of Turquino Peak, where they negotiated food and rest with the *guajiros*. Guevara counted the mouths to be fed and waited with the peasants for the food to be cooked, so as to take it back to his troops. In the meantime, his hosts served up three portions and invited Che and his escort to sit down and have lunch while the rest of the food was prepared. Che refused. He gave orders that the three portions should be put into a large dish, so they could be shared among all later on. The peasants' invitation would not have given him a larger share; it would merely have allowed him to save some time by eating earlier. But even this was unacceptable to him. All the food was carried to the bivouac and the troops stood in line to be served, Che among them.

There were few journalistic reports about Che himself during those months. A *New York Times* correspondent, Homer Bigart, was sent to the Sierra Maestra in 1958. He was accompanied by a Uruguayan journalist, Carlos María Gutiérrez, who later became a friend and aspiring biographer of the *comandante* slain at La Higuera. The Uruguayan recalls a sense of easygoing camaraderie in the camp. He found Che relaxed and natural, but with a series of defenses well in place to avoid any undue closeness or complicity. Physically, he was "very thin, with a sparse beard that barely framed an almost childlike face."[63] Only the later events of 1958 would begin to age Guevara, transforming him into the iconic figure of the triumphant entry into Havana.

For his part, Bigart reported to the U.S. Embassy in Havana on his conversations with Guevara, emphasizing his "rather strong anti-U.S. sentiment." He also described his encounter with Fidel Castro, whom he asked how he could depend so much on an anti-U.S., Communist Argentine. Fidel answered that "in reality Guevara's political convictions did not matter as it was he, Fidel Castro, who set the course for the guerrillas."[64] Indeed, Che still did not cut an awesome figure; the Argentine journalist Jorge Masetti, who also visited the camps in February 1958, remarked: "The famous Che Guevara seemed to me a typically middle-class Argentine youth. He also struck me as a rejuvenated caricature of Cantinflas."*

Ernesto Guevara still set aside time for reading and, according to one recruit, various girlfriends. He continually asked for books from the cities, including on one occasion Will Durant's *History of Philosophy,* as well as works by Proust, Hemingway and Faulkner, Graham Greene and Sartre, and the poetry of Milton, Neruda, and Góngora.[65] His asceticism was renowned, but never reached extremes; as Joel Iglesias describes it,

> In Las Vegas de Jibacoa, Che met a black or rather mulatto girl with a very lovely body, called Zoila. Many women were crazy about him, but in that sense he was always very strict and respectful, but he liked that girl. They met and were together for some time.[66]

The girl's name was Zoila Rodríguez García and she doubtless, at age eighteen, reminded him of the "beautiful mulatto girls" of his youthful days in Porto Alegre and Trinidad. One may deduce from her account that the relationship lasted several months, from early 1958 until August, when Castro developed the plan to "invade" the center of the island and Guevara resigned himself to leaving her. According to the young woman, Che's fascination with the exotic remained the same, if not stronger:

> He was looking at me the way boys look at girls and I became extremely nervous. . . . He had a slightly mischievous look. . . . As a woman I liked him immensely, especially his look, he had such beautiful eyes, such a calm smile that he could touch any heart, move any woman. . . . He awoke in me a very great and very beautiful love. I pledged myself to him, not only as a combatant but as a woman.[67]

*Jorge Ricardo Masetti, "Los que lloran y los que sufren," quoted in Ernesto Guevara Lynch, *Mi hijo el Che* (Barcelona: Editorial Planeta, 1981), p. 42. Cantinflas was a famous Mexican comic actor, somewhat similar to Charlie Chaplin in his character and demeanor.

His military and organizational experiments in the Sierra were often emulated. Raúl Castro, in particular, reproduced many of Che's innovations in the Frank País Second Front, opened in March 1958 on the Sierra de Cristal. Che made a qualitative change in the war, shifting from a strategy of "hit-and-run to a combat of positions, which must resist enemy attacks so as to defend rebel territory, in which a new reality is being built."[68] Of course, Guevara sometimes rushed ahead of himself. As Franqui says, he had good strategic sense, but little tactical intuition. He positioned his column prematurely, in an area that lacked the military conditions needed to defend occupied territory and installations. Fidel applied many of Che's innovations, but in a better-thought-out fashion. Without Fidel, many of Che's ideas would have failed. An ominous precedent was being set; in the words of Carlos Franqui:

> If Che acted so differently when he was only two steps away from Fidel, outside of the Sierra this phenomenon was exacerbated for better or for worse. Insofar as the distance or situation was greater or more dissimilar, the difficulties and complications grew more serious.[69]

The idea of stable camps was attractive to Castro for many reasons. Stationary bases, subject only to sporadic movements while waiting for something to happen, presented a number of tactical benefits. Wrapped in Che's conceptual packaging, the idea was even more attractive. Until the failed general strike of April 9, 1958, and the subsequent army offensive, the guerrilla leader in fact lacked a military strategy for taking power. His meager forces did not permit it. As a result, his only goal was to overthrow the regime through a general strike. After the strike failed, Castro moved to lay the blame on the "plains" leadership. In one of the revolutionary war's many paradoxes, Fidel Castro became far more powerful after the failure of the April strike which he had in fact planned and ordered. By successfully pinning responsibility for the debacle on the 26th of July national leadership, he opened up a vacuum of power which he was then able to fill. As Che noted after the failed strike and subsequent finger-pointing within the movement, "From that time on, the war would be conducted politically and militarily by Fidel, in his double capacity as commander-in-chief of the rebel forces and secretary-general of the organization."[70]

A stormy meeting took place on May 3 in the Altos de Mompié, at which the movement's leaders hurled accusations at each other over the strike fiasco while each attempted to absolve himself. This gave rise to a double shift within the rebel coalition. On the one hand, the moderate, civilian elements from the plains were displaced by Fidel and his group. Che contributed decisively to this ouster, participating for the first time in a meeting of the national leadership. Together with Fidel, he acted as public prosecutor against the leaders from the plains: Faustino Pérez, René Ramos Latour, Marcelo Fernández, and David Salvador. Coincidentally, there was a gradual shift in alliances. The Popular Socialist Party (PSP) began to acquire a presence it had previously lacked. In this realignment as well, Che played a crucial role. His column, along with the Second Front headed by Raúl Castro, was chosen to incorporate the newly recruited Communist cadres.

The first eight months of 1958 were a time of consolidation, both for the Fidelista guerrilla forces and for Ernesto Guevara's role in the war. From the general strike of April 9 and its failure until the desperate, broad-ranging, and ultimately futile counteroffensive by the army in May, the rebel forces in the Sierra lived through their worst hours. Their survival was in itself a guarantee of victory. Che participated in the defense against the Batista onslaught, though not in any spectacular way; his column fought at the battle of El Jigüe on July 20, and at Santo Domingo. But it was Fidel Castro who ensured the success of the resistance; with obsessive concentration he moved troops, arms, supplies, and resources from one sector to the other in the Sierra, requesting reinforcements, scolding his colleagues, and making all the major decisions. The dangers of the moment were reflected in Castro's extreme irritability. He even went so far as to heap insults on Celia Sánchez, his closest and most loyal collaborator until her death in 1980. The following letter, dated June 18, 1957 (just one day before that which Fidel Castro would call the most critical of those months), at the height of the army offensive, illustrates another telling fact. There is not a single known letter in which Fidel Castro expresses the slightest anger, reproach, or exasperation at Che during all the time he spent in the Sierra. In contrast, the letter to Celia reveals his irritation:

> Whenever you feel like it, you look at things in the most whimsical conceivable way. Some of your attitudes make me fear that you shall gradually go completely blind. I think in my treatment of you I have always maintained a fundamental respect for the forms. . . . In yesterday's letter you have violated all these considerations. I will not write to you in the language I might use with any other companion. . . . Unlike you, I do not write with the purpose of disappointing, or wounding, or worrying you, or without any concern at all. . . . Do I have any hopes that you will understand me? None at all! Because when I have written to you with greater clarity, you have chosen to understand whatever has best suited you.*

---

*Fidel Castro, letter to Celia Sánchez, June 18, 1957. Huber Matos, who fought under Che's command in the Sierra for several months, has a similar recollection: "Fidel always tried to impose his authority, raising his voice or saying insolent things or trying always to be right. However, I never saw him clash with Che. Fidel sometimes behaved in an insulting or despotic way with his subordinates. There were exceptions. Che was one of them. I never

Batista's offensive in the Sierra Maestra was to last seventy-six days, involving over 10,000 troops. The guerrilla fighters, in contrast, barely totaled 321 men. The government forces suffered over 1,000 casualties; in addition, the rebels captured 400 prisoners, 500 modern rifles, and 2 light tanks. After the offensive failed, the outcome of the war became self-evident. The fall of Batista was now merely a matter of time. Who would replace him, and how, would depend on strength, skill, and daring.

The period in question also witnessed a game of hide-and-seek between Castro's men and the United States government, as the regime weakened and a revolutionary victory became more plausible. The series of coy encounters, contacts, and controversies included messages that crossed each other; press interviews; incidents at Guantánamo, the U.S. base; kidnappings of American citizens; and attacks on property owned by U.S. companies. The guerrillas and their allies sought to stanch the flow of arms and munitions to Batista, as he tried to preserve it; the CIA dabbled in helping varying factions of the 26th of July Movement. Che's role in this minuet with the U.S. was minor. For the moment, he stood in the diplomatic shadows, and he was neither a spokesman or negotiator nor a decisive influence in one direction or another.

He did, however, have a major impact, both substantive and lasting, on the switch in alliances that followed the breakdown of the Pact for Unity at the end of 1957. From then until mid-1959, when the revolutionaries had already taken power, a ferocious internal struggle raged within the 26th of July and the opposition front. This bitter conflict included, but also extended beyond, differences between the Sierra and the plains, revolutionaries and liberals, partisans of a military junta and defenders of a fight to the end. A gradual realignment emerged. Fidel Castro moved further and further away from his former liberal allies—Prío, Chibas, Pazos, the Student Movement, the 26th of July's former national leadership—and drew closer to cadres of his Rebel Army and of the Popular Socialist Party. This was not a rapid or clear-cut process by any means. It did not have a definite beginning or end, nor did it necessarily derive from any plan concocted by Fidel beforehand and then deliberately executed.

The first contact between Castro and the PSP took place at the end of 1957 when a Communist labor leader, Ursinio Rojas, arrived in the Sierra. He informed Castro that the Party leadership had decided to allow its members to join the Rebel Army. One such recruit was possibly Che Guevara's first link to the Cuban Communists. Pablo Ribalta arrived to join his col-

---

saw him talk to Che in a rude or ugly way." Huber Matos, transcript of interview with English journalists, London, October 1995, mimeo made available to the author.

umn, along with a certain Hiram Prats. A young but experienced cadre from the PSP, Ribalta had traveled abroad and carried out Party work in Prague, as an aspiring soldier of the international Communist movement. He would stay by Che's side for half a decade until he was appointed Cuba's ambassador to Tanzania. There he would serve as liaison between Havana and Guevara's expedition in the Congo. In mid-1957, he recalls, Che "asked for somebody with characteristics like mine: a teacher, with some political instruction and experience in political activism."[71] Che could have added a further characteristic: someone of African origin. According to Ribalta, Che instructed him to keep secret his membership in the PSP, and especially his leadership position within the Communist Youth. Ribalta obeyed him to the letter. The other members of the column learned of his Communist affiliation only in November of the following year.[72]

Strangely enough, the Americans were slow in detecting Che's pro-PSP leanings.* The two intelligence reports that mention him during this period include the relevant facts: his close contacts with the Soviet mission in Mexico, the ideological orientation of Hilda Gadea, and his vehement anti-imperialism. But they still fail to draw the logical conclusion. On the rare occasions when Che's name is linked to Communist influence within the 26th of July Movement, the connection is far from clear. Thus, for instance, a cable from the U.S. consulate in Santiago, dated February 21, 1958:

> The reporting official has asked several Cubans to respond to allegations that one of the most trusted lieutenants of Fidel Castro, Dr. Ernesto Guevara, an Argentinian, is a Communist or Communist sympathizer. They invariably respond with vehement denials, but admit that they know nothing of his background and prefer to avoid the conversation altogether, suggesting that Dr. Guevara is an idealistic adventurer.[†]

---

*In the undated intelligence report previously cited, the Americans concluded: "It seems clear, then, that even though he is not a member of the Communist Party, Guevara is a Marxist in his thinking, and does maintain some contacts with Communist circles." At this stage, the Americans seriously underestimated both Che's Communist leanings (not so much in terms of the Party as its ideas) and his growing links to the PSP. Quoted in "Possibility of Communist Connections," Department of State, National Archives, lot 60 D 513, MER 1137, box 7–8.

† Dispatch from the U.S. consulate at Santiago de Cuba to the Department of State, "Foreign Relations of the United States, 1958–1960," vol. 6, p. 35. According to Tad Szulc, the vice-consul at Santiago (possibly the author of this cable) was a certain Robert Wiecha, a CIA agent who delivered large sums of money to the 26th of July—either as part of the Eisenhower administration's policy or on the initiative of the CIA itself. See Szulc, *Fidel*, pp. 469–471. In an interview with Georgie Anne Geyer in 1987, Wiecha denied having given money to Fidel or his group, though he acknowledged his sympathy, as well as the CIA's in general, for Castro and the rebels. There is still some mystery as to somebody else from the CIA, or Wiecha himself, giving funds to rebels that did not strictly belong to Fidel's group. See Georgie Anne Geyer, *Guerrilla Prince* (Boston: Little, Brown, 1991), p. 189.

Che drew even closer to the Communists in August of 1958, when his troops were separated from their mother column. Castro ordered Guevara and Camilo Cienfuegos to "invade" the center of the island and split it in two militarily. At that time, Che drew even further away from the national leadership of 26th of July Movement and the liberals, incorporating ever more Communists into his guerrilla band. During the final discussions on the agrarian reform law—the most far-reaching legislation enacted by the guerrillas in the Sierra—Guevara laid the basis for an even closer alliance. He now stood clearly for the PSP and the most radical theses, and against the "plains," the liberals and more cautious positions. But this phase belongs to a different tale: that of victory and the emerging legend, when Che, together with Fidel Castro, becomes the very emblem of the Cuban revolution. In this saga, his face is identified forever with the jubilant islanders, numbering in the hundreds of thousands, that greeted their triumphant entry into Havana in the early, heady days of January 1959.

Chapter 5

Our Man in Havana

By August 18, 1958, Fidel Castro knew he had won the war against Batista. The failure of the army's offensive and the rebels' earlier breakout from the Sierra Maestra to another mountain range, the Sierra de Cristal, had tipped the balance. The regime was cornered and crumbling fast. The key was to ensure the victory of those rebels hiding in the cities and mountains, rather than a military junta or any compromise solution imposed by Washington. To achieve this, Castro devised the most astute and decisive military move of the war. He called for an "invasion" of the island, by two columns setting off from the Sierra Maestra. Their mission was to travel westward, to initiate combat in the center of Cuba, to cut the island in two, and to start the march toward Havana.

With his brother leading the Second Front, Castro had few commanders left for the two spearheads in the guerrillas' counterattack. Camilo Cienfuegos had distinguished himself since the *Granma* landing by his bravery, ingenuity, and easy relations with combatants and civil population alike. He was a natural candidate, though he had never held an autonomous command. The other logical choice was Che Guevara, who for almost a year had led his own column (recently renamed the Ciro Redondo after a *Granma* expeditionary fallen in combat). His leadership skills and military boldness were well known. And Fidel Castro trusted him enough to give him a task whose political implications were even more complex than its military ones.

Che's mission was to cross endless miles of enemy territory with only 150 new recruits, far from the shelter of the mountain range. But he also had to "coordinate operations, plans, administrative decisions, and military organization with other revolutionary forces operating in the province [of Las Villas], who will be invited to merge into a sole Army Corps, so as to structure and unify the Revolution's military efforts."[1] In other words, Che would have to convince or oblige the other opposition forces operating in Las Villas and the Sierra del Escambray to accept his preeminence. These included battalions from the 26th of July Movement, as well as isolated groups from the Revolutionary Student Directorate, the Popular Socialist Party (PSP), and the Second National Front of the Escambray, which had split off from the student organization and was led by Eloy Gutiérrez Menoyo. Che was thus assigned three goals. From a military point of view, he was to attack and defeat the enemy in the center of the country. He was to maintain unity and discipline under singularly adverse conditions, without the sheltering mantle of Fidel Castro. Finally, he had a political mandate requiring both negotiating skills and the exercise of authority.

True, Castro had few choices in assigning these tasks. But this does not detract from Guevara's achievement during his three years with the Cuban leader. He started out a mediocre physician, a wandering foreigner lacking any political and military experience, and became the third most important figure in an undertaking of epic proportions. Perhaps the Cubans on board the *Granma* resented his arrogance, his ironic and haughty reserve, his isolation and foreignness. Maybe the least radical elements of the 26th of July, in the mountains and plains, mistrusted his pro-Soviet stance and growing affinity with the long-discredited Cuban Communists. And those closest to Fidel Castro, including his brother Raúl, may have had their moments of envy when they saw the camaraderie and loyalty that bonded the two men. However, none of these feelings could overshadow Guevara's enormous contribution to the struggle, his bravery, discipline, organization, and levelheadedness. The very traits that at first the Cubans tended to dislike eventually made him indispensable. His Argentine and European sense of order, his punctuality and formality, his respect for the rules, his insistence on honoring promises and commitments, were not Caribbean virtues by any means. Indeed, it was their rarity which made them so precious during the final phase of the war.

At the end of August 1958, Che was forced to separate himself from some of the people he held dearest: Camilo Cienfuegos, his most trusted friend in the Sierra Maestra, and Zoila, his girlfriend of several months. He also demanded of his troops an explicit decision regarding the "invasion." He warned them that they were risking their lives: up to half of them might die. Almost 80 percent of them were young men lacking combat experience, mere boys newly recruited from Minas de Frío.

Che embarked on his mission on August 31 with 148 men. During forty-six days they would endure all the hardships of isolation in a tropical climate: hunger, thirst, mosquitoes, cyclones and floodwaters, unsafe roads, an indifferent population, and continual harassment by Batista's army. They marched over 300 kilometers, suffering through swamps, torrents, and constant privation. They were forced to abandon their transport trucks after the army cut them off from gasoline supplies, and had to perform the entire trek by foot or on horseback. Though only six men died (or three, according to some accounts), their tribulations soon became the stuff of legend. This was partly thanks to General Francisco Tabernilla Dolz, Batista's joint chief of staff, who on September 20 announced the annihilation of the "invading" force and the death of Che Guevara. The ordeal finally ended on October 16:

> When the situation was at its most tense, when only insults, pleas and tantrums could make the exhausted people keep marching, a single faraway vision animated their faces and infused the guerrillas with new spirit. That vision was the blue line of the mountain range of Las Villas.[2]

Thus ended the first phase of Che's independent mission. Victory was less than three months away. Strangely enough, there is no mention of asthma attacks during this entire period—the "invasion," the battle of Santa Clara, the entry into Havana—either in Che's notes or his companions' recollections. Of course, the episodes may have taken place with their usual intensity during those weeks without Che's recording them in his diary. But there are other possible explanations for a lull in the illness. A first, physiological, one involves the level of adrenaline generated by continual combat-readiness. If adrenaline is the best-known bronchodilator, and the human body is its best supplier, it is not absurd to speculate that the tension arising from constant danger should have provided Che with the best possible antidote, his own adrenaline.

Another possible reason is the absence of situations that were likely to bring on attacks. Once Che left the Sierra and was no longer busy running the camps with their constant problems, contradiction disappeared. Even when he had to settle disputes among the different factions opposing Batista, Guevara chose the ideal political-military tactic, which was also the optimal antidote to his ailment: combat. The link between asthma and ambivalence would thus seem to have worked both ways.

This was the real beginning of Che Guevara's autonomous command. During this stage he acquired loyalties and habits, and the fame that would accompany him even in death. He set up an escort consisting of José

Argudín, Alberto Castellanos, Harry Villegas ("Pombo"), and Hermés Peña. The first three formed part of his international team in Argentina, Bolivia, and the Congo. Eliseo Reyes Rodríguez ("San Luis"), Carlos Coello ("Tuma," whose remains were found in Bolivia in 1996), and Alberto Fernández ("Pachungo"), other companions during this phase, would all die in Bolivia.

These six weeks also saw the emergence of a lasting and characteristic trait in Che Guevara: intransigence toward the weakness of others. However essential to the brand of leadership he exercised, this trait would prove a liability under more normal conditions. He could not tolerate errors in his subordinates; he scolded, insulted, and punished them. Joel Iglesias recalled one such incident at the height of the "invasion":

> Several comrades got off the truck, which was stuck . . . while others refused to get off and push it. Che got into a very ugly mood, addressing them with very harsh and violent words, in my opinion, and with an angry expression. He strongly criticized their behavior in those moments. He was something to hear and see when he was indignant.[3]

Che's decency (and nobility) always led him to apologize after a few hours or days. And he never demanded of his subordinates anything that he would not impose upon himself. But these abstract qualities irritated people in the real world: others did not share his sense of destiny, intellect, or willpower. His explosions of anger toward his followers, whose devotion knew no limits, became part of his unwritten story. During the "invasion," his expeditions to the Congo, and especially in Bolivia, his outbursts were legendary. Though rarely unfair or based upon an authoritarian position, they were always extreme and devastating. His rages, or "outpourings," as they were eventually termed by his companions, were followed by moments of contrition—but they were still continual. In this regard, one cannot neglect the possible influence of his frequent epinephrine or adrenaline injections. These bronchodilators have no long-term effects, but can generate sudden increases in blood pressure, anxiety, and "rushes" lasting up to thirty minutes. Though appropriate from a medical standpoint, the medication may have contributed to his drastic mood swings.*

The column's arrival in Las Villas forced Che to focus on the task of unifying the opposition forces. He had also to institute administrative procedures to fulfill the great promises of the coming revolution—especially land reform. During those months Guevara, Cienfuegos, and other rebel leaders undertook an extensive process of land distribution, beginning with a sus-

---

*I owe this hypothesis to an enlightening conversation with Dr. Roberto Krechmer, one of Mexico's most eminent authorities on childhood asthma. Mexico City, July 6, 1996.

pension of rental payments on small plots and tax exemptions for small farmers (for instance, coffee producers). The spread of these practices soon required a legal framework, which became the Sierra Maestra's Law no. 3 on agrarian reform, dated October 10, 1958.

For Che, the incorporation of peasants into the guerrilla war acquired a purifying dimension, over and beyond its military or political significance. The guerrilla fighter "joins" the people as they, in turn, join the rebel army. As the "people," in rural areas, consist of peasants, their affiliation with the revolution became a defining moment. In his own words,

> Simultaneously with the incorporation of peasants into the armed struggle due to their demands for freedom and social justice, a magical word arose which mobilized the oppressed masses of Cuba in their struggle for land ownership: Land Reform.[4]

In areas like the Sierra Maestra—which is where Che had his first encounter with the problems of land and rural poverty—the farmers' principal demand was land ownership and the cancellation of rents. This was not necessarily the main concern of day laborers toiling on the sugar and tobacco plantations in other areas. But in the zones where Che Guevara came to know the peasants' way of life, land was essential. As a result, agrarian reform was crucial to the process of merging the peasants with the guerrilla camp. That is why Che called the Rebel Army a "peasant army," and the 26th of July a "peasant movement."[5]

For Che, who had been acting on his own initiative only since mid-October in Las Villas, land distribution and rent cancellation were of central importance. They also strongly influenced his approach to various matters, including relations with the Communists and other forces. The reform in question was a limited, rather timid endeavor. It did not contemplate cooperatives or any communal or collective forms of tenancy. Che pushed for a more radical project—though not precisely an incendiary one, either. In his words, the legislation finally approved was "incomplete."[6] But for now Castro sided with the more moderate wing of the 26th of July, led in this domain by Humberto Sorí Marín, a somewhat conservative lawyer who would become minister of agriculture in the new regime and was executed a couple of years later for conspiring against the government.

Though some commentators have suggested that the Communists adopted a moderate position regarding agrarian reform, in fact they identified with Guevara's views and sought a more frontal attack on *latifundia* ownership. Che in turn empathized with their isolation in July 1958, and he opposed the expulsion of Communist leader Carlos Rafael Rodríguez from the La Plata camp where Fidel was staying. Rodríguez, who was sent to negotiate his party's support for the guerrillas, held a position on the agrarian reform that was similar to Che's. The 26th of July leaders Faustino Pérez, Manuel Ray, and Carlos Franqui demanded the ouster of Rodríguez; Guevara, Raúl Castro, and Camilo Cienfuegos defended him. Che declared that "in the Sierra the only people who should be expelled are U.S. journalists. If we persecute the Communists, we will be doing up here what Batista is doing down there."[7]

Ray was the first economist called in by Castro to draft the agrarian reform decree, together with Sorí Marín. As Guevara would later describe the process:

> Our first action [in Las Villas] was to issue a revolutionary decree establishing the Land Reform, which stipulated . . . that the owners of small plots of land would stop paying rent until the Revolution examined each case. In fact, we were advancing with the Land Reform as a spearhead of the Rebel Army.[8]

The process naturally generated friction with other opposition groups in the area, less enthusiastic than Che over unilateral reforms and reluctant to establish such precedents. The debate on land distribution was finally settled in May 1959 by the First Law for Agrarian Reform, and then again in 1964 by the Second Law, largely along Che's lines. From the beginning, he insisted on two essential components: destroying the *latifundia* and eliminating prior cash payment of compensation to landowners.

In 1958, however, the discussion was superseded by the need to unite the forces opposing Batista. Che's mandate was unequivocal: he was to bring everybody together in Las Villas. The task was difficult, but not impossible. His way of achieving this unity reflected developments in his own action and thinking that would become decisive in the following months. During the march from the Sierra Maestra to the Escambray, Che held two meetings with PSP militants that illustrated his growing ties to the Communists. In a note to Fidel dated October 3—ten days before completing the dreadful expedition across the plains—Guevara complained bitterly about the 26th of July:

> We were unable to make contact with the 26th of July organization, as a couple of so-called members of theirs rejected my request for help and I received it only . . . from members of the PSP, who told me they had asked for help from the Movement's organizations, and had received the following reply. . . . If Che sends over a request in writing, we'll help him; if not, that's too bad for Che.*

*Ernesto Che Guevara, letter to Fidel Castro, "Sobre la invasión," quoted in Ernesto Che Guevara, "Pasajes de la guerra revolucionaria," in *Escritos y Discoursos,* vol. 2 (Havana: Editorial de Ciencias Sociales, 1977), p. 277. In the ongoing efforts of many biographers to rewrite the story of Che's life, some have tried to detect an early hatred of the Communists in Che, creating the image of a "good" Che who was always anti-Communist,

Che probably believed that Castro, having signed a unity pact with all the anti-Batista forces except for the Communists in Caracas on July 20, needed to be coaxed into an alliance with them. The long weeks Carlos Rafael Rodríguez spent in the Sierra helped accomplish this, and helped forge a strong but ultimately unsustainable friendship between the Argentine and the Cuban Communist. They exchanged books, including Mao's *On Guerrilla Warfare,* and discussed the land reform bill at length. Carlos Rafael Rodríguez expressed his admiration for Che Guevara that July: "He is the most intelligent and able of all the rebel chiefs."[9] While probably true, the praise also reflected a growing political closeness. The association acquired a more personal touch in September, when a Communist cadre from Santa Clara, Armando Acosta, joined the column as Che's virtual right-hand assistant.* Aside from Pablo Ribalta (whose incorporation was described in the previous chapter), the PSP had also sent Guevara another cadre in February of 1958. Sergio Rodríguez was assigned to the column to "supply pencils, ink and paper to print the newspaper *El Cubano Libre.*"[10] The political overtones of the company Che increasingly kept were quite obvious. As Enrique Oltuski, a Jewish engineer of Polish origin who was the clandestine leader of the 26th of July in Las Villas, recalls:

> I knew Acosta, who was the PSP delegate in Las Villas; suddenly I see him as part of Che's column. We knew Che's inclinations and I was not surprised. Che was playing along with all this.[11]

The enlistment in October 1958 of Ovidio Díaz Rodríguez, secretary of the Popular Socialist Youth in Las Villas, strengthened Che's growing links to the Communists. He recalls that Che preferred to keep his relations with the PSP as discreet as possible. One day a Party member arrived bearing a small present for Che (a little can of Argentine maté) and loudly proclaimed, "Look, Comandante, here is a gift from the Party leadership." He accepted it without a word, but later instructed Ovidio to tell the Party not to send such indiscreet comrades.[12]

---

as opposed to the "bad" Fidel, who was one from the beginning. Horacio Rodríguez, for example, takes this same passage to prove the exact opposite of the interpretation offered above. The "Movement's organizations" are identified with the PSP leadership, and the text is thus transformed into a complaint against the PSP. The interpretation presented here was corroborated by Che himself, in an exchange with Enrique Oltuski: "So far we have received little help from the Movement. The ones who have done a lot for us are the PSP." Enrique Oltuski, "Gente del llano," *Revista Casa de las Américas* (Havana), vol. 7, no. 40, January–February 1967, p. 52. See Horacio Daniel Rodríguez, *Che Guevara: ¿Aventura o revolución?* (Barcelona: Tribuna de Plaza y Janés, 1968), p. 122.

*According to Carlos Franqui, Acosta joined Che's column from the Sierra and "in violation of Communist Party discipline." Carlos Franqui, *Diario de la revolución cubana* (Barcelona: R. Torres, 1976), p. 604.

By November, Che was more explicit than ever in his opinions about the various groups opposing Batista. In a bitter reproach to Faure Chomón, head of the Revolutionary Student Directorate in Las Villas, he pointedly informed him that "in official conversations with members of the Popular Socialist Party, the latter have taken an openly supportive stance and placed their organization in the plains at our disposal."[13] Che's evaluation of the groups rested, understandably, upon a clear-cut value judgment. The Communists had accepted Che's leadership without reservation when he arrived in Las Villas. Other sectors had been slower, more reluctant, or frankly opposed to him. But the PSP joined forces with Che as promptly as it did with Raúl Castro and his Second Front, unconditionally accepting him and his lieutenants as leaders.

Guevara's ties to the Popular Socialist Party are among this period's thorniest subjects. A few of the *condottiere*'s biographers prefer to emphasize his distance vis-à-vis the Communists, citing a couple of derogatory statements. The best-known is, "The Communists are able to train cadres who will let themselves be ripped to shreds in a dark dungeon without a word, but not cadres who will take a machine-gun nest by assault."[14] Che's other famous statement (also from this period) expresses a similar criticism: "the PSP had not seen clearly enough the role of guerrilla warfare, or the personal role of Fidel in our revolutionary struggle."[15] Several scholars—including Fidel's latest biographer—have even gone so far as to insist that the Argentine was not a Communist at the time.* However, according to a combatant in the Sierra who joined Che's column in August 1957,[16] Che himself told her of his ideological leanings shortly after they met:

> I cannot forget the first night he talked with me. . . . He spoke of my religious ideas and that made me ask him if he was religious. No, he answered, I cannot be religious because I am a Communist.[17]

This tangled set of assertions deserves further analysis. Che's differences with the Communists derived from tactical, and at times personal, considerations: they do not know how to fight, and they do not train their people

---

*Che "was not yet a Communist, either according to his own account or that of other witnesses." Robert E. Quirk, *Fidel Castro* (New York: Norton, 1993), p. 197. Hugh Thomas, the most distinguished historian of the Cuban Revolution, makes a similar statement: "However, in 1959 Guevara expressed himself with a certain ambiguity. He was not a Communist and had never been a member of the Party." It is worth recalling that Thomas's masterful text was first published in 1971. He could not have known, or made reference to, the wealth of material, letters, interviews, and documents on Che's political and ideological leanings as we have presented them in these pages. See Hugh Thomas, *Cuba: la lucha por la libertad, 1958–1970*, vol. 3 (Mexico City: Grijalbo, 1974), pp. 1347–1348.

to do so. Consequently, they do not recognize the importance of the armed struggle, or the role played by Castro and his Rebel Army in the fight against Batista.* But Guevara's objections are neither strategic nor ideological. He considers himself a communist with a small c, in the truest sense of the word at that time: a soldier in the international struggle for socialism led by the Soviet Union. He does not perceive himself as a Communist with a capital C—as a member of the Cuban Party—mainly because of his views on guerrilla warfare. But once this dispute was resolved by victory in January 1959 and the subsequent unanimous endorsement of the armed struggle, Che and the Communists emerged as natural allies. Nothing separated them any longer. Only later would the vicissitudes of revolutionary government, geopolitics, and Latin American revolution lead to renewed confrontation.

Perhaps the most interesting debate Che had between his arrival at the Escambray and the battle of Santa Clara was reflected in his exchange with Enrique Oltuski. Oltuski's fate would take many a turn. The youngest minister of the revolutionary government at age twenty-eight, he would soon be fired and jailed, only to reappear later at the Ministry of Industry under Che Guevara. In the early nineties he was still working with the Cuban government in the area of natural resources.

The give-and-take was both substantive and impassioned, Che's letters revealing as always his state of mind and political development. The correspondence centered on the two men's dissension over agrarian reform. Oltuski favored a gradual distribution of land, while Guevara pressed for an immediate confiscation and allocation of plots. Among his many objections to the expropriation of large landholdings, Oltuski argued that such a radical step would lead to confrontation with the United States. The dialogue between them is worth quoting:

OLTUSKI: All the idle land should be given to the *guajiros* [peasants], while heavily taxing the *latifundistas* in order to buy their lands with their own money. Then the land would be sold to the *guajiros* at cost, with payment facilities and loans for production.

CHE: What a reactionary idea! How can we charge people for the land they work? You are the same as all those other people from the plains.

OLTUSKI: For crying out loud, what do you want to do? Give it to them? So they

---

* Theodore Draper makes the same distinction between Castro and the Communists: "The dividing line between Castro and the Communists had been reduced to a single topic: the armed struggle. To achieve an alliance, the Communists had to bridge that difference." Theodore Draper, *Castroism: Theory and Practice* (New York: Praeger, 1965), p. 34.

can let it go to seed, as they did in Mexico? Men must feel that it takes an effort to get what they have.

CHE *(shouting as the veins in his neck stand out)*: You're full of it!

OLTUSKI: Anyway, we must disguise things. Don't believe for a moment that the Americans are going to sit idly by and watch us do things so openly. We have to play it smart.[18]

CHE *(scathingly)*: So you are one of those who believe we can make a revolution behind the backs of the Americans. What a shitface you are! We must make the revolution within a struggle to the death against imperialism, from the very outset. A true revolution cannot be disguised.[19]

The dialogue included a topic that later became a source of minor but undeniable friction between Che and Fidel Castro. Only a couple of months earlier, the future *caudillo* had strongly rebuked Raúl Castro for kidnapping several U.S. citizens—engineers from the Moa and Nicaro mining complexes, and a few Marines. Fidel considered the U.S. embargo on arms sales to Batista vital to the revolution. The time was not yet ripe for a showdown with Cuba's neighbor to the north. Castro scolded his younger brother, who immediately released the prisoners. The arms embargo was maintained, but the Cubans were unaware that the kidnappings had kindled a heated debate over the embargo in Washington. The following passage from a classified State Department document reflects the tenor of that debate:

Our Embassy at Havana has recommended that the policy on arms shipments to Cuba be reviewed in the light of the kidnappings. . . . [They] believe that we should permit the Cuban Government to purchase arms in the United States to enable that Government to take military action to crush the Castro revolt or as an inducement to Batista to hold acceptable elections. . . . The principal reasons favoring such a change in policy are that the refusal to sell arms weakens the constituted Government of Cuba and that reports from our consuls who negotiated the release of the Americans in Oriente Province indicate possible communist influence in the forces of Raul Castro. The reasons against permitting sales of arms to Cuba include the considerations that arms shipped to the Batista Government in the past have not permitted the Government to deal effectively with forces weaker than those the 26th of July group can now muster, the bulk of the Cuban people are disaffected from the present regime and Batista is scheduled to leave the office of President next February unless he retains power by force, and open support to the present Government as evidenced by sales of arms would likely harm the United States position in most of the other American republics. On balance, ARA [the State Department's American Republics section], believes that the reasons against resuming arms shipments outweigh those favoring such a course of action.[20]

What distinguished Fidel Castro from Che and Raúl was his spectacular sense of timing. His lieutenants tended to discount the importance of opportunity and tactics; for him they were decisive.

Che had another discussion with Oltuski, equally charged with passion and indignation, about confiscating funds from the wealthy denizens of Las Villas. Guevara ordered Oltuski to rob the bank of a town called Sancti Spíritus, but the local leader refused outright, arguing that such an act was simply crazy, and would turn many people who currently supported the rebels against them. Besides, it was unnecessary; they had access to bountiful funds, which Oltuski offered to share with Che. Oltuski was also certain that Fidel would not approve of the operation.[21] Che replied with one of his fearsome tirades: "[If] the people's leaders threaten to resign . . . let them. Furthermore, I demand it right now, as we cannot allow the deliberate boycott of a step so beneficial to . . . the Revolution." He then pulled rank on Oltuski: "I see myself in the sad necessity of reminding you that I have been named commander-in-chief. . . ." Guevara concludes by establishing a connection between land distribution, bank robbery, and the class content of the revolution:

> Why is it that not a single *guajiro* has found fault with our idea that the land is for those who till it, and the landowners have? And isn't this related to the fact that the struggling masses agree to robbing the banks, because none of them has a penny in them? Haven't you wondered about the economic roots for that respect toward the most arbitrary of all financial institutions?[22]

Che perceived the struggle from a perspective all his own. In a "true revolution," he often said, alienating the bankers, landowners, or Americans was of no importance. It could even prove useful, triggering reprisals that would help radicalize the revolutionary process. This in turn would clean the ranks of the anti-Batista forces, more neatly defining the course of those who stayed.

Guevara was able to indulge in these verbal and conceptual luxuries first of all because he was *not* the commander-in-chief. Real responsibility resided in Fidel Castro, for whom Che was a sort of left flank or critical conscience. Secondly, his being a foreigner made it much easier for him to adopt extreme positions, since he was not exposed to recriminations from childhood friends, aging aunts, or former classmates—factors that undoubtedly influenced the Cuban leaders. Finally, in contrast to them, Guevara had an unclouded strategic vision as well as precise long-term goals. He fought for socialism, he wanted Cuba to join the Soviet bloc, and he considered confrontation with the United States indispensable. The decisions made by Che in Las Villas were both lucid and consistent with this perspective. But they clashed violently with the aspirations and tactics of the reformist Cuban leaders from the plains.

Che's time in Las Villas was not devoted entirely to polemics. He displayed brilliant political skills in the mission entrusted him by Fidel Castro. Slowly but surely, he reached agreement with the different opposition groups: the 26th of July Movement in Las Villas, the student organization, the Communists, and even the Second National Front of the Escambray, led by Eloy Gutiérrez Menoyo and Jesús Carrera. He had a dangerous dispute with Carrera, however. The small splinter group from the 26th of July Movement operated within a certain zone. When Che's troops tried to enter it, they were asked for a password, which they did not have. Guevara himself was challenged by Carrera. Fortunately, he was able to reach an understanding with Gutiérrez Menoyo before things got out of hand.* In a letter to the student leadership dated November 7, Guevara rejected any alliance with Gutiérrez Menoyo. In the latter's view, however, the incident had no further consequences:

> Che may have had some resentment against the officers I sent, the ones who stopped him, and especially Comandante Jesús Carrera. He sent me a letter, complaining about Jesús Carrera. When I met with Guevara I told him that he had no right to complain because Comandante Jesús Carrera was following orders from me. In other words, when anybody enters our zone there must be an agreement on passwords, in order to avoid confrontation. This is territory liberated by us, where our guerrillas operate. In consequence, if in the evening or at night you ask troops for the password and they can't give it, then they are enemy troops. This is an elementary thing, which he later understood perfectly.[23]

Che's accords with the different groups, including that of Gutiérrez Menoyo, were partly expressed in the Pact of El Pedrero, which was signed in early December at a village near Guevara's general headquarters. Though the pact involved only Che and the Student Directorate, represented by Rolando Cubela, it symbolized a wider agreement with the other opposition forces. Members of the PSP, led by Felix Torres, joined the unit commanded by Camilo Cienfuegos, and Gutiérrez Menoyo himself reached an "operational pact" with Guevara. Weeks later, Castro would strongly re-

*In a text published in February 1961 in *Verde Olivo,* Che described his contact with Gutiérrez Menoyo the following way: "On January 1, the revolutionary leadership ordered all troops to be placed under my command in Santa Clara. The Second National Front of the Escambray, through its leader, Gutiérrez Menoyo, immediately accepted. There was no problem." Ernesto Che Guevara, "A Son of the Revolution," *Verde Olivo* (Havana), February 12, 1960. A few lines below, he denounced the behavior of Gutiérrez Menoyo's troops on entering the capital, but that is another matter.

buke his subordinate for the accord, accusing him of having revived a corpse.[24] On December 26, just before the final victory, Castro warned Che:

> At this time the situation in Las Villas is my major worry. I do not understand why we are making precisely the same mistake that made us send you and Camilo to the province in the first place. Now it turns out that, far from having solved it definitively, we have made it worse.[25]

Carlos Franqui harbors no doubt about the meaning of this message: "In his note to Che, Fidel vigorously disapproved of the importance given to the Student Directorate," not to mention Gutiérrez Menoyo.[26] Despite this criticism, the agreement did help achieve Castro's goal, which was to unite all the opposition forces and bring them under his command. Gutiérrez Menoyo—who spent twenty years in a Cuban jail after the Revolution— describes the cordial relationship he had with Guevara:

> Once that incident was put behind us, I met with him. We signed the pact for agrarian reform, and the operational pact, which he even took a picture of. It must be in the archives, locked up until they decide to tell the true history of Cuba, and not just a part of it. After that, our relations were fine; they operated on the northern coast while we were on the southern one. We even sent arms to reinforce Camilo Cienfuegos's position at the siege of Yaguajay.[27]

The unity among opposition forces in Las Villas allowed Che to disrupt and effectively block the elections scheduled for November 3 by Fulgencio Batista. As its military situation crumbled, the dictatorship was increasingly pressured by its reluctant allies to seek a political solution to the war. The most obvious, supported by the U.S. and important business sectors, was to organize early elections which would not include Batista. They would pave the way for a decorous retirement by the former sergeant, and usher in a new government. They would also foreclose any possibility—no matter how remote—of Fidel Castro and his Rebel Army reaching power. Castro understood the maneuver perfectly, and put all his effort and imagination into foiling the plot. He appealed to the population not to vote, to sabotage the elections in urban areas and disrupt them in the countryside. Eighty percent of the electorate answered his plea. In Che's words,

> The days before November 3 were days of extraordinary activity: our columns mobilized in all directions, almost completely blocking voters' access to the voting booths in those areas. In general terms all transport, from Batista's soldiers to merchandise, was stopped. There was practically no voting in Oriente; in Camagüey the percentage was a bit higher, and in the western zone . . . the population obviously stayed home.[28]

During those final weeks of the struggle, Che's fierce asceticism began to yield before the hard realities of administration, alliance politics, and the idiosyncratic reactions of the local population amid exceptional circumstances. For instance, after taking the village of Sancti Spíritus, Che tried to ban alcoholic beverages and the lottery. The villagers revolted, and Che was forced to back down on his attempts to impose on them his own habits and experience from other Latin American countries. He also tried to regulate relations between men and women within his column, especially as it grew in size during the struggle against Batista. There, too, he had to give in to the temptations of the tropics and the reality of combat conditions: sexual puritanism did not exactly flourish among the youthful, irreverent troops. Che finally reconsidered, authorizing relationships as people saw fit.*

In early November, at El Pedrero, Guevara met the woman who would become his second wife. His principal companion for the rest of his life, she would give birth to four of his five recognized children. Aleida March was a young and pretty clandestine militant of the 26th of July Movement in Las Villas. Pursued by the police, she took refuge at Che's camp in the Escambray. Just twenty-two, she was an exceptionally attractive woman; a Cuban who knew her well recalled days after Che's death that "she was one of the most beautiful women in Cuba and her preference for Che could not but provoke some resentment against that damned Argentine who had carried her off as a war trophy in Santa Clara."[29] A bright university student with a white, urban, upper-middle-class background, she soon became his closest friend and assistant. She was at his side without interruption in the last few weeks of the war and during his entry into Havana.

Yet Aleida did not bewitch Guevara with the exoticism of a Hilda Gadea or a Zoila Rodríguez; rather, she seemed a watered-down version of Chichina. Undeniably beautiful, and more similar to Guevara than the other women who were close to him, she lacked the complex otherness of Chichina. Che was deeply in love with her and the intensity of his passion lasted for years. But a distance grew between them almost from the outset. Some attribute it to the Revolution; others to the fact that Aleida soon lost her good looks. Others still point to a feminine possessiveness which survived her husband and extended to his children, his records, and his mem-

---

*As Che wrote in a later text, "One must . . . avoid all disruptions that might undermine the troops' morale but, following the rules of guerrilla warfare, one must allow people without previous commitments who mutually love each other to contract marriage in the sierra and lead a married life." Ernesto Che Guevara, "La guerra de guerrillas," in *Escritos y discursos,* vol. 1 (Havana: Editorial de Ciencias Sociales, 1977), p. 133. Che evidently considered his own marriage to Hilda Gadea emotionally canceled, though formally intact; so he does not appear to have been excessively strict in this regard.

ory. Years later, Pepe Aguilar, Che's childhood friend from Alta Gracia, who kept closely in touch with him until his departure from Cuba, accurately described Aleida's dilemma: "She was difficult to get on with, and besides she was terribly jealous of everyone and everything that had been close to Che before she knew him."[30]

By November and December 1958, Che was able to cut communication routes through the center of Cuba, blocking transport across the island. His luck held despite constant combat and unnecessary risks. His only injuries occurred while jumping from a rooftop: he seriously twisted his wrist (necessitating a plaster cast) and cut himself just above the eyebrow. Both injuries became part of his legend, as the photographs depict him entering Havana with a bandaged arm and a scar on his forehead.

Military victories followed one another in quick succession. The town of Cabaiguán, where Che's troops captured ninety prisoners, seven machine guns, and eighty-five rifles, fell on December 21. A couple of days later they took the city of Placetas, also with weapons and prisoners. Batista's troops were openly demoralized, less willing to fight with each passing day. His soldiers surrendered even when they had the military advantage; they sensed how the civilian population was increasingly hostile to them, and sympathetic to the rebels. Che's column's relentless advance led him to conceive and prepare the assault on Santa Clara, a city of 150,000 inhabitants, the capital of Las Villas province, and the largest urban community in central Cuba. It would witness the greatest battle of the war, sounding the death knell of Batista's dictatorship and consecrating Che Guevara as a revolutionary hero and military strategist.

The principal barracks of Santa Clara housed over 2,500 soldiers and ten tanks. Another thousand troops were stationed on the city outskirts. Guevara launched his attack with 300 men—most of them exhausted, undernourished, and inexperienced. He was informed, in addition, that enemy reinforcements were on their way from Havana by rail. The armored train, which would become part of the Guevara legend, consisted of two locomotives and nineteen cars; it carried fourteen machine guns and 400 well-equipped soldiers. Che knew that the battle might last several weeks. As late as December 28, he suspected that it would take a month.[31] With the city surrounded and Batista's forces quartered in their barracks, on the dawn of December 28 Che's column began moving into Santa Clara. The *comandante* himself traveled in a jeep at the halfway point of the column. His men were divided into several platoons. They arrived at the university, then went on to capture a radio station; on the way, they came upon a light tank, which killed five guerrilla fighters and wounded several others. At the same time, the soldiers from the armored train, perched on the hill, opened fire on the column.

During the morning, rebel student reinforcements arrived by another highway and approached the Leoncio Vidal army headquarters, where most of the army troops were concentrated. In the meantime, Batista's air force was bombing and strafing Che's men, as frightened city residents took shelter in their homes. The military requested more reinforcements, but rebel troops outside the city and on the highways were able to block them; air support from Havana was also called in, and failed equally to materialize. At sunset of the first day of the battle, the soldiers were still quartered in their barracks. Then, under the cover of darkness, the civilian population began building barricades against the army tanks, as more rebels entered the city during the night, in small groups. With the army grounded and the passive complicity of the population, Che was able to disperse his forces throughout the center of Santa Clara. The field was ready for the next day's combat.

Che understood that the crux of the battle consisted of stopping the armored train, preventing army troops and tanks from leaving their garrison, and mobilizing the civilian population. According to Oscar Fernández Mell, a physician and officer in the Rebel Army, if instead of taking refuge within the city, the enemy had organized its defense from higher, fortified positions, the Rebel Army would have required more time to take the provincial capital. It would also have suffered more casualties.[32] The secret lay in the army's refusal to fight; that was the crucial element Che had to work with. When the officers commanding the armored train succeeded in evading combat and approached the army headquarters in search of protection, they found that the tracks had been removed the day before. What followed was a spectacular derailment. Three of the twenty-two cars fell off the track, overturning immediately; the others were pounded by rebel fire and Molotov cocktails. The troops inside the train were caught in an unbearable combination of heat, bombs, and gunfire. They soon begged for a truce, and negotiated their surrender with Che that afternoon.

The train episode was decisive. Thanks to the weapons they were able to capture, Che's troops entered Havana several days later with much more firepower than any other opposing group—including, especially, the Student Directorate and the Second National Front of the Escambray. Gutiérrez Menoyo suggests a different interpretation of the train affair because his group was the most adversely affected by the surrender to Che. According to him, the capture of the train was a decisive operation whose history has not been fully clarified. The train was under the command of a Lieutenant Rossel; Gutiérrez Menoyo recalls he was the first person to whom the military broached the issue of surrender. He offered guarantees for the troops, and a promotion for Rossel; the soldiers decided to surrender to Menoyo. Then, recalls Gutiérrez Menoyo, "Lieutenant Rossel's brother spoke to Che Guevara. I don't know what he offered that I didn't, but the fact is that they surrendered the train to him. Cuba still commemorates this as the heroic assault on the armored train, but that train was surrendered."

The capture of the train allowed the rebels to launch their final offensive against Santa Clara and then Havana. As Gutiérrez Menoyo remembers, "I discussed this two or three times with Guevara and asked him, what did you offer that I didn't? He only laughed and never confessed the truth to me. If they had surrendered the train to me, there was an incredible amount of supplies there and that would have allowed us to launch the final offensive. Che never gave me a specific answer."[33] Antonio Nuñez Jiménez, who was a member of Che's column and has written about the armored train, categorically denies this account. He insists that Gutiérrez Menoyo had nothing to do with the train, and that there was a derailment rather than a surrender.[34] In a strange footnote to history, Fulgencio Batista asserts that the train was indeed surrendered by Rossel, "who deserted after having received 350,000 dollars or one million dollars from Che Guevara." In his view, the train was not captured but bought.[35] Conflicting testimony abounds on the issue. Ramón Barquin, the only Batista officer to be jailed by the dictator for conspiring against him, states that the train was handed over as part of a deal; Ismael Suárez de la Paz (Echemendia), the 26th of July's man in Santa Clara, swears there was no such arrangement, just a straightforward surrender.[36]

Che asked Aleida March to stand before the derailed train, saying, "Aleida, I'm going to take a picture of you for history."[37] The episode was indeed crucial to the final outcome. The booty was enormous: six bazookas, five 60-millimeter mortars, fourteen machine guns, one 20-millimeter cannon, 600 automatic rifles, and one million rounds of ammunition.[38] It was the largest seizure of enemy weapons of the entire war. Almost 400 soldiers were taken prisoner. News of the capitulation spread rapidly through the city and into army headquarters, with devastating effects on morale and an explosive impact on the inhabitants of Santa Clara.[39]

Combat continued on December 30. Guevara's forces advanced, but not without difficulty. At police headquarters they met with strong resistance from 400 Batista troops who refused to submit, fearful of reprisals from the civilian population: the troops had engaged in summary executions for minor offenses and treason, as well as torture, in the previous weeks. This bastion, along with the Leoncio Vidal garrison and its 1,300 troops, were Batista's last hope in Santa Clara. As the sun rose upon the final day of the year, the army had not yet surrendered and the guerrilla offensive seemed to stagnate. But police headquarters was soon overrun, leaving only the military garrison. That was the situation when the New Year dawned on Santa Clara.

Negotiations for the garrison's surrender began at sunrise, but were immediately overshadowed by events in the rest of the island. During the New Year celebrations, Batista fled the island in a scene made famous by dozens of subsequent films. The impact in Santa Clara was decisive: "Of course [when] Batista left, there emerged favorable conditions so that on the fourth day of the attack on Santa Clara the war was over."[40] An improvised military junta, led by General Eulogio Cantillo, still attempted to avert the army's complete collapse and the rebels' final victory. Cantillo broadcast by radio an order to all base commanders throughout the country, instructing them not to give up and insinuating that he had reached an agreement with Fidel Castro in Oriente: "What we have just done here in Columbia [Havana's principal military base] has the approval of Dr. Fidel Castro."[41]

For his part, Castro broadcast a radio proclamation from the outskirts of Santiago. He denounced the attempted coup d'état, rejecting any negotiation with the besieged garrisons, and instructed Che and Camilo Cienfuegos to proceed to Havana immediately. Minutes before Che's ultimatum to the Santa Clara officers expired, troops began streaming out and throwing their weapons to the ground. The battle was over. The population took to the streets in celebration, acclaiming Che and his bearded revolutionaries, who immediately began the march to the capital. The Revolution had triumphed.

It is up to historians to determine just how decisive the battle of Santa Clara really was. The biographer must ask different questions. Was the revolutionary triumph in the capital city of Las Villas due to Che's military genius, or did it have more to do with politics and psychology? Santa Clara, together with resistance in the Sierra against the Batista offensive of May–June 1958, was the only battle of the war really worthy of the name. Without it, Batista might not have fled. And if the dictator had stayed on, his army might not have collapsed as it did after his New Year's Eve departure. The existing balance of military power—still unfavorable to the rebels—might have lasted longer. Without the seizure of the armored train, the Leoncio Vidal garrison would probably not have capitulated. Without the booty from both victories, Che's column would not suddenly have become the strongest unit in the rebel army. Without Santa Clara, this astounding CIA analysis (drafted one month before Castro's triumph) might have come true:

> Castro has failed to convince the majority of the Cuban people that his personality and program, in preference to Batista's, are worth fighting for. Cuba continues to enjoy relative economic prosperity, and a large part of the population, probably concerned that revolution would jeopardize their well-being, appears to hope that there can be a peaceful transition from authoritarian to constitutional government.[42]

It is also true, however, that only six guerrilla fighters died in the battle of Santa Clara, in a war in which Batista's army lost fewer than 300 men. Moreover, the Batista army's destruction was imminent; as Castro said to Che on the eve of the battle, "The war is won, the enemy is collapsing entirely."[43] Without Santa Clara, the process would have taken longer, with fateful consequences in many areas. But the final outcome would have been the same. Che Guevara's troops were not the sole military factor involved, nor was the struggle exclusively military. Granted, one should not minimize the sacrifices made by thousands of Cubans to topple a corrupt and heinous regime, nor should anyone underestimate the military aspect of Batista's overthrow. But all accounts agree that the victory of January 1959 was not only or even primarily a military one. Che's role was doubtless crucial in the final days of the war. His composure, determination, lucidity, and spirit of sacrifice were invaluable in Santa Clara. Without his leadership skills, his implacable centralization of all decisions, his detachment and sense of strategy, victory would have been impossible under such adverse conditions. Guevara's complete concentration on the requirements of the struggle, his disdain for any sentimental distractions, stand out in this passage from his memoirs:

> I rebuked a soldier for falling asleep in full battle, and he replied that he had been disarmed for having fired without orders. I answered with my customary dryness: "Go win yourself another rifle, go up to the front line unarmed . . . if you are capable." In Santa Clara, [I was] encouraging the wounded . . . a dying man touched my hand and said, "Do you remember, *comandante?* You sent me to get a weapon . . . and I won it for myself." It was the soldier who had fired without orders, who would die minutes later, and he seemed happy to have proven his bravery. That's what our Rebel Army is like.[44]

Nonetheless, there were other considerations involved in the battle of Santa Clara. Acknowledging them does not detract from Che's accomplishments; rather, it highlights them. First of all, Batista's troops refused to leave their barracks; when they did venture out, they declined to fight. Morale was abysmally low. The soldiers were full of misgivings: they did not receive requested reinforcements, had lost the support of the United States, and felt—quite rightly—that their officers might betray them at any time. In contrast, the rebel fighters were devoted to their cause, had genuine (if limited) combat experience, and one crucial advantage: the enthusiastic support of the civilian population, which proved decisive in the street-by-street combat for the city. Finally, though Che was the highest commander in the field, he also had two critical human elements in his favor. He was backed by superb lieutenants, men like Rolando Cubela, Victor Bordón,

Fernández Mell, and Faure Chomón, among others, and by the faraway figure of Fidel, who continued to design the overall plan of the war.

The victory of Santa Clara was thus due to the many talents of Che Guevara, but also to a fortunate (though far from random) convergence of circumstances, which did not necessarily stem from his virtues as a military leader. Absent these circumstances, the Argentine's military acumen would doubtless have played a lesser role. A misunderstanding of this delicate balance and an overestimation of Che's military prowess would prove fateful in his life and death. With its corollary overemphasis on the struggle's military aspects, this faulty interpretation would also prove disastrous for the prospects of revolution in Latin America. Both fallacies were unavoidable, once the leaders of the 26th of July Movement were caught up in the whirlwind of that memorable New Year's Day of 1959, when history for once smiled upon the noble cause of ordinary people. Che was the symbol of that cause and of its victory. He appeared in newsreels and picture magazines, the military commander ready to take Havana by storm. While Castro found himself at the other end of the island plotting strategy, Che was in the trenches, his men tired, wounded, and jubilant like him. In those days of celebration, Guevara was the emblem and the conqueror.

Fidel Castro's orders were categorical. Che and Camilo were to proceed immediately to Havana. Che would take the military base located at the fortress of La Cabaña, Camilo that of Columbia. The commanders of the 26th of July Movement were to enter the coastal city alone, before anybody else, and wait there for Fidel Castro to conquer Santiago. From there he would embark on his historic march the length of the island, arriving at the capital one week later. Fidel's instructions were straightforward on another score, as well. His two subordinates were to exclude from the triumphant entry into Havana the Student Directorate, the PSP's Communists, and other forces like those of Gutiérrez Menoyo. Once there, they were to seize the weapons stored at Havana's two fortresses.* Castro's specific mission assignments were, however, both devious and dexterous—a complex maneuver by one of the most wily and skillful politicians of the twentieth century.

Carlos Franqui wonders why Castro sent Che to La Cabaña. Columbia was the head and heart of the tyranny and its military power; La Cabaña was a secondary post. Che had taken the armored train and the city of Santa Clara; he was the second leader of the Revolution. Camilo was an outstanding warrior, but nevertheless Che's lieutenant in the provinces; he

---

*Fidel Castro, letter to Ernesto Guevara, December 26, 1958, quoted in Franqui, *Diario.* The first forces to enter the capital were those of Gutiérrez Menoyo and the student organization. Despite Fidel's orders, they occupied the university and the presidential palace.

had to lead a furious battle against the Yaguajay garrison, 100 kilometers further from Havana than Santa Clara. Che was the right man to take Columbia. Why did Fidel entrust Camilo with the chief mission, and Che with the back-up command?[45]

None of Che's or Fidel's biographers has really explained the *caudillo*'s decision. Yet it was crucial for the events that followed.* Franqui is right: the second most important leader of the Revolution was relegated to a secondary task, while the glory of the first entry into Havana and the capture of Batista's main headquarters were assigned to a man of indisputable heroism but lesser political importance. There are several possible explanations. The most obvious is the fact that Che was a foreigner. Another, slightly more far-fetched, is that Fidel had already decided to try—and execute—Batista's partisans at La Cabaña, and needed somebody there who would not hesitate to do so. In this perspective, he also wanted a foreign scapegoat in case there was a bloodbath. Franqui offers another explanation, which is more logical though somewhat confusing. Guevara was the second leader of the Revolution, and the most radical one. To assign him Columbia would have made him even more powerful, which was not in Fidel's interest for several reasons. Che had an agenda of his own. He had already disobeyed orders by forging a close alliance with the Student Directorate. Furthermore, he was too close to the Communists, which could alienate the Cuban liberals and Americans. Camilo, in contrast, was not a threat to Fidel. He was younger, less experienced, more "fun-loving" than Che. He did not represent any problem for Fidel's allies, or for his potential enemies. The leader at Fidel's side during his public appearances was always Camilo. Guevara stayed inside the fortress, far from the limelight.[46] In this interpretation, there was no coincidence in the celebrated scene where Fidel addressed the masses at Columbia. As a dove straight from Cuban *santería* alighted on his shoulder, the *caudillo* asked the famous question, "¿Voy bien, Camilo?" (How am I doing, Camilo?) And the guerrilla fighter answered, "Vas bien, Fidel" (You're doing fine, Fidel).

In any case, Camilo entered Havana on the morning of January 3 to the cheers of a jubilant, adoring population. Che arrived at the capital more discreetly, at dawn of the following day, accompanied only by Aleida and his closest collaborators. He came in as he had fought the war: tired, dirty, uncombed, practically in rags. On January 7, he left for Matanzas to receive Fidel—whom he had not seen since August—on his way to Havana. They entered the capital together aboard a tank, and were received by ecstatic,

---

* Guevara's biographers sidestep the matter entirely. Szulc, Quirk, and Geyer, who have narrated the life of Castro, simply ignore the issue. Jean-Pierre Clerc insinuates that Che's marginalization was due to his foreign nationality. Jean-Pierre Clerc, *Fidel de Cuba* (Paris: Ramsay, 1988), p. 178.

delirious crowds. The photographs of this meeting between a people and its heroes captivated not only the eye of editors around the world, but the imagination and sympathy of admirers everywhere. Che's shy smile enraptured thousands, then millions of Cubans, Latin Americans, and citizens of the world who identified him with a revolution that was also theirs. There was no question as to the legitimacy of the *guerrilleros'* struggle or the justice of their triumph. Nor was there any doubt as to the freshness, spiritual integrity, and boundless charisma of the bearded young men in olive green. Smiling, talented and ingenious, courageous and pure, they seemed ready to storm any heaven, conquer any winter palace.

It would have taken phenomenal modesty and maturity to avoid the key political and conceptual mistakes that would later prove so costly for Cuba and the entire continent. How could Fidel not be convinced that victory was his, and his alone, amid the cheers of hundreds of thousands of Cubans as they hung, fascinated by his oratorical genius, upon his every word, expression, and gesture? How could he resist the temptations born of the contrast between his youthful boldness and the rancid mediocrity of the old political class, represented in the new government by several cabinet ministers and the president himself, Manuel Urrutía? It was only natural that there should be an imaginary reconstruction of events: "the Sierra" had won, not "the plains"; the 26th of July had done it all, without any important allies; its leaders had carried the day, thanks to their exceptional wisdom and intuition. And Fidel, the *líder máximo,* had played strictly by the rules, taking power fair and square. The consequences of this assessment of victory were barely perceptible in those days of celebration. Soon, however, as the island paradise began to crumble, the flaws in the simplistic analysis surged forth.

In conceptual terms, the "revisionist" view of the war would reach its highest expression in Che's later writings, pregnant with his talent and his vision. They would inevitably bear the mark of his worldview and his notion of history, summarized in this stunning declaration addressed to the Argentine writer Ernesto Sabato: "The war transformed us completely. There is no deeper experience for a revolutionary than the act of war; not the isolated act of killing nor of bearing a gun or even of one form or another of combat but the total act of war."[47] There, the many-faceted, complex process of the Sierra would be transformed into a magnificent, straightforward epic that could be repeated anywhere with bravery and integrity. Only Fidel, Che, Raúl, and Camilo had the moral authority to write the official history of the war. Fidel lacked the time, patience, and literary or theoretical penchant. His brother learned and practiced from early on the virtues of silence; for almost forty years he would be the man in the shadows. Camilo had no vocation for writing, and soon ran out of time: he died in November when his plane disappeared over the sea; his body was never recovered. The only one left was Che, who was indeed singularly suited for the task.

But he carried only the cultural and intellectual baggage he had brought with him to Havana. He did not know the capital. The only Cuban city familiar to him was Santa Clara in ruins; the political, intellectual, and cultural life of Havana, among the most vital in Latin America, was totally alien to him. It was inevitable that he should emphasize those aspects of the war that he had lived firsthand. Military matters, peasant issues, radical ideas would overshadow other concerns in his analysis—not only of Cuba, but of all Latin America:

> We have demonstrated that a small group of men who are determined, supported by the people, and without fear of dying . . . can overcome a regular army. . . . There is another [lesson] for our brothers in America, economically in the same agrarian category as ourselves, which is that we must make agrarian revolutions, fight in the fields, in the mountains, and from here take the revolution to the cities, not try to make it in the latter without a comprehensive social content.[48]

Che would maintain this position, though further qualified and refined, until the end of his life. Hence, its impact throughout the continent, and its failure. The Guevarist description of what occurred in Cuba was incomplete, and even false to some extent. He wrongly extrapolated the supposed lessons of Cuba to other latitudes, and ignored one central point: what happens once can rarely be repeated.

This interpretation is based upon a long conversation Che had with Carlos Franqui five years later, in 1964, in which their different approaches to the history of the war became apparent. Guevara attached decisive importance to guerrilla warfare and the countryside; Franqui to politics and the cities. Che focused on how the Student Directorate was decimated in the cities, making the subsequent leadership position of the Sierra unavoidable, while Franqui emphasized the significance of the student movement. Che took shelter in radical ideas and the rules of guerrilla warfare, while Franqui stressed the integrity and importance of the clandestine struggle. Finally, Che underlined the guerrillas' military action and their role in the army's surrender. Franqui then replied:

> I know, Che, that without the support of the clandestine struggle in '57 the guerrillas would have been liquidated. Without the organized support of the peasants of the 26th [of July], not that of the other peasants, the

Granma nucleus would not have regrouped. Without the arms sent from Santiago and Havana, as your war chronicles acknowledge, Che, without our actions in all the island, which paralyzed the tyrant's military and repressive apparatus, without the reinforcement of men, medicines, food, without the help of the exiles, the guerrillas alone would not have won.[49]

After Che's victory march into Havana with Fidel, the course of events accelerated. On January 7, Che and Aleida moved into an army officer's residence at La Cabaña. It was his first comfortable home since Buenos Aires. Che's parents, sister, and brother Juan Martín arrived in Havana on January 9, in a Cubana de Aviación airplane sent by Camilo Cienfuegos to repatriate the Cuban exiles of Buenos Aires. Che met them at the Rancho Boyeros airport and immediately took them to the Havana Hilton (soon to be renamed the Havana Libre). The family reunion was a happy one, darkened only by uncertainty about Che's future as expressed in his parents' questions: What are you going to do? Will you go back to medicine? Why don't you come home to Argentina?

Two weeks later, Hilda Gadea and their daughter arrived from Lima, anxious to see the Revolution and their new homeland. The situation became more and more tense for him. Aside from his difficult political duties, Guevara had to tend to his Argentine family with their burden of memories and ambivalence, the presence of the two Hildas, and his affair with Aleida. A physical breakdown was almost inevitable. It soon came, along with agonizing inner doubts about his destiny.

A conversation between Che and his father reveals the persistence of his wanderlust: "I myself don't know where I will lay my bones to rest."[50] Antonio Nuñez Jiménez, who entered La Cabaña with Che and negotiated the Leoncio Vidal garrison capitulation in Santa Clara, recalls the same trait in Guevara:

He told me about it the day we reached Havana, on January 3, 1959, as we penetrated into the fortress of La Cabaña. Crossing the Havana tunnel in a jeep, he said to me: "My mission, my commitment to Fidel ends here, with our entry into Havana, because the agreement I had with Fidel was to participate in Cuba's guerrilla struggle and then have the freedom of choice to go somewhere else and do what I had done in Cuba."[51]

Che's parents and siblings remained until February 14. His mother, Celia, would return alone on May 1. They thus accompanied their son on February 2, when the Council of Ministers issued a general decree, largely for Che's benefit, granting Cuban nationality by birth to those foreigners who had spent at least two years fighting the dictatorship. Their extended stay allowed them to appreciate the changes in Ernesto both physically and, especially, psychologically. Che was by now a mature man of almost thirty-one years, with a daughter, two women, and a job to do. His face reflected the intensity and wear of the previous two years. In mid-January he suffered a violent asthma attack which obliged him to leave Havana for many weeks and seek solace at a summer villa near Tarará, not far from the capital.

Before departing he had to supervise, either at close quarters or from his window at La Cabaña, the executions of Batista's collaborators. Justifiable as these executions may have seemed at the time, they were carried out without respect for due process. Estimates as to their exact number vary, especially for those executions carried out at La Cabaña in the first days of the year. Cables from the United States Embassy, dated January 13 and 14, place the figure at 200.* Historians' and biographers' estimates range from 200 to 700 victims.† Years later, Fidel Castro would place the number executed between 1959 and 1960 at 550. Some took place outside Havana: over 100 were ordered shot in Santiago by Raúl Castro in early January.‡

After a certain date most of the executions occurred outside Che's jurisdiction. In mid-January, partly due to a wave of protest from the U.S. media and Senate, Castro decided to hold public trials in the sports stadium of Havana. They became notorious after the sentencing in mid-January of Major Jesús Sosa Blanco, a particularly ruthless Batista functionary in the province of Oriente, and of colonels Grau and Morejón. Though Fidel's decision was a disaster for the image of the regime, it released Che from any authority over the fate of his prisoners at La Cabaña. He had previously ordered dozens of executions, curiously abetted by Herman Marks, another "internationalist," a former convict from Milwaukee who had joined Che's ranks in the Escambray.[52]

Conflicting views exist of Che's role in the executions at La Cabaña. Some exiled opposition biographers report that the Argentine enjoyed the rituals of the firing squad, and that he organized them with gusto—though

*Smith (Havana) to Secretary of State (Dept. of State), January 14, 1959 (Confidential), and Foreign Service Dispatch, Earl Smith/Embassy to Dept. of State, January 13, 1959 (Confidential), dispatch 725. In a cable dated December 29, 1959, the Embassy's estimate rose to "over 500." Braddock/AmEmbassy to Dept. of State, December 29, 1959, "Indications and Manifestations of Communism and Anti-Americanism in Cuban Revolutionary Regime."

† This figure is cited by, among others, Father Iñaki de Aspiazú, a Basque Catholic priest, who researched the matter in depth and from a stance sympathetic to the revolutionary regime. See Aspiazú, *Justicia revolucionaria,* quoted in Leo Huberman and Paul Sweezy, *Anatomy of a Revolution* (New York: Monthly Review Press, 1960), p. 70.

‡ Daniel James asserts that Guevara told Félix Rodríguez at La Higuera, on the eve of his execution, that Che himself had sent 1,500 enemies of the Revolution to their death. See Daniel James, *Che Guevara* (New York: Stein and Day, 1969), p. 113. But Rodríguez does not mention this in his memoirs, or in his report to the CIA, or in an interview with this author in Miami in 1995.

they acknowledge that the orders came from Fidel Castro. Others relate that Guevara suffered at every execution, pardoning as many prisoners as he could—though he did not hesitate to carry out orders when he felt they were justified. This was the case for José Castaño Quevedo, the head of Batista's anti-Communist forces. Che sent him before a firing squad despite pleas for his pardon by the Catholic Church and other sectors of Cuban society. In contrast, his behavior regarding Huber Matos was more nuanced. Expelled from the Rebel Army in November 1959, accused of treason by Fidel Castro, and sentenced to thirty years in jail, Matos recalls today, nearly a decade after leaving a Cuban prison, that Guevara

> . . . was in communication with my relatives so they would know that he did not approve of the death penalty for me, that he even thought my problem had been erroneously managed by Fidel. And he suggested that we present an appeal immediately after the conclusion of the trial.*

Guevara's responsibility for events at La Cabaña—though it cannot be diminished, as Che himself never tried to do—must nonetheless be seen within the context of the time. There was no bloodbath; nor were innocent people exterminated in any large or even significant numbers. After the excesses of Batista, and the unleashing of passions during those winter months, it is surprising that there were so few abuses and executions. It is also true, however, that Che had no major qualms about the death penalty, or summary and collective trials. He was ready to give his life for his ideals and believed that others should be as well. If the only way to defend the revolution was to execute its enemies, he would not be swayed by any humanitarian or political arguments. He had nothing but contempt for the (doubtless hypocritical) criticism brandished by the press in New York or the establishment in Washington. The revolution took precedence. He never wondered about or agonized over the link between means and ends, past and future actions, historical precedent and harmful consequences for the future.

Guevara's asthma during this period, reflecting his many conflicts, was far more severe than was usual for him. The triggers, beyond his general physical weakness, may have been the customary ones. Though Che belonged to the winning faction, he had been partly ousted from the slot in the pecking order he deserved. In addition, he was the object of worrisome comments on the part of Fidel Castro. Alternatively, this recurrence of his

---

*Huber Matos, interview with English journalists, London (transcription made available to the author, 1995). According to Franqui, "At a certain point Raúl and Che demanded Matos's and the other conspirators' execution. But then Che changed his mind when he saw the courageous way in which they all stood up to Fidel." Carlos Franqui, interview with the author, San Juan, August 20, 1996.

asthma may simply have reflected his state of exhaustion. He suffered an onset of emphysema, as well as fatigue, weakness, anemia, and stress.*

As a result, Che moved into a house by the sea at Tarará, twenty kilometers from Havana. It became the center of his political and ideological activities through the spring of 1959; visitors recall his presence there beginning January 17, and he stayed until May.† There the so-called Tarará Group began meeting regularly: a sort of shadow government which, parallel to the new regime's visible authorities, started building an alternate social, political, and economic masterplan.‡ Though Che was largely bedridden at the beach until early April, as he confessed to his friend Alberto Granado, he was lucid and able to review documents.** Many of the major decisions taken by the revolutionary government during its initial year were first debated in Tarará. It was also there that Che drafted his earliest strictly political writings, beginning with his most famous book (after the Bolivian diary): *La guerra de guerrillas,* or *Guerrilla Warfare* in its English translation.

His departure from the capital was soon publicized by a critic of the regime, who questioned the assignment of a luxurious seaside residence to the notoriously austere Comandante Guevara. In response, Che published an open letter to the 26th of July's daily newspaper in which he explained his ailment and his need for rest, but he kept silent about his other reason for leaving La Cabaña:

> I wish to explain to the readers of *Revolución* that I am ill, that I did not catch my illness in gambling dens or spending nights in cabarets but by working more than my system could endure, for the Revolution. The doctors recommended a house in a place removed from daily visits.[53]

Che's additional motive for quitting La Cabaña, aside from his need for rest due to illness—which was highly uncharacteristic of him—derived precisely

---

*The radiological report from the armed forces' medical service says "double and diffused pulmonary emphysema." See Adys Cupull and Froilán González, *Un hombre bravo* (Havana: Ediciones Capitán San Luis, 1995), p. 392.

† "Che lived in a modern and comfortable summer residence on the beach of Tarará. . . . I visited him there on January 17, 1959." José Pardo Llada, *Fidel y el Che* (Barcelona: Plaza y Janés, 1989), p. 123.

‡ The first revolutionary government included no members of the PSP and few leaders from the 26th of July Movement—quite to the contrary, it comprised many liberals and traditional moderates, starting with the president, Manuel Urrutia. The speed with which the Batista regime collapsed, and Castro's intuitive caution, made this inevitable; but his vision for the future, as well as Che's, made a parallel government equally unavoidable.

**"I thought of going with Fidel to Venezuela. Later events kept me from doing so; I thought of going shortly afterward, and an illness is keeping me in bed." Ernesto Guevara, letter to Alberto Granado, quoted in Alberto Granado, *Con el Che Guevara de Córdoba a la Habana* (Córdoba: Ediciones Op Oloop, 1995), p. 87.

from the essential task he fulfilled in Tarará, far from inquisitive eyes and ears.

The very existence of the Tarará Group remained relatively unknown until the 1980s.* The seaside deliberations, which continued in Castro's house at Cojímar after Che's recovery, focused on several matters. Two of the lesser issues deserve special mention: the establishment of state security in Cuba and the first Cuban attempts to export revolution abroad. On January 14, Che met with Raúl Castro, Camilo Cienfuegos, Ramiro Valdés (his closest collaborator in the Sierra and during the "invasion"), and Víctor Piña of the PSP, to begin building "a body with secret characteristics that will be responsible for the security of the revolutionary state."[54] Very soon, Valdés would be entrusted with the army's G-2, and Efigenio Amejeiras with the police, while Raúl would work with the army and cadres from the Sierra to fulfill the security needs of the new state. Osvaldo Sánchez, a member of the PSP leadership who was in charge of the Party's Military Committee and one of the first Communists to have made contact with the guerrilla fighters in the Sierra, was assigned to accompany Valdés.[55] Angel Ciutah, a Communist veteran of the Spanish Civil War later exiled in Moscow, also lent a hand, having been sent to Cuba by the Soviet security apparatus. According to Carlos Franqui, he would play a key role in the construction of the notorious Cuban security machinery, thanks partly to his ties to Che, whose profound sympathy for the Republican cause in Spain dated back to his earliest childhood.[†] By November, when Huber Matos (the first son of the Revolution to be devoured by it) was arrested, tried, and sentenced to thirty years in jail, the new state security apparatus was in full operation. Che played a central role in its establishment, along with several of his collaborators—some Cuban and some foreign, including the sinister Frenchman Alberto Lavandeyra and Ciutah himself.

A second task, of great significance for Che's future though not terribly relevant at that time, centered on revolutionary expeditions to other countries. In 1959, the new Cuban regime helped organize attempts to export the revolution to Panama, Nicaragua, the Dominican Republic, and Haiti. Castro's government proudly acknowledged its involvement in attempts to

---

*Hugh Thomas, for instance, lists the authors of the Agrarian Reform Law, but omits any mention of the house at Tarará or of the secret meetings held in it. Carlos Franqui was equally unaware of the group's deliberations. Carlos Franqui, interview.

† Carlos Franqui, interview with the author. It is unlikely, though, that Che knew of, or participated in, Ciutah's apparent links to the Mercader brothers, Joaquín and Ramón, despite Franqui's claim in his books. Ramón murdered Leon Trotsky in Mexico in 1940, spent twenty years in a Mexican jail, and then traveled to Prague through Havana in 1960; Joaquín was also a member of the Soviet security services.

overthrow Anastasio Somoza and Rafael Trujillo, while denying any role in the other two nations. Che played a role in all four.*

In April, a group of 100 exiled Panamanians and Cubans landed in Panama. The revolutionary government denied any responsibility for it, but Raúl Castro made a lightning trip to Houston to meet with Fidel during the latter's tour of the U.S. and Latin America, to report on the situation and be scolded once again by his brother. In June an officer of the Rebel Army and former combatant of the Sierra Maestra, Delio Gómez Ochoa, led an invasion of the Dominican Republic. The ten Cubans and 200 domestic opponents of Trujillo were massacred just hours after having disembarked.

The Dominican expedition coincided with a similar attempt in Haiti. During the first days of January, a Haitian writer named René Despestre came to Havana from Port-au-Prince. A day after his arrival, Che received him at La Cabaña. They talked at great length about poetry, Jacques Roumain and the *Governors of the Dew*, Haiti and Latin America. Che was soon convinced of the need to overthrow François "Papa Doc" Duvalier, the newly inaugurated dictator of Hispaniola's French-speaking half. Among other misdeeds, he had been a staunch supporter of Batista. The writer organized a meeting between Che and Louis Desjoie, an elderly Haitian senator of the center-right who had run against Papa Doc in elections held during the mid-fifties. They agreed to organize and train a revolutionary contingent. During the months of April and May about fifty Haitians, both white and black, received military instruction in Cuba in the province of Oriente. According to Despestre, Che visited them and partly supervised the operation. The invasion of Haiti, including thirty Cuban veterans from the Sierra Maestra, was scheduled to take place a few days after the incursion into Dominican Republic, though it was planned more as an assault action than as an extended campaign of guerrilla warfare. The operation was canceled after the Dominican fiasco—though Desjoie had already begun to hesitate in light of the radicalization of the Cuban process.[†]

Lastly, on June 1, planes from Costa Rica airlifted a large number of "internationalists" into Nicaragua. After several skirmishes, they were ex-

---

*A secret report by the U.S. Department of Defense, dated April 15, 1959, states: "Guevara also has control of the so-called liberation groups staging in Cuba presumably for two eventual invasions of Nicaragua, Haiti and the Dominican Republic. He favors those with communist leadership and opposes others." Department of Defense, "Working Paper for Castro Visit: Summary of the Present Status of the Cuban Armed Forces," April 15, 1959 (Secret), RG 59, lot file 61d248, Reg. Affairs 1951/1952, box 16.

† This account is from René Despestre himself, who over and beyond the license one would expect from a poet, seems to be a reliable source. Interview with the author, Princeton, N.J., October 27, 1995.

pelled to Honduras. There they were captured by Honduran troops, who found on them a letter from Che Guevara to the Cuban authorities, asking them to help the Nicaraguans before their departure from Cuba.[56] Thirty years later, the Sandinista leader Tomás Borge would recall the rout of June 24, 1959, in Honduran territory, when one of the Nicaraguan guerrillas

fell firing an M-3 submachine gun. He had adopted it since the two planes had arrived from Cuba with a shipment of arms sent by Che Guevara, which was possible thanks to the complicity of [Honduran] president Ramón Villeda Morales, an admirer of Che's.*

But meetings in Tarará and Cojímar were chiefly devoted to three larger issues: land reform, Castro's alliance with the PSP, and the construction of the revolutionary army. Che played a key role in all three. As Antonio Nuñez Jiménez described the discussions twenty years later, "During two months we held night meetings in Tarará where Che was recovering his health. . . . Our work was secret."[57] The fact that these three tasks were all deliberated upon in the same place and with the same persons involved has confused many observers ever since.

The radicalization of the regime during the first few months of the year, and especially after May 1959, was not due to any great Communist influence. The government's alliance with the old PSP was an effect, not a cause, of its shift toward more extreme positions. The left wing, the Communist school of thinking, was in fact personified and promoted by two figures totally alien to the PSP: Raúl Castro and especially Che Guevara. Fidel Castro obviously oversaw the entire process, and made decisions for reasons of his own. But like any highly intuitive politician, he was sensitive to pressures, influences, opinions, and arguments presented to him by those he trusted with regard to training the new army and land distribution, although somewhat less in the area of relations with the Communists, and the person he most trusted was Guevara.

Land reform was the most controversial item on the economic policy agenda and in Cuba's relationship with the United States. Che first outlined his radical stance toward land reform during a lecture delivered on January 27 at the Sociedad de Nuestro Tiempo. His presentation has often been cited due to its content and its contrast with the public positions of Castro and his government at the time.[58] But its significance goes even further than was assumed by analysts like Theodore Draper, who did not know then

---

*Tomás Borge, *La paciente impaciencia* (Managua: Editorial Vanguardia, 1989), p. 149. Borge also mentions that Che "gave us 20,000 dollars . . . that were used in the guerrilla struggle of Rio Coco and Bocay." Ibid., p. 167.

about the Tarará meetings. The Tarará deliberations on land reform included figures like Alfredo Guevara, a young Communist filmmaker who had been—and continues to be—a close friend of Fidel Castro since his university days; Oscar Pino Santos, an economics journalist with links to the Party; Antonio Nuñez Jiménez, a geographer who joined Che in Las Villas, also close to the PSP's Marxist approach; Vilma Espín, the wife of Raúl Castro; and Che Guevara. They all worked together for several months, outside the margins of the official government institutions, excluding even the minister of agriculture, Humberto Sorí Marín, who had drafted the revolutionary agrarian reform decree issued in the Sierra Maestra in 1958. Alfredo Guevara recalls their work as follows: "We would meet every night until dawn at Che's house, then Fidel would come and change everything. Nobody knew what we were up to."[59]

In his January 27 lecture and in an interview with two Chinese journalists published years later, Che was very explicit as to the shortcomings of the previous reform. He described the guiding principle of the new and definitive distribution of land: to replace *latifundia* with cooperatives. Che's interview with the Chinese is significant because of its date.[60] He granted it on April 16, a full month before the new law was passed; but he asserted categorically that the law would be enacted, describing its content and major dispositions in full detail. The law was conceived in his home and under his auspices. Its purpose was not to distribute small plots to the peasants, but rather to nationalize or transform the great sugar, coffee, tobacco, and other plantations into cooperatives.

Guevara's project was more political than economic. He sought to destroy the *latifundia* as a power base for the oligarchy and foreign landowners, rather than to redistribute wealth by dividing the land into thousands of small plots. Che realized that such a reform would imply a major confrontation with Cuban landowners, especially the sugar producers, and with the Americans. He also believed that, under the existing compensation scheme, land expropriation would be a long and tedious process. Finally, he understood that the mechanism intended to implement the law, the future National Institute of Agrarian Reform (INRA), could become a powerful means to radicalize the Revolution.

The economic problem was a very real one. The Cuban economy could not prosper on sugar alone. In 1925, the sugar harvest had surpassed five million tons; in 1955, it barely exceeded four million. In the meantime, the population had increased by 70 percent, and its requirements had grown even more. Diversification and industrialization were thus the catchwords of the day not only among revolutionaries and Marxists, but even within the technocratic and business community. But exports made up 40 percent of the national income, and sugar accounted for 80 percent of total exports. Thus, there could be no diversification, industrialization, or even higher growth rates without transforming the country's agricultural structure.* As long as Cuban and foreign capital centered on sugar cane, allowing for high short-term profits with a stable market and attractive prices, and the sugar sector continued to dominate the island's economy and politics, there could be no future for Cuba. Che's real agenda was thus to break the power of the oligarchy, diversify the economy, and raise peasant incomes. It was critical, then, to expropriate the *latifundia,* collectivize land ownership, and diversify crops and exports. In Che's lucid analysis,

> When we propose an agrarian reform and enact revolutionary laws to achieve this goal quickly, we give special consideration to land redistribution, the creation of a strong domestic market and a diversified economy. For the moment, the purpose of agrarian reform is to promote sugar production and improve production techniques. In the second place, we must allow farmers to have their own plots, promote the opening of virgin land, and cultivate all arable land. Thirdly, we must increase production, and reduce our imports of basic grains . . . we must undertake national industrialization . . . which requires the adoption of protective measures for new industries, and consumer markets for new products. If we open the doors of the market to *guajiros* without any purchasing power, there will be no way to expand the domestic market.[61]

Che was fully aware of the implications of his position, and the direction in which it pointed. It was part of a long-term strategy which was self-evident to him and which, furthermore, would be in harmony with future revolutionary processes in other countries:

> Cuba's anti-popular regime and its army have now been destroyed, but the dictatorship's social system and its economic foundations have yet to be abolished. Many people from before are still working within the nation's structures. To protect the fruits of the revolutionary victory and allow for a continuous development of the revolution, we must take another step forward.[62]

---

*A mission from the World Bank visited Cuba in 1950 and concurred with this diagnosis and consequent remedies: "Cuba's development should move toward the following objectives: 1. To make Cuba less dependent on sugar by promoting additional activities—not by curtailing sugar production. 2. To expand existing—and create new—industries producing sugar by-products or using sugar as a raw material. 3. Vigorously to promote non-sugar exports in order to reduce the emphasis of the country's exports on one product. Among the most promising possibilities for achieving this aim are the promotion of mineral exports and the export of a variety of crude and processed foodstuffs. 4. To make further progress in producing in Cuba, for domestic consumption, a wide range of foodstuffs, raw materials, and consumer goods now imported." World Bank, *Report on Cuba,* quoted in Huberman and Sweezy, *Anatomy,* p. 108.

The agrarian reform enacted on May 17, 1959—just days after Fidel Castro returned from a successful trip to the United States, Brazil, Uruguay, and Argentina—was moderate in certain aspects, but its implications were not. It sanctioned the expropriation of large sugar and rice plantations and allowed for compensation through high-interest-paying but long-term bonds. The United States nonetheless denounced the law in no uncertain terms, in a diplomatic note dated June 11. The sugar companies' stock prices fell on the New York Stock Exchange, and firms whose assets had been confiscated—including United Fruit and the King Ranch—immediately prepared reprisals. The cattle ranchers of Camagüey, who were also affected, entered into all sorts of conspiracies; the region would remain a hotbed of counterrevolutionary activity for years to come.

Following the protest unleashed by the Agrarian Reform Law, President Manuel Urrutía resigned on July 13, after a tactical and short-lived abdication by Fidel Castro from his post as prime minister. Many liberals were subsequently expelled from the government by Castro, leading to a much closer alliance with the Communists. The crisis was largely triggered by Che's emphasis on radical land reform, promoted during the meetings at Tarará and then Cojímar. The establishment of the National Institute of Agrarian Reform (INRA) in accordance with his plans completed the process. It was responsible for rural health, housing, and education; it was empowered to set up centers supplying machinery and services to peasants; and it was entrusted with the industrialization of the countryside.* The INRA's first operational director, under the formal presidency of Fidel Castro, was Nuñez Jiménez, a close collaborator of Guevara's since Santa Clara. Che himself was the first administrator of the Department of Industries, a virtual Ministry of Industry within the INRA.

During his recovery at Tarará and until his voyage around the world in June, Guevara was also entrusted with another task central to the Revolution: the training of the new army, especially in ideological terms. At the fortress of La Cabaña, Che had already launched a series of educational projects. The leadership's central thesis left little room for doubt. In the words of Raúl Castro, "The Rebel Army is a political army whose objective is to defend the interests of the people."[63] Che formulated its goals with greater precision and frankness:

*In the words of Nuñez Jiménez, "The INRA, presided over by Fidel, was the bastion from which the Revolution was carried forward in those first few months. It was the body that finished off the bourgeoisie and imperialism. It was not expedient to suddenly change the Council of Ministers. Our people were not yet ready ideologically for us to stage an open battle between the Revolution and the counterrevolution, which was waiting in ambush within the government itself. Fidel replicated in the INRA the major functions of the Revolutionary Government." Antonio Nuñez Jiménez, *En marcha con Fidel* (Havana: Editorial Letras Cubanas, 1982), p. 309.

We must move rapidly toward restructuring the Rebel Army, because we improvised an armed corps of peasants and workers, many of them illiterate, without culture or technical training. We must train this army for the high duties entrusted to its members, giving them a technical and cultural education. The Rebel Army is the vanguard of the Cuban people.[64]

The new armed forces became the main pillar of the revolutionary regime, and would remain so. This was partly due to the mission Che entrusted to them, and his way of instilling in them a certain ideology and motivation.

Guevara soon organized courses for both officers and troops. Following the model of Raúl Castro's Schools for Troops Instructors in his Second Front (led by members of the PSP), Che inaugurated at La Cabaña what would later become the Schools for Revolutionary Instruction (EIR). Armando Acosta and Pablo Ribalta, Che's companions during the "invasion," and Angel Ciutah formed the core of instructors, along with several other Soviet-Spanish veterans. The idea of linking the army's ideological training to the Communists at La Cabaña made sense. Che's differences with the PSP were mainly tactical; at the time, he was an orthodox Marxist-Leninist. Many of his best cadres were members of the PSP, and he did not have unlimited human resources to devote to the army training program. He had to work quickly, using whoever was available. Conviction and convenience coincided once again in Che's decisions.

It soon became public that a radical ideological training program was underway at La Cabaña. A first indication that something important was happening in the fortress appeared in a note from the American Embassy dated March 20:

> The Embassy has been receiving increasing reports during the past few weeks of Communist penetration of La Cabaña Fortress, under the command of Major Ernesto "Che" Guevara. These reports cover the personnel which Guevara has brought in, the orientation of the education courses which are being given to the troops stationed there, and the manner in which the revolutionary tribunals at Cabaña have functioned. It has been very difficult, however, to obtain specific, concrete evidence of Communist penetration in that important military installation.[65]

The cable later refers to a series of art exhibits, ballet performances, and poetry recitals organized by the Department of Culture at La Cabaña.*

*In a cable dated April 14, 1959, the U.S. Embassy confirmed that "Much of the strength of the Communist effort in Cuba is directed toward infiltration of the Armed Forces. La Cabaña appears to be the main Communist center, and its Commander, Che Guevara, is the most important figure whose name is linked with Communism. Guevara is definitely a Marxist if not a Communist. He is a frequent guest speaker before the Communist front organizations. Political indoctrination courses have been instituted among the

Another report drafted by the Department of Defense at about the same time mentioned the establishment of a new body within the armed forces. It stated that the Department of Culture, also known as G-6, had created a unit whose ostensible purpose was to teach illiterate recruits how to read and write, but it also offered Marxist instruction. The report concluded that "penetration of the Army has been especially effective in the Havana area because of the position as commander of the Havana garrison of Ernesto 'Che' Guevara, a leftist if not an actual Communist, and probably still the Number Three man in actual power in Cuba."[66]

During those months, Che was also involved in a third task. In early January, Fidel Castro began consolidating his fragile alliance with the Popular Socialist Party. The basis for it lay in the partnership that had developed in the Sierra Maestra during the visit of Carlos Rafael Rodríguez, along with the incorporation of PSP cadres into Che's column and Raúl Castro's Second Front. It also stemmed from the creation in October 1958 of a Unified National Workers Front (FONU), which brought together PSP trade unionists and 26th of July militants. The process was not without friction and contradictions, giving rise to countless polemical articles in the PSP's *Hoy* and the 26th of July's daily *Revolución;* the "rapprochement" was also secret.

According to Fabio Grobart's account to Tad Szulc in 1985, beginning in January 1959 the top leaders of the Sierra and the PSP held a series of clandestine meetings either at Che's dwelling in Tarará or Fidel's house in Cojímar. Castro was accompanied by Che, Camilo Cienfuegos, Osmany Cienfuegos (the guerrilla leader's brother, a sometime member of the PSP, who had remained in Mexico during the war), Ramiro Valdés, and, occasionally, Raúl Castro. The PSP was represented by Carlos Rafael Rodríguez, its secretary-general, Blas Roca, and Aníbal Escalante, a member of the Politburo. According to Grobart,

> We began to hold meetings as soon as Fidel, Che, and Camilo arrived here. We were not informing the militants, only a small group in the leadership. The success [of the negotiations] was linked to the need of preventing the Americans from having a banner for an intervention, as they had done in Guatemala, and we had to go on maintaining the secret that had prevailed until then and had contributed to the success.[67]

Problems arose very quickly when labor union elections were held at the end of January. As the former pro-government leadership of Cuba's

---

soldiers under his command at La Cabaña. Material used in these courses, some of which the Embassy has seen, definitely follows the Communist line." Foreign Service Dispatch, Braddock/AmEmbassy to Dept. of State, April 14, 1959, "Growth of Communism in Cuba" (Confidential), *Foreign Relations of the United States, 1958–1960,* Department of State Central File, LBJ Library.

Confederation of Workers (CTC) disintegrated, both the PSP and the
26th of July began jockeying for control of the old labor organization.
The 26th of July mounted a fierce attack on the PSP, obliging it to esca-
late its salary demands in order to regain its traditional leadership of the
labor movement. The controversy was highly publicized. It took up entire
pages of *Hoy* and *Revolución* throughout the summer, and lasted most of
the year. Finally, in November 1959, the PSP was soundly defeated in elections for the CTC congress. Only Fidel Castro's intervention kept the
Party from being evicted entirely from the labor movement. But the rivalry
and friction between the union activists of the PSP and the 26th of July did
not obscure the fundamental unity that was gradually being forged by the
leadership on both sides. Che played a major role in this process.

The reason he helped build the alliance with the Communists was not
personal sympathy with them—though, aside from Raúl Castro, Che was
the leader who had the most PSP aides. Rather, it was based on strong
political affinities; Che was, in a sense, *the* Communist within the 26th of
July, as much as Raúl Castro; moreover, as Carlos Franqui recalls "Raúl
was in fact more discreet than Che."[68] The strength and presence of PSP
cadres was due to their convergence with Che, not the other way around.
Arnoldo Martínez Verdugo, a former secretary-general of the Mexican
Communist Party who spent several months in Havana in early 1959,
remembers how as early as then Che protected the PSP. One day at a Party
office an official from the Commission of Recovered Properties knocked
on the door, bearing an order from Che to take over the buildings. The
Party member in charge warned him immediately, "Sit down. You don't
seem to know where you are; we are a revolutionary party that fully participated in the January 1st victory." He picked up the phone, Che himself
answered, and the PSP kept its branch.[69] Over and beyond agrarian reform
and the new army training program, Che was moving ever closer to the
classic positions of Latin American Marxism. The fact that he would later
break with these positions, and with the Cuban Communists and their
Soviet backers, does not invalidate the fact that he shared their views completely for almost four years.

In several public appearances during those months, Che gradually drew
away from the traditional stances of the 26th of July, distinctly drifting
toward the movement's left wing. In the first days of January, there was still
a certain amount of confusion in Cuba and in U.S. government circles as to
Che Guevara's ideological position.* By April, and especially after Che

*When the Argentine ambassador in Washington met with Undersecretary of State Roy
Rubottom on January 6, he told him that he "had spent two hours with General Montero,
who is a friend of Guevara's father. The Ambassador said that he had asked the General
about young Guevara. The General had said that the Guevaras are an old and conservative

granted a long television interview to the program *Telemundo Pregunta,* his views began to attract greater attention in Havana and U.S. Embassy circles. The Embassy had it basically right:

> Ernesto "Che" Guevara, Chief of La Cabaña Fortress, if not an out and out Communist, is so closely oriented toward Communistic doctrine as to be indistinguishable from one. . . . Che Guevara and Raul Castro because of their political orientation, coupled with their popularity and the effective control which they exercise over the armed forces, represent the single most important danger of Communist infiltration within the present government. The extent of their influence over Fidel Castro is not known, but is probably considerable. It may be an important factor in Fidel Castro's reluctance to align himself clearly with the free nations in the East-West struggle.[70]

In his television interview, Che displayed vast rhetorical and diplomatic skills when asked about his ideological leanings, his opinion of the Soviet Union, the PSP, the land reform, Cuba's participation in an uprising in Panama, and so on. Despite his verbal maneuvers, however, it was obvious to anyone watching the program that Che was not only close to Communist positions but supported both the idea and the reality of an alliance with the PSP. He probably expressed the same views in private conversations: Guevara was not given to concealment.

This is confirmed in a report delivered to the U.S. Embassy by a Cuban tobacco grower in May 1959.* Dr. Napoleón Padilla was a member of the Tobacco Forum, a group established by the revolutionary government to improve the industry's production and working conditions. The government's representative was Che himself, so Padilla was able to observe him closely for several weeks. According to his report, Guevara even offered to make him manager of the state cigarette company he was planning to create. Padilla stated that Che was violently anti-American, opposing the sale

---

family of San Juan, and that the boy's sentiments are entirely democratic and not at all communistic. He had fought against Peron, and then had gone to Peru, where he married a Peruvian girl. The Ambassador said he was repeating this to Mr. Rubottom because he knew there had been some thought that Guevara had communistic tendencies." Department of State, "Memorandum of Conversation Between Roy Rubottom and Argentine Ambassador Barros Hurtado" (Confidential), January 6, 1959, *FRUS, 1958–1960.*

*The report included comments by Che on the fall of Arbenz in Guatemala—a topic very much in fashion in Cuba during that period. According to the Embassy informer, Che believed that freedom of the press had been a decisive factor in the defeat of 1954. It should have been curtailed, in his view; and Cuba should avoid making the same mistake. Thanks to Rolando Morán's earlier conversations with Che at the Argentine Embassy in Guatemala, we know that the young Guevara did indeed hold this opinion (see footnote on page 71, Chapter 3).

of any U.S. products in Cuba—including those actually made in the country, like Coca-Cola, Keds sneakers, and American cigarettes; he did not want any U.S. capital in Cuba, or good relations with Washington. He described the Rebel Army as the "defender of the proletariat" and "the main political wing of the people's revolution." Padilla also asserted that the new army was to be a major source of "indoctrination" for the Cuban people. Though it would also engage in useful public activities, its main task was to defend the Revolution—which would inevitably come under attack by the United States, as it was essentially contrary to American interests.[71]

Padilla's report includes exaggerations—Che "often talked of the way he controls Fidel Castro"—and personal interpretations—"Guevara and Raúl Castro want to create a Soviet system in Cuba"—but its main thrust seems plausible. Che did, indeed, hold the views ascribed to him and expressed them quite openly. At the same time, however, Fidel Castro was making his way along the East Coast of the United States, trying to convince the American establishment and the general public of his "good" intentions in a number of areas: land reform, communism, and the Soviet Union, among others.*

This glaring inconsistency has various possible origins. Castro, with his extraordinary talent for showmanship, may have tried to placate his American hosts by telling them exactly what they wanted to hear, in order to gain more time before the inevitable confrontation with Washington. For almost forty years, Castro has proven repeatedly that he is fully and easily capable of sustaining two or more contradictory positions simultaneously. In this interpretation, Fidel said one thing up north while his brother and Che said another on the island, totally aware of what they were doing.

Or perhaps Fidel had not yet defined the course of the Revolution, and was seeking a middle ground—unstable and temporary, but effective for a

---

*"In the Department's opinion the Castro who came to Washington was a man on his best behavior who carefully followed the advice of his accompanying Ministers and accepted the direction of an American public relations expert. The result achieved by Castro in terms of a favorable reception by the public and the information media may therefore be considered as contrived. At the same time, we should not underestimate the effect on Castro of the friendliness and openness of the American people and officials and their willingness to hear his plea for an understanding of the Cuban revolution. When he departed from Washington for Princeton on April 20 he was certainly warmer in manner toward the Department officials who bade him farewell than he was in his greeting to them upon his arrival. By his apparent frankness and sincerity he succeeded in allaying much of the criticism which had arisen against him in the general press and public. With regard to his position on communism and the cold war struggle Castro cautiously indicated that Cuba would remain in the western camp." Robert Murphy (Deputy Undersecretary of State) to Gordon Gray (Special Assistant to the President for National Security Affairs), May 1, 1959, "Unofficial Visit of Prime Minister Castro to Washington—a Tentative Evaluation" (Confidential), *Declassified Documents Catalog,* Washington, Jan./Feb. 1989, file series no. 137, vol. 15, no. 1.

time. Finally, the possibility exists that Castro was saying whatever people wanted to hear, with the conviction of a master politician who fully trusts his own powers of persuasion. When Fidel spoke with his companions in the United States—Regino Boti and Felipe Pazos, among others—and accepted their words of caution and restraint, he did so just as sincerely as when he agreed with Raúl and Che that the Revolution must proceed rapidly in a more radical direction. Some eventually felt betrayed by him; others saw their suggestions and aspirations made reality. But when talking with Fidel, they all swore he was telling them the truth. That was simply the way he functioned.

The relationship between Fidel and Che grew closer during those months, though it went through several minor difficulties. Their styles were too dissimilar for there not to be occasional friction. Fidel talked unceasingly, while Che was extremely reserved. Fidel was a politician who carefully calculated his myriad, oratorically torrential public declarations; Che expressed openly and publicly his sporadic utterances. Fidel lived in a continual, luxuriant chaos, while Che was highly organized, disciplined, and austere. Che believed in well-defined political goals; Fidel was always pondering his course and was able to adjust, qualify, or reverse it at a moment's notice. When he left the Sierra, Fidel returned to a familiar world; indeed, he was in his element. Che, in the meantime, was confronted with a completely new environment; his friends and family, his youth, were all far away.

Comments attributed to Fidel during those months, especially during his trip to the United States and immediately after his return to Cuba, must have hurt Guevara. Since January, there had been rumors of critical or sarcastic statements by Fidel. Lázaro Ascencio, a veteran of the Escambray who had dinner with Castro in Cienfuegos during his triumphal march from Oriente to Havana, recalls a strange comment by the *líder máximo*. Speaking of Comandante William Morgan (a companion of Gutiérrez Menoyo who would later be executed), Fidel declared that he should leave Cuba. When Ascencio disagreed, Castro attacked Che Guevara: "All these foreigners are mercenaries. Do you know what I'm going to do with Che Guevara? I'm going to send him to Santo Domingo and see if Trujillo kills him. As for my brother Raúl, I'm going to send him to Europe as a minister or diplomat or ambassador."[72] The rumor became so widespread that a journalist asked Che on January 6 whether "it is true that you are going to lead an expedition to liberate Santo Domingo, and that you're going to finish off Trujillo."[73]

Later, and perhaps more realistically, Jules Dubois, an American journalist who had interviewed Fidel Castro in the Sierra and was in contact (to say the least) with U.S. intelligence, delivered a report to the State Department. He had been assured by people close to Castro that the latter was convinced of "Communist" infiltration and propaganda within La Cabaña, and that he was going to deal with it immediately. The first step would be to expel Che Guevara from the country. He planned to use as a pretext an official invitation from President Gamal Abdel Nasser of Egypt, to commemorate the expropriation of the Suez Canal. Castro even predicted that Guevara, during his travels through the Middle East, might well suffer a severe and prolonged attack of asthma.[74]

Though the exact wording may be fictitious, Castro must have expressed himself along these lines. Yet his comments may have been a test or a disinformation ploy, in one of the grand maneuvers that Fidel Castro has systematically used to mislead and confuse his interlocutors for nearly four decades. Che was doubtless familiar with his friend's subterfuges—but he also knew that Fidel could be ruthless in his alliances and loyalties. Throughout all his years in power—and even as a university student—Castro had always been a staunch supporter of his friends while they remained out of politics, and a man fully capable of turning on them, no matter how close to him, if they entered the political fray and expediency required it.

During those innocent and memorable days of victory, Che may well have believed more in a well-intentioned maneuver by Fidel than in his duplicity or sudden indifference. But he must also have suspected that there was some truth to the rumors. Behind them lurked a typical Fidelista logic. A vicious struggle was underway between what Carlos Franqui has called the nationalist wing of the 26th of July Movement and the pro-Communist one led by Che and Raúl. As Franqui notes, "Fidel Castro, being a much more skillful politician than his brother or his favorite deputy, thought that if he confronted the United States prematurely, it would have been fatal for the Revolution. That's why he wanted everybody to keep believing in his classical anti-communist stance."[75] Several conflicts erupted between them all—for instance, regarding agrarian reform: when Raúl and Che encouraged land takeovers, Fidel delivered a violent speech against such acts. On one occasion at the Havana Comptrollers Court, the conflict between the Castro brothers became so bitter that Raúl "ended up in tears."[76] Things became even more disconcerting in the context of Castro's trip to the United States, which Che had opposed.* During the voyage, Fidel's moderate advisers held full sway. Castro's statements in Washington and New York added to the uncertainty that Che probably felt despite himself. But he stayed at his post and fought his battles. The First Law for Agrarian Reform enacted in May was a partial victory; he achieved other triumphs: the departure of Sorí Marín from the government, followed weeks later by the

---

*"Che . . . did not agree with the idea of the trip, though he was careful not to say so." Hugo Gambini, *El Che,* p. 231.

resignation of Manuel Urrutía from the presidency and the Revolution's radicalization in July 1959.

On June 2, Che Guevara celebrated his second wedding. Having finally broken his relationship with Hilda and obtained his divorce, Ernesto was free to marry Aleida. Till her death, the Peruvian activist believed she lost her husband to Aleida: "When a man falls in love with another woman, there is nothing a wife can do."[77] Herein perhaps lies the cause, logically enough, of the strain and antipathy that prevailed between her daughter, Hilda Guevara, and Aleida, till the former's death in 1995.[78] The marriage took place at the home of one of his bodyguards, Alberto Castellanos, and once again Raúl Castro was one of the witnesses. The couple left immediately for Tarará: not very far, not very different, and not for very long.* Nonetheless, the honeymoon had a strong impact on Che Guevara. Later, during a trip to India, José Pardo Llada shared a room with him and committed the indiscretion of reading a letter from Che to his wife. He found it extremely explicit sexually, "absolutely pornographic."[79] After his relationship with Hilda, followed by the hardly romantic conditions prevailing in the Sierra, the experience of spending days alone with an attractive and worldly Cuban woman must have made a strong impression on the stern guerrilla fighter.

On June 5, Castro confirmed his decision to send Che on a lengthy trip to the Middle East, India, and Japan. Guevara left a week later, to discover a completely alien world, accompanied by a dear and familiar companion: his love of otherness. He spent three months away from Cuba, in an exotic voyage replete with contradictions and uncertainties. It was the first in a long series of missions around the globe that were useful for the Revolution and captivating for him. But always they were darkened by a sense of exile—no matter how necessary, important, or temporary. All of these voyages would contain a mystery. His last one, to Bolivia, would bring about his death.

---

*Jean Cormier, doubtless due to a mistake on the part of his sources, notes that Aleida was pregnant at the time of the wedding. He insinuates that Che married her because of the Sierra decree obliging any guerrilla fighter who made his companion pregnant to marry her. Jean Cormier, *Che Guevara* (Paris: Editions du Rocher, 1995), p. 265. Che's first child with his second wife, Aleidita, was born in November 1960; her mother cannot have been pregnant with her in June 1959. The only other possibility is that Aleida March lost the first baby (voluntarily or not).

Chapter 6

The "Brain of the Revolution";
the Scion of the Soviet Union

Che left for Africa on June 12, 1959, with his bodyguard, José Argudín, and two government officials, Omar Fernández and Francisco García Valls. They were joined in Cairo by a mathematician, Salvador Vilaseca, and in India by the journalist José Pardo Llada. The trip included countries either politically or economically important to Cuba—Japan, Yugoslavia, India, and Egypt—and others less significant, like Ceylon, Indonesia, Pakistan, Sudan, and Morocco. The true nature of the expedition was never entirely apparent, though speculation abounded. After Che's victories on the domestic front, perhaps Fidel decided it was best to remove him temporarily from the public eye. Indeed, the first great crisis of the Revolution arose during his absence. Following the resignation of President Urrutia, several moderate or liberal ministers departed the government and the regime shifted to the left. On July 26, a huge celebration took place in Havana commemorating the assault on the Moncada. But nobody could blame Guevara for the government's radicalization: he was thousands of miles away.

Certainly the pressures on Guevara were mounting, imposed by Cuban and American critics alike. The serious setbacks suffered by the moderates and the concerns of the United States were increasingly—and with some reason—attributed to the growing influence of Che and of Raúl Castro. But if the trip was indeed a form of "semi-exile," as Pardo Llada has stated, it did not last for long.* When he returned in September, Che took charge of the INRA's Department of Industries and, weeks later, the National Bank of Cuba.

Perhaps Che was the only close aide Fidel could count on to represent the Revolution abroad. Raúl Castro, who attended a special session of the OAS Council of Ministers in Santiago, Chile, on August 15, made a poor showing. He was unprepared, poorly dressed, and maladroit. Furthermore, Che's responsibilities did not require his full-time presence. Fidel could manage without him for a time. Besides, the victorious rebels had no diplomatic skills or international expertise whatsoever. They might have imagined that the three-month trip would be of prime importance to the Revolution, though in fact, it was perfectly dispensable. Finally, there was the Argentine's personal fascination with the rest of the world. After six months in Havana, he probably yearned for new horizons. The ports of call on the itinerary were too attractive to resist, in his first encounter with the world beyond Latin America.

In Cairo, President Gamal Abdel Nasser, by then a hero of Arab and pan-Islamic nationalism, received Guevara with full honors. Che toured the Pyramids and Alexandria, where he spent a night in the royal palace of Montaza. He visited the Aswan Dam, still under construction, as well as the Suez Canal and Port Said. During his two weeks in Egypt he forged a close bond with Nasser, which would lead him to return five years later. The Suez Canal crisis of 1956 and Britain's boycott of Egyptian cotton made a strong impression on him: "[they] provoked an extremely dangerous situation from which [Egypt] was able to emerge thanks to the appearance of a buyer that purchased the entire harvest, which was the Soviet Union."[1] He might have reached the same conclusion regarding Aswan. When Eisenhower and John Foster Dulles decided to terminate U.S. funding for the dam, Nasser turned to Khrushchev. A year later, the United States boycotted Cuban sugar, and Esso, Shell, and Texaco refused to refine Soviet oil in Cuba. In both cases, the Soviet Union stepped into the breach.

The U.S. State Department considered the visit to Egypt a success for the Cubans,[†] but Nasser himself was left with a different impression. Che was

---

*In Carlos Franqui's opinion, two factors were at work here: "Each time someone in Cuba fell from favor, he was sent abroad; it was a way of displacing them, and besides, maybe Che had a real interest in getting to know those countries." Carlos Franqui, interview with the author, San Juan, August 20, 1996.

† "In that country [Egypt] the mission was apparently successful." Memorandum from the Deputy Director of Intelligence and Research to the Secretary of State, "Che Guevara's Mission to Afro-Asian Countries," August 19, 1959, quoted in *Foreign Relations of the United States (FRUS), 1958–1960,* vol. 6, p. 590.

doubtless careful not to argue with his hosts. Salvador Vilaseca recalls that Guevara specifically pointed out to him a number of delicate matters, and instructed the members of his delegation as to what they should not talk about, in each country. For instance, Cuba had carried out a radical land reform, but in Egypt the visitors were ordered not to discuss the issue because, according to Che, many Egyptian leaders were large landowners. As Vilaseca recalled: "Our goal was not to fight but, on the contrary, to make friends."[2]

However, in his memoirs (actually written by Mohammed Heikal), Nasser relates a brief exchange precisely about land reform, following a rather strange question posed by Che Guevara:

> "How many Egyptian refugees had to flee the country?" When President Nasser answered that they had been very few, and that most of them were "white," naturalized Egyptians of foreign origin, Che became upset. "That means," he said, "that your revolution has not accomplished much. I measure the depth of change by the number of people it affects, who feel that there is no place for them in the new society." Nasser explained that he was trying to "liquidate the privileges of one class, but not of the individuals in that class. . . ." Guevara insisted on his point of view and, as a consequence, not much came of the visit. President Nasser paid scant attention to the Cubans and their policies.[3]

In India, Che's group devoted twelve days to tourism (Agra and the Taj Mahal), to the economy (with visits to airplane factories and research centers), and to sociology (the poverty in Calcutta). The stifling heat provoked repeated asthma attacks. Despite Che's efforts, Pardo Llada considered the trip unproductive. He describes a long dinner with Nehru at the former residence of the imperial viceroys, during which Che tried to coax the founder of the republic to express a substantive opinion about any one of the topics of the day—but in vain.[4] The U.S. intelligence services similarly found little of value in the visit to India, noting that "no trade relations were established with India, where the Cuban mission met with little success."[5] Che's culture and sensitivity allowed him, however, to explore the complexities of Hindu civilization. He also learned lessons that he would take back to Cuba—not necessarily apt, but logical nonetheless: "the basis for a people's economic development is determined by its technical advances."[6]

Che made "a good impression" in Japan, according to the Americans, though again he did not achieve any trade or financial agreements.[7] The twelve-day stay combined work (visits to factories, ports, businessmen), tourism (Mount Fuji, sumo wrestling), and political activity (Hiroshima, Nagasaki). The visit was educational, enriching his own sense of culture and preparing him for the political tasks ahead: "We must recall that determination is far more important in the modern world than the existence of raw materials. . . . There is no reason for our country not to develop its iron and steel industry."[8] The secret of Japan's success, in Che's view, was willpower. To emulate it, a country needed only to deploy the same prodigious combination of desire and discipline. Of course, Che's travel notes, published after his return to Cuba in *Verde Olivo,* the armed forces magazine he had just founded, did not allow for much depth or subtlety. But his social and cultural sensitivity far outweighed his economic or even political understanding.

Che's apparent admiration for Sukarno's regime in Indonesia further illustrates this dichotomy. He established the following analogy: "Of all the countries [we] have visited, the Republic of Indonesia is perhaps the one that has developed in recent times a social historical project most like ours."[9] Drawing a parallel between the Cuban and Indonesian struggles for national liberation, he discovered in Sukarno "a genuine national hero." The latter, "interpreting the popular will and the true needs of the people," denied the "counterrevolutionaries' right to sow discord and attack the regime which is the expression of the people's armed struggle."[10] Guevara bestowed upon the Indonesian leader an arguable privileged status when he asked rhetorically, "Is Fidel Castro not a man of flesh and blood, a Sukarno, a Nehru, a Nasser?"[11]

Whatever the requirements of protocol, Che reveals in these passages a basic misperception of people and events, a certain gullibility, and the wishful thinking that would lead to his African debacle of 1965. Sukarno was indeed a national leader who arose from his country's fight for independence; at the Bandung Conference of 1955, he played a central role in creating what later became the Nonaligned Movement. But like many leaders of Afro-Asian decolonization (with the major exceptions of Ho Chi Minh, Nehru, Nyerere, and Nasser), he was essentially a devious and corrupt reactionary. It was far more important for him to defend the privileges of the new elite he belonged to than to organize and eventually depend upon the needy masses of his country. He combined fiery rhetoric and an undeniable advancement of Indonesia's national identity with an extravagance and ostentatiousness of pharaonic proportions. His authoritarianism finally led to a bloody countercoup by General Suharto in 1965, and the massacre of half a million Communists. And he was not the only Third World leader to pull the wool over Che's eyes. Indeed, Guevara's adventure in the Congo would consist largely of the successive traps he fell into. The expedition never recovered from the procrastination· and corruption of Congolese leaders like Gaston Sumialot, Laurent Kabila, and Christopher Gbenye, who were supposedly struggling for their country's liberation.

In the end, Che did realize how mistaken he was, but by then it was too late. In an unpublished letter addressed to Fidel Castro from the shores of Lake Tanganyika in October 1965, Che criticized the Congolese leaders who had just been received in Havana like kings and in whom he had deposited all his trust:

> Sumialot and his companions have sold you an enormous bridge. It would take me forever to enumerate the huge number of lies they told you. . . . I know Kabila well enough to have no illusions in his regard. . . . I have some background on Sumialot, like for example the lies he told you, the fact that he has not set foot on this godforsaken land, his frequent drinking bouts in Dar-es-Salaam, where he stays in the best hotels . . . they are given huge amounts of money, all at once, to live splendidly in every African capital, not to mention that they are housed by the main progressive countries who often finance their travel expenses. . . . The scotch and the women are also covered by friendly governments and if one likes good scotch and beautiful women, that costs a lot of money.[12]

By the time Che grasped the type of allies he had shacked up with in the Congo, his expedition was in fact just about over. The explanation for this tragic misunderstanding lies not only in his ignorance about the situation on the ground, but also in his obsession for discovering nonexistent political virtues in an always bewitching otherness.

Che was enormously attracted by the cultural and ethnic diversity he found, by "the multitude of brothers in this part of the world who await . . . the right time to consolidate a bloc that will destroy . . . colonial domination."[13] His commitment to revolution, politics, and the armed struggle was too strong for him to see beyond the ideological wrapping of those people he admired. Yet his love of the differences he unearthed in each civilization, race, literature, architecture, and history prevented him from reducing everything to politics. Beginning with this trip, Che always sought two things in his travels: political affinity and cultural diversity. Since he could not find the latter in either Europe or Latin America—he was, after all, a Latin American with a European heritage—he would increasingly invent the former, concocting political analogies where in fact there were none. The Congolese leaders *had* to be revolutionary because they were culturally different. The native Indians of Bolivia *had* to be ready to take up arms. Mao and the Chinese leaders *had* to be willing to promote world revolution, especially in Africa. Che never ceased to be disappointed because he never ceased to hope, endlessly renewing his search for political parallels.

His passage through Ceylon and Pakistan was unremarkable, aside from its slightly quixotic tinge. It is difficult to understand how the third most important leader of the Cuban Revolution could spend three days visiting places like Colombo and Karachi while the new regime struggled against both internal and external threats. In contrast, his week in Yugoslavia seemed more relevant. This was Che's first voyage to a Socialist country—albeit an atypical one—and he discovered many things worthy of his interest, if not his praise. It was for him "perhaps the most interesting of all the countries [we visited]."[14]

Interesting and somewhat surprising. Although it was "avowedly Communist,"[15] only 15 percent of the land had been collectivized. It enjoyed "a very great freedom of criticism, though there is only one political party ... and the newspapers ... logically follow government guidelines within a certain margin for discussion and disagreement. ... I can assert ... that in Yugoslavia there is a wide margin of freedom within the limitations imposed by a system whereby one social class dominates the others."[16]

Guevara formulated the first of a long list of objections to Yugoslav-style self-management: too many luxury products on the market, and no long-term economic strategy. In his words: "I cannot insist strongly enough on emphasizing the larger course of industrialization which must be carried out in a country as poor and underdeveloped as Yugoslavia."[17] He felt somewhat deceived by the Yugoslavs; Che's traveling companion Omar Fernández recalled in an interview thirty years later how Guevara asked Tito for weapons during a long lunch at his Brioni game preserve. Tito refused, explaining that his country did not produce enough arms. A few days later, Che read in the press that Yugoslavia was selling weapons to an Arab country. "Great neutrality!" he exclaimed.[18]

As in Bolivia five years earlier, Che made no mention of the link between Yugoslavia's geopolitical stance and its internal regime. He does not appear to have assimilated the connection between moderate reforms, greater freedom, and national consensus on the domestic plane, and less friction with Washington. Indeed, there is no comment at all about contradictory U.S. stances. In Egypt, for instance, Che failed to perceive that an important element in the devolution of the Suez Canal to Egypt lay precisely in the U.S. condemnation, in November 1956, of the Anglo-French invasion of Port Said. Without it, the Tel Aviv-London-Paris coalition might well have reversed the Canal expropriation and toppled Nasser. Che did not acknowledge any link between the "peculiar" domestic traits of Yugoslav "communism" and Tito's virtual neutrality in the East-West conflict. He could have rejected Yugoslavia's "goulash" socialism (a forerunner of the Hungarian variety), or he might have praised the domestic margin of freedom allowing for international neutrality. He chose simply to neglect Tito's role on the world stage.

In fact, Che did not want to raise any matter which might have weakened his own position or that of Fidel Castro in the Cuban struggle. To recognize the possibility of combining neutrality and "communism" (even if the term had to be redefined) might have undermined Cuba's resistance vis-à-vis the United States. It might also have blunted the Manichaeism needed for the coming, entirely desirable, confrontation with Washington. One might even speculate that Che, in his first political writings after the Revolution, was careful in what he said and how he said it, subordinating his views to the political requirements of the moment. Without concealing the truth, he might well have adjusted it in the light of Cuba's political situation.

So Che Guevara was by now fully committed to the Revolution: all else was secondary. The best proof of this lies in one of his letters to the most important woman in his life—his mother, Celia. In it, he explains why no one should be surprised if he adapts the content of his writing to his political goals. It is worth quoting in its entirety, as it reveals Guevara's evolution better than any description:

> My old dream of visiting all countries is now coming true. . . . Though, without Aleida, whom I could not bring due to one of those complicated mental states I have. . . . A sense of the big picture as opposed to the personal has been developing in me. I am still the same solitary person who continues to seek his path without any help, but now I have a sense of my historical duty. I have no house, wife, children, parents, or brothers; my friends are friends as long as they think like me, politically, and yet I am happy, I feel important in life—not only a powerful inner strength, which I always felt, but also an ability to influence others and an absolutely fatalistic sense of my mission which frees me from all fear. I don't know why I am writing you this, perhaps I am just missing Aleida again.*

It might seem strange that a newly married man should confide to his mother that he does not have a wife, even in figurative terms. But the letter reveals far more than a possible problem in the marriage. It suggests that Che had decided to devote his life to a cause. His loves, friendships, all personal matters, would henceforth be subordinated to his "mission," his "historical duty." He missed Aleida—he mentioned her twice—but she, too, was relegated to the background; she would not play a central role in his life. And his "fatalistic sense," which "frees me from all fear" and would lead him to his death at La Higuera, now possessed him entirely. Perhaps he was exaggerating to his mother the importance of this new element. But he now

*A photocopy of the original text, written on Air India stationery, was given to Chichina Ferreyra by José González Aguilar. Chichina lent the photocopy to the author. The letter is not dated, but according to the itinerary it must have been written on July 2 or 3, 1959.

had a clear idea of death and a personal destiny. Nothing he did from this point on would escape the imprint of these ideas: Che was convinced that he was challenging death, and that he had a fate.

On September 10, he was back in Havana. Many changes awaited him, and he was soon caught up in a whirlwind of events. He returned to his post at the INRA, heading the Department of Industries, where his work had acquired far greater importance than before. Many of Cuba's sugar mills had been expropriated and placed under INRA jurisdiction, which meant that Che was actually taking on the most important sector of the country's economy.* At first, both Fidel and Nuñez Jiménez, the INRA's operational director, were careful to keep Che's designation a relative secret†; no public announcement was made. But Washington was already fully aware of the setback to U.S. interests:

> Contrary to our earlier hopes, moderating forces (the National Bank group especially) have for the present at least lost out in contest for influence over Castro. Our bitter enemies, Raul Castro and Che Guevara, are very much in the saddle. They can be counted on to speed up radical agrarian reform as well as measures designed to destroy or cripple U.S. mining, petroleum and public utility interests.[19]

The government soon announced Che's designation as director of the National Bank (Cuba's central bank). His performance is well documented; he was in charge of the island economy for over four years. For better or worse, one of the Revolution's most important fronts was entrusted to an Argentine physician who was a pro-Soviet radical with scant knowledge of economics. But, as pointed out in Chapter 4, he had a very clear idea of his goals and a sense of discipline and organization sorely lacking in Cuba at the time.

The decision to place Che at the head of the central bank did not take place as has often been reported. In the consecrated anecdote, Fidel Castro asked during a meeting who among those present was an economist; Che replied that he was, only to explain later that he had misheard the question, understanding "Communist" instead of "economist." Castro knew perfectly

---

*And not only of its economy: on September 30 a reliable source informed the U.S. Embassy in Havana that Che had presided over two meetings of military leaders in which Raúl Castro had also been present. See AmEmbassy Havana to Secretary of State, dispatch 509, October 5, 1959 (Confidential), U.S. Department of State Files, vol. 9, 814–817, p. 2.

† The attempt at concealment was futile. In a cable dated September 2, 1959 (one week before Che's return), the new ambassador, Philip Bonsal, reported to Washington that Guevara "might have an important role in the industrialization programs." Philip Bonsal to Roy Rubottom, September 2, 1959 (Confidential), in *FRUS, 1958–1960*, p. 594.

well that Che had little or no expertise in economics, but the real economists he had available were not trustworthy in his eyes. Among the people he did trust, Che was the most knowledgeable. He had read some economics, and already had two months' experience at the INRA. Furthermore, his mission abroad had included some trade negotiations. Fidel's decision to put him in charge of the money supply and financial policy for the new companies within the INRA made sound political sense. Furthermore, the death of Camilo Cienfuegos in November and the definitive designation of Raúl as defense minister left him little choice.

The moment was also ripe for Fidel to send a message to the United States and the Cuban oligarchy about who was running the country, and how. Washington understood, well before the Cabinet changes at the end of November, that its allies in the National Bank had been defeated. Che's appointment to the Bank was accompanied by other changes, all in favor of his close associates and to the detriment of liberal moderates. Fidel also named Raúl minister of defense and his brother's secretary, Augusto Martínez Sánchez, minister of labor, as a sop for the PSP, after its resounding defeat at the CTC labor congress. The changes followed the arrest and imprisonment of Huber Matos, whose trial was indeed the trigger for Fidel's new shift toward the left. It also marked the first appearance of Cuba's new apparatus for state security and terror. Matos was accused, along with others, of conspiring against the Revolution. The evidence against him was of the Soviet variety, characteristically fabricated by the intelligence services; it was built on rumors, letters, telephone taps, and anonymous accusations. The truth of the conspiracy has never been proven. But it was abundantly clear that Matos opposed Fidel's course. No further proof was necessary.

Che headed the central bank for fourteen months. He was responsible for Cuba's monetary policy, foreign-currency reserves, and macroeconomic strategy. He was also involved in building up the army, in Cuban diplomacy, and writing. He took courses in mathematics, economics, aviation, and (toward the end of this period) Russian. But his main activity was in the Bank, where he acquired a reputation for order, punctuality, and an enormous capacity for work. He would arrive at his office toward mid-morning, staying until two or three a.m. every night. His desk was always in order; he was quick at dispatching paperwork, and the classic verbosity of his Cuban subordinates was for a time banished from some government offices.

That year also saw the consolidation of two other features in his daily life: his eternal irreverence, and interminable nighttime discussions. These were both conspiratorial and conversational: anybody could visit him at the Bank to talk about anything at all. His irreverence reached its peak with the issuance of Cuban currency notes signed "Che." When criticized for this by a Cuban correspondent, he replied:

> If my way of signing is not typical of bank presidents . . . this does not signify, by any means, that I am minimizing the importance of the document—but that the revolutionary process is not yet over and, besides, that we must change our scale of values.[20]

Che's iconoclastic bent was also reflected in his informal dress and protocol. He always received visitors in his olive-green fatigues, his feet often resting upon the desk, obliging those he did not like to wait for hours, while maintaining with his subordinates a relationship based upon equality and camaraderie. Like many of his traits, this irreverence was only partly spontaneous: he sought to project a certain image to others, and confirm it to himself. But he never allowed his apparent informality to affect the substance of his work. On the contrary, Che's tenure at the Bank would be recalled for his seriousness in studying documents, his hard work, promptness, and efficiency.

Many also recall his impressive intellectual versatility and inclination for universal ideas. He was interested in everything: issues, countries, personalities. At the top of his list were Argentines, be they revolutionaries or intellectuals. During those years, Che had "friends" throughout the Latin American, European, and American left—from Jean-Paul Sartre and Simone de Beauvoir to C. Wright Mills and John Gerassi; from René Dumont and Charles Bettelheim to Ernesto Sabato and Lázaro Cárdenas. He would receive them in his offices at midnight, maté and cigar in hand, relaxed and always avid for information, ideas, and messages. Countless projects, conspiracies, and complicities were hatched during those nocturnal meetings, as well as abiding loyalties and affections which would survive Che's demise.

Because of his meager familiarity with economics, his early decisions at the Bank were cautious and fairly orthodox. He first concentrated on building up the country's hard-currency reserves, initially restricting foreign luxury goods and then all purchases abroad. He stepped up sugar exports in the first quarter of 1960, and tried to limit imports requiring cash payments either through barter or long-term agreements. The need to save hard currency, to escape the bondage of purchases in dollars or other strong currencies, the apparent benefits of barter, or a "ruble zone," marked the beginnings of his work in government. He was obsessed by Cuba's lack of resources; his fascination with alternatives to the dollar as an international exchange currency would distort his views on more than one occasion.

Ideological concerns led him to make a series of mistakes. For example, he immediately cut salaries and benefits for Cuba's highly specialized government bureaucracy, which was (as in many Latin American central banks), honest, competent, conservative, and well paid. Ernesto Betancourt, deputy director of the Bank when Che took over until his resignation three weeks later, recalls him with affection and respect as being naive and businesslike simultaneously. The way he handled the thorny problem of wages at the Bank illustrates this combination. Betancourt's secretary at the time made $375 a month; Che came along, stating: "The highest salary we should pay here is $350; nobody should make more than 350." The administrative head of the Bank explained that employees had already bought their houses, and had a standard of living based upon higher salaries, and would simply leave if their salaries were cut. Che replied: "I don't care, let them leave, because we'll bring in longshoremen or cane cutters to do their field work here and we'll pay them that salary." Subsequently he grasped the blunders made by the "proletarians," and changed course.[21]

Something similar happened when Che precipitously sought to have Cuba withdraw from the International Monetary Fund. Faced with the obligation to send instructions about a Cuban vote through its regional director at the Fund, Che decided to go against the experts' technical advice. Betancourt recalls the following revealing exchange:

"No, look, we are going to withdraw anyway from the Monetary Fund because we are going to join the Soviet Union, which is technologically 25 years ahead of the United States." So I said to him, "*Comandante,* if the government has decided to withdraw from the Monetary Fund, that's fine. I want you to understand one thing, though: we currently have a 25-million-dollar loan from the Monetary Fund, which we will have to pay if we withdraw, and we only have 70 million dollars in our hard-currency reserves. It is not a good idea for us to use that money now, because we are at the end of the year and we won't have any dollars coming in until the sugar harvest begins in January." Che confessed: "Oh, I didn't know that, I was told that they hadn't lent us anything." I said to him, "What you have been told is wrong. The agency that has never lent anything to Cuba, either now or under Batista, is the World Bank; but the IMF has." Che changed his mind; but Cuba still left the IMF a full year later.[22]

Che was not yet imbued with the economic theories that a group of Marxist Chileans, Mexicans, and Argentines would soon foist upon him. Nor was he yet familiar with the Soviet ideas he would later adopt. He tried to function with the sitting team at the Bank; but its members decided to leave—first for their homes, and then Miami. His aides would gradually take up the slack. Due to both the arrest of Matos and the removal of Felipe Pazos, as well as their own reluctance to follow Che's policy at the Bank, most of the senior Bank officials resigned. Although Che learned economics quickly* he still needed technicians, and began to recruit as many as he could. They gradually adopted his priorities, which were ethical and political rather than economic. Betancourt recalls the process as follows:

> Che was never a fully integrated Marxist. He was a typical Latin American leftist, with some rudiments of Marxism—but he was not trained by the Party. The proof is that he arrived at the Bank and, recognizing that he had a limited knowledge of Marxist economics, asked Juanito Noyola (a Mexican Marxist economist)—who did have that background—to teach him. Che was very organized, very systematic in everything he did, and so he simply took classes with Juanito twice a week so that Juanito could explain to him the basics of Marxist economics.[23]

Then, as now, the principal progressive recipes for Latin American economic development were few in number and fairly diffuse. They consisted essentially of industrialization through import substitution; the diversification of import and export markets; a central role for the state in the economy; and the need for significant land reform—more or less radical, depending on the country. These all formed what might be called the consensus of the U.N. Economic Commission for Latin America (ECLA). The Latin American left distinguished itself from ECLA by its emphasis on four essentially quantitative criteria: faster industrialization, greater diversification, more radical land reform, and a more powerful state in the economy and society.

At first, Che's economic views did not go far beyond the ECLA consensus. He contemplated measures similar to those proposed by his leftist advisors like Noyola, the Chilean Alban Lataste, the Ecuadorean Raúl Maldonado, and the Argentine Néstor Lavergne, and others. Among them, as Maldonado recalled, nationalizing the island's foreign trade—which represented half of the domestic product—figured prominently. Che's aim for the National Bank consisted precisely in its transformation into a sort of Foreign Trade Bank.[24] He would gradually conclude that the state monopoly of all trade with the rest of the world was a necessary condition for the type of institutional relationship he would seek to negotiate with the Soviet Union toward the end of 1960 during his visit to the socialist countries.

However, these strictly economic criteria would soon be overtaken by his political strategy for confrontation with the United States and the Cuban

---

*According to one of his Argentine aides, Néstor Lavergne, "Che took an economics seminar largely dedicated to studying [Marx's] *Capital*. It was conducted by Anastacio Mancilla, a Spanish-Soviet doctor, a refugee who was really a brilliant expert in Marxist economics." Néstor Lavergne, interview with the author, Buenos Aires, February 16, 1995.

oligarchy. This was the weak point in Guevara's ideology—or its strong point, depending on one's view. Until the end of his life, Che believed that the economic sphere should be secondary, in politics as in life. He operated from an ethical and humanistic stance rather than a Marxist or historical one; Che always called for the abolition of mercantilistic relations among people, and insisted that society should be governed by something other than money. Hence the escalation of his conflict with the Americans in several areas: the sugar quota, the refinement of Soviet oil, arms purchases from Europe and then the U.S.S.R., and the expropriation of American assets. On all these fronts, he decided to negotiate as little as possible, and only when necessary. This forced the Cuban regime even further to the left, leading to a gradual break with the United States which Che perceived both as an end in itself, and a powerful platform for change. By this stage, Fidel was much closer to his stance than before. As Che saw it, "the presence of an enemy stimulates revolutionary euphoria and creates the necessary conditions for radical change."[25]

In a secret document dated March 23, 1960, the U.S. Director of Central Intelligence emphasized Che's role in his government's antagonism toward the United States:

> Under the direction of Fidel Castro's brother Raul, and under the influence of Che Guevara, the armed services, police, and investigative agencies have been brought under unified control, purged of Batista professionals as well as other outspoken anti-Communist elements, and subjected to Communist-slanted political indoctrination courses; a civilian militia composed of students, workers, and peasants is being trained and armed.[26]

To counterbalance this confrontational attitude toward the U.S., Che sought closer relations with the Soviet Union in a move that he considered both desirable and necessary, due to the conflict with the United States and the urgent need to find other buyers for Cuban sugar. He also tacitly hoped that these first two tactics would expand the state's function in the Cuban economy—both as a goal in itself, and as a way to banish economic criteria from the realm of human relations. If the state controlled everything, then relations among people would improve as they became free of the problems arising from money, salaries, exchange, competition, and rivalry.

The land expropriation program had accelerated in the last months of 1959 as a result of grassroots peasant pressure for land and Fidel Castro's shift toward the left. Compensation payments were still pending; when they did occur, they fell far short of U.S. requirements. They were not prompt, adequate, or immediately effective. Other internal and external pressures mounted throughout 1960, especially between January and July, when two crucial events took place. First, the U.S. canceled its purchase of the government's sugar quota. Then Castro expropriated the foreign-owned oil refineries after they refused to refine the Soviet oil that had replaced Venezuelan supplies. Che played a decisive role both in bringing on the July crisis and in finding and implementing a Soviet solution to it.

Relations with Moscow had been intensifying from the outset. In October 1959, Antonio Nuñez Jiménez was approached by a character central to this account: Aleksandr Alexeiev, an intelligent and sensitive man who thirty-five years later maintained an immense affection for Cuba and its people, as well as the Revolution which brought him into contact with history and the tropics. He arrived in Havana on October 1 as an official of the Foreign Ministry. Alexeiev was traveling with a delegation of Soviet journalists and also had a journalist's visa. Though he was regarded as a correspondent, he never concealed his true mission.* He quickly arranged a meeting with Fidel in order to deliver a gift and establish contact on behalf of his government. But he first met with Che, whom he considered "almost a Communist"[27]: "He was the first Cuban leader to receive me, on October 12, 1959, at INRA."[28] According to Alexeiev, "our assessments of numerous different world events were identical, with no substantive divergencies."[29] Che quickly set up a meeting with Castro on October 16.

Their conversation gave rise to an important idea. After the Soviet Deputy Prime Minister Anastas Mikoyan attended the United Nations General Assembly in November, he was scheduled to inaugurate a Soviet industrial exhibit in Mexico. The suggestion was made that the exposition could then travel to Havana, where it would be officially opened by Mikoyan. Alexeiev flew off to Mexico to take up the matter with Mikoyan, who promptly accepted the invitation. Tentatively, November 28 was chosen as the date. But the Cubans then decided they preferred that the Soviet visit not coincide with a religious conference scheduled for those days and postponed it to the following year. Che's man Ramiro Valdés and Héctor Rodríguez Llompart, an aide of Carlos Rafael Rodríguez, were shipped off to Mexico to reschedule everything.† Days later, the Cuban government announced that Anastas Mikoyan would inaugurate the Soviet Industrial Exposition in Havana on February 3, 1960.

---

*According to several sources, Alexeiev had been working for the Soviet intelligence services since the Second World War. This account was corroborated by Karen A. Khachaturov, former director of the Soviet news agency Novosti, who has been similarly described by others. Interview with the author, Moscow, November 1, 1995.

† This account comes from Alexeiev, "Cuba depués," pp. 63, 65. Antonio Núñez Jiménez attributes the whole idea to Camilo Cienfuegos. See Nuñez, *En marcha con Fidel* (Havana: Editorial Letras Cubanas, 1982), p. 318. According to Georgie Anne Geyer, the idea for the exhibit came from Fidel, while Mikoyan's visit was suggested by Alexeiev. See Georgie Anne Geyer, *Guerrilla Prince* (Boston: Little, Brown, 1991), p. 250.

At this point a curious Soviet personage appeared on the scene: Nikolai Leonov, the KGB officer who had met Raúl Castro in Vienna in 1953 and Che in Mexico in 1956. He accompanied Mikoyan to Mexico in 1959 as his interpreter and bodyguard. When Mikoyan subsequently traveled to Cuba, Leonov went with him, entrusted among other things with a delicate task: to choose gifts for their Cuban hosts. To Che and Raúl, he presented an odd selection: "for Che, who likes arms, we bought two weapons: a very fine pistol and another high-precision sports model, along with ammunition. For Raúl I bought a chess set, as he was a very good chess player."[30] Upon his arrival in Havana, Leonov visited Che's home in Ciudad Libertad, where—to the Russian's surprise—he had to be awakened at mid-morning. They met as old friends, perhaps with greater affection and familiarity than was warranted by their earlier, fleeting acquaintance in Mexico. Only four years had passed since their previous encounter, but what a difference. As Leonov remembers, when they opened the box with the weapons, "he tried them without firing them; he liked them."[31]

Che was highly active in the negotiations with Mikoyan, especially concerning the amount, time frame, and strategic significance of Soviet cooperation. After welcoming Mikoyan at the airport with Fidel, Che attended their next meeting in secret; it was of historic importance. Leonov described it as follows:

Che was present at the key conversation, which took place at a little fishing place Fidel had on the Laguna del Tesoro. We made the trip in a Soviet helicopter which was part of the exhibition. Fidel brought Che along as the second member of the Cuban delegation. The Russian delegation consisted of Mikoyan and the Soviet ambassador in Mexico and myself as an interpreter and note-taker, as we were not using tape recorders for the sake of security. The helicopter landed outside the little fishing cottage, where we all stayed. The conversation took place in an absolutely spectacular setting: we were not indoors, but walking along wooden bridges over the swamp, amid the croaking of the bullfrogs and the sounds of the tropical night. The conversation centered on two or three basic points: the establishment of relations; it was February and we had no embassy. Mikoyan said that in order to be in contact we needed to open embassies both here and there, to have formal contact, and this was quickly agreed upon. Then another matter arose, that of loans; and here Che Guevara participated, supporting Fidel's position. The essence was that Mikoyan had instructions to promise only 100 million dollars. Fidel said it was too little, that 100 million dollars would not be enough to begin reorganizing all economic activity, and this during a full-fledged conflict with the United States. What he was planning was the economic reorganization of Cuba within the Socialist camp, and 100 million dollars was too little. Mikoyan said: "Well, let's use the 100 million and then we'll go on talking to obtain more." Che said, "When taking a historic step it is better to have a far deeper commitment, providing greater security for the future; it's no joke to reorient a country from one side to the other. If you drop us halfway with 100 or 200 million dollars, we won't solve anything."[32]

According to Alexeiev, "Che was the principal architect of Soviet-Cuban economic cooperation,"[33] though not in all of its aspects. For instance, the possibility of Soviet arms sales to Cuba was not discussed during Mikoyan's visit.* As Alexeiev recalls it, Castro secretly asked the Soviet Union for arms (via Alexeiev) only one month later, after the explosion of the French ship *La Coubre* in Havana on March 4, 1960. Over a hundred Cubans were killed and an entire shipment of rifles and ammunition was destroyed. Raúl negotiated the terms the following July in Moscow.[34]

Thanks to Mikoyan's visit, the revolutionary regime accomplished several of its goals. It obtained a loan of 100 million dollars, no strings attached, and it consolidated the Soviet Union's commitment to continue buying sugar. (A small transaction had been negotiated earlier, and in reality Moscow had been purchasing Cuban sugar since Batista's time.) In addition, the two countries established diplomatic relations. Faure Chomón, the former Revolutionary Student Movement leader who had fought at Che's side in Santa Clara, was named Cuba's first ambassador to the Soviet Union. Sergei Kudriavtsev, earlier entrusted with an espionage mission in Canada, represented his country in Havana. Finally, the Cubans ensured the receipt of Soviet oil shipments in significant and increasing volume, in exchange for Cuban sugar.

Cuba's oil situation was desperate indeed, and the problems it raised constituted Che's first confrontational international experience. The American refineries in Cuba imported crude from Venezuela, sold it to clients in pesos, and charged the National Bank in dollars so as to pay their Venezuelan suppliers. Che began delaying payment to the companies, which in turn started to pressure him. The first shipment of Soviet oil arrived at Havana on April 19, 1960. Negotiations with the American companies were at a standstill. Their representative, Tex Brewer, complained bitterly of Che's threats and obstinacy. Finally, Che agreed to a last payment on debts outstanding, on the condition that the refineries buy 300,000 barrels of Soviet oil. The companies refused to refine the Soviet crude, with the complicity of the U.S.

---

*"There was definitely no talk of weaponry. We discussed advisers, advisers of all sorts, both civil and in other types of construction . . . and that was the third item we discussed. And that was all because Che, if I recall, had to return to Havana. The conversation left everybody quite pleased." Nikolai Leonov, interview with the author, Moscow, October 28, 1995.

Treasury and without consulting the American Embassy in Havana. On June 6, Ambassador Philip Bonsal described to his superior in Washington, in an "eyes only" report, a meeting he had held with Brewer:

> The policy of his company (ESSO) had been, on the assumption that the US Government would take no stand in the matter, that it would be inevitable to refine the Russian crude: as desired by the Cuban Government. The assumption, however, turned out to be contrary to fact. At a meeting held perhaps on June 3 in Secretary Anderson's office with Tom Mann representing the Department and Mr. Barnes (CIA), Texaco and Standard (ESSO) were told by Secretary Anderson the following: That a refusal on their part to refine Russian crude in Cuba would be consistent with over-all US policy toward the Cuban Government. On the basis of this statement of US Government policy, Standard (ESSO) and Texaco have decided to refuse to refine Soviet crude. The effect of this policy . . . will be to present the Cuban Government with the alternative of either accepting the decision or of assuming full responsibility for the operation of the refineries and for the procuring of the necessary crude from Russian or other available sources. I think the companies will be intervened and that the Government will make every effort to increase shipments of Russian crude. On the other hand, if the Government manages to operate the refineries and to maintain an adequate flow of products, it will have gained a significant victory, comparable to that of Egypt when it demonstrated its ability to operate the Suez Canal.*

A cable from the British ambassador to the Foreign Office, dated June 22, emphasized Che's role in the negotiations and their final outcome. Guevara stated unabashedly that the Soviet Union "is a Power which has the petroleum, the ships to transport it, the willingness to transport it and the decision to do so." Her Majesty's ambassador drew the appropriate, if un-American, conclusion: "If this is so, I cannot see that diplomatic pressure and threat of withholding supplies altogether would be of any avail."[35]

Castro proceeded accordingly, ordering the refineries to process the

---

*Philip Bonsal to Roy Rubottom, June 6, 1960 (Secret, Eyes Only), *FRUS, 1958–1960.* That the companies were used to promote a U.S. confrontation with the revolutionary regime is confirmed by another report, written by the Royal Dutch Shell representative after a meeting at the Foreign Office in London: "Mr. Stephens explained that he hoped H.M.G. might be able to join the American, Dutch and Canadian Governments if joint diplomatic action were taken. He considered that as the State Department had definitely promoted the action of the American Companies as a powerful economic contribution towards Castro's downfall it was for them to act first, even before the Cubans took specific action against the companies." Foreign Office 371/148295, Record of Meeting, June 20 in Sir Paul Gore-Booth's Room (Confidential), item 8, June 21, 1960, Public Record Office, London.

Soviet oil or face the consequences. Their nationalization on June 29 was decreed by Che Guevara, who had won his first international battle. The collision course he had chosen was the right one: the inevitable confrontation with Washington had radicalized the masses, and raised their consciousness; Moscow's support had proven both reliable and decisive.

Days later, the Eisenhower administration suspended the purchase of Cuban sugar. Che and Castro, invoking their agreement with Mikoyan in February, asked Khrushchev to take on the equivalent of the U.S. quota, if only for symbolic purposes. Thanks to the earlier negotiations and Nikita Khrushchev's sympathy for the Cuban Revolution (which was not necessarily shared by the rest of the Soviet leadership), the next day the Kremlin announced that it would buy the total amount of the U.S. quota for that year.[36] There was another reason, however, for Khrushchev's decision. Moscow was fully engaged in its struggle with China—though in Cuba there was little information about or awareness of the issue. The first public clash between the two giants of socialism had taken place just weeks earlier, at the Congress of the (Workers) Communist Party of Romania, held in Bucharest on June 21. Khrushchev privately described the Chinese delegation as "crazy," "Trotskyist," and "warmongers."[37] The Central Committee of the Soviet Communist Party met two weeks later and adopted Khrushchev's proposal to withdraw all Soviet technicians from China. As the French journalist K. S. Karol noted in 1970, the Soviet Union's support for Cuba was the perfect alibi for its anti-China offensive. Nobody could accuse the Soviets of being soft toward the United States, or failing to support the Third World, at a time when they were saving Cuba from international ostracism and economic disaster.[38]

From early 1960, Che had launched a campaign against the sugar quota, presenting it as a form of slavery which forced Cuba to keep producing sugar cane. He was now proven right, and could boast of his victory.* He alone sought the elimination of the quota, promoted an alliance with the Soviet Union, conducted the economic negotiations with Mikoyan in February, and finally succeeded in substituting Moscow for Washington. On July 9, at the height of the conflict with Washington over oil and sugar, Khrushchev announced that the Soviet armed forces would defend Cuba with missiles, if necessary. Castro confirmed the announcement, but warned that it should be interpreted "metaphorically."

---

*Che even believed that the United States would not be able to cancel its sugar quota: "It is impossible for them to cancel it, for Cuba is the United States' largest, most efficient, and cheapest supplier of sugar. . . . It is impossible for them to eliminate the sugar quota." Ernesto Che Guevara, *La guerra de guerrillas*, in Ernesto Che Guevara, *Escritos y discursos,* vol. 1 (Havana: Editorial de Ciencias Sociales, 1977), p. 182.

Guevara, never one to be left behind, immediately declared that "Cuba is now . . . a glorious island in the center of the Caribbean, defended by the missiles of the greatest military power in history."[39] A few days later, the two Cuban leaders backed down from their belligerent tone. Fidel clarified that Cuba's independence rested upon the justice of its cause, not on Soviet missiles. Che announced that any attempt to transform Cuba into a Soviet satellite would be resisted to the last man.[40] Regardless, once the brief brouhaha subsided and private visits to the U.S.S.R. by Nuñez Jiménez in June and Raúl Castro took place in July, it was only natural that Guevara should lead the regime's first official delegation to the Soviet Union in October 1960. It was to be the culmination of Che's love affair with real, live socialism.

As Fidel and Che drew closer to the Soviet Union, tensions with the United States were exacerbated. The revolutionaries had already acquired a safety net for Cuba's sugar sales and its oil supply, and soon would also acquire weapons. They could now proceed to harden their domestic positions, in a crackdown which Che supported and, to some extent, inspired. It was he who set up Cuba's first "labor camp" in those months, in Guanahacabibes.[41] He spent a few days there, establishing one of the most heinous precedents of the Cuban Revolution: the confinement of dissidents, homosexuals, and, later, AIDS victims. His retrospective justification was frank, concise, and thoroughly regrettable:

[We] only send to Guanahacabibes those doubtful cases where we are not sure people should go to jail. I believe that people who should go to jail should go to jail anyway. Whether long-standing militants or whatever, they should go to jail. We send to Guanahacabibes those people who should not go to jail, people who have committed crimes against revolutionary morals, to a greater or lesser degree, along with simultaneous sanctions like being deprived of their posts, and in other cases not those sanctions, but rather to be reeducated through labor. It is hard labor, not brute labor, rather the working conditions are harsh but they are not brutal. . . .*

*Ernesto Che Guevara, *Actas del Ministerio de Industrias,* Bi-Monthly Meeting of January 20, 1962, in Ernesto Che Guevara, *Obras completas,* vol. 7 (Havana: Ministerio del Azúcar, 1968), p. 166. The minutes of meetings at the Ministry of Industries were drafted for four years by Juan Valdés Gravalosa, the ministry's technical secretary. They made up the final volume in a first edition of Che's complete works in seven volumes, edited by Orlando Borrego, a close aide of Che's and minister of sugar after 1964. The edition's run consisted of 120 copies, which were distributed only to high officials. It remains unavailable to the general public. The texts in volume 7 were omitted from subsequent editions of Che's complete works. They made up a virtual diary of over 700 pages, which reflects the evolution of Che's thinking at the ministry. The author expresses his gratitude to the Cuban (who must remain anonymous) who lent him a copy of the document in its entirety, and to José Valdés Gravalosa for verifying its authenticity in Havana on August 25, 1995. The document will be referred to hereafter as the *Ministry of Industries Minutes (Minutes).*

Freedom of the press was curtailed. The government shut down several newspapers, and nationalized the principal press agencies. It also pressured the university to toe the line; independent-minded professors proceeded to leave the country. Of course, the authorities' radicalization affected both sides: liberals and dissidents from the 26th of July Movement joined Batista's ex-henchmen, who were preferred by the CIA, in combatting their new enemies—the Castro brothers and Che. Counterrevolutionaries stepped up their opposition through sabotage, burning the sugar crops, murdering literacy workers in the Escambray mountains, and organizing armed expeditions from abroad. The United States, for its part, also made a series of irrevocable decisions, resolving to overthrow Fidel Castro by any means. Preparations began for what would become the Bay of Pigs. Everyone was caught up in the rush of events—but some knew where it was leading, while others did not.

Che was one of those who knew, and this gave him enormous political power. In a secret cable in July, Ambassador Bonsal reported a rumor that Che was sponsoring a sort of coup d'état, at a time when stories circulated about a serious illness befalling Fidel Castro. He did not venture to give further details, but explained, "I am convinced that Guevara is the real leader of this country at this time, though he would not be able to govern for long without Fidel."[42] On August 8, *Time* magazine devoted its cover story to Che Guevara, calling him the "brain" of the Revolution, while Fidel was its heart and Raúl its fist.[43] As Henry Luce's magazine pontificated,

> Wearing a smile of melancholy sweetness that many women find devastating, Che guides Cuba with icy calculation, vast competence, high intelligence and a perceptive sense of humor.[44]

So when Che Guevara arrived in Moscow for an official visit on October 22, he had the world and Cuba at his fingertips. His goal, in principle, was to ratify and extend Soviet-Cuban cooperation. This was the second stop in a two-month journey—once again, a long absence from Cuba. He left behind Aleida (who was eight months pregnant), a precarious economic situation, and a series of pending "internationalist" projects. No matter. As in his youth in Buenos Aires, he was sailing under the banner of Henry the Navigator and Caetano Veloso: "To navigate is necessary, to live is not."

The trip had been well planned. On September 1, Che had notified the new Soviet ambassador that he would head the Cuban mission to Moscow.[45] His first concrete goal was to ensure that the U.S.S.R. would buy the sugar that the U.S. was meant to purchase in the following year. Guevara presented his concerns to the Soviet ambassador: the United States would not be buying the 3 million tons of sugar projected for 1961, and so

Cuba hoped that the U.S.S.R. would fill the gap.[46] He accompanied Cuba's request with the possibility of its joining the Socialist bloc, and proposed a series of "conferences or meetings with representatives of other Socialist countries in Moscow." He suggested several other important items for the agenda, like Cuba's request for Soviet banking specialists (a contradiction in terms), as Fidel was planning to nationalize all private banks by the end of the year. Lastly he wished to propose the resale of Cuban gasoline, derived from Soviet oil surpluses, to countries like Canada—a scheme which would last until the late eighties, providing substantial hard-currency revenues.[47]

The first stop on the trip was Czechoslovakia, where Che had his first direct taste of a Warsaw Pact country. There he signed a cooperation agreement which included a 20-million-dollar loan and the establishment in Cuba of a Czech automotive plant (basically for trucks and tractors). Then on to the U.S.S.R., where Che stayed for just over two weeks. The Cuban delegation visited all the obligatory sites: the Lenin Museum, the Moscow subway, the Lenin and Stalin mausoleums, Red Square on the anniversary of the October Revolution, eight Moscow factories, and a Sovkhoz on the outskirts of the capital. They also attended a philharmonic concert and two performances of the Bolshoi Ballet. The visit included talks with Khrushchev and Mikoyan—to discuss, among other things, the election of John F. Kennedy, which had just occurred. In Leningrad, they visited the Smolny Institute, where Lenin launched the Bolshevik Revolution, as well as the battleship *Aurora,* the Hermitage, and the Winter Palace, before heading for Stalingrad and Rostov-on-the-Don.

In brief, Che was given the standard tour for friends of the heroic Soviet Union. Careful examination of his schedule suggests that because there were few substantive aspects to the trip, his time therefore had to be filled with activities and amusements. Perhaps he was not meant to have any free time, so he would not see things or people other than those programmed for him.[48] Either way, Guevara was unable to break away from his hosts, and did not get a chance to see any typical Soviet housing, the countryside, Siberia, or the less glorious sides of daily life in the U.S.S.R. The Soviets thought that just fine, explaining that he did not "make contact with the humble man in the street, because he was not one of those populists." Che spent his time in conversations with officials, where he could "solve problems for his government that he could not resolve in the street."[49]

On November 16, he left Moscow with his admiration for the fatherland of socialism intact. Of course, certain details disconcerted him. At a supper for friends at Alexeiev's home, he noted that the dinner service was made of the finest china, and asked, "Do the proletarians really eat on dishes like this?"[50] Carlos Franqui recalls an episode even more revealing of Che's ideological bent at the time:

> Upon my return to Havana, I had a run-in with Che Guevara at a Council of Ministers meeting. I talked about our experience in Prague with the "tuzeras" (the Czech girls in the hotels). And the stores for the "tuzex" (Czech Nomenklatura officials). Che, who had been there at the same time as us, heading a delegation, contradicted me: "Those are lies. You and your prejudices." "I'm not lying, Che. Nor am I prejudiced. I'm just not blind like you, who see everything in rosy colors." "I say it's a lie. I was there just as you were, and I didn't see anything."*

His naïveté was understandable if inexcusable: he did not know the Socialist world; he had not followed the great debates in Western Europe about the Eastern bloc, and his contacts with Marxist intellectuals from abroad were just beginning. The lack of a militant past made its weight felt. Che did not even notice the vigorous debates stimulated by the Khrushchev thaw. Less than a year after his visit, the Russian capital would see the publication of Alexander Solzhenitsyn's *A Day in the Life of Ivan Denisovich,* along with other heretical works. During his stay in Moscow, the city hosted the Congress of 81 Communist and Workers Parties of the World, where Chinese and Soviet representatives engaged in a ferocious fratricidal and irreversible struggle. Che remained oblivious to it all. He rejected Cuban ambassador Faure Chomón's advice against placing a floral tribute at Stalin's tomb; he went anyway. There were both Soviet and Cuban reasons not to do so: barely a year later, in November 1961, the body of the Little Father of the People would be transferred from Lenin's mausoleum to its current burial place in the walls of the Kremlin.

It was in Moscow that Che was first flustered by the intensity and complexity of the incipient conflict between China and the Soviet Union. Before his departure from Havana, Soviet diplomats there had insisted on holding a "roundtable" meeting of Socialist countries in Moscow. Their reasons were obvious: the U.S.S.R. wished to divide purchases of Cuban sugar among its allies. Of the 3 million tons Che had asked the Soviets to buy,

---

*Carlos Franqui, *Retrato de familia con Fidel* (Barcelona: Seix Barral, 1981), pp. 186–187. Maybe Che was a bit less naive than Franqui suggests. Raúl Maldonado recalls how Alberto Mora, one of Guevara's young aides at the time, was accosted, or perhaps even sexually harassed, by a charming young Moscovite during their stay. He proudly informed his boss how he had resisted her perverse and repeated advances, only to be pistol-whipped by Che's lacerating Argentine irony: "What kind of a fairy are you?" Raúl Maldonado, interview with Paco Ignacio Taibo II, made available to the author by Taibo, Mexico, March 16, 1996.

Khrushchev had approved only 1.2 million tons. The other countries were asked to purchase the remaining 1.8 million.

The real problem, however, was China's participation in the roundtable. Anatoly Dobrynin, the Soviet undersecretary of foreign affairs entrusted with the matter, summoned the Chinese ambassador in Moscow to inform him of Che's visit and invite him to attend the roundtable. For his part, Che sent a note to Faure Chomón from Prague, instructing him to invite all the Socialist countries, and especially China.[51] In a sense, Che fell into the Soviet trap. Moscow wanted Sino-Cuban cooperation to take place under its sponsorship. Of course, the Chinese were not taken in. Dobrynin informed Deputy Minister Pushkin on the day of Che's arrival that, despite Moscow's insistence, "there is as yet no reply from Beijing" on Chinese participation in the roundtable.[52] Indeed, China did not attend the meeting.*

This was not Che's only faux pas within the complexities of the Sino-Soviet confrontation. According to Nikolai Leonov, who was Che's interpreter and shadow during his Russian trip, Che requested that he accompany him to Beijing and Pyongyang. Guevara was worried that he would not find a Spanish-language interpreter in North Korea; Beijing, of course, angrily refused him an entry visa even for transit.[53] The interpreter/spy did, however, go to North Korea with the Cuban delegation. Once there, he was forced to stay at the Soviet Embassy, while the Cubans were at an official residence. This was quite logical: neither the Chinese nor the Koreans wanted a KGB agent in the Cuban delegation, even if he was supposedly just an interpreter.

The Congress of 81 Communist and Workers Parties of the World began while Che was in Moscow and concluded after his "side trip" to Beijing and Pyongyang. The Soviets' purpose in holding the meeting was to have the international Communist movement condemn the "war-mongering and reckless" theses of Mao Zedong. When Che returned from China and learned of the conference's conclusions, he declared, "We did not participate in drafting the communiqué from the Communist and Workers parties, but we fully support it." He also asserted that "the declaration by the parties [is] one of the most important events of our time," and emphasized the "militant solidarity of the Soviet people and the Cuban people." And he further backed the Soviet position, stating that "Cuba [must] follow the example of peaceful development provided by the USSR."[54]

The Congress was Khrushchev's first attempt to excommunicate the Maoists from the Communist church. Though he was not entirely success-

---

*According to Che, the countries that signed the Multilateral Payments Accord were "all the socialist countries of Europe and the People's Republic of Mongolia." Ernesto Che Guevara, "Comparecencia televisada de la firma de acuerdos con los países socialistas," January 6, 1961, in Guevara, *Escritos y discursos,* vol. 5, p. 8.

ful, China found itself isolated and surrounded. Its only ally, Enver Hoxha of Albania, walked out of the Congress on November 25. Che was in the dark regarding the falling-out between China and the Soviet Union, and regarding the Congress itself, despite the attendance of a Cuban PSP delegation headed by Aníbal Escalante:

> The fact that Che Guevara knew nothing of the Conference of 81 was explicitly confirmed to me by a member of his entourage in Moscow. It seemed surprising to me, as the conference had dramatic moments and its outcome was uncertain until the last minute. . . .
>
> Incredible as it might seem, the hardly united family of the Communist parties followed its habit, amid this huge fight, of keeping its "secrets only for initiates." Even Che Guevara, a progressive revolutionary who was a friend *par excellence* of the Socialist bloc, had no right to be informed of the situation, even partially. These methods would eventually have an impact on Che who, after having been one of the warmest supporters of the USSR in Cuba, became one of its harshest critics.[55]

Guevara spent almost two weeks in China. He met Zhou Enlai and an aging but still lucid Mao Zedong. The Great Helmsman, partially overshadowed by Liu Shaoqi, was still paying for the enormous mistakes of the Great Leap Forward with a virtual internal exile. It would end only five years later when he declared "war against the general headquarters" and launched the Cultural Revolution. Che held three meetings with Mao. According to a recent biography—which provides no sources—the Chinese leader confided his willingness to support the struggle of Patrice Lumumba in the Belgian Congo. Che would leave Beijing convinced of the purity of contemporary Chinese Marxism-Leninism.[56] China pledged that it would buy one million tons of Cuban sugar in 1961, and Che was feted by Zhou Enlai at the Great Hall of the People. In his speech there, Guevara drew several analogies between the Cuban and Chinese revolutions, extolled the example of Chinese communism, and stated that it had opened "a new path for the Americas." All of this led the U.S. State Department—and undoubtedly several Soviet analysts as well—to conclude that Che had taken sides with Beijing in the Sino-Soviet conflict—an evaluation that was premature and superficial, but prophetic.[57] Before leaving, Che received news on November 24 of the birth of his first daughter with Aleida. His absence from Cuba confirmed his proclamation to his mother: the only thing that counted for him was the Revolution. Everything else was secondary.

Depending on the source, Che's visit to Moscow, Beijing, and Pyongyang has been variously perceived as a success, a failure, or none of the above. The Americans considered it rather positive for Cuba, though they doubted whether the accords reached would actually bear fruit: "[CIA Director] Mr.

[Allen] Dulles reported that Che Guevara had returned to Cuba with many agreements which, if they were fulfilled [which was unlikely, in Dulles's view], would result in over half of Cuba's trade taking place with the [Socialist] Bloc."[58] The British held a different view:

> One of my colleagues is said to have been told by the Cuban Ambassador [in Moscow] that Guevara's mission left for Peking disappointed with the practical results of their visit to Moscow, despite the extreme warmth of their public reception. Another of my colleagues claims to have been informed by sources close to Khrushchev that Soviet policy is now to avoid any action which could seriously jeopardize relations with the [incoming] Kennedy administration and that Cubans have therefore been told to avoid undue provocation, while keeping the kettle nicely on the boil. . . . The Cubans are now suffering from a serious shortage of dollars. . . . The Soviet Government . . . has, so far, been unwilling to do anything to relieve the dollar shortage. . . . Guevara may make another effort to secure dollars from the Soviet Union when he returns to Moscow from Peking.[59]

Che undoubtedly impressed his interlocutors. They did not expect a visitor from a Caribbean island to show such a substantive and orderly approach to his work. He knew the value of time; he kept his delegation on a short leash and followed the protocol's schedule to the hour and minute. As Leonov recalls, "Contrary to Mexican and Latin American custom, he was very punctual; he hardly seemed Latin American at all."[60]

All the same, some of his economic views were so outrageous that they can only have mystified his hosts:

> He wanted to transform Cuba into an industrialized state overnight. Cuba has no metal which might serve as a basis for . . . machinery and transport. He intended to make Cuba into an exporter of metal and sheet steel in the Caribbean area. All the Soviet technicians opposed this; they said it was economic folly, that there is no coal or iron ore in Cuba, that everything has to be shipped there and that makes iron production much more expensive. Besides, Cuba does not have a skilled labor force. Che could not find arguments strong enough to convince them. They gave him more and more calculations showing that it would be anti-economic. The discussion lasted days. He insisted. He explained that this would help him create a working class and a market. . . . He insisted on the social, or rather the strategic, aspects, while the Soviets looked at economic calculations, costs, markets: You don't even have a market for an iron and steel plant, for one million tons a year. Imagine, in 15 years you'll have 15 million tons of steel! What will you do with it?*

---

*Nikolai Leonov, interview with the author, Moscow, Oct. 28, 1995. As Anatoly Dobrynin recalled years later: "Guevara was impossible, he wanted a little steel mill, an

After visiting China and North Korea, Che returned to Moscow, where, on December 19 (two months after his arrival), a joint communiqué was finally signed and issued announcing the sugar accord. During his stopover in East Berlin, he found another client for Cuba's principal export. The only other event of note during his visit there was that he met a young German-Argentine translator, Tamara Bunke. She would die six years later, under the name "Tania," in a hail of machine-gun fire while crossing the Rio Grande in Bolivia; her association with Che began then, long before she joined him in the Andean highlands.*

Finally home in Havana, Che presented the results of his trip on television. He sought to dispel any doubts regarding his prolonged absence and the unusual wait for the joint communiqué with the U.S.S.R. He explained that the negotiations had dragged on owing to their complexity. They had implied shifting practically all the country's foreign trade, from one day to the next, toward an economic bloc which had nothing in common with Cuba: not its climate, weights and measures, language, or culture. Che also explained, quite convincingly, why the Socialist countries had finally agreed to his requests, how he had persuaded them, and why the accords were so advantageous to Cuba after its break with the United States. He projected an image of calm rationality and expertise; indeed, his screen presence was second only to Fidel's, and all the more surprising in a person without any previous television experience.

Che returned to Cuba with the same ideas—or perhaps even more adulatory than before—about the Socialist bloc. He expressed an admiration that was probably sincere, but hardly consistent with the facts. For instance, his comments on China, just a year after the catastrophe of Mao's Great Leap Forward with its devastating impact on the economy, society, and politics, were very similar to the idealized views held by many visitors to China in those deluded years:

> Naturally, one cannot pretend that the standard of living in China is like that of developed countries in the capitalist world, but there are absolutely none of the symptoms of misery that one sees in other Asian countries which we have had a chance to visit, even far more developed ones like Japan. And one sees that everyone eats, everyone is dressed—dressed

---

automobile factory. We told him Cuba wasn't big enough to support an industrial economy. They needed hard currency, and the only way to earn it was to do what they did best—grow sugar." Richard Goodwin, *Remembering America* (New York: Harper and Row, 1989), p. 172.

*According to Saverio Tutino, the *Unità* correspondent in Havana, Tania was invited to Havana shortly afterward by Armando Hart, at Fidel Castro's initiative, to "keep Che happy." Saverio Tutino, *Guevara al tempo di Guevara* (Rome: Editori Riuniti, 1996), p. 31.

uniformly, it's true, but everyone is decently dressed—everybody has work, and an extraordinary spirit.*

Che's evaluation of the Socialist countries as a whole, though shared by millions of Communists around the world, was also at odds with the understanding many former devotees now held of socialism as it really existed. Undoubtedly, his purpose was not to deceive the Cuban public. He believed in what he said, but was unwittingly painting himself into a corner. The gap between his beliefs and reality was so abysmal, and his intellectual honesty so deep, that his disillusionment would be devastating when it finally came. His sincerity could only lead to tragedy; as the following passage reveals, his expectations were simply too high:

> The human spirit in those [Socialist] peoples convinces us that we definitely cannot count on friendly governments except, above all, in those countries of the world. And besides, their strength, their high rates of economic development, the dynamism they show, the development of all the people's potential, convince us that the future definitely belongs to all the countries who struggle, like them, for peace in the world and for justice, distributed among all human beings.[61]

Che did not dedicate all his time at the National Bank to the economy, or to negotiations with China and the Soviet Union. He had two other activities during those fourteen months, which would prove important not only for him but for Cuba and Latin America. First of all, he helped launch the concept of volunteer work; secondly, he published his most influential work, *Guerrilla Warfare* (*La guerra de guerrillas*), vowing that Cuba would export the Revolution to the entire continent. The theses contained therein would prove Che's most enduring legacy.

Volunteer work projects began in Cuba on November 23, 1959. The first one took place at the Ciudad Escolar Camilo Cienfuegos, in Caney de Las Mercedes, in the province of Oriente. Che's influence was evident both in the project's goal—to build a school named after the late Camilo—and in the fact that the construction team was headed by Armando Acosta, Che's Communist companion from Las Villas. Over several months, every Sunday Che would fly his official plane to Las Mercedes, where along with the shoe industry workers from Manzanillo and a hundred or so soldiers from the Rebel Army he helped build the school that carried his friend's name.[62] But he had in mind a much vaster program.

---

*Ernesto Che Guevara, "Comparecencia televisada," p. 14. Che's comment on his visit to North Korea is even more illuminating: "Of all the Socialist countries we visited in person, Korea is one of the most extraordinary. It is perhaps the one that impressed us the most of all." Ibid., p. 19.

Che himself set an example in the sugar harvest that December. He also worked in construction and textiles, and helped unload ships from Socialist countries. Beyond the fact that he enjoyed mixing with ordinary Cubans, there was also the personal challenge of working amid the dust of machinery and sugar cane, classical triggers for asthma attacks. But his real purpose was political. He believed that the best incentive for labor should be revolutionary emulation; it was crucial that Cubans be involved in the Revolution. Volunteer work was, for him, a pleasurable activity "that is done with joy, to the rhythm of revolutionary songs, amid a fraternal camaraderie and human contacts which invigorate and dignify all involved."[63]

Volunteer work also served to awaken revolutionary fervor and teach the basics of revolution:

> It was a school to raise awareness, an effort made by society and for society as an individual and collective contribution, [which] develops a higher awareness allowing us to accelerate the process of transition. . . . Volunteer work is a part of that educational undertaking.[64]

Volunteer weekends soon became the fashion throughout the island. Some Cubans enjoyed them, others hated them. Songs were written in their praise, making their way as far as Chile: a tune by Isabel Parra extols "los domingos solidarios del trabajo voluntario"—the Sunday solidarity of volunteer work.

Guevara's endeavor had two effects. On the one hand, he became known as a leader willing to make sacrifices like everybody else—and this out of genuine commitment, not obligation. On the other hand, he became a role model, paving the way for the expansion of volunteer labor. The footage of Che cutting cane, weaving, carrying sacks of rice, and digging ditches soon became part of his iconography. His popularity grew apace. None of the other revolutionary leaders could equal his enthusiasm for working on weekends.

Problems arose when the idea was pushed beyond its original purpose. Cuba's need to boost its sugar production eventually transformed the initial concept into a way of exploiting workers. Volunteer work began as a political, ideological, and cultural precept, admirable in its goals. When used as a means to extend the workday and reduce real salaries, it became counterproductive and harmful to the economy. Che would later understand this:

> Volunteer work should not be seen in terms of its economic significance for the State today; volunteer work is essentially a factor that can develop workers' awareness more than any other.[65]

As would become apparent in 1970, when Cuba failed to reach its stated goal of a 10-million-ton sugar harvest, nothing dislocates an economy as much as a massive transfer of labor from one sector to another, even (or especially) if it is done "voluntarily."

In time, the apparent—but illusory—economic benefits of volunteer labor transformed it into an obligation. People who failed to "volunteer" were penalized in various ways, ranging from social ostracism to accusations of being "counterrevolutionary." Che did not live to see all this. His contribution to the altruism of the Cuban Revolution is one of the most lyrical pages in its history. But the perversion or distortion of his tenets would haunt him to the end: his death was partly due to his own misguided application of them.

Che's role in the government became even more varied. Aside from his formal duties in economic policy and diplomacy, he became increasingly involved in his true passion: promoting revolution in Latin America. He began to meet systematically with Latin American leaders, acquiring a better understanding of different political currents and also clearer opinions. He gradually focused on three fronts: regional reactions to U.S. aggression, the behavior of the traditional left, and propagating the lessons of the Cuban Revolution.

After the August 1960 meeting of the Organization of American States in Costa Rica, it became obvious that Washington would try to enlist the support of Latin American governments in its anti-Communist, anti-Soviet crusade, just as it had against Guatemala in 1954. By 1960, Che had developed a sophisticated geopolitical analysis of the region. The following report of a conversation between Che and the Soviet ambassador in Cuba reveals a complex and subtle approach to the motives—and logic—underlying the different political stances of regimes in the region:

Che said: The governments of these countries are playing a game on two levels. Verbally they oppose intervention in Cuban affairs, but they vote with the Americans against Cuba. The reactionary governments of Latin America appear to stand firm vis-à-vis Washington, in order to pressure the Americans into giving them loans and other forms of assistance. They try to use the existence of a revolutionary Cuba to blackmail the United States. The U.S., fearing a repetition of the Cuban revolution in other countries, has begun providing more assistance in order to forestall the development of a revolutionary process in the region. But Latin America is at the boiling point, and next year we can expect revolutionary explosions in several countries, beginning with Peru and Paraguay. These processes will undoubtedly be accelerated if the United States, supported by reactionary governments, dares to take action against Cuba. Of course, any revolutionary uprisings in these countries will probably be crushed by the U.S. armed forces, who will be summoned by these countries' reactionary governments. In such cases the Soviet Union and other Socialist countries would unfortunately not be able to help the people of countries like Argentina, Uruguay, Chile, or Peru.[66]

Che grasped only too well the attitude of the United States and its allies in the region. The Alliance for Progress, launched by John F. Kennedy months after this conversation with Kudriavtsev, would pursue these very goals: to prevent new revolutionary outbreaks by channeling resources toward the countries south of the Rio Grande. Che was also right—to a lesser degree—about the position of Latin American governments. He foresaw that they would maintain a certain resistance vis-à-vis Washington as long as that allowed them to secure more aid, and if the confrontation did not extend beyond certain limits. And he was equally prescient in predicting that the U.S.S.R. would not be able to support other countries as it had Cuba—as Chile would discover ten years later. But Guevara overestimated Latin American resolve—even when buttressed by economic interests—in the face of an escalating conflict between Havana and Washington. With the exception of Mexico, all the region's governments eventually submitted to the U.S. *diktat,* curtailing their commercial and diplomatic relations with Cuba.

Moreover, Che was totally wrong about the imminent "explosions" within Latin America. They simply did not happen—either in Peru or Paraguay, or indeed even in Chile, which would follow a very different path ten years later. Still another decade would transpire after Salvador Allende's election in Chile before any further revolutionary uprisings occurred in Central America. Precisely because his analysis of the region was accurate, Che's projections were mistaken. The United States would indeed provide military support and economic backing to the governments in place, transferring to them huge amounts of aid compared with the past. Thanks in part to that strategy, which would later be termed "counterinsurgency," the revolution did not come to Latin America.

The happy ending envisaged by Guevara also failed to materialize because of another factor, which he accurately analyzed: the bankruptcy of the existing left. Che expounded his views of the Latin American left during a conversation with the Soviet ambassador, who was perhaps surprised by his frankness. As Kudriavtsev reported,

Guevara began talking in a brusque tone. He said: the leaders of the left in Latin America do not take advantage of revolutionary situations, they behave like cowards, they do not go to the mountains to begin the struggle against their corrupt governments. Leftist parties in other countries of Latin America, Che emphasized, have far better conditions for an armed struggle

and victory than the Cuban people. We are certain that the active struggle
against American imperialism, which Cuba is pursuing, will soon revolu-
tionize the masses in the countries of Latin America. There, finally, we will
see truly revolutionary leaders capable of leading the people against their
current corrupt and reactionary governments, and of achieving victory.
That is why, Guevara emphasized, we believe that any attempt by the Cuban
government to negotiate our differences with the U.S. will be unsuccessful.
On the contrary, it might be interpreted by the peoples of Latin American
countries as a sign of Cuban weakness. We must overcome the fatalism that
is so widespread among the peoples of Latin American countries, in the
sense that it is impossible to fight against American imperialism.[67]

It is surprising that Che already held this opinion of traditional leftist
parties in Latin America. His assessment was quite valid: there was nothing
revolutionary about them. And his prediction about the emergence of new
leaders within the Latin American left would prove correct. Thanks to the
example and support of the Cuban Revolution, younger, more radical and
libertarian figures and groups surfaced throughout the continent. Che was
right to believe that Cuba's firm stance before the United States would set
an example for a new generation of leftists in the hemisphere.

Still, the heart of his analysis did not come true. The impoverished
masses of Latin American did not follow the new leaders who emerged from
the Cuban crucible. Despite all their efforts and sacrifice, the Communist
parties did not become the harbingers of revolution. Nor did the partisans
of Castro and Guevara who proliferated in the jungles and universities of
Latin America; they, too, failed to arouse the masses forsaken by the
Communists. Once again, Che was right in his analysis, and wrong in his
conclusions.

What is finally most impressive is his prescience and constancy. From the
beginning, he sustained the same ideas, based on similar diagnoses and
linked to the same hope. This can be seen most clearly in *Guerrilla Warfare*
(*La guerra de guerrillas*), whose prologue appeared in early 1960 in the daily
Revolución; the complete text was published in the second half of that year
by the Ministry of the Armed Forces. The day after the preface appeared,
Fidel Castro called the newspaper's director, Carlos Franqui, and demanded that he not publish the rest of the text. Franqui asked him to reach
an agreement directly with Che. He then informed the Argentine (with
whom he did not have very cordial relations) of the call, and the latter
agreed to suspend publication.[68]

The controversial—even for Cuba—text's most important and famous
ideas, laden with consequence for Latin America, appear on the first page;
Che was by now remarkably concise and rigorous. He began by asserting

that the Cuban Revolution had contributed three great lessons to the "mechanics of revolutionary movements in America":

1. Popular forces can win a war against the army.

2. It is not always necessary to wait for all the conditions to be present [to make] a revolution; the insurrectional *foco* can create them.

3. In the underdeveloped Americas the terrain of the armed struggle must be primarily the countryside.[69]

He added a couple of warnings, both complementary and contradictory, which also became virtual—though ephemeral—canons for the armed struggle in Latin America:

> When a government has come to power through some form of popular election, whether fraudulent or not, and it maintains at least the appearance of constitutional legitimacy, guerrilla activity cannot take place, because the possibilities for civic struggle have not yet been exhausted. . . . Guerrilla warfare is a struggle of the masses, a struggle of the people; the guerrilla as an armed nucleus is the fighting vanguard of the people, its great strength resides in the mass of the population.[70]

The conceptual gaps in these passages would soon be filled by the *comandante*'s many commentators. The first, while not the most significant, reveals how difficult it is to interpret Guevara's tenets, especially when they are a matter of life or death for so many people. Che's third thesis can be understood to imply that all of Latin America is underdeveloped, and that any struggle within it must always begin in the countryside. Alternatively, it can be taken to refer only to those parts of Latin America which are underdeveloped; in other areas, guerrilla warfare should not be limited to the countryside. In practice, the first interpretation has systematically prevailed (except in those countries where it cannot be applied—Uruguay, for instance, where Montevideo accounts for over half the population). Taken at face value, the thesis is false, if not dangerous. Large sections of Latin American society would surmount many of the worst traits of their underdevelopment—including the prevalence of rural population and poverty—precisely in those years, or soon afterward. Many men died—including two of Che's close friends, his bodyguard Hermés Peña and the Argentine journalist Jorge Masetti—because they went off to fight in the jungles of Latin America, inhabited at the time only by guerrillas and armies.

Che's approach to the war in Cuba, which underlies his cardinal ideas, is itself open to discussion. It prejudges the central question of the debate: did the 26th of July guerrillas defeat the army militarily, as suggested in regard to the battle of Santa Clara, or did Batista lose what was essentially a political contest without his army being defeated? Che focused all of his attention and expertise, and the weight of his authority, on the military aspects of the struggle in Cuba and Latin America. He presupposed that the core of the struggle consisted in the confrontation between two armies, with one loser and one winner. But in the thirty-five years since *Guerrilla Warfare* was published, this miracle has been repeated only once—in Nicaragua in 1979. And even there, things did not quite happen as Che predicted.

There is also a contradiction between Che's second thesis regarding the conditions for a *foco* (or incipient guerrilla base) and his warning about elections. If guerrilla warfare can create the conditions for revolution, then it makes no difference whether they are present *ex ante;* a *foco* can begin independently of the circumstances. Hence, the existence of a "democratic" regime ceases to be an obstacle. There can be insurrectional *focos* even in those countries where a constitutional regime is in power—for instance, Venezuela or Colombia. And indeed, many such *focos* appeared throughout the continent very soon afterward, regardless of Che's warning—indeed, with his blessing and backing.

Many of his other ideas in *Guerrilla Warfare* had already been expressed in speeches or in his accounts of the war. In the text they are reformulated in a more systematic way: the guerrilla fighter who distributes land as he crosses mountains or jungles is an "agrarian revolutionary"; "the guerrilla fighter is the Jesuit of warfare"; the guerrilla fighter must fight only when he is certain of winning; and the guerrilla army must be transformed gradually into a regular army; but these are all reflections of Che's experience in 1957 and 1958.

The text also includes a number of technical, somewhat eccentric tips about the most appropriate weapons for guerrilla warfare, the importance of proper footwear, and so on. It is replete with highly perceptive insights and reflections, and instructions so detailed that they can easily wreak confusion and havoc despite their great precision. A good example is Che's indications regarding the ideal physical and psychological profile of the guerrilla fighter—down to the usefulness of smoking a pipe, "as it allows one to make full use of tobacco from cigarettes, at times of scarcity, or whatever is left of cigar stubs."[71] Che had no reason to suspect the impact all this would have on thousands of young university students in the ensuing thirty years, as they cheerfully marched off to be massacred, with or without pipes. No author should be held responsible for his readers' sagacity—or lack thereof. Nor could Che have foreseen that one of his later disciples, the Mexican rebel Subcomandante Marcos, would take the precept of the pipe to levels of international media fame that Guevara would never have imagined.

Che's more substantive ideas include the following passage on the inverse correlation between a terrain's suitability for guerrilla warfare and for human habitation; it illustrates his uncanny knack for applying the intelligent, knowledgeable, and cultivated layman's insight to disciplines or areas generally reserved for the square-minded and otherwise ignorant specialist:

> All favorable environments, all facilities for human life tend to make man more sedentary. The opposite occurs in guerrilla warfare: the more facilities there are for man, the more nomadic and uncertain the life of the guerrilla fighter. In reality, they follow the same principle. . . . Everything that is favorable to human life with its accompanying communications, urban and semi-urban nuclei with large concentrations of people, terrain easily accessible to machinery, etc., places the guerrilla fighter at a disadvantage.[72]

The book also includes important observations about the relationship between the people and the guerrilla warriors—a link that Che considered vital, as noted in previous chapters. Partisans and peasants educate and transform each other mutually; the latter instruct and influence the former, radicalizing them and teaching them the realities of their world.

There are also many references—predictable, but by no means obsequious—to Fidel's leadership:

> Fidel Castro embodies the highest attributes of the combatant and statesman; it is to his vision that we owe our voyage, our struggle, and our victory. We cannot say that without him the people would not have triumphed, but this victory would doubtless have cost more and been less complete.[73]

Sadly, myriad Latin American enthusiasts would soon forget that not everyone can be Fidel Castro, and that the chances for success fade rapidly without a bold, visionary, and multifaceted leadership like his. Many would infer that anyone can become a Fidel Castro. Others, including Che, would conclude that the *caudillo*'s many talents could be replaced with other virtues—a fatal mistake for Guevara and countless others.

Beyond these reflections (and others regarding the role of women, sanitation, indoctrination, and so on), *Guerrilla Warfare* must be judged in terms of its impact rather than its intent. It is, after all, a manual. Unavoidably brief and simplistic, it carries the risk of being read too quickly by enthusiastic and innocent students of revolution. Both insightful and accessible, it helped mobilize the youth of Latin America on behalf of just causes. It taught that in order to win, one must dare to try, and in order to dare, one must have faith. Che endowed two generations of young people with the tools of that faith, and the fervor of that conviction. But he must also be held responsible for the wasted blood and lives that decimated those generations. His all too costly errors included his emphasis on technical and military matters; the lessons he drew from watching only half of a very complex film; his belief that the enormous obstacles to social change can be overcome by sheer willpower; his neglect of social, economic, and political conditions in much of Latin America, beginning with his native Argentina and Brazil; and finally, his underestimation of his own impact, his uniqueness. His death allowed him to sidestep a question he could never have answered: why so many university students from the region's emerging middle classes sallied forth so innocently to their slaughter. These are some of the debts that he owes to history.

Che left the National Bank on the eve of the Cuban Revolution's greatest victory: the Bay of Pigs, on April 22, 1961. His months at the Bank did not mark him physically, aside from a few pounds he put on because of trips and lack of exercise. The added weight might also have been a side effect of cortisone, then newly introduced as a treatment for asthma. Ricardo Rojo recalls that he found Che overweight in mid-1961; when he asked him why, Guevara replied that it was the fault of the cortisone.* Indeed, asthma specialists who have examined photos of him in those years detect the classic "moon face" and chubbiness of cortisone users.

Overweight or not, Che's charm endured, as can be seen in a beguiling anecdote. Despite a trace of bad humor and fatigue due to work and illness, as well as his characteristic slovenliness, his face was beautifully rendered by a Cuban photographer who had the talent and luck to snap his picture by accident on a day of glory and mourning in Havana. Not for the first time, fortune helped create an iconic image of Che Guevara. The picture, taken by pure chance, traveled around the world. Made into a poster, it haunted the social imagination of an entire era. It hung in college dormitories and was borne aloft in demonstrations by millions of students. It recorded the Christlike image of the living Che, eventually joining the equally Christlike photo of his corpse in Vallegrande.

The picture became emblematic because it was both starkly iconographic and completely spontaneous. Che happened to cross Alberto Korda's lens for a fleeting moment, on his way to someplace else. Korda describes the event:

> On the day after the explosion of the *La Courbe,* there was an improvised ceremony on the corner of 12th and 23rd. Fidel Castro presided, and gave a speech honoring the victims of the sabotage. The street was full of people, and flowers rained upon the caskets as they passed by. I was working as a news photographer for the daily *Revolución.* . . . I was slightly below the

---

*"It's not laziness, no, there's no time for that here." Ricardo Rojo, *Mi amigo el Che* (Buenos Aires: Legasa, 1994; first edition, 1968), p. 102.

level of the dais, with a 9-mm. Leica camera. I used my small telephoto lens and took all the people in the first row: Fidel, Jean-Paul Sartre, and Simone de Beauvoir. Che was not visible; he was standing behind the rostrum. But for a moment there was an empty space in the front row, and in the background the figure of Che appeared. He unexpectedly entered my viewfinder and I shot the photo horizontally. I immediately realized that the image of him was almost a portrait, with the clear sky behind him. I shifted the camera to a vertical [position] and shot a second photo. It all happened in less than ten or fifteen seconds. Che left and didn't appear again. It was a coincidence.[74]

It was cold that day in Havana. Guevara was wearing a zippered plastic jacket, lent him by a Mexican friend. It was not his usual attire, and made him look slimmer than he was. The newspaper neglected to publish Korda's photograph; there were already enough pictures of the ceremony.

Six years later, the Italian publisher Giangiacomo Feltrinelli stopped in Havana on his way from Bolivia to Milan; he looked up Korda, searching for some pictures of Che. According to Korda, the Italian was convinced that Che would never leave Bolivia alive. Without paying a cent, he chose the 1960 photo of the *La Courbe* ceremony. Weeks later, when Guevara died, Feltrinelli produced the most thumbtacked poster in history. It was immediately taken up by the mourning students of Milan and brandished in angry demonstrations. It became the other half of an iconographic diptych. Freddy Alborta's picture of Che's corpse in the laundry room of Nuestra Señora de Malta robbed millions of young people of their idol. But Korda's photo returned to them a living Che: gaze fixed upon a distant horizon, hair in the wind, face clear against an open sky.

Chapter 7

"Socialism Must Live, It Isn't Worth Dying Beautifully."

Che Guevara was not born to be a banker. On February 21, 1961, he was named minister of industries, which essentially meant taking over the entire Cuban economy. He would remain in the job until his departure from the island in early 1965. There he won his first great ideological-economic battles; and there he suffered the defeats that eventually led him to seek other paths toward power and glory. Perhaps he knew that his time at the ministry was limited. The secretary who had worked with him since his time at La Cabaña, Manuel Manresa, recalled his words when he took the ministerial post: "We are going to spend five years here, and then we will go. When we're five years older, we'll still be able to do guerrilla warfare."[1] During his three years at the ministry, he accumulated a series of victories. He put his seal on almost every aspect of the Cuban Revolution. His children were born, his books were written, and the seeds of his myth were gradually sown.

His shift away from the National Bank more or less coincided with the most important and joyous moment of the Revolution. The Bay of Pigs—or Playa Girón, as it is known in Cuba and Latin America—consecrated Cuba's victory against the Kennedy administration and the Miami conspirators. It also proved Guevara right. Between April 17 and 21, 1961, a small army and a large militia, rapidly armed by the USSR and masterfully directed by Fidel Castro and his lieutenants, put down a bold but absurd attempt, plotted by the White House and CIA, to overthrow the revolutionary regime. The expedition was defeated thanks to the regime's popularity and leadership, the exiles' mistakes, and the indecision of John F. Kennedy—but also, in Che's view, thanks to Cuba's international alliances.

Before the invasion, Che had again linked the island's defense to the Soviet nuclear umbrella: "[The imperialists] know they cannot attack directly, that there are rockets with atomic warheads which can be deployed anywhere."[2] Just before the expedition, the veterans of the Sierra Maestra made a sharp ideological turn to the left. On April 16—the day before the attack—Fidel Castro made a fiery speech before a tense and angry crowd in Havana, proclaiming the Socialist nature of the Cuban Revolution. The imminent invasion did not cause this shift; it merely hastened it. Since the previous October, the government had nationalized practically all the companies owned by the Cuban business community and U.S. interests, in two broad sweeps: 376 Cuban companies on October 13, and 166 U.S. properties on October 24. Che revealed the full intent and definitive nature of the process in a conversation with Julio Lobo, the richest and most powerful sugar producer in Cuba. Guevara summoned Lobo to the Bank and said to him, "We are Communists, and we cannot allow you to go on as you are, representing as you do the very essence of capitalism in Cuba."[3] He told Lobo that he could either leave, or else join the Revolution—in which case Che would make him director-general of the country's sugar industry. He would also lose his plantations, but retain the usufruct of his favorite mill. Lobo replied that he would think it over, and took the next flight to Miami.

Strictly speaking, Che played a minor part in the Bay of Pigs episode and in confirming the regime's Socialist character. But he played a major role in defining the course that shaped these events. His ideas inspired the resolutions adopted by the revolutionary leadership; his predictions all proved true during that spring filled with hope and optimism. Two days before the Bay of Pigs, the Soviet cosmonaut Yuri Gagarin became the first man in space. Three months later, he would accompany Castro and Guevara in celebrating the anniversary of the Moncada assault. The future belonged to socialism. Everything seemed possible, and many of the decisions taken in subsequent years stemmed—inevitably and understandably—from the conceit of the Cuban leaders who had "defeated imperialism." By mid-1963, their mistakes and recklessness would translate into shortages, internal division, and tensions with the USSR. But for over two years, Che Guevara had an opportunity rarely granted to a revolutionary and intellectual: to experiment freely with an entire economy, a society, and even, in a sense, with human nature. His place in the iconographic skies of the twentieth century is due, above all, to his emphasis on the latter—his attempt at social engineering.

It all began with the Bay of Pigs. The Eisenhower administration had been contriving to overthrow Castro by force since March 1960. The CIA recruited groups of Cuban exiles in Miami and trained them in various parts of Central America, especially Guatemala. This was no coincidence, since it was the scene of one of the Agency's greatest victories in the Cold War, the overthrow of the Arbenz government seven years earlier. Several operators in this new U.S. undertaking, including David Atlee Phillips, had participated in the 1954 coup. When John Kennedy succeeded Eisenhower on January 20, 1961, plans for the invasion were already far advanced and diplomatic relations already broken. The only thing missing was the green light from Washington.

The plan was relatively simple, and ludicrous. It relied on a series of faulty and biased analyses asserting that the Cuban population, weary of the regime's terror and privations, would welcome a brave and prestigious expeditionary force. According to CIA informers, division and unrest prevailed within the rebel armed forces; they would not hesitate to rise against the government. The plan called for the "freedom fighters" to establish a beachhead near the Escambray mountains where there was some armed opposition to the regime. There they would receive foreign (that is, United States) recognition and support, and deploy a massive propaganda campaign. This would suffice to topple the government, or at least involve it in a civil war which would quickly become internationalized.

The plan never called for more than a limited U.S. commitment. The United States would organize the Miami plotters, arm and train them, and supply them with the ships needed to sail from Central America. It would also provide the planes required to destroy the meager Cuban air force before it got off the ground. But there would not be any direct or explicit involvement. The State Department opposed it and Kennedy, despite his indecision, finally accepted the counsel of his diplomatic advisers. U.S. participation depended on the exiles setting up a provisional government, which would then call for assistance.

Kennedy's misgivings led him to implement several changes in the plan. The landing point was shifted to the Bay of Pigs, in the Zapata Marsh—a strange choice, as it was Fidel Castro's favorite fishing spot (and the site of the meeting with Anastas Mikoyan described in the previous chapter). The regime had invested a great deal of money in vast, outlandish schemes to develop the area. The destitute peat-and-tar collectors, the marsh's only inhabitants, were among the favorite sons of the Revolution, owing to their poverty and marginalization, and to Fidel's special affection. But neither the CIA nor the exiles knew this—or if they did, they did not share their knowledge with Kennedy or his principal advisers.[4] Nor did they explain to the newcomer at the White House that, in choosing the Bay of Pigs, he had eliminated a key contingency plan for the invaders in case they were unable to hold their position on the coast. They could no longer seek protection in the Escambray mountains, as Castro had done in the Sierra Maestra.[5] The new beachhead was miles away from the sheltering range, separated from it precisely by the impenetrable Zapata swamp.

On the U.S. side, the Bay of Pigs was a tragicomedy of errors. Reluctant to appear weak before the old cold warriors of the CIA and the Pentagon, Kennedy felt obliged to push ahead with the expedition. But he refused to provide it with the resources to succeed. The first air strike was launched from Nicaragua, and was immediately denounced at the United Nations by the Cuban Foreign Minister. Kennedy then postponed a second air strike (meant to destroy the Cuban air force on the ground) until the invaders' brigade had captured a landing strip near the Bay of Pigs, so he could plausibly claim that the marauding B-26 bombers had taken off from there. But the brigade was unable to secure the strip. Short of ammunition, it could not be resupplied because the ships anchored at sea could not approach the coast, defended as it was by the Cuban air force. The latter had not been destroyed, after all, because Kennedy did not authorize the second air strike.* The Bay of Pigs, as seen from Washington, was nothing but a series of misunderstandings. The CIA spurred Kennedy on, convincing him that the Cuban population would rise up in arms, and Kennedy in turn deceived his intelligence services. The operators in the field never believed that the President of the United States would stand by passively while an expeditionary force of almost 1,500 men, armed and trained by his own government, went down to defeat. But he did.

From the Cuban viewpoint, the Bay of Pigs proved two things: the Revolution's popular support, and Fidel Castro's political intuition. The Cuban leadership evidently knew about the bizarre landing before it happened. Its intelligence services had infiltrated the community of conspirators in Miami, and even the exiles concentrated in Guatemala. Cuba was ready to resist, and attempted to speed up arms deliveries from the Socialist bloc. But the Soviet MIG-17s, tanks, and armored transports did not arrive quickly enough. Nor was there enough time to train a regular professional

---

*Since January, a CIA memorandum had warned: "The Cuban air force and naval vessels capable of opposing our landing must be knocked out or neutralized before our amphibious shipping makes its final run into the beach. If this is not done we will be courting disaster. . . . The CIA wanted maximum air power; the State Department wanted it kept at a minimum so that the planes could ostensibly originate in Cuba." Peter Wyeth, *Bay of Pigs, The Untold Story* (New York: Simon and Schuster, 1979), p. 135.

army; the Rebel Army consisted of only 25,000 men. Castro had no choice but to arm the population. He would never have done so had he not been certain of their loyalty and support. The resulting 200,000 militiamen played a central role in Cuba's victory. They allowed Castro to deploy lightly armed, mobile forces to all possible landing points, forming a huge early-warning network. The militia's training was entrusted to the Department of Instruction of the Rebel Armed Forces, headed by Che since 1960. His contribution to the victory was thus crucial. Without the militias, Castro's military strategy would not have been viable; without Che, the militias would not have been reliable.

As a U.S. historian has said, Castro had enough political instinct that "when Kennedy firmly excluded the use of U.S. forces against Cuba, Castro believed him."[6] He comprehended that the White House plan—and the CIA blueprint it was based on—was to duplicate the Guatemala operation of 1954. It would include an indirect invasion, a beachhead, and a provisional government, followed by foreign assistance and recognition. Castro realized that the invading force had to be crushed immediately, before all this could happen. He would have to deploy all his forces at the invasion beachhead as quickly as possible. He also needed to make the best possible use of his tiny air force (fifteen dilapidated B-26s, three training T-33s, and six Sea Furies) to sink or disperse the expedition's supply ships, thus cutting off its reinforcements, communications, ammunition, and the fuel for its amphibious vehicles. To a large extent, the battle of the Bay of Pigs was won in the air.

Of course, Castro also had a strategy in the event of a direct American invasion. Raúl Castro would be in charge of defending Oriente province, Juan Almeida the center of the island, and Ernesto Che Guevara Pinar del Río, Havana, and the Occidente province as a whole. Thus, Che did not see combat at Playa Girón itself. Moreover, his sidearm accidentally went off when he dropped it a day before the battle, wounding him in the cheek, at the Consolación del Sur headquarters in Pinar del Río. He was forced to spend almost twenty-four hours in hospital, and was weakened for several days. In any event, Castro, convinced that Girón was the counterrevolutionaries' principal theater of operations, concentrated all his forces there from the second day. Everything would be won or lost at the Bay of Pigs. As it turned out, Fidel won. The native Cubans lost 161 men, and the Miami exiles 107. But 1,189 invaders from the ill-fated 2506 Brigade were taken prisoner. Castro would later send them back to Kennedy, in exchange for 52 million dollars in food and medicines.

Months later, Che Guevara thanked Kennedy's envoy to the Punta del Este Conference for the Bay of Pigs fiasco. "Thanks to you," he said only partly in jest, "we were able to consolidate the revolution at a particularly difficult time."[7] He was right. The Bay of Pigs allowed the regime to close ranks and tighten a few screws, mounting the formidable state security apparatus that would become the Committees for the Defense of the Revolution and the machinery of the Interior Ministry. In addition, from then on the government would—quite justifiably—be able to lambast all its opponents as U.S. agents or puppets. As the British ambassador informed the Foreign Office:

> Fidel Castro has managed in 1961 to lead his country well and truly into the communist camp against the wishes and instincts of the majority of people. This was a tour de force which, I believe, not even the prodigious Fidel Castro could have brought off had it not been for that blue-print for disaster, the April invasion—an operation which, as seen from here, made the Suez campaign look like a successful picnic. . . . I doubt whether United States prestige has ever been lower in any country than it was here shortly after the invasion.[8]

Between April 15 and 17, over 100 thousand presumed conspirators against the regime were detained in Havana and taken to the Blanquita Theater, La Cabaña fortress, the Matanzas baseball stadium, and Príncipe Castle. Their leaders were shot immediately or shortly afterward. The shift toward greater rigidity, or "dogmatism" as it would later be called, became even more acute. As Che confided to the Soviet ambassador, Sergei Kudriavtsev, "Cuba's counterespionage agencies were going to repress the counterrevolutionaries in a decisive way, not allowing them to raise their head again as had happened before the attack."[9] The government formalized its alliance with the Popular Socialist Party, which rapidly took advantage of the situation to attempt a takeover of it, the new Integrated Revolutionary Organizations (ORIs), the nucleus of the new party. As the British ambassador noted:

> Already an interlocking network of revolutionary committees, organisations and movements such as the Committees of the Defense of the Revolution, Rebel Youth Movements, Revolutionary Women Societies, have spawned over the countryside forming cells in factories, collective farms, army, militia and trades unions. Such evidence as we have shows that they have been carrying out their functions with a great deal more resolution, order and discipline than was ever expected of Cubans. Through them the Government operates and organises everything from the nationwide literacy campaign to village protest meetings, from the implementation of security measures against counterrevolutionaries to the distribution of ration tickets. Through them the Government stays close to the people and knows

what they are thinking. Through them again it is able to correct "wrong thinking," stop dissatisfaction before it spreads and use all just and unjust means of persuasion for the good of the cause.[10]

Above all, the Bay of Pigs allowed the regime to reassert its economic and political course, and to face down the United States in the eyes of the rest of Latin America. Che was entrusted with two tasks in the latter regard. First, he headed the Cuban delegation to the Punta del Este Conference in Uruguay. There Douglas Dillon, the U.S. Secretary of the Treasury, announced the details of the Alliance for Progress, which had been launched with great pomp on March 13, 1961. Che was quick to denounce the entire initiative. Strengthened by the Bay of Pigs, he castigated Dillon and the so-called Latin American Marshall Plan, as well as the "weak and sycophantic" governments of Latin America. Castro also asked Guevara to try to make contact with the U.S. administration, preferably through one of Kennedy's university-based, "best and brightest" young eggheads. Che accomplished both tasks with skill and assurance, though also with his characteristic hyperbole and intransigence.

The Cuban government had resolved some time before to attend the conference. Che communicated the decision to Kudriavtsev on July 26, though he asked him to keep it secret. Cuba's intention, he said, was to highlight the differences between the U.S. aid program, to be unveiled by Kennedy's envoy, and Soviet assistance to Cuba.[11] Che's designation as head of the delegation followed the same rationale as in his previous missions abroad. He was the only high-level Cuban leader, aside from Castro himself, qualified to play an international role; Raúl Roa, the foreign minister, lacked the charisma for such missions.

By now, Guevara had sized up perfectly the rationale of Washington's behavior. As he saw it, the Cuban Revolution was a major threat to U.S. interests in Latin America. The solution for the United States was to contain it by tolerating a lesser evil. The lesser evil involved transferring large amounts of resources to Latin America, while promoting limited social and political reforms to forestall any revolutionary aspirations within the Americas. As Che had foreseen almost a year before in his conversation with the Soviet ambassador in Havana,[12] the U.S. government's actual plan, derived from this strategy, was transparently obvious:

Give priority help to Latin America, especially during the next ten years, for improvement in health and education, reform of tax systems and administration, housing improvement, better and more equitable land utilization, construction of roads and other public facilities, establishment of productive enterprises and for better distribution of income.

Devote special attention to the improvement of rural areas and of living conditions of subsistence Indian and campesino groups.

Urge and assist all countries to establish long-term, balanced development plans.[13]

Che recognized that the U.S. strategy was ingenious, and accordingly designed an effective and far-reaching response. His plan reflected both the times and the prospects of the Cuban economy as he assessed them. This was the period when Nikita Khrushchev threatened to "bury" the Americans, and to surpass in ten years their production of steel (then considered by the Soviets the paradigm of modern industry). The Kremlin's thesis of peaceful coexistence had unleashed a fierce competition between the two superpowers, especially in terms of economic performance. Thus Che's reasoning at Punta del Este. The most incontrovertible proof of Cuba's superiority over the other countries of Latin America (until they consummated their own revolutions) would be its economy. Thanks to the Revolution, socialism, and Soviet assistance, the island would attain levels of development and well-being unknown in the rest of the region, despite U.S. aid. Che chose this area above all others because it was the most important for Marxists at the time, because it was his area of responsibility, and because it seemed the best way to solve the critical problems of Latin America.

He arrived in Montevideo on August 4. He was received by a youthful crowd (huge in some accounts, disappointing in others) that escorted him to Punta del Este, a beach resort frequented by the oligarchy of the Plate River region. Normally shut down during the southern winter, it had been refurbished for the conference. Che's trip was like a triumphant return home. His family and friends from school and university came from Argentina to see him. One of them recalls the scene: "He asked about his friends, though just the ones he was interested in, and the people he had loved, particularly Chichina and her uncles."[14]

Once again, he traveled without Aleida. It was a chance for him to bask in his mother's love and youthful memories, and in the adulation of personal and political groupies of both sexes. In a secret memorandum that Richard Goodwin sent to John Kennedy after meeting Che at a party, he reported that when the latter arrived "the women threw themselves at him."[15] His trip, then, had its social side, too, as he met with friends and family for long conversations in the hotels and casinos of the south Atlantic resort.

Guevara's speech at the Conference of the Inter-American Economic and Social Council addressed several important issues. First of all, he repeatedly reminded the other Latin American delegates that they should thank the Cuban Revolution for whatever U.S. assistance they might obtain:

This new phase is beginning under the sign of Cuba, a free land in America; and this conference and the special treatment your delegations have received and whatever loans are approved, all bear the name of Cuba, whether their beneficiaries like it or not.[16]

He was absolutely right, but his position could hardly ingratiate him with the other Latin American delegations. Guevara then compared the funds pledged by Dillon—20 billion dollars in the following decade, a substantial figure—with the amount proposed by Fidel Castro—30 billion dollars—in a speech in Buenos Aires two years earlier. He reflected that "with just a little more effort, [you] can reach thirty billion."[17] But, he noted, so far the U.S. Congress had approved only 500 million dollars to finance the Alliance for Progress. His message was not terribly diplomatic, but it made its point. The United States had realized that its options in Latin America were limited: either money or revolution. This could actually work in favor of submissive governments, if they did not allow themselves to be shortchanged by the "Yankees"—which would eventually happen anyway. Thus, in Che's opinion, the Alliance was doomed to failure.

Guevara presented a second, prescient idea in his list of demands. It was practically the original formulation of what later became the Third World agenda, taken up by many other countries subsequently regardless of their ideological affiliation. This was the first time that a developing country presented an international economic agenda to the industrialized world as a whole, on behalf of the entire Third World. The list included stable prices for the raw materials exported by poor countries; access to rich-country markets, and a reduction in tariffs and nontariff barriers to trade; financing without political conditions; financial and technical cooperation, and so on. All these ideas had been presented earlier by organizations like the Economic Commission for Latin America; they were also similar to the demands of Third World countries in later years. But Guevara's precision and eloquence gave them an exceptional prominence at Punta del Este. According to Dillon's report to Kennedy:

Dear Mr. President: Guevara speech was a masterful presentation of the Communist point of view. He clearly identified Cuba as full-fledged member of bloc talking of our sister Socialist Republics. Since he attacked Alliance for Progress in its entirety and everything conference is trying to do, he made little substantive impression on delegates. However, he was aiming over their heads at people of Latin America, and we cannot from here estimate how successful he was in this effort.[18]

The core of Guevara's speech lay in his comparative approach, as well as his impassioned and exorbitant predictions:

The growth rate cited as a great success for all America is 2.5%. . . . We are speaking of a development [rate for Cuba] of 10% without the slightest fear. . . . What are Cuba's plans for 1980? Well, a per capita income of 3000 dollars, more than in the United States today. . . . They should leave us alone; let us develop, and in twenty years we'll all come here again, and we'll see whether the swan song was revolutionary Cuba's, or their own.[19]

But, in fact, Che's position, in general terms, was moderate and conciliatory. During the ten days of the conference, he repeatedly emphasized Cuba's willingness to remain within the inter-American community, join the newly established Latin American Free Trade Association (LAFTA), refrain from sabotaging the Alliance, and try to reach an understanding with the United States. He even engaged in an outright falsehood to project a conciliatory, reasonable, and diplomatic image: "What we can give is a guarantee that not one rifle will leave Cuba, not a single weapon will leave Cuba [to be used] in any other American country."[20]

Perhaps the promise applied only to the future, as the exact opposite had been happening in the immediate past—indeed, under Che's direct supervision. But the pledge was not upheld in the following months or years either. In fact, preparations were already underway for several guerrilla expeditions to Venezuela. The Cubans could argue, as they did, that their promise depended on Washington's keeping its commitments, and that U.S. violations justified theirs. But in Punta del Este there was an unusually large gap between Che's rhetoric and his own awareness of the facts.

Over and beyond the self-persuading mechanisms that the Cuban revolutionaries have always used to justify their political shifts, Che's mandate at the conference was to try and temper his government's confrontation with Washington and the rest of Latin America—either in reality or in appearance. His speech was cautious with regard to the United States, especially in view of the huge expectations aroused by the international press. Observers had almost expected Guevara to mow down the delegates with his machine gun; they hoped he would call for a continental uprising, and curse the day the United States was born.*

The head of the U.S. delegation seems to have concluded that Che's moderation gained him significant support among the Latin Americans, and he attributed it to very specific reasons:

---

*A speech by Che a few days before the Bay of Pigs partly justified these fears. He referred to the Americans as "the new Nazis of the world . . . they don't even have the tragic greatness of those German generals who thrust all of Europe into the worst holocaust the world has ever known, and destroyed themselves in an apocalyptic ending. These new Nazis, cowardly felons and liars . . . [have been] vanquished by history." Ernesto Che Guevara, "Discurso a las milicias en Pinar del Río," April 15, 1961, quoted in Ernesto Che Guevara, *Escritos y Discursos*, vol. 5 (Havana: Editorial de Ciencias Sociales, 1977), p. 73.

Guevara has had no success in upsetting conference but I do not believe this was his primary purpose. He has by maintaining relatively moderate position during working sessions of conference made it considerably more difficult for any early action. . . . I am convinced that his primary purpose here was to forestall such action. In this I am afraid he has had considerable success.[21]

Similar motives might have led Che to meet with Richard Goodwin, Kennedy's young adviser and a junior member of the U.S. delegation at Punta del Este. Though the encounter was immediately taken up by the press, its content was not made public until 1968, when Goodwin published an article about it in *The New Yorker*. Over twenty years would pass, however, before Goodwin's memorandum to Kennedy was declassified. The account that follows is based on it.

The meeting was promoted by the Cubans, according to both Goodwin's report and several Brazilian and Argentine journalists and diplomats who were present as it got under way.* The episode began when an Argentine diplomat relayed a classic Che Guevara challenge to Goodwin: "Che said he sees that Goodwin likes cigars; he bets you wouldn't dare smoke Cuban cigars." Goodwin replied that he'd love to smoke Cuban cigars but that "he couldn't get them." That night two magnificent mahogany inlaid boxes of the finest Cuban cigars were delivered to his hotel room—one for him, the other for President Kennedy.† Along with them came a note with the best wishes of Comandante Ernesto Che Guevara. The next day, Goodwin received a message: Che wished to speak with him.[22]

A number of go-betweens attempted during the conference to bring Che and Goodwin together—with Che's approval, if not at his request. A new meeting was scheduled for the last day of the conference, but Dillon canceled it. But the public animosity between the two countries, especially after Cuba refused to vote in favor of the final declaration, made any such casual encounter impossible. After the conference ended, another effort was made to bring them together, this time successfully, during a party at the Montevideo home of a Brazilian diplomat. There the two officials finally met, first in a group and then privately in a small sitting room. The exchange lasted three hours. Goodwin's memo seems to corroborate that Che took the ini-

*Other journalists have provided a different version. One journalist present at the beginning of the meeting, Daniel Garric of *Le Figaro*, asserted that "President Kennedy had sought the meeting, and Guevara did not present any objections." Daniel Garric, *L'Europeo*, Milan, September 14, 1967, quoted in Gregorio Selser, *Punta del Este contra Sierra Maestra* (Buenos Aires: Editorial Hernández, 1969), p. 111.

† To this day, Goodwin keeps in his house in Concord, Massachusetts, the more elaborate box designated for Kennedy; he kept it quite visible in his offices at the White House and the State Department during the time he worked there. Goodwin, interview with the author, Concord, Mass., May 5, 1995.

tiative for the meeting, as he led the course of the conversation. The American limited himself to listening, taking note of Che's remarks for his report to Kennedy. Guevara, he says, expressed himself in a relaxed manner, without any polemics, propaganda, or insults—and often humorously. He "left no doubt that he felt completely free to speak on behalf of his government, and rarely made a distinction between his personal observations and the official position of the Cuban government. I had the impression that he had carefully prepared his comments; he organized them very well."[23]

The United States should understand, said Che, that the Cuban process was irreversible and Socialist in nature; that it could not be defeated through internal divisions or breaks, or in any other way aside from direct military intervention. He spoke of the Revolution's impact in Latin America, warning that Cuba would continue cultivating its links with the Eastern bloc based upon "the existing natural sympathy, and shared convictions about the appropriate structure of the social order." He then acknowledged the problems facing the Revolution: counterrevolutionaries and sabotage; the hostility of the *petite bourgeoisie;* the Catholic church; the lack of spare parts due to Cuba's conflict with the United States; and the shortage of hard currency. He emphasized the deficit in Cuba's foreign trade balance. The development process had been pushed too quickly, and hard-currency reserves were dangerously low. Cuba could no longer import the basic consumer goods required by its population.[24]

Predictably, Guevara stated that Cuba wished to seek a rapprochement with Washington, and was willing to take important steps toward that end. He proposed that Cuba pay for confiscated U.S. assets with tradeable goods; that it refrain from making military or political alliances with the Socialist bloc; and pledged to hold elections once the "single" party had been institutionalized. He even promised, laughingly, "not to attack Guantánamo." So far, nothing new. The plot thickened when Che broached the matter of promoting revolution in the rest of Latin America. He never admitted that Cuba had armed, trained, and sponsored guerrilla groups in other countries—after all, Brazilian and Argentine diplomats were present. But, he insinuated, he realized that any arrangement with Washington would imply the suspension of such activities, and Cuba would approach the subject on that basis.

When Goodwin returned to Washington the next day, he met with Kennedy and, at the President's request, drafted his memorandum. It circulated among the highest levels of the U.S. government; however, Goodwin recalls that Kennedy never responded to it in any formal or explicit way.[25] The memorandum recommended that the United States follow a more moderate policy toward Cuba—less "obsessive"—but one based, nonetheless, on covert activities and "the sabotage of crucial points in the industrial plant like the refineries." The government should "study the problem of an economic war against Cuba" through economic pressure, military maneuvers, disinformation, and propaganda campaigns.[26] But the text also recommended that the U.S. maintain an "underground" dialogue with Cuba, arguing that if Che—the most Communist-oriented government official— wished to explore the possibility of talks with the United States, "there might be other Cuban leaders even more willing to reach an understanding with the United States." This would perhaps reveal "divisions within the highest leadership."

Cuba's initiative did not prosper. It surfaced at an unpropitious time for Kennedy. The government of Rómulo Betancourt in Venezuela was under severe pressure from both the left and the military; a reconciliation with Cuba would have strengthened the left and led to a coup d'état. In addition, Castro had become too powerful, and any sign of détente would have been perceived as a victory for him. This in turn would "oblige the United States to resign ourselves to the existence of a Communist, anti-American government in Latin America, which would have made other movements elsewhere more attractive."[27]

As long as the Cubans do not open their own archives—if they exist— and the last informed persons still living refuse to speak, there is no way of ascertaining exactly what Fidel Castro and Che Guevara intended in seeking a dialogue with Washington. Guevara certainly minimized the importance of the meeting when he returned to Cuba and reported on his mission:

> We were invited by some Brazilian friends to an intimate gathering, and there was Mr. Goodwin. We had a meeting, . . . a social conversation between two guests at the house of their host, . . . neither one representing our respective governments at that moment. I was not authorized to have any sort of conversation with a United States official, nor was he. . . . In sum, it was a short, polite, indifferent exchange, as befits two officials from countries that are officially enemies, aren't they, which had no importance until some journalist or someone, some official, . . . gave it all that publicity. That was all.[28]

It is especially strange that Che, who a few months before the Bay of Pigs had assured the Soviet ambassador in Havana that any reconciliation with the United States would harm the cause of revolution in Latin America, should suddenly have changed his mind. And it is hardly likely that Fidel Castro would believe Kennedy open to any compromise with Cuba, when he had rejected it upon taking office—and even less so, after the Bay of Pigs. The CIA's explanation, and that of Douglas Dillon, for the shift in Cuban policy—though not for the encounter with Goodwin—was to speculate that

Castro was trying to avoid being ostracized at an upcoming meeting of the OAS. They also pointed to the growing economic crisis in Cuba.[29] Though the Cuban leadership might simply have been naive, its intention in speaking with Goodwin and sending a message to the White House may have lain elsewhere. It was perhaps an attempt to convince Brazil and Argentina (critical in the upcoming OAS condemnation of Cuba) of the regime's good will toward the United States. Alternatively, it might have been intended as a message to the Soviet Union, which had possibly insisted that Cuba try to reach an agreement with the United States before it entered the Socialist bloc and took shelter under Moscow's nuclear umbrella.

Khrushchev did not approve of Fidel's announcement of the Revolution's Socialist character in April. According to U.S. intelligence, Che asked him for missiles during his trip to Moscow at the end of 1960, but Khrushchev flatly refused.[30] It is also known that Castro's fervent adoption of Marxism-Leninism, barely hinted at on July 26, 1961, but fully explicit by December 1 of that year, was not well received by the Soviet leadership. The Kremlin harbored doubts about taking on a fragile Cuban economy. It is thus quite likely that Moscow jawboned the Cubans to exhaust all possibilities of dialogue with the United States, especially just two months after the unsuccessful Vienna summit between Kennedy and Khrushchev. In this hypothesis, Castro and Che obeyed Soviet instructions. They put forward their most anti-American leader, Che Guevara, to try and make contact with Washington, choosing a discreet but sufficiently public occasion to do so. Che presented quite reasonable proposals, in case the Americans themselves informed the Soviets about the conversation. When it became clear that, after so much effort, there would be no response from Washington, Khrushchev was left with no alternative but to help the Cubans.

Another possibility involves Che's mission to Argentina during those days. He traveled secretly from Montevideo to Buenos Aires for a lightning visit with President Arturo Frondizi. If one believes the rumor that circulated before the Bay of Pigs, Frondizi had proposed to Kennedy that he mediate the conflict with Cuba, along with his Brazilian colleague President Janio Quadros. The initiative went nowhere, but the idea lingered. When Frondizi noted Che's moderate stance, he probably thought the time was ripe to launch a new attempt at mediation. Their meeting, at the presidential residence of Los Olivos, lasted seventy minutes. Afterward, Che had a thick Argentine steak with Frondizi's wife and daughter and visited his own aunt María Luisa, before returning to Montevideo. It was his first sojourn in his native land since 1953, and would be his last. The mission was kept secret, as agreed—but not for long. Twenty-four hours later it erupted into a public scandal, precipitating the resignation of Argentina's foreign minister. Che Guevara's brief stay in the city of his youth caused such an uproar

that the coup d'état which toppled Arturo Frondizi less than a year later
was attributed by many to his visit.

Frondizi confusedly explained in a 1992 interview that John Kennedy
had asked him to meet with Che. The U.S. President wished to "repair relations with Cuba after the fiasco of the Bay of Pigs. Kennedy and [Brazilian
President] Quadros and I believed that Guevara was a Communist who was
a friend of the United States, while Fidel Castro was the USSR's man."[31]
The reasoning is both wayward and unlikely: there is no indication that
Kennedy ever believed anything of the sort.

Quadros, who awarded Che the High Order of the Cruzeiro del Sur two
days later in Brasilia, also suffered from the Guevara hex. He resigned the
presidency of Brazil one week later, in a strangely impulsive gesture that has
never been explained. A recently published book by his press secretary
describes some of the political complexities involved, and Che's behavior at
the award ceremony:

> Janio briskly greeted Cuba's revolutionary hero in his traditional olive-drab
> uniform. Che was tired and sleepy—he had traveled all night—and seemed
> terribly uncomfortable during the ceremony. Quadros awkwardly put the
> ribbon around his neck and gave him a box containing the diploma and
> medal. After Guevara's brief thanks, there was a strained silence. Janio
> invited Che to come into his office and, perceiving his discomfort, turned to
> his chief of protocol and instructed him, "Minister, take that ribbon off
> Guevara. . . ." The next day a rumor began to circulate that several military
> officers planned to return their decorations to the government, in protest
> over its tribute to Guevara. The rumors were true.[32]

In Havana, Che faced new and serious challenges. The most important
was the economy, whose performance Che himself had called the yardstick
of the Revolution in Punta del Este. It was in a nosedive. The other challenge was political: the time had arrived to institutionalize the Revolution
by creating a sole party with a vertical structure.

After the Bay of Pigs, Castro and the revolutionary leadership initiated
the long and difficult process of building a political organization. In July
1961, Fidel announced the establishment of the Integrated Revolutionary
Organizations (ORIs). They represented the convergence of three currents:
the 26th of July Movement, the Revolutionary Student Organization—or
what was left of it—and the Popular Socialist Party. In his speech of July
26, commemorating the assault on Moncada, Fidel baptized the incipient
party with a descriptive though not very exciting name: the United Party of
the Socialist Revolution. Despite his announcements, time passed and the
party failed to materialize. It was being organized by those few people avail-

able for the task—basically the Communists of the PSP, since those of the 26th of July and the student organization were busy with government and defense activities. And the Communists, led by Aníbal Escalante (the number two man since the 1940's), immediately set about building a traditional, old-style Party. They gradually took over the entire process, setting the rules of the game and placing their own men in leadership positions. Castro began to praise them in public in a rather disconcerting way. Not very plausibly, he announced his definitive conversion to Marxism-Leninism in December 1961. When Cuba was suspended from the OAS at the end of January 1962, at another meeting in Punta del Este Fidel issued a Second Havana Declaration, reiterating even more forcefully the Socialist character of the Revolution.

But the disputes within the revolutionary movement concerning the composition, nature, and goals of the new party were intensifying. A first ORI governing council was named on March 9. It consisted of thirteen *Fidelistas* and ten Communists, though some of the former were more loyal to the Party than to Fidel. The following weeks witnessed several attempts to restructure the leadership. Various public incidents, and a prolonged disappearance of Fidel, Raúl, and Che, pointed to a bitter internal struggle.* It came to a head on March 27, when Castro issued a violent diatribe against Aníbal Escalante, accusing him of "sectarianism" (which encompassed all conceivable political sins) and ousting him from the ORI leadership. This led to a general easing of the hard, orthodox, Stalinist line which had prevailed in Cuba for several months.

Che had never approved of the ORI's creation under the aegis of the PSP and Escalante. Along with Juan Almeida, Raúl Castro, and Osmany Cienfuegos, he played an active though discreet role in the investigation of Escalante's activities, which led to his ouster from the new party.[33] In an interview with an Egyptian magazine four years later, Che explained:

---

*A well-informed Western ambassador described the outcome in a confidential report to his capital, as follows: "The evidence suggests that a period of withdrawal from the public view was used by Castro both to rally the support of his personal followers and to prove to the old Communists that they could not maintain themselves in power without him. Finally, as an apparent compromise old Communists were given important positions in the economic sphere, most notably Rodríguez as President of INRA . . . while the new Communists were ceded a clear majority in the Directorate of ORI. Castro, with this majority support, was then able to drive out old Communist Aníbal Escalante, who was made the scapegoat for the policy of working to place control of the Revolution exclusively in the hands of old Communists, which Castro terms 'sectarianism.' " Ambassador George P. Kidd, Canadian Embassy, Havana, to Under-Secretary of State for External Affairs, Ottawa, May 18, 1962 (Confidential), Foreign Office Archive, FO371/62309 Ref. 8664, Public Record Office, London. The term "old Communists" refers to the PSP leaders; the "new Communists" are Fidel's men from the Sierra Maestra wing of the 26th of July Movement.

Escalante gradually began to take over all important positions. He used iso-
lationist ideas which did not allow the building up of a popular party. . . .
Some of them reached leadership positions and enjoyed various privileges—beautiful secretaries, Cadillac cars, air-conditioning, keeping the
warm Cuban atmosphere outside.[34]

Despite the accusations against Escalante, little changed. Che did not yet
distance himself from the Communists, though he began to view them differently. Something similar would occur a few months later with the Soviet
Union—after the October crisis, especially once he detected the difficulties
inherent in Socialist assistance to Cuba. The two issues were not unrelated.
For many observers and participants, it was no coincidence that Castro
launched his offensive against Escalante just a week after he instituted
rationing for a large number of basic goods. The step was necessitated by a
shortage of imports, due to pressure on the foreign-trade balance and a
trade deficit with the U.S.S.R. Under the leadership of Ernesto Guevara,
the Cuban economy was sinking rapidly.

Che was a man in a hurry—and not just in terms of the economy. As
Fidel Castro confided to Régis Debray in January 1967, he was always one
step ahead of the beat, both on the dance floor and in history.[35] Che's triumphant claims in Uruguay were only the tip of the iceberg. In Cuba he set
foolishly ambitious goals, both for himself and for the island's unhinged
economy. Not without reason: the backwardness, shortages, poverty, and
neediness of the masses, now dignified and emboldened by the Revolution,
seemed to require immediate action—even if it eventually proved unsustainable. In Che's view, with "85 percent of the economy in the hands of the
people, as well as all the banks, essential industries, and 50 percent of agriculture,"[36] the planning phase could now commence.

In mid-1961, he announced an ambitious four-year plan with outlandish
goals:

the adoption of an annual growth rate of 15%; to be self-sufficient by 1965
in food and agricultural raw materials except in those areas where material
conditions make it impossible; to multiply tenfold production of fruits and
other raw materials for the canning industry . . . ; to build 25000 rural
homes and 25000 to 30000 urban homes . . . ; to reach full employment
within the first year of the Plan . . . ; to keep consumer and wholesale prices
stable; to attain a harvest of 9.4 million tons of sugar by 1965; to achieve an
overall growth of food consumption of 12% annually.[37]

In a nutshell, Che sought to double living standards by 1965. The objective was to produce in Cuba most of the products previously imported; to
increase consumption, if only of basic goods; and to extend education and

health coverage to the entire population—all without reducing sugar output. The goals were admirable in themselves, but mutually incompatible. Che paid a heavy price for his lack of training and experience as an economist, but also for his eternal political flaw: there always prevailed in him a gap between strategy and tactics, the long and the short term, the grand vision and the daily workings of bureaucracy. Thus came about the collapse of the Cuban economy toward the end of 1961 and especially in 1962–63, as a consequence of both structural factors and management errors, largely acknowledged by Che himself in 1963.

The first error was to seek industrialization at top speed. Based on the Stalinist experience of the 1930s in the Soviet Union, it was further inspired by Cuba's victory at the Bay of Pigs, by Socialist-bloc assistance, and by political haste. Even if the Eastern-bloc countries had delivered on time the factories needed to produce previously imported goods, creating the new working class Che prayed for, two critical problems persisted. The first, and most intractable, was the shortage of raw materials. Where was Cuba to obtain the coal and iron to produce steel, the oils to make soap, the material for clothing, the leather for shoes? A certain quota of raw materials could be covered by the Socialist camp, but many had to be imported from hard-currency countries. And there were no foreign reserves—which was precisely the second problem. This had two causes. One was the very success of the Cuban Revolution: consumption rose substantially, thanks to the downward redistribution of income and wealth, as well as literacy and vaccination campaigns. The second reason, like so many things in Cuba, had to do with sugar.

Notable advances had been achieved in education. Before 1959, 40 percent of all children aged six to fourteen did not go to school. By 1961, the proportion fell to 20 percent. That year's literacy campaign reduced illiteracy from 23 percent to 3.9 percent (though these figures might not be entirely reliable). Altogether, almost 270 thousand teachers participated in the campaign, including 120 thousand adults.[38] By 1965, the percentage of children enrolled in school surpassed the Latin American average by 50 percent, and was higher than in any other country of the region.[39] Cuba built hospitals and clinics, organized vaccination campaigns, and made an enormous effort to train physicians, in order to replace those gone to Miami. All of this cost a great deal of money, generated further demands and aspirations, and provided few economic returns in the short term. But the political benefits were considerable, helping the Revolution overcome a severely trying economic situation.

Many foreign observers dismissed these advances. Some particularly perceptive ambassadors, however, like that of Britain, detected them and drew the relevant conclusions:

Since our own lives have become so much less pleasant, western diplomats here tend, I think, to forget how this section of the population sees the Revolution. Our social contacts are restricted to the few remaining upper middle-class counter-revolutionary Cubans—all naturally enough burnt up with prejudice and wishful thinking. We see little or nothing of the enthusiasm of peasants living in their new settlements, of the working class using former luxury clubs and the new public beaches for the first time, their children enjoying absurdly well-equipped kindergartens and sports grounds. Still more important are the natural and perfectly healthy emotional reactions of youth, most of it under-privileged, responding to a call to work together for a brighter future and a cause they believe to be just. We are badly placed to assess the strength of these emotions, of their convictions and of their feelings of loyalty.[40]

The problem resided in the meager domestic supply of goods and services, in the face of an ever-greater demand. This led to increasing imports which ate into already depleted foreign-currency reserves. Furthermore, exceptional projects like the literacy campaign or creating militias and sustaining them in a state of combat-readiness (independently of their social and political effects) also drew resources away from the domestic production of basic consumer goods.* Such goods soon became unobtainable in Cuba. Almost a year before rationing was introduced, on April 14, 1961, Che confided to the Soviet ambassador that it would be necessary, though politically disastrous, to ration cooking oil and soap.[41] There had also been food shortages since the end of 1960.

A second factor complicated things even more: sugar, as always in Cuba's history. Output was falling, due to drought, the early harvest of unripe cane in 1961, a more or less deliberate decision to reduce cultivated areas, and a shortage of manpower following the land reform: the *guajiros* who had received land refused, quite sensibly, to continue cutting cane.† Between 1961 and 1963, cultivated areas fell by 14 percent, mill capacity by 42 percent, and yield per hectare by 33 percent. In 1961, owing to inertia and the unseasonable harvest of immature fields, sugar production reached a record

---

*"The almost permanent mobilization of many young men in the army or the people's militias had a negative impact on the performance of industry in general." Ernesto Che Guevara, quoted in MID-1904-30-1-62, Sergei Kudriavtsev, "Memorandum of Conversation of December 8, 1961, with the Minister of Industry Ernesto Guevara," December 18, 1961 (Secret), Archives of the Foreign Ministry, Moscow.

† In fact, Che tried to moderate Fidel Castro's initial antisugar compulsion. Carlos Franqui recalls a meeting in 1961 in which Che objected to Fidel's publicly censuring cane production "because with Fidel's influence on cane in Cuba, there was a real danger that if he spoke against it, it would disappear. He made his antisugar speech anyway and the consequences were disastrous." Carlos Franqui, interview with the author, San Juan, Puerto Rico, August 20, 1996.

6.8 million tons; in 1962, it plummeted to 4.8 million, and in 1963 to 3.8 million. A study by English and Chilean economists with full access to the files of the Ministry of Industries described the catastrophe as follows:

> The unpredictable factors in the decline of 1962–63 were, first of all, the drought and, secondly, a deliberate government policy aimed at reducing sugar production to promote the longstanding objective of agricultural diversification. This decision . . . perhaps the single most important mistake in agrarian policy since the Revolution, was made at a time of great success, just after the 1961 harvest and the Bay of Pigs victory.[42]

The problem derived, in part, from an indisputable fact: the U.S.S.R. was not willing, or able, to bankroll Cuba's extravagance indefinitely. As Theodore Draper concluded, the Cubans had behaved after 1960 as if the Soviets had extended "not a $100 million five-year credit but an unlimited account."[43] The Soviets were calling in their debts. The Cubans' propensity for profligacy and negligence—fully shared by Che—is evident in a letter from the Minister of Industries to Soviet Deputy Premier Mikoyan, dated June 30, 1961. It includes a shopping list exorbitant in its cost and ambitiousness, requesting among other things: "an increase in the capacity of the first cast-iron processing plant, built by the U.S.S.R., from 250 thousand to 500 thousand tons; an increase in oil refining capacity from one to two million tons a year; chemical-industry and cellulose plants, valued at 157 million rubles; a thermoelectric plant for Santiago de Cuba, with a capacity of 100 thousand kilowatts; a variety of technicians and specialists."[44]

The combination of all these factors had a devastating effect on the economy, leading to an acute imbalance in Cuba's foreign accounts. Growing domestic consumption, plunging sugar exports, and a limited availability of hard currency bred an unsustainable deficit in the balance of payments, with far-reaching consequences for the future of the Revolution. The basic problem, as described by Hugh Thomas, was never solved—neither then, nor thirty years later. To escape the monoculture of sugar, Cuba needed to industrialize. To do so it required foreign currency, and the easiest way to obtain it, then as always, was by selling sugar. Perhaps Cuba could have saved hard currency by selling other commodities on a large scale. But the market for such an expansion was that of the U.S., which was now closed.[45]

Over and beyond these structural factors, a series of contingent circumstances also wreaked havoc with the Cuban economy. According to agronomists favorable to the regime, half the total production of fruit and vegetables was left unharvested in 1961 and 1962; bottlenecks in labor, transport, and storage had a calamitous effect on consumption and living standards. In March 1962, Fidel Castro had no choice but to decree rationing for a broad variety of staples: rice, beans, eggs, milk, fish, chicken, beef, oil, toothpaste, and detergent. Che had already presented an initial *mea culpa* on television, recognizing that he had designed "an absurd plan, disconnected from reality, with absurd goals and imaginary resources."[46]

Moreover, aid from the Socialist bloc did not fulfill Cuban expectations. Though the Soviets and their allies delivered what they had promised in terms of quantity, the quality and timeliness of their assistance left much to be desired. Their factories, consumer goods, and industrial inputs were less advanced and of far lower standards than Che had foreseen. Already in 1961, in a meeting with the Soviet ambassador, he unburdened himself. His criticism was directed at the countries of Eastern Europe, but one may assume it was also directed at the Soviet Union:

> Guevara noted that certain difficulties in the economy were being created
> by several Socialist countries. The Czechs, for example, have imposed a very
> tough trade policy on the Cubans, which in Che's opinion sometimes resem-
> bles a relationship among capitalist and not Socialist countries.[47]

Finally, a number of administrative choices executed by Guevara him-self—based upon his theoretical views—obstructed his management of the economy. They included highly centralized decision-making within Cuban state industries, and his attempt to abolish currency transactions among state-owned companies. The magnitude of the bureaucratic apparatus in his hands was mind-boggling: the entire sugar industry, the telephone and power companies, mining, and light industry—over 150,000 persons and a total of 287 companies, including chocolate and alcoholic-beverage facto-ries, printing presses, and construction firms. Che's schemes regarding cen-tralization and intercompany relations were evident from the moment he entered the Ministry, though they would not become points of friction with Soviet and Communist technicians until 1963–64, when they would be roundly defeated.

Initially weak, centralization became more and more pronounced. But from the instant the Ministry of Industries was established, every company had to transfer its total revenues to the Ministry's accounts; in return, each firm received the funds required to continue operating, for both current expenditures and investment. No company was allowed to keep cash. In addition, there were no monetary transactions among companies—so there was no possibility of a market. The Ministry's visionary projects for expan-sion bore no relation to reality:

> There were complicated plans to exploit the mineral deposits of Oriente so
> Cuba would become self-sufficient in steel, to build machinery of all types,

including mechanical sugarcane cutters, to create a new oil refinery, build new electrical facilities, expand the chemical industry, produce paper from cane trash and rubber from butane. . . . Since Cuba had such large nickel reserves, why should it not be the second largest producer in the world?[48]

Che's remarkable order and discipline served him well at the Ministry; but they also had their serious disadvantages. He expected others to impose the same degree of organization, punctuality, and attention to detail upon themselves as he imposed upon himself, and sincerely believed this would somehow resolve the Ministry's countless technical problems. One of his assistants recalls how Che administered the agency. He would arrive exactly at eight, and everybody had to be present at the morning meeting. At 8:10 he would close the Council door and nobody else could then enter, not even the deputy minister; and he would end at 12 sharp, even if someone was in the middle of saying, "I know how to overthrow imperialism in two days." At noon precisely Che would say, "Gentlemen, I'll see you in the afternoon." He had an amazing capacity to summarize meetings, presenting the conclusions of a three-hour session in ten minutes, and was in general exceptionally well organized: "Che did things nobody had done in Cuba before."[49] As another colleague, who had in other respects serious grievances against Che, remarked: "Che brought Cuba an administrative competence and diligence it had never achieved before, or ever since."[50]

This discipline existed alongside a compulsion to organize and micromanage everything, regardless of the damage done by similar efforts in the USSR and Socialist countries—which were, in many ways, better placed to succeed. According to the same aide, the Ministry's general policies were discussed at bimonthly meetings lasting the entire second Sunday of every other month, beginning at two in the afternoon and sometimes ending at two or three in the morning on Monday. Factories were grouped together by companies; the companies belonged to sectors, and the sectors supervised the companies. The person responsible for the mechanical sector, which consisted of nine companies, had at his fingertips all the production figures of the companies, as well as all the factories in the companies. He was accountable to a deputy minister of light industry, who had four sectors, and that deputy minister reported to the minister, who controlled all three departments: light industry, heavy industry, and industrial management. On the second Sunday of each month, rain or shine, Che discussed anomalies company by company—why it had not reached its production goals, in what category, and so on.[51]

The real origins of this extreme centralization and the ensuing complicated relations among companies were not exactly the ones Che suggested later on, during the dispute with his opponents. When the expropriations began, in 1960, some nationalized companies possessed ample funds of their own, while others were either flat broke or had very meager cash flows. At the INRA's Department of Industries, and especially at the National Bank, Che decided that all companies should deposit their resources in accounts at the central bank so they could be distributed according to the strategic priorities of the Revolution. The idea was not absurd, especially if one considers that revolutionary cadres tended to be better qualified at higher levels—say, at the National Bank—than within individual companies.

However, Che overestimated the administrative strengths bequeathed by Cuban capitalism to the Revolution, proclaiming real but insufficient reasons to promote centralization: the island's excellent communications (highways, telex, telephones), as well as its advanced accounting practices and the small size of the country. Once the decision was taken, it was easy to justify with all sorts of considerations that would make centralization more viable in Cuba than in the USSR. For instance:

> We are a small, centralized country with good communications, a single language, an ideological unity that is growing ever stronger, a unified leadership, an absolute respect for the highest leader of the Revolution, where there are no discussions, there is a unified management whose power nobody disputes. . . . The entire country is mobilized on behalf of a shared goal, if our cadres were obliged to travel due to any serious administrative problems, it would not take them more than one day because we even have planes; and there are telephones, telegraphs, now we are going to link all the companies through a telephone and microwave system.[52]

This was the logical and justifiable origin of what eventually became known as the Budgetary Financing System, which Che would later defend against Carlos Rafael Rodríguez and the Soviet technicians. But he soon began to advocate an extreme form of centralization and a total ban on monetary transactions among companies. His arguments rested more on Marxist theory than on economics, and revealed a peculiar indifference to actual conditions in Cuba. The bleeding of the middle classes, the administrative chaos that follows any revolution, the scarcity of goods due to the U.S. embargo, the lack of hard currency and experience, were all potential obstacles to the system envisaged by Che. The clockwork mechanisms with which he proposed to fine-tune the economy, which was indeed relatively small and manageable, simply did not exist in Cuba—or in any other country, capitalist or Socialist.

In February 1963, Che formulated his first justification for the system's excessive centralization in an article entitled "Against Bureaucracy" ("Contra el burocratismo"). Owing to its origins, the Revolution had initially spawned a sort of "administrative guerrilla warfare" in which everybody did as he pleased, "disregarding the central leadership apparatus." It had become necessary to "organize a strong bureaucratic apparatus" to implement a "policy for operational centralization, strongly curtailing the initiative of administrators."[53] Later, in 1964, Che would recognize that the system had serious drawbacks: a lack of cadres, excessive bureaucracy, incomplete information for decision-makers, and severe deficiencies in distribution.[54] But at the outset he was adamantly in favor of centralization, and a number of other ideas which helped exacerbate an already disastrous economic situation.

The task Che set himself was in all likelihood unrealizable. Rapid, intensive industrialization had been feasible in Stalin's Soviet Union thanks to its resources as the largest country in the world. However, it had taken a huge toll in human suffering, and had led to the weak economic foundations which would become apparent only years later. Mao's Great Leap Forward in China had also had disastrous consequences, at a human cost intolerable to a Western country like Cuba. Che could not possibly win with the cards he had been dealt. He assumed, wrongly, that Soviet aid and sheer determination (his own and that of his followers) would overcome the obstacles ahead. A less ambitious project might have achieved more lasting results and avoided painful setbacks before they occurred. But Che was incapable of a more limited vision. What's more, the political course he and Castro had chosen, both internally and externally, did not allow for more moderate plans. Given the international context, Cuba's resources, and the political goals of the Revolution, most of Che's theses were bound to triumph at first, only to be abandoned later—though their replacement no longer coincided with his ideas or sensibility.

The failure of Che's policies during those first years was reflected in his own rigorous process of self-criticism. In the initial phase, his vision was superficial and simplistic—though still more focused than that of the other leaders. Thus, at the first national meeting for production held on August 27, 1961, he threw down a challenge to his audience:

> You have received me with a warm round of applause. I don't know if you did so as consumers or simply as accomplices. . . . I believe it was more as accomplices. At [the Ministry of] Industries we have made mistakes that have resulted in considerable shortages in supplies for the population. . . . At every turn we have had to change directors, replace administrators, send others to improve their cultural and technical capacities, and others to improve their political positions. . . . The Ministry has often issued orders without consulting the masses, it has often ignored the labor unions and ignored the great working masses . . . and at times the decisions of the working class . . . have been taken without any discussion with the leadership

of the Ministry. . . . There is currently a shortage of toothpaste. We must explain why. In the last four months, production has been paralyzed; yet there was a large stock. The urgent measures required were not taken, precisely because there was a large supply. Then, the stock began to shrink, and the raw materials did not arrive. . . . Then the raw materials arrived, a calcic sulfate which did not have the required specification to make toothpaste. . . . Our technical comrades at the companies have made a toothpaste . . . which is as good as the previous one; it cleans just the same, though after a while it turns to stone.[55]

The audience at this meeting also witnessed one of the few public disagreements between Che and Fidel. After Guevara declared there was a "crisis in production," Castro announced that "there is no crisis of production," despite the criticism and complaints of his own economic officials. Rationing would be instituted six months later.

In 1962, Guevara increasingly questioned the Revolution's economic performance, especially at the Ministry's bimonthly meetings. He repeatedly criticized the Ministry itself and the evolution of the economy, though his analysis remained shallow and shortsighted. Che still believed that any problem could be solved by dint of enthusiasm, revolutionary fervor, and unbending determination. Charles Bettelheim, a French Marxist economist who held a heated debate with Che in 1964, recalls that Guevara systematically tried to talk his way through errors and problems. He would race from factory to factory, haranguing his audience.[56] When this did not work, he would stubbornly insist until he persuaded his public—or had to rush off to solve another problem.

Che explained his approach as follows:

As for the problem of enthusiasm, the lack of enthusiasm, the need to rekindle revolutionary enthusiasm, there is the concept of emulation. We have completely neglected emulation. It is fast asleep, it must be awakened at once. Emulation must be the basis that constantly moves the masses; there must be people who are constantly thinking of ways to rekindle it. It is not that difficult to look for ways, other ways, to engage people in the struggle.[57]

Che returned to this again and again, in a strange combination of realism and utopianism. He recognized the failings of the Revolution—and called for more of the same, though with greater dedication. He did not relinquish his beliefs or theoretical analysis. Only in 1964 would he seek a more complex explanation for the impasse reached by the Cuban Revolution. For the time being, however, he continued to express both lamentations and exaltation:

[Cuba is] the first Socialist country of Latin America, the vanguard of America, and there is no *malanga,* there is no yucca and there is none of anything else; and here [in Havana] rationing is more or less decent, but go to Santiago and there are four ounces of meat a week; everything is lacking and there are only bananas, and half the lard; here in Havana we have twice as much of everything. All of these things are hard to explain and we have to explain them through a policy of sacrifice whereby the Revolution, and the leaders of the Revolution, march ahead of the people.[58]

In mid-1963, Guevara began to formulate more explicit and substantive criticisms in his writing, speeches, and interviews. He anticipated the consequences, recognizing that any viable alternative to the policies followed in 1961–62 was indeed abhorrent—but necessary. Yet rather than continuing to strive for an impossible goal, or living ambivalently with an unavoidable but unacceptable situation, he preferred to flee—to Africa, Bolivia, and history. Any other course would have been despicable in his eyes. If Guevara had effected the changes in economic policy that were required, he could have stayed in Cuba with full honors, his position and prestige intact. But resigning oneself to the imperatives of realpolitik and economics is not the stuff of which myths, or heroes, are made. He soon perceived the quandary into which he, and the Revolution, had fallen. Guevara described it, with brutal frankness, to the Soviet ambassador as early as mid-1962. After requesting that construction proceed more quickly on an ironworks in Oriente whose opening had recklessly been announced for October, and about which Che had already written to Mikoyan, he admitted:

Our government has already made many different promises to the people, which it unfortunately cannot fulfill. I would not like our promise to build an iron and steel industry as the keystone of the country's industrialization to be in vain. Of course we should be more careful about the promises we make, and tell the people only about things we can really accomplish. But if the promises are already made, they must be fulfilled.[59]

In a speech delivered at a planning seminar in Algiers on July 13, 1963, Che noted a series of conceptual—not practical—errors that had given rise to Cuba's disastrous economic situation. First he placed them within a theoretical framework: "Essentially, in terms of planning we did two contradictory things, which were not compatible. . . . On the one hand, we copied in detail the planning techniques of a sister country; on the other, we remained spontaneous in many decisions, especially the political ones with economic implications, that needed to be taken daily in the process of government."[60] He provided an example of the lack of analysis and information that beset the Revolution during its initial years. The government had first proposed an annual growth rate of 15 percent, and then studied the ways to achieve it; but, "for a monoculture country, with all the problems I have told you about, to grow 15 percent was simply ridiculous."[61]

He then criticized more specific aspects of the regime's early economic policy. First of all, Cuba attempted to become self-sufficient in an array of intermediate and consumer goods that could be acquired more cheaply from friendly countries. Secondly, "we made the fundamental mistake of disdaining our sugar cane, trying to carry out an accelerated diversification, which led us to neglect the cane plantations, which together with a severe drought which afflicted us for two years, caused a serious fall in our cane production."[62]

Finally, Che revealed:

> In terms of income distribution, at first we gave too much emphasis to pay-ing fairer salaries, without sufficiently considering the real state of our economy. . . . We have a phenomenon where, in a country that still has unemployment, we lack labor in agriculture . . . and every year we have to levy volunteer workers.[63]

The new course—concentrating on sugar—resulted from policies dia-metrically opposed to those followed thus far. It was the only option, but not the one favored by Che. He grasped—possibly before anyone else—that the Revolution's economic policy was unsustainable, and he admitted it publicly, with his characteristic honesty and sincerity, so unusual in Cuba. But in 1962 he had not yet fully assimilated the implications of the disaster; he did not yet realize how distasteful the alternative would be. Not until Cuba signed a long-term sugar agreement with the U.S.S.R. on January 21, 1964, did he recognize that the only road still open to Cuba was unaccept-able to him.

Though his disenchantment with the Soviet alliance began in 1961, it would reach its climax only in the first days of 1965. Its real trigger was the Cuban missile crisis of 1962, when the world came closer to the nuclear precipice than ever before or since. Che's participation during those days in October extended through three phases: decisive before the crisis, almost nonexistent while it lasted, and extremely forceful in its aftermath.*

Che had invoked the Soviet nuclear umbrella several times in 1961. His major premise rested upon an indisputable reality: as long as the United States persisted in its attempts to overthrow the Havana regime by force,

---

*In recent years there have been many lectures and seminars about those memorable "Thirteen Days." While not everything has been clarified, a great deal of information has become available that was previously unknown. The following pages are based largely upon recent sources; they attempt to reconstruct Che's participation, rather than the crisis as a whole.

Cuba had the right and obligation to defend itself by all available means. Cuba had militias, a regular army, a flimsy air force, and huge popular support, but even all together these were not very formidable. The deployment of Soviet short- or medium-range missiles in Cuba would be a powerful deterrent. From this perspective, Cuba would become a sort of nuclear tripwire for Soviet ballistic weapons. Any attack against the island would be countered by the USSR from Cuba, in a rationale similar to that for the U.S. missiles stationed in Germany and Turkey. The Cubans were understandably convinced, until the summer of 1962, that Kennedy, the CIA, and Miami would seek revenge for the Bay of Pigs at any cost, in a new invasion attempt.

John F. Kennedy had assured several Latin American leaders—from Rómulo Betancourt of Venezuela, in December 1961, to Adolfo López Mateos of Mexico, in June 1962—that the United States "did not foresee for the time being any unilateral action against the Castro regime."[64] But Havana believed the exact opposite—or at least it wanted the Soviets to think so. Castro pointed to a conversation between Kennedy and Alexei Adzhubei, a journalist and political operative of Khrushchev's who was also the Soviet premier's son-in-law and the director of *Izvestia*. According to Adzhubei, during a three-hour lunch at the White House on January 31, 1962, Kennedy conjured an analogy with Hungary to justify his policy toward Cuba. Adzhubei concluded (in a report to Khrushchev forwarded to Castro) that the U.S. President was once again bent on toppling the Havana regime by force of arms.* Recent statements by Soviet sources continue to suggest that it was the Adzhubei report which led the Cubans to insist on the issue of their defense. As a result, in the last days of April or early May 1962, Khrushchev convinced himself that Washington was determined to destroy the Castro regime.[65]

Aleksandr Alexeiev—named Ambassador to Cuba in May 1962 after Kudriavtsev had earned Fidel's animosity—recounts a meeting he attended

*The Americans have always questioned the veracity of Adzhubei's account, but they have not yet declassified their own official memorandum of the conversation. The history of Kennedy's conversation with Adzhubei began with a report by French journalist Jean Daniel, published shortly after JFK's death. Daniel quoted Fidel Castro as saying that the Adzhubei report convinced him of a new U.S. invasion plan. In December 1963, Kennedy's press secretary, Pierre Salinger, and McGeorge Bundy, his National Security Adviser, both asserted (the former in public, the latter in a private memorandum to columnist Walter Lippmann) that Kennedy never used the Hungarian analogy as Adzhubei interpreted it. Kennedy never meant it as a threat, but as an example of how a superpower can become nervous when it sees a hostile group emerge near its border. Both Salinger and Bundy insisted that Kennedy was categorical in his statement to Adzhubei, when he said that the United States had no intention of invading Cuba. See McGeorge Bundy, Memorandum for Walter Lippmann, December 16, 1963, and Transcript, White House News Conference with Pierre Salinger, December 11, 1963, pp. 9–10.

in the Kremlin. He was summoned to an office next to Khrushchev's. The meeting included the premier himself, Deputy Premier Anastas Mikoyan, Frol Kozlov (secretary of the Communist Party's Central Committee), Minister of Defense Malinovsky, Foreign Minister Andrei Gromyko, and Marshal S. S. Byiruzov, the commander of the Soviet strategic missile force. In Alexeiev's words,

> Khrushchev started off by asserting, "We can only help Cuba by taking a very serious step. If Cuba agrees, we will place medium-range missiles on the island." Then he asked: "How will Fidel take the news?" Mikoyan replied that Castro would never agree, as his strategy was based on the force of Latin American and world public opinion. If USSR missiles and bases were stationed in Cuba, it would place itself in the same situation as U.S. semidominions. Everyone fell silent except Malinovsky, who exclaimed, "How can a Socialist revolution not accept our help; even the Spanish Republic accepted it!" They all decided to send a delegation to Cuba, consisting of Rashidov [Sharif Rashidov, the party leader of Uzbekistan], Byiruzov, and myself. Khrushchev warned us before we left: "We do not want to lead Cuba into an adventure, but the Americans will accept the missiles if we install them before their elections in November."[66]

The Soviet delegation arrived in Havana in early June. They were met at the airport by Raúl Castro, who was still unaware of the purpose of their visit. Byiruzov was even traveling incognito, under the guise of an engineer named Petrov. Alexeiev confided to Raúl that Petrov was actually the commander of Soviet ballistic-missile forces, and that he requested an urgent meeting with Fidel. The latter received them immediately. Alexeiev took notes, both in order to translate and for the historical record; according to those notes, the Soviets began by stating that Khrushchev believed the strongest way to help Cuba was to place missiles on the island. Fidel replied that the idea was very interesting, but not necessary to save the Cuban Revolution. Conversely, if such a step could strengthen the Socialist bloc, it was worth thinking about. In any case, he could not answer immediately.[67] Another meeting took place the following day. Cuba was represented by Raúl and Fidel Castro, Che Guevara, President Osvaldo Dorticós, Carlos Rafael Rodríguez, and Emilio Aragonés. Fidel gave the Cuban reply: yes— not to bolster the Cuban Revolution, but the Socialist bloc. As Castro would admit thirty years later,

> We did not like the missiles. If they had been only for our defense, we would not have accepted them. Not so much because of the danger, as the damage they might inflict on the image of the revolution . . . in Latin America. The missiles made us into a Soviet military base, which would have a high polit-

ical cost for our image. If the issue had been only our defense, we would not have accepted the missiles.[68]

Fidel Castro decided to send Raúl to Russia in order to finalize the compact. Shortly afterward the Cuban defense minister traveled to Moscow, where he received from Marshal Malinovsky a draft text which he examined page by page. The agreement proposed sending 42,000 Soviet troops and forty-two 24-meter missiles to Cuba. Khrushchev asked that the delegation refrain from contacting Havana by radio or telegraph, in view of the danger of American interception. The element of surprise was crucial. In August, Alexeiev returned to Cuba with the revised text in his portfolio; he transmitted it to Fidel Castro, who found it too technical. He asked the Soviets to specify how Cuba asked for their help, and to include a more political preamble. As the covenant could not be negotiated through regular communications channels, somebody had to fly to Moscow. Fidel decided to send Che and his closest aide, Emilio Aragonés, the secretary-general of the incipient Unified Revolutionary Party.

These facts are not disputed by Soviet sources. But American participants, even thirty years later, retain a very different perception of the crisis. Meetings in Cambridge and Hawk's Cay in 1987, Moscow in 1989, and Havana in January 1992 brought together several of the principals involved, allowing them to review their interpretations. Robert McNamara (U.S. Defense Secretary at the time), McGeorge Bundy (National Security Adviser), and Theodore Sorensen (Kennedy's top political aide) have stated that none of them ever fathomed Khrushchev's motivations. They always supposed that they involved the strategic balance, Berlin, the U.S. bases in Turkey, or internal struggles within the Kremlin, rather than Cuba itself. Sorensen, for example, speculated that if Khrushchev did not act publicly, signing an open agreement with Cuba, he must have had some more mysterious motive.[69]

American sources also differ—both among themselves and with their Cuban and Soviet counterparts—as to the true nature of U.S. policy toward Cuba. In Bundy's words, "I remember that in the fall of '62 there was great frustration about Cuba and considerable confusion about what we should do. In my opinion, covert action is a psychological salve for inaction. We had no intention to invade Cuba, but it seems . . . that there was a very solid picture in Moscow that we were going to do something more than we were."[70] McNamara explained, for his part, "Let me say that we had no plan to invade Cuba, and I would have opposed,the idea strongly if it ever came up. . . ." He then qualified his statement, saying, "Okay, we had no intent. . . . That's my point. We thought those covert operations were terribly ineffective, and you thought they were ominous. We saw them very differently."[71]

Sergo Mikoyan (who accompanied his father, Anastas, to Cuba in November 1962) states categorically that the notion of installing missiles on the island originated with Khrushchev, who saw no other way of fore-stalling a U.S. invasion.[72] When McNamara asked Andrei Gromyko in 1992 why the Soviets deployed missiles with nuclear warheads in Cuba, the for-mer foreign minister replied with brutal clarity that "[the Soviet] action was intended to strengthen the defensive capability of Cuba, and to avert the threats against it. That is all."[73] According to Mikoyan, Khrushchev first insinuated the convoluted, half-baked scheme to his father at the end of April 1962. The deputy premier dissented, arguing that the Cubans would reject it, and the Americans would find out and raise hell. He was aston-ished by Fidel's acceptance, and by Biryuzov's pledge that the missiles would be deployed in secret. Sergo Mikoyan does not deny that the Soviet military might have had ulterior motives; but, like the other Soviets, he swears that the main reason for sending missiles to Cuba was the defense of Cuba, though, of course, Malinovsky and others talked of the strategic bal-ance. The problem was that Khrushchev did not think through the U.S. reaction. He believed that after they were informed of the missiles, U.S.-Soviet relations would improve.[74]

Perhaps Khrushchev was seeking an inexpensive way to improve his country's nuclear balance with the United States. Perhaps the Soviet mili-tary wanted to test the Americans' defense and intelligence systems. But if Khrushchev used Castro, it worked both ways. Though the initiative for the missiles might have originated in Moscow, Fidel and Che had pulled the Soviet missile card several times; Carlos Franqui even asked Khrushchev about it in Moscow.* Oleg Daroussenkov, Che's Russian teacher in Havana (later in charge of Cuban relations at the Central Committee of the Soviet Communist Party), was astounded by his first conversation with Guevara and the Soviet Embassy's economic attaché, Nikolai Kudin, in July 1961: " 'All right, Kudin,' Che asked, 'are the Americans going to attack us or not?' The Americans were just over the horizon, and Che seemed to be say-ing that the missiles were needed so they wouldn't come in."[75]

So the idea did not suddenly appear out of the blue; many people had already conceived it. Fidel Castro emphasized in 1992 that he himself had refrained from mentioning it in his speeches, while suggesting that Khru-shchev and "several comrades" (perhaps including Che) had discussed it

---

*One Che biographer asserts, without providing sources, that Che said in 1960, in Moscow, "This country is willing to risk everything in an atomic war of unimaginable destructiveness, to defend a principle and protect Cuba." Philippe Gavi, *Che Guevara* (Paris: Editions Universitaires, 1970), p. 96.

publicly.[76] Actually, Castro did refer to the missiles at least once in 1960, as noted in the previous chapter.

In any case, when Che and Emilio Aragonés arrived in Moscow to revise the agreement in September, they found that Khrushchev was on holiday in the Crimea. Welcomed by Leonid Brezhnev, already an important figure in the USSR hierarchy, they were promptly brushed off and told: "No, no, go and see Nikita, take the plane and go there, I don't want to know anything about this. Take it up with Nikita."[77] The Cuban envoys left immediately for Yalta. In their meeting with Khrushchev, they threshed out the crucial issue of secrecy. Like Mikoyan at the time and Sorensen thirty years later, they questioned whether it was feasible, or even desirable, to keep the operation shrouded clandestinely. Their discussions with the Soviet premier took place on a pier at the edge of the Black Sea, where all sat huddled together in the early autumn chill: Khrushchev, Malinovsky, a military interpreter, Che, and Aragonés. The Cubans' main concern was to persuade Khrushchev that the missile operation in Cuba could not be kept secret for long. Their intelligence had already collected data about Cuban émigrés traveling to the United States to visit their families, or writing to relatives, reporting that missiles were being deployed. Several had discovered a truck loaded with missiles. Khrushchev turned a deaf ear, simply concluding, "We must hurry."[78]

Che maintained that the two countries should sign a public military treaty.[79] Khrushchev replied that this was not possible, especially as the balance of military forces was detrimental to the USSR. He promised he would send the Baltic fleet to North America if the Americans found out and anything happened, in order to restore the balance to some degree.[80] Fidel Castro later corroborated this account, indicating that he himself instructed Che and Aragonés to insist that the military accord be made public—and, if necessary, the missiles' deployment as well. Khrushchev declined. As Castro was intent on "letting Nikita take the final decision,"[81] the course was set. Khrushchev ended the meeting with characteristic bravado and bluff: "If the Yankees find out about the missiles, I will send the Baltic fleet."[82]

Che and Aragonés had their doubts. They wondered if it would really be possible to deploy the Baltic fleet beyond its home waters for the first time since 1905, but they finally acceded to the Soviet decision.[83] Khrushchev then accepted all the Cubans' amendments to the text, "down to the last comma."[84] Yet when Che returned to Havana in mid-September after a week's absence, he was uneasy. If the project could not be made public, was it sustainable? In the words of Aragonés,

> The problem was not sending the missiles. They said the missiles were to protect Cuba's independence from an American attack. But it would have

been sufficient to have a solemn declaration by the Soviet State, saying that if [the United States] attacked Cuba it would be an attack on the Soviet Union. The piece of paper would have been important, though of course the missiles were far more important than the piece of paper. We in Cuba wanted a public pact, because that nut Khrushchev took the decision together with only six members of the Cuban Communist Party leadership: Fidel Castro, Raúl Castro, Che Guevara, Blas Roca, Carlos Rafael Rodríguez, and Emilio Aragonés. Nobody else knew anything about it.*

Che did not yet mistrust the USSR; he did not even imagine that Khrushchev might withdraw the missiles in the event of a confrontation with Washington. Nor had he fully assimilated the Soviets' pathetic nuclear inferiority compared with the United States. He still believed there was an essential parity between the two superpowers. Guevara even scolded Aragonés for expressing his reservations; the Argentine was firmly convinced of Soviet resolve. On the way back, they encountered several Cubans in Czechoslovakia to whom Aragonés complained about the agreement. Che retorted, "How can you say that!" Guevara had bought the deal, lock, stock, and launching pad.[†]

In retrospect, Khrushchev's position was less harebrained than it seemed at the time, and Che's predictions proved only partially accurate. It is now known—because Soviet participants insinuated as much at the Moscow meeting of 1989, and Fidel Castro stated so categorically at the Havana conference of January 1992—that twenty of the forty-two Soviet missiles deployed in Cuba were armed with *nuclear warheads.* And six tactical missile launchers, loaded with nine missiles with *nuclear tips,* were ready to be used in the event of a U.S. invasion.[85] They entered Cuba without Washington's realizing it. Arthur Schlesinger and Robert McNamara, who both attended the Havana conference, almost fell off their seats when they heard this.[86] Furthermore, the number of Soviet troops sent to Cuba was much larger than the Americans suspected. They estimated 4,500 in early Octo-

---

*As Castro later stated: "The USSR could have declared that an attack on Cuba would have been the equivalent of an attack on the Soviet Union. We could have had a military accord. We could have achieved our goal of defending Cuba without the presence of the missiles. I am absolutely convinced of it." Fidel Castro, "Transcripción de sus palabras en la conferencia sobre la Crisis de Caribe," Havana, January 11, 1992, Foreign Broadcast Information Service, quoted in The National Security Archive, Lawrence Chang and Peter Kornbluh, eds., *The Cuban Missile Crisis* (New York: The New Press, 1992), pp. 336–337.

† Emilio Aragonés, interview. It is worth noting an element that careful readers will already have noticed: the accounts given by Emilio Aragonés and Aleksandr Alexeiev are virtually identical, including details, sequence, and causal explanations. Needless to say, there is no longer any communication between them. Aragonés lives in Havana, a semi-outcast retiree; Alexeiev, now elderly and ill, spends much of his time in a *nomenklatura* hospital on the outskirts of Moscow. The two men's accounts are remarkably similar, because they were both marked by the events in question—and because they are true.

ber, 10,000 at the height of the crisis, and 12,000 to 16,000 at its end. In reality, 42,000 soldiers entered Cuba, disguised with winter clothing and even snow skis. Castro has confirmed this figure, also put forth by Alexeiev and Mikoyan.[87] In other words, the Soviets were able to deploy missiles, atomic warheads, troops, and sophisticated antiaircraft equipment in Cuba before American intelligence caught on. So much so that Walt Rostow, then a State Department adviser, reported to President Kennedy in a "top-secret and sensitive" memorandum dated September 3, 1962 (less than a month before the crisis) that "on the basis of existing intelligence the Soviet military deliveries to Cuba do not constitute a substantial threat to U.S. security."[88]

The problem was not keeping the missiles secret, but what the Soviets were willing to do with them once they had been introduced into Cuba. Neither Khrushchev nor the missile commander in Cuba dared give the order to fire when the confrontation escalated. True, Soviet military officers in the field were authorized to launch the missiles with nuclear warheads; and the U-2 spy plane shot down over Cuba on October 27 was attacked under instructions from the Soviet base in Cuba—not Moscow. The crisis intensified; Kennedy, on learning that there were Soviet missiles on the island—and others on the way—ordered a naval blockade, demanding their withdrawal. Khrushchev first blustered, then blinked (in Dean Rusk's famous phrase). On October 28, he yielded to the U.S. ultimatum. The missiles were to be withdrawn under United Nations scrutiny (which Castro never accepted). In exchange, the United States promised the U.S.S.R. not to invade Cuba—a pledge never made in writing—and to withdraw its (obsolete) missiles from Turkey, in a *quid pro quo* Washington never acknowledged.

Castro felt terribly insulted, cheated, and spurned by the U.S.S.R.—both because of its surrender and because he learned of its decision on the radio. Enraged, he called Khrushchev a "sonofabitch, a bastard, an asshole."[89] He soon recovered his dignity, but was unable to deter the missile withdrawal. A couple of days later, he declared at Havana University that Khrushchev "had no *cojones.*"[90] That very day, Fidel rejected the U.S. promise not to invade Cuba and submitted five demands: an end to the blockade and other forms of harassment by Washington, an end to exile activities against his government from the U.S., an end to all overflights, and the return of Guantánamo.

The cry that echoed through Havana in those days—*"Nikita mariquita, lo que se da no se quita"* (Nikita you fairy, what you give you can't take back)—reflected the general mood in Cuba, among both the people and the revolutionary leadership. Khrushchev's decision proved costly. It was immediately criticized by the Chinese, who termed it "the worst treason since that of German Social-Democracy at the beginning of the First World War,"[91] and by the premier's enemies within the Soviet Union. Though his removal in October 1964 was not a direct consequence of the Caribbean fiasco, it must have played some role. Khrushchev attributed enormous importance to relations with Cuba, and also to China's criticism of Moscow. This is amply illustrated in an extraordinary letter he sent Castro on January 31, 1963, made public only in January 1992. Thirty-one pages long, it is laced with barely disguised diatribes against the Chinese, and a few ominous observations about Cuba. Khrushchev insists that Castro visit the U.S.S.R. in the spring, inviting him to fish, hunt, and walk with him in the country-side, to heal the wounds of October. In his words,

> . . . it seems to me that this crisis has left a mark, although barely visible, in the relations between our states. Speaking frankly these relations are not what they were before the crisis. During the Caribbean crisis, our view-points did not always coincide, we did not see the different stages of the cri-sis in the same way. . . . I will not hide from you, it would be senseless to do so, that any imprudent step or even any roughness in our relations could today generate several problems. One ill-advised step or one wrong sentence could make us, and you, think. It is possible that under normal conditions, no one would attach any importance to this; but under the conditions that have now been created, I would say that serenity and self-control are neces-sary. I have already told you, comrade Fidel, that there now exists, in our relations with you, a certain amount of resentment, and that this harms the cause, and naturally, harms Cuba and harms us. Allow me to tell you with-out beating around the bush: this harms our party and our country, but these difficulties cannot benefit you either. . . .[92]

Castro accepted Khrushchev's invitation. During his stay in the U.S.S.R. he renegotiated several economic and military accords, and put aside the anger and tensions of the previous October and November. He did not have much choice; Khrushchev could not continue helping Cuba while it accused him of caving in to United States intimidation. Indeed, the Soviet premier had already dispatched Mikoyan to Havana in November to sue for peace and attempt to restore the Soviet Union's badly tarnished image before his Chinese rivals and world public opinion. For three weeks, "Moscow's Cuban" (as he was known at home) tried to convince the Cubans to accede to the different parts of the agreement with Kennedy and, especially, to tone down their criticism of Khrushchev. He succeeded only in part.

Che Guevara was largely absent from the decisions taken during the Octo-ber crisis as such. As at the time of the Bay of Pigs, he was sent to Pinar del Río as commander of the entire western region, ready to repel a U.S. inva-sion or, if necessary, to lead the subsequent guerrilla struggle. Rafael del

Pino, a pilot hero of the Bay of Pigs, was summoned by Fidel Castro on the second day of U.S. overflights to advise him on air force strategy. According to Del Pino, who served as Fidel's personal aide throughout the crisis (even sleeping next door to his headquarters), Che did not meet with Castro until the crisis subsided on October 28.[93] They may have been in contact by telephone, but as the Cubans lacked scramblers to encrypt their communications, they can hardly have sustained any substantive exchanges.[94] The persons closest to Fidel during the crisis, according to Del Pino, were the Communist Flavio Bravo and the army's head of intelligence.[95]

Che may not have participated in the intricate details of the Cuban missile crisis, at least not in its October phase; however, he played a significant role in its aftermath. According to Guevara's biographer Ricardo Rojo, Che was with Fidel when he learned of the Soviet decision, kicking the wall in a fit of rage.[96] Che was more resigned to the outcome, but, unlike Castro, he was sickened by the implacable realities of world politics during the Cold War.* He was not as discreet as Fidel in concealing his distaste, confessing his anger to the British Communist Party daily paper (though the interview was not published in its entirety) as follows:

> If they attack, we shall fight to the end. If the rockets had remained, we would have used them all and directed them against the very heart of the United States, including New York, in our defense against aggression. But we haven't got them, so we shall fight with what we've got.[†]

Che's intolerance for ambivalent emotions was catching up with him. He had been in an angry mood since the end of the crisis, as he admitted to his closest Soviet friend, Oleg Daroussenkov. After the missile crisis, when they enjoyed target practice together and talked things over, Che "complained that he could not discuss anything with those big shots, meaning

---

*Che's letter to Anna Louise Strong in Beijing, on November 19, 1962, reflects his terrible ambivalence: "The situation here in Cuba is one of combat alert; the people await an attack on a war footing. . . . If we come to lose (which will happen after selling our lives very dear) people will be able to read in every nook of our island messages like those of Thermopylae. But anyway, we are not studying our pose for a final gesture; we love life and we will defend it." Ernesto Che Guevara, letter to Anna Louise Strong, November 19, 1962, quoted in Ernesto Che Guevara, *Cartas inéditas* (Montevideo: Editorial Sandino, 1968), p. 14.

† Ernesto Che Guevara, "Interview with the *Daily Worker*," November 1962, reproduced in *Foreign Broadcast Information Service Propaganda Report, Changing Pattern of Fidel Castro's Public Statements,* December 7, 1962, pp. 23–24. The report asserts that the first three sentences quoted here were not included in the published text of the interview, though the *Daily Worker* correspondent did transmit them to London. Ibid., p. 25. Carlos Franqui has corroborated this omission, suggesting that Castro may have spoken to Guevara on the phone in this regard, perhaps regretting how Che always said what he thought. Carlos Franqui, interview with the author, San Juan, Puerto Rico, August 20, 1996.

Khrushchev. One day they say one thing, and the next day another. Khrushchev had assured him that if anything happened he would send the Baltic fleet to Cuba—and where was the fleet? Guevara was furious."[97]

Che must have perceived the Soviet surrender as a betrayal; to some extent, he regretted that the crisis had not culminated in a final sacrifice:

> [We have] the harrowing example of a people ready to sacrifice itself to nuclear arms, that its ashes might serve as a basis for new societies; and, when an agreement is reached without even consulting it, and the atomic missiles are withdrawn, it does not breathe a sigh of relief, it does not give thanks for the respite. It enters the fray to make heard its own, unique voice; its own, unique fighting stance; and beyond that, its determination to struggle, even alone, against all dangers, and even the atomic threat of Yankee imperialism.[98]

Che was present at all the discussions with Anastas Mikoyan except one. Most of his initial comments were devoted to emphasizing the pernicious effects on the Latin American revolution of the Soviet cave-in. And also to cracking macabre jokes, that nonetheless contributed to making everybody relax, up to a point. On one occasion, the Soviet interpreter Tikhmenev had Castro insultingly comparing Mikoyan with U Thant; Mikoyan blew up, first, mistakenly, with Fidel, then with his translator, upon realizing that the offense was attributable to Tikhmenev, not to Castro. Che suggested a brief break, unholstered his Makharov automatic pistol, and placed it at Tikhmenev's side. He then quietly suggested that the interpreter shoot himself, since after Mikoyan's outburst there really was no future for him in the translation business.[99]

The final exchange between Che, Mikoyan, and Alexeiev (made public in 1995 by U.S. and Russian researchers) is of exceptional interest. It reveals Guevara's frame of mind, and the chasm already separating him from the Soviet leadership. As a conclusion to Che's golden years in Cuba, and a preamble to the decisions and disillusions ahead, it is worth quoting in its entirety:

> GUEVARA: I would like to tell you, Comrade Mikoyan, that, sincerely speaking, as a consequence of the most recent events an extremely complicated situation has been created in Latin America. Many communists who represent other Latin American parties, and also revolutionary divisions like the Front for People's Action in Chile, are wavering. They are dismayed . . . by the actions of the Soviet Union. A number of divisions have surfaced. New groups are springing up, factions are springing up. The thing is, we are deeply convinced of the possibility of seizing power in a number of Latin American countries, and practice shows that it is possible not only to seize it, but also to hold power in a range of countries, taking into account practical experience. Unfortu-

nately, many Latin American groups believe that in the political acts of the Soviet Union during the recent events there are contained two serious errors. First, the exchange [the proposal to swap Soviet missiles in Cuba for U.S. missiles in Turkey—ed.] and second, the open concession. It seems to me that this bears objective witness to the fact that we can now expect the decline of the revolutionary movement in Latin America, which in the recent period has been greatly strengthened. I have expressed my personal opinions, but I have spoken entirely sincerely.

MIKOYAN: Of course, it is necessary to speak sincerely. It is better to go to sleep than to hear insincere speeches.

GUEVARA: I also think so. . . . The USA, by achieving the withdrawal of Soviet missiles in Cuba, in a way received the right to forbid other countries from making bases available. Not only do many revolutionaries think this way, but also representatives of the Front of People's Action in Chile and the representatives of several democratic movements. Here, in my opinion, lies the crux of the recent events. Even in the context of all our respect for the Soviet Union, we believe that the decisions made by the Soviet Union were a mistake. . . . I think that the Soviet policy had two weak sides. You didn't understand the significance of the psychological factor for Cuban conditions. This thought was expressed in an original way by Fidel Castro: "The USA wanted to destroy us physically, but the Soviet Union with Khrushchev's letter [to Kennedy on November 27, accepting the missile withdrawal—JGC] destroyed us legally."

MIKOYAN: But we thought that you would be satisfied by our act. We did everything so that Cuba would not be destroyed. We see your readiness to die beautifully, but we believe that it isn't worth dying beautifully.

GUEVARA: To a certain extent you are right. You offended our feelings by not consulting us. But the main danger is in the second weak side of the Soviet policy. The thing is, you virtually recognized the right of the USA to violate international law. This did great damage to your own policy. This fact really worries us. It may cause difficulties for maintaining the unity of the Socialist countries. It seems to us that there already are cracks in the unity of the Socialist camp.

MIKOYAN: That issue worries us too. We are doing a lot to strengthen our unity, and with you, comrades, we will always be with you despite all the difficulties.

GUEVARA: To the last day?

MIKOYAN: Yes, let our enemies die. We must live and let live. . . . Comrade Guevara evaluated the past events in a pessimistic tone. I respect his opinion, but I do not agree with him. I will try during the next meeting to convince him, though I doubt my ability to do that. . . . I am satisfied by my meetings with you. . . . Basically, we have come to an agreement on the protocol. Besides that, I must say that I thought that I understood the Cubans, and then I listened to Comrade Che and understood that no, I still don't know them.

ALEXEIEV: But Che is an Argentine.

MIKOYAN, to Che: Let's meet and talk a little. . . . Our stake in Cuba is huge in both a material and moral [sense], and also in a military regard. Think about it, are we really helping you out of [our] overabundance? Do we have something extra? We don't have enough for ourselves. No, we want to preserve the base of socialism in Latin America. You were born as heroes, before a revolutionary situation ripened in Latin America, but the Socialist camp still has not grown into its full capability to come to your assistance. We give you ships, weapons, people, fruits and vegetables. China is big, but for the time being it is still a poor country. There will come a time when we will show our enemies. But we do not want to die beautifully. Socialism must live. Excuse the rhetoric.*

Already, the Christlike image of a beautiful death could be read on Che's face. Perhaps Mikoyan, a cultivated Russian Armenian, remembered the scene of Prince Andrei's first wound in *War and Peace*. Napoleon inspects the battlefield after his defeat at the Berezina and while contemplating the inert body of Andrei (who is actually still alive), exclaims to nobody in particular, "*Quelle belle mort!*"

*"Memorandum of Conversation: Anastas Mikoyan with Osvaldo Dorticós, Ernesto Guevara and Carlos Rafael Rodríguez," November 5, 1962 (Top Secret), quoted in Cold War International History Project *Cold War Crises,* Bulletin No. 5, Spring 1995, Woodrow Wilson International Center for Scholars, Washington, D.C., p. 105. The quoted text is from the archives of Russia's Foreign Ministry. It has undergone two translations: Alexeiev's translation of his notes of the conversation, from Spanish to Russian, in 1962; and from Russian to English, in 1995.

Chapter 8

With Fidel, Neither Marriage Nor Divorce

T here was more to Che's life than sugar quotas and missiles, though. This period saw his family grow, along with his fame and love of continual movement. His first son was born in 1962 and named after Camilo, Che's comrade from the Sierra Maestra; a third daughter, Celia, was born in 1963. Aleida, who had accompanied Che on most of his travels within Cuba, now tended to stay at home. The comfortable—though far from luxurious—family residence at 772 47th Street, between Conill and Tulipán streets in the Nuevo Vedado quarter, was filled with children, papers, books, and (according to neighbors) a ferocious German shepherd. Yet Guevara spent little time there, what with his trips abroad and in the interior. In the words of his eldest grandson (who recalls his mother's account), "he was never home."[1] Che had not formed the kind of bourgeois family he so dreaded in Buenos Aires, but his household was much what it would have been anywhere. He continued to cultivate his love of reading, and spent long hours writing letters, articles, and essays (which he published at a frantic pace), as well as his diaries.

Che remained as ascetic as always, strictly imposing upon himself the ethical norms of the Revolution and trying to avoid any abuse of power or privilege. But Aleida, confronted daily, like many Cuban housewives, with the ordeal of long lines and shortages, sometimes used Che's official car, escort, and influence to fulfill the minimal requirements of subsistence. Che would send her to the market by bus, explaining irritably, "No, Aleida, no, you know that the car belongs to the government, it is not mine, and you cannot take advantage of it. Take the bus, like everybody else." Ricardo Rojo, who stayed with the family for a couple of months in early 1963, recalled how according to both Aleida and Che's mother, Celia, Che was bent on obtaining from his government position only the indispensable. The house he lived in, a mansion confiscated from a rich emigrant, was empty, despite the countless gifts he received during his international travels. Che simply remitted the presents, ranging from art objects to craftswork and electrical appliances, to youth training centers throughout the island, still wrapped.[2]

His main preoccupation during this period (over and beyond his administrative and diplomatic activities) was the revolution in Latin America and, increasingly, Africa. If his chief concern after the missile crisis was the adverse effects of the Soviet surrender on the rest of Latin America, that was because of his growing obsession—theoretical, political, and personal—with one goal: to replicate the Cuban model in other latitudes, with all available means and at all costs. Che had presented the conceptual foundation for this in a 1961 essay in which he briefly first described those features of the Cuban Revolution which he believed made it unique in Latin America: the figure and "earth-moving force" of Fidel Castro, and the way "imperialism was taken by surprise." He then presented a series of conditions which he considered common and/or constant in Latin America: the submissive attitude of the bourgeoisie, the existence of *latifundia,* and a poverty-stricken peasantry—"a phenomenon to be found in all the countries of Latin America without exception, and which has been the basis for all the injustices committed here"—and the hunger of the people. Finally, Che summed up the significance of Cuba's victory as "the possibility of triumph and the inevitability of triumph." In a succinct conclusion, he claimed:

> The possibility of triumph of the popular masses in Latin America is clearly expressed in the path of guerrilla warfare, based upon a peasant army, an alliance between workers and peasants, the defeat of the army in a direct confrontation, the taking of cities from the countryside. . . .[3]

Che recast these ideas in a more far-reaching essay which appeared in *Cuba Socialista* in September 1963 under the title "*La guerra de guerrillas: un método.*" In it, he restated his previous arguments and insisted that the armed struggle in Latin America was both feasible and necessary. But the text was different from earlier versions, such as *Guerrilla Warfare,* because by 1963 the Cuban regime was far more intent on "exporting the revolution." Certainly, there had been many occasions in the past when Che or other Cuban leaders engaged in undercover practices like sending arms and funds, training guerrillas, obtaining documentation, advising on logistics, and so on. But this had been more a matter of ideological inclination than state policy. After Cuba was expelled from the Organization of American States (OAS) in 1962 and found its diplomatic relations with most Latin American countries severed, things changed. There was no longer any reason for the Cubans to desist from their revolutionary endeavors in the region—seen as seditious or subversive by the governments involved. Indeed, the caveats imposed on the creation of a *foco* in the original manual *Guerrilla Warfare* vanished in this one; for example, there is no further mention of the obstacle constitutional governance can represent for a guerrilla movement.* Furthermore, by 1963 Che had greatly consolidated his position within the Cuban government. Thus, his essays were perceived in many Latin American capitals as far more than the personal views of a Cuban intellectual or guerrilla fighter, albeit an important one. They were seen as an expression of Cuban state policy. Above all, the great difference between 1960–61 and 1963–64 was Che's personal involvement. He was now directly committed to Cuba's revolutionary adventures.†

His first guerrilla love, quite naturally, was his native Argentina. The roundabout road Che would follow there began in a meeting with his compatriots in Cuba, many of whom gathered in Havana for Argentina's independence-day festivities on May 25, 1962. Though the traditional roast was lacking, they sacrificed a rather scrawny calf which, together with their customary maté, sufficed for the occasion. Che had been invited to speak by the Institute for Cuban-Argentine Friendship. Having agreed with some

---

*See, for example, Matt D. Childs, "An Historical Critique of the Emergence and Evolution of Ernesto Che Guevara's Foco Theory," *Journal of Latin American Studies* (Cambridge University Press, London), no. 27, 1995, pp. 593–624. This shift in Guevara's arguments was not necessarily reflected in the way his followers interpreted his point of view.

† A further, conclusive sign of the difference is that, this time around, Che's essay received a Soviet response. An article signed by Dimitri Levonov appeared on November 11, 1963, in the Spanish-language *Revista de la URSS,* under the title "La coexistencia pacifica fortalece el frente de la lucha contra el imperialismo" (Peaceful coexistence reinforces the front in the struggle against imperialism). According to the British Embassy in Havana, "the article might in fact be read as a reply to Guevara's article on guerrilla warfare of last September in *Cuba Socialista,* with which it is in marked contradiction." Havana Telegram to Foreign Office, Counter-Revolutionary Activities, January 10, 1964 (Confidential), Foreign Office, FO371/174003, Public Record Office, London. A top-secret cable from the Soviet Embassy in Havana branded the essay "ultrarevolutionary bordering on adventurist." According to the embassy, Che "ignores basic tenets of Marxism-Leninism." Embassy Cable no. 47784, January 28, 1964 (Top Secret), Russian National Archive, Center for the Conservation of Contemporary Documents, File no. 5, List no. 49, no. 655, Moscow.

reluctance—for he knew what a hornet's nest awaited him—he addressed
the entire Argentine community of Havana, including Perón's representative John William Cooke, Tamara Bunke (the young teacher and translator
who had joined the Cuban Revolution the previous year), two hundred
technicians sent by the Argentine Communist Party, as well as a number of
artists, scientists, and writers living in Havana.* Che's speech reflected both
his strengths and his weaknesses, his successes and his failures. As an
Argentine militant at the scene recalled: "The Communist Party, which had
sent a special plane to Havana after the victory of the Revolution packed
with activists and experts, had bad relations with Cuba; Cuba believed in
revolutionary violence, and the Party did not. Many of the Argentines
began to receive training for the militias, deepening the conflict, because the
Party elders thought Cuba was training militias within the Party, thus
undermining the leadership. This led to a tense situation, verging on a
break, particularly when the delegate from the Party was recalled from
Cuba. So Che was venturing into very troubled waters, and rapidly found
himself in a delicate position: 'I will speak at the celebration on May 25, but
only if they don't pose any conditions.' "†

On the one hand, he was absolutely certain that armed struggle was the
only way to bring revolution to Argentina; the only means to defeat the army
and oligarchy was to unify all those political forces capable of joining in the
struggle. But one of those forces, the Communist Party, was led by a notorious Argentine-Soviet *apparatchik,* Víctor Codovilla (indirectly involved in,
among other nefarious acts, the first attempt on Trotsky's life in Mexico City
in 1940). Codovilla rejected Che's *foco* theories, and the other opposition
forces squabbled among themselves for a leadership position which they did
not, in many cases, deserve. Either they featured talented personalities who
nonetheless represented very little—as in the case of Cooke, despite his personal association with Perón‡—or they were simply peopled by fans of the
Socialist or Castroist left, with scant links to Argentine society.

Cooke, who had already distanced himself from Peronism if not from
Perón himself, and who was exiled in Madrid, also addressed the crowd. On
that spring day in Havana, he made a fiery speech supporting Guevara's
position, recalling that all the great heroes of Latin American liberation had
been "guerrilla fighters."[4] Che, never one to beat around the bush, appealed

---

*They came to almost four hundred, according to one of them. Carolina Aguilar,
quoted in Marta Rojas and Mirta Rodríguez, *Tania: La guerrillera inolvidable* (Havana:
Instituto Cubano del Libro, 1970), p. 108.

† Amalio Rey, interview with the author, Córdoba, November 25, 1994.

‡ "In September of 1961 [Cooke] no longer spoke as a Peronist . . . but as a Communist." Ernesto Goldar, "John William Cooke de Perón al Che Guevara," in *Todo es historia*
(Buenos Aires), vol. 25, no. 288, pp. 26, 27.

for unity among traditional enemies, calling for them to rise up in arms— which many did not even have or want to have:

> We believe we are part of an army fighting in every part of the world, and we must ready ourselves to celebrate another 25th of May not in this generous land, but in our own country and with new symbols, with the symbol of victory, the symbol of the construction of socialism, the symbol of the future.[5]

The words, gestures, and especially the intentions of Comandante Guevara could only alarm the many Communists in the audience. His calls for convergence with the Peronists and among all revolutionaries, and for guerrilla warfare and revolutionary violence, inevitably antagonized the Communist Party. There was an uproar the next day, and heated arguments among the delegates.[6] The Communists were enraged, and even censured Che's speech in their publications. Guevara suddenly found himself an outcast, caught between his revolutionary goals and a dismal lack of supporters to achieve them with. His only alternative was one which Cuba—and he himself—would be forced to choose for years to come: the promotion of more or less explicit divisions within the Communist parties of Latin America, training militants in Cuba without the knowledge or consent of their leaders, and plotting for the militants' takeover of their organizations.

A private letter written by several Argentine Communists living in Cuba to one of the Party's leaders in Moscow illustrates the bad blood between Che and some of his compatriots:

> Our relations with our famous countryman Ernesto Guevara are going from bad to worse, and all of this because of the incidents involving our beloved Party. We took it up with Cooke and his wife and the whole group that the Cubans were training. Their defender was none other than Guevara; he was financing them. Among the members of the future "commandos" there was a group of Trotskyists who were going around claiming that when they have the chance to apply what they are learning they will make no fine distinction between "gorilas" (the anti-Peronist military) and "Stalinist Communists."[7]

That takeover rarely if ever materialized, but the attempts aroused infinite mistrust and resentment among Party leaders. Che gradually realized that if he hoped to mount a guerrilla war in Argentina or anywhere else, he would have to do so alone—that is, with individual recruits, and on the margins of existing groups.

A case in point was Tamara Bunke, who often accompanied him to parties or volunteer-work celebrations, or to welcome foreign delegations.

Some of the Argentines who attended the independence festivities met a couple of days later to discuss the incidents and determine their future course. Several of them—not including Tamara—expressed disagreement with Che. Imbued with her Communist parents' spirit of sacrifice and the recklessness that would lead her to her death in Bolivia five years later, Tamara stormed out, exclaiming, "I'm leaving, I'm not going to waste my time here."[8]

Che would have to make his revolution in Latin America with the Tamaras of the hemisphere--and without the Codovillas. From an individual viewpoint, this had its advantages; in terms of politics and popular support, it was a disaster. This was especially true in the case of Argentina, where neither the Socialist Party, nor the Communists, nor Perón was prepared to join in a delusional armed struggle. When Cooke returned to his country two years later, Che was left even more isolated in his Argentine aspirations. But he did not give up. In the days following that 25th of May, 1962, he confided his true intentions to more sympathetic compatriots living in Havana, who visited him at the Ministry. They found him with a map of his native land spread out on his desk. Che brought out some maté and they spent four or five hours sipping it like true Argentines, exchanging countless anecdotes. One above all impressed his interlocutors. "Revolution," said Che, "can be made at any given moment anywhere in the world." "Anywhere in the world?" they asked. "Even in Argentina or La Paz?" Pointing with his finger at the city of his youth, Che proclaimed: "Even in Córdoba there can be guerrilla warfare."[9]

Several Latin American countries possessed the central traits Che had described in *Guerrilla Warfare* as impediments to the armed struggle: constitutional government, elections, etc. But those obstacles now loomed larger, as they were buttressed by the Soviet Union's growing reluctance to countenance Cuban adventures, and especially by the refusal of Communist parties in the region to engage in guerrilla warfare. Preliminary attempts had failed in Venezuela, Nicaragua, and Guatemala. Repression—even by democratic governments—was intensifying. The dangers for large mass organizations inspired or led by the Communists were growing. Under these conditions, the parties' willingness to take up arms—never overwhelming to begin with—faded day by day. The Communists asked Moscow on occasion to intervene and temper the Cubans' revolutionary fervor. But the Soviets, who already had enough troubles with their tropical partners, preferred discretion over any public rift—for the moment. So the natural candidates for armed struggle in Latin America—the Communist cadres—became increasingly reluctant, and Che Guevara increasingly irritated.

Faced with this growing resistance and the ever-repeated objection that the time was not ripe, Che revised his original views in the September 1963 essay on guerrilla warfare. Before, he had insisted that the creation of a guerrilla *foco* required a series of conditions, including the absence of a constitutional elected government. Now he claimed that those conditions could be self-created: the *foco* could breed the prerequisites for its own existence. Did this new idea derive from a new theoretical viewpoint? Or was it the total absence of those conditions in reality, along with Che's stubborn insistence on making the revolution here and now, which led to a retroactive justification of the *foco*'s self-generation? Without a doubt, it was the lack of real revolutionaries that led Che to theorize that they were no longer necessary. At the end, he would perish surrounded by the silence of absent Bolivian *campesinos* and Communist cadres, as his *foco* in Ñancahuazú created everything but the conditions for victory.

Within this troubled and contradictory political context, there occurred another crucial event in the history of the Cuban Revolution: Fidel Castro's lengthy visit to the USSR in the spring of 1963. He spent over forty days there, reaching agreements with the Soviet leadership which would have countless implications for the island's economic and political future. Despite an explicit invitation to Che from the Soviet ambassador (discussed later in the chapter), he did not accompany Fidel—though the trip was to include important commercial and industrial negotiations well within his areas of responsibility. Indeed, according to French journalist K. S. Karol, Guevara learned of Fidel's accords with the Soviets only after the fact.[10]

So much the better: the principal result of the trip was to confirm Cuba's sad fate as a single-minded producer of sugar, along with a few other raw materials and farming products, within the Socialist bloc's division of labor. Thus did Fidel explicitly renounce a project which had in fact been abandoned months earlier: the island's industrialization. Che did not forgive the USSR for its October betrayal as readily as did Castro, nor was he as quick to accept Cuba's dependence on the Soviets.*

Fidel's visit dissipated the tensions and recriminations of the previous October. He was spontaneously acclaimed, honored, and feted by the people of Russia, Uzbekistan, Ukraine, and Georgia, as well as by the Soviet leadership—though they were perhaps less sincere. In turn, he had nothing but praise and admiration for the fatherland of socialism, especially after his return to Havana on June 3, 1963. If during October and November 1962 there had been some parallels between the Cuban and Chinese views of Khrushchev, they were now banished from Castro's political discourse.

---

*Commenting upon Khrushchev's fall in November with his friend and teacher Anastacio Cruz Mancilla, Che said: "I will never forgive Khrushchev for the way he resolved the missile crisis." "Memorandum of Conversation of November 6, 1964, of E. Pronski with Havana University Professor Anastacio Cruz Mancilla," November 13, 1964 (Secret), Russian National Archive, File No. 5, List No. 49, Document No. 759.

There were still occasional flourishes, remarks, or gestures (for instance, on July 26, 1963) which some observers saw as pro-China and somewhat anti-Soviet.* But Cuba's alignment with the USSR was increasingly evident, despite its attempted neutrality in the Sino-Soviet dispute. In exchange, the Soviets paid lip service to the cause of armed struggle in Latin America, while entangling any real aid in so many clauses and reservations that Latin American Communist parties could well decide to abstain from military activity without contravening any Soviet dispositions.

Che's doubts as to the wisdom and decency of a hasty reconciliation with the USSR were aggravated by a new though recurrent factor: Fidel's incessant flirtations with Washington, which always allowed contradictory interpretations; indeed, that was their very *raison d'être*. In the spring of 1963, a U.S. television journalist, Lisa Howard, interviewed Castro and found that he seemed amenable to an understanding with President John F. Kennedy. Washington promptly signaled its refusal. The journalist persisted in her efforts, leading in September 1963 to preliminary talks between Cuba's permanent representative to the United Nations, Carlos Lechuga, and the U.S. journalist and diplomat William Atwood.

All of this occurred thanks to the good offices of Howard, who had a close relationship with René Vallejo (Fidel's personal aide and physician); he had helped set up her meeting with Castro in May. He offered to send a plane to the United States, to bring a Kennedy envoy back to Havana to negotiate. When Washington rejected the offer, Vallejo—with Howard and Atwood listening in on the call—proposed by telephone to travel secretly to the United States himself in order to launch negotiations. Kennedy's death in November put an end to the initiative. It is impossible to say whether it would have prospered, and if Castro was really willing to make the concessions demanded by Washington to re-establish normal relations.

Significantly, however, the following argument emerged in several conversations between U.S. and Cuban representatives:

> Castro is unhappy about his present dependence on the Soviet bloc, the trade embargo is hurting him, and he would like to establish some official contact with the U.S.; even though this would not be welcomed by most of

*The FBI, which for some strange reason was also interested in Cuba, but whose ideological expertise was severely limited, commented in a secret intelligence report: "Castro has, since July 26, 1963, demonstrated discontent with and coolness toward the Soviet Union, while exhibiting a tendency to favor the Chinese communists in their dispute with the Soviet Union. Cuban diplomatic officials have even indicated that Cuban leaders are completely disappointed in their treatment by the Soviets, that the Cuban Government is closer than ever to the Chinese communists, and that this is known to the Russians." Federal Bureau of Investigation, "Current Intelligence Analysis" (Secret), November 27, 1963, p. 2, NSF, Country File, Cuba, Gordon Chase File, LBJ Library.

his hard-core Communist entourage, such as Che Guevara . . . there was a
rift between Castro and the Guevara-Hart-Almeida group on the question
of Cuba's future course. . . . Guevara and the other communists were
opposed to any deal, and regarded Castro as dangerously unreliable."*

The analysis was not necessarily valid, nor was there a rift between Fidel
and Che during those months. To the contrary, they may even (albeit for different reasons) have agreed on the necessity of reinforcing Cuban support
for revolutionary groups in Latin America—Che as a matter of principle
and due to his disillusion with the USSR, and Castro because he had not
found the understanding he sought, either with Moscow or with Washington. Intensifying internal difficulties may also have contributed to Fidel's
enhanced activism in the jungles and swamps of the region. But it was one
thing to equip revolutionaries and quite another to confront the USSR.
Che, who increasingly believed the two went together, simply could not tolerate the ambivalence implicit in Fidel's juggling with both. Castro thrived
on the game; Che abhorred it.

In early 1964, Che granted a television interview of his own to Lisa
Howard, reiterating Castro's views. Top White House officials congratu-
lated Howard for the program, even while recognizing Guevara's poise and
skill.[†] Watching the rushes of the interview thirty years later, one can only
admire Che's charm, assurance, and inner strength; even in crossing the set
to light a cigarette for the journalist, he moved with incomparable elegance
and grace. Despite being tired and overweight, he was still a man of exceptional beauty. The Christlike expression of his death was already there: the
ineffable, veiled sadness in his eyes portended an accepted tragedy; he is
already, as Dolores Moyano Martín, a friend from his youth, wrote with
Dostoyevsky's portrait of Nechaev in mind, "a doomed man," even if he
has not yet "severed every tie with the civil order."[11] There were still battles
ahead, but at some unconscious level Che may have known that he had lost
his war in Cuba.

A few days after Castro's return from the Soviet Union, Guevara packed

---

*Quotations are taken from several documents pertaining to the U.S.-Cuba exchange,
which took place between September and November 1963. See William Atwood's memorandum to National Security Adviser McGeorge Bundy. Dated November 8 (Secret), it reports
on Atwood's contacts with Lisa Howard, Carlos Lechuga, and René Vallejo in Havana.

† Cf. especially Gordon Chase's memorandum to McGeorge Bundy, dated March 25,
1964, where Chase comments on the program's excellence and suggests that Howard's
request that he write the ABC Vice-President for News to that effect be granted. Chase to
Bundy (Top Secret, Eyes Only), March 25, 1964, Memorandum, The White House (copy
LBJ Library).

his bags again and left for Algeria in early July to attend the first anniversary celebrations of its independence. He spent three weeks there, touring the country extensively. On his way to Algiers, he had time to reflect upon the changes and events of the previous months: Cuba's reconciliation with Moscow, Castro's critical advances to Washington, the island's dire economic crisis, his own disagreements with the rest of the governing team, and his gradual removal from economic policy-making.

At a planning seminar in Algiers, Che acknowledged Cuba's failure to achieve industrialization and trade diversification, as well as the island's economic debacle. His views were not that different from those of Fidel, the Russians, or the Cuban Communists. But his doubts were one thing; quite another was the course the Revolution was starting to adopt in economic and foreign policy terms. Algiers marked the beginning of three important projects for Che Guevara: one economic, and two in international policy. He was already preparing the escape route he would follow less than two years later.

The first of Che's foreign initiatives targeted Argentina and would founder. But the second involved Africa and Algeria, and would endure. The young Algerian republic was faced with an ominous and debilitating crisis on its western borders. King Hassan of Morocco, both on his own initiative and pushed by French and American intelligence services, had declared war on his neighbor over the territories of the eastern Sahara. Ahmed Ben Bella, the hero of the clandestine struggle against France and first president of Algeria, had no means of defense, but he and his government enjoyed considerable international support. They had a longstanding friendship with Cuba, whose saga had closely paralleled their own. A high-level Cuban delegation had attended their declaration of independence in July 1962, and Ben Bella had visited Havana on the eve of the missile crisis. During his visit, Castro and Guevara had offered technical, medical, and, if needed, military support to defend the newborn Maghreb State. The first Cuban medical mission of fifty-five members arrived in Algiers on May 24, 1963, just five weeks before Che. It was natural, then, that the Cubans should rise to the defense of their friends when Moroccan troops took several Algerian border posts in September 1963, unleashing the so-called War of the Desert. Moroccan superiority in weapons and training boded ill for the Algerians.

According to Cuba's ambassador in Algiers, he himself transmitted Ben Bella's urgent appeal for help to Cuba. Castro agreed within the spirit of adventure and internationalism which had characterized the Cuban leadership since the Revolution. Ben Bella has a slightly different version. In his view, it was the Cubans who offered to help:

When I went to Havana in September 1962, Castro strongly insisted that Cuba had a debt with Algeria, contracted before independence, which he wanted to pay. When Che came to Algeria, he also insisted on paying it—but in kind, with sugar. And a boat loaded with sugar was about to sail from Cuba in October, to pay the debt. When Hassan attacked us, I did not ask for anything; but Foreign Minister Abdel Aziz Bouteflika saw Ambassador Serguera and spoke with him. And the Cubans put a battalion of 800 men with 70 tanks into the sugar boat. I found out about this several days later, when Serguera came to see me and showed me a sheet of paper, torn from a school notebook, advising him that the sugar boat was also carrying 800 men and 70 tanks. But they never saw combat, for in those very days Hassan called for negotiations. That was because we sent 300,000 civilians to the border to occupy it, and the Americans pressured Hassan into desisting.[12]

In the Cuban version, reconstructed by the Italian-American historian Piero Gleijeses, at Ben Bella's request Castro sent an advance group of Cuban officers to Algeria, rapidly backed by other units totaling 686 men and a large number of tanks.[13] Though the Cubans would have preferred to keep the operation secret, it was reported by the world press shortly after the landing at Oran. A few days later, Ben Bella began talks with King Hassan and on October 19, in Bamako, the capital of Mali, signed a cease-fire. The Cubans remained in Algeria for six months, delivering the military supplies they had brought and training a large number of troops.

Jorge Serguera, Cuba's first ambassador to Algeria and Che's aide in all of his African expeditions, believes Cuban assistance played a key role in Ben Bella's victory over Morocco:

Of course [Hassan] asked for negotiations. He had only three tanks and we took over sixty. Our help was decisive. Algeria could not have negotiated on its own, pressured as it was by the Americans, pressured by the English, and pressured by everybody.[14]

Thus, the growing complicity between Cuba and Algeria, whether in providing military supplies and training to guerrillas in Latin America, or acting jointly in Africa. This had been Cuba's first expedition in Africa, and Che had played a central role in it, as he would in the next four years. Cuba's political relationship with Algeria and Che's personal bond with Ben Bella became the pillars of Cuba's African policy, and the starting point of all Guevara's projects there in the future.

The understanding between the two countries was such that the arms shipment discovered in Venezuela at the end of 1963, which would serve as a pretext for OAS sanctions against Cuba, probably originated in Algeria. As Ben Bella revealed in an October 1987 interview with the French

Trotskyist daily *Rouge,* Che asked him on behalf of Fidel and the Cuban leadership to send arms and trained cadres to South America; Cuba could no longer do so, as it was under close observation. Ben Bella immediately agreed.* On November 28, 1963, the Venezuelan government revealed that it had discovered a 3-ton weapons cache in the coastal province of Falcón, including eighteen bazookas, four mortar guns, eight recoilless rifles, twenty-six machine guns, and one hundred assault rifles bearing Cuban insignia. According to available information—ambiguous but revealing— the reunified guerrillas of Venezuela had convinced the Cubans (including Che) to send them the arms they needed to overthrow the Caracas regime. Cuba simply rerouted some of the light arms it sent to Algeria, as they were no longer needed following the cease-fire signed by Hassan and Ben Bella.

Despite Che's increasing involvement in African politics, this was for now only a sideshow in relation to his other pet international project, the creation of a guerrilla *foco* in Argentina. There was a link between the two though: Jorge Masetti, the Argentine journalist who interviewed Che in the Sierra Maestra in 1958. As early as January 10, 1962, the Cuban cargo ship *Bahía de Nipe* had docked in Casablanca to deliver a large weapons supply to the National Liberation Front (FLN) and transfer Algerian casualties to Cuba.[15] Masetti was there to receive it.

He had stayed on in Cuba after the Revolution and—with the support of Che and others, including Gabriel García Márquez—founded Prensa Latina, the Cuban news agency (which also indulged in other activities). In 1961, Masetti resigned from Prensa Latina, due to strained relations with both the Cubans and the Argentine Communists working at the agency. At the end of that year, he negotiated the first Cuban arms shipment to Algerian guerrillas and their provisional government. He remained in Algeria until its independence several months later, then returned to Cuba. In November 1962, leaving behind a newborn son, he left again for the Maghreb to receive military training.

After a failed attempt by Che and John William Cooke to bring Perón to Havana and transform him into a patron for the armed struggle in Argentina, Che finally resigned himself to waging the revolution in his native country with a handful of supporters: a group of heroic and misguided Argentines, and the Cubans closest to him. When Guevara arrived

---

*In Ahmed Ben Bella, *Connaître Che Guevara,* Cayenne (French Guyana), October 1987, p. 53. Gleijeses quotes Ulises Estrada and other members of the Cuban expeditionary team, in Piero Gleijeses, "Cuba's First Venture in Africa: Algeria, 1961–1965," *Journal of Latin American Studies,* no. 28, London University, Spring 1996, p. 188. Efigenio Amejeiras, head of the Cuban mission in Algeria, gave a similar account to Paco Ignacio Taibo II and others in September 1995 in Havana. Taibo, as on other occasions already cited, shared the interview with the author.

in Algeria in early July 1963, he first dealt with the forlorn Cuban physicians in Sétif who had not yet received their stipend, and attended the planning seminar mentioned earlier. Then he met with Masetti, by now the designated *comandante* of the future Argentine *foco*.

With his training in Cuba and Algeria, and some combat experience in the latter country,[16] Masetti set about recruiting Communist dissidents and university students from Argentina, who were all on the margins of traditional leftist organizations. He was soon forced to include several Cubans in the expedition due to the sparsity of local recruits. Three of them participated in it directly; another two were involved only in its preparation. Hermés Peña, one of his bodyguards, died in the Argentine jungle of Salta. Alberto Castellanos, Guevara's driver (at whose home Che and Aleida had been married), was captured and spent four years in jail in Argentina. José María Martínez Tamayo ("Papi"), the first advance man for the Argentine affair and Che's highest-ranking personal aide, accompanied him to the Congo and helped prepare the expedition to Bolivia, where he died a few months before Che. He landed in La Paz in July 1963 to lay the groundwork for the others. And Cuba's current Minister of the Interior, General Abelardo ("Furri") Colomé Ibarra, was sent by Raúl Castro (under whom he still serves, as his closest collaborator) to "coordinate the entire operation."[17]

Furri first went to Buenos Aires with one of the Argentines, the painter Ciro Bustos. From Buenos Aires he traveled to Tarija, Bolivia, the jump-off point for the guerrilla expedition into northern Argentina. There they all regrouped: Masetti, Martínez Tamayo (who carried the money), Furri (in charge of weapons), Hermés Peña, and Alberto Castellanos, entrusted with logistics and security for Che Guevara, who in all likelihood had already decided to join them.

Masetti had probably made a first secret trip to Argentina in 1962, along with Hermés Peña.* One year later, during the summer of 1963, the aspiring guerrillas arrived in Bolivia disguised as members of an Algerian trade mission. Between September and December they journeyed several times in and out of Argentina, seeking volunteers for the Salta *foco*.† Castellanos joined them in September. In late 1963 (September, according to some

*Masetti's son Jorge places his father's return to Argentina in 1962. Masetti last appeared publicly in Cuba at the televised trial of the Bay of Pigs prisoners; he then disappeared from Cuba. Cf. Jorge Masetti, *La loi des Corsaires* (Paris: Stock, 1992). He confirmed this account in a telephone conversation from Paris with the author on September 5, 1996.

† Ricardo Rojo notes that he, Masetti, and Che met several times in Havana between early February and mid-April 1963. Rojo's recurring chronological imprecisions render his account somewhat unreliable. Ricardo Rojo, *Mi amigo el Che* (Buenos Aires: Editorial Legasa, 1985; first edition, 1968), pp. 171–172.

sources), they made their final entrance into Argentina; neither Masetti nor Peña would leave the country alive (by early 1964 the entire affair was over). They were never able to recruit more than a handful of inexperienced youths, devoted but completely unfit for guerrilla warfare. Their tale would impact Argentine public opinion just enough to draw the armed forces' attention—but not enough to awaken the slightest glimmer of sympathy.

There are three indications that Ernesto Guevara intended to leave Cuba and direct the armed struggle in his own land. First, the leaders of the Argentine expedition all belonged to his inner circle: two of his bodyguards, his best journalist friend, and his closest Cuban aide. Castellanos asserts that the head of Che's escort, Harry ("Pombo") Villegas, was not included because he was of African origin and, as Che declared, "there are no blacks where we are going."[18] Guevara's fourth bodyguard, José Argudín, was excluded because (according to Castellanos) he had seduced the wife of Peña during the latter's absence.[19] Che's two subsequent expeditions would also include his bodyguards or the old guard dating back to the Sierra and the "invasion": Pombo, Papi, and Tuma (Carlos Coello). And it was inconceivable, given Che's nature, that he should ever have contemplated sending his closest aides on a dangerous mission without eventually joining it himself.

In the second place, when Che summoned Castellanos to the Guantánamo officer-training school and announced that he had decided to entrust him with a task which could well last twenty years, he said: "I will go soon. You go and wait over there, you go and set up the group and have them wait for me."[20] By January 1964, Papi and Castellanos had arrived in Tucumán to contact possible Argentine recruits (mainly Trotskyists, Castellanos recalls). Among other things, they carried twenty thousand dollars for one Dr. Canelo in Tucumán. As Castellanos describes it,

> Then Papi told me that Che would not be going just then, that he would send a message to . . . Masetti, but he told me that Che wasn't going just then because it was too complicated, that he'd go a little later. He did not say why. At least he didn't tell me. No, just that he couldn't go at that time, that we should wait for him, continue exploring, and that . . . we should not recruit any peasants until we began fighting.[21]

Thirty years later in Havana, Castellanos ruefully remembers that he never harbored any doubt that his boss fully intended to join the guerrilla group in Salta. As for the presence of Colomé, one of the men closest to Raúl Castro, and the reasoning behind the mission, there was no margin for confusion. Furri was always linked to Raúl, from the time of the Sierra

Maestra and the Second Front. Raúl was involved in the operation because it was Che's mission; Che was already planning to leave the island.*

Finally, there was the enigma of Masetti's *nom de guerre* in Salta: "Comandante Segundo" or "Segundo Sombra" (Second Shadow). Both names have been interpreted as a wink to Guevara: either because the first *comandante* was going to be Che, or because Segundo Sombra is a central figure in nineteenth-century Argentine literature, along with Martín Fierro—an occasional nickname of Che's. In any case, the double meaning is sufficiently explicit to suggest that Ernesto Guevara was determined to join the guerrillas in Argentina between late 1963 and early 1964. His instructions to Castellanos—"do not recruit any peasants for the moment, just devote yourselves to exploring the area"—reinforce this interpretation. Combat was to begin only after Che's arrival.

Perhaps Guevara's decision to participate in the Salta team was triggered by Castro's extended visit to the Soviet Union in May 1963, or perhaps by Che's own trip to Algeria. Either way, his state of mind was limpid and manifest. After his departure from Algiers in July, he stopped in Paris for a couple of days. There he reflected upon his future in Cuba, in view of Fidel's reconciliation with the USSR and the growing controversy surrounding his management of the economy. He also delivered a talk at the Maison de l'Amérique Latine on the Boulevard Saint-Germain. There he met Carlos Franqui, who had been living in intermittent exile in Algeria and Europe for some time. Relations between them were strained; they had clashed several times in Cuba over a number of issues, but had just celebrated a virtual reconciliation in Algiers, where Franqui had interviewed Ben Bella and mounted an exhibit of Cuban art he had brought from Paris. According to Franqui's memoirs, the two now discovered many affinities: "We were both friends of Ben Bella. [Che] was seeking another path. He considered the Cuban situation very difficult, despite an apparent lull in sectarianism and the missile crisis. It was one of our best meetings."[22]

Che put his arm around Franqui's shoulders and the two went walking along a deserted boulevard in the Paris summer, cooled by the chestnut trees and the last cobblestones paving the avenues of the French capital. Guevara tried to persuade the journalist to return to Cuba, without denying the problems there and his own frictions with Castro. It was then, in the heart of the Latin Quarter, that Che gave vent to a feeling which would soon lead him away from his closest friend and dearest companion-in-arms: "With Fidel, I want neither marriage nor divorce."[23] The phrase aptly expressed

*In the words of Castellanos, "Many people say it's a lie, but Che was going to leave here in 1963; he even sent me to wait for him. I had not said this before." Alberto Castellanos, interview with the author, Havana, January 23, 1996.

Che's quandary; it enclosed an unsustainable ambivalence, an intolerable mingling of contradictory feelings. Flight to the Argentine guerrilla operation had to wait; the Revolution's internal difficulties loomed too large at the end of 1963. But in the following year a new path opened up for Guevara—much sooner than he could have guessed.

Jorge Masetti's guerrilla campaign ended in tragedy. Wracked by internal dissensions that led to executions of its own members, and isolated from the cities, his group was easy prey for the government. In addition, representative democracy had returned to Argentina in October, with the election of Arturo Illía as president. This was no tinhorn dictatorship Masetti was fighting. The correspondent's dreams, dating back to the Sierra Maestra, were no match for the ruthless competence of the Argentine gendarmerie. His column was destroyed after being undermined by its own divisions and excesses, infiltrations, army persecution, and the hardships of the terrain. Castellanos was captured on March 4, 1964; he was defended at his trial by Gustavo Roca, a Córdoba friend of Che's, who had asked his compatriot to help his friends. No one knew of the link between Castellanos and Guevara until the latter's death in Bolivia, when a photograph of Che's wedding with Aleida was published and Castellanos appeared in it as their host. As for Masetti, he was simply swallowed up by the Salta wilderness. Castellanos has his own explanation, straight from *The Treasure of the Sierra Madre,* for the fact that Masetti's body was never found, though Che sent several envoys to search for it. He was carrying over $20,000, plus a large sum of Argentine money and two Rolex watches. The police probably found him; if he was not already dead from exposure, they killed him, took the money, split it up, and reported he had disappeared. If the body showed up, the money had to show up as well.[24]

In many ways, the Salta operation was a dress rehearsal for the Bolivia escapade three years later. In Cochabamba, Papi may have met the group of Bolivian Communists charged by Mario Monje, the Party's Secretary-General, with promoting the armed struggle in the region: the Peredo brothers, Rodolfo Saldaña, and Luis Tellería. Along with Papi, they would be entrusted with preparations for Che's expedition in 1966. It is possible that Tamara Bunke (or Tania), who arrived in Bolivia in October 1964, was initially sent to investigate Masetti's whereabouts and fate, as well as that of any survivors, rather than to organize a new guerrilla campaign in Bolivia.*

---

*This hypothesis has been suggested by Ulises Estrada, who was Tania's companion for a year—she mentions him in letters to her parents—and who also believes Che's original intention was to join the Argentine expedition: "Two Cuban officials were in Masetti's column; Che always saw that guerrilla attempt as something for later, as a mother guerrilla which he would later join. Tania was part of all of that." Ulises Estrada, interview with the author, Havana, February 9, 1995.

Ciro Bustos, who was arrested along with Régis Debray in Bolivia in April 1967 upon leaving Che's camp, and who was responsible for linking the Bolivian struggle and a future Argentine one, was already present at the Salta saga. He traveled from Havana to Buenos Aires with Furri, and even visited Castellanos in jail on several occasions.[25]

Che may have decided not to participate in the early stages of the Salta expedition, but there is no doubt that he intended to join it sometime soon. The deaths of Masetti and Peña, and the capture of Castellanos, must have dealt him a terrible blow. This was not the first but the second time that close friends had perished in combat, under circumstances which might well have included him. He had taken leave of Julio Roberto ("el Patojo") Cáceres in Havana in December 1961, his travel companion and fellow-photographer on the streets of Mexico City. A portrait of el Patojo would later hang in Che's Ministry offices; Cáceres died fighting in Guatemala, only weeks after joining a guerrilla group. Why did they have to expire putting into practice his ideas and methods? He would either share their fate, or prove that death was not the only possible outcome.

There is then no mystery enshrouding the increasing strain in Che's relations with the Communist parties of Latin America and the Soviet Union during 1963. Since Cuba was entering a period of creeping alignment with the Soviet Union, inevitably, Che's situation became more and more untenable. In April 1963, the Soviet ideologue Mikhail Suslov declared that the Communist parties of Latin America "would be wrong to pin all their hopes on the armed struggle . . . revolution cannot be accelerated or made to measure, nor can it be promoted from abroad."[26] There was no explicit break, for the moment. But as Che's economic and international views drew further and further away from those of the Soviet, Cuban, and Latin American Communists, the veiled discrepancies and discreet recriminations drifted toward a harsh and bitter contest of wills. So before analyzing the broad economic policy battles between Che and his "orthodox" colleagues, it is necessary to examine some of his chief differences with the Soviet Union.

Before Castro's departure for Moscow in April 1963, Che met with the Soviet ambassador to review the trip's technical aspects. He commented that, in general, Khrushchev's letters to the Cuban leaders generally showed wisdom and sensitivity; in contrast, a recent memorandum on trade was "disturbing" and amounted to a provocation. When Aleksandr Alexeiev asked Guevara if he would like to accompany Fidel, Che jokingly wondered aloud how useful that would be, as he was perceived by Moscow as an "ugly duckling" and a "troublemaker."[27] Alexeiev replied:

> I know the opposite is true, because in my country you are appreciated precisely for your honesty and sincerity, your firmness in defending your ideas,

even though they are sometimes wrong, and for your courage in recognizing your mistakes; and a certain taste for troublemaking is not a defect in our eyes.[28]

A further moment of tension surfaced that April. According to a U.S. military intelligence report, important segments of the Cuban militias began to be dismantled during those weeks. At the same time, military facilities at San Antonio de los Baños outside the capital and at San Julián in Pinar del Río were placed under Soviet control. The Cuban air force commander of the former base was arrested for refusing to transfer it to the Soviets. He was freed thanks only to Che's personal intervention.[29]

Toward the end of 1963, when the Sino-Soviet conflict escalated and the USSR stepped up its pressure on Cuba to distance itself from Beijing, Che found himself complaining bitterly to his Russian friends about the Soviet "bureaucrats." He proposed to his Russian teacher and friend Oleg Daroussenkov that the Soviet Embassy organize a chess tournament and invite him, so as to ease relations with various officials who considered him "fervently pro-China." As Che explained,

> Several Soviet comrades tend to think that my views on topics like guerrilla warfare as the principal means for the liberation of Latin American peoples, or the issue of financial self-management as opposed to the system for budgetary financing, are Chinese positions and conclude that Guevara is pro-China. Can't I have my own opinion on these issues, independently of what the Chinese think?*

Che was increasingly irritated by the Chinese issue. He reluctantly adopted Cuba's position of neutrality: "We cannot even publish [an article by Paul Sweezy about Yugoslavia] because of our position of absolute neutrality, as we cannot intervene in any area involving the Chinese-Soviet conflict."[30] Che was troubled by the harassment of China's supporters in Cuba and elsewhere, and felt that the global onslaught against Beijing was exces-

---

*MID-463-26.XII.63. Oleg Daroussenkov, "Memorandum of Conversation of December 20, 1963, with Minister of Industries Ernesto Guevara," December 26, 1963 (Secret), Ministry of Foreign Affairs, Moscow. Beginning in mid-1963, when Cuba was formally excluded from the Socialist bloc, all cables from the Soviet Embassy in Havana were also sent to the Central Committee department in charge of relations with the Socialist countries. The head of this department was none other than Yuri Andropov. The first direct accusation leveled at Che of being pro-Chinese appears in Soviet cables in February 1963. It comes from a high official of the Hungarian Communist Party, who spent several weeks in Havana: "Some Cuban leaders (Che Guevara, Vilma Espín) are under strong Chinese influence." "Memorandum of Conversation, February 28, 1963, of Istvan Tempe," March 4, 1963, Russian National Archive, p. 419n, File No. 5, List 49, Document No. 653.

sive.* In an earlier conversation with Daroussenkov, he had gone to great pains to deny the existence of what the Soviet official called an "anti-Soviet propaganda campaign by the local Chinese Embassy."

The Russian envoy accused the Chinese Embassy of "spreading anti-Soviet literature, with a written request that it be distributed to the various Soviet specialists working in Cuban organizations."[31] Che defended it, arguing that everything was actually a provocation by another Socialist-bloc embassy (which, though he did not say so, was probably that of Albania). He himself had discussed the issue with the Chinese ambassador, who had denied any involvement whatsoever. The propaganda leaflets were even examined by the Cuban security laboratories and found not to be of Chinese origin. They had arrived in Cuba by some embassy's diplomatic pouch, and various Cuban Trotskyists helped distribute them, together with a Trotskyist Argentine official from the Ministry of Industries who was under scrutiny.[32] In fact, Che was being associated with China despite himself, although he did not disguise his admiration for Mao (he called him a wise man) or his gratitude to the People's Republic:

> The Chinese leadership has behaved in a way that is difficult for us to criticize. They have given us considerable aid, that we cannot neglect. For example we asked the Czechoslovaks for arms; they turned us down. Then we asked the Chinese; they said yes in a few days, and did not even charge us, stating that one does not sell arms to friends.[33]

The geopolitical, ideological, bureaucratic, and affective barriers all around him were closing in. If in 1963 he traveled little, in 1964 he spent entire months away from Cuba. His pattern of flight was overtaking him once again.

The disagreement among China, the U.S.S.R., and Guevara was not just ideological. Nor did it center exclusively on the issue of support for revolutionary movements in other countries—important though that was. The underlying dispute involved economic policy. In January 1964, Fidel Castro returned to Moscow to negotiate new Cuban sugar deliveries; he confirmed the island's long-term concentration on cane. Che agreed in principle, and

*Years later, Sergo Mikoyan recalled the following scene in Geneva, during an UNCTAD conference: "Che nodded toward a Chinese man seated on a bench and smiled, saying that some considered him pro-Chinese. These poor people were here to follow all his movements and contacts. And indeed, the inscrutable and silent Chinaman was still there three hours later when, after going for a walk and having a long talk in the room, we finally left Che seated before a pile of documents." Sergo Mikoyan, "Encuentros con Che Guevara," in *América Latina,* Academy of Sciences of the USSR, Latin American Institute, No. 1, 1974, p. 193.

was willing to reverse the shift away from sugar begun in previous years; but he opposed the unavoidable consequences of that decision.

Nor could he have been pleased by the implications of Fidel's second trip to the U.S.S.R. A confidential U.S. analysis of the mission emphasized that the U.S.S.R. had strongly—and successfully—pressured Castro to restrain "his natural impulse to promote violent revolution." Especially, the Soviets sought to prevent Cuba from intervening in any way in the Panama crisis that erupted in January 1964.* In addition, they wanted Cuba to put its economic house in order, and, if it would not condemn China as the Soviets wished, at least to show a less neutral position in the conflict between Moscow and Beijing.[34] Castro did not bow to all the Soviet demands; but, as pressure on him grew in the following months, so did his concessions. If one is to believe a report from the Brazilian government to U.S. Secretary of State Dean Rusk, the Soviet ambassador in Brasília had told Brazilian President Castelo Branco that:

> Fidel Castro has broken his link with Beijing; the Cuban government had suspended its relations with China and was peacefully disposed toward other countries, especially Brazil and the United States. The weapons found in Venezuela last November, which caused Cuba's expulsion from the OAS . . . might have been sent by the Chinese. Many of the revolutionary pamphlets and other guerrilla propaganda attributed to Cuba actually came from Chinese sources.[35]

Che's distress over Cuba's pro-Moscow drift may have derived from the same dilemma shared by the millions of young people who paraded his picture during myriad mass demonstrations of the late sixties. They wanted the same ends, but not the means; they accepted the goals, but not the steps needed to attain them. In his Algiers speech Che clearly acknowledged that the shift away from sugar had been a mistake, but he rejected the next logical step, which was to reemphasize sugar cultivation. He did so because the economic changes underway in the U.S.S.R. during the Khrushchev era awakened in him sharply negative reactions; together with the disagreement over international trade and the revolution in Latin America, they made him increasingly antagonistic toward the U.S.S.R.

*Indeed, the Americans recognized that "There is no conclusive evidence linking Castro with direct responsibility for the rioting. There is nothing to show that the Cuban leader was in consultation with Panamanian Castroists in the planning and direction of the recent disturbances or that he delivered material support for use in the riots." INR to Secretary, "Castroist and Communist Involvement in the Panamanian Disorder," RAR-3, Bureau of Intelligence and Research, Department of State (Secret), January 31, 1964, NSF, Country File, Cuba, vol. 1, LBJ Library.

The Guevarist criticism of existing socialism was by now explicit, though not public, and it was indeed close to the doubts and reservations expressed by the Chinese. It stemmed from a "leftist" position, blaming many Soviet shortcomings on the "rightist" course adopted by Khrushchev. Also echoing the Chinese experience, Che drew away from the U.S.S.R. due to delays in assistance and broken promises. During 1963, Che was doubly disappointed by the U.S.S.R. Guevara soon surmised that Moscow was both less able and less willing to provide assistance than he had assumed.*

His estrangement was based upon a radical position which today might be termed fundamentalist—and which was hardly distinguishable from the Chinese critique of Russian revisionism. At a Ministry of Industries meeting on October 12, 1963, he articulated his views with greater precision than ever before or after; as far as is known, his comments went unreported. Che was by now fully aware of the enormous economic difficulties confronted by the U.S.S.R. But, for him, the solution did not lie in any liberalization or Gorbachev-style reform. Rather it was to be found in greater economic centralization and in banishing market forces from all transactions except trade with capitalist countries. Guevara's assessment was categorical:

> Agricultural problems in the Soviet Union today come from somewhere.
> . . . Something is wrong. . . . It occurs to me, instinctively, that it has to do
> with the organization of the kolkhozes and sovkhozes, decentralization, or
> else material incentives and financial self-management, aside from various
> other problems, naturally, such as giving private plots to members of
> kolkhozes; in sum, with the little attention they have paid to moral incentives,
> especially in the countryside, concerned as they were by the countless
> problems they faced. . . . So the Soviet Union now has an agricultural catastrophe
> similar to ours, and this indicates that something is wrong. . . . There
> are more signs every day that the system serving as the basis for Socialist
> countries must be changed.[36]

Che was clearly taking sides in one of the most heated, ongoing debates in the Soviet Union. On one side were backers of Khrushchev's economic liberalization, who favored reforms aimed at economic decentralization and more flexible planning, in a sort of premature *perestroika* generally identified with the economists Memtchinov, Trapeznikov, and especially Yefsei G.

---

*A CIA report in 1965 noted that industrialization in Cuba had failed due to a shortage of equipment, raw materials, and skilled labor; a lack of experience in heavy construction; and a lack of discipline in budgets and economic planning. Central Intelligence Agency, Intelligence Memorandum, Cuba: "Delay and Misdirection of the Industrial Production Program, 1960–1965," November 1965 (Secret), p. 1, NSF, Country File, Cuba, W. G. Bowdler File, vol. I, no. 8 report, LBJ Library.

Liberman; on the other side were opponents to reform. The problem for Cuba, as Che saw it, was that Soviet influence no longer served to radical-ize or advance socialism, but rather to undermine it. In his view, the in-evitable next step would be "goulash socialism," as the Chinese had labeled it, in view of its Hungarian origins.

Che considered the new Cuban emphasis on agriculture and sugar to be a betrayal of the industrialization process. He related Cuba's growing links to the Soviet Union with that country's process of decentralization, so-called financial self-management, and material incentives—all in contrast to the budgetary system he advocated, which was linked, instead, to moral incentives and centralization in investment and decision-making. Guevara tended to shove all these elements into the same bag, though his opponents were not necessarily aware of the binding links among them. For their part, the Cuban company managers and high officials who supported the Soviet-inspired reforms were in a sense disciples of Liberman without realizing it. As a Russo-French economic consultant of the Cubans at the time recalls: the champions of company autonomy and financial self-management were responding to the daily realities of administration, and not to any directives from Liberman or the Soviet Union.[37]

Che assessed all these issues in terms of a theoretical debate about the role of the so-called law of value in socialism. The term, taken from classi-cal English economic theory and Marx's *Capital,* served as a euphemism for what is now called the market. In Guevara's view, the Soviet Union had fallen under the sway of the law of value, or the laws of the market. Identi-fying the prevalence of the law of value with his bêtes noires—centraliza-tion, material incentives, and self-management—Che believed that:

> The budgetary system is part of a general conception of the construction of socialism and must thus be studied in context. The budgetary sys-tem . . . [implies] a certain way of guiding the economy . . . and all the rela-tions within it, along with all the relations among moral incentives and material incentives in building socialism. All these things are linked together. Financial self-management must include material incentives as its fundamental pillar, along with decentralization and a whole organization of planning in accordance with these relations. . . . In the budgetary system there must be another type of planning, another conception of develop-ment, another conception of material incentives.[38]

As the French and Soviet economists who advised Che during the fateful years of 1963 and 1964 noted, his concerns were not just economic. Victor Bogorod and Charles Bettelheim, two French Marxist economists who assisted the Cubans in the early sixties, agree that Che was not really interested in economics; the part of his work that he most enjoyed was his daily contact with workers and staff.[39] His real goal was to abolish all market and monetary relations based on value, both among state-owned companies and within the population as a whole. The underlying rationale for his apparently technical positions on the budgetary system, his views on moral incentives and on the concentration of management in state industry, is to be found in the last essay he wrote, the one that will be best remembered: "El socialismo y el hombre en Cuba" ("Man and Socialism in Cuba," 1965). But his conception of the "new man" that the revolution had to create was not fully developed until 1965; the disputes of 1963 and 1964 took place on a purely economic battleground—one in which he could not win, due to his lack of technical knowledge and the international context.

Alban Lataste, a former aide from Chile who accompanied Che on his first trip to the Soviet Union and later parted ways with him, defined three indispensable tasks in which Guevara would ultimately fail:

> 1) To apply the principle of individual and collective material interest in economic policy; 2) To perfect the regime of real and nominal salaries, so as to achieve a true equivalence between effort and remuneration; 3) To improve the pricing system both as an element to redistribute national income and as a factor in economic calculations.[40]

Che's failure derived precisely from his tendency to see alternatives in global, abstract terms. Every little disagreement was for him a matter of principle, the reflection of a deeper divergence. His opponents openly criticized him for elevating every discussion to the category of high principles of philosophy or doctrine, even with regard to minor technical details of management or problem-solving.[41]

Later, after Che left his economic policy post in Cuba, some of his ideas were retrieved by the leadership. This was due partly to another dispute between Castro and the Soviet Union, and partly to a relative improvement in the economy. Che's internationalist ventures were also presented as harking back to his domestic-policy positions—not in economic, but in moral and ethical terms which the Revolution attempted to revive as its independence vis-à-vis the U.S.S.R. waned. But, as one of his principal intellectual opponents in those years, Carlos Rafael Rodríguez, noted, the economic and accounting policies implemented in the late 1960's "had nothing to do with Che."[42] Fidel Castro himself commented in 1987:

> Some of Che's ideas were at times incorrectly interpreted, and even wrongly implemented. There was never any serious attempt to put them into

practice, and during a certain period even ideas that were diametrically
opposed to Che's economic thinking were adopted.*

In his Algiers speech in July, 1963, Che expressed his regret at having forsaken the sugar industry and adopting policies leading to a disastrous balance of payments. He related the economic debacle to problems in Socialist
planning, as well as excessive ambition and idealism. However, though he
acknowledged his mistake in underestimating the importance of sugar,
he did not resign himself to a future of monocultivation for Cuba. Indeed,
he saw things very differently:

> The single-product structure of our economy has not yet been overcome
> after four years of revolution. But the conditions are there for what in
> time might become an economy solidly based upon Cuban raw materials,
> with a diversified production and technical levels that will allow it to com-
> pete in world markets. We are developing our own lines of production,
> and we believe that . . . by 1970, we will have laid the foundations for
> our economy's independent development, based primarily upon our own
> technology and our own raw materials, mostly processed with our own
> machinery.[43]

Time would show that the agreements Castro signed with the Soviets in
1963 and implemented in early 1964 were effectively locking Cuba into its
role as a sugar producer and an importer of consumer goods, energy, and
light machinery. Granted, there was little choice; the monocultivation of
sugar was probably the only path, or the only available path.† But it was not
Che's, nor one he could tout abroad, especially in Latin America. As Canadian Ambassador George Kidd noted, with his usual perspicacity:

> It seems that Cuba's leaders now intend to make the island a tropical New
> Zealand for the Communist world rather than a Switzerland for the
> Caribbean. . . . It is no doubt sensible for Cuba to be responsive to the
> needs of its principal customer. . . . [But] it is hard to see how such an eco-
> nomic programme can have much appeal to the left-wing nationalists in
> Latin America who are clamouring for rapid industrialisation largely of the
> disastrous kind Cuba undertook in the initial revolutionary period.[44]

*Fidel Castro, "En el acto central por el XX aniversario de la caída en combate del
Comandante Ernesto Che Guevara," *Cuba Socialista* (Havana), November–December
1987, p. 93. "One of the greatest heresies committed in this country was to assume that
what we were doing between 1967 and 1970, the economic disruption that prevailed, took
place . . . in the name of Che."

† The Socialist countries had even asserted that they would fulfill aid commitments
through 1964 but could promise nothing beyond that, as reported by the London *Financial
Times,* July 29, 1964.

Though everybody now agreed on Cuba's need to produce more sugar, there was no consensus on the course to be followed. This was the focus of Guevara's first significant disagreement with Castro and the rest of the government. As in other instances, he was partly right. As a lucid and knowledgeable critic of Cuban agricultural policy recognized a few years later, it was undoubtedly reasonable to reemphasize the agricultural economy, though perhaps without abandoning so many industrial projects. Che may not have been that wrong in pushing industry as much as he did. It may have seemed logical to reestablish the priority of sugar. But, as French agronomist René Dumont wondered, was it necessary to go beyond the realistic threshold of 8.5 million tons?[45] Whether these nuanced, balanced stances were compatible with Che's character and approach was another matter.

The dispute over sugar and industrialization came up in a private conversation between Che and Daroussenkov, concerning the renewed emphasis on agriculture and the delivery of a monumental steel mill promised by the USSR. Already a bitter debate was underway in Cuba about its construction. In a confidential 1963 cable to the British Embassy from the Foreign Office, London sent Counselor Eccles (probably the MI5's man in Havana) a summary of British intelligence's evaluation:

President Dorticós has now said that because of the need to develop agriculture, industrialisation will have to wait until after 1965. Che Guevara, the Minister for Industry, has complained that many of the industrial installations being delivered are unsuitable for Cuba because they require imports of raw materials costing nearly as much as it would cost to import the finished product. Dr. Castro has declared that the task of industry was to assist agriculture by producing fertilizer and agricultural machinery; and he has indicated that the building of a large steel-works with Soviet assistance, previously regarded as one of Cuba's biggest projects and greatly publicised in the Cuban press, could be postponed or abandoned because there were more important things to do.[46]

Che did not openly contradict Castro, but he did not spare his reservations in a conversation reported by Daroussenkov to Moscow:

When I asked how one was to take the statement by Fidel Castro . . . that agriculture would be the basis for Cuba's development in the next few decades, and that it might be more beneficial from an economic point of view to invest money not in building a steel mill but in irrigation, the chemical industry, and the construction of agricultural machinery, Guevara answered that the question of building the steel mill has not yet been decided. There are many arguments in its favor, he said. Under the current international circumstances, any country that does not have its own steel will face continual difficulties in developing its economy. . . . The Soviet Union is trying to fulfill our needs, but sometimes it cannot do so for the simple reason that it, too, has difficulties in some types of production that we lack. Let us take tin as an example. We have very good prospects to develop the production of canned fruits, but to do so we need large quantities of a special tin that the Soviet Union cannot send us. Cuba needs to develop its ship-building industry. We live on an island. Our trade is maritime, and we have virtually no merchant or fishing fleet of our own. But to build modern ships one needs steel, and where are we to get it? Of course we cannot import it from across the ocean. . . . Some people, he continued, say that as Cuba does not have coke of its own the cost of steel would be very high, and so the Cubans should not develop their steel industry. But they forget that one can use progressive technology and an advanced production technology, so the import of coke is no longer a problem. For example, Japan's steel industry functions not only with imported coke but also ore, and it successfully competes with other countries. In a word, the question of building the steel mill or not has not yet been resolved, and we will strongly insist on its construction.[47]

The problem was not only one of development strategies. Cuban farming, directed from the INRA by Carlos Rafael Rodríguez since 1961, was governed by principles strongly opposed by Che Guevara. Material incentives, the financial self-management of companies, high salary differentials, and relatively decentralized investment programs prevailed in the rest of Cuban agriculture, excluding the sugar industry. Those who worked more were paid more*; each company kept its own resources, transferring only its surplus to the INRA or the banks. In a word, the law of value was playing a central role in Cuba's socialist agriculture outside sugar. Even after the second land reform of October 1963, 30 percent of all land remained in private hands. Bestowing priority on agriculture thus implied an unqualified preference for its most characteristic features. Converting it into the pillar of the Cuban economy, as was the case, effectively doomed the kind of socialism Che desired for his adopted country. Though he agreed that a centralized system like that which prevailed in industry could exist alongside material incentives, which were current throughout the economy, he believed moral

*The following conversation between Che and Alexeiev illustrates the growing controversy on the subject: "Guevara told me that at this time in all industrial branches work norms would be introduced with the help of Soviet experts. He disagreed with progressive salaries and declared that he would only apply moral incentives. I told him he was wrong thinking that it was possible to increase productivity without material incentives. He replied that at this point the aim was not to increase productivity but to raise consciousness and to introduce new technologies." Aleksandr Alexeiev, "Memorandum of Conversation December 25, 1963 with the Minister of Industry Ernesto Guevara," January 29, 1964 (Secret), Russian National Archive, File No. 5, List No. 49, Document 760.

incentives were not compatible with the financial self-management applied in agriculture: "Moral incentives cannot work with financial self-management; they cannot advance two steps together, but trip each other up and fall. It is impossible."[48]

In other words, the full implementation of the law of value would reinforce the status quo, the existing relations between agriculture and industry, cities and countryside, and among the different regions. As Che succinctly put it, "It is now evident to me that wherever we use the law of value we are actually, through indirect methods, letting capitalism in through the back door."[49]

The "great debate," as it came to be called, was summed up in a recent study as follows:

> Ernesto Guevara and others contended that Cuba could not allow the law of value to determine investments without reneging on the possibility of overcoming underdevelopment. Industry did not enjoy the comparative advantage of agriculture and, therefore, was not as "profitable." Self-finance planning would tend to reinforce uneven development and specialization. The budgetary system of centralized planning allowed the state to plan for the economy as a whole, correct past inequalities, and promote more balanced development. The fact that Cuba was a small country with limited wealth and an open economy compelled the state to harness its most abundant resource: the will, energy and passion of the Cuban people. Self-finance planning advocated material incentives on the grounds of efficiency and rationality. Yet material incentives privatized conscience, and inefficiency was not restricted to economic resources. Moral incentives would develop conscience as an economic lever and further the creation of new human beings.[50]

When on July 3, 1964, Che lost his direct tutelage of the sugar industry, which would now have its own ministry—albeit headed by Orlando Borrego, one of his closest advisers—he could hear one shoe falling.* At the same time, President Osvaldo Dorticós replaced Regino Boti at the Ministry of the Economy, and was also named head of the Central Planning Council. This amounted to a second attack on Che, not because he had a poor relationship with Dorticós but because a second power center was being established in Cuban economic policy—as important as his own. Che pursued the debate throughout 1964, publishing three essays on his major areas of disagreement with the Soviets, the old Cuban Communists, and the

---

*At first, Che did not give much importance to the emergence of the new ministry: "There are to be two new ministries. . . . One of them, naturally, is that of Sugar under Borrego, which is nothing more than an offshoot of the existing Ministry. . . ." Ernesto Che Guevara, Meeting of July 11, 1964, *Ministry of Industries Minutes,* p. 508.

new Cuban technicians: centralization, the budgetary system, and material incentives. Charles Bettelheim would note thirty years later that there was always a bureaucratic bias in Che's analysis. He regarded the Cuban economy from the perspective of the large companies within the Ministry of Industries, where there could indeed be appropriate forms of oversight and control. But for the countless small firms that had been nationalized in 1963, no centralized direction was feasible; there was not enough administrative capacity, nor enough cadres or resources. Che saw the forest, but not the trees; he did not acknowledge that the changes wrought in the Cuban economy and society worked against his system.[51]

He continued to develop his views during this period, within the Marxist discourse of the time but also with undeniable sincerity:

> The consciousness of men in the vanguard . . . may perceive the right path to carry a socialist revolution to victory . . . even if . . . the contradictions between the development of the forces of production and the relations of production which would make a revolution necessary or possible are lacking.[52]

In this reply to Bettelheim, Che concluded that even if Cuba was not "ready" for the precise and comprehensive planning he would have wished, or the moral incentives and extreme industrial centralization he advocated, it made no difference. What counted was the prevalence of an advanced consciousness among the Cuban leadership and the most enlightened sectors of the people, for the process to be forced through. This stance permeated all his views: about sugar and industry, the budget and centralization, moral and material incentives. His positions were not strictly economic; they were essentially political, and stemmed from a central premise: consciousness (which for Che meant willpower) is the driving force behind change. Administration comes later, and is entirely secondary.

Che was right, to a certain extent. If the degree of political awareness and mobilization he called for had existed, it would perhaps have been possible to run an economy as simple as Cuba's like clockwork: centralize everything in a few hands, and structure prices, salaries, and investment in light of moral criteria. Indeed, that level of activism seemed ready to dawn at certain moments of the Revolution: the Bay of Pigs, the missile crisis, the literacy campaign. It was Che's misfortune that this higher consciousness always faded, and that his own passion and dedication were not shared by all—nor could they be, as he all too often failed to understand.

The debate went back and forth from centralization to the budgetary system to the central management of investment, salaries, and banks; then it would shift back to moral versus material incentives, its original starting point. Carlos Rafael Rodríguez stated over twenty years later that he and Che "had small differences in our conception of incentives."[53] From a distance, the discrepancy between Che and the other economic policy-makers was more a matter of degree than substance, though this did not prevent furious arguments. Che once stalked out of an INRA meeting so abruptly that even his bodyguards were left behind, according to a Soviet technician. A man so hotheaded could hardly debate matters of historical importance with any degree of calm.[54]

The Cuban government mounted a retroactive whitewashing campaign to minimize its differences with Che, insisting that they were only a matter of emphasis. Thus, Rodríguez notes that Che never sought to eliminate material incentives—which is true. Nor did the old Communists demand that moral incentives simply be eliminated. But the dispute—whether a matter of substance or degree—was very real. For Che, moral incentives were the key; for the others, it was material incentives.* The cycle ended with Fidel Castro's second trip to Moscow in January 1964. Cuba's alignment with the USSR was now virtually complete, and in a sense beneficial to the island, as its depleted economy was able to accumulate foreign-currency reserves, take advantage of high international sugar prices, and ensure a long-term market for its produce.

And so Che Guevara began his final year in Cuba relatively marginalized from the daily running of the economy. But he continued laboring in other areas of government and in his private activities. In early 1963, he turned again to volunteer work. During the sugar harvest of that year, he broke records in cane-cutting and consecutive hours of labor, providing a twofold example. First, he strengthened the government's revolutionary resolve and proved that Cuba's leaders could still sustain the effort and sacrifice they demanded of the people; secondly, he showed that volunteer work helped solve the daunting problem of scarce manpower. After 1963, the sugar harvest fell precipitously; when the government decided, in 1964, to reemphasize sugar production, it came up against a shortage of labor. The countryside was not entirely deserted, but the rural population had fallen and the machinery promised by the Soviets (and eagerly awaited by Che, who even experimented with several designs) never arrived. By that time Guevara's conception of volunteer work was gradually

---

*The following passage makes the point very succinctly: "The discussion of 'moral incentives' is being made the center of all issues, and moral incentives in themselves are not the center. . . . Moral incentives are the predominant . . . form which incentives must take in this phase of the construction of socialism . . . but they are not the only form. . . . Material incentives are also valid." Ernesto Che Guevara, *Minutes,* p. 345.

changing; he acknowledged that it could not be sustained without adequate planning:

> Last Sunday I went and lost my time at volunteer work, and something happened that had never happened to me during volunteer work, except for cane-cutting, which was that I kept looking at my watch every fifteen minutes to see when my hours would be up so I could leave, because it didn't make any sense.[55]

Volunteer work was a partial solution. Others were mandatory military service, instituted in December 1963 (the first recruits were called up in March 1964), and legislation on labor norms and salary classifications, promulgated in the first half of 1964. The consolidation of the armed forces and reorganization of the militias served the same purpose, and strengthened the leadership as a whole. But they also undermined Che's influence. Indeed, neither the exiles in Miami nor the Mafia in the United States considered him as important as they once had; the price on his head fell to $20,000, while Fidel Castro's was worth $100,000.[56]

Che continued to write essays and grant interviews to the international media; along with Fidel Castro, he remained the most effective spokesman for the Cuban Revolution—and perhaps the most credible. But the revolutionary process was foundering in Latin America, despite efforts in Venezuela, Guatemala, and Peru. He felt alone, caught in a dead end. As he wrote to the director of a primary school in the provinces, "Sometimes we revolutionaries are alone; even our children see us as strangers."[57] With each passing day, there was less for him to do in Cuba. Increasingly, he yearned for movement, for a radically different situation less fraught with ambivalence. Fully aware of his predicament, at the end of March and before leaving on a new trip to Africa and Europe, he spoke with Tamara Bunke in his office for several hours. She had by now completed her training as a Cuban intelligence agent, and Guevara gave her the following instructions: "Go and live in Bolivia, where you will establish relations within the armed forces and the governing bourgeoisie, travel around the country . . . and wait for a contact who will signal the moment for definitive action."[58] The contact would be Che himself, two and a half years later.

Aside from his defeat in economic policy and Cuba's alignment with the U.S.S.R., other, more personal factors were pushing him to leave. On March 19, 1964, a woman named Lilia Rosa Pérez gave birth to a son of his in Havana. He was the only child conceived out of wedlock that Che would ever acknowledge, though there is partial evidence of others. Lilia Rosa was an attractive Havana woman about thirty years old who had met Che in Santa Clara in 1958, and then again at La Cabaña in 1959; in 1996 she still attended the annual commemoration of the occupation of the fortress on January 2. Faithful to his heritage, Omar Pérez (named after Omar Khayyam, author of the *Rubaiyat,* an edition of which Che gave to Lilia Rosa) is a dissident poet and translator who has, for opposing the regime and refusing military service, done time in one of the labor camps his father founded.* He has the eyes, eyebrows, and smile of his father; on the few occasions he has a reason to be glad, his face lights up just as Che's did. He does not speak of his lineage, though he has Guevara's long, straight black hair, prominent brow, and sad, mysterious expression. His gestures, look, and reticence also betray his antecedents.

Toward the end of the eighties, Lilia Rosa appeared one day at the home of the companion of Che's daughter, Hilda Guevara Gadea, with a pile of books by Guevara and others full of handwritten inscriptions. Lilia thus confessed her past relationship with the *comandante,* and introduced Omar, who became a close friend of Che's firstborn. Hildita, as she was known in Cuba, was already beset by cancer, alcoholism, and depression, the latter partly brought on by the ostracism she had always suffered from Che's official widow and children. Until her death in August 1995, she and Omar would share an especially dear part of their father's inheritance: his rebelliousness, individualism, and lack of favor with official circles. Hilda Guevara never had any doubt that Omar was her brother; she treated him accordingly, and asked her children to consider him as such. Omar's story is well known in Cuba, as is that of Che's other presumed illegitimate offspring.[†] Omar's case is different, however, for a simple reason: Che's Mexican grandson, Canek Sánchez Guevara, told this author (in both Havana and Mexico, in a private conversation and a taped interview) that his mother, Hilda, introduced Omar to him in those terms, and loved him as a sibling.[59] The many reports about Omar, his physical likeness to Che, and the account by Che's daughter, all confirm his birthright.[‡]

It is not known if Che was aware of his son's birth in 1964, but in any case, this situation must not have been an easy one for him. He had always opposed his colleagues' frequent affairs as a matter of principle, and had succeeded in avoiding the erotic temptations of power in the tropics. But something happened in mid-1963, if not before, that can only have exacerbated his growing restlessness in Cuba.

---

*Lilia Rosa Pérez kindly indicated the origins of her son's name, as well as the circumstances under which she met Che, in a letter to the author dated November 2, 1996.

[†] One in particular, Mirko, was even under investigation for a time during the eighties.

[‡] Lilia Rosa, in the cited letter to the author, confirmed the story while noting that she had not taken the initiative to reveal it. Lilia Rosa López, letter to the author, November 2, 1996.

Hence his more moderate and flexible attitude in the Ministry of Industries, as was evident in the case of an official named Mesa, a director of the
Toy Company in the Ministry. A married man with children, Mesa fell in
love with his secretary and was spotted with her in dubious circumstances.
The case was presented to Che on July 11, 1964, four months after the birth
of Omar. His response was revealing:

> No one has yet established in human relations that a man must live with one
> woman all the time. . . . I said I didn't know why all the discussion was nec-
> essary, because I consider this a logical case that can happen to anybody,
> and we should perhaps analyze whether the sanction . . . is not extreme. . . .
> Obviously, if something happens, it is because the woman is willing; other-
> wise, it would be a serious crime, but this doesn't happen without the
> woman's consent. . . . We have tried not to be extreme in these matters.
> There is also a degree of Socialist saintliness in this area, and the real truth
> is that if one could enter into everybody's conscience we would have to see
> who would cast the first stone. . . . We have always advocated not going to
> extremes, and especially not making of this a capital matter, or making it
> public; this could go so far as to destroy homes which could have survived,
> as these are quite natural, normal things that happen.[60]

So Che was restive; his predicament and his eternal wanderlust led him,
as always, to travel. On March 17, he left for Geneva as head of the Cuban
delegation to the first United Nations Conference on Trade and Development (UNCTAD), whose Secretary-General was his compatriot Raúl
Prebisch. Che spent most of his month abroad in Switzerland, with brief
stopovers in Prague and Paris, and a couple of days in Algiers to see his
friend Ben Bella. His speech at the United Nations was substantive and historic, presenting several of the concerns that would dominate his thinking
and public statements in the following year.

The hall at the Palais des Nations erupted into applause as Guevara
made his way to the podium; he was already a legendary figure.[61] He began
by castigating the conference for excluding several delegations—China,
North Vietnam, and North Korea—and for inviting others with dubious
credentials, like South Africa. Then he staked out his position, in ideological and political terms:

> We understand clearly—and express frankly—that the only correct solution
> to the problems of humanity at this time is the complete elimination of the
> exploitation of dependent countries by developed, capitalist countries, with
> all the consequences implicit in that fact.[62]

Che's speech was short, ironic, and rhetorical ("the imperialists will
insist that underdevelopment is caused by underdeveloped countries"), but

lacking in vision and proposals. It was respectful of the Socialist countries, but no more. Guevara repeatedly emphasized the plight of poor nations, the peoples "struggling for their liberation," "the needy of the world," with hardly any mention of the Soviet Union. In contrast, he subtly presented the problem that was beginning to obsess him, and which would set him increasingly at odds with the Cuban regime.

He noted the worsening terms of trade, whereby the price of raw materials exported by developing countries tended to fall, while that of goods and services exported by industrialized countries tended to rise. This meant that poor nations were forced to export more and more in order to maintain the same volume of imports. He observed that "many underdeveloped countries reach an apparently logical conclusion": in their trade relations with Socialist countries, the latter "benefit from the current state of affairs."[63] He then explained that this reality must be acknowledged "honestly and bravely," granting that it was not entirely the fault of the Socialist bloc. And the situation changed when countries reached long-term agreements, as Cuba had with the Soviet Union. Yet his term for Cuba's sugar pact with the USSR— "relations of a new type"—while reflecting his conviction that it was not the same to do business with Socialists as with capitalists, was hardly enthusiastic. He resented the way he was mistreated by the other Socialist delegations; he simply was no longer part of the family, if he ever had been:

> Guevara complained of the poor impression he brought back of the contacts with Soviet comrades and the other Socialist countries in Geneva, who did not trust him. The Cuban delegation was isolated; the delegations of Eastern Europe would meet and talk things over and only afterwards, for appearances' sake, notify the Cubans of their decisions. The Cuban delegation was isolated.[64]

Guevara's days in the Calvinist city of Jean Jacques Rousseau had an element of mystery. Very few heads of delegation stayed for the entire month of the UNCTAD meeting. Che had a tense relationship with many of his fellow Latin Americans; according to a member of the Mexican mission, he was not even invited to meetings of the regional group.[65] He stayed at a modest hotel near the lake, with a large security detail, and sometimes visited with the Mexican delegates to drink tequila and sing tangos and boleros. He expressed a certain nostalgia for Mexico, asking about people and events there and recalling his time with an affection he acquired only after he left for Cuba. One day, a Mexican delegate saw him walking alone on the banks of Lake Geneva, pausing for a long time on a rock at the water's edge and contemplating the Salève in the distance; perhaps he was reflecting upon the hard decisions that awaited him in Cuba.

A lightning trip to Algeria—officially to attend the first Congress of the

National Liberation Front—allowed him to review events in Africa with Ben Bella. By now, the African struggle for liberation had become a leitmotif in Guevara's speeches: in Geneva, he evoked Congolese independence martyr Patrice Lumumba several times. Renewed combat in the Congo and the growing weakness of the central government were the issues of the day. He met in Algiers with some of the Congolese exile leaders, and became convinced that the 1961 rebellion, crushed since the assassination of Lumumba, was about to erupt again.*

Che's interest was not merely academic. In January he had Pablo Ribalta, a close aide of African-Cuban origins from his Sierra Maestra days, appointed the Cuban ambassador to Tanzania. The newly formed republic included the island of Zanzibar, where Cuba had had relations with the Nationalist Party; it had been training combatants and militants from the island.[66]

On his way back to Cuba, Che stopped in Paris, where he had lunch with Charles Bettelheim on the Boulevard Saint-Michel. He finally admitted that he had been wrong in his appraisal of the Soviet Union and in trusting its promises on aid and development. He returned to Havana at the end of April—back to the economic controversy and his administrative duties at the Ministry. Though he continued to discharge them diligently, he seemed bored and listless. His interest in economic matters was fading, and he had less influence in government deliberations. In the meantime, the team of Soviet advisers at the National Bank was gaining the upper hand. According to a British Embassy cable,

> Some observers see the recent strengthening of the Soviet team of advisers at the Cuban National Bank and other evidence of assumption by the Russians of more detailed responsibility for getting the Cuban economy to work, as a sign that both the Soviet and Cuban Governments have committed themselves reluctantly to a greater degree of Russian control.[†]

---

*Che's evaluation was similar to that of a CIA national intelligence estimate dated August 5, 1964 (drafted in the spring of that year), which began by saying: "In recent months, regional dissidence and violence have assumed serious proportions, even by Congolese standards, and produced the threat of a total breakdown in governmental authority. The difficulties confronting Prime Minister Tshombe are enormous." Director of Central Intelligence, "Special National Intelligence Estimate: Short-Term Prospects for the Tshombe Government in the Congo," August 5, 1964 (Secret), *Declassified Documents Catalog,* Research Publication (Woodbridge, Conn.), vol. 16, #5, Sept.–Oct. 1990, file series no. 2439.

† Havana Telegram No. 48 to Foreign Office, Cuban Political Situation, November 23, 1964 (Restricted), Foreign Office Archive FO371/174006, Public Record Office, London. Che was already on bad terms with Bank officials, especially its Soviet advisers: "You know that we have always had rather strained relations with the Bank, practically since I left the Bank. It has always been, through its Czech and Soviet advisers, the champion of financial self-management." Ernesto Che Guevara, Meeting of July 11, 1964, *Minutes,* p. 530.

Ernesto Guevara Lynch and his son, the future Che, c. 1930.

With his caddy friends, Altagracia, 1938.

The Guevara family, 1938 (with the young Ernesto at far left).

With his girlfriend Chichina Ferreyra, Malagueño, 1951.

Che, far right, and Raúl Castro, center, Veracruz, Mexico, 1955.

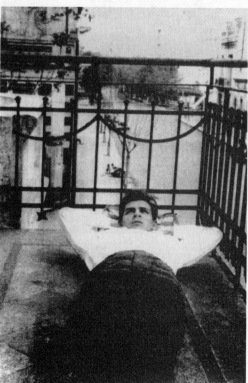

At his family's apartment, 1951.

Climbing Popocatepetl, Mexico, 1955.
Che turns to face the camera.

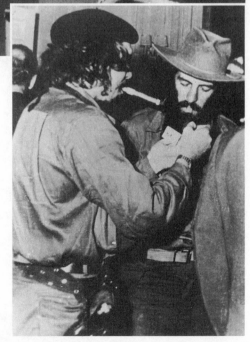

Perhaps the first picture of Che (right) with Fidel Castro, at the Miguel Schultz Immigration Detention Center, Mexico City, summer 1956.

With Camilo Cienfuegos, Havana, 1959.

With his mother, Celia,
a month after victory,
Havana, 1959.

Playing golf at the Havana
Country Club, 1960.

Playing baseball, Havana, 1960.

With his second wife, Aleida,
Havana, 1959.

With his first wife, Hilda, and their
daughter, Hildita, just after the
couple's separation, Havana, 1959.

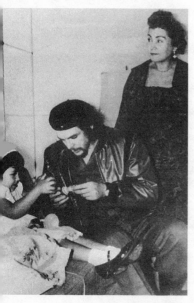

With Fidel, both putting on weight.

With Fidel and Raúl Castro on the eve of the Bay of Pigs.

With Mao Zedong (right), Beijing, 1960.

With Ahmed Ben Bella,
Algiers, 1963.

At the Ministry of Industries,
Havana, 1963.
*(Photo courtesy of Magnum
Photos Inc., © 1963 René Burri)*

With Aleida and three of his children, at home in Havana, 1964.

With Aleida and Cuban president Osvaldo Dorticós at the Havana airport on Che's return from Africa, March 15, 1965: one of the last public photographs of Che in Cuba.

Reporting on his trip to Africa at the Ministry of Industries, Havana, March 1965.

The last-known photograph of Che with his family, April 1965.

Top: In the Congo, summer 1965.
(Photo courtesy of Archive Photos)

Bottom: Disguised as a bureaucrat
before leaving for Bolivia; Havana, 1966.

The last photograph of Fidel and Che together, on the eve of his departure for Bolivia, October 1966.

In disguise in La Paz, Bolivia, November 1966.
(Photo courtesy of Der Spiegel*)*

In Bolivia.

CIA Bolivia Station Chief
John Tilton (right) and
Bolivian President René
Barrientos, 1967.

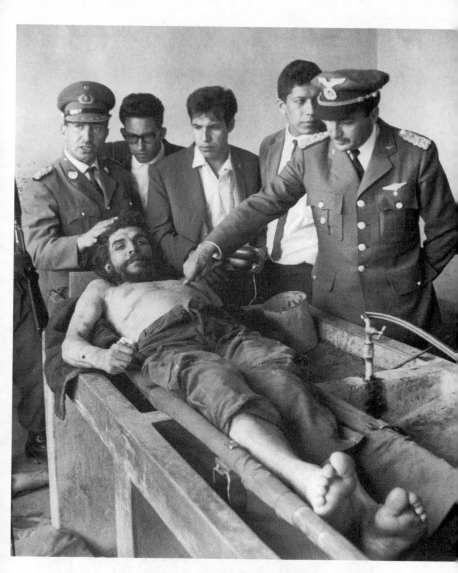

After execution, October 9, 1967.
(Photo by Freddy Alborta Trigo)

By November, Che was ready to ship off again, now as Cuba's representative to the anniversary of the Russian Revolution. The visit was particularly important as Khrushchev had just been ousted, and replaced by the troika of Leonid Brezhnev, Alexei Kosygin, and Nikolai Podgorny. Though there had been no love lost between Khrushchev and the Cubans since the missile crisis, the new Moscow leaders were completely unknown to them. Che's trip was a success in terms of protocol, but devoid of substance. Several witnesses remember him on the flight from Murmansk to Havana: he was euphoric, tipsy, and unusually chatty about his private life. It was during this trip that he confessed to Oleg Daroussenkov that he had agreed to marry Hilda Gadea after a few too many drinks.[67] It was also then, while sitting between the secretary-general of the Mexican Communist Party, Arnoldo Martínez Verdugo, and that of the Bolivian Party, Mario Monje, that he made his marvelous comment to Salvador Cayetano Carpio, leader of El Salvador's Communist Party: "Here you have me, Carpio, sitting between a monk [*monje*] and an executioner [*verdugo*]."[68]

On his return to Havana, Che convened one of his last official meetings with aides at the Ministry. After recounting with brutal frankness his impressions of the Socialist countries, he explained why he was against the so-called "economic reforms" underway in Eastern Europe and the USSR. His comments are worth quoting, both because they have not been published and because they reflect the dilemmas Guevara faced on the eve of his new odyssey:

> In Moscow I had a meeting with all the [Cuban] students who wanted to talk. So I invited them to the Embassy. I found myself face to face with about 50 of them. I was prepared to wage a huge battle against the self-management system. Well, I have never, during a mission of this sort, had a public as attentive, concerned, and able to understand me. Do you know why? Because they lived there, and many of the things I have told you, and tell you here in theoretical terms because I don't know any better, they know very well. They know because they are there, they go to the doctor, they go to the restaurant or to stores to buy something, and incredible things happen in the Soviet Union today. . . . Paul Sweezy says in an article that Yugoslavia is a country headed toward capitalism. Why? Because in Yugoslavia the Law of Value reigns supreme, and more so every day. Khrushchev said that [what was happening in Yugoslavia] was interesting, he even sent people to study there. . . . Well, what he saw in Yugoslavia that seemed so interesting to him is far more developed in the United States because it is a capitalist [country]. . . . In Yugoslavia they have the Law of Value; in Yugoslavia they close factories because they aren't profitable; in Yugoslavia there are delegates from Switzerland and Holland looking for unemployed workers so they can take them back to their own countries . . . as foreign labor in an imperialist country. . . . This is what is happening in Yugoslavia.

Poland is now following the Yugoslav path, of course, collectivization is being reversed, they are going back to private land ownership, establishing a whole series of special exchange systems, cultivating relations with the United States. . . . In Czechoslovakia and Germany they are also beginning to study the Yugoslav system in order to apply it. So we have a whole series of countries changing course, in the face of what? In the face of a reality which we can no longer ignore—which is, though nobody says it, that the Western bloc is advancing faster than the people's democracies. Why? That is where, instead of getting to the bottom of it, which would solve the problem, a superficial answer has been sought, which is to reinforce the market, introduce the Law of Value, reinforce material incentives.[69]

By this time, Che had an uninhibited and definitive opinion of the Socialist countries. They were losing the race with the West not because they had followed the axioms of Marxism-Leninism, but because they had betrayed them. As they realized they were falling behind in the battle with capitalism, they shifted to a diametrically different course—mistakenly, in Che's view. His position, especially when viewed against the backdrop of the simmering Sino-Soviet conflict, was coming dangerously close to the edge. The Communists he met on the plane from Moscow and Murmansk had just sojourned in Beijing. They had joined Carlos Rafael Rodríguez on a Latin American mission to China hoping to mediate between the two Socialist powers, following a proposal by Martínez Verdugo at the meeting of Latin American Communist parties in Havana. The Cubans were pivotal in the Latin American Communists' decision to go to China and mediate: they organized the trip and may even have instigated the Mexican proposal, while ensuring that Rodríguez would figure as spokesman. According to Martínez Verdugo, Mao received them hospitably but exclaimed, "You are here because the revisionists sent you; we do not agree with you, but we welcome you all the same."[70] The effort at mediation floundered, as would that undertaken by Che two months later.

One of the reasons for these attempts was that Che, Cuba, and the Socialist powers were about to be sucked into the African maelstrom. In the summer of 1964, Pierre Mulele, Lumumba's minister of education and his spiritual and political heir, had rekindled the Congolese rebellion in the central-western region of Kwilu. A National Liberation Committee had accomplished the same in the east and north, near Stanleyville. They all rose up in arms against the regime imposed three years earlier by the United Nations, Belgium, and the CIA. The Congolese government was on the verge of collapse, and Washington and Brussels stood ready to help it. When the rebels captured Stanleyville in August, Belgium and the United States became seriously alarmed. Two months later, they flew in several battalions of paratroopers to crush the uprising, retake the city, and regain control over the eastern part of the country. Another ostensible goal was to prevent a repeat of the bloodbath that had occurred when the rebels entered Stanleyville, taking hostage the U.S. consul, dozens of U.S. missionaries, and three hundred Belgian citizens and, according to some reports, executing 20,000 Congolese from the urban middle class.[71]

This new rebellion in the Congo, which will be examined in further detail in Chapter 9, had a twofold effect on Che and the Cubans. First, it persuaded them that Lumumba's anticolonialist struggle had finally revived. Second, the intervention of Washington and the colonial powers seemed to confirm the anti-imperialist nature of the reborn rebellion in Africa. Thus Guevara's wholehearted commitment to the Congolese cause; he immediately stepped into the breach to uphold what he saw as a just and ongoing struggle for freedom.

Che's African campaign began in New York, where the travel arrangements were made. It would continue in Africa at the end of 1964 and throughout all of 1965. On December 9, just three weeks after his return from the USSR, he packed his bags again, this time on his way to the United Nations. His designation as head of the Cuban delegation to the Nineteenth General Assembly, at its very end, made no great impression in Havana. Along with his UNCTAD mission several months earlier, it was seen by some as a sign of his fading authority:

> Che Guevara's appointment to lead the Cuban delegation at the United Nations seems less important. Guevara similarly represented Cuba at the UNCTAD conference at Geneva; and in any case his political advice seems to carry less weight than ever.[72]

As he embarked upon the path that would lead him to glory elsewhere, Che also entered his twilight phase in Cuba.

Guevara's eight days in the United States—the first since visiting Miami fifteen years earlier—afforded him little respite. His activities were varied and somewhat eccentric. An old friend, Laura Berquist of *Look* magazine, organized a meeting with New York intellectuals and journalists. Berquist was a childhood friend of Bobo Rockefeller, the widow of Winthrop, former governor of Arkansas; she owned a splendid townhouse across the street from the Cuban mission to the UN. The location was ideal for a security detail overwhelmed by anti-Castro demonstrations, and for a gathering of New York leftists eager to meet with Che. His interpreter was Magda Moyano, the sister of Dolores, Guevara's neighbor in Córdoba and a cousin of Chichina Ferreyra. She and Che shared memories of their now faraway youth.

He also appeared on the Sunday television program *Face the Nation*. His performance was so skillful and convincing that several Latin American governments protested to the White House over the CBS invitation.* Guevara met secretly with Democratic senator Eugene McCarthy, and talked at length with Arab and African delegates in the UN corridors and delegates' lounge. He was already preparing for his next trip which, beginning on December 18, would take him to nine countries in three months and impel him to leave Cuba forever.

Che's UN speech was fiery in both its tone and its content. He reiterated Cuba's traditional stance toward the United States—including the five points of October 1962—and Cuba's denunciation of the OAS and its Latin American "puppets." The new element, however, was his emphasis on Africa. Like his Geneva address, it would be recalled as a sign of his drift away from the USSR and Socialist countries. But this time he was more explicit. Though still somewhat elliptical, he skipped the euphemisms of his Geneva speech:

> We must also clarify that concepts of peaceful coexistence must be well-defined, and not only in relations involving sovereign States. As Marxists, we have maintained that peaceful coexistence among nations does not include coexistence between exploiters and the exploited, between oppressors and the oppressed.[73]

But Che's most forceful passages were those about the Congo, and especially the airlift operation of Stanleyville:

> Perhaps the children of Belgian patriots who died defending their country's freedom are the same ones who freely murdered millions of Congolese on behalf of the white race, just as they suffered under the German boot because their Aryan blood count was not high enough. . . . Our free eyes now look toward new horizons, and are able to see what our condition as colonial slaves kept us from seeing only yesterday: that "Western civilization" conceals under its lovely façade a gang of hyenas and jackals. That is the only possible name for those who have gone on a "humanitarian" mission to the Congo. Carnivorous animals, feeding on defenseless peoples: that is what imperialism does to man, that is what distinguishes the imperial

---

*"Numerous LA delegations have protested what they feel to be unnecessarily helpful US publicity to Fidel Castro result of CBS TV interview of Guevara. . . . LAs also miffed no US press coverage LA replies to Che Guevara in GA." Department of State, Incoming Telegram, Cuba: Che Guevara CBS Interview, December 14, 1964 (Confidential), NSF, Country File, Cuba, Activities of Leading Personalities, Cuba, no. 62 cable, LBJ Library.

"white." . . . All the free men in the world must stand ready to avenge the crime of the Congo.[74]

In his conversations with Americans, he staunchly defended the Cuban Revolution and refused to acknowledge any split with Fidel Castro. On television, he refrained from taking sides in the conflict between China and the USSR, highlighting instead the need for unity. He let slip some of his reservations regarding the Soviets, but with such discretion that observers were forced to read between the lines.* Tad Szulc, who participated in the *Face the Nation* program and then chatted with Guevara at length, noted "Che's gradual withdrawal from economic policy-making, and his growing concentration on contacts with the Third World, evidently in concurrence with Castro. Guevara seemed to enjoy this mission."[75]

There was a curious element in Che's conversation with Eugene McCarthy, the liberal senator from Minnesota who three years later would become the principal opponent of the Vietnam War in the United States, forcing Lyndon Johnson to renounce any attempt at reelection in 1968. They met at the insistence of Lisa Howard, the journalist who had previously interviewed Che and Fidel in Havana and had undertaken to mediate between Cuba and the United States. She had attempted to persuade her contacts in the Johnson administration to meet with Che during his trip to the United Nations, while doubtless making the same proposal to him. Washington was less than receptive to her ploy:

> The Che Guevara matter has gone up to George Ball. The idea for now is to use a British delegate at the United Nations to make the contact. (Ball and everybody else agree that we should stay away from Lisa Howard.) The Englishman would say to Che tomorrow: "An American colleague informs me that a press source has told him that you have something to say to an American official. My American colleague is not at all sure of the accuracy of this report. Is it true?" If Che answers "yes," the British contact would say something like, "I got the distinct impression that my American colleague is willing to listen to what you say, but I would have to check back with him to make sure." Ball and others in State agree fully that we should not appear to be taking the initiative. In this regard, if the modalities of setting up this operation can be done only by indicating eagerness, the talk isn't worth it. . . . I doubt whether Che has anything to say that we do not already know, but a chance to listen to him might be worthwhile.[76]

---

*The first foreign official Che met with in New York, Enrique Bernstein of Chile, later reported to the U.S. Embassy in Santiago that Che had completely embraced "the position of Beijing." WTDentzer/AmEmbassy Santiago to ARA/DOS Washington, December 21, 1964 (Confidential), NSF, Country File, Cuba, Activities of Leading Personalities, Document no. 57, LBJ Library.

As the encounter with Washington officials did not materialize, Che agreed to Howard's plea for him to meet briefly with McCarthy at the journalist's apartment. According to the senator's report to George Ball the next day, the Cuban *comandante* was bursting with self-confidence. He assured McCarthy that the Alliance for Progress would fail, and that Central America and Venezuela were on the brink of revolution. He then reviewed the most sensitive items on the bilateral agenda—U.S. overflights, the sale of medicines, Guantánamo, the CIA's involvement in Cuba, and so on. The most striking thing about the memorandum of this conversation, declassified just recently—indeed, the identity of Che's interlocutor was revealed only in 1994[77]—is the candor, if not impudence, with which Che boasted of Cuban support for revolution in Latin America. According to McCarthy's notes,

> Guevara did not attempt to conceal the subversive activities which Cuba was undertaking. He explicitly admitted that they were training revolutionaries and would continue to do so. He felt that this was a necessary mission for the Cuban Government since revolution offered the only hope of progress for Latin America.[78]

This happened just as Fidel Castro was trying to trade his support for Latin American revolution in exchange for peaceful coexistence with Washington,* and when the new Soviet leadership appeared willing to ease tensions with the United States. At that precise moment, Che used the highest-level contact Cuba had had with the United States in years to boast of Havana's international ventures. The episode can only evoke his behavior fifteen years earlier, at the immigration bureau in Mexico City, when the brash young Argentine doctor proclaimed himself a Communist, damning the consequences.

His animosity toward the United States had by now reached new heights. Che openly expressed his feelings during a speech in Santiago, Cuba, before leaving for New York:

> We must learn this lesson, learn the lesson about the absolutely necessary abhorrence of it [imperialism], because against that class of hyena there is no other help than abhorrence, there is no other medium than extermination.[79]

This growing anger at the U.S. was perhaps a symptom of how the world was closing in on him. Throughout 1964, especially in the final weeks of the year, Che had displayed a growing restlessness and need for change. Many

---

*In a long interview with Richard Eder of the *New York Times,* Castro "proposed an agreement to cease helping the guerrillas in Latin America" if Washington suspended its own assistance to the Cuban exiles in Miami. *New York Times,* July 6, 1964, front page.

friends and acquaintances sensed that he was on the brink of a threshold in his life. Though none predicted a tragic outcome, many had political and personal glimpses into the change ahead. An official at the British Embassy had been cabling premonitory reports to London since 1964: "It would not surprise me if Guevara himself were soon to receive a more appropriate post—or a sinecure designed to free him for his important duties as liaison with other Latin Americans."[80] Another observer who predicted a shift in Guevara's existence was Gianni Corbi, an Italian journalist for *L'Espresso* who visited Cuba during the summer of 1964 and spent countless hours in conversation with Che: "I should not be at all surprised to see Che Guevara and his buddies, those traveling salesmen of the permanent revolution in Latin America, shake the dust of Castro's Cuba off their feet and head for the hills. When next heard of, they'll be heading partisan bands in the barren peaks of the Andes."[81] For the moment, his destination was Africa.

Che's time in Cuba was drawing to a close. Though he would return for several months in 1966, in convalescence and in training for Bolivia, his Cuban saga came to an end, for all practical purposes, after his trip to New York in December 1964. The African and Algerian chapters of his history remained to be written. But the die was cast, particularly in that small space where two of the great epics of our age had intersected: his own, and that of Fidel Castro.

During that long year of 1964, when he lost both friends and battles, undertaking endless struggles over topics crucial to the fate of the Revolution, Che discovered two indisputable facts about his role in Cuba. One was that Castro held him very dear, indeed; he would back him in all his projects for Argentina, Algeria, Venezuela, and now Africa. Fidel never disputed the place Guevara had carved out for himself, or reproached him for his errors or outbursts. Che could nurture no grudges on that account. But Guevara also understood that Fidel, consummate politician that he was, did not really commit himself to Che's stances. He had to wage his own battles, and suffer his own defeats. Without ever disputing his sporadic victories, Castro never extended Che Guevara his full consent. At times, he even sided with his opponents, either because *révolution oblige,* or because he simply did not agree with Che's ideas.

Moment by moment, battle by battle, Che gradually realized he was alone: neither with nor against Fidel. But Castro was everywhere; lacking his support, Che had nothing, no ground to stand on. His situation was untenable: the slogan of neither marriage nor divorce with Fidel became unsustainable for Che. Nothing could have affected Che more than this tangle of ambiguities and contradictions—the half-tones of his twilight in Cuba. Once again, it was time to leave.

Chapter 9

_____

Che Guevara's
Heart of Darkness

I n the words of Ahmed Ben Bella, former president of Algeria, "We arrived in the Congo too late."[1] Ernesto Che Guevara would spend the next-to-last year of his life supporting a struggle that was already over, in a dismembered country at the heart of a continent torn by age-old divisions and foreign incursions both tragic and comic. The latest intervention pitted revolutionary Cubans led by Guevara against Cuban-born pilots recruited by the CIA, thousands of miles from their birthplace. Certainly, there was a rebellion in the Congo; unquestionably, it was the most important armed uprising in sub-Saharan Africa since its struggle for independence.* But by the time Che began preparing for his Congo expedition, the rebellion had been crushed by Belgian paratroopers, Rhodesian and South African mercenaries, and U.S. transport planes. Opération Dragon Rouge was the code name for the new and old colonial powers' attempt to retake the city of Stanleyville.†

_____

*The time lag is worth noting: the period encompassing independence, the death of Patrice Lumumba, and the "Katanganese gendarmes" had drawn to an end almost five years before.

† Place names in the former Belgian Congo were changed in the 1970s. The country itself, previously known as Congo-Leopoldville, was renamed Zaire. The capital, Leopoldville, became Kinshasa. The capital of the eastern provinces, originally called Stanleyville, was

The crisis erupted in July 1964. The tentative peace and territorial integrity forcibly imposed by the United Nations, Washington, and Brussels in the early sixties were coming apart at the seams. Once the danger of secession by the mining region of Upper Katanga was averted, the Organization of African Unity (OAU) lost all interest in maintaining a UN mission in the Congo. The UN withdrew in mid-1964, frustrated by its costly and discredited task. It left a vacuum behind, which was rapidly filled by the social and political forces already present at the beginning of the decade.

Uprisings inspired by the memory of the martyred independence hero Patrice Lumumba immediately flared up in the western part of the country. One of them, beginning in January 1964, was led by Pierre Mulele. Lumumba's first minister of education, Mulele had spent time in exile in Beijing, and obtained Mao's support. His was "the first great peasant uprising in an independent African country."[2] According to an admiring biographer, it was as well "the first great people's revolution against neocolonialism in postindependence Africa."[3]

The incumbent prime minister of the Congo soon resigned. In his stead, President Kasavubu named the discredited leader of the independence wars, Moise Tshombe, who enjoyed the support of the Société Générale of Brussels (a sort of tutelary body for the Congolese semicolony). Tshombe was despised by the leaders of the OAU, especially its most radical ones—the so-called Group of Six, consisting of Nasser, Ben Bella, Kwame Nkrumah of Ghana, Sékou Touré of Guinea, Julius Nyerere of Tanzania, and Modibo Keita of Mali*—who still blamed Tshombe for Lumumba's death. The rebellion quickly spread eastward, led by several of Lumumba's former aides, and by a more recently arrived and dubious revolutionary, Gaston Soumaliot. They had all previously formed a Committee for National Liberation (CNL) supported by the USSR, Cuba, and the OAU itself. Beginning in early 1964, the CNL had established bases in neighboring Rwanda-Burundi (one country at that time), on the western shores of Lake Tanganyika. By July 1964, the important mining town of Albertville had fallen; in August the rebels took Stanleyville, the provincial capital named after the *New York Herald* journalist of Livingstonian fame, where, according to several Western authors, they unleashed a reign of terror that killed 20,000 Congolese.[4] The CNL's strategy of operating from Rwanda-Burundi proved decisive: its base there was the only one to survive the rebel defeat in late 1964. That is where Che would arrive the following April.

---

rebaptized Kisangani. Elisabethville became Lubumbashi, and Albertville, Kalemie. This account will use the former names, which were current during Che's lifetime.

*According to Ben Bella, these leaders had a group of their own within the OAU; they regularly consulted and conspired among themselves. Ahmed Ben Bella, interview with the author, Geneva, November 4, 1995.

In sum, there were two rebellions, two leaderships, and two guerrilla campaigns in the Congo: that of the CNL in the north and east, and Pierre Mulele's in the west. The former had greater African, Soviet, and international support; the latter was better organized, had more ideological depth and consistency, and was probably more deeply rooted in Congolese society. Mulele was a natural leader, and Lumumba's only plausible heir. But his movement never extended beyond his tribal base (Bapendes and Bambundas) and region (Kwilu and the northeastern part of the country). In contrast, the CNL conquered a larger territorial base, but its leaders soon gained a reputation for corruption, cowardice, and internal squabbling. The radicalism of the two movements was very relative. The CNL leadership maintained relations with both Belgian Foreign Minister Paul-Henri Spaak and the CIA station chief in the Congo, Lawrence Devlin.[5] Even so, the rebellion came to represent a significant threat to Belgium's economic interests—embodied by the archetypical Union Minière du Haut Katanga, longtime owner of the Congo's immense mineral riches—and to the geopolitical interests of the United States, which could not possibly allow Soviet gains in Africa during its own presidential election campaign. It also posed a problem for the South Africans and ex-Katanganese, who feared reprisals for their atrocities in the early part of the decade: massacres, murders, and assaults.

The CIA soon decided to help crush the rebellion with the help of anti-Castro pilots. So did South Africa, with several hundred mercenaries led by the notorious and movie-famous "Mad Mike" Hoare, as did Belgium with up to 450 combatants, initially sent in as advisers. By November 1964, after a campaign which succeeded in isolating the rebels in Stanleyville, there was little left to do. The death blow was Opération Dragon Rouge, when Belgian paratroopers were dropped into the east of the country by U.S. planes and reconquered the eastern capital.

The results were to be expected: a bloodbath, including the massacre of thousands of Congolese by South African mercenaries and the cold-blooded murder of about eighty Western hostages. The international outcry was deafening, but the mission had succeeded. Though the rebels, called "simbas," would survive in the area for years, by November 1964 they were largely dispersed; and when, in March 1965, "the white mercenaries captured the town of Watsa on the far eastern frontier . . . the rebellion was declared defeated. . . . After the Dragon Rouge parachute operation in November 1964, the rebellion was not a serious threat."[6] The Stanleyville operation and its bloody aftermath were eloquently and passionately denounced by Che at the United Nations. Many saw the Stanleyville defeat as just one more phase in the struggle; in fact, it proved to be the last mass rebellion in the eastern Congo for decades, until 1996.

The uprising in Kwilu dragged on until late 1968, when Pierre Mulele finally surrendered, theoretically in the context of a negotiated peace, to Mobutu Sese Seko. He was promptly dismembered, and his remains readily fed to the crocodiles of the Congo River. In reality, however, his movement had been condemned by internal tribal divisions since March 14, 1965. On that day,

> a grave defeat shattered Mulele's prestige and any faith in the future of the movement. The unity of Mulelism was broken; many youth abandoned the guerrilla movement. It was Mulele's only decision based on tribal consider-
> ations, but it had disastrous repercussions for him.[7]

Thus Ben Bella's lament that progressive forces had arrived too late in the Congo. Che, too, was late. For this reason, and many others, his expedition was doomed from the outset. Guevara threw his support behind a struggle that had already been soundly and definitively crushed. When he left New York's Kennedy Airport for Algiers, the first stop in a multi-city African tour, on December 18, 1964, the uprising in the eastern Congo was already over. His entire African saga went against the current; that was its fatal weakness. At the same time, it was rooted in undeniably historical events: the first armed, massive, revolutionary uprisings against the postcolonial regime, in a country at the heart of the African continent so important to the rest of the world that everybody, from Washington to Beijing, strove to control it. The country would prove so ungovernable and unfortunate that thirty years later it came to symbolize the epitome of a failed decolonization. Ravaged by AIDS, corruption, violence, and desperate poverty, it would gradually lose any semblance of nationhood; on its eastern borders, in the Great Lakes region, it would register one of the cruelest tragedies of hunger, genocide, and migration in modern times.

Che's African tour was planned from New York, by the Cuban Ambassador to Algiers, Jorge Serguera. None of the missions in Cuba of the countries Che visited were notified of his movements.[8] The Soviets were not consulted either. Comandante Guevara started off with a full week in Algiers, where he mapped out the remainder of what would be a three-month trip. He reviewed the situation in Africa with Ben Bella, and met with Congolese and liberation-movement leaders from the Portuguese colonies of Angola, Mozambique, and Guinea-Bissau. It soon became apparent to him that the struggle in the Congo faced two serious challenges. First, it required a united and centralized leadership; military operations had to be coordinated jointly. In the next three months, as he traveled through eight African countries, Guevara would return to this idea time and again, always in vain.

The second challenge was equally complex. Essentially, it involved ensuring and harmonizing Soviet and Chinese assistance to both factions: that of Mulele, helped by the Chinese, and that of the National Liberation Committee, supported by the Soviets. The Sino-Soviet conflict complicated the situation in Africa enormously; it also interfered with aid, which was not very timely or smooth to begin with. Thus Che's emphasis on a third task during those months: persuading Ben Bella and other African leaders to fill in for tardy or inadequate Soviet and Chinese assistance as much as possible.

On December 26, Che left Algiers for Bamako, the capital of Mali. The idea probably originated with Ben Bella, who considered Modibo Keita the senior and most respected member of the Group of Six.[9] Che's visit did not receive much attention: the joint communiqué was not signed by any member of the Politburo or senior minister. President Keita usually took holidays at Christmas, and there was no public welcome for Che in the streets of Bamako. Even press coverage was scant. The visit was in all likelihood scheduled at the last moment.

In Mali, Che stressed that Cuba had been wrong to align itself so closely with the Soviet Union and China; this was one of his observations to the minister who received him.[10] On January 1, Che traveled to the People's Republic of the Congo (Brazzaville), where he announced that twenty young men would receive military training in Cuba. There he also forged one of the closest alliances Cuba would ever enjoy in Africa. A few months later, a detachment of Cuban troops commanded by Jorge Risquet would arrive in Brazzaville to serve as presidential guards for President Jean-François Massemba Debat. Some of the soldiers who accompanied Che to the Congo in April 1965 later joined this unit, which would stay on long after the Argentine's departure. Guevara's meeting with Agostinho Neto, head and founder of the People's Movement for the Liberation of Angola, would also have long-lasting effects: Cuban troops left the former Portuguese colony only in 1992.

Che also visited Guinea, from January 7 to 14, renewing his friendship with Sékou Touré, who was, along with Ben Bella, the African leader most sympathetic to the Cuban Revolution. He was received more effusively than in Mali, except when he traveled with the president's entourage to meet with Leopold Senghor, the President of Senegal. The poet of *négritude* and his aides were "indignant" at Guevara's inclusion in talks among African leaders. Che renewed his call for support to liberation movements in Africa, emphasizing the need for unity in the "struggle against imperialism." The Congolese and other movements had to be united within and among themselves, and should draw closer to the Socialist countries, especially the two great powers. But not too close; in a secret cable, the CIA reported that Che's motivation in Africa was to warn "their friends" not to get in too deep with the Soviet or Chinese communists. According to Guevara, while Cuba was as dedicated as ever to socialism, Cuban officials were very unhappy about the depth of interference in their internal affairs of the USSR and communist China. Guevara said that it was too late for Cuba to do anything about it but that the Cubans felt it was not too late for the Africans to redress the situation. Guevara added that the Cubans were especially concerned about their friends the Algerians, and that he was proceeding directly to Algiers to deliver the same message to Ben Bella.*

From there, it was on to Ghana, where Che talked at length with Kwame Nkrumah, the classic archetype of Africa's charismatic and corrupt independence leaders. He also met Laurent Kabila, the Congolese leader from the region bordering on Lake Tanganyika where Che would establish his guerrilla base three months later.† Thirty years later, Kabila, Che's chief interlocutor in the Congo, would lead the Tutsi rebellion in eastern Zaire, in the midst of one of the late twentieth century's worst humanitarian crises; in May 1997 he finally achieved power in the country he had sought Che's help to liberate in the mid-sixties.

In late January, Guevara returned to Algiers to compare notes with Ben Bella and decide what to do next. He was increasingly inclined to participate directly in the Congolese struggle. In an interview with the official FLN daily *Algers Ce Soir,* he declared that while the Congo was an African problem, Cuba was morally committed to its struggle. By now, Che's views on Africa, the Congo, and his own destiny were fairly well defined. As Ben Bella recalls, Guevara had reached the conclusion that "Africa was the continent in the world most favorable for great changes; Africa set the course for the renewal of the anti-imperialist struggle."[11] In the words of Jorge Serguera, Africa was for Che a sort of no-man's-land which the great powers had not yet carved up into spheres of influence, and where victory was still possible.[12]

---

*Central Intelligence Agency, Intelligence Information Cable, Statements of Ernesto Che Guevara on the Primary Purpose of His Mission to Africa (Secret). The cable quotes information dated late December 1964, and is itself dated January 15, 1965, NSF, Country File, Cuba, vol. 4, LBJ Library. Its main thrust is supported by the fact that Che publicly expressed his anger at the Soviet Union six weeks later, precisely in Algiers. This account of Che's warning against close relations with the USSR and China was repeated in a report by the State Department's Intelligence and Research section, signed by Director Thomas Hughes, and addressed to the Secretary of State. Knowing the professionalism of Hughes and Adrian Basora, who wrote the reports on Cuba during those years, it is difficult to imagine that they would have given credence to any dubious information. See INR/Thomas Hughes, April 19, 1965, NSF, Country File, Cuba, Activities of Leading Personalities, no. 18 memo, LBJ Library.

† At least this is the account provided by Oscar Fernández Mell, who met Kabila in Dar-es-Salaam and spent four months with Che in the Congo. Oscar Fernández Mell, interview with the author, Havana, August 24, 1996.

For several reasons, Congo-Leopoldville seemed to Che the country, or
rather the territory, with the best chances for success thanks to the formidable guerrilla movement in the west and the unified forces of the Committee of National Liberation in the east. Furthermore, as the United
States became increasingly involved in Vietnam, it was unlikely that it
would intervene in the struggle in any direct or significant way. Finally,
though the Congo was a landlocked nation with no outlet to the sea other
than Cabinda, it had many neighbors: Congo Brazzaville, the Republic of
Central Africa, Sudan, Uganda, Zambia, Tanzania, Rwanda-Burundi. It
was a sort of African Bolivia. This was only one of many analogies
between the two countries, and Guevara's two expeditions.

Another decisive element in Che's approach to Africa, in Serguera's view,
was its geostrategic situation. According to the Cuban ambassador to
Algiers, who would later be accused of having "dragged" Che into Africa by
painting a rosy picture for him,[13] Guevara gambled that the Soviet Union
would tolerate Cuban support for the struggle in Africa, even if this was not
quite the case in Latin America. Moreover, a success in Africa might induce
Moscow to view more favorably Cuba's support for the revolution in Latin
America.[14]

As his African odyssey progressed, Guevara became more aware of certain factors, while neglecting or rejecting others. His initial motivations
were gradually buttressed or replaced by others. As Serguera describes it,
Guevara was profoundly moved by the poverty, backwardness, and racial
and colonial oppression which had characterized Africa since conquest and
colonization. He also observed at first hand the divisions among progressive forces and the mediocrity of their leaders, believing unavoidably perhaps that he could help to shape events, albeit with limited resources. He
underestimated two vital points, nonetheless: the capacity of the United
States to intervene in a similar way (that is, to wield enormous influence at
scant cost), and the fact that the internal divisions among political leaders
were a reflection—indirect but faithful—of profound tribal and ethnic fractures. The weakest link in the chain, however, was Che's conception of "the
people": there was no such thing in most of Africa. This would become evident in the course of Cuba's subsequent interventions in Brazzaville,
Angola, and Ethiopia. Che was wrong to assume that opposition to the
colonial powers (or, after decolonization, "imperialism") would suffice to
coalesce groups that had always been enemies, with nothing in common
save the borders imposed upon them by the great powers.

During those months, Che visited Cairo twice: once very briefly on February 11, on his way back from China; and a second time in March, when he
spent a couple of weeks on his way back to Cuba. There is a record of his
conversations with Nasser, thanks to notes taken by Mohammed Heikal and

published one year after the Egyptian president's death.* First of all, Nasser detected in Che a "deep personal anguish" and great sadness. Che did not discuss his inner concerns; he told Nasser only that he was going to Tanzania to study the prospects of the liberation movements in the Congo. But Nasser sensed in him little enthusiasm for the project. When he returned from Tanzania along with Pablo Ribalta, Cuba's ambassador in Dar-es-Salaam, Guevara recounted to Nasser his visit to the guerrilla camps in the vortex of the Congo-Tanzania-Burundi. He had made up his mind to personally direct Cuban assistance to the Congolese rebels: "I think I will go to the Congo because it is the hottest place in the world today. With the help of the Africans through the Committee in Tanzania, and with two battalions of Cubans, I believe we can strike at the heart of the imperialists' interests in Katanga."

Nasser expressed his astonishment and attempted to dissuade him, explaining that a white, foreign leader commanding blacks in Africa could only come across as an imitation of Tarzan. Nonetheless, Che tried to convince the President of the United Arab Republic to help the Congo rebels. Nasser agreed, but refused to send troops: "If you go to the Congo with two Cuban battalions and I send an Egyptian battalion, it will be seen as a foreign intervention and do more harm than good."

After several lengthy conversations, Nasser wondered how sure Che was of his plans. As Guevara confessed to him, "I have thought of going to the Congo, but in view of events there I am inclined to accept your opinion that it would be harmful. I have also thought of going to Vietnam. . . ." Anyway, as Che declared during their final conversation, he would not stay in Cuba. Nasser was struck by Guevara's preoccupation with death; he had remarked to the Egyptian that "The decisive moment in a man's life is when he decides to confront death. If he confronts it, he will be a hero whether he succeeds or not. He can be a good or a bad politician, but if he does not confront death he will never be more than a politician."

Some of this jibes with Ben Bella's memories. Che shared with him, too, his intention to join the struggle in the Congo. The Algerian, for his part, was bent on persuading Che to renounce his delusional project—or at least not to don a prophet's robes and play messiah with the African people. The racial issue was far too delicate, he explained: "The situation in black Africa was not comparable to that prevailing in our countries; Nasser and I, we warned Che of what might happen."[15]

In Cairo, Guevara conversed at length with the Congolese leaders who had been exiled after their defeat at Stanleyville. Gaston Sumaliot lived on

*Heikal's recollections should be read with caution—not because Heikal is falsifying the truth, but because he inevitably furnishes a somewhat blurred image of events. Still, the thrust of Nasser's commentary dovetails with other descriptions of Che at that time. Mohammed Heikal, *The Cairo Documents* (Garden City, N.Y.: Doubleday, 1973).

the island of Zamalek, where he received Che several times. Guevara met again with Laurent Kabila, one of the National Liberation Committee's two vice-presidents; the other was Pierre Mulele. Kabila was supposedly leading a guerrilla campaign in an area of Congo-Leopoldville bordering on Lake Tanganyika. Here a new and unfortunate contradiction arose. Mulele's absence and the collapse of the front at Stanleyville undermined the exiled rebels' efforts to secure funds and assistance. Their solution was, temporarily at least, to exaggerate the significance of Kabila's army in the Great Lakes region, which was in fact sorely lacking in combatants, arms, and revolutionary morale. Indeed, its only true military asset lay in its potential to establish a rebel sanctuary in Kigoma, across the lake in Tanzania.

When Che visited the camps from Dar-es-Salaam in mid-February, he perceived these difficulties as well as the fierce divisions among factions in the area. But he did not recognize that the groups on the western shores of Lake Tanganyika did not constitute a combat front in any real sense. Thus can be explained his insistence on sending Cuban troops to train and reinforce the Congolese—though not to fight alongside them, much less instead of them, as would in fact occur. Later, Che would spend long and frustrating months in the Congo waiting, in vain, for Laurent Kabila to lead his own troops into combat. Even when he finally departed from Africa, Guevara remained somewhat confused about all of this, though he had by then grasped what was actually happening in other areas:

> There are two zones in which one might say there is an organized attempt at revolution: the area where we are, and part of the province held by Mulele, who remains a big mystery. In the rest of the country there are only isolated bands surviving in the jungle; they lost everything without even fighting, just as they lost Stanleyville without a fight.*

In reality, the struggle in Che's area depended almost entirely upon the Cubans. As for Mulele's uprising, it was dying a slow and painful death. The revolution in the Congo was over before it even began.

Three Cuban sources have confirmed that Che decided to join the Congo rebellion before he returned to Havana. The first is Cuba's former ambassador to Tanzania Pablo Ribalta, dispatched to Africa by Che as his advance man in February 1964. Ribalta believes without a doubt that Che had determined to take the revolution beyond Cuba ever since his trip to the United Nations.[16] According to Serguera, the second source, "There was already a

---

*Ernesto Che Guevara, "Pasajes de la guerra revolucionaria (el Congo)," unpublished manuscript, Havana, p. 86. As was noted in Chapter 1 (see footnote, p. 5), Che's text, based upon his field journals in the Congo, remains unpublished, though it has been quoted by various authors. The authenticity of the manuscript has been ratified by several readers familiar with the original text.

conspiracy afoot when he left Algiers, he was already determined to go to the Congo."[17] The third source is Colonel Dariel Alarcón Ramírez—"Benigno," one of the three survivors of the guerrilla campaign in Bolivia—who from the time he enrolled in the Congo expedition until the day of Guevara's capture in Bolivia played a crucial role in Che's life and is an invaluable witness for the following two years. Benigno states in his memoirs[18] that he ran into Che in Algeria late in 1964. He believes that Che resolved to go to the Congo while still in Algeria:

> I believe he made the decision in Algeria because it was then that Che was first accused of being pro-China and a Trotskyist. He sent me from Algeria to the Congo: go with Ribalta and wait [for me] there.[19]

So by mid-January 1965 Che was obviously inclined to head for Africa permanently. Three elements were missing for a final decision. One was his trip to Beijing at the end of January. Another was his speech—famous because it marked his break with the USSR—at an economic planning seminar in Algiers on February 24, 1965. The third was his week in Tanzania, when he visited the supposed guerrilla camps in the Congo and verified the ideal rearguard position tacitly provided by the republic founded by Julius Nyerere.

The trip to Beijing took place at a time of growing tension between Cuba and China. Fidel Castro had increasingly aligned himself with the USSR in the Sino-Soviet conflict during the previous year. Cuba's neutrality first tilted toward an effort at mediation—the Latin American Communist Party mission headed by Carlos Rafael Rodríguez and cold-shouldered by Mao— and then culminated in a virtual identification with Moscow. Though frictions remained, Cuba's affiliation was now self-evident. Its progressive alignment between 1964 and 1966 has been described as follows by the most distinguished scholar of Cuban foreign policy:

> Seven days later—just after Guevara's charges in Algiers about Soviet collusion with capitalism—Raúl Castro went to Moscow to attend the meeting of Communist parties. The meeting was boycotted by China, which finalized the split in the international Communist movement. Cuba, which had not responded to previous invitations to attend meetings of Moscow-oriented Communist parties in March and June 1964, at last did so, siding with the Soviets against the Chinese. On March 13, Fidel Castro warned the Chinese that "division in the face of the enemy was never a correct strategy, never a revolutionary strategy." Rapid deterioration of Sino-Cuban relations followed, along with momentary improvement in Soviet-Cuban relations. By mid-1965, China was flooding Cuba with its own propaganda, aimed especially at military officers. China also announced that it would buy [less sugar than expected], and . . . sell Cuba [less rice than had been

agreed]. It refused to extend further credit to Cuba. . . . On January 2, 1966, in his opening address to the Tricontinental Conference, Fidel Castro denounced the Chinese government.*

A meeting of Communist parties in Havana in November 1964 was crucial, both for the Soviets and the Cubans. The latter achieved a stronger commitment and greater backing from the Communist parties of Latin America.[20] This was not insignificant, if one recalls Che's perpetual complaints about their lack of support. In exchange, the Soviet and Latin American party leaders wrested two major concessions from the Cubans. First, local parties would be in charge of coordinating and unifying pro-Cuba groups throughout the continent, in order to build broad political fronts and campaigns on a continental scale. Secondly, the meeting's final declaration included a strong condemnation of "public polemics and fractionalized activities," in an oblique but obvious denunciation of China and its supporters in Latin America.[21] Perhaps Castro considered that the deeper purpose of the conference was to avoid division and promote unity without taking sides. But Mao and the Beijing Communists saw the conference resolution quite differently, as part of the Soviet Union's "revisionist" offensive.

Some Latin Americans, and possibly the Cubans themselves, realized that the explicit condemnation could create problems with China; thus the November 1964 mission to Beijing, in order to soften the blow. It wrought the opposite effect. Perhaps due to the inclusion of old Communists like Rodríguez and the Chileans, the November démarche exacerbated China's irritation and failed in its attempt at mediation. Even worse, an open dispute erupted between Rodríguez and Mao Zedong. When they discussed the situation in Latin America, Mao had nothing but disdain for the Cuban Revolution. Mario Monje, Secretary-General of the Bolivian Communist Party, recalls the Great Helmsman's contemptuous attitude and the Cuban's reaction: "Mao said it was an expression of *petit-bourgeois* nationalism. Carlos Rafael leaped up, declaring that he would not permit such statements about the Cuban Revolution, or any doubts to be cast on Comandante Fidel Castro."[22]

---

*Jorge Domínguez, *To Make a World Safe for Revolution: Cuba's Foreign Policy* (Cambridge: Harvard University Press, 1989), pp. 68–69. This view was also held by the Intelligence and Research Section of the U.S. State Department: "In the winter of 1964–1965, Cuba moved definitely toward the Soviet side of the Sino-Soviet dispute. On four key issues—relations with the Chinese communists, Cuban-U.S. relations, Latin American revolution, and Cuban economic problems—the Soviets were able to pull Castro substantially toward their own positions." Thomas Hughes to the Secretary, INR Research Memorandum 21, The Cuban Revolution: Phase Two, August 10, 1965 (Confidential), pp. 9–10, NSF, Country File, Cuba, W. G. Bowdler File, vol. 1, no. 46 memo, LBJ Library.

Nonetheless, Che and the Cubans (perhaps for different reasons) decided to undertake a second attempt at mediation, for Cuba's sake, or Che's, in the worst of cases. Guevara had several direct and immediate reasons to try. He wanted to see for himself whether the November run-in between Mao and the Latin Americans had been the fault of the Chinese or of Carlos Rafael Rodríguez, his chief adversary in Cuba.[23] In Havana, Castro confided to Monje that "we decided Che should go because we knew about your problems in Beijing, so we sent the person closest to us to find out the truth, and it was confirmed. Che verified the confrontation that took place; it was China's fault, period."[24]

In addition, Che knew it would be very hard for him to shake off his pro-China stigma, which he had been complaining about since 1963. Any open conflict between Havana and Beijing—as would take place in the coming months—entailed a serious and perhaps insurmountable dilemma for Che Guevara. He had learned long since to flee this type of predicament. The ambivalence in being the only pro-Chinese Cuban—or the only one who was not anti-Chinese—at the height of political and ideological tensions was probably unbearable for him.* Better by far to avoid confrontation than be consumed by it.

Che also realized that any Cuban initiative in Africa, at least in the Congo and Tanzania, could not dispense with Mao's approval. Beijing had amassed a great deal of experience in the area: its technical assistance—for instance, helping to build a railroad from Tanzania to the Atlantic—had been well received. Nyerere possessed an enduring affection for China's leaders; Zhou Enlai would visit Dar es Salaam in October 1965. Pierre Mulele, the most strongly rooted leader among the Congolese rebels, was also a sinophile. So without a green light from China, there could be no African expedition—either for Cuba or for Che.

Havana decided to try its hand as a go-between again in late January 1965. The mission comprised this time the Secretary of Organization of the new Cuban party, Emilio Aragonés, a friend and close aide of Che's, and Osmany Cienfuegos, who had the full trust of Fidel Castro; no members of the former PSP were included. Che was still in Algiers according to the official organizers of his trip, interior deputy-minister and intelligence chief Manuel Piñeiro's team in Havana. After waiting for him in vain for more than a month in Algiers, where Piñeiro's team presumed him to be,

---

*Pro-China Latin Americans and the Chinese themselves did little to ease the situation. A U.S. military intelligence report noted in March 1965 that a pro-China group in Peru— the Movement for Reformist Unity—had distributed to its militants Che's essay "La Guerra de guerrillas: Un método," subtitled "Una interpretación de la Segunda Declaración de La Havana." Department of Defense Intelligence Report No. 2230027265, Cuban-Supported Political Subversive Activity, March 25, 1965 (Confidential), Miami.

Aragonés and Cienfuegos traveled to Paris; there they finally hooked up with the errant Argentine.* They spent several days in the French capital, resting and meeting with various contacts, and waiting for a flight for Beijing. Then they left for Pakistan (to avoid a stopover in Moscow, which might have offended the Chinese) on their way to Beijing.

By most accounts, the trip was an unmitigated disaster. Mao initially refused to receive the delegation. Discussions with Liu Shaoqi, President of the Republic, and Deng Xiaoping, Secretary-General of the Party, led nowhere. Any chance of a reconciliation between Moscow and Beijing, even any easing of tensions, was now out of the question. Zhou Enlai agreed only to send one boat with weapons to the Congolese rebels, on the understanding that they would be trained by Cuban advisers. Perhaps the Cubans did not realize—they had no reason to—that the most populous country in the world was on the eve of one of its recurrent convulsions: the Great Proletarian Cultural Revolution, which Mao would shortly launch. In that context, there could be no agreement with the USSR or with Cuba.

As Emilio Aragonés remembers, the Chinese held fast to their basic opinion, which was that

> The Cuban Communist Party had wrongly aligned itself with the Soviets. We were not evil, we were good, we were Communists, but we had been taken in. We did not accept that, nobody had taken us in, they were the ones who were confused.[25]

Despite Che's careful preparations and brilliant opening presentation, the mission foundered. Aragonés hoped the Chinese would come around to the Cuban view, with all its solid argumentation and indisputable principles. Indeed, when the Cubans rose from the first meeting they were ecstatic, certain that they had dispelled Beijing's inaccurate impression of their alignment with the Soviet Union. They were astounded when Deng Xiaoping launched into the same litany on the very next day, as if nothing had occurred. The Cubans were speechless; they were not yet familiar with the Chinese negotiating style, which basically consisted of repeating the same thing over and over again regardless of any objection. Che might have won a few debates; that did not mean he had carried the discussion. When Liu Shaoqi complained that the Cuban government had invited to Havana Gilberto Vieyra, the Colombian Communist leader who had compared Mao to Hitler, Che replied with his biting *porteño* irony: "If you have rehabilitated

---

*Emilio Aragonés, interview with the author, Havana, February 10, 1995. Aragonés's quip that Piñiero did not really know where Che was or when he was due to arrive in Algiers confirms that Che organized his African trip very much on his own, with only Serguera's help, informing Havana as little as possible of his movements and intentions.

Pu-Yi, the last emperor, why shouldn't we rehabilitate a poor Colombian Communist?"[26] The remark had no perceivable effect whatsoever.

Despite these underlying disputes, the Chinese treated their Cuban guests with their traditional exuberant hospitality. They even insinuated toward the end of the visit that a request to see Mao might be well received. On closing the last meeting, the Chinese delegation inquired if Che and his companions had any further wishes, aside from touring the Great Wall. They were really proposing an encounter with Mao, who would presumably forgive and absolve them. Perhaps the Cubans made a mistake in not accepting the offer, though it would have meant recognizing that the Cuban Communist Party had been "taken in" by the "revisionists." As Aragonés recalls, "Che, Osmany and myself decided to ask nothing further, so as not to allow them that satisfaction."[27]

After his ten days in Beijing, Che arrived in Dar-es-Salaam on February 13. He was welcomed at the airport by a second-level minister, and the visit was relegated to inner pages by the local press. Perhaps Julius Nyerere already had an inkling of what was afoot. Che soon perceived the effects of his failed mission to China. The official dinner, hosted by the foreign minister, was attended by all the African ambassadors and the Soviet representative, but there was nobody from the Chinese Embassy.[28] In any event, Che promptly began discussing with Congolese leaders the technicalities of Cuban assistance. He explained to Kabila that the problem in the Congo affected the entire world, not just Africa; in consequence he offered "on behalf of the government to send about thirty instructors and whatever arms we could. He accepted them gladly, recommending that we hurry, as did Sumaliot; the latter leader also suggested that the instructors be black."[29]

Che then talked at length with the freedom fighters, to gauge for himself their willingness to enter combat. It was a large meeting, with over fifty participants from about ten countries. Che responded to their appeals for help with caution and firmness:

> I analyzed the requests they had expressed, almost unanimously, for financial help and training. I explained the cost of sending people to Cuba, the amount of money and time required, and the little certainty that they would return as combatants useful to the movement. . . . So I proposed that training take place not in our faraway Cuba, but in the nearby Congo, where the struggle was not against a puppet like Tshombe, but against United States imperialism. . . . I spoke to them of the fundamental importance . . . of the liberation struggle in the Congo. . . . Their reaction was more than cold; though most refrained from making any comments, some asked for the floor to reproach me violently for my advice. They argued that their people, mistreated and debased by imperialism, would claim if there were victims

that they would have died not for their own country, but to liberate another State. I tried to make them see that this was not a struggle bounded by any border, but a war against a common enemy, present everywhere . . . but nobody saw it in this light. It became clear to us that there was a long way to go in Africa before achieving a truly revolutionary leadership, but we were glad to have met people who were ready to fight to the end. From that time, our task was to select a group of black Cubans, volunteers of course, and send them to reinforce the struggle in the Congo.[30]

There were precedents. Since 1961, Cuba had been grooming revolutionaries from Zanzibar. There were also training camps for the Algerian People's Army in the Kabilia mountains, where ten Cuban technicians were instructing Algerians and Africans from several countries including Tanzania.[31] Che's many talks with Congolese leaders in Algeria and Africans in Mali, Brazzaville, and Conakry also established an antecedent. The content and conditions of Cuban assistance were gradually taking shape. Initially it was intended to include arms, communications equipment, and thirty advisers who would have no combat role. Cuba also pledged to help coordinate and unify the different groups operating in the Congo, and enlist the support of other African countries if necessary: Algeria, Egypt, Congo-Brazzaville, and so on.* There was no mention of Che himself conducting the operation; on the contrary, the Cuban presence would be as discreet as possible, so as not to attract attention or reprisals by the Western powers. The future Cuban advisers soon began their drills on the island. Rafael del Pino recalls that he was ordered as early as January to commission a group of black air force officers from Pinar del Río to a special location.[32] With or without Che, the groundwork for the operation was already underway. Only a few personal decisions of Che's were still pending.

Che returned to Algiers from Southeast Africa to attend an economic seminar of the Afro-Asian Solidarity Conference. He met once again with Ben Bella to review his experience in China, and discuss the next step. At that point, Che had probably not quite yet decided to leave Cuba for the Congo. He wrote as much in his journal, noting that he had not shared with Kabila his intention of leading Cuban operations in Africa.[33] He was only

---

*According to U.S. military intelligence, there was a further agreement: "Guevara on his trip through Africa made propositions for the delivery to GOC of Cuban prisoners that had been fulfilling [U.S.] missions in the Congo. Cosme Toribio (T), a Cuban exile pilot, is a prisoner of the Congo Rebel Troops. Fidel Castro had Guevara propose that Toribio be turned over to the GOC as a condition for Castro to initiate the sending of 400 to 500 men to the Congo to fight with the Congo rebels." Department of Defense Intelligence Report No. 2210002365, Proposed GOC Aid to Congo Rebels, March 23, 1965 (Confidential), Miami.

at the halfway point of his journey, and several decisive events had not yet occurred—in particular, the Algiers speech in which he would break with the Soviet Union, on February 24.

One of the factors leading up to the speech was probably the signing in Moscow, on February 17, of a long-term agreement on trade and payment mechanisms between Cuba and the Soviet Union. The accord included a higher volume of bilateral trade, as well as a substantial increase in Cuban sugar deliveries. Negotiations had dragged on for three months, suggesting tensions and reluctance on both sides. The Cubans were especially concerned by the high prices charged them for Soviet machinery and equipment. There were even rumors that Castro had dismissed his chief negotiator, the economist Raúl Maldonado. Whatever his mood, though, Fidel had no choice but to cut a deal, despite Che's opposition and the fact that Moscow was clearly taking advantage of Cuba's dependence on it.

Guevara's Algiers speech began with a reiteration of his traditional views. But then, in the next paragraph, Che embarked on a genuine diatribe against the Socialist countries:

> The development of those countries now entering the path of liberation must be paid for by the Socialist countries. . . . We must not talk any more of a mutually advantageous trade based on prices which the law of value . . . imposes on backward countries. What is the meaning of "mutual advantage" when [some countries] sell at world prices the raw materials that cost backward countries infinite sweat and suffering, while they buy at world market prices the machines produced in large, mechanized factories . . . ? If we establish this sort of relations between the two groups of nations, we must agree that the Socialist countries are, to a certain extent, accomplices of imperial exploitation . . . and of the immoral nature of this exchange. The Socialist countries have a moral duty to cease their tacit complicity with the exploiting countries of the West.[34]

Che formulated a series of precise but utopian proposals, calling for solidarity among Socialist countries to finance development in the Third World and openly denouncing the behavior of the Socialist bloc. He then returned to the matter of relations with the capitalist countries, warning against the fallacies of joint ventures or competition among neighboring underdeveloped countries. He concluded with an eloquent and passionate appeal to delegates to "institutionalize our relations," to create some sort of unity among Third World and Socialist countries. And he also touched upon his main concern of the moment: the supply of arms to liberation movements. Again, he castigated the Socialist countries—even while acknowledging that their support for Cuba had been exemplary:

If it is absurd to believe that a company director in a Socialist country at war is not going to have his doubts about sending the tanks he produces to a front where there is no guarantee of payment, it is equally absurd to examine the payment possibilities of a people fighting for its liberation. . . . Arms should not be merchandise in our world; they must be delivered at no cost, and in whatever quantities are needed and possible, to those peoples that require them to fire against the common enemy. That is the spirit in which the USSR and the People's Revolution in China have given us their military support. . . . But we are not the only ones.[35]

As Ahmed Ben Bella recalls, Che knew exactly what he was doing.* He was aware of the shock he would cause, and the problems he would spark for Fidel Castro and the Cuban Revolution. The implications and repercussions of his speech were evident. The Soviets already mistrusted him, due to his real and imagined ties with China, his trips to Beijing and Africa, and his persistent opposition to their recommendations concerning the Cuban economy. Che also knew of the links between Cuba and the Soviet Union, and how they had grown tighter since the beginning of his world travels in early November. He realized that his criticism of the USSR would be badly received in Havana, opening a serious rift between himself and Fidel Castro. Time would tell just how serious it would be.

As in Mexico in 1956 and New York in 1964, Che's outburst revealed powerful unconscious urges. Provocation was his preferred form of expression during moments of great tension; his solution was always to seek the most exacerbated and gratuitous extremes. This is perhaps the only way to understand the speech he made in Algiers: icily provocative, it was born in that small space between anguish and reason.

Che was forced to spend two cold and dark days in Shannon, Ireland, in mid-March on his way back to Cuba; the stopover due to mechanical difficulties allowed him to reflect upon his future. Rafael del Pino piloted the Cubana de Aviación Britannia sent to bring him home. Che rarely flew alone, yet this time no one accompanied him. Osmany Cienfuegos was on the same flight, but traveling separately; he had come from a preparatory meeting for another conference of Communist parties in Moscow. Che finally sought out Del Pino to talk, answering his query about Africa with, "Africa is really fucked; the people there are so difficult, so different." He explained that people in Africa had no sense of nationality; each tribe had its own chief, territory, and

*"We discussed his speech all night; he was fully aware of what he was going to say. He was an enormously charming man, but terribly dogmatic and stubborn in his ideological positions." Ben Bella, interview.

nation even though they all lived within a single country. Guevara concluded, "It's very difficult, but there is some possibility that they will adopt the revolution, because the Cubans are good at that. . . ."*

His ruminations in Ireland and in flight rested on more upbeat prospects for the Revolution that he and Castro had wrought. The situation in Cuba had improved. Even the U.S. State Department detected encouraging signs in the sugar harvest and the country's economic performance.[36] The circumstances that had prevented him from leaving for Argentina the year before were hence no longer valid. Similarly, though he had lost many ideological and policy battles, at least he was satisfied that his opponents had not won either. Carlos Rafael Rodríguez had just been removed as director of the INRA, and its new head (under Fidel Castro himself) was a young Fidelista, Raúl Curbelo, without any links to the old Communist guard.

Che could now depart, if he so wished; and he nurtured powerful political and personal reasons for doing so. Distinctly marginalized from economic policy-making, he no longer even attended negotiations with the Soviets. All of his theses had been defeated. In March a rumor circulated that, due to Foreign Minister Raúl Roa's illness, Guevara would be chosen to replace him.[†] The scuttlebutt seems implausible: after Che's denunciation of the USSR in Algeria, he could hardly be expected to function as chief diplomat to a Socialist-bloc country. The more likely explanation was that transmitted to the Italian Communist Party by Saverio Tutino, the Havana correspondent for *L'Unitá*. Aside from being the shrewdest foreign journalist on the island, Tutino had unsurpassed contacts among the Cuban *nomenklatura*— including Manuel Piñeiro, the intelligence chief—and had the political and intellectual capacity to understand the vicissitudes of the Cuban situation. His interpretation was cited in a long cable from the British Embassy to London: Castro had decided to remove Che from all economic duties—as had indeed already occurred in fact, what with Guevara's travels and the prior transfer of Che's closest aides. But, out of friendship, respect, and necessity, Fidel had offered Che a high political position in recognition of his rank and

---

*Rafael del Pino, interview with the author, Washington, D.C., September 30, 1995. Cienfuegos had accompanied Raúl Castro to Moscow. The distance Del Pino observed between him and Che during the flight was perhaps a sign of things to come when they returned to Havana.

† The rumor appeared in two secret cables, one from the British Embassy in Havana, the other from the British Embassy in Washington, D.C., to the Foreign Office. The second cable notes that the information originated in the State Department; in the first cable, the rumor is given little credence. See Lord Harlech to Foreign Office, No. 581, March 10, 1965 (Secret), FO/371/AK1015, Public Record Office, London, and Mr Watson to Foreign Office, No. 186, March 13, 1965 (Secret), FO/371/AK1015, ibid. There is also a U.S. cable about it: Central Intelligence Agency, Intelligence Information Cable, "Alleged Current Activity of Che Guevara," June 2, 1965 (Secret), NSF, Country File, Cuba, Activities of Leading Personalities, #14 cable, LBJ Library.

trustworthiness. According to Tutino, Che had agreed to resign from the Ministry of Industries, but rejected any other post because, though his ideas had been defeated, he still believed in them. It would have been wrong, dishonest, and futile "to work for something in which he did not believe."[37]

In addition, Che seems to have resigned himself momentarily to the fact that, given the annihilation of the guerrillas in Argentina and the precariousness of movements in Colombia, Venezuela, and Guatemala, there was scant hope that revolution could succeed in Latin America without triggering an immediate U.S. intervention. A British report based on previous analyses by the United States noted that in Algiers, "even the indomitable Che Guevara seemed pessimistic about the possibility of more Cubas emerging in Latin America." The United States, he said, "would intervene to prevent it."* In contrast, there were many reasons for reckoning that Moscow's vehement opposition to any further Cuban ventures in Latin America would not apply in Africa. After all, the Soviets themselves shipped arms to the Congo rebels, if only not to lose face vis-à-vis China. And U.S. involvement in the Congo and neighboring countries, though not insignificant, could not be compared to its interest in the Americas. If there was nothing useful left for Che to do in Cuba, and his prospects in Latin America seemed just as bleak, then the logical next step was Africa. His mind was made up. The only thing lacking was to discuss things with Fidel, obtain his support, and get to work.

But even a full-fledged revolutionary does not live off politics alone. Two other factors impelled him to escape. The first, already mentioned, was his ruined marriage; his home life was a shambles. As he admitted to Nasser, "I have already broken two marriages."[38] Once again, he had been absent when Aleida gave birth—this time to his son Ernesto, on February 24, 1965. Che was consumed anew by his fever for movement, and the troubled, precarious state of his affective relations, far from tying him down, was pushing him further and further away. Another loss, no matter how unexpected, was confirmed in Paris at the end of January: his Córdoba friend Gustavo Roca, who defended the survivors of Jorge Masetti's guerrilla campaign in the Argentine courts, recounted the sordid details of the debacle in Salta. The

* British Embassy in Havana, Research Memorandum, "Che Guevara's African Venture" (Secret), undated, Foreign Office Archive FO371/AK1022, Public Record Office, London. Aside from a few additional comments such as that quoted above, this report is identical to one by the Intelligence and Research Section of the Department of State in Washington, under the same title, dated April 13, 1965, and registered as RAR-13 (copy LBJ Library). This only confirms that U.S. and British intelligence services cooperated very closely in Cuba, as in many other countries. See Thomas Hughes to the Secretary, Che Guevara's African Venture, INR/DOS, April 19, 1965 (Secret), NSF, Country File, Cuba, Activities of Leading Personalities, no. 18 memo, LBJ Library.

news must have affected Guevara deeply, with both pain and a predictable sense of guilt. It was no longer possible for him to keep sending others into combat while remaining safely on the sidelines.

Finally, there was Che's relationship with Fidel Castro. He had sworn that there would be neither marriage nor divorce, but this balance became increasingly precarious the longer he stayed in Cuba. Guevara could not countenance the changes Castro was effecting, or promoting, on the island. Nor could he break with him, or wish to. He never imagined himself playing the role of a Trotsky, or even an anti-Trotsky, as a marginalized leader who nonetheless defends himself while he still possesses the means to do so. As he waited in Ireland for his plane to be reoutfitted, he wondered how to resolve these many dilemmas. There was not much time left.

Guevara landed in Havana on March 15, three months after his departure; Fidel, Raúl, President Dorticós, and Aleida were at the airport to greet him. But something was wrong: instead of holding a press conference or delivering a televised report on the results of his trip, Che disappeared for several days. He spent forty hours talking with Fidel, Raúl, and several others. There is no eyewitness account, thus far, of that stormy exchange: neither Fidel nor Raúl has spoken of the meeting, even to their closest friends. And if Che kept notes, his widow has not made them public. However, two indirect witnesses have provided their version of events. It is thus possible to surmise the content of the meeting, particularly since we know, as mentioned earlier, that when Che landed in Havana his decision had already basically been made. His conversation with Fidel might have been a catalyst, a trigger, but it was not the cause of Che's departure from Cuba. Less than a month later, as the United States Congress approved the Gulf of Tonkin Resolution formally inaugurating large-scale U.S. involvement in the Vietnam War, Che would leave the island.

Che's aide Benigno has provided the following reconstruction of a heated dispute between Raúl and Che, and Fidel's refusal to take sides. It is a highly plausible account, due to the quality of the source,* to the fact that it corresponds with what is known of Fidel's position vis-à-vis Guevara,

---

*On October 9, 1996, the Bolivian daily *La Razón* published Che Guevara's evaluations of his men's performance during the guerrilla campaign in Bolivia; the document was captured together with Che's diaries in October 1967, but had never been made public. Che's evaluation of Benigno reads as follows: "11-3-67 (three months): Very good, a simple young man, with no duplicity, strong, modest and extremely hard-working, always with his morale up; 11-6-67 (six months): Very good, has had some minor problems in food distribution; in everything else, first rate; 11-9-67 (nine months): Very good, he is learning, has totally overcome his former minor problems." Compared to the evaluations of other men, Benigno's rating constitutes an example of admiration and trust on Che's part comparable only to that which he extended to one or two other combatants.

and to its similarity with a discussion between Carlos Franqui and Raúl Castro the year before, when the latter accused Che of being pro-Chinese.* Because the report is unpublished it is worth reproducing verbatim, as narrated by Benigno, without any stylistic changes or deletions (aside from idiomatic repetitions):

> Che was accused of being a Trotskyist and pro-Chinese. When he came back from Algeria, I know there was a strong discussion between him and Fidel, which upset him very much: he even left for Tope de Collantes for about a week, with very serious asthma attacks. I know this from Comrade Argudín, one of his personal bodyguards. Argudín was working as his bodyguard. He told me about it because we were comrades in Che's escort and I was away. He told me: "Shit, I'm worried." "What's going on?" "I overheard a very big argument between el Fifo and Che." So I asked him, "What about?" He said: "They were discussing Chinese policy and discussing another Soviet leader"—for he was semi-literate. So I mentioned the names of several Soviet leaders. He said, "No, it was one that's already dead. The one they call Trotsky, and they said to Che that he was a Trotskyist. Raúl said that. Raúl was the one who said he was a Trotskyist, that his ideas made it clear that he was a Trotskyist." Argudín told me that Che got up very violent, as if he were about to jump on Raúl, and said to Raúl: "You're an idiot, you're an idiot." He said he repeated the word idiot three times; then he looked over at Fidel, says Argudín, and Fidel did not respond. . . . When Che saw that attitude, he left very upset, he slammed the door and left. And then, a few days later, he decided suddenly to leave for the Congo. He went to Tope de Collantes for a week, to a sanatorium in the center of the country. He had several terrible asthma attacks, apparently because he was so upset. I remember it perfectly, just as I am telling it to you word for word. Argudín and I had things worked out this way; if we were present at some big meeting I would tell Argudín what had happened. When he was on duty he told me. . . . So he told me about a week later, two days before I took the boat to Dar-es-Salaam.†

*Carlos Franqui, *Retrato de Familia con Fidel* (Barcelona: Seix Barral, 1981), pp. 464–470, especially p. 466. In an interview, Franqui provided the author with a more detailed and relevant version of the same dialogue between Raúl, Che, and Franqui, at the Palace of the Revolution, on January 1, 1964: "Then suddenly Raúl exclaims, 'You and Che are pro-Chinese'; when I heard that I was stunned in relation to Che; Raúl got that from a French magazine *Révolution*, edited by the lawyer Vergés, who without Che's permission published an article of Che's and a picture of my exhibition. Of course Raúl knew Che was sympathetic to the Chinese." Carlos Franqui, interview with the author, San Juan, P.R., August 20, 1996.

† Benigno interview. A false document, known as the R-Havana Report, attributed to East German intelligence, mentions a serious psychosomatic ailment afflicting Che in those days. It never happened, but the asthmatic attacks mentioned by Benigno could explain the rumor, and his days of rest or seclusion at Tope de Collantes could have been confused with a prolonged hospitalization. See Frederic Hetman, *Yo tengo siete vidas* (Salamanca: Loguez Ediciones, 1977), p. 128.

Carlos Franqui has furnished his own description of the dispute and its causes. His source is Celia Sánchez, Fidel Castro's assistant, companion, and confidante, who died in 1980:

> What is certain is that Guevara was received at the airport when he returned by Fidel Castro, Raúl, and President Dorticós, energetically reprimanded, accused of indiscipline and irresponsibility, of compromising Cuba's relations with the USSR; Fidel was furious over his irresponsibility in Algiers, as he said to many, including myself. Guevara acknowledged that what they said was true, that he had no right to say that on behalf of Cuba, that he accepted his responsibility, but that that was his way of thinking and he could not change it. That they should not expect a public self-criticism, or any private apology to the Soviets, and with his Argentine humor he said that the best would be for him to punish himself, that he would go and cut sugarcane.[39]

Raúl Castro had just returned from Moscow. On the very day of Che's anti-Soviet diatribe in Algiers, Fidel's younger brother had met with the new leadership in Moscow, along with Osmany Cienfuegos. The two were attending a preparatory meeting for the international (minus China) Conference of Communist Parties, scheduled for the following month of March. Raúl evidently received acerbic complaints about Che's performance from the Soviet leaders, not only about his economic positions in Cuba and insolence in Algeria, but for his repeated marks of sympathy toward China. So it turned out that Raúl Castro, who had always favored Cuba's ties to the Socialist bloc, who had obtained arms and then missiles to defend the island, had supported greater alignment with the USSR and opposed China, was the man to whom the Soviets presented their long list of grievances against Guevara. Shortly after the argument, on March 18, Raúl traveled to Poland, Hungary, Bulgaria, and again, on two occasions, to Moscow, to placate the Soviet leadership and participate in the conference.* Both Raúl, in principle, and Fidel, pragmatically, understood that Cuba would have to take sides in the Sino-Soviet conflict. On top of that, all the personal resentments between Raúl and Che had reached a head: Che had lost his battle and nobody, not even Fidel Castro, could save him.

It was almost certainly at that time that a unit of about a hundred men, commanded by Che, was formed to train and support the Congo freedom fighters and, if necessary, to fight at their side—though never in their stead.

---

*According to the CIA, Moscow pressured Fidel Castro to send his brother to the Parties' Conference; the Cuban leader agreed. Central Intelligence Agency, Directorate of Intelligence, Castro and Communism: The Cuban Revolution in Perspective, Intelligence Memorandum, May 9, 1966 (Secret), p. 18, NSF, Country File, Cuba, Bowdler File, vol. 2, box 19, no. 71 report, LBJ Library.

Perhaps some of the combatants were selected before the hasty decision to send them was actually made; others, like the subordinates of Rafael del Pino in the air force, were called up a few days before Che's return to Cuba. Del Pino was instructed to pick out the "blackest" troops from the Holguín base, especially those with anti-aircraft combat experience, since a large number of anti-Castro Cuban pilots were already in action against the Congo rebels. Del Pino selected fifteen pilots, including Lieutenant Barcelay, who, under the name of Chango or Lawton, would save Che's life eight months later on the banks of Lake Tanganyika.

There were many considerations involved in Cuba's resolution to dispatch an expeditionary force into the heart of Africa. If there was any doubt in Che's mind, it was dispelled by Fidel's attitude. Not because they had fallen out, or because Castro had reprimanded him for his anti-Soviet outburst in Algiers, his pro-Chinese position, or his three-month leave from government duty, but because of Fidel's conscious noninvolvement in the successive watersheds of the revolution involving Che. The fact that Castro had not sided with him, and had allowed Raúl's accusations to stand, left Guevara with little choice. It was time to leave. Fortunately, the path was now open: there was a struggle in which he could participate in a dignified and effective way. There was even a chance that the Soviets and their friends would increase their support for the revolution in Latin America if the African expedition succeeded.[40] Besides, Cuban penetration on the continent was not limited to Che's presence in Congo-Leopoldville; a few months later, another Cuban contingent was sent to Congo-Brazzaville. By mid-1966, over six hundred Cuban officers and troops were operating in Africa. In the summer of that year, a group of them stationed in Brazzaville saved President Alphonse Massemba-Debat from a coup d'état.

Furthermore, the Congo rebel groups, though not ideal, had the great merit of existing. They embodied the first postcolonial struggle in independent Africa, and thirsted for assistance from Cuba. Che's initial contact with them had not been in vain. Their cause was a good, if temporary, substitute for what he had really sought since 1963: a return to his native Argentina, regardless of the local conditions. According to Emilio Aragonés—who would soon join Che in the Congo—two obsessions clashed. Che wished to return to his country of origin, and Fidel Castro wanted to save him from death at the hands of the Argentine army.

I knew that his dream was to go to Argentina: that was his ultimate goal. I believe Fidel encouraged or facilitated Che's trip to Africa in order to save him from a trip to Argentina. Fidel knew that the Argentine army was not the same as Tshombe's soldiers. Fidel found the solution in an expedition to Africa, where there was less danger from a Yankee intervention. I think

Fidel sold him on Africa, I think Che came back enamored of Africa because he spoke with all the African leaders and came out of there very enthusiastic. It seems to me that Fidel wound him up because there was less risk, rather than sending him off to Argentina he delayed him in Africa, where things would be different because there would not be such a brutal reaction, nor could there be in any other country, nobody would pay much attention to something happening in the jungle. This is a subjective view, I have not discussed the matter with Fidel. What Fidel wanted was to gain time. Fidel could not go against the deal they had made in Mexico, but he was trying to make sure by any means that Che would not be killed.*

The pact in Mexico referred to by Aragonés allowed for a separation, but certainly did not cause it. Fidel Castro has recalled several times how, when Che joined the *Granma* expedition, they agreed that the Argentine would be able to follow his path regardless of any consideration of state or political obligation. Thanks to this pact, Che could leave without remorse; though in fact over the next year and a half, he would anguish repeatedly over quitting the government on an island with such severe shortages in qualified, devoted cadres. If anything made Che think twice about leaving, it was the prospect of jumping ship with a masterful captain but few and mediocre lieutenants. The friends' discussion during March concluded with these words—Che's bitter and categorical, Fidel's reluctantly resigned:

All right, the only alternative left me is to leave here for wherever the hell, and please, if you can help me in any way in what I intend to do, do so immediately; and if not, tell me so I can see who can. Fidel said to him, "No, no, there is no problem there."[41]

Che prepared for his departure. On March 22, he convened his last meeting at the Ministry of Industries and delivered a couple of talks—one in general terms, and one within the governing council. At both meetings he recounted his experience in Africa and highlighted the similarities between Cuban and African culture, emphasizing the African roots of modern Cuba. He did not say that he was leaving for Africa. From the outset, he agreed with Castro that they would explain his absence by saying that he had gone to cut sugar cane in the province of Oriente. The deception was quite plausible: everybody knew that Che had a penchant for volunteer work. The main point was to gain time.[†]

---

*Aragonés, interview January 23, 1996. During the course of three interviews and almost ten hours of recorded conversation, Aragonés repeated this interpretation, almost obsessively, several times.

† Saverio Tutino, the previously cited well-informed Italian journalist, does not discard the possibility that for a week or two Che may have actually marched off to the cane fields,

Che's cover could not last forever. Soon, it would be necessary to account for his whereabouts, but by then he and his expeditionary force would be in the hills of Africa. Before leaving, he sent books, gifts, and elliptical letters of farewell to his friends. He also selected the aides who would accompany him: among them, Víctor Dreke, a black combatant from the old Student Directorate; Papi (José María Martínez Tamayo); and Pombo (Harry Villegas, who this time could be included precisely because he was black).

Almost all the 130 Cubans who landed on the shores of the Great Lakes were black, and many of them volunteers, but not all went entirely of their own free will. A large number of "volunteers" were completely unaware of their geographic and political destination. Evidently, security had to be tight. But the ignorance of the "internationalists" about their mission would have dire consequences. So Che would conclude at year's end, devastated by defeat and dysentery:

> In Cuba very few of our principal military or mid-level cadres with good training were black. When we tried to send primarily black Cubans, we sought them out among the best elements of the army, with some combat experience. The result is that our group has . . . a very good combat morale and precise tactical knowledge in the field, but little academic training. . . . The fact is that our comrades had a very scant cultural background, and also a relatively low political development.[42]

As Aragonés would exclaim months later in the Congo, "Shit, Che, nobody knows what the hell we're doing here"; no wonder the Cuban troops were soon overwhelmed by discontent, rage, and indiscipline. But Che was, as always, in a hurry. The whole process of selection, training, and transport lasted less than a couple of months. At daybreak of April 2, 1965, Che's head shaved and with a dental prosthesis in place, he, Dreke, and Papi departed from Havana's José Martí airport for Dar-es-Salaam. As Castro would reveal twenty years later: "I myself suggested to Che that he should gain some time and wait; but he wanted to train cadres, develop through experience."[43]

The account of Celia Sánchez quoted by Franqui, whereby Che left Cuba without taking leave of Castro, rings true.[44] In mid-April, Franqui was summoned by Castro late one night to his house on Calle Once, where the *comandante* was deeply distressed, pacing back and forth like a lion in a cage. He had seen him in that state only twice before: at the Miguel Schultz immigration bureau in Mexico City and in the Sierra Maestra in June 1958,

---

imposing a sort of self-punishment on himself for having violated instructions in Algeria by speaking on his own behalf. Still, he had no regrets. Carlos Franqui concurs with this hypothesis: "I think it's true, knowing him." Carlos Franqui, interview.

when Batista's counteroffensive came within half a kilometer of his general headquarters. Castro ordered him to seek out Italian publisher Giangiacomo Feltrinelli, who was about to return to Milan from Cuba, to tell them that rumors of Che's death in the Dominican Republic were false. Che was alive and well, he said, and had gone to Vietnam. Franqui dissuaded Castro, explaining that the story would create more suspicions than it would dispel. But he understood two things: Che was not in Vietnam, and Fidel was enormously upset at his friend's departure.

With or without a hug from Castro, Guevara finally departed Havana, leaving Celia Sánchez a good-bye letter for Castro: "Afterwards, Celia told me Fidel was quite upset because he had not been able to see Che before his departure; he had so much work those days."[45] The departure of the other combatants—who would arrive in Tanzania little by little—was also arranged in haste, as were the arms shipment and messages to the families and governments involved. A first unit, commanded by Che, landed at the Tanzanian capital on April 19. Four days later they embarked upon their trek across the savannah to Kigoma, a godforsaken village on the lakeshore facing the Congo.[46]

Che's insistence on a secret operation contrasted with Fidel Castro's political need to keep his principal partners informed. The itinerary followed by most of the combatants was fairly straightforward, passing through Havana, Moscow, Algeria, Cairo, and Dar-es-Salaam.[47] Che's trip, however, was more roundabout and lasted seventeen days, in order to avoid arousing undue curiosity—including in friendly countries. Even in his journal, Che noted that he could not divulge the stops on his slow passage to Tanzania. According to a Cuban intelligence source who worked at the Cuban Embassy in Prague, Che, Dreke, and Papi arrived in Prague directly from Havana, and remained there for several days without the Soviets' knowledge. It is possible that they then traveled less directly, through Belgium, Paris, and Madrid.* Whatever the road, the effort was in vain: during those very days, Fidel Castro shared with the Soviet ambassador in Havana one of the best-kept secrets in the world.

Aleksandr Alexeiev had visited Che at the Ministry of Industries in late March, asking whether he would be accompanying Fidel and the diplomatic corps to the sugar harvest in Camagüey. Che replied that he wouldn't, as he was off to Oriente "to cut cane for real, not make-believe." Alexeiev cautioned him gently but a bit late, "There's no sense in fighting, Che." To which Che answered, "All the same, I'm not going." When the Soviet

---

*This is the opinion of a strange figure, a former intelligence agent of the Francoist dictatorship in Spain, who has blended utter fantasy in his memoirs with kernels of fact and insight. See Luis M. González-Mata, *Las muertes del Che Guevara* (Barcelona: Argos Vergara, 1980), p. 19.

ambassador met with Fidel in Camagüey on April 18 or 19, he was still disturbed by Che's tense attitude. Fidel took him by the arm, leading him away from the others, and whispered:

> Che did not go to cut cane; he's left for Africa. Che believes Africa is a no-man's-land, where neither Europe, the USSR, or the United States has hegemony; it's the right place for Cuba. You know he is a revolutionary and this is how he can help the world. Don't transmit this to Moscow by radio or in code, but I want you to know it and inform your leaders in person whenever you can.[48]

According to Alexeiev, the USSR never discussed or protested Che's presence in the Congo, at least not through its diplomatic mission. Moscow evidently considered that if Fidel had decided Che should go to the Congo, it was all right with them. Oleg Daroussenkov, Nikolai Leonov, and other Soviet diplomats in Cuba at that time corroborate that the USSR knew what was going on, but never raised any objections or interfered with Cuba's African venture. Fidel's deference to the Soviets undoubtedly placated them, as did Raúl's when he attended the Conference of Communist Parties in April. In contrast, Che did not even tell his mother about his plans, which would lead to a series of misunderstandings.

While in Havana in March, Che had met with Gustavo Roca, who would soon return to Buenos Aires. He asked him to remit a letter to his mother, who was dying from cancer. Celia received the letter, dated March 16, at the hospital in mid-April. Part of its content is known thanks to her reply, sent to Cuba with Ricardo Rojo, a copy of which he saved and published in 1968. Che wrote to his mother that he intended to leave the revolutionary government and go off to cut cane for a month; then he would manage a factory for the next five years. He warned his mother not to travel to Cuba for the moment, and told her about his family and the birth of his son Ernesto, in a perfunctory tone for which Celia would bitterly reproach him. Her reply never reached Guevara; the mail service in the Congolese guerrilla camps left much to be desired.

Celia questioned him sharply: wasn't there a better use for her eldest son's talents than cutting cane or managing factories? Celia's condition worsened in mid-May. She asked Rojo to call Che in Havana; Aleida, who answered, reported that Che was in Cuba, but not accessible by phone. A couple of days later Aleida returned the call, only to say that her husband had not been in touch. Che's family in Argentina was heartbroken; his mother died two days later. His siblings would not know until much later where their eldest brother was, or why he could not contact his mother on her deathbed. Che's younger brother Roberto did not learn of his trip to the Congo until the end of 1967, when he met with Fidel after Guevara's execution in Bolivia.[49] Even when his mother was dying, Che followed the law of the revolution; Soviet diplomats knew more about his movements than his own family in Buenos Aires.

Between Che's disappearance on March 22 and October 5, 1965, when Fidel read publicly his letter of farewell from Cuba, countless rumors proliferated concerning his whereabouts and his relationship with Castro.* Cuba's intelligence services added to the confusion through a disinformation campaign. So the word spread that Che had gone to fight the U.S. marines in the Dominican Republic; or that he had been seen by a priest in the state of Acre, in Brazil; or that he lay ill in a Cuban sanatorium; or that Castro had had him shot. U.S. intelligence also floated stories, in the hope that someone would slip up and tell the truth—but to no avail, except in the Congo itself. The Cubans' expertise in this area, and Che's obsession with secrecy, functioned more than adequately until July, and even then the CIA refused to believe its field officers' reports.

In contrast, the substantive rift between Castro and Che became increasingly public. Embassies and intelligence services alike reported and analyzed it in depth, though somewhat late in the game. The best summary is to be found in a CIA intelligence memorandum drafted on October 18, 1965, a few days after Fidel revealed Che's decision to lead a revolution elsewhere.[50] Aside from listing previous disagreements among Che, the Soviets, and the Communists, the U.S. report examined Che's growing distance from Castro. It began on January 21, 1965, when the Cuban leader announced that the best five thousand cane-cutters would receive prizes, such as motorbikes, trips abroad, and first-class holidays in Cuban hotels, effectively putting an end to moral incentives. Already in December 1964, the government had announced a pilot program of contractual salaries, profit sharing, and prizes for workers. Later, during his 26th of July speech in Santa Clara, Fidel Castro (with a huge portrait of Guevara as a backdrop) denounced moral incentives and administrative centralization. His presentation was polished and well-reasoned, and its central message was clear:

> Nor [can we have] idealist methods which conceive of all men obediently following the concept of duty, because in real life we cannot think like that . . . nor choose those paths which seek, above all else, to awaken selfishness in men. . . . It would be absurd to try [to convince] the great mass of

---

*Che's disappearance also evoked doubts and criticism among some of Cuba's supporters abroad. The U.S. left-wing publication *Monthly Review,* edited by Paul Sweezy and Leo Huberman, asked: "Is Fidel Castro aware of what is really at stake in the Guevara case? Does he realize that every day he delays in clearing up the mystery, he contributes to the anguish and doubts of honest revolutionaries, and to the joy of his enemies?" Quoted in Léo Sauvage, *Le Cas Guevara* (Paris: Editions La Table Ronde, 1971), p. 49.

men who cut cane to make their best effort out of duty, regardless of whether they make more or less.[51]

Fidel resumed his attack on September 28, asserting in a speech that he favored "local development and administration."[52] Finally, among the list of divergences between Che and Fidel there was the structure of the Central Committee in Cuba's newly founded Communist Party; the announcement of its creation was the occasion Fidel chose to make public Che's letter of renunciation. This was largely unavoidable, as Guevara was not among the members of the Central Committee; indeed, in his farewell letter he had discarded his Cuban citizenship. But his closest aides at the Ministry of Industries were not included in the Party's governing body either. Furthermore, the only cabinet ministers left out were those most identified with Che: Luis Alvarez Rom, the minister of finance allied with Che in his dispute with the National Bank; the minister of sugar, Orlando Borrego; and Arturo Guzmán, who replaced Che at the Ministry of Industries. Salvador Vilaseca, the mathematics professor who was a close friend of Che's, was also excluded. Che's economic-policy team had been politically annihilated.

Guevara did not take his succession of economic policy defeats quietly. He responded in two steps: first, in an interview with the Egyptian publication *Al-Tali-'ah,* in April 1965, which has never been published in Cuba; and, second, in his most famous essay, "El socialismo y el hombre en Cuba" (Socialism and Man in Cuba), originally published in Uruguay in March 1965, and written during his official African tour. In the Egyptian interview, Guevara launched his offensive on two fronts—one directly related to Cuba, and the other to the Sino-Soviet conflict. He was categorical about material incentives, saying that Yugoslavia "has given preference to material incentives," and that they should be "liquidated." He rejected the idea that workers should participate in setting salaries, and all profit-sharing and prize schemes. In his words,

An "automatized" industry which distributes high revenues only among privileged workers is denying those resources to the community as a whole. The efforts of those workers in high-revenue companies are like the effort invested by farmers in their own plots of land. Such conditions create a privileged group and strengthen capitalist elements.[53]

This was a direct response to the decisions taken in Cuba over the previous months. Che also expressed his contradictory feelings about Yugoslavia's international position, and his exasperation with the Communist movement worldwide: "We differ in two ways from the Yugoslav experiment: in our reaction to Stalinism, and our opposition to having the Soviet Union dictate to us its economic and leadership ideals."[54] Though some of the meaning may have been lost in translation—from Spanish to Arabic to English—it was clear that Che's criticism of Yugoslavia was similar to China's. Che did not share in Tito's emphatic anti-Stalinism; on the contrary, his view was closer to that of the Chinese, who saw in Tito's and Khrushchev's anti-Stalinism a fatal sign of revisionism.

In "El socialismo y el hombre en Cuba," Guevara returned to the issue of moral incentives and responded to some of the criticism he had received:

> The temptation to follow the beaten path of material interest, as the motor for accelerated development, is very great. The danger is that the trees can prevent us from seeing the forest. By pursuing the illusion of achieving socialism with the blunted arms bequeathed us by capitalism (merchandise as economic unit, profitability, individual material interest as driving force, et cetera), one could well arrive at a dead end. So to build communism, one must make a new man together with the material base. It is very important that we choose the right instrument to mobilize the masses. That instrument should be of a moral nature, fundamentally, without neglecting the appropriate use of material incentives, especially of a social nature. As I have said, at times of extreme danger it is easy to magnify moral incentives; but to keep them effective, we must develop a consciousness where values acquire new categories.[55]

Guevara went on to describe the past errors of the Cuban government, and the special features of the Revolution—though the two were not necessarily related, in his view. He avoided making any link between the *caudillo*-style leadership of Fidel Castro—which he praised—and the "revisionism" he condemned. This is perhaps why he found it difficult to criticize the revolutionary process as a whole, in any effective or constructive way. If one compares his statements about Fidel with his analysis of the mistakes committed in Cuba, the Guevaran predicament becomes apparent. He is in effect denouncing the errors while celebrating their causes:

> In large public gatherings one may observe something like a dialogue between two tones, whose vibrations provoke new ones in the listener. Fidel and the masses begin to vibrate in a dialogue of increasing intensity until reaching a climax in a sudden finale, crowned by our cry of struggle and history. It is difficult, for somebody who has not lived the experience of the Revolution, to understand that close dialectical bond between the individual and the masses. . . . In our country, we have not made the mistake of a mechanistic realism, but have gone to the other extreme. And this is because we have not understood the need to create a new man. . . . The reaction against nineteenth-century man has made us fall anew into the decadence of the twentieth century. This is not too serious a mistake, but we must overcome it, so as not to open a channel for revisionism.[56]

Finally, Che commented briefly but insightfully on his own journey as a revolutionary, and the ties between the new man and himself. The new man is, in a sense, the Cuban Communist: the veteran of the Sierra Maestra and volunteer work, of the Bay of Pigs and the missile crisis, of international missions and solidarity. In a word, he is very much like Che Guevara. Che never lacked a capacity for self-analysis, or a clear idea of his own destiny; indeed, the fantasy of a chosen fate had obsessed him since his youthful nights in Chuquicamata and the Peruvian Amazon. For him, the new man and the revolutionary leader are fused into one exemplary individual; he comfortably identifies himself with a new man who has yet to see the light of day in Cuba, and never will:

> In our ambition as revolutionaries, we try to advance as quickly as possible, clearing paths . . . by our example. . . . The leaders of the Revolution have children who, in their early babbling, never learn the word for father; women who are ready to sacrifice their lives in order to take the Revolution to its ultimate goal; friends who are strictly comrades in the Revolution. There is no life outside it [the Revolution]. In these conditions, we must have a large measure of humanity, a large sense of justice and truth. . . . Every day we must struggle to transform that love of a living humanity . . . into actions which will serve as an example.[57]

Che soon found himself forsaking these Marxist polemics and testamentary preoccupations, as well as the intrigues of Havana and his economic failures. Once again, he was on the road, lured by the enrapturing mystery of Africa and the excitement of combat. After minor incidents and rising impatience, in the last days of April he finally arrived at the freedom fighters' camp in Kibamba, where he and his companions were received with military honors. There, on the western shores of Lake Tanganyika, the Cubans introduced themselves: Dreke, or "Moja" (number one in Swahili); Martínez Tamayo, or "M'Bili" (number two); and Che, or "Tatu" (number three), registered as interpreter and physician. They would spend seven months in the area, waiting for a war that never came.

From the outset, they faced a disconcerting dilemma: whether or not to divulge to the Congolese and Tanzanian leaders the true identity of "Tatu." Laurent Kabila, head of the rebels in the zone, preferred Che's presence to remain secret. Accordingly, Cuba's ambassador in Dar-es-Salaam, Pablo Ribalta, did not reveal it to President Nyerere until after Che's departure in November. But the envoy was pulled in opposite directions. On the one hand, Che had entered Tanzania without the consent of local authorities, and he wanted the ambassador to inform the central government as soon as possible. On the other, Havana repeatedly instructed him not to reveal Tatu's identity. Ribalta was in despair over these contradictory demands.[58]

The reasons for this indecision were obvious. The news that over one hundred Cuban advisers had arrived could in itself internationalize the conflict. The fact that they were led by Che Guevara would, in addition, attract countless South African mercenaries, as well as U.S. and Belgian reprisals—which would quickly neutralize any conceivable advantages ensuing from Cuban solidarity. Since Kabila was still in Cairo with his lieutenants, where a conference supporting the Congo rebellion had established a Supreme Council of the Revolution presided over by Gaston Sumialot, Che had, by default, an excellent justification for entering the Congo without telling anybody:

> To be frank, I was afraid that my offer of support might cause extreme reactions, and that some of the Congolese or the friendly government [of Tanzania] might ask me to stay away.[59]

He soon realized that he was spending most of his time waiting for a shoe to drop: the arrival of Kabila or his aides; the refurbishing of a deserted camp; the authorization to move onto another hill; the landing of visitors or supplies from Havana. He worked as a doctor and helped train the Congolese troops. As he complained in his journal, "we had to do something in order to avoid complete idleness. . . . Our morale was still high, but some comrades began to grumble as they saw the days pass in vain."[60] In early May the rest of the Cubans arrived; so did Kabila's deputy, who reiterated his chief's orders to keep Che's identity secret; Che was learning patience and humility the hard way.

In the meantime, he was initiated into the mysteries of the *dawa:* the magical belief of Congolese fighters in a potion which *mugangas* (sorcerers) rubbed over them, and which had the supernatural power to protect them from enemy bullets—but only if they believed in it. Guevara reflected that while *dawa* might boost courage in combat, it could also work against the Cubans if there were many casualties and the Cubans were held responsible because of their lack of faith.

He discovered the political and personal consequences of his bizarre situation almost immediately. First he was felled by an acute tropical fever which caused in him an "extraordinary fatigue, so I didn't even want to eat": his health, always fragile, was no match for the natural hardships of the terrain. Then Kabila's deputy, who was nominally serving as the struggle's temporary leader in the field, decided to proceed with an absurd project: to attack Albertville, a large mining town about 200 kilometers south of the main guerrilla camp. The conditions for doing so were sadly missing, as was the chain of command needed to rescind his order. Neither Kabila nor his deputies were in any position to lead: not only were they absent most of the time, they lacked the capacity. And there was nothing Che could do: he was not the leader. Predictably, he suffered constant asthma attacks, losing one-fourth of his body weight. He was in the kingdom of ambivalence, as it was aptly described by Oscar Fernández Mell, his comrade-in-arms from Santa Clara, who was sent by Fidel to watch over him: "He was not there as leader, or anything; his role was one that he especially hated: to send people, without going himself."[61]

At the end of May an envoy from Havana arrived, bringing the news of Celia's imminent death in Buenos Aires. Che's state of mind may be surmised from his journal's May summary:

> The main defect in the Congolese is that they don't know how to shoot. . . . Discipline here is very poor, but it seems that things are changing on the front. . . . Today we can say that the apparently greater discipline on the fronts was false. . . . The main feature of the People's Liberation Army is that it was a parasite army which didn't work, didn't train, didn't fight, and demanded supplies and labor from the population, sometimes by force. It is clear that an army of this sort can be justified only if it occasionally fights, like its enemy counterpart. . . . But it didn't even do that. . . . The Congolese Revolution was irreparably doomed to failure owing to its internal weaknesses.[62]

According to Che's journal, this state of affairs prevailed throughout the region, not just at the camp in Kibamba. The findings of the reconnaissance missions sent by Che to other localities—Baraka, Lulimba, Katenga—were discouraging. They unearthed drunkenness, dissipation, and laziness, and absolutely no disposition to fight or even resist. At the same time, the camps teemed with weapons: shipments from the USSR and China (via Tanzania) were flowing in. In June, Zhou Enlai visited Nyerere in Dar-es-Salaam, promising greater support for the Congo rebellion and providing Kabila, once again, with a pretext to remain far from the combat zone. Time was passing, without any prospect of action: two months already, "and we had still done nothing." The only plausible military target was still Albertville, far beyond the reach of the Congo revolutionaries and their Cuban advisers. In truth, Che was cornered. When the troops of South African mercenary leader Mike Hoare and his small air force concluded operations along the border with Sudan and Uganda and headed south, there would be no way to repel them.

In part simply to do something, and also to forestall a possible defeat, Che and Kabila agreed in an exchange of letters quoted in Che's journal to attack the village of Front de Force or Bendera, about forty kilometers south, near a dam not too far from Albertville. Che would have preferred to restrict hostilities to the town of Katenga, smaller and more accessible. But

Kabila insisted on Bendera, despite the risk of alerting Tshombe's forces to the Cuban presence. Che was anxious to participate directly in the attack, but had to restrain himself, lacking Kabila's express authorization. Instead, Dreke was given command of the fewer than 40 Cubans and 160 Rwandan soldiers assigned to capture Front de Force.

The attack in the last days of June was a military disaster; even worse, it disclosed the Cubans' involvement. Four of their soldiers died; the bodies were recovered by the mercenaries. The Cuban combatants had failed to follow Che's strict orders to strip themselves of all personal belongings and documents before engaging the enemy. When the South Africans examined the bodies and supplies, they discovered their nationality and sent a report to U.S. advisers in the Congo.* Lawrence Devlin, the CIA station chief, confirmed his suspicions: the rebels near Albertville were receiving Cuban support.[†] The news spread rapidly: it was published by the press in Dar-es-Salaam a couple of weeks later, and the mission's cover was effectively blown. In his journal summary for June, Che wrote: "This is the worst state of affairs so far."[63] Laurent Kabila persisted in his passivity; but each time Che suggested that he inform the Tanzanian government of his presence, Kabila refused.

The defeat at Front de Force further undermined the Cubans' morale. Bitterly resentful, they now realized that the Congo rebels would not fight: they either dropped their rifles and fled, or else shot into the air. Several members of the expedition expressed their desire to return to Cuba. Most painful for Che was the case of "Sitaini" ("the Chinaman"), an aide from the time of the Sierra Maestra, who argued that he had not been told how long the war would last (in Che's view, three to five years). Because Sitaini was a member of his personal escort, Guevara could not allow him to leave; yet forcing him to stay against his will proved counterproductive. For the first time, Che was confronted—in the flesh, and under combat conditions—with the effects of his own intransigence. The others could not, or would not, keep pace with him; they lacked the determination, the vision and mystique, to bear the adverse conditions of the Congo.

Che finally met with Kabila at Kigoma on July 11. The African stayed only a few days, as he had to return to Dar-es-Salaam in order, he said, to

---

*In his memoirs, Mike Hoare recalls how his men discovered the passport and diary of a fallen Cuban soldier; the passport described the itinerary to Africa and the diary, among other things, lamented how "The Congolese were too lazy even to carry a 76 mm howitzer and its shells." See Richard Gott, "The Year Che Went Missing," *The Guardian Weekend* (London), November 30, 1996, p. 30.

[†] The U.S. Embassy did not disclose the presence of Cuban corpses until July 6; only on September 21 did it confirm that there were 160 Cubans operating in the Congo. The U.S. estimate was off by about forty. See Godley/AmEmbassy/Leopoldville to SecState, September 21, 1965 (Secret), NSF, Country File, Congo, vol. 11, no. 7 cable, p. 49, LBJ Library.

confront Sumialot, who was passing through the Tanzanian capital.[64] Kabila's new departure was the last straw for the Cuban troops; their morale was now completely crushed. Quite justifiably, they were unable to comprehend why their leaders never even appeared in the area of operations, much less participated in or commanded them. Tensions within the Cuban camp were growing apace: two physicians and several members of the Communist Party threatened to leave, and Che reacted violently (though less so, he thought, than on previous occasions). He decided to leave for the front, only to meet with the veto of the African leaders for the obvious reason, in his view, that they would lose face when their troops perceived that the man from Cuba was willing to go to the front and they were not.[65]

The situation improved slightly at the end of July, when an ambush mounted by twenty-five Cuban and twenty-five Rwandan troops met with success. Yet several Cubans still wanted to return home. Che described his own position with ironic sadness: "I'm still here on a scholarship."[66] By August 16 he no longer cared about Kabila's authorization, but simply left for the front. That same night he arrived in Bendera, exhausted and feeling like a "delinquent." There he uncovered vast supplies of weapons, but the rebel forces were completely dispersed along the Albertville highway. At least he felt closer to events, participating in an ambush and a shoot-out near Front de Force. The adrenaline was flowing again. His August summary was the most optimistic so far:

> My scholarship days are over, which is a step forward. In general this month has been very positive: besides the Front de Force operation, there has been a qualitative change in the people. My next steps will be to visit Lambo in Lulimba and visit Kabambare, then convince them of the need to take Lulimba, and keep going along that path. But for all this it is necessary that this ambush and subsequent operations be successful.[67]

Che's debacle in the Congo did not go unnoticed in Havana, though reports were fragmentary, and distorted by their bearers' illusions. After the first defeat at Front de Force, Che sent a letter to Fidel through Antonio Machado Ventura, the Cuban physician and high official who had arrived in May bringing the news of Celia's illness. When he received the letter in Havana, Castro summoned Emilio Aragonés and General Aldo Margolles to a meeting with Osmany Cienfuegos and Manuel Piñeiro. The latter had not yet intervened in Che's African adventure in any way; indeed, months earlier, Piñeiro had sought out Aragonés at his Party offices with a Mexican journalist from *Siempre* magazine, asking about Che's whereabouts; Guevara had already been in the Congo for a month.

When Aragonés arrived, Fidel said to him, "Read this." Che's terrible predicament was brutally expressed in the letter. He described the disaster of Front de Force, where the Africans had fled and Che had lost several officers. During the retreat, a group of deserters had assaulted a soft-drinks truck. Fidel interpreted the letter accurately—far from being a cry of despair or regret, it was a lucid and professional analysis. Others, like Piñeiro, considered it unduly pessimistic; his reaction, according to Aragonés, was: "Shit, he's gone crazy." Fidel thought it over, and decided to order Aragonés and Fernández Mell to Africa. He did not send them to rescue Guevara but to help him. And if there was nothing to be done, they should bring him back to Cuba.[68]

Fernández Mell retains a slightly different version of events. When Manuel Piñeiro went looking for him at the beach where he was enjoying his summer holiday, he felt he was being given a chance to join his friend and former commander in combat. Indeed, Piñeiro's description of events in the Congo was not particularly negative:

> I talked with Piñeiro and Piñeiro told me the exact opposite: that [the expedition] was a phenomenal success, that the Force Bendera operation had been a success and that everything was going well. That's what I was told, and I left with that impression because Aragonés did not tell me anything either, or tell me anything about Che's letter. I didn't even know the letter existed.[69]

Between the end of August and November 21, when the Cubans were expelled from the Congo, Aragonés and Fernández Mell never left Che's side. Guevara did not welcome them with any great pleasure, construing their arrival as a bad omen for his mission.* They were both surprised to find that "Che was practically a prisoner in his own base, they didn't let him move even after he had asked for permission 200 times."[70] Che was gradually losing his self-control: his outbursts were becoming more frequent, against both the Congolese and those Cubans who had "given up," demanding of them and himself rising levels of effort and sacrifice. He often applied to them the most terrible punishment of all, leaving them without food for one, two, or three days. This, he argued, was the most effective sanction in guerrilla warfare.

The two emissaries were astonished when Fernández Mell, as the expedition's chief of staff, asked Che to order boots for his troops from Kigoma and received from him the laconic reply, "The blacks go barefoot, the Cubans must do the same." When the chief of staff asked for vitamins and

---

*"When I learned who was coming, I was afraid they would arrive with a message urging me to return to Cuba." Guevara, "Pasajes . . . (el Congo)," pp. 66–67.

salts, Che's response was, "Do underdeveloped peoples have access to vitamins?" Fernández Mell tried to argue, but met only with sarcastic comments and criticism. He did observe, however, that the troops were losing
respect for their leader and were ready to do almost anything to escape. One
night by the campfire, a combatant handed a note to Aragonés. It read:
"Comrade, you are a member of the Party Secretariat just like Che. Che is
blinded; you must get him out of here."[71] Such insubordination was unacceptable in guerrilla warfare, but Che's brooding isolation was even more
damaging.

The Cuban envoys also confirmed that the military situation, precarious
to begin with, was rapidly deteriorating. The slight improvement in August
had led only to a more forceful response by the government and the South
Africans. According to Major Bem Hardenne, the Belgian chief of staff of
OPS/SUD (Belgium's military mission in Albertville), careful intelligence
work with the prisoners suggested that the rebels were stronger than originally estimated: "The certainty that there are numerous Cubans on Congolese soil aggravates the rebel threat against the cities of Albertville and
Kongolo."* The Belgians resolved then to retake the initiative and launch
an offensive as soon as possible, preferably before the end of September.
Led by Mike Hoare's Fifth Battalion of South African commandos—
a total of 350 men—within two months they surrounded the rebels at
their Kibamba base. The mercenaries were confronting their most severe
challenge thus far in the Congo; the rebels, especially the Rwandan soldiers, were defending themselves more energetically. Moreover, as Major
Hardenne also noted, the Congolese government troops demonstrated the
same limitations as their enemy counterparts: at the first shot they simply
threw down their arms; they never aimed, took to their heels at the earliest
opportunity, and spread the myth that the rebels were invincible. Despite all
this, the two battalions—the South African mercenary unit and the Congolese troops commanded by Belgians—advanced relentlessly toward the
lake. Unable to destroy or capture the rebels, they would soon drive them
across the border and back into Tanzania.

Just as Guevara had feared, news of the Cuban presence soon reached
the Congolese authorities and the CIA. According to Major Hardenne,

---

*Major Bem Hardenne, "Les Opérations Anti-Guerillas dans l'Est du Congo en
1965–1966," February 1969, mimeograph, pp. 19–20. The CIA and State Department also
saw the significance of the Cuban presence: "Although reported number of Cubans et al
probably exaggerated, it not surprising their presence disturbs OPS/SUD. Even small number these 'advisers' in combat leadership role and actively participating in fighting can provide rebel units the backbone necessary to take on not only ANC but also be sharp thorn
in ODO side. It confirmed that Cubans took active part in at least one engagement." God-
ley/AmEmbassy/Leopoldville to SecState September 21, 1965 (Secret), NSF, Country File,
Congo, vol. XI, no. 7 cable, LBJ Library.

The South Africans report that the rebel units display discipline and aggressiveness, and that they move in the field like well-trained troops. They have not detected any Cubans, but are certain of their presence because several messages in Spanish were intercepted by the Fifth Commandos' portable radios.[72]

At the battle of Baraka in late October, where the rebels suffered hundreds of casualties, the South Africans detected several white Cubans leading the opposing forces, but were unable to capture any. For its part, the local CIA station was by now positive that Tatu was none other than Che Guevara, but it was never able to convince the top brass in the United States. Lawrence Devlin, the station chief who years later would be accused of masterminding the assassination of Patrice Lumumba in early 1961, had suspected it even earlier. He showed photos of Che to twelve prisoners, who stated that they had talked with Tatu in Kibamba and later in Bendera; in the pictures he alternately wore a mustache or a beard, or was clean-shaven. Eleven of the twelve soldiers recognized Tatu, making his identity virtually certain.[73] Shortly afterward, Devlin confirmed Che's presence thanks to war diaries seized from fallen rebels. But CIA headquarters never listened.[74] Fernández Mell surmises that the Americans did not care whether Che was in the Congo.* Che was worried that they would find out,[75] but perhaps he was wrong; had his presence been made public,

> Che might have developed into the guerrilla leader that he really was, instead of always fearing that Kabila shitface and the Tanzanian government. Perhaps that . . . prevented Che from becoming in Africa the great guerrilla fighter and political figure that I knew.[76]

Gustavo Villoldo, a Cuban exile who fought at the Bay of Pigs and was sent to the Congo by the CIA to help the Tshombe government, recalls that he knew Che was in the Congo, and became infuriated on learning later that the Cubans had escaped. He confronted his recruiter, declaring that he hadn't come all the way to the Congo to fight the Castro regime, only to see the Cubans return home safe and sound.[77] The most fervent desire of the anti-Castro Cubans (who were all white, according to Devlin) was to simply exterminate the Castroists (who were all black, except for Che, Papi,

---

*The lack of U.S. concern or emphasis on the Cuban presence lends credence to this idea: a CIA report dated August 26, 1965, summarized the situation in the Congo as follows: "However, several thousand rebels do hold a considerable redoubt on the northwestern shore of Lake Tanganyika. The insurgents there are well armed, probably accompanied by at least a few Cuban and Chinese advisors, and seem better trained and more resolute than were their counterparts in the northeast." Central Intelligence Agency, Intelligence Memorandum, Situation in the Congo, August 26, 1965 (Secret), NSF, Country File, Congo, vol. 11, no. 106 memo, LBJ Library.

Benigno, Fernández Mell, and Aragonés). For their part, most of the latter
had only one wish at the end: to escape. Aside from a few machine-gun
exchanges involving aircraft and troops along the Albertville highway, the
two bands of Cubans never came face to face.[78]

Che spent the months of September and October exploring the area. He
visited Fizi, Baraka, Lilamba, and other towns, whose local bosses and
troops unfailingly asked for Cuban funds and soldiers. While traveling on
foot from town to town, Che found himself under fire from the mercenary
and anti-Castro air force several times, though he was never in any real danger. He constantly debated whether to disperse his small unit—as he noted,
he never deployed more than forty men fit for combat, owing to illness and
disciplinary problems—so as to restructure the Congolese combatants, or
else concentrate his troops in order to develop an effective fighting force. By
the end of September, however, this was a moot question; the rebel group
was disintegrating anyway. Che bitterly reproached himself for his own
blindness: "Our situation was getting more and more difficult and the
notion of building an army was slipping through our fingers, with all its
arsenal of weapons, men, and munitions. Still imbued with a sort of blind
optimism, I was incapable of seeing it."[79] One of the reasons for his misguided confidence was that no one dared tell him the truth: "Nobody ever
confronted him."[80] Even senior officers feared that any doubts or questions
they raised would be diagnosed as signs of cowardice. For his part, Che
always thought in terms of his experience in the Sierra Maestra: he expected
the Congolese to react similarly, and they never did.*

Fidel's envoy, Health Minister Machado Ventura, returned at the beginning of October, bringing news of a much-trumpeted visit by Gaston
Sumaliot to Havana in September and a message from Fidel. According to
Che, Castro advised him "not to despair, he asked me to remember the first
period of the struggle and recalled that these problems happen, emphasizing that men are good."[81] The fact that Che had never fully revealed the
hardships he faced had evidently reinforced the impression in Havana that
he was behaving with undue pessimism. On October 5 he wrote a long letter
to Fidel, whose main paragraphs are worth quoting at length:

I received a letter from you which aroused contradictory feelings in me, as
on behalf of proletarian internationalism we make mistakes that can be
very costly. Besides, I am personally worried because, either due to my lack
of seriousness in writing or because you did not fully understand me, it

*Emilio Aragonés, interview with the author, August 24, 1995. Aragonés still wonders
how Che could have been so deluded: "I don't know if he really believed it, or if he said so
in part because he didn't want to leave, he didn't want it to fall apart, I don't know. But a
man as intelligent as he can hardly have believed it would work."

might appear that I suffer from the terrible disease of pessimism without cause. When your Greek present [Aragonés] arrived, he told me one of my letters had given the impression of a condemned gladiator, and the Minister [Antonio Machado], when he gave me your optimistic message, confirmed your opinion to me. You will be able to talk at length with the bearer of this, and he will give you his impressions firsthand. . . . I will say only that here, according to those close to me, I have lost my reputation for objectivity because I am unduly optimistic in the face of the existing, real situation. I can assure you that if it weren't for me this lovely dream would have disintegrated entirely amid a general catastrophe. In my previous letters I had asked you not to send lots of people, but cadres. I said we are not short of weapons, aside from a few special ones; on the contrary, we have too many and not enough soldiers. I especially warned you not to give out funds except in very small amounts and only after many requests. None of these things have been taken into account, and extravagant plans have been made which risk discrediting us internationally and putting me into a very difficult situation. . . . Forget about sending more men to ghost units; prepare me up to one hundred cadres, who should not all be black . . . treat the issue of the boats very tactfully (do not forget that Tanzania is an independent country and we have to play it clean there). Send, as soon as possible, some mechanics and a man who can navigate to get us across the lake at night in relative safety. . . . Don't repeat the mistake of giving out money. . . . Have some trust in my judgment and do not judge by appearances. Shake down those in charge of transmitting accurate information, who are not capable of untangling these knots and present utopian images that have nothing to do with reality. I have tried to be explicit and objective, concise and truthful. Do you believe me?[82]

Che refers, at the end of this letter, to a problem which would pursue him until the end of his life at Quebrada del Yuro, a couple of years later. Since the middle of 1965, the person in charge of follow-up, support, communications, and logistics for him was Manuel Piñeiro, undersecretary of the interior and chief of his own so-called "Liberation Section." Aragonés's departure from Cuba deprived the Party of this responsibility; and Osmany Cienfuegos traveled too often to accomplish the task. In early August, two of Piñeiro's aides arrived in Dar-es-Salaam. One was Ulises Estrada, in charge of African affairs; of African origin, in the mid-seventies he would become Cuba's ambassador to Jamaica, from which he would be expelled for mischief-making and interference. The other was a minor official called Rafael Padilla. It is to them that Che referred when he warned Castro to beware of reports from Tanzania. Those familiar with Piñeiro's team (which would later become the Americas Department of the Communist Party) over several decades, know that it had, among many qualities, two enormous defects.

Anybody whose responsibility it is to export the revolution must believe in it. And those who request a constant flow of money, arms, morale, and diplomatic support from the government for their revolutionary efforts abroad cannot be bearers of bad tidings or pessimists. Piñeiro and his team were always strong supporters of the struggle in Africa and Latin America; their faith and enthusiasm never flagged. But the other side of the coin lay in their inevitably deluded, ingenuous, or frankly falsified assessments about the real situation abroad. The work of the "Ministry of the Revolution" was always hampered by exaggeration, an underestimation of obstacles, and an incapacity to gauge the real balance of power. Che suffered the consequences of these illusions, so dear to the revolutionary establishment. They were not fatal in Africa; in Bolivia, they would be.

The second defect of the Cuban services assigned the role of promoting insurrection all over the Third World was their lack of experience. This was unavoidable in a young revolution willing to undertake anything but lacking the cadres to do so. The officer in Havana trying to follow events in the Congo, Bolivia, El Salvador, or Nicaragua relied upon his agents in the field; Piñeiro depended upon both, and Fidel on Piñeiro. But in 1965, Ulises Estrada had never set foot in Africa, and neither had his superior in Cuba. The information from the front was a disaster, and the conclusions drawn from it by Piñeiro, Raúl Castro, and Fidel Castro were completely groundless. That is why Che asked Castro in the letter quoted above not to believe reports from Dar-es-Salaam; that is why Che landed in Bolivia a year later under adverse conditions which precluded any possibility of success.

Aside from the internal divisions in the Cuban camp and the interminable string of defeats, Che's state of mind was also affected by his health, which was deteriorating day by day. He was plagued by chronic diarrhea, probably dysentery. His determination and resistance were fading quickly, and his decline was reflected in his treatment of both Congolese and Cubans—even those closest to him:

> His state of mind was not even at half capacity. I think that is why he was even more susceptible to asthma; he had a diarrhea which lasted almost two months, plus the asthma which afflicted him constantly. He was fading day by day and was always in a bad mood. I don't mean to say that he treated us badly, no, but we always saw him alone with his book, reading, and we no longer saw in him that earlier disposition; he stopped meeting with us as he had at the beginning. We realized this was not the Che we knew. We asked ourselves, "What's wrong with Che?" . . . one of us went to ask him and was scolded for his trouble.[83]

The last straw was the news Che received sometime between the 6th and 10th of October: in Havana, Fidel Castro had made public Che's letter of farewell. This was the famous declaration in which he took his leave of Cuba and Castro, resigning from all his posts and titles and his Cuban citizenship; in which he renounced all power and began his public pilgrimage toward crucifixion, after giving up all his worldly possessions. In the letter, Guevara recapitulated his years on the island and assumed full responsibility for his future actions, whatever they might be. The logic behind Fidel's reading of the text was impeccable: he was then announcing the composition of the Central Committee of the Communist Party, and no one would have understood Che's exclusion from it without some sort of explanation. Furthermore, the international campaign of rumors about him was out of control; the pressure was becoming untenable.* Over and beyond the beauty of Guevara's text—it is probably his most austere and deeply felt piece of writing—its publication triggered a chain reaction around the world, especially among the small circle of sick Cubans on the run in the Congo.

Aragonés and Fernández Mell have differing accounts of how Che learned about Fidel's publication of his letter.[84] The former swears that he found out through a report on Radio Beijing. The latter asserts that Dreke told him, after receiving a packet of letters and magazines from Havana. The two senior Cubans recall Che's bewilderment and resignation on hearing the news. In the personal reflections which conclude his journal, Che suggests that the letter had a devastating effect on his troops. It made "the comrades see me as a foreigner among Cubans, as when I started out in the Sierra many years before; at that time, I had just arrived, and now I was leaving. Many things that had been shared were now lost. . . . This separated me from the troops."[85]

But the most serious consequence of the publication was not Che's estrangement from the Cuban soldiers. A greater dilemma was that his bridges were now effectively burned. Given his temperament, there was now no way he could return to Cuba, even temporarily. The idea of a public deception was unacceptable to him: once he had said he was leaving, he could not go back. A direct eyewitness, Benigno, recounts a far more dramatic scene than the previous comments suggest:

When Dreke arrived and said that there had been a public event in Cuba where Fidel had read the letter, Che was sitting on a log . . . he had fever, aside from his asthma and diarrhea. He leapt up and said, "Say that again,

---

*"At a given moment it became inevitable that we publish the letter, as all that campaign without any answer or explanation to world opinion was doing a great deal of damage, and there was no other alternative than to publish the letter." Fidel Castro, quoted in Gianni Miná, *Un encuentro con Fidel,* Office of Publications of the State Council, Havana, 1988, p. 327.

say that again. How was that?" Dreke was taken aback and said, "No, Tatu, look, it was like this and this is what I was told." Then he began to explain it to him, and Che started pacing back and forth muttering things that we couldn't make out: "Shit-eaters," he said, "they are imbeciles, idiots." We started to move away, because when he was upset we used to leave him alone like a lion, we didn't want to cast a shadow. Nobody wanted to be around because we had already had the experience of seeing him angry.[86]

Che's problems were multiplying, and seemed to have no solution. Even an event which might have filled him with joy and nostalgia—his first and only combat in the Congo—was a disaster. The camp, with its deposit of gunpowder and equipment (mortars, radios, and so on), was attacked on October 24. Guevara hesitated between withdrawal and resistance, finally choosing the latter. But the Congolese took to their heels as usual, and Che himself had to sound the retreat, after holding out on a hill for several hours. The gunpowder, equipment, and position were lost; the Congolese had once again proved unfit for combat. As Che concluded in his journal: "Personally, I felt terribly depressed; I felt responsible for the disaster due to my lack of foresight and weakness."[87] Perhaps by then Che had reached the same conclusion as the Africa specialist at the U.S. National Security Council, who reported on October 29, 1965, that "the war in the Congo is probably over."[88]

From that time, Che's relations with his Cuban troops went into a tailspin. None of them believed in victory anymore, and most (about half, in Che's estimate) would have returned to Cuba if given the choice. There were complaints on all sides: some wondered why, if revolutions could not be exported and the Congolese refused to fight, they were there in the first place. Aragonés reminded Che that he had been a Cuban much longer than Che had, and strongly suspected that the troops' grumbling was increasingly directed against their leaders. As Aragonés recalls, Che's instructions approached the absurd: he demanded that the rebels requisition food from the enemy, but the enemy had no food, and, in fact, there was no enemy: "so we all ate yucca with no salt." The Cubans were outraged when the Congolese refused to continue carrying supplies, screaming that they were not trucks to run around loaded with equipment. Toward the end of his stay, as Che was reading one of his many books at a camp outside the Kibamba base, the telltale sound of an approaching bombardment led him to instruct Fernández Mell: "Make sure they put a Cuban at the door of each hut so the Congolese won't escape." He returned to his book and a few minutes later the government forces attacked. The Cubans could not tell by which route the South Africans advanced and the Congolese fled; so Che could not decide in which direction to retreat. When the firing and shelling made it impossible to stay in place, Che ordered, "Let's leave by that path down there, and hope they'll come the other way."[89] There was nothing left by now but such "hopes."

Beginning in October, three factors contributed to the Cubans' final departure from the Congo. Their situation was deteriorating daily. Che no longer attempted to deny its seriousness, especially as the mercenaries and the Congolese army continued their advance toward the lake, retaking villages once under rebel control. In his October summary, his last in the Congo, Che admitted frankly, "A month of disasters without any extenuating circumstances. To the disgraceful fall of Baraka, Fizi, and Lubonja . . . we must add . . . total discouragement among the Congolese. . . . The Cubans are not much better, from Tembo and Siki [Aragonés and Fernández Mell] to the soldiers."[90] So, regardless of any external considerations, Guevara's adventure in the Congo was drawing to an end: Che either would flee, would be captured, or would die on the shores of Lake Tanganyika. The Cubans were surrounded by mercenaries to the north and south; on the west was a mountain, and to the east the lake.

But two additional factors also shattered Che Guevara's African dreams. Thanks to Che's letters and his envoys' reports, Fidel Castro was forced to conclude that the African expedition was foundering. He promptly shipped communications equipment to Tanzania and sailors with suitable boats to prepare for an eventual retreat. And he dispatched Osmany Cienfuegos to persuade Che to recognize defeat, abandon the expedition, and save himself.[91] Finally, Fidel wrote a letter which Che received on November 4:

> We must do everything, except for the absurd. If in Tatu's view our presence becomes unjustifiable and futile, we must think of retreating. We must act in accordance with the objective situation and our men's frame of mind. If they believe we should stay, we will try to send whatever human and material resources they consider necessary. We are worried that you will make the mistake of fearing that your attitude will be considered defeatist or pessimistic. If you decide to leave Tatu can stay the same, either returning here or staying somewhere else. We will support any decision. Avoid annihilation.[92]

The letter expressed Fidel's unmistakable hope that Che would leave, and offered him a way out: either returning to Cuba or undertaking a new mission somewhere else. Castro could imagine that Che would not come back after his farewell letter, but he did not want Che to leave immediately for Argentina. In fact, Fidel was already devising an alternative for his uncomfortable companion.

Further events in October dealt a final blow to Che's heroic and absurd attempt to lead a revolution in the heart of Africa. On October 13, 1965, just before an OAU summit meeting scheduled in Accra, President Kasavubu dismissed Prime Minister Tshombe. One month after Che's departure, Kasavubu would in turn be overthrown by Mobutu.* But for now, having disposed of Tshombe, the Congolese leader adopted a more conciliatory stance toward his neighbors: he had fulfilled their central condition for peace with the organization. For its part, the group of radical states had lost any reason to continue supporting the rebels; indeed, several leaders had already ceased to do so. Ben Bella was deposed by Houari Boumedienne in June; Obote of Uganda had already suspended his assistance; and Nkrumah of Ghana would fall a few months later. Julius Nyerere, the rebels' foremost supporter, found himself practically alone, without any real rationale for continuing to support a struggle which was disintegrating anyway.

Nyerere even proposed to Kasavubu that he meet with the rebel leadership immediately after the Accra summit. The Congolese president opened talks with Congo-Brazzaville as well, aimed at reducing its aid to Pierre Mulele's rebellion in Kwilu. By the end of October the situation in the region had changed radically: the front of progressive countries was crumbling in tandem with the front by the lake. The missing link was for Nyerere to ask the Cubans to depart, along with the South African mercenaries, in accordance with the Accra resolutions on nonintervention. He did so at the beginning of November. Mike Hoare left the Congo that month, though his men lingered on through the following year. On November 1, the Cubans received a message from Dar-es-Salaam: Nyerere formally requested that Cuban assistance be discontinued. This effectively cut off all aid to the Congo rebellion—or what was left of it. As Che noted, "it was a death blow to a dying revolution."[93]

But the exhausted and undernourished Argentine was not yet ready to capitulate. As long as the South African mercenaries were still operating in the Congo, he felt it would be unfair to leave unless the Congolese rebels themselves asked him to. The only leader to be found in the area was Masengo, Kabila's lieutenant; he and Che met in mid-November, as the

---

*Several authors suspect that the CIA and Lawrence Devlin were involved in the ouster of Kasavubu on November 25, though not necessarily in that of Tshombe. Some believe, however, that the two events were part of a single operation. See, for example, Ellen Ray, William Schapp, Karl Van Meter, and Louis Wolf, eds., *Dirty Work: The CIA in Africa,* vol. 2 (Syracuse: Lyle Stuart, 1979), p. 191. The tight relationship between Devlin and Mobutu is corroborated by the following incontrovertible comment by U.S. Ambassador Godley: "Devlin is closer to Mobutu than any non-Congolese I know." AmEmbassy Leopoldville to SecState, November 25, 1965 (Secret), National Security File, Country File, Congo, vol. 12, cable no. 47, LBJ Library.

mercenaries closed in around them. Che presented the alternatives: "Resistance and death, or retreat." Masengo objected, "No, I don't agree. If we are not capable of contributing a Congolese fighter, a single one, beside each Cuban in order to die together, we cannot ask the Cubans to do so." Che's response was, "Fine, but the decision has to come from you and has to be perfectly unambiguous. Whatever you decide we should do, we will do it, but the decision is clearly yours."[94]

The nearest hill had already been captured by the enemy. The last, sacrificial battle seemed imminent. The Cubans insisted on a formal request for their departure: "You must give us a document saying that you believe the Cuban advisers should withdraw, as their presence here has exacerbated the repression." Che reiterated, "Look, they are already here, the issue for us is to be ready for a final confrontation. The situation is clear: resistance and death, or retreat."[95] Finally the Congolese agreed, and the Cubans prepared to board the boats that would carry them to safety.

Che strove one last time to keep his dream alive. Just as they were about to embark, he advised Aragonés and Fernández Mell that he would rather stay behind with a few men and begin a long march—over 1,500 kilometers through the Congo to Kwilu—to join Mulele in the west and resume the struggle. His friends were stupefied. Fernández Mell threw his hat on the ground and finally lost all patience. Aragonés, older and wiser, argued, "Listen, Che, I have obeyed everything you have said here without discussion, to the letter, as your subordinate. But Che, let me tell you this: don't even think that you can dare to tell me to leave while you stay here."[96] Che relented, but only outwardly; he still had one card to play.

Quick to find a last pretext, he then proposed: "I'll stay here with five strong men to recover our dead or missing in action. . . . The idea of leaving completely and departing as we had arrived, leaving behind defenseless peasants and armed but defenseless men, given their little capacity to fight, defeated and feeling that they had been betrayed, hurt me deeply."[97] The boats were filling with women and children, families from the rebel villages fleeing the mercenary advance. Lawton, the Cuban in charge, was horrified to see his precious boats filled with civilians pleading not to be left behind, while his commander refused to embark. Che withdrew to his last line of defense: the women and children must go first. Lawton objected that he had other orders, explaining to Che: "Look, those blacks belong here in the jungle, they are willing to live here. These blacks are not whom the mercenaries are after. They are after you and the black Cubans." Che insisted, "When they get here, they are going to massacre these people." Lawton retorted, "Yes, but my orders are that those who must not be massacred are yourselves, and I have to get you out. I respect you, but I am here under orders

from Fidel; if I have to tie you up to take you out of here, I will."* Che
acceded.

As Che wrote at the beginning of his Congo journal, the entire venture
was the history of a failure.[98] There were many reasons. Some he accurately
recorded; others escaped him, and have become apparent only after thirty
years. As Ben Bella lamented, Che arrived in the Congo too late. His
rhythms, impulses, and inner demons were not those of the struggle in
Africa. He tried to replicate in the Congo his epic of the Sierra Maestra, but
neither the copy, nor the original, was rooted in reality. But perhaps the
cruelest negation of his delusion lies in a peculiar footnote, which may serve
as an epitaph to this chimerical episode.

Three authoritative sources have posed the same question and offered
different answers, in a bizarre re-creation of Machiavelli's *Mandragola*.
How was it possible for one hundred Cubans and dozens of Rwandan and
other rebel fighters from Kibamba to cross, in the light of dawn, and under
zealous pursuit by their adversaries, a lake which was intensively patrolled
by speedboats from South Africa, the CIA, and the Congolese army?

Benigno raises the issue with greater precision. The Cubans were ready
to fight to the last man, as they traversed the lake in their leaking and over-
crowded vessels, surrounded by enemies who were fully aware of their
schedule and itinerary. But they did not have to. Either nobody saw them,
or those who did decided not to attack.† The outcome was hardly believable:
the Cubans, though surrounded, were able to escape safely.

The Belgian military mission was furious; they were not convinced that
the Cubans had left for good. Devlin offers a plausible explanation in the
African context: "I assigned a boat to prevent the Cubans from crossing the
lake; but it broke down, and the Cubans got away. I will never forgive
myself."[99] Major Hardenne recalls his own perplexity:

Weather conditions had improved, so the command post and OPS/SUD
were directing operations from a plane. They realized that the Cubans were
fleeing on several boats, crossing the lake or navigating southward along the

---

*This remarkable exchange was related to the author by Benigno (interview cited) and
corroborated separately by Aragonés and Fernández Mell (interviews cited). The fact that
there are three sources justifies this verbatim account, with the license authorized by the
passage of many years and traditional Cuban hyperbole.

† Benigno, interview. "I was very surprised by a place we passed at dawn. I thought it
was impossible for us to get by without being seen, because we passed between two sloops,
we had to turn off the motors and all of us dove into the water, those who knew how to
swim dove in and pushed the raft to pass between the two sloops that were there. I at least
expected them to start shooting at us any second. It was humanly impossible for them not
to see us."

coast. For reasons that will never be explained, the ANC planes and boats piloted by mercenaries were not only not there despite orders, but did not respond to calls from the plane. . . . This bad execution of orders allowed the Cubans to escape.[100]

But Jules Gérard-Libois, who has been studying the wars in the Congo for thirty years at the Centre de Recherche et d'Information Socio-politique (CRISP) in Brussels, finds incomprehensible the failure of the Belgians, South Africans, and anti-Castro Cubans to prevent Che from leaving the Congo. In his view, OPS/SUD ordered the Congolese battalions under its jurisdiction to let the Cubans get out alive. The two Belgian CIA pilots were confined to their hotel rooms. According to Gérard-Libois, the CIA station chief in Albertville confessed to two Belgian officers that he had received instructions to avoid any incident with the Cubans before December 1. The CIA ordered its aircraft and boats to effect an "operational destruction of the enemy," but the order was not obeyed.[101]

Gérard-Libois relates the mystery to another event that was taking place at the same time, on the other side of the planet: the so-called Camarioca immigration agreement between Cuba and the United States. Negotiated through the Swiss ambassador in Havana, it contemplated the emigration, over several months, of tens of thousands of Cubans wishing to leave the island. During the first year of the agreement's application, more than forty-five thousand Cubans would fly to Florida.

On October 27, Castro had announced that he was willing to allow those who wished to leave to do so; the only problem, he said, was that Washington refused to grant them entry visas. Castro's speech eventually led to the agreement, made public through simultaneous press releases in both capitals on November 4. Gérard-Libois believes that the accord—on a terribly delicate issue, which would resurface during the Mariel exodus of 1980 and in the summer of 1994, with the Cuban raft people—led the United States to avoid any conflict which might have blocked its implementation. In this perspective, it seems logical that Washington should have instructed its missions abroad to avert any friction or confrontation with the Cubans during those weeks, until the Camarioca agreement had been fulfilled. Obviously, the U.S. government had not foreseen that its general guidelines would allow Che Guevara to escape. Officers in the Congo may well have misinterpreted the instructions, and allowed the encircled Cuban fighters to flee from Kibamba.

None of the U.S. officials involved in these mysteries and contradictions recalls any such indication, or gives the interpretation much credence. Devlin says he never received any such order and, at the request of this author, consulted with his former subordinates in Albertville (particularly Richard Johnson, the CIA base chief); they do not remember anything of the sort either. Gustavo Villoldo swears that he never would have followed such an order if he had received it—but he did not. William Bowdler, the U.S. diplomat who negotiated the Camarioca agreement, does not remember any such trade-off or unilateral decision by Washington.[102]

However, the mystery remains: how and why was Che allowed to leave the Congo? It would be only one of many ironies in his life if he survived his African expedition thanks to this strange coincidence. Perhaps the two years of borrowed time left him were the result of an uncanny convergence of interests involving Fidel Castro, the immigration and diplomatic authorities of the United States, the CIA, and South African mercenaries, all coming together on the shores of Lake Tanganyika. If his life had ended there, his sacrifice would have been just as noble, and his myth still one of the greatest in our century. But it would have been different.

Che himself wrote the best appraisal of his role in the Congo campaign. He concluded the next-to-last and still unpublished book of his life with a stark evaluation of his performance in Africa:

My hands were tied by the somewhat unusual way I entered the Congo, and I was never able to overcome that disadvantage. My reactions were uneven; for a long time I had an attitude which might be termed complacent and, at times, I had very offensive and hurtful outbursts, perhaps due to something innate in me. The only people with whom I had appropriate relations were the peasants, for I am more accustomed to a political language, direct explanations and teaching through example, and I think I would have been successful in that field. As for relations with my men, I think I sacrificed myself enough that no one can reproach me in any personal or physical aspect, though I was able to satisfy my two great addictions in the Congo: tobacco, which I hardly ever lacked, and reading, which was always abundant. The discomfort of having tattered boots or a dirty change of clothes, or eating the same food as the troops and living in the same conditions was not a sacrifice for me. Especially, the fact that I could withdraw into my reading and flee from daily problems tended to separate me from the men, aside from certain aspects of my character which make intimate communication difficult. I was hard, but I don't think I was excessively so, or unfair. I used methods which are not practiced in regular armies, such as leaving [soldiers] without eating; it is the only effective method I know in guerrilla warfare. At first I tried to apply moral coercion, and failed. I wanted the troops to see the situation the way I did, and I failed. They were not ready to look optimistically toward a future hidden by the black fog of the present. I was not brave enough to demand the ultimate sacrifice at the moment of truth. This was an internal, psychic block in me. For me it was very difficult to stay in the Congo. From the point of view of a fighter's dignity, it was the right thing to do. From the point of view of my future, though it was not the best thing to do, that made no difference at the time. While I struggled to make a decision, I knew how easy it would be to make the ultimate sacrifice—and this worked against me. I think I should have imposed that final gesture upon a few chosen combatants; just a few, but we should have stayed. I have emerged believing more than ever in guerrilla warfare; but we failed. My responsibility is great; I will not forget this defeat or its valuable lessons.[103]

Chapter 10

Betrayed by Whom in Bolivia?

L ife had stopped smiling on Che Guevara, but his prodigious willpower and luck held out long enough for one last adventure. The man who emerged from defeat and despair in the Congo still possessed inner strength and convictions, though he was not unscathed. Having lost more than forty pounds, he now weighed less than one hundred and ten; his asthma and dysentery had taken an enormous toll.* Even worse, the discouragement and gloom caused by failure had rapidly turned into depression. Being cooped up for several weeks in a tiny bedroom and office set up for him on the first floor of the Cuban Embassy in Dar-es-Salaam did not help. He began to recover from his various illnesses and dejection only as plans for the future gradually took shape. His secretary during those months in Tanzania recalled: "I don't think he left in a spirit of defeat, but rather with a critical attitude toward the organization's political leadership, with a spirit of love and compassion toward the Congolese brigades."[1]

During the time he spent with Pablo Ribalta, the Cuban ambassador to Tanzania and his old comrade in arms, in the Tanzanian capital, Che made

---

*According to his secretary in Tanzania, "he was skinny, pallid, underfed." Colman Ferrer, interview with the author, Havana, August 25, 1995.

two crucial decisions: he would not return to Cuba, and his next destination was Buenos Aires. As Benigno recalls, "He did not want to go back to Cuba in the least."[2] The reason was understandable: Fidel Castro's public reading of his farewell letter rendered it impossible. Che would not have violated his pledge for anything, even if it had been possible for him to return to the island in secret. Having renounced all he had in Cuba, he could not go back vanquished and humiliated. The course taken by the Cuban economy was foreign to him; his supporters had been left out of the new Communist Party's Central Committee; and his international strategy had foundered in the harsh realities of Africa. He had nowhere to go. So he decided to seek out his original starting point—not as a prodigal son rejoining family and country, but to make the revolution where he had always hoped: in Argentina.

Angel Braguer, "Lino," who dealt with Bolivian affairs for Cuban intelligence, had no doubts. After his recovery in Dar-es-Salaam, Che's sole desire was to head for Buenos Aires, with or without preparation, resources, or company:

> He planned it in a very heroic way, practically without any conditions. It was very similar to staying on the shores of Lake Tanganyika, almost without support. It was like staying to fight on the banks of the river, on open ground, against superior forces about to win.*

Che's final months in Africa were largely devoted to an ongoing dispute with Havana. Guevara wanted to leave immediately; Castro resorted to a series of stratagems and pretexts to keep him from going and being killed by the Argentine gendarmerie, which Emilio Aragonés so justifiably feared. One of the first weapons Castro used was Aleida, Che's wife; another was Ramiro Valdés, Che's closest friend in Cuba and his children's guardian in the event of his death. Ribalta later recalled Aleida's trip to Tanzania: "His wife arrived in Dar-es-Salaam. They were staying at the Embassy. Che was very friendly, very happy, they talked about the children, they hugged. . . . She stayed until later."[3] As a source in the Cuban security machinery retold it,

> There was an ongoing struggle with Fidel to keep [Che] from going to Argentina and [make him] come back to Cuba. Fidel sent Aleida and others to see him. Che wanted to leave directly for Buenos Aires. Fidel invented

---

*Angel Braguer, "Lino," interview with the author, Havana, January 24, 1996. Benigno presents the same account in his memoirs, published in Paris in 1995, which provoked various heated reactions on the part of Cuban officials. Benigno, *Vie et mort de la Révolution Cubaine* (Paris: Fayard, 1995), p. 108.

Bolivia for him, using all the resources [there], to convince him to return to Cuba and not go to Argentina.[4]

Che was drawn by degrees to the idea of Bolivia, or in any case to a stopover there before going to Argentina—but not Cuba. In the southern fall, he dispatched José María Martínez Tamayo ("Papi") to Bolivia to prepare his trip to Argentina; he also instructed Pombo and Tuma to travel to Bolivia to recover some old suitcases filled with dollars, left over from previous adventures, and to wait for him on the Argentine border. However, the two aides stopped in Cuba, where the authorities convinced them to change their plans—at least until July, when they finally landed at La Paz.[5]

While waiting, Che spent his free time writing—his favorite activity, apart from combat and literature. Working from notes taken in the Congo, he began drafting the manuscript repeatedly quoted in the previous chapter—"Pasajes de la guerra revolucionaria (el Congo)." Colman Ferrer, a young secretary at the Cuban Embassy in Dar-es-Salaam, served as his assistant. Che dictated his text, Ferrer transcribed it, then Guevara revised and corrected the final manuscript. In the words of Ferrer, Che basically spent the days "marking time, preparing the conditions for a change of scenery." As Oscar Fernández Mell recalls it,

> One of Che's great virtues was the way he enjoyed reading, though he also had more exacting tastes and ways of spending his time. He could read for hours; he had a good time even when he was alone.[6]

He was extremely meticulous in his work. In Ferrer's words, "he was careful in the things he was going to write, avoiding any mistakes. He took great care, he analyzed and reread the transcription repeatedly."[7] The book left little time for other activities: "He wrote day and night. His only distraction was an occasional game of chess with me. One day when I was about to checkmate him, he looked at me as if he had not realized what was happening; it was obvious that he wasn't really in the game."[8]

Finally, at the end of February or beginning of March 1966, Che agreed to leave for Prague and plan the next phase of his life, desisting from flying to Argentina.* The person assigned to accompany him to the Czech capital was Ulises Estrada, Piñeiro's officer for African affairs.† Che would spend

---

*Several sources place the date at the end of February: Fernández Mell, who stayed on in Dar-es-Salaam, Ulises Estrada, who accompanied Che to Prague via Cairo, Colman Ferrer, who spent that time working with Che on the "Pasajes . . . (el Congo)" manuscript, and Pablo Ribalta.

† "But everybody returned to Cuba and he stayed on alone in Tanzania, and then I decided to get him out of Tanzania and take him to a safe place until he decided what he was going to do." Ulises Estrada, interview with the author, Havana, February 9, 1995.

more than four months there, recovering from illness and depression—Castro sent his own physicians to treat him—and preparing the new expedition. The Cuban official from Piñeiro's team who received him, José Luis Ojaldo, initially found him an apartment in the city, then moved the group to a house approximately twenty kilometers away in the direction of Lidice. Estrada stayed about a month with Che before being replaced by Juan Carretero, later known as "Ariel," the bearer of coded messages between Bolivia and Havana, and Alfredo Fernández Montes de Oca, alias "Pacho" or "Pachungo," with whom Guevara would travel to Bolivia in November.

Estrada recalls his weeks in Czechoslovakia in varying shades of gloom: the Central European winter, Che's somber mood, their uncertainty about the future. It was not by any means a happy or hopeful time:

> I stayed with him until he decided to return to Cuba. We were living in a worker's apartment, where Che could supposedly have some peace and quiet. We lived a bit on tenterhooks. We hardly went out, and when we did, with comrade José Luis, we went to the outskirts of Prague, to restaurants outside the city, in the countryside. I attracted a lot of attention, the waitresses wanted to touch my hair, and [Che] said to me, "Look, I hope I won't be found out because of you, you attract a lot of attention. Everywhere we go people look at you. You have the privilege of being black; in other parts you are discriminated against but here they admire you, so I'm going to ask Fidel to send me someone else.*

These were perhaps the worst months of Che's life: dark and solitary, permeated with uncertainty. According to an uncorroborated but plausible report, Che spent weeks recovering from intoxication induced by a Soviet-made medication for asthma whose expiration date had passed. Beset by illness, he was also subject to pressures from all sides. Life had deprived him of those certainties that had allowed him until then to resist contradiction and determine his own fate. The months dragged by, punctuated only by efforts to keep his presence secret and to organize from afar his next attempt at revolution. The Czechs were never informed that Guevara was in their country—or at least, this is his companions' opinion to this day. Che's obsession with secrecy made his movements hard to detect, but it seems doubtful, given the precedents, that Castro would have kept his famous friend's whereabouts from Moscow. Moreover, the maneuvers must have awakened some suspicion. Why were there suddenly so many Cuban conspirators in the heart of Central Europe?

---

*Estrada, interview. Paco Ignacio Taibo II, in his biography of Che, quotes similar passages from these same interviews. Taibo and the author shared part of the information obtained by either one. In this case, the interview was granted to the author, who then gave it to Taibo.

Castro was willing to try anything to induce Guevara to postpone his
return to Buenos Aires, or at least to prepare for it appropriately.* Aleida
joined in the chorus, visiting Che again in Prague, as did Ramiro Valdés,
whom Benigno met in Moscow between flights; he believes it was Ramiro
who finally convinced Che to return to Cuba.[9] Another visitor to Prague
was Tamara Bunke, Tania, the Argentine-German translator turned Cuban
intelligence agent, according to Ulises Estrada,† who was her lover for over
a year.‡ After the Cubans lost touch with Tania in La Paz, she was indirectly
summoned to Prague to evaluate her work and prospects in Bolivia:

> ... Tania was left without communications for a year in La Paz. Finally
> contact was made with her first in Mexico and then Czechoslovakia. Her
> codes were changed when she was in Czechoslovakia. She went to Czecho-
> slovakia where she was retrained and taught the codes, the radio schedule,
> and other operative things. It all took place in Prague.[10]

According to Ulises Estrada, the Cubans found a farm outside Prague
where they could hold their meetings with Tamara Bunke; this is where Che
"spent time with Tania."** Gossip about a romance between her and Che
became even more insistent, though it did not begin in Prague. Indeed, the
scuttlebutt had been circulating for years, due to the pair's many joint activ-

---

*In an interview with Gianni Miná in 1987, Fidel Castro confirmed that Guevara
refused to return to Cuba: "[Che] did not want to go back because it was very painful for
him to return after the publication of the letter. . . . But I finally convinced him to comeback, it was the best way to achieve the practical goals he had set for himself." Fidel Castro,
quoted in Gianni Miná, "A Meeting with Fidel," Office of Publications of the State Council, Havana, 1988, p. 327.

† Estrada, interview. Based upon documents recovered from Bolivia by the CIA and per-
haps other intelligence material, Che biographer Daniel James was able to reconstruct
Tania's itinerary. She left Bolivia in mid-February 1966 via Brazil, arriving in Mexico on
April 14 and then "disappearing" after April 30. Though James surmises that she went to
Cuba to receive instructions from Che, it is now known that Guevara was still in Prague and
that she actually traveled to Czechoslovakia, though she might have made a stopover in
Havana. Daniel James, Che Guevara: Una biografía (Mexico City: Editorial Diana, 1971),
pp. 268–269.

‡ Estrada, interview. Tania refers to Estrada in a letter to her parents dated April 11,
1964, saying that she hoped "they won't steal my little Negrito before I return, then I am
going to marry him. . . . I don't know if this will produce little mulattos. . . . [He is] skinny,
tall, quite black, typically Cuban, very affectionate. . . ." Marta Rojas and Mirta Rodríguez,
Tania: La guerrillera inolvidable (Havana: Instituto Cubano del Libro, 1974), p. 195.

**Tania's visit to Prague is also confirmed by the secret archives of the East German
Communist Party (SED). They include a letter to Tania's parents from an Argentine writer
at the magazine Problemas de la paz y del socialismo. Dated April 27, 1969, it says in part:
"We had met your daughter, as you recall. . . . During her stay in Prague she visited us
several times." Institut für Marxismus-Leninismus beim Zentral Komitee der SED, Zentrales Parteiarchiv, SED Internationale Verbindungen, Argentinien 1962–72, DY 30/IV
A2/20/694, Berlin.

ities in Havana. Some sources in the Cuban intelligence services even speculated that Guevara's real reason for dismissing Estrada was to have Tania to himself in Prague. This is not impossible. Nor should one neglect the rumor that Che and his wife had a serious dispute during one of her visits, precisely about Tania. Be that as it may, these missions, maneuvers, and promises gradually shaped the expedition to Bolivia. Everybody involved— Aleida, Castro, Ramiro Valdés, Manuel Piñeiro, Che's closest subordinates, and Tania—offered an alternative.

It was no easy feat. In order to prevent Che from risking his life in Argentina, there had to be an alternative course that was both feasible and close or adjacent to his native land. The first choice was Venezuela. Carlos Franqui claims that Fidel Castro used his good offices with the Venezuelan guerrillas to try to persuade them to receive Guevara; they refused.[11] This is confirmed by Teodoro Petkoff, a Venezuelan guerrilla leader who was in jail at the time and is now a minister of state.[12] Germán Lairet, a former representative of the Fuerzas Armadas de Liberación Nacional in Havana, notes that a precedent existed: the Cubans had been trying to integrate Che into the Venezuelan guerrilla movement since 1964.* But the movement was faltering: internal divisions, a government counteroffensive, and the international context made it a dangerous option for Che. Furthermore, the Venezuelans themselves opposed his involvement because, according to Petkoff, it would have confirmed accusations that the guerrillas constituted a foreign presence there. In early 1967, with Che in Bolivia and the Venezuelan guerrilla campaign breathing its last, Fidel Castro launched a fierce attack on its leaders, accusing them of having betrayed the struggle. So Venezuela was not an option.

Another possibility was Peru. The 1963 guerrilla campaigns of Luis de la Puente and Hugo Blanco had held out some promise. But Blanco's semi-Trotskyist movement in Valle de la Convención came to an abrupt end when he was arrested on May 29, 1963. Weeks later, another revolutionary group, headed by the young poet Javier Heraud, was liquidated as it entered Peru from Bolivia, at Puerto Maldonado. There was also a more typical Castro-style *foco,* led by De la Puente, which launched a somewhat successful offensive in June 1965, but its ranks were decimated between September 1965 and early 1966, when its leader was killed in combat. One final attempt, a new front headed by Héctor Bejar, failed in December 1965. Moreover,

*Germán Lairet, telephone conversation with the author, October 1996. Régis Debray wrote exactly the opposite in 1974: it was the Venezuelans, particularly Teodoro Petkoff's brother Luben, who invited Che to their country. In this account, Che refused because he did not want to "get onto a train that was already moving." See Régis Debray, *La critique des armes,* vol. 2, *Les Epreuves du Feu* (Paris: Seuil, 1974), pp. 21–22. The two accounts are not necessarily incompatible: it is possible that Fidel approached the Venezuelans in 1966 precisely because they had already expressed their interest in 1964.

Peru's Communist Party had systematically opposed all of these efforts, arguing that conditions were not ripe and the armed struggle was not the best way. The Cubans, despite their original intentions, informed the Peruvians of their government's decision "to begin the struggle first in Bolivia, and later in Peru."* The circumstances were not appropriate; they invited the Peruvians to continue working jointly with them, sending men to Bolivia to set up a *foco* there and extending it later back home.

There were few places left. The traditional animosity between Fidelistas and Communists in Latin America posed real problems, both in the field and in winning Che over. Worse still, the entire operation had to be presented to him as temporary—as a mere stopover on the way to his native country. This led to the idea of creating a mother guerrilla force, which would give birth to various offshoots—mainly, of course, in Argentina. These reasons, and the resources available to the Cubans in Bolivia, made it the best choice.† All that remained was to convince the Bolivians and Che himself.

Bolivia offered a number of advantages for the creation of a guerrilla *foco*. There was already, within the Communist Party (PCB), a nucleus of cadres linked with Cuba. Similarly, a small group of Bolivian students had received training in Cuba in 1965. Some of them would die with Che; others would remain in Havana during his Bolivian epic. In the view of Mario Monje, Secretary-General of the Communist Party at the time, a peculiar relationship had developed between the PCB and Havana since 1962. In 1962, the Peruvian Communists sent a group of students to visit Cuba, where they received military training without the Peruvian Party's knowledge or consent, as often happened. Once armed and ready for combat, they returned to their country via Bolivia, the best clandestine route. When the Cubans asked Monje to help them out, he replied that they should

---

*Harry Villegas ("Pombo"), "El verdadero diario de Pombo," *La Razón* (La Paz), October 9, 1996, p. 17. Until 1996, the only available text of Pombo's diary was an English version retranslated into Spanish, delivered apparently by the CIA to the New York publishing house Stein and Day in 1968. In late 1996, the Central Bank of Bolivia, which holds the documents pertaining to Che's Bolivian campaign, allowed two journalists access to the vault in order to review and publish some of the texts. The original version of Pombo's diary was one of them.

†According to Mario Monje, Secretary-General of Bolivia's Communist Party, Che explicitly said to him: "The only place where we have a serious structure is Bolivia, and the only ones who are really up to the struggle are the Bolivians, and I did not have that in Argentina, which is in a period of latency, or in Peru, where things are only beginning." The Bolivian replied, "But that structure is not for you; you are taking advantage of a structure which you have not built." Mario Monje, interview with the author, Moscow, October 25, 1995. This account coincides with what the Argentine Ciro Bustos told his Bolivian interrogators concerning a conversation with Che during the Bolivia campaign. See "Account by Ciro Roberto Bustos of his Stay with Guevara's Guerrillas in Bolivia," quoted in Jay Mallin, ed., *Che Guevara on Revolution* (Miami: University of Miami Press, 1969), p. 200.

address themselves to the Peruvian Communist Party. The Cubans retorted, "The Peruvian Party sent these people to Cuba, and now refuses to take responsibility for them."[13]

The plot thickened. Monje traveled to Havana, meeting several times with Manuel Piñeiro and finally with Fidel Castro. For the Bolivian Party to sidestep that of Peru, and help a Cuban-trained group of guerrillas to start fighting without the consent of its Peruvian counterpart, broke all the rules governing relations among "sister parties." Fidel did all he could to convince Monje:

> Look, we have had our experience. We're not going to prevent these young people from having theirs. If I ask you, independently of your views, to help these boys travel through your country, giving them the opportunity that we had, why shouldn't they have the same opportunity? They are young, as we were. Why don't you help them get through on behalf of proletarian internationalism?[14]

This led to the creation of a special clandestine military apparatus within the PCB, exposing it to very real risks in its relations with other Latin American parties. The Cubans soon started over, asking Monje to help mount the Salta expedition of Jorge Masetti. One of Che's aides visited Monje and declared without further ado, "This is a request from Che, I am here on his behalf. And I want you to help send people to Argentina."[15] Monje replied that he could not undertake such a commitment alone; he would have to inform the rest of the leadership, especially Jorge Kolle, the Party's Number Two man, who would replace Monje as secretary-general in 1968. When Kolle learned of the request, he objected: "There you go again, first in one place and now in another. We have to tell the Argentine Communists that the Cubans are meddling in their country." Monje agreed, but asked, "If they send people, what can we do? Che is behind this, and they've asked me to take on the logistics."[16]

It is worth recalling that the Communist Party of Argentina was strongly opposed to the Castro line in Latin America; its leader, Víctor Codovilla, had taken a vehement stand against Guevara and his theories. This mattered little to Fidel, however; he personally reiterated the request, emphasizing that it was Che's operation. And as early as mid-1963 he offered the following analysis of Bolivia:

> I am very sorry for you and for Bolivia, because it is very difficult to conduct guerrilla warfare over there. You are a landlocked country, you've already had a land reform, so your fate is to help revolutionary movements in other countries. One of the last countries to achieve liberation will be Bolivia. Guerrilla warfare is not possible in Bolivia.[17]

Che had maintained the same position, to Monje's surprise, during a conversation with him in Havana in 1964:

> I've been in Bolivia, I know Bolivia and it is very difficult to have a guerrilla struggle in Bolivia. There has already been a land reform, and I don't think the Indians would join a guerrilla struggle. That is why you must help operations in other countries.[18]

As stated, Che's aide, José María Martínez Tamayo (Papi), arrived in Bolivia March 1966. He immediately began preparations for Che's new expedition, based upon all these precedents and his old friendship—dating back to the Masetti affair—with several Bolivian Communists, including the Peredo brothers (Inti and Coco), Jorge Vázquez Viaña (el Loro), Rodolfo Saldaña, Luis Tellería Murillo, Orlando "Camba" Jiménez, and Julio "el Ñato" Méndez. Despite Fidel's and Che's misgivings, many factors pointed to a successful operation in Bolivia. There was already a unit of young guerrillas with Cuban links within the country. The PCB's leadership recognized that Havana (despite some contacts with pro-China dissidents) had never interfered in the Party's affairs or tried to mount a guerrilla *foco* in Bolivia— as it had in Peru, Argentina, Venezuela, Guatemala, and Colombia. The Bolivian Communists were at least formally receptive to the arrangement.

But this did not imply that Monje, Kolle, or the other national leaders (in contrast to the Party's youth movement) supported the armed struggle, or that they enjoyed a broad margin of freedom vis-à-vis Moscow, allowing them to align themselves with Havana. Indeed, the secret archives of the Soviet Union include the minutes of a 1966 Politburo meeting of the Party's Central Committee, approving a payment of $30,000 to the PCB in 1966, and of $20,000 to the Bolivian Party's electoral arm, the National Front.[19] This was a considerable sum, given the Party's tiny dimensions—enough to cover many of its expenses, and thus a powerful form of persuasion.

Still, Monje and the rest of the leadership were less reluctant than other Latin American groups to embark on the military road to power. In fact, Monje received guerrilla training in Cuba during the first half of 1966. He placed the PCB's small secret-operations unit at the disposal of the Cubans, and several of its members (including the Peredo brothers) spent weeks or months training on the island. Bolivia seemed a natural alternative to Che's Argentine project. It had historical ties with the Cubans and a favorable geography which included five borders, valleys and mountains, tropical and snow-covered regions. The presence—or absence—of the political conditions needed to trigger a revolutionary process never figured as a central issue. The main point was to find a project for Che, and to have the requisite resources at hand.

During his stay in Prague, Che continued to negotiate with Cuba, even as he pushed forward with preparations for South America. The more he insisted on going to Argentina, either directly or after a short stay in Bolivia, the more Havana tried to persuade him to return to Cuba, and proceed to Bolivia only when everything was ready. Guevara described his dilemma in a dialogue with Monje on December 31, 1966:

CHE: You know that I left Cuba in an elegant and dignified way. Fidel insisted several times that I return, but I was cooped up in an apartment in Czechoslovakia, trying to find a way out. I couldn't go back to Cuba, I couldn't show my face there again. That option was closed for me.

MONJE: And why did you find the solution here? You've fallen into a trap here.[20]

Perhaps one of the greatest misunderstandings—or deceptions—in Che's Bolivian saga was the confusion between traveling through Bolivia and actually creating a *foco* there. According to Castro, Mario Monje was responsible for the betrayal that led to Che's death. The Bolivian agreed to support Guevara's quest for revolution, and then reneged on his promise. Monje, however, claims that he acceded to a very different request. When he saw Castro in May 1966 on a flight from Santiago to Havana, Fidel said to him:

Listen Monje, I am grateful for the help you've given us, you've always fulfilled everything we have asked for. Now there is a mutual friend of ours who wants to return to his country, and I ask you personally to choose the people who will protect this man. No one can doubt his rank as a revolutionary. He wants to return to his country. This has nothing to do with Bolivia.[21]

Monje immediately agreed. This time he was not dealing with Peruvians or Argentines, but with a leader of the Cuban Revolution whose destination was Argentina. He did not hesitate to commit himself; he knew that the man in question was Che Guevara. The rest of the PCB leadership was not aware of this, but was nonetheless well disposed toward the Cuban request,* as Jorge Kolle confirms:

We thought it was a repeat of Masetti's expedition. Though we did not have a script, we were involved in a series of events that gave us a certain percep-

---

*Beginning in August 1966, Kolle suspected that the Cubans had something afoot. At a Congress of Uruguay's Communist Party held that month in Montevideo, he confided to the host leader Rodney Arismendi that there was "a guerrilla project aimed at the Southern Cone, in which the Cubans are playing a central role." See Régis Debray, *La guerrilla del Che* (Mexico City: Siglo XXI, 1975), p. 79.

tion of what was happening and where things were headed. Ñancahuazú is in an area close to Argentina, it's closer to Argentina or Paraguay than to La Paz. There is no population to feed a guerrilla campaign, in a province which is almost as big as Cuba: 82,000 square kilometers and 40,000 inhabitants. We thought the idea was to set up a base to send a group to Argentina.[22]

The PCB lent the Cubans the four cadres who had previously worked with them: Roberto "Coco" Peredo, Jorge "el Loro" Vázquez Viaña, Rodolfo Saldaña, and Julio "el Ñato" Méndez, and also, marginally, Luis Tellería. The first three were dispatched to Havana almost immediately to receive further military training; they returned in July via Prague, where they probably met with Che. Back in Bolivia, they recruited a group from the Communist Youth and sent them to train in Cuba, along with Coco's brother Inti Peredo. The operation had already extended far beyond its original scope of expediting Che's getting to Argentina; the goal was now to establish a mother guerrilla movement in Bolivia. The "Upper Peruvian," as Monje was known for his inscrutable nature, now believes that Fidel deliberately deceived him—as he very likely did.

There is, however, another hypothesis. When Castro made the deal with Monje, he might well have believed that Che would indeed merely pass through Bolivia on his way home. After all, he had perhaps not yet convinced him to stay in Bolivia. It is not evident that Fidel initially misled Monje. Similarly, the Bolivian Communists never directly expressed to the Cubans their opposition to the armed struggle. When Pombo and Tuma landed in La Paz toward the end of July and held their first meeting with members of the Party, they were assured that Monje would join the armed struggle—and if he did not, the rest of the Party would.[23] At the same meeting, Monje himself promised Che's representatives at least twenty guerrilla fighters. When the Cubans tried to ascertain what would happen if Che joined the operation, he responded, "If that were the case, I would fight by his side no matter what."[24]

None of them put their cards on the table. On the contrary, everyone indulged in a game of deception, as Kolle confessed later:

> I am proud of having misled them completely. One day I was pro-guerrilla; the next day they perceived me as anti-guerrilla. In other words, I misled the Cubans.[25]

Che remained in Prague until July, if we are to believe William Gálvez, author of an as-yet unpublished official Cuban biography of Che.* Regard-

---

*"Cuando el Che se llamó Ramón," interview with William Gálvez in *Cuba Internacional*, no. 296, 1995, p. 31. General Gálvez supposedly wrote an account of Che's stay in

less of the dates, the indisputable fact is that he finally decided to return to Cuba. He was received by Raúl Castro, who appeared at the old Rancho Boyeros airport on a mission of peace and reconciliation. Che immediately traveled to a rest home at San Andrés de Taiguanabo, at the foot of the Cordillera de los Organos. There he spent several weeks recovering from his Congo ordeal. He also launched preparations for the new expedition, hoping to avoid the errors which had doomed his mission in Africa. But as a friend lamented years later, his obsessive attempt to do things differently this time led him to commit countless other mistakes. What he did in Bolivia he should have done in the Congo, and vice versa.

On this occasion, Che handpicked his team. With help from René Tomassevich, Piñeiro's staff, and Raúl Castro, he selected his men from a carefully prepared list. Many who wished to be included were not—Ulises Estrada, Emilio Aragonés, Alberto Mora, and Haydé Santamaría, among others. Che began contacting revolutionaries in Bolivia, deciding where, when, and with whom he would start operations. Several questions arose immediately. Should the campaign center on the Alto Beni in the northwest of Bolivia, and especially in a small semitropical area called Los Yungas, or in the southwest, in the basin of the Rio Grande, near the oil center of Camiri? Should he rely upon the Bolivian Communist Party which, according to Fidel Castro and Manuel Piñeiro, was now fully devoted to the armed struggle? Or was it better to seek an alliance with the Maoists, including a group headed by Oscar Zamora, whom Che had met in Havana in 1964 before Zamora was expelled from the PCB for his pro-China leanings? Was it preferable to cast his lot with the Cuban establishment, especially the staff of Piñeiro and Raúl, which had so seriously let him down in the Congo with its irresponsibility and incompetence? Or should he mount his own network for communications, support, logistics, and intelligence? He struggled with these choices from July to November, when he finally left Cuba for good. But he never reached any explicit conclusions, aside from the location of the *foco.* And even here, his decision was more the result of circumstance than of conscious deliberation.

---

the Congo, which was even granted a Casa de las Américas award in 1995. Though it has still to appear in print, it is without a doubt the first book ever awarded a prize before being written. This is probably due to the same obstacles which, ever since 1967, have prevented any Cuban from writing a Che biography—and which have even blocked the publication of documents such as the "Actas del Ministerio de Industrias" or "Pasajes de la guerra revolucionaria (el Congo)." Benigno for his part notes that Che returned to Cuba in April 1966, but this is probably too early. This chapter of Che's life is still enshrouded in mystery within Cuba. The Cuban "chronologists" provide no information whatsoever about these months, though they state that Che returned on July 20. See Benigno, *Vie et mort,* p. 113, and Adys Cupull and Froilán González, *Un hombre bravo* (Havana: Ediciones Capitán San Luis, 1995), p. 309.

The process of selection was soon complete. The team included many of the cadres linked with Che since the "invasion" from the Sierra Maestra in 1958, several who had accompanied him to the Congo, and others from the Ministry of Industries. They were secluded in a training camp in the province of Occidente, then transferred to Che's villa in San Andrés. There, in September, René Tomassevich led the guerrillas to the terrace, where they met a bald, elderly man of medium height, clean-shaven and wearing glasses, who promptly started screaming at them, calling them incompetent "shit-eaters" unfit for guerrilla warfare; several of them grew increasingly irritated. Finally, Jesús Suárez Gayol (el Rubio), deputy minister of industries and a companion of Che's since the battle of Santa Clara, saw through the disguise and hugged his old boss.[26] The twenty or so recruits were filled with pride and joy: the honor of being chosen for the mission outweighed any doubts or fears they might have harbored. They did not know that most of them would die in the wilderness of Bolivia.

Their training went into high gear after Fidel Castro's birthday on August 13. Che began by laying down the law: the men would have to forget about their officers' rank, for in Bolivia they would be mere foot soldiers. Shooting practice started at six in the morning, one hour after reveille. There was one hour's rest at eleven, and then a forced march of twelve kilometers in the nearby hills with a twenty-kilo rucksack. The men were entitled to another hour's rest at six in the afternoon, followed by courses in general culture: languages, history, mathematics. Finally, at nine there were two hours of Quechua, the indigenous language of Bolivia. Che's reasoning was obvious: in order to avoid a repeat of the Congo, he needed guerrilla fighters well versed in political and military affairs, who understood their mission and were ready to die for it: a battalion of Che Guevaras.

Visitors dropped in every weekend: either high officials or Fidel Castro, who came several times. Castro explained to the guerrillas the purpose and logic of their mandate, which was to distract the United States. As Castro put it, Cuba's obligations as a sugar producer were taking up too much of the population's time and energy. This was undermining efforts in education and economic diversification. Each combatant cost Cuba ten thousand dollars; "imperialism" should be made to pay a hundred thousand dollars for each fallen warrior. The struggle in Bolivia would be to the death, and would last from five to ten years. Its real goal was to reduce the pressure on Cuba.

Fidel's reasoning, though not absurd, was actually an ad hoc justification for a decision based on other factors. True, there was an important (if recent) precedent: Cuba's support for revolutionary movements in the rest of Latin America. But there was a slight difference in the case of Bolivia. Unlike Venezuela, Nicaragua, Haiti, or even Colombia, it had no rebel movement of its own. The Cubans would serve as a revolutionary spear-head, not as reinforcement. The PCB's apparent willingness to engage in the armed struggle did not mean there was a *foco* already in existence. Che and the Cubans did not sweep down upon Bolivia to join a process already underway but to initiate, single-handedly, a guerrilla movement. This was an extreme interpretation of Guevara's view that pre-existing conditions were not necessary; they could be created from outside. For the first time since the invasion of the Dominican Republic in 1959—which had witnessed the massacre of the entire expeditionary force—a large number of Cubans were being sent to fight in Latin America despite the total absence of a local movement.

The guerrilla campaign in Bolivia was intended and designed for Che Guevara. Since there had to be a *foco,* it was better to bestow an ideological basis on it than to establish it in a void. Thus the ex post facto rationale of distracting imperialism and breaking the U.S. stranglehold on Cuba. A revolutionary victory elsewhere in Latin America would indeed provide the island with much-needed respite. But if the struggle was identified with Cuba, the price to pay would be as high as the benefits accrued. This is what happened with the Sandinistas in Nicaragua ten years later, though in relative terms the Cuban presence there was more significant than in Bolivia. Cuba derived undeniable benefits from its involvement in Nicaragua; it also paid a very high price.

Bolivia was Castro's last gamble: he would either win or lose all. If the expedition prospered, or the mother *foco* ignited a successful revolution in a neighboring country, U.S. pressure on Cuba would recede. If it failed, Castro would resign himself to an indefinite alignment with Moscow, until the United States called a truce or a new opportunity emerged. Roughly coinciding with Che's time in Bolivia, Castro's tone and attitude toward the Soviet Union underwent an undeniable change: he renewed his support for revolution in Latin America and, in early 1968, endured the worst crisis yet in his relations with the USSR, when it virtually suspended oil shipments to Cuba. The price to pay appeared only after Che and the *focos* in other countries had been defeated. In August 1968, when the Soviets invaded Czechoslovakia, Fidel had to bow and accept an event which would change forever the course of socialism in Cuba and the world. This was the real consequence of Che's debacle in Bolivia. The future of Latin America might well have been quite different if the Argentine revolutionary had not been killed at La Higuera. But effects are not causes: Bolivia was a compromise solution for Che, not a strategic goal for Cuba.

Preparations for the expedition intensified. A number of Bolivians arrived for training in Cuba while Pombo, Papi, and Pachungo looked after the final details in Bolivia. Tania, back in La Paz after her trip to Prague, served as liaison. She hid the Cubans, established contact with local groups, and took charge of the mission's logistics: money, safe houses, documents, and weapons. Very quickly, however, the Cubans understood that their Bolivian expedition was no picnic, and that something was terribly wrong in the Andean crests and valleys.

Their relations with the Bolivian Party became increasingly torturous. After Monje and the PCB leadership realized that the Cubans did not just intend to use their country as a transit lounge en route to Argentina, but hoped to establish themselves in Bolivia itself, they were outraged. When the Cubans requested the twenty men they had been promised, Monje feigned surprise. He was having "problems," he explained, with his Central Committee, which was "opposed to the armed struggle." Guevara's lieutenants sensed "great uncertainty about [the Bolivians'] decision to join the armed struggle." The situation was at an impasse. Nothing could be done; all plans were put on hold: "there is apathy, and little enthusiasm, over all this." The Cubans concluded, "we are the ones doing all the organization, and they are not helping us."[27] Their reports to Havana were received with surprise and disappointment: "they are crazy [over there] because nothing is ready here."[28]

Things got worse late that southern winter, when an enigmatic figure arrived on the scene: the French writer Régis Debray, who had already traveled in Bolivia during 1964 partly on his own, partly as an emissary sent by pro-China groups in Paris to recruit Bolivian Maoists. Now he had been dispatched by Fidel Castro with a slightly different mission. He was to study the different regions of Bolivia to determine the best location for a *foco*. His other task was to initiate talks with the pro-Chinese labor unionists of Moisés Guevara, who had broken both with the PCB and the Maoist group led by Oscar Zamora—with whom he also spoke.* Debray's mission was thus twofold: to find the optimum site for a *foco,* but also to persuade Che that the Bolivian venture was possible. Debray's links to Castro were well known: during those weeks, his book *Revolution in the Revolution?* was published with Castro's endorsement.

To Mario Monje, it was Debray's appearance in September, along with the presence of Pombo, Papi, and Tuma in La Paz and Cochabamba since July, that tipped him off to the real nature of unfolding events. Fidel's original story of smuggling a high-ranking Cuban into Argentina did not square with the arrival of important figures like Debray and Che's lieutenants. As Jorge Kolle also recalled, "We had known Debray for a long time; we knew about his links to the Venezuelan guerrillas and his ideas which were aligned with those of the Maoist dissidents."[29] When the Boli-

---

*"I spoke with Zamora; I went to discuss the guerrilla movement with him. He said yes." Régis Debray, interview with the author, Paris, November 3, 1995.

vians detected his presence at Los Yungas, they realized that the Cubans "were misinforming us, they had not given us the whole script."[30] The day Monje glimpsed Debray in Cochabamba, he became furious and demanded of Papi and Pombo,

> "What is Régis Debray doing in Bolivia? You know him, but we have no contact with him. He has come for you to start a guerrilla struggle." "No," said the Cubans, "we have nothing to do with him." Monje replied, "That remains to be seen. You are trying to develop a guerrilla struggle here, and you are not respecting the plan."*

A new series of arguments broke out, pitting Monje and most of the PCB leadership against Castro and Piñeiro, with Che as a more or less innocent bystander. The Cubans were playing a double game. They wanted Monje to participate in an armed struggle which he did not support and did not believe possible.† Simultaneously, they were attempting to infiltrate and divide Bolivia's Communist Party, reinforcing partisans of military action like the Peredo brothers, Jorge and Humberto Vázquez Viaña, and the youth movement led by Loyola Guzmán. It was only natural that Che and the Cubans should have identified with that sector of the party: links of solidarity, affection, and shared experience, as well as broad ideological affinities, bound them together. But so that their friends would not be forced to choose between the armed struggle and the party line, it was vital that Che and the Cubans also maintain cordial relations with the PCB leadership.‡ The radical break would come later, leading to open hostility on the part of the PCB. For the time being, however, comity seemed an indispensable part of the plan—and the only way to achieve it was through duplicity and deceit. Che and his companions were right to believe in the courage and dedication of the Communists, whether the youth movement or pro-Castro

---

*Monje, interview. Debray confirms that he did not know Papi or Pombo. Debray, interview with the author, Paris, November 3, 1995.

† Despite the huge resentment between them, Monje and Kolle have similar perceptions of that time. Kolle asks, "How were we going to get involved in a project we had opposed? During our entire lives, we always supported the Cuban Revolution, and we were ready to do anything, even be called traitors, cowards, whatever, in order to protect the Revolution. But one thing is the historical fact of the Cuban Revolution; quite another is the vicissitudes of individuals in history." Jorge Kolle, interview with the author, Cochabamba, October 29, 1994.

‡ Che was aware of the problems he raised for those Communists willing to join the armed struggle. In one of the earliest entries in his campaign diary, he notes: "I warned the Bolivians about their responsibility in violating party discipline in order to adopt another line." Ernesto Che Guevara, "Diario de Bolivia," new annotated edition, published in Carlos Soria Galvarro, ed., *El Che en Bolivia, Documentos y Testimonios,* vol. 5 (La Paz: Cedoin, 1994), p. 63. This is the most recent edition of the journal, and the most complete in its annotations.

dissidents—but they paid a high price for their cultivation of the PCB at the expense of other groups. Their efforts cost them time and energy that could have been better spent elsewhere, and their role was inevitably tainted by mystery and ambiguity.

Monje soon started weaving his own traps and tricks. First he tried to change the location of the Cuban base, shifting it away from the more advantageous setting of the Alto Beni and Los Yungas, in order to achieve his own goal: to get Che and the Cubans out of Bolivia as quickly as possible. The difference between the initial site in the northwest and Ñancahuazú in the southeast was obvious. The former had no outlets; ideal for a struggle within Bolivia, it was unsuited for a mother column meant to branch off into other countries or to cross quickly and secretly into Argentina, which the second location was quite appropriate for. Next Monje convened the Party's Politburo and solemnly announced: "Gentlemen, the guerrilla struggle is beginning in Bolivia in September or October. Régis Debray is studying the terrain in Bolivia."[31] Then Monje decided to travel to Havana, either to ratify his initial agreement with the Cubans—or else to cancel it entirely.

Concurrently, Fidel and Piñeiro were concealing from Che the full complexity of the issues and positions involved. On the eve of his departure, Che did not know that Monje was insincere in his pledge to join the armed struggle; or that the Bolivian was also, to some extent, being misled; or that the Communists behind the plan represented only a marginal faction within the PCB. Castro's motives were fairly straightforward: in contrast to Argentina, what made Bolivia attractive as a possible place for a *foco* was that Cuba possessed serious and significant political assets there. It would have been counterproductive to share with Che the intricacies, dubiousness, and precariousness of those assets or resources; Guevara would merely have concluded that he should go to Argentina after all. But this gave rise to a chain of misunderstandings, euphemisms, and simulations which all pointed in one direction: to unleash the armed struggle in Bolivia, at almost any cost. Later, the same web of deceptions would converge on a tragic outcome: complete failure, and the heroic or simply brutal death of the participants.

The final weeks at San Andrés de Taiguanabo were devoted to further training, and to preparing false biographies for the Cubans. Of the twenty-one guerrilla fighters, some, like Che, would pose as Uruguayan; others, as Peruvians or even Bolivians.[32] They eventually included five members of the Party's Central Committee and two deputy ministers of state. Guevara devised the preliminary plan and a long-term schedule, that would never be followed. The strategy was to open two fronts, one near the city of Sucre and the other in the Alto Beni. By December 20, all the Cubans and sixty

Bolivians would be in place; this initial nucleus would establish, not a *foco,* but a school for Latin American guerrillas. Their camp would be secret, isolated, and impenetrable; they would not attempt to infiltrate inhabited areas, recruit peasants, or obtain supplies. In early 1967, a call would be issued to most of the revolutionary leaders of Latin America, asking them to send their best cadres using routes facilitated by Monje and the PCB.* Several national columns would then break out toward their respective countries, for training and reconnaissance purposes rather than combat. After various rehearsals, they would slip into the neighboring nations, with Che leading the Argentine column.[†] Before this, however, the guerrillas would make their first public appearance in Bolivia on July 26, 1967, attacking a military base at Chuquisaca, in Sucre; this would furnish them with their first combat experience.[33] There is an obvious parallel here to the Sierra Maestra—for instance, the creation of a mother column dividing into several smaller ones.

D-day was set for October 15. The training camp at San Andrés was dismantled and the guerrillas began departing for Bolivia in small groups, all traveling in roundabout and complicated ways. The operation was successful in terms of secrecy; but it required an enormous effort that was short-lived. As Che confessed to Renán Montero, one of his urban cadres in La Paz, the Bolivian government's security measures were far less strict than he had suspected; all the energy and trouble devoted to penetrating the country in secrecy were partly unnecessary.[‡] Or perhaps, Che's exertion had another purpose: the Soviets probably did not find out immediately about the mission to Bolivia; this time, Castro did not discuss the matter with Ambassador Alexeiev. Still, a secret CIA report stated a year later that Castro "informed Brezhnev that Ernesto Che Guevara with men and material furnished by Cuba had gone to Bolivia in the fall of 1966."[34]

---

*Some parts of this deluded plan might have been feasible. A confidential report by the Intelligence Section of the U.S. Department of Defense noted, on March 16, 1967, that a group of Panamanian revolutionaries planned to sail in secret from their country to Argentina, where they would receive military training at a camp commanded by Ernesto Guevara. Department of Defense Intelligence Report, Alleged Training of Panamanian Revolutionaries in Algeria, Colón, March 16, 1967, report number 2230024967 (Secret).

[†] The plan has already been described by Régis Debray in *La guerrilla del Che* (Mexico City: Siglo XXI, 1975), p. 75. Benigno confirms it in *Vie et mort* (p. 127); his corroboration is important because it comes from somebody who was actually at the training camp.

[‡] Renán Montero, Iván, interview with the author, Havana, August 25, 1995. This interview was the only one in this book that could be neither recorded nor conducted with a witness present. Renán Montero had never spoken of his role in Bolivia, much less in Nicaragua, where he fought beginning in 1961 with Tomás Borge and the group of Sandinistas armed by Che; he was later deputy chief of state security from 1979 to 1990. A foreign correspondent accompanied this author to a house where Montero was staying, ratified that he was indeed Montero, and can vouch for the fact that Montero agreed to be interviewed by the author. However, he was not present at the interview itself.

Nonetheless, Che's effort took its toll. A few days before his departure from Cuba, an incident took place that illustrated his obsession with secrecy, as well as his mood and that of his companions. Aleida often visited Che at the camp, but on the eve of his departure, when the other combatants had been refused permission to take leave of their families, Ramiro Valdés drove her so she could spend some time with her husband. Che was furious; he insulted Valdés and forbade Aleida even to exit the car. In the midst of the altercation, Fidel arrived. When he realized what was happening, he persuaded Che to allow all the guerrillas to see their loved ones before flying off, arguing that it would not pose any great threat to security. Guevara relented, and finally allowed Aleida to stay with him in San Andrés.* The outrageous demands Che placed on both himself and others would play a central role in the Bolivian debacle.

The disinformation campaign mounted for the Bolivian expedition was extremely effective. If the same amount of time and effort had gone into other areas, the mission's outcome might have been different. Ramiro Valdés and the Interior Ministry fabricated a cover for each of the combatants; supposedly, they were off to study in the USSR. They received fake letters, postcards, and documents in order to deceive their families, and were even asked for a list of the presents their wives and children might expect from the Socialist bloc.

It is said that just before the departure, Che and Fidel held their last private conversation while sitting on a log in the ravine of San Andrés.† An official from the Interior Ministry who attended the training program but was excluded from the mission at the last minute overheard part of their conversation, and deduced the rest from their body language. Castro did the talking, while Che was sullen and withdrawn; Castro was vehement, Guevara quiet. At last Fidel ran through all the problems, both inherent and circumstantial, in the Bolivian expedition. He emphasized the lack of communications, Monje's hesitations, the organizational weaknesses of Inti and Coco Peredo. He intended to dissuade Guevara, or at least induce him to postpone his trip. Both finally stood up, gave each other several slaps on the back: less than blows, more than a hug. Fidel's gestures revealed his des-

---

*Benigno, *Vie et mort,* pp. 131–132. The son of Jesús Suárez Gayol (el Rubio, the first Cuban to die in Bolivia), together with his wife, Marial, confirmed the general tenor of this anecdote, during a conversation with the author in Havana in January 1996.

† This legend, confided to the author by a source who preferred not to be identified but who has proven reliable in the past, does not necessarily contradict the account given by Fidel Castro himself. In his interview with Gianni Miná in 1987, Castro described how, "on the day he left," he played a practical joke on Che, inviting him to have lunch with several Cuban leaders; nobody recognized Guevara. This was not, however, the last time Che and Fidel were alone together; for on this occasion, Che appeared in secret before his own companions.

peration at Guevara's stubbornness. They sat down again for a long while, in silence. After a while, Fidel got up and left.

Che was overtaken by impatience, for the last time in his life. He realized—though perhaps incompletely—that the plans for Bolivia were unraveling. Mario Monje's sabotage became increasingly explicit as he discovered the mission's true scope. His meetings with Pombo along with Debray's movements confirmed his suspicions, as had his colleagues' trips to the island: the Cubans were planning to mount a *foco* in the Alto Beni. As previously noted, Monje decided to render the location unusable by revealing it in the right quarters. In doing so, he forced Che's lieutenants to shift from the Alto Beni and Los Yungas to another area entirely: the canyon of Ñancahuazú in southeastern Bolivia. The new location was completely unsuited to guerrilla warfare, though perhaps adequate to conceal an isolated school for cadres or to launch an expedition to Argentina.* Monje now acknowledges that he was behind the shift to Ñancahuazú, though he knew it might become a trap; he wanted to push Che as close to Argentina as possible, effectively forestalling the armed struggle in Bolivia.†

Debray adds a further complication. In his view, the best political text he has ever written was precisely the report Fidel requested of him and which he delivered to Piñeiro, where he explained why the Alto Beni was an ideal location for guerrilla warfare, due to its climate, geography, urban and rural political history, and so on.‡ However, Debray believes that Che never received the report; nor did he ever assimilate the enormous differences between the Beni region and the southeast.** In April 1968—several months after Che's death—a meeting was held in Havana reuniting the three recently arrived Cuban survivors plus the youngest Peredo brother,

*Monje states that he explained this to Che during their conversation on December 31, 1966: "We bought this property first of all as a transit point toward the south, a place to concentrate troops and then transfer them. Strategically, it is a very bad location. Not only because the mountains are bare and rugged, but because there are no inhabited settlements. It's a kind of trap, unsuited for guerrilla warfare. You have to get out of there immediately, because you will lose. This is a bad choice from the point of view of the armed struggle; [we chose it] for another purpose entirely." Monje, interview.

† Another person close to the guerrillas, Humberto Vázquez Viaña (brother of Jorge, el Loro), maintains that Monje opposed the Alto Beni in part because it was home to Maoist peasant organizations controlled by his arch-enemy, the pro-Chinese Oscar Zamora. See Humberto Vázquez Viaña, "Antecedentes de la guerrilla del Che en Bolivia," Institute of Latin American Studies, University of Stockholm, research paper, Series #46, 1987, p. 27.

‡ Debray, interview. Debray adds: "I completed the report and gave it to Piñeiro. I did not speak with Che."

**It is still not clear to Debray whether his report was shelved for chronological reasons—by the time he finished it, Che was already on his way to Bolivia—or political reasons, due to Piñeiro's and/or Castro's reluctance to pass it on to Guevara. He was later told that his report would be used in opening a second and third front, in the Alto Beni and Chapare. Debray, interview.

Antonio, the brother of Jorge Vázquez Viaña, Humberto, Juan Carretero or Ariel, and Angel Braguer or Lino. Pombo explained, "We thought the plan was to develop the struggle in the north. . . . We were not going to conduct operations in Ñancahuazú."[35] Addressing Ariel, he added: "Che was tricked. We had been told this was an area for settlement, and it wasn't. We should review the reports, they must be somewhere."[36] This suggests, as Humberto Vázquez Viaña concluded, that the location was chosen without any previous research; in short, Pombo and Papi knew next to nothing about the terrain.* Furthermore, Che made no secret of his dissatisfaction with his envoys' performance. Papi Martínez Tamayo relates in the unexpurgated edition of Pombo's journal how Che once complained that "his big mistake had been to send him [to Bolivia], as he was useless." Papi recalled that Che's criticism had hurt him enormously; for he was there "not because he was particularly interested in Bolivian affairs, but out of personal loyalty to Che."[37]

This was doubtless another consequence of the Congo debacle: Che mistrusted Cuban intelligence, choosing instead to rely upon his own team. None of Piñeiro's men were sent to Bolivia in advance[†]; none of the officials previously stationed at the Cuban Embassy in La Paz were asked to help; Debray's opinion was not taken into account; not even Furri, the confidante of Raúl Castro who helped prepare the Salta expedition, was heeded by Che. After the intelligence fiasco of the Congo, he was wary of everyone save his closest aides; but, as he acknowledged to Monje later in the year, they were military men, not political operators. Even so, while Che was in Cuba all the information from Bolivia was filtered through Piñeiro's team; Piñeiro himself (Barbaroja, or Redbeard), Armando Campos, and Juan Carretero visited him almost every weekend. As Benigno put it, "Everything Che received went through Piñeiro. . . . They sent [Che] information

---

*Vázquez Viaña and Aliaga Saravia, *Bolivia: Ensayo de revolución continental,* provisional edition, July 1970, pp. 18–19. Benigno suggests another explanation for Papi's acceptance of Ñancahuazú: "Papi was a man with many illusions. These illusions had to do with his personal situation. Over in Lagunilla [near Ñancahuazú] he had met some girls; Coco Peredo was with one and Papi with the other, and that led them to have closer relations in the area." The idea seems a bit far-fetched, but becomes more plausible in the light of Che's personal evaluation of Papi, which remained unpublished until early 1996: "7/2/67 (three months). He has not reached top physical condition, nor does he have the ideal character. He has some bad habits and is somewhat resentful, apparently because his privileged position in the C. has been very diminished in the current constellation." "7/5/67 (six months) Bad. Though I talked with him, he has not corrected his deficiencies, and is effective and enthusiastic only in combat conditions." Carlos Soria Galvarro, "El Che evalúa a sus hombres," *La Razón* (La Paz), October 9, 1996.

† "Piñeiro's unit was supposed to support Ernesto in his activities in the Congo, or Argentina, or, finally, in his operation in Bolivia; but they did not prepare a network in Bolivia, either. There was nobody from Piñeiro's team here." Jorge Kolle, interview.

about everything that was being done in Bolivia, supplies, logistics, and he received nothing but wonderful news."[38] Guevara was right to mistrust Cuban intelligence, for they committed the same mistakes they had made in the Congo.

In August, Che instructed Pombo, Tuma, and Papi to purchase a place in the Alto Beni; the PCB cadres went along. However, pressured by Monje and the need to maintain cordial relations with the PCB, they, too, had opted for the southeast. When they informed their leader that they had bought a property in Ñancahuazú and were already squirreling away weapons there, they presented him with a fait accompli. Che acquiesced. He had not seen Debray's text, and his own intentions were still somewhat vague—was his intention to create a *foco* in Bolivia, or just to pass through on his way to Argentina? There was no time to review the plan.* If Che had overruled his envoys in Bolivia, he would have had to start over from scratch. This would have entailed delaying his departure to Bolivia, as he could not remain in urban areas indefinitely; he would have to travel to a camp very quickly, to avoid leaks and betrayals. But there would be no camp if there were no farm, and there would be no property if he did not take advantage of the one already acquired by the PCB. Rather than wait, Che decided to leave Cuba as soon as possible. Quite justifiably, he feared that any further delay might jeopardize the entire project: either Monje and the PCB would compromise him by revealing the entire plan, or Castro would abort the mission when he realized that preparations were not going smoothly. As Angel Braguer, "Lino," recalls, "there was no time to mount anything else."†

When Che arrived in Bolivia, he discovered that the twenty guerrillas requested by Fidel and reluctantly granted by Monje were nowhere to be found. Instead of repairing relations with the Bolivian Communists, or with Oscar Zamora's pro-Chinese faction (which ultimately decided to keep its distance from the expedition), or even reorienting the entire mission toward the Bolivian miners and popular movement, Che decided to recruit his men through the dissident Maoist splinter group led by Moisés Guevara. This required casting a wider net, with slacker requirements and greater chances for mistakes and infiltrations; recruits enticed by money or promises were more likely to desert after their first brush with combat. However, more

---

*In contrast to Debray, Angel Braguer, "Lino," asserts that "Che did read the Frenchman's study, but he accepted the fait accompli in the southeast because he was in a hurry and, especially, he did not want to get into any more fights in Cuba." Braguer, interview.

†Lino, interview. According to Ciro Bustos, Che told him during a conversation at the camp that when Papi Martínez Tamayo traveled to Cuba in September, he said that Che should hurry up and enter Bolivia, or else he would never enter. See Ciro Bustos, "Account of His Stay," p. 201.

careful screening procedures would have delayed the entire operation, since the campaign could not begin without Bolivian combatants, and Monje's forces were now reduced to only four or five cadres, some of whom were delegated to the cities. The only people left were discouraged Peruvians and overzealous Cubans. The mission had to incorporate more Bolivians. All of these obstacles might have led anyone else to rethink the whole project, or in any case delay it. But Che characteristically decided to outrun the problem. He opted to proceed with the plan as scheduled with the resources at hand. A more sensible and prudent man, with more time and patience at his disposal, might have stopped at the edge of the cliff.

Before leaving, he bade farewell to Aleida and the children. Disguised as a bald, fat, and short-sighted Uruguayan bureaucrat named Ramón, he had dinner with his daughters without revealing his identity. They would learn it only later, when reports of his death were confirmed. On October 23, he flew from Havana to Moscow, together with his traveling companion, Pachungo. From there he skipped over to Prague, then by train to Vienna, Frankfurt, and Paris, where he took a plane for Madrid and São Paulo, finally reaching Corumbá, on the border between Bolivia and Brazil, on November 6. After crossing uneventfully, he and Pachungo were met by Papi, Renán Montero, and Jorge Vázquez Viaña. They then journeyed by jeep to Cochabamba and La Paz. Vázquez Viaña, intrigued by his passenger's features, was shocked to discover that he was the legendary Comandante Guevara; he'd had no idea.

For a long time, Che's itinerary was an object of uncertainty and conflicting accounts. First of all, there were discrepancies in the passports he used. When the Bolivian army entered his camp and recovered a large number of documents, they found two fake Uruguayan passports with identical photographs, one bearing the name Adolfo Mena González, the other Ramón Benítez Fernández. They both contained entry and exit stamps issued by the Madrid airport, with different dates in October. Che was also sighted a number of times in various parts of the world. Betty Feigín, the former wife of Che's Córdoba friend Gustavo Roca, recalls that her husband told her in September or October 1966 that he would be away for several days. Upon his return, he claimed that he had met with Guevara in Tucumán or Mendoza. Betty's sister Nora, who had known Ernesto in his youth, swears that she saw Ernesto walking in shirtsleeves along Monjitas Street in the Chilean capital, near the golf club, in the southern spring of 1966. Though disguised, he was recognizable to anyone who knew him well. Nora waved, but Che signaled that she was not to express any recognition or greeting, and so she continued on her way. When she related the incident to her husband, he asked her to forget the matter entirely; otherwise, he would be obliged to notify the Argentine National Intelligence Service attaché in Santiago.*

It was also rumored that Che passed through Córdoba, even staying at the home of a Beltrán family on the outskirts of the city. None of these assertions should be dismissed, considering the absurd veil of secrecy still imposed by Cuba on the details of those weeks. Several authors, ranging from the Argentine Hugo Gambini to the Bolivians González and Sánchez Salazar, mention various stopovers in the course of Che's trip to Bolivia. General Alfredo Ovando, the highest-ranking Bolivian officer in the campaign to capture Che, announced months later that he had entered Bolivian territory between September 15 and 22, 1966, and that he returned on November 24.[39] Daniel James asserts that Che zigzagged through Bolivia and several other Latin American countries during the first half of 1966. He quotes an article from the Mexican daily *Excélsior* published on September 14, specifying the precise day of Che's entry into Bolivia—two months before the generally accepted date.[40] However, there have been so many published accounts, and so many attempts to mislead researchers, that one may safely conclude that Che's itinerary from Cuba to Bolivia was in all likelihood the one revealed by the captured documents.

In any case, he finally completed his long journey and arrived at the Ñancahuazú camp in early November. He discovered that none of the carefully laid plans had been executed: there were few weapons, and no Communists other than those he already knew; Monje was not even in the country; the team's communications equipment was virtually useless, and the area presented innumerable problems.[†] Che's optimism allowed him to overcome some of these setbacks, though when Benigno arrived on December 10, he found him "in a state of horrible impatience and in a very bad mood."[41] But nothing mattered: the excitement of being in the mountains, ready for combat, finally free of the ambivalence of Prague and Cuba, helped Che to forge ahead. No obstacle seemed too great, and the well-

---

*Nora Feigín, telephone conversation with the author, Washington, D.C., September 22, 1995. Gustavo Villoldo, one of the three Cuban-origin envoys sent by the United States to Bolivia, confirms (when expressly questioned) that Che was indeed in Chile. Gustavo Villoldo, interview with the author, Miami, November 21, 1995. Reyna Carranza, Gustavo Roca's second wife, has confirmed to the author that her husband did indeed tell her several years later that he had met Che at the Mendoza airport in Argentina (almost on the Chilean border), and that Che had blond hair, wore glasses, and was returning from Chile. But Roca died in the 1980's and his papers were destroyed when he fled Argentina after the 1976 military coup; there is no way of knowing whether Roca made the story up, or his widow has embellished it somewhat. Reyna Carranza, interview with Marcelo Monjes, at the request of the author, Córdoba, September 19, 1996.

† In Benigno's words, "There is no food, no medicines, no weapons." Benigno, interview.

trained Cuban recruits were able to accomplish their initial aims despite a series of hindrances.

The country in which Che had chosen to light the fires of Latin American revolution was no longer the one he had known in 1953. Bolivia's chronic political instability had gradually given way to an incipient institutionalization, as represented by the more or less democratic election of President René Barrientos in July 1966. Its relations with the United States, born of Milton Eisenhower's mission in 1953 when Che was hitchhiking through the Andes, had developed into close ties of aid and complicity. By the mid-seventies, American military assistance per capita was the highest of all Latin America, and second only to U.S. aid to Israel. Over one thousand Bolivian officers had been trained at Panama's School of the Americas. Cooperation between the two armies reached such heights that when Barrientos requested a U.S. Air Force plane for a vacation trip to Europe, his petition was instantly granted.* There was no doubt of Bolivia's submission to the United States; but the nationalism of its 1952 revolution had given that submission an idiosyncratic bent.

Bolivia was still, first and foremost, a very poor country—after Haiti, the most backward in all of Latin America. A large part of the population lived in rural, marginalized, and poverty-stricken areas. But, as in Mexico, its poverty was very special: the peasants had received land thanks to an agrarian reform; the workers belonged to powerful labor unions that were alternately banned and rehabilitated with astounding frequency. The country's natural resources—mainly tin, antimony, and petroleum—had been nationalized by the revolution. The armed forces, always ready to take a hand in government, held the Latin American record for military *pronunciamientos;* but they displayed a peculiar combination of nationalism and pro-U.S. conservatism reminiscent of Brazil. The Nationalist Revolutionary Movement of Víctor Paz Estenssoro had withdrawn from the government; the Confederation of Bolivian Workers, or COB, was in the opposition; and Bolivian civil society enjoyed a vigor and pluralism that few other countries in the region could boast.

Finally, the election of Barrientos, an air force officer who was a founder and strong supporter of the armed forces' Program for Civic Action, reflected still another unique feature of Bolivian politics. Since 1952, the coexistence of the old army, trained early in the century by the Germans,

---

*Hurwitch/AmEmbassy La Paz to Ruehcr/SecState, January 4, 1966 (Secret), NSF, Country File, Bolivia, vol. 4, box 8, LBJ Library. The CIA station chief at La Paz recounts in his unpublished memoirs that President Barrientos once feared he had suffered a heart attack; the CIA immediately sent a cardiologist from the United States. "Barrientos was too good a friend of the United States to neglect a possible illness." John Tilton, unpublished memoirs, graciously lent to the author by John Tilton, chapter 9, "Chasing Ol' Che," p. 113.

with peasant and worker militias had led to a close linkage between the military and the peasant *caciques* involved in land reform. Ever since the Alliance for Progress, the Program for Civic Action had "allowed the armed forces to take the political initiative in fulfilling the local needs of the population. . . . for instance, building schools and roads in rural areas."[42] Barrientos was fluent in Quechua and was genuinely popular among the peasants, not because of any personal charisma, but thanks to that precedent and tradition. Shortly after taking office in 1966, he signed a Military-Peasant Pact which, among other things, pledged that:

> The Armed Forces will enforce respect for the conquests achieved by the majority classes, such as the land reform, basic education, the workers' right to unionization. . . . For their part, the peasants will firmly and loyally support and defend the Institution of the Military at all times. They will place themselves under military orders against all subversive maneuvers of the left.[43]

The complexities of politics and culture in Bolivia went far beyond the cartoon vision of the country held by many Cubans. They tended to see it as a prototypical banana republic, bursting with mining resources and an impoverished population just waiting to be liberated. In fact, a strong indigenous composition did not interfere with a widespread nationalism, especially among the armed forces; this would frustrate many of the expectations harbored by Che Guevara. The country presented a further paradox. On the one hand, it possessed a highly politicized, radical labor movement, concentrated in the powerful Confederation of Bolivian Workers, of leftist and occasionally Trotskyist inspiration. The miners' unions, in particular, wielded enormous influence despite their status as a minority due to their central role in the economy. In 1965, mining represented only 2.7 percent of the working population, but accounted for 94 percent of exports, which in turn constituted a high proportion of GDP: "Thirty thousand tin miners fed a country with five million inhabitants."[44]

On the other hand, the left itself was extremely weak; its foundations had been undermined by the revolution of 1952. The Communist Party, Maoist groups, and civil organizations, though not insignificant, were fiercely divided. Hence the CIA's evaluation of Bolivia, in a secret report of 1966, as a country hardly ripe for revolution. The American intelligence service rated Bolivia as the last among nine countries unstable enough to warrant U.S. intervention.[45]

Such was the country where Che hoped, in November 1966, to implement a project radically different from his original plan. There would be no guerrilla movement in Peru, and things had not worked out quickly enough in Argentina; so Bolivia was chosen as the cradle for Latin American revolution. And it would all happen in Ñancahuazú, the worst possible place for a guerrilla *foco*. Here there were no communications or landless peasants; on the contrary, the few and dispersed inhabitants were more like settlers, having benefited from land reform. Nor was there much vegetation, wildlife, or water—all indispensable factors in guerrilla warfare. Instead of a well-organized support team, Che found a reluctant Communist Party, with devious leaders and a few enthusiastic but marginal cadres. Yet less than three months after his arrival in the Rio Grande basin, the training camp and school for Latin American guerrillas unwittingly became a deadly combat theater.

Che's expedition never recovered from its ill-starred beginnings. It lurched from crisis to crisis, starting with the guerrillas' arrival in early November and concluding at La Higuera in October 1967. The details of the Bolivian saga are well known, thanks to Che's diary and numerous other accounts. This analysis will consequently focus on the campaign's successive tribulations, and Guevara's increasingly desperate and contradictory reactions to them. His fate was fast approaching. Che did not have a death wish, but since his early youth he had yearned for a Christlike destiny: an exemplary sacrifice. He would soon achieve it.

The first crisis was the unexpected resolution of the Communist Party's ambivalence. Its endless hesitations were no longer tolerable, as they became a real threat to the expedition. The weapons never arrived; the urban network was never formed; the combatants never appeared; and Mario Monje was traveling in other parts of the world. Returning to Havana in June from a trip to Moscow, he refused to stop in Prague, probably believing that the Communists would try to unite him with Guevara so that the *comandante* could pressure him personally.[*] Castro intercepted him in Havana on his way back from the Bulgarian Communist Party Congress in December 1966. Monje, he said, would be guided to Che's camp upon his arrival in Bolivia—though Castro did not divulge the camp's location or tell him it was in Bolivia.[†]

On his return to La Paz, Monje called an urgent meeting of the Party leadership. Announcing that he had been invited to meet with Che at his

[*]Somebody said to me, I'm not sure if it was Piñeiro, How are you going back to Bolivia? I'm going back Moscow-Prague-La Paz. Do you know why I'm asking? We might have some information for you in Prague. So I arrived in Moscow, and said to them, Get me a direct flight to Bolivia. I don't want to go to Prague. These people in Prague have something up their sleeve." Monje, interview.

[†] Monje, interview. In a coded message from Castro to Che dated December 14, 1966, and found among Che's papers when he was captured on October 8, 1967, Fidel notified Che that he had "misinformed" Monje as to the camp's location. See Soria Galvarro, *El Che*, vol. 4, p. 299.

camp, he requested that the Politburo and Central Committee convene as soon as he came back. Monje knew that there could be no agreement with Che. His goal consisted in preserving the Party's unity at any cost, as its Castroist faction—the youth movement, the clandestine-operations unit, and so on—would obviously support the Cubans and join the armed struggle.

On December 31, Tania escorted Monje to Guevara's headquarters, by then a full-fledged base with the capacity to house and feed about a hundred men, with several secondary camps removed from the "calamine house," as it came to be known because of its corrugated-tin roof. The base also included an auditorium for lectures, a bread oven, and a defense system, complete with communications equipment and caves for food, supplies, medicine, and documents.

The meeting was bound to be tense. If Che's plan hinged on help from the Bolivian Communist Party, and that help was no longer forthcoming (aside from the participation of a few heroic individuals), then the entire project was meaningless. According to Monje, Che led off the discussion by acknowledging that he and Fidel had duped him:

> We have, in reality, deceived you. I would say it was not Fidel's fault, it was one of my maneuvers as he made the request on my behalf. I initially had other plans and then changed them. . . . Forgive the comrade with whom you spoke, he is very good, absolutely trustworthy, but not a politician, that is why he did not know and could not explain my plans. I know that he was very rude to you.[46]

The "comrade" was Papi Martínez Tamayo; the initial project was to travel to Argentina. This hypothesis has already been suggested: perhaps Castro initially suspected he would not be able to dissuade Che from his original scheme. Monje's version is also plausible: Che himself admitted that the Cubans had deceived him. Their true intent may always have been to create a guerrilla *foco* in Bolivia, aware that neither Monje nor the other Communist leaders would ever agree.

Che then proposed that Monje become part of the armed struggle as its political leader; he himself would retain military command. The Bolivian agreed to resign from the Party and join the guerrillas, on three conditions: one, the creation of a broad continental front, beginning with a new conference of Latin American Communist parties; two, that the armed struggle should go hand in hand with insurrection in the cities, under the coordination of the Communist Party; a national political front should be established including groups throughout the country, united under a single revolutionary command; and three, that the struggle not be limited to guerrilla warfare; it should include other activities. The military command would be subordinate to the political leadership, headed by himself. Monje would not accept a foreigner in that position, no matter how illustrious or experienced; the top leader must be a Bolivian. If one believes the journals of some of Che's aides, Monje also insisted that the pro-Chinese group of Oscar Zamora be excluded, and Che agreed, admitting that he had been wrong about Zamora from the outset.[47]

Che wrote in his diary, however, that the three demands seemed dishonest and contrived to him. What the Bolivian really wanted was a complete break; thus he fabricated conditions that he knew were unacceptable.* Che warned Monje that resigning as Secretary-General of the PCB would be a mistake. As for Monje's international requirement, Guevara was partly indifferent, partly skeptical: it resembled transforming poachers into gamekeepers. And he rejected categorically the condition regarding the struggle's leadership: "I could not possibly accept it. I had to be the military commander, and could not accept any ambiguities in that area."[48]

This was Che's fatal mistake, in the view of Emilio Aragonés. A more politically minded person would have accepted Monje's requirements, leaving it for later to find a way around them. Fidel, for instance, would have agreed.† But Che almost preferred to do without Monje: perhaps he still believed in the fantasies of Cuban intelligence, which continued to insist that most of the members and leaders of the Communist Party would rally to his cause and leave their Secretary-General behind. This might explain the following entry in his journal: "Monje's attitude might delay developments in one sense, but in another helps free me from any political obligations."‡ But Che was completely mistaken. Just eleven days later, Monje obtained the full support of his Politburo and Central Committee, which drafted a unanimous collective letter to Fidel Castro reiterating their position vis-à-vis Che Guevara.**

---

*"My impression is that when he realized . . . I had decided not to yield on strategic matters, he focused on them in order to force a break." Guevara, *Diario,* p. 73.

† Monje asserts that Castro sent a message to Che in December, before the meeting, advising him to "make any concessions, except those having to do with strategy"—such as the matter of leadership. Monje, interview.

‡ Guevara, *Diario,* p. 72. In his monthly summary, Che notes resignedly, "The party is against us and I don't know where this will lead, but it will not stop us and might even be beneficial in the long run (I am almost sure of this). The more honest and combative people will be with us." Ibid., p. 88.

**"The Bolivian revolution and armed struggle must be planned and directed by Bolivians. Our leadership has no excuses to make, and takes very seriously its responsibility in this area. Within this requirement, it does not underestimate or reject any voluntary help it might receive from revolutionary cadres and experienced military from other countries. This view of the Political Commission was unanimously backed by the Central Committee." Quoted in Soria Galvarro, *El Che,* vol. 1, p. 51.

All was not lost, however. When PCB Number Two man Jorge Kolle and Communist labor leader Simón Reyes met with Castro in Havana at the end of January in an attempt at reconciliation, Fidel notified Che that he would be "hard with them"; they then decided to revise their attitude, in view of Castro's emphasis on the project's continental nature. In a sense, this was a new deception; any alternative plans for other countries were by now purely imaginary, if they had ever existed: the Peruvian project had long been abandoned, nothing was happening in Argentina, and the Brazilian option had always been a fantasy. Fidel tried to play down Che's intransigence, explaining that Che wanted to lead the Bolivian guerrillas precisely because it was part of a regional strategy. He brought all his gifts of persuasion into play, largely in vain. The meeting was acrimonious in tone, according to a secret report sent to the German government by a member of the Politburo, Ramiro Otero:

> A partisan struggle was imposed on the Bolivian Communist Party by its comrades from Cuba and other countries. The PCB wrote a letter to Fidel Castro, asking that it be allowed to determine the when and the how of the struggle. Fidel reacted negatively. The result: the Party's propaganda apparatus was completely dismantled, the party banned, the members of the Politburo detained . . . Comrade Otero sees contradictions between Guevara and Fidel Castro. He believes "Che" is more intelligent, but more dangerous politically.*

While in Havana, the Bolivians nominally pledged to extend Che logistical support at least, and if possible to send him more people. As late as the beginning of February, Pombo noted in his diary that the guerrillas were still expecting a new Monje visit.[49] According to Benigno, as many as thirty-six Bolivians trained in Cuba could have joined the expedition, but never did.[50] Any further discussion of the agreements reached in Havana soon became irrelevant, however, once fighting broke out on March 23. New trips by Communist leaders were simply out of the question.

The Congo was still casting its long shadow. After eight months of waiting inertly in the African savannah because he lacked the authority to act, Che could not tolerate any ambivalence in this regard.† In another context

---

*"Informe sobre la situación en Bolivia (en base al informe de la delegación del PC Boliviano en conmemoración de la VII Reunión Partidaria en la RDA," Institut für Marxismus-Leninismus beim Zentral Komitee der SED, Zentrales Parteiarchiv, SED Internationale Verbindungen, Bolivia 1963–70, DY 30/IV A2/20/142, Berlin.

† This interpretation is shared by one of Che's companions in the Congo and Régis Debray (*La guerrilla*, p. 103). It also coincides with Che's own version, according to Mario Monje: "He told me about his experience in Africa, . . . the problems he had had there, how he depended upon forces that couldn't be mobilized, and how there were contradictions he couldn't resolve." Monje, interview.

he might have accepted a leadership council, or some compromise solution that would have satisfied Monje without surrendering to him full command. But after his calvary in the Congo, Guevara was unwilling to make any concessions.

The talks ended in complete disagreement. Monje asked to address the Bolivian Communists who had already joined the guerrillas to explain his stance. Che agreed, adding that all those who wished to leave the camp and return with their leader could do so; none did. Monje presented his position, but soon found his worst fears confirmed: the Cubans had "turned" his people during their training in Cuba, especially the Peredos. He ended his talk with a prescient warning:

> When the people find out that this guerrilla movement is being led by a foreigner, they will turn their backs on it and refuse to support it. I am sure it will fail because it will be led by a foreigner instead of a Bolivian. You will die heroically, but have no chance whatsoever of winning.[51]

Che did not blink, but attempted to minimize the effects of Monje's decision. As Benigno recalls,

> He tried not to show it—but imagine, this forced him to change his entire plan. He called us together and said, "Well, this is over before it even began. There is nothing left for us to do here." He gave both the Bolivians and Cubans a chance to leave if they so wished, and if any Cubans wanted to go over to the Bolivians they could do that. Nobody would be seen as a traitor or a coward.[52]

After the failed talks with Monje, attempts to recruit other groups were stepped up—especially the faction led by Moisés Guevara. In the meantime, Che decided to organize a reconnaissance and training march scheduled to last between ten and twenty days; it would drag on for weeks. Che left four men at the camp to receive visitors and recruits, and formed three teams for the mission: a vanguard unit of five men, led by Marcos (Antonio Sánchez Díaz); a main unit commanded by Che himself, consisting of eighteen men; and a rearguard of six men under Joaquín (Juan Vitalio Acuña). The twenty-nine guerrillas—fifteen Cubans and fourteen Bolivians—would return in rags, exhausted and discouraged.

The expedition, originally meant to be of relatively short duration, extended over six interminable weeks. The men trekked through canyons, rushing streams, uninhabited villages, and roads, exploring rocky crags and mountain passes as far north as the Rio Grande and the Río Masicuri. Two new recruits, Benjamin and Carlos, drowned without ever having fired a shot. The dense, thorny vegetation, mosquitoes and other insects (including the "boro," a fly which deposits its eggs under the skin), the lack of wildlife to hunt, heavy rains and swollen rivers made up a terrain very different from that of the Sierra Maestra. The explorers had to clear their way with machetes. By the third day, several guerrillas were without boots, and all suffered from hunger and thirst after their food supplies ran out; lack of discipline and petty thievery prompted Che to begin meting out the worst punishment of all, suspending food rations. The guerrillas had to sacrifice a horse they had bought just two days before, leading to "an orgy of horse-meat," as Che called it, and the resulting intestinal ravages. Logically, tensions soon rose to dangerous heights, with constant arguments and quarrels. The reconnaissance mission was useful in that it exposed all of these problems; but it proved very costly for an incipient guerrilla campaign. Tragedy struck on March 17, when a raft overturned in a torrential river: rucksacks, ammunition, and six rifles were lost, and one man drowned—the best Bolivian in the rearguard, according to Che.

The group finally returned to the base on March 20, devastated by six weeks of hunger, thirst, exhaustion, and conflict. Visitors were shocked by Che's appearance: emaciated, his feet and hands swollen, he had lost more than 20 pounds. Back at the camp, he found "terrible chaos"; moreover, the secrecy so vital to the camp, guerrillas, and the *comandante* himself had been violated. Desertions within Moisés Guevara's group, the suspicions of local residents, the diligence of the CIA and Bolivian intelligence services, and encounters with several oil technicians from Camiri had finally alerted the Bolivian army. It immediately headed for Ñancahuazú.

A series of events took place between March 11 and 17 that proved fatal. Seven men belonging to the Moisés Guevara faction had finally enlisted in mid-February: one would accompany Che until his death and, like him, would be executed; three others would betray him during those fateful days in March. Though nobody surmised it at the time, the Interior Ministry's Bureau for Criminal Investigation was tailing Moisés Guevara; in March he was followed to Camiri. When he climbed up to the camp, accompanied by Tania and Coco Peredo, he was tracked by the police. A report was duly remitted to the army's Fourth Division stationed in Camiri.[53] On March 11, two of Moisés Guevara's men commissioned to hunt for the day, Vicente Rocabada Terrazas and Pastor Barrera Quintana, quietly slipped out of the main camp, dropped their weapons, and fled toward Camiri. On March 14, they were captured by the police and handed over to the Fourth Division. The two men proceeded to recount everything they knew about the guerrilla base, describing its location, composition, and, especially, Che Guevara. They furnished the authorities with his aliases, entry dates into the country, and other details. Neither of them had ever seen him, as he was away on the reconnaissance mission when they arrived.* Rocabada even confessed that he learned Che's identity on January 12, before entering the camp, when Moisés Guevara first asked him to join the guerrillas.

The handful of Cubans in Bolivia were thus condemned by two devastating errors. First, Moisés Guevara was lax in his recruitment procedures: he exaggerated his group's real strength to Che and, in order to save face, enlisted whomever he could, even offering volunteers money or stipends. He also misrepresented the strength of the guerrilla force to prospective recruits. The latter were further offered the incentive of fighting under the legendary Che Guevara. The men thus enlisted not surprisingly deserted at the first opportunity. This was not just Moisés Guevara's fault, however. Once freed of his obligations to the Communist Party and eager to enlist more Bolivians, Che himself pressured Moisés to hasten the pace of recruitment. As he noted in his January summary, "the slowest part has been the incorporation of Bolivian combatants."[54]

Secondly, Che's absence caused lapses in the Cubans' discipline, despite their long training at San Andrés Taiguanabo; elementary security norms were violated. They were indiscreet with both Moisés Guevara's men and other visitors to the camp. There was an enormous, almost obsessive, amount of picture-taking, involving Che himself. Rocabada and Barrera's betrayal, and the precise and detailed information they provided, led the army (already alerted to the possible presence of armed men in the area) to order a patrol to investigate the "calamine house" at Ñancahuazú. The guerrilla camp was half-empty; thirty men were away on the reconnaissance mission. The others retreated to secondary bases, leaving only a single guard in their main camp: Salustre Choque Choque, one of Moisés Guevara's recruits. When the army patrol arrived, the Bolivian surrendered without a fight and, on questioning, confirmed the information previously supplied by his two companions. Five hundred meters from the house, the military found the remains of a temporary camp, including six suitcases full of clothes with Cuban and Mexican labels.

The army benefited from the testimony of deserters. But Bolivian army chief of staff General Alfredo Ovando revealed several months later that his men had already detected five foreigners in the area since late February. The outsiders had reportedly inquired of local inhabitants about fords across the Rio Grande; they were later seen swimming, and drying large wads of U.S. and Bolivian money in the sun. In addition, the reconnais-

---

*The text of the interrogation, which confirms that this was the first reliable information to reach the army about Che's presence in Bolivia, appears verbatim in Gary Prado Salmón, *La guerrilla inmolada* (Santa Cruz: Grupo Editorial Punto y Coma, 1987), pp. 80–82.

sance platoon led by Marcos was separated from the other two groups and returned to the camp before them. This led to an incident at the Tatarenda water station, when Marcos boasted of his guerrillas' prowess before an oil technician named Epifanio Vargas. His suspicions aroused, Vargas followed the platoon and then rushed to Camiri with the news.

Furthermore, since the creation of the guerrilla *foco* in November, a local resident named Ciro Algarañaz had demonstrated immense interest in the daily life of the camp. He even offered to help the supposed farmers, assuming that they were cultivating coca crops and producing cocaine. Algarañaz assigned one of his laborers to watch the calamine house. When the armed forces arrived in March, they corroborated all the suppositions and information delivered by Algarañaz and his hired hand.

So there were many clues signaling the presence of armed men by the time the chief of the army's Fourth Division dispatched his patrol to investigate the farm. Marcos and his vanguard group ran into the army patrol; after killing a soldier they promptly retreated, dodging combat and abandoning the farm. The military returned to Camiri, humiliated but bearing a priceless trophy: confirmation of the existence of a rebel group in the Ñancahuazú canyon. The war was starting in the worst possible conditions. The recently regrouped guerrillas did not even have time to rest, incorporate their new recruits, attend to visitors, or bolster their supplies. They were immediately confronted with the consequences of having lost their cover.

Marcos had already exasperated Che during the march by his constant bickering with the others, and especially with Pachungo (who was also the object of several of his leader's outbursts). When contact was re-established and Guevara learned of Marcos's retreat and the army's discovery of the calamine house, he exploded in anger. A guerrilla must never retreat without fighting; there can be no victory without combat, as Che noted in his journal. According to Régis Debray, Che was furious, screaming, "What's going on here? What sort of a fuck-up is this? Am I surrounded by cowards and traitors? I never want to see your Bolivian shit-eaters again, they're punished until further orders."[55] No matter that the defensive position was intended to mount an ambush; no matter that a long discussion took place among Marcos, Rolando, and Antonio (Orlando Pantoja) about the strategy to be followed.

Depressed by the string of misfortunes, worn out by hunger, thirst, and illness, and ravaged by his chronic intestinal problems and all the jealousies and intrigues, Che made one of the most critical and questionable decisions of his life. Despite his experience and the unspoken but evident disapproval of his subordinates, he organized an ambush against the military unit that would doubtless appear in the wake of the discovery by army headquarters of the rebel camp and the death of a Bolivian soldier. The guerrillas were not at all prepared to initiate hostilities. Their lack of cohesion, and the very nature of the whole long-term strategy, argued against the notion of immediate combat. Though the initial skirmish had exposed them, there still would have been time to escape and avoid contact with the enemy. Che chose the opposite course.

His decision was deliberate and unavoidable, according to both Humberto Vázquez Viaña, a member of the urban network, and Gary Prado, the Bolivian officer who captured him at the Yuro Ravine. Vázquez Viaña believes that the time and place were those originally planned, and that Che had no intention of letting months go by before submitting his cadres—neophyte Bolivians and reckless Cubans—to the test of combat. In his view, the expedition did not founder merely because it was premature, but as a result of a myriad other factors.[56] Prado believes Che's decision was appropriate given the circumstances: the alternatives—fleeing without fighting, or disbanding his group—were less attractive. Flight would not remedy their discovery by the army, and dismissal was not a viable option.[57] However, Fidel Castro himself has stated that premature hostilities exacted a heavy toll.* Given the Bolivian army's initial disarray and its natural tendency to elude combat, the guerrillas could have abandoned the field and started over later without any major problem. U.S. intelligence repeatedly emphasized that the Fourth Division's patrols, based in Camiri, pursued the guerrillas half-heartedly at best.†

On March 23, half the army unit of eighty men sent to Che's camp was attacked by the guerrillas in the Ñancahuazú gorge, in a textbook ambush. Overflights by the air force alerted the rebels; long experience allowed Che and his companions to execute the operation perfectly. Seven members of the armed forces, including one officer, were killed immediately; fourteen more surrendered, among them four wounded. The guerrillas did not suffer a single casualty. Their booty encompassed sixteen rifles and two thousand rounds of ammunition, three mortars, two Uzi machine guns, one submachine gun, and two radio outfits. From a strictly military and tactical point of view, the exercise was a complete success: it was a first, victorious com-

*The CIA also believed that the Cubans were overtaken by events: "Moreover, this professionalism has been attained even though the guerrillas were discovered by accident well before they felt themselves ready to begin actual operations." Central Intelligence Agency, Directorate of Intelligence, Intelligence Memorandum, The Bolivian Guerrilla Movement: An Interim Assessment, August 8, 1967 (Secret), NSF, Country File, Bolivia, vol. 4, box 8, Intelligence memo, LBJ Library, p. 4.

† "After considerable prodding, [Bolivian] Army patrols began to follow up reports of groups of bearded strangers in southeast Bolivia. On 23 March, an Army patrol stumbled into a guerrilla hideout." Central Intelligence Agency, Intelligence Memorandum, Cuban-Inspired Guerrilla Activity in Bolivia, June 14 (Secret), National Security File, Intelligence File, Guerrilla Problem in Latin America, box 2, no. 6, Memo, LBJ Library.

bat experience for the guerrilla unit, both effective and economical. But in its aftermath, the small and isolated group of poorly armed and ill-fed men would have to confront an entire army which, while undeniably mediocre, would enjoy growing U.S. support.

Denial was no longer possible: a full-fledged guerrilla war was underway in Bolivia, involving both natives and foreigners. Its location, strength, and tactical capacity were now fully recognized. All the guerrillas' previous plans, so meticulously designed, were overtaken by events. Further meetings with the Communist Party leadership, the recruitment of new Bolivian cadres, the coordinated creation of an urban network, and a timely publication of the guerrillas' goals, became unthinkable. On April 14 the Communist Party was banned, forcing even those militants distanced from the leadership, like Loyola Guzmán (the youth leader in charge of finances for the urban network), to go underground. They would no longer be able to fulfill the missions assigned them in the cities.

Régis Debray believes today that the skirmish was not entirely negative. Though it by no means constituted a strategic triumph, Che was glad that his troops were no longer idle. Combat helped harden the men, raising their morale and clarifying the situation.[58] It is worth recalling the context of Guevara's unfortunate decision: the climate of apathy and defeat among his men, and his own state of mind. He had become increasingly taciturn and introspective:

> Sitting to one side on a hammock, smoking a pipe under his plastic shelter, he read, wrote, thought, sipped maté, cleaned his rifle, listened to Havana Radio on his transistor at night. [He gave] laconic orders. He was absent. Locked within himself. A tense atmosphere in the rest of the camp. Disputes, national sensitivities, discussions about the tactics to be followed, all exacerbated by exhaustion, the lack of sleep, and the continual hostility of the jungle. Anyone else would have mixed with the troops, talking or joking with them. Che applied a bare discipline, without any niceties or personal relationships.[59]

Before Che's return from the reconnaissance mission, three important figures showed up at the camp: Régis Debray, Ciro Bustos, and Tania. Tania was not supposed to be there; her mission resided in guiding recruits and visitors to the guerrilla hideout, then returning to La Paz. But this time she burned her bridges. Either deliberately or unconsciously—in a mixture of fantasy, guilt, desire, an obsession with guerrilla warfare and her probable love for Che Guevara, negligence, and nervousness—the Cuban intelligence agent left her jeep at the calamine house, which would be taken over by the army days later. In it she had abandoned telephone directories, clothes, and other belongings that facilitated her identification by the military.

As Che would write in his journal, Tania had been "individually spotted; two years of good and patient work have been lost." According to the German magazine *Der Spiegel,* Che slapped her when he returned from the reconnaissance march and found her at the camp decked out in guerrilla attire.[60] One of his few links to the urban network was lost; the others would vanish in the following weeks, leaving the guerrillas completely isolated.

Who was Tania? Why did she insist on joining a guerrilla campaign for which she was not trained, and which she could have served better in the city? A number of myths arose after her death three months later, when she quickly metamorphosed into a "heroic guerrilla warrior" exalted by the Cubans. According to one hypothesis, she was actually a double agent for the KGB or the East German Ministry for State Security (MFS). This interpretation was based on flimsy evidence and mainly on an interview with a former East German agent, Gunther Mannel, which was published on May 26, 1968.[61] Mannel, who defected in 1961, recalled recognizing Tania when he saw a picture of her after her death. He had been her handler in East Germany, and claimed that she had worked for the MFS since 1958. Her specialty lay in waiting on foreign visitors—which was how she met Che in Berlin during his first stay there in 1960; in addition, she was a master at the trade traditionally associated with female spies in the literature. According to Mannel, in 1960 the KGB decided to expand its presence in Cuba; he was entrusted with recruiting Tania for that purpose. This he duly accomplished in a Berlin train station.[62] This version of events has never been confirmed, and Mannel did not supply any further details. Daniel James reiterated the story in his biography of Che, offering intelligent but unsubstantiated conjectures.

Markus Wolfe, the renowned head of East German counterintelligence, immortalized as Karla in the novels of John Le Carré, was interviewed in 1995 by the producers of a documentary on Che Guevara. He stated categorically that Tania never worked for the MFS.[63] Moreover, Wolfe never mentioned her in any of his public interviews or during his trial in Germany after the fall of the Berlin Wall; he refers to her in his memoirs, published in 1997, but abstains from implicating her as his agent. Of course, he could have been lying; or perhaps, having now reached his eighties, he could no longer recall the names of all his subordinates. But Tania was a notorious figure and it seems implausible that he would forget a Mata Hari of her stature, if indeed she had been under his control.

It is in fact quite likely that Tania, like thousands of other young people from Germany and the East bloc, was indeed approached at one time by her country's intelligence services. With her excellent Spanish and her Argentine origins, she was a natural candidate for international espionage. She may even have traveled to Cuba in August of that year while still under Wolfe's orders. But there is no evidence, either in the German and Soviet archives or in her behavior in Bolivia, to suggest that she was a provocateur or double agent. It is of course possible that she simply fell in love with Guevara, and that this made her commit a series of mistakes unworthy of an agent with her training and experience.

Ulises Estrada maintains, three decades later, that she was infatuated with Che and wanted to be by his side at any cost.* Like Michèle Firk in Guatemala in the 1960's and the admirers of Subcomandante Marcos in Chiapas today, she aspired to be a guerrilla fighter—not just a bureaucratic liaison between leaders and combatants in La Paz, escorting people to hotels and helping them establish contact, a mere witness to important decisions and heroic deeds. Her sights were set on a greater goal: to participate in guerrilla warfare. When hostilities broke out, her wish was fulfilled; she was unable to return to La Paz in her previous identity, and was forced to stay in the camp.

Were she and Che lovers? It is impossible to say. The surviving witnesses of this period have given contradictory reports. Only five people who might have a well-founded opinion are still alive; among them, Pombo and Urbano are Cuban apparatchiks with no independent say in the matter. Two of the others, Debray and Bustos, have refused either to suggest that they were lovers or to deny it. Debray is skeptical, because he doubts that in the jungle Che had the energy required for anything more than a platonic relationship.[†] Bustos has never addressed the issue. Benigno was unclear in his book, but in a later interview asserted that they did have an affair— though he provides no conclusive arguments to back his claim.[64]

There are two elements in favor of this interpretation. First of all, the precedents: Tania and Che met in late 1960, attended countless meetings and parties together, and were both in Prague during the spring of 1966; everything indicates, at the very least, that she was in love with him. In the second place, when Tania's body was recovered in August, rumors circulated that she had been three months pregnant at the time of her death. However, there is no record of an autopsy. Some have speculated that the autopsy may have been carried out by the same physician who amputated Che's hands after his death, a Bolivian named Abraham Baptista Moisés.[‡] If Tania was pregnant,

*Interview with the author.

[†] Interview with the author, Paris, November 3, 1995.

[‡] According to the head of the CIA's Country Team in Bolivia, Gustavo Villoldo, "Tania was not subjected to an autopsy. She was not pregnant. Nothing was really known, primarily because there was no autopsy. There was a rumor that she was pregnant, but I do not believe it was true." Conversely, Félix Rodríguez, the other CIA agent on the ground in Bolivia, has stated in interviews, including one with the author, that Tania was pregnant. Villoldo, interview.

the father may have been Che Guevara. But there is no definitive evidence regarding all of this, and one may suppose that, if there were, some trustworthy witness would have surfaced in the course of the last thirty years.* It seems plausible that Tania was simply a revolutionary groupie, quite naturally fascinated by the larger-than-life guerrilla fighter she met in Berlin. The situation could easily lend itself to temptations and misinterpretations. But it appears unlikely that Che rediscovered the enchantments of his earlier Argentine loves in the austere and somewhat masculine figure of Tania.

Ciro Bustos, the second important visitor to the camp mentioned earlier, arrived at the camp with Tania in March. He was not the first Argentine summoned to Bolivia. During the first days of February, a leader of the Argentine journalists' union, Eduardo Josami, was contacted by Tania in La Paz and then conducted to Camiri. There he learned that Che had left camp on his reconnaissance mission and would be back in two weeks. Josami opted to depart and return a month later, rather than awaken suspicions in the area. As things turned out, he never made it to the base. He now recalls that "the purpose of the trip was never clear to me." He was shocked at the "precariousness" of the rebels' situation, and was concerned that so many journeys back and forth in the jeep with Tania and two other Peruvian recruits would finally alert the armed forces.† They did.

In contrast, Bustos did eventually reach Ñancahuazú. He had known Che since 1963, at the time of Jorge Masetti's failed expedition. Tania had invited Bustos to the camp in January; he arrived on March 6, along with Régis Debray. A mediocre painter and naive leftist, Bustos had been assigned his mandate by Che long before. He was to prepare Guevara's return to his native country, organizing Communist dissidents and factions, Peronists, and even Trotskyists in order to assemble an armed group in Argentina. Bustos was not scheduled to spend much time in Bolivia; he was to leave quickly and discreetly. Instead, he ended up spending three years in the Camiri jail, along with Régis Debray.

The Frenchman was on his third trip to Bolivia in as many years, but this time his mission was more purely political in nature. His purpose was to transmit messages and analyses from Fidel Castro to Che Guevara, and back. In addition, Debray was meant to serve as liaison between Che and

*Benigno notes that if she was three months pregnant, Che cannot have been the father; the guerrillas were split into two groups on April 20, and Tania died on August 31. According to Benigno, the father was Alejandro, a member of the rearguard with whom Tania had a love-hate relationship. Benigno, interview with the author, Paris, November 8, 1996.

†Eduardo Josami, written communication to the author, November 5, 1996. He was referring in particular to Juan Pablo Chang Navarro, el Chino, a Peruvian activist who visited Che, was stranded with the guerrillas when fighting began, and died in October of that year.

other revolutionaries in Latin America; his next destination was São Paulo, to coordinate Guevara's plans with those of Carlos Marighela.[65] His stay at the camp was likewise intended to last only a few days, so he could leave Bolivia as quickly as possible.

The three visitors spent less than a month with Che at the guerrilla base. Their departure would trigger another, debilitating crisis that would divide the guerrilla forces in two. But it was preceded by several additional events which shattered any hopes of rest or tranquillity. First, the guerrillas' communications equipment broke down; then a series of desertions and indiscretions took place, furnishing the Bolivian army with a gold mine of information.

Communications were the Achilles' heel of Che's expedition. The guerrillas had brought two huge, heavy American transmitters still operating with vacuum tubes and dating from the Second World War, which required an autonomous generator. According to one of the officers in charge of Bolivian affairs in Cuba,

> They had a radio transmitter which never really worked, an enormous machine with its own motor which they were never even able to install. They never had communications with the outside world. The only radio they had was a six-band receiver with which they listened to Radio Havana, but they were unable to transmit anything.[66]

One of the two devices got wet and stopped working in January; it had to be buried in a cave. As for the other one, two of its tubes were broken, and El Loro, Jorge Vázquez Viaña, was commissioned to buy new ones in Santa Cruz. Instead of purchasing a box of them he only bought two, and deposited them on the floor of the jeep. The tubes were totally useless by the time they reached the guerrillas' headquarters after 1,600 kilometers of bad roads.[67] The guerrillas ran out of gas for the generator in March; they were never able to obtain any more. Their two other radios, designed for short-wave aficionados, soon broke down as well. They had a radio-telegraph—but lacked the codes needed to operate it:

> Everything was improvised. The communications equipment is supposed to work, but when you get there it doesn't work at all, it's a piece of shit. You buy walkie-talkies that are supposed to be the best in the world and they turn out to be useless, they're really toys for children. Then the batteries run out and there are no more batteries.[68]

Beginning in February, Che lost contact with La Paz, Havana, or anywhere else, save to receive messages. He could not transmit reports, pleas for help, or war communiqués.* When the urban network disintegrated and thus communications by messenger were severed, all links to the outside world were lost. Che was alone. Cuba became aware of this situation in February; from then on, Havana's only news from Bolivia stemmed from press reports. Che's support team on the island obtained no direct information, except when messengers arrived from the camp during the first few months and through the urban network liaison, Renán Montero, when he returned to Cuba in March. Given the central importance of communications in guerrilla warfare, isolation was an ominous sign indeed. Havana did not seem unduly alarmed.

The onset of hostilities and the guerrillas' exposure caused new desertions and led the armed forces to the rebel camps. At a general meeting on March 25, Che scolded everybody, and lashed out at Marcos and removed him as head of the vanguard; he offered either to demote him to foot soldier or ship him back to Havana. He then declared that three of Moisés Guevara's recruits were useless, as they contributed nothing and refused to work. They requested permission to go home; Che determined to dismiss them as soon as possible. In the meantime, if they refused to do their duties they would be deprived of food, along with another Bolivian recruit named Eusebio, "a thief, a liar, and a hypocrite"; he, too, asked to leave.

On April 7, the Bolivian army's Fourth Division occupied the rebels' main camp. Their field hospital, medicines, oven, and countless belongings were taken over, providing military intelligence with a lode of data. Even so, the army suffered another defeat on April 10: two ambushes along the river leading to the camp resulted in nine dead, a dozen wounded, thirteen prisoners, and considerable booty for the guerrillas, including weapons, hand grenades, and ammunition. Rolando's group displayed great tactical skill by not retreating after the first ambush; rather than strike and flee, it struck twice. This was the most inspiring episode of the war for the guerrillas; it demoralized the government, encouraged rebel supporters, and thoroughly disconcerted the regime of René Barrientos.

The situation was indeed alarming for the Bolivian authorities. In just two weeks, they had suffered eighteen dead and twenty wounded, and lost considerable amounts of supplies. During the same period, the guerrillas had only one casualty—Jesús Suárez Gayol (el Rubio). Morale among the armed forces was falling rapidly. Officers exaggerated the number of rebels—some spoke of five hundred—and their military prowess. Barrientos toured the area and promised to crush the uprising as soon as possible;

---

*"No, we were never able to transmit a single message from the mountains. Ever. We always received, but were never able to transmit anything. It wasn't possible." Benigno, interview.

but his nervousness and erratic behavior were obvious to all. Only with time and considerable U.S. prodding did General Alfredo Ovando finally take charge of the government's response. He realized that the war would inevitably drag on, requiring foreign arms, training, and intelligence; he would need elite fighting units that could be effective against irregular forces.

Though the military were certain of Che's presence, they preferred to speak of Cubans and foreigners in general. They avoided mentioning him by name whenever possible: "The first reports about the possible presence of Che Guevara have been handled with great care; we did not make them public, but [have] contacted the intelligence services of other countries to see if they can be confirmed."[69] The United States did not want the news to spread either, and tried to keep out the international press.* The authorities' discretion served them well. As Mario Monje pointed out in a letter to the Central Committee of the PCB in 1968, the fact that Che's identity was kept secret might have protected him, but it also prevented militants from joining an uprising led by the *comandante,* now a legend throughout Latin America.

How and when was Che's presence in Bolivia definitively ascertained? Gustavo Villoldo, who first arrived in Bolivia in February and returned in late July to head the CIA's Country Team, became convinced of Guevara's role thanks to three infiltrators in the urban network mounted by the Cubans and Communist Party. Villoldo refuses, to this day, to reveal the names of the two Bolivians and one Peruvian, who still live under CIA protection. He adds, "I can tell you that we placed a series of assets and those assets began giving us the information we needed to neutralize [the uprising]. That entire mechanism, that logistical support . . . left the guerrillas completely isolated. We completely penetrated the urban network."[70]

Larry Sternfield, the CIA station chief in Bolivia until April 1967, has confirmed that he knew of Che's presence before the Bolivian authorities, thanks to mid-level Bolivian sources working for the CIA.[71] John Tilton, Sternfield's successor, has corroborated this in his unpublished memoirs: "Barrientos had called me at home that night to ask about a rumor that Che Guevara was in the country. I arranged a meeting and told him I thought the rumor was true."[72] It is not surprising that the CIA establishment at Langley was reluctant to believe its station chief in La Paz; it had reacted similarly in regard to Lawrence Devlin's reports about Che in the Congo.

---

*"[The press] received all kinds of guarantees and confidences from the U.S. Embassy and military advisers from Washington assuring them that the Bolivian panic was all a maneuver to get more military assistance from the United States." Andrew St. George, "How the US Got Che," *True* Magazine, April 1969, p. 92.

Tilton still resents the obstacles he confronted when he tried to transmit his suspicions to CIA headquarters.

By the time Debray and Bustos were captured on April 20, the armed forces already possessed all the information supplied by the deserters and their semiprisoner Salustio Choque Choque, and were already convinced that the guerrillas' leader was Che Guevara.* In addition, the Bolivian Communist cadre Jorge Vázquez Viaña, El Loro, was wounded and captured by the army on April 24. Some have said that he was trying to flee; others, that he was simply careless. After surgery in a military hospital, he was interrogated by a CIA agent who went by the nom de guerre of Eduardo González. To complicate matters further, there were two CIA officers operating in Bolivia under the same name: González, who arrived first; and Gustavo Villoldo who, as previously noted, disembarked in July and would later appear in photos alongside Che's corpse at Vallegrande.† It was the former González, now deceased, who interrogated Vázquez Viaña, Debray, and Bustos. González set a trap for El Loro, presenting himself as a journalist from Panama; Vázquez Viaña spilled everything he knew, down to the last detail.[73]

During his first week of interrogation and beatings, Debray stuck to his story: he was a journalist who had come to Bolivia to interview the guerrillas; he had heard rumors of Che's presence, but had not actually seen him. Subsequently, he would acknowledge having interviewed Che, but maintained that the *comandante* was no longer in Bolivia. Armed with El Loro's information, González confronted Bustos. The latter was the first to succumb, drawing portraits of the guerrillas and giving a full description of the camp, complete with maps and access routes. Bustos broke down when his captors showed him the photographs of his two daughters whom they threatened to kidnap. Lacking the integrity and stamina needed to resist interrogation, Bustos was not even beaten.

On April 18, Che himself triggered a new crisis for the guerrillas. Forced by the revelations of the deserters to relocate, ensure the safe departure of his guests Debray and Bustos, and seek new supply routes, he decided to separate his forces. Intended as a temporary measure, the division would prove both lasting and fatal. The group was too small to be split; its two halves, lacking any form of communication, would spend the next four months seeking one another in the Bolivian wilderness. Though they came

*"The capture of Debray and Bustos was not essential in finding out about Che; that was already known." Villoldo, interview.

† The distinction between the two agents named González was communicated to the author by Gustavo Villoldo during an interview in Miami on November 22, 1995. It was corroborated by Larry Sternfield in a telephone conversation with the author on November 4, 1996.

within a few hundred meters of each other and even opened fire among themselves upon several occasions, they never re-established contact.

Originally, Che's intention was to provide a safe escape route for Bustos and Debray. Both men offered, perhaps reluctantly, to join the guerrillas when they grasped how difficult it would be for them to depart from the area, now surrounded by the army. Che objected that Debray would be more useful elsewhere, relaying messages to Fidel and organizing foreign support. An international campaign had become all the more necessary when hostilities broke out and the urban network collapsed. Che noted in his diary that Debray had been too "vehement" in his request to leave the camp, but he finally agreed. He left his second in command, Joaquín (Juan Vitalio Acuña) with seventeen guerrillas, including Tania, who could no longer return to the city, several sick men, and four of Moisés Guevara's recruits, who were meant to be dismissed as soon as possible. With the remaining thirty combatants, Che headed south toward Muyupampa; he hoped to capture the town and dispatch his two visitors in the ensuing confusion. Then his group and Joaquín's would rejoin, avoiding any contact with the enemy.

The army, however, reached Muyupampa first. Guevara's vanguard, in the meantime, met with a Chilean-English journalist who had supposedly been led to the guerrillas by some children. George Andrew Roth made a deal: in exchange for an interview with Inti Peredo, if set free he would return to Camiri with Debray and Bustos, vouching for their status as journalists.* The arrangement did not work out; Debray and Bustos were arrested by the police regardless, and handed over to the army's Fourth Division. They were interrogated with the violence typical of Latin America's armed forces, and probably would have been killed had their arrests not become known, setting off an outcry in the world press. Pressure from the CIA (which was not acting out of altruism, but simply in the hope of obtaining more information) also helped. Both men were judged and sentenced to thirty years in jail. They were released only in 1970, when a new government came to power in Bolivia.

Che had failed to establish alternative, back-up meeting points with his rearguard in case the original rendezvous was foiled by the army or unexpected circumstances. The lack of communications—either between the two guerrilla units or a third party (La Paz or even Havana) made it impossible for the two detachments to regroup. When army maneuvers forced Che to march north, away from the original meeting point with Joaquín, all con-

---

*Roth did not mention this tradeoff in his own account; he notes only that the guerrillas asked him to fulfill this task. George Andrew Roth, "I Was Arrested with Debray," in *Evergreen* magazine, April 20, 1967.

tact was lost. Still, he never stopped hoping for a reunion. When his companions begged him to change strategy, he became furious: "We once dared to say to him, 'Why don't we stop searching for Joaquín and let them fend for themselves?' He didn't even let us finish. He threw a huge tantrum."[74] Because the area was sparsely populated and its few inhabitants were reluctant to speak with the guerrillas, out of fear or hostility, in the absence of direct communication only luck would have brought the two groups together again. And Che's expedition was singularly unlucky.

Why did Che fail to set up a contingency rendezvous? The mystery remains unanswered thirty years later. In the most profound analysis written by a Bolivian officer, Gary Prado Salmón speculates that Che erred because he overestimated his own forces, while underestimating the army's.[75] The key should more likely be sought in Che's state of mind at that time; he was wracked by fatigue, asthma, ill humor, and innumerable other problems. In his war diary, he recorded constant asthma attacks and depression. None of this was conducive to intelligent, prudent, or farsighted decisions.

Che had hoped, during those weeks in April and May, to forge links with peasants in the area—though he knew it would not be easy. He achieved exactly the opposite. The death of two civilians created ill feeling among local residents; the armed forces' anti-Communist propaganda proved effective; and the communiqués issued by the newly formed National Liberation Army, as Che baptized his band of warriors, went largely unheeded by an increasingly censored press. The local population barely sold supplies to the guerrillas, and only with great reluctance. And they immediately reported any contact to the authorities.

On April 15, Havana published an essay by Che in *Tricontinental* magazine, in which he famously called for "the creation of two, three, several Vietnams." He also exalted violence and mortal sacrifice—or martyrdom, some would say—in unusually explicit terms:

> Hatred as an element of struggle; unbending hatred for the enemy, which pushes a human being beyond his natural limitations, making him into an effective, violent, selective, and cold-blooded killing machine. This is what our soldiers must become; a people without hatred cannot triumph over a brutal enemy.[76]

Che's article was also openly anti-Soviet and propagandistic in tone.* The magazine published six photos of him, two in civilian clothing and four in

*"There is a shameful reality. Vietnam . . . is tragically isolated. In a bitter irony, the solidarity of the progressive world with . . . Vietnam is like the plebeians' encouragement to gladiators in the Roman circus. The point is not to wish a victim well, but to share his fate." Ernesto Che Guevara, "Mensaje a la *Tricontinental*," quoted in *Obra revolucionaria* (Mexico, D.F.: Ediciones ERA, 1969), p. 642.

olive-green fatigues. As he noted in his diary on April 15, "now there should be no doubt of my presence here." At that point, the Bolivian army's counterinsurgency campaign turned into a manhunt. All local resources were mobilized toward a single goal: to capture and/or kill Che Guevara. Soon, thousands of soldiers were combing a huge and inhospitable area, tracking down less than forty weak and hungry men, split into two isolated groups.

The United States had been involved since the beginning. True, two of the three Cuban CIA agents, Félix Rodríguez and Gustavo Villoldo, did not fully join the counterinsurgency offensive until June; they landed in El Alto, outside La Paz, on July 31. But analysis meetings had been taking place in Washington since April. According to Andrew St. George, the journalist who interviewed Fidel and Che in the Sierra Maestra, on April 9 a high-level committee met for the first time in the American capital to work out a response to reports of Che's presence in Bolivia.* The conclusive proof of Che's location, according to St. George, was a photo of the bread oven at Ñancahuazú: its rounded clay design replicated the ovens of Vietnam and Dien Bien Phu.

After a visit to La Paz by U.S. General William Tope, Washington concluded that "these people have a tremendous problem but we are going to have great difficulty in getting together on even how to approach it much less find a solution."[77] On April 29, U.S. officers and twelve soldiers, led by Ralph "Pappy" Shelton, headed for Bolivia. They immediately began a nineteen-week training course for several hundred Bolivian troops. The latter would become the first group of Rangers in Bolivia; less than six months later they would capture Che Guevara and defeat his guerrilla expedition.

Yet the months of May and June were not all bad for the rebels. At the end of May, they occupied three villages in a single day, in a show of ubiquity and professionalism which demoralized the army once again. But while Che's guerrilla fighters had an abundance of courage and tenacity, they showed less and less tactical creativity. Indeed, Che hardly conducted any offensive actions at all in Bolivia: he never attacked any military facilities, either with commandos or with larger units, or any communications routes near urban settlements. Most of the time, he simply reacted to the army's assaults with ambushes and defensive maneuvers, or by occupying villages.

*St. George, "How the US," p. 93. The first White House document to confirm Che's presence is dated May 11, and says: "This is the first credible report that Che Guevara is alive and operating in South America." Walt Rostow to the President, May 11, 1967 (Secret). The first available CIA report stating categorically that Che was in Bolivia is dated June 14; it is a summary which obviously recapitulates previous information. Central Intelligence Agency, Cuban-Inspired Guerrilla Activity, June 14 (Secret).

During this period, he lost several men who were both valuable and dear to him: San Luis, or Rolando, on April 25, whom he had known since the Sierra Maestra and who was perhaps the best military man on the team; Carlos Coello, or Tuma, whose death he mourned deeply; and Papi, on July 30, 1967, in a minor skirmish. Though Papi had disappointed him repeatedly, his death was still a terrible blow. If his men kept being picked off at that pace, without any new recruits to take their places, his guerrilla war was doomed. No matter how successful his forces were in striking at the army, they would eventually be worn away. This was already obvious to the leadership in Cuba; public news of the guerrilla casualties was a clear indication that disaster was fast approaching.*

Until mid-year, though, the military balance of power was not necessarily unfavorable to the revolutionaries. According to a secret memorandum written in mid-June by the U.S. National Security Adviser, Walt Rostow, to Lyndon Johnson,

> They [the guerrillas] have so far clearly outclassed the Bolivian security forces. The performance of the government units has revealed a serious lack of command coordination, officer leadership and troop training and discipline.[78]

However, the rebels' advantage was misleading. Che's real weakness lay elsewhere. The local inhabitants of the area he crisscrossed for months on end never supported him, never welcomed him, never understood the meaning of his expedition. Not a single peasant joined the guerrillas, neither in late June when the group came into closer contact with the population as the area of operations shifted, nor when Che practiced as a dentist in several villages. The guerrillas also could not profit from the mining crisis that broke out in mid-June, when workers at the Siglo XX, Huanuni, and Catavi mines went on strike supported by the student movement. The existence of a strong labor movement was one of the reasons Che had chosen Bolivia in the first place. Separated from the miners by the Andes and over a thousand kilometers, without any political ties or means of communication, the guerrillas stood by helplessly as the government massacred dozens of demonstrators on the day of San Juan. The uprising soon subsided.

Two additional crises beset the expedition between April and August. The first had to do with the urban network. It had never really functioned, and ended up in the hands of dissident Communists. In the height of paradox, despite their Party's distaste for the armed struggle, they were nonethe-

*Lino, interview. Lino acknowledges, however, that Havana did not know Joaquín's group had been isolated until it was announced that the rearguard had been annihilated on August 31.

less persecuted and repressed by the government for their links with Che when the PCB was banned. Mario Monje harassed some of the Communists who sympathized with the guerrillas; the government took care of the rest. The Party's leadership contributed neither supplies, arms, medicines, nor assistance to the guerrillas, much less combatants. Once Tania joined the rearguard and Debray was captured, there was only one foreigner left to work the cities: Renán Montero, or Iván, whose role in Che's Bolivian venture remains a mystery. There could be only one conclusion for the Cubans in the field: "If somebody was not sent through to make contact with the city, the prospects looked very poor to us. Logically, we discussed it among ourselves, we could not possibly tell Che."[79]

Montero was originally a Cuban; thanks to his services during the Sandinista revolution, he would later obtain Nicaraguan citizenship. He was probably the only Cuban within the network who was not part of Che's old guard; he belonged to the Cuban state security services, though not to Piñeiro's group. His assignment in Bolivia, following his arrival in September 1966, was to, along with Tania, receive the Cubans, including Che. He and Tania argued incessantly, mainly—according to Ulises Estrada—because of Renán's romantic intentions and Tania's rejection.[80] Tensions between them soon reached dangerous heights, if we are to believe Pombo's diary. After the combatants had been safely escorted to Ñancahuazú, Montero's mission was to become a businessman, as Che noted in his diary, and penetrate Bolivian society. Iván attained the latter aim, seducing a young woman related to Barrientos. Encouraged by Che, he became engaged to her.

Renán Montero suddenly vanished at the end of February or early March. He left Bolivia, traveled to Paris, and appeared in Cuba at the end of April, as noted in a coded message from Havana to Che.[81] In Montero's own account, the reason for his departure was quite simple: he needed to have his papers in order. His passport and visa expired after six months in Bolivia. Since he had received no further instructions from Che—communications between the city and the guerrillas had been severed for weeks—he decided to proceed according to the preestablished plan: he left the country to renew his papers.[82] This explanation is either disingenuous or deceitful. As Benigno noted, "He would not have left on his own initiative. The decision was not his to make. I have no doubt that he received instructions. He was sent to France in order to recover and then come back, but for reasons unknown he did not. I never understood the true story of Renán."*

---

*Benigno, interview. Lino, in contrast, believes that when communications were cut between Havana and Bolivia, Montero decided to leave on his own. Already ill with acute amebiasis, he was extremely depressed by Che's refusal to enlist him in the guerrilla group.

According to Montero, he was still in La Paz when Tania departed from the capital for the last time in early March with Bustos and Debray.* Consequently, he knew that she was now "burned," useless as an urban contact. He was also aware of the newly begun hostilities, and the intractable problems faced by the Communists since they had been forced underground. Finally, his marriage plans were well advanced and had provided him with a number of high-level contacts, who could easily have helped him with his papers: "Three or four days after the first battle, I saw Barrientos and the family took the opportunity to back my request for land in the Alto Beni."[83] Under those circumstances, it seems unlikely that he would abandon his post and fly to Paris just to renew his papers.

The other reason, mentioned both by Montero and by Che himself in his diary, was illness. But this explanation does not fit in with the custom of the times, which was to suffer any adversity and overcome any weakness for the sake of the cause. In his journal, already quoted, Pombo states that Papi Martínez Tamayo had expressed his misgivings about Montero to Che as early as January: "Iván will not stay, because he has his doubts about the situation." This soon proved true. Even if Montero decided to return to Cuba on his own initiative, a question remains: how did Havana react to his departure from Bolivia, when he was the only contact left in the urban network? Montero himself acknowledges that he "spent several long months waiting in Cuba," from early April until September; he expected to be sent back to Bolivia, but "it was decided that I should not, for security reasons. Once the guerrilla's presence was revealed, it would have been dangerous."[84]

At that time, guerrilla cadres were supposed to die at their posts. Any other conduct was seen as a lack of discipline or even treason, and brutally punished. Not only was Montero never penalized for leaving his post; he still enjoys, thirty years later, the favor and protection of the Cuban government. Given that his own explanation is highly implausible, there are two other hypotheses: either somebody tipped him off, advising him to leave Bolivia and re-establish contact with Havana from another safe country, or else he received ambiguous instructions from Cuba, which he interpreted as authorization to leave. One way or the other, from the time he arrived in Havana (or Paris), the Cuban leadership held all the information it needed to conclude that Che's mission had failed. Its source was Iván, and this has been his insurance policy for the last thirty years: Renán Montero knew that Castro, Raúl, and Piñeiro knew that Che's expedition was floundering.

---

* Montero, interview. Debray, however, recalls that Montero never showed his face during those early days in March, and he always believed that Montero had already left Bolivia by then. He argues that the reason Tania was forced to take him and Bustos up to the mountains was precisely because Renán had already left; the argument is plausible, and Renán's claim that he was still in La Paz sounds somewhat weak. Debray, interview.

The next-to-the-last coded message Che received from Havana informed him that a "new comrade" would "soon" be taking Iván's place; the new comrade never arrived.

The second crisis eventually cost Che his life in Bolivia. It derived from a handicap that had pursued him from childhood: his asthma. Considerably aggravated since the onset of hostilities in April, it was now accompanied by other illnesses. In May he wrote,

> When I began the hike, I had a terrible colic with vomiting and diarrhea. It was controlled by demerol, and I lost consciousness as I was carried in a hammock; when I awoke I was much better, but covered in my own filth like a newborn infant.[85]

The illness severely affected his mental agility and capacity for decision-making. On two different occasions (June 3 and when planning the departure of Debray and Bustos), Che noted in his diary that "my brain did not work quickly enough," "I didn't have the courage," "I lacked the energy."[86] The vegetation, climate, his generalized weakness, and, especially, the scarcity of medicines, finally defeated Guevara. Each decision, each internal dispute and casualty, exacerbated his condition. Che resorted to a variety of potions and home remedies. Hanging from a branch, he asked his men to beat him on the chest with a rifle butt; he tried smoking different herbs in a desperate search for ephedrine. He stopped eating foods that might trigger an attack, and injected himself endovenously with novocaine or cortisone. When he could no longer walk, he rode a mule. Unable to carry his rucksack, for the first time he had to be helped. Though his determination never flagged, his body had reached its limit.

From June 23, Che's diary contained daily references to his asthma, the lack of medicines, the futility of other remedies, and his despair at finding any relief. This led him to a decision which initially offered some hope: taking the locality of Samaipata, at a crossroads between Santa Cruz and Cochabamba. It was the largest town to be occupied by the guerrillas during their calamitous trek through the Bolivian southeast. The assault was every bit as professional as their first ambush: while some of them harangued the population, the rest fanned out scavenging for supplies and medicines; Che remained hidden in a van appropriated by his men. However, either they could not locate the medicines or there were simply none available. The purpose of the entire operation was defeated: "In terms of supplies, the action was a failure. . . . Nothing of use was bought, and none of the medicines I needed was found."[87]

Mario Monje drew his own conclusions from the fiasco at Samaipata. Initially, he was encouraged by the fact that the guerrillas had descended

into the plain, as this meant they had broken through the military encirclement and were headed for the Chapare zone, far better suited to an
armed struggle. But, when the press reported that the guerrillas were returning south, he exclaimed at a meeting of the Party leadership, "Gentlemen,
Che will not leave here alive. The entire group is going to be exterminated.
They have made the worst possible mistake; we must send somebody to
Cuba and tell them to save Che."[88] After a long discussion, it was decided
that Monje would go to Havana and present his plan for Che's escape. He
traveled through Santiago, Chile, where he shared his project with the
Chilean Communists, asking them for assistance in reaching the island.
Their reaction surprised him: first of all, they were incredulous; then, they
hesitated in their response. Monje was stuck in Santiago for several months;
he never reached Cuba, mainly because the authorities in Havana did not
respond to requests for safe passage or a visa. If the Chilean Communists
were reluctant to send him on his way, their passivity arose from the
Cubans' own reticence. They would never have acted as they did on their
own.*

After the failed attempt to obtain medicines in Samaipata, Che dispatched Benigno, the strongest man remaining on his team, to the caves of
Ñancahuazú over two hundred kilometers away, to recover the asthma
medication buried there since the previous November. But the caves were
discovered by the Bolivian army as he approached them. The announcement was the worst news yet during that worst month of the war. Already,
on July 31, eleven rucksacks, the last medicines, and a tape recorder used to
copy messages from Havana had been lost; that marked the end of communications from the outside world. On August 8, Che yielded to despair, stab-
bing his mare in rage; he was overwhelmed by asthma attacks, diarrhea, and
the unending string of setbacks, as he confessed in his diary.[89] A Bolivian
officer, Captain Vargas Salinas, asserts that the Peredo brothers had in fact
assumed command since August and that Che had even attempted suicide.
This has not been corroborated in any other diary or account.†

The army's discovery of the caves was "the worst blow they have dealt us;
somebody talked. Who? That is the question."[90] An informant led the military to the cave near the first camp, which contained documents, photo-

*This explanation was suggested to the author by Volodia Teitelboim, the Chilean
writer and Communist leader, during a conversation in Mexico City on November 12, 1996.
By 1967, Teitelboim was already one of the top leaders in the Chilean Communist Party,
and would have been informed of any decisions taken at the time.
† Mario Vargas Salinas, *El Che, Mito y Realidad* (Cochabamba-La Paz: Editorial Los
amigos del libro, 1988), p. 57. Vargas Salinas was the retired general who announced to the
press in November 1995 that Che's body had not been cremated but buried, thus triggering
a long, costly, and thus far futile search.

graphs, supplies, medicines, and weapons. According to three survivors—two guerrillas, one in the government—the informant was Ciro Bustos.* Che had recruited him due to his links with the Salta expedition; he trusted him without knowing him very well. In Debray's view, Bustos was the one who led the military to the base: "He would disappear, we could only exchange a few words in the courtyard. But I knew what he was telling them, because I could see what our interrogators knew."[91]

Benigno also believes that Bustos guided the army to the caves. Che had brought him from Argentina so he could then return, describe the guerrilla operation, and attract Argentine recruits. That is why he showed off the caves to him in the first place—for they were not known to all: "He would go out walking with Bustos and show him the caves; some were known to the Bolivians, others were not."[92] According to Villoldo, Bustos's descriptions of the guerrillas—he drew sketches of them for the army—and of the camp and its vicinity were "very important."[93] Villoldo confirms that Bustos took them to the cave, though he also recognizes, "I cannot explain why [he did this], since his life was not in any danger. I cannot say he acted from a lack of conviction, and he was very attached to Che."[94]

When the cave was found, Che's medicines were lost; Benigno's effort had been in vain. The government also recovered photos of many of the guerrillas, including Che. They were taken to the OAS as proof that Comandante Guevara was indeed in Bolivia. Che, in contrast, never brandished his identity; he never resorted to his increasingly mythic image to appeal for local or international support. At a conference of the Latin American Solidarity Organization (OLAS) held in Havana on August 15, neither Osvaldo Dorticós nor Fidel Castro revealed Che's whereabouts, much less his desperate plight. They made no effort to launch a campaign to help or save him. Either the deluded optimism of Piñeiro's team was still in place, despite the countless and ominous warning signs emanating from Bolivia, or else the Cubans had resigned themselves to a tragic outcome. It was not far off.

After three months of blindly and stubbornly following Che's orders to the letter, and tarrying in the area where they had separated, Joaquín's rearguard finally headed north, five members short of its original strength.

---

*On five occasions in the course of a year, the author attempted to interview Ciro Bustos by telephone at his home in Malmö, Sweden, as well as in writing. He always refused to answer any questions on this matter. For their part, the Cubans think it was one of Moisés Guevara's men, Chingolo, who led the army to the cave. See Adys Cupull and Froilán González, *La CIA contra el Che* (Havana: Editora Política, 1992), p. 96. However, it does not seem that Chingolo and his companions would ever have seen the cave, or that they were present when it was dug. Apparently the Cubans take this version from the confession extracted, under torture, from Paco or José Castillo Chavez, the only survivor of Vado del Yeso, where Che's rearguard was annihilated. See "Paco cuenta su historia," *Presencia* (La Paz), August 2, 1996.

Tensions had sprung up within the group since the beginning. Tania got on terribly with the others. She was struck or insulted on several occasions by the Cubans, who accused her of having provoked the separation. On August 30, the rearguard attempted to ford the Rio Grande with the guidance of a peasant named Honorato Rojas, who had helped the guerrillas once early in the year. Inexplicably, Joaquín asked him for advice on how to cross the river—though he had already forded it, without assistance, many times. A signaling system was set up: that afternoon, Rojas would display a white apron at an appropriate crossing point if the coast was clear. Just after leaving Joaquín, however, Rojas came upon a military patrol commanded by Mario Vargas Salinas, the Eighth Division's head of intelligence, and promptly informed him of the guerrillas' intentions. Vargas Salinas mounted an ambush across the river, at the ford indicated by Rojas, and simply waited. On the afternoon of August 31, just before the sunset which would have protected them, the guerrillas started wading across the river at Vado del Yeso. With water up to their chests and their rifles held high, they were mowed down instantaneously. Ten died, including Joaquín, Tania, Moisés Guevara, and Braulio. Several bodies were swept downstream, and only recovered days later, swollen and disfigured.

Two Bolivian guerrillas were captured; one died of his wounds, the other yielded a detailed description of the rearguard's long pilgrimage. Codenamed Paco, he later spread the rumor that Tania had cancer in her reproductive organs, which delayed her periods and accounted for the bloodstains on the sanitary napkins she used.* Paco also made public the constant squabbles within Joaquín's group, especially as a result of Tania's emotional crises. As Lyndon Johnson's National Security Adviser informed him four days later, "After a series of defeats at the hands of the guerrillas, the Bolivian armed forces on August 30 finally scored their first victory—and it seems to have been a big one."[95]

With the liquidation of the rearguard, Che's time finally ran out. Vado del Yeso was the end of the road not only for those who died in the river but also for the entire guerrilla expedition in Bolivia. Isolated, decimated by casualties, illness, and desertions, their leader wracked by asthma and depression, surrounded by an increasingly energetic and professional army, they had no escape. Only five weeks remained before the fully predictable conclusion. Before narrating Che's death, though, and the Christlike aura that derived from it, it is important to attempt to convey an understanding of what happened, and why.

---

*"In reality, Tania suffered a lot because she had a cancer that didn't let her sleep." Paco, quoted in Vargas Salinas, *El Che,* p. 102. See also "Tamara Bunke, Drei Leben in einer Haut," *Der Spiegel,* no. 39, September 23, 1996.

After we dismiss the prevailing fantasies—that Che is still alive; that Che had died earlier; that Che never went to Bolivia—there are two possible explanations for the tragedy.* One rests upon the hypothesis that the Cuban government initially helped Che to a limited degree, only to forsake him later for geopolitical reasons. The other assumes that Havana always maintained good intentions, and that the outcome was simply the result of monumental incompetence and inexperience. It is worth summarizing both theories, leaving the final judgment to readers and to history.

This much we know: Fidel sold the Bolivian undertaking to Che in order to avoid his being killed in the broad avenues of Buenos Aires or the jungles of rural Argentina. It is also well established that Che's original idea of a continent-wide movement spreading from Bolivia was soon reduced to the small area of the Rio Grande's basin in the country's southeastern region. There is equally no doubt that the resources at Che's disposal were pathetically inadequate: neither the men, the weapons and communications, nor the expedition's allies fulfilled his expectations, much less the needs of the expedition. At the outset, these deficiencies may possibly have been unknown both to Che and to the Havana leadership, including Fidel Castro. But any hypothetical misjudgments or confusion became implausible after March 1967. By then, the Cubans were fully aware that Monje and the PCB had refused to make any concessions; that combat had begun prematurely; that communications had broken down; that the urban network had never functioned; and that the United States had joined the fray. Even if they were ignorant of the guerrillas' separation into two groups and the isolation of Joaquín's rearguard, it was obvious to anyone familiar with these circumstances—which were either public knowledge or easily deduced from published reports—that Che's campaign was doomed.

Based on these premises, there were two possible courses of action open to the Cuban leadership: either to make a greater support effort, or else to launch a rescue operation. The human and material resources required were available in both cases. Thanks to Lino, Benigno, and the coded communiqués of Ariel (Juan Carretero), it is known that between twenty and sixty

---

*One of the most extravagant and intelligent fantasies appears in a novel by Joseph Marsant entitled *La séptima muerte del Che*. Originally published in Paris, it was translated into Spanish and published in 1979 by Plaza y Janés. Marsant is a nom de plume for Pierre Galice, who was a cultural attaché at the French Embassy in Havana during the late sixties. His central thesis is that Manuel Piñeiro planted one of his men in Che's team in order to betray the Argentine. The most likely candidate would have been Braulio, or Orlando Pantoja Tamayo, who did in fact come from the team of Piñeiro and Ramiro Valdés at the Ministry of the Interior. The purpose was to blame the Soviets for Che's death, so as to induce a break between Castro and Moscow. Intelligence sources from another West European country have commented that Galice was extraordinarily well informed—as is evident in his text—and that his story has some truth to it, fantastic though it might seem.

Bolivians trained in Cuba were prepared to return to their country and open a second front, or reinforce their comrades in the southeast.* They included Jorge Ruiz Paz, El Negro, and Omar. Opposition to Monje and Kolle's policy of passivity within Bolivia's Communist Party raised the possibility of greater cooperation in the future, and publicizing Che's presence would have aroused enormous sympathy and solidarity throughout the country, the hemisphere, and the world. Such an effort would have sought to endow Che with the means he really needed for his project, once it became obvious that those originally planned were insufficient.[†] The cost would have been high, but worth it.

However, raising the stakes in Bolivia would have bestowed upon Cuba a far higher profile in Latin America than was compatible with its evolving ties to Moscow and its economic quandary. It was one thing to send a few more men to Venezuela—and be caught red-handed once again; it was quite another to declare war on a sister republic, in order to reinforce a guerrilla expedition led by a former Cuban Minister of State. Regardless of the outcome, Cuba could simply not afford such a luxury—even if its leaders and people had been willing. And in any case, Moscow was not willing, and it was now calling the shots.

From several sources, beginning with a secret note from Walt Rostow to President Lyndon Johnson, we know today that a vicious conflict had surfaced since the beginning of the year between Cuba and the Soviet Union over the island's Latin American policy. Dated October 18, ten days after Che's death, the memo reads in part:

> Herewith a fascinating report on a sharp exchange of letters between Castro and Brezhnev over Castro's sending Guevara to Bolivia without consulting the Soviets. The exchange was one of the reasons for Kosygin going to Havana after Glassboro.[96]

Indeed, had the Cubans contemplated the possibility of upping the ante in Bolivia, the stormy visit of Alexei Kosygin to Havana on July 26, 1967,

---

*According to Lino, over sixty Bolivians had been trained in Cuba and were ready to leave for Bolivia to reinforce Che; they never received the order. Lino, interview. In the next-to-the-last coded message sent Che from Havana, in July 1967, he was informed that "we are preparing a group of 23 persons, the great majority from the ranks of the Bolivian Communist Party's youth movement." See Soria Galvarro, *El Che,* vol. 4, p. 307.

[†] In a postmortem assessment of the Bolivian insurgency dated May 1968, the CIA estimated that the Cubans allocated less than $500,000 to the entire enterprise; needless to say, the agency analysts considered that "the number of men as well as Cuban financing and planning were totally inadequate for the scope and aims of the Cuban operation." Central Intelligence Agency, Directorate of Intelligence, Cuban Subversive Policy and the Bolivian Guerrilla Episode (Secret), Intelligence Report, p. 40.

surely dissuaded them from any further Andean fantasies. Moscow and Havana had been arguing over Che Guevara since the early part of the year. How did the Soviets uncover one of the world's best-kept secrets (again)? One can barely fathom the Byzantine complexity of the deceptions and conspiracies that still surround the final months of Guevara's life. Mario Monje has always maintained that during his return trip from Bulgaria in November 1966, he stopped nowhere except in Havana, where he met with Castro. But Benigno claims in his memoirs, published in Paris in 1996, that in fact Monje spent several days in Moscow at the time, informing the U.S.S.R. of Che's intentions and obtaining the Kremlin's tacit permission to leave Che to his own devices. In a letter to this author dated October 1996, Monje confirms that he did stop in the Soviet capital for financial reasons: the Bulgarians were paying for his plane ticket, and his pre-established itinerary included Moscow. In a subsequent phone conversation, Monje revealed that he made two stopovers in the Russian capital: one on his way to Bulgaria, and one on his way back. Benigno adds that a Spanish-Soviet colonel of the KGB nicknamed Angelito, who was in charge of expediting the discreet arrival of Cubans and Latin Americans at Moscow's Sheremetevo airport, informed him that Monje was received by a Central Committee official who whisked him off to the capital by car. The Bolivian, he says, stayed in Moscow for a week.*

Monje's layovers in the Soviet capital confirm Benigno's statement and also establish a context for Monje's meeting with Che.[†] Though he denies it adamantly to this day, it seems inconceivable that Monje would not have informed the Latin America specialists of the Soviet Party's Central Committee, or of the KGB, about the Cuban expedition in his country.[‡] As noted previously, Monje received large sums of money from the Soviet Union at that time; he has also resided in Moscow since 1968 and has always manifested greater loyalty to the fatherland of socialism than to Cuba. What is more, Monje likely consulted Moscow about his response to the Cubans' request for assistance. Perhaps the Soviets did not pressure him to deny sup-

*Benigno, interview with the author, Paris, November 18, 1995. Impeccably informed sources inside the CIA at the time have told the author that in their view, Monje was a KGB asset, not simply an ally or friend of the Soviet Union.

[†] Benigno concludes that during his stay in Moscow, "Monje revealed the entire plan to the Soviets, who then pressured Fidel, and that is how we lost contact; Che was told nothing, he was abandoned." Benigno, *Vie et mort,* p. 170.

[‡] This view is held by several Latin American old Communist leaders who know Monje and were interviewed by the author. They include the Mexican Arnoldo Martínez Verdugo and the Chilean Volodia Teitelboim. Nonetheless, Oleg Daroussenkov, then stationed in Moscow and in charge of Latin American affairs for the Party, does not recall Monje's passage through Moscow, much less having spoken with him about Che. Oleg Daroussenkov, telephone conversation with the author, Mexico, December 19, 1996.

port to Che's endeavor*; one may suppose, however, that they backed his decision to keep any such assistance to a bare minimum. And even if Monje did not mention Che to his hosts, it is highly probable that during a visit by Dorticós and Raúl Castro to Moscow between October 7 and 22, Fidel's brother revealed Guevara's decision to fight in Bolivia either to Defense Minister Grechko or to the KGB. It seems difficult to imagine Raúl Castro's hiding a secret of this magnitude from his Russian colleagues.† Hence the following hypothetical but plausible version of events.

In January, after Monje's visit, the Cuban ambassador to the U.S.S.R., Olivares, is summoned to the Kremlin, where he is severely rebuked and treated for the first time as the envoy of a satellite country; he is advised that Havana should stop provoking the United States; indeed, the diplomat surmises that perhaps the Soviets fear an American strike, and are washing their hands of the affair. The ambassador immediately flies home to report on the situation, giving rise to a series of efforts to deceive the Soviets, as well as a furious speech by Fidel Castro on March 13, directed mainly against the Venezuelan Communist Party, but also at the Soviet Union: "This revolution is following its own guidelines. It will never be anybody's satellite. It will never ask permission to uphold its own positions." But tensions rise as soon as the Soviets discover that Che is indeed in Bolivia and that the Americans have decided to oppose him.

In a high-level exchange of letters between Moscow and Havana leading up to the Kosygin visit, the U.S.S.R. accuses Cuba of having violated previous agreements: those reached at the Conference of Latin American Communist Parties in November 1964, as well as a series of bilateral accords. The Central Committee of the Communist Party of the Soviet Union particularly regrets that Cuba has proceeded without consulting Moscow; it states that in consequence Cuba should not hold the U.S.S.R. responsible if the United States were to carry out reprisals against the island for its mischief in Latin America.‡ Cuba replies that the U.S.S.R. is weakening the

---

*This is the opinion held by a low-level former official in charge of Latin America at the Central Committee of the Communist Party of the USSR: "We were sure it would not work, but we did not meddle; there was no attempt on our part to convince the PCB not to help." Konstantin Obidin, interview with the author, Moscow, October 31, 1995.

† The CIA's assertion that Cuba informed Moscow of Che's intentions as early as "the fall" of 1966 seems to validate this supposition. The CIA stated in an October 1967 memo that "In 1966 Brezhnev strongly criticized the dispatch of Ernesto Che Guevara to Bolivia. . . . In the fall of 1966 Castro informed Brezhnev that Ernesto Che Guevara with men and materiel furnished by Cuba had gone to Bolivia."

‡ In addition to being mentioned in the memo from Rostow to Johnson quoted above (see note 94), and in the CIA intelligence cable quoted above, the existence and the substance of the letter from Moscow to Havana have been corroborated by Oleg Daroussenkov, the highest-level official in Moscow working for the Central Committee in charge of Latin America, in a telephone conversation with the author, Mexico City, December 19, 1996.

cause of revolution in the hemisphere by cutting deals, extending credits, and establishing diplomatic relations with "bourgeois governments" in Latin America that were murdering and torturing revolutionary activists.* Moreover, Moscow is sabotaging the Bolivian expedition by pressuring Monje not to cooperate. Che, the Cubans explain, left of his own volition; they could hardly not help him, though his mission was not government-sponsored.

When Kosygin traveled to the United States in July to address the United Nations and to meet with Lyndon Johnson in Glassboro, New Jersey, both the Cubans and Soviets concluded that a visit to Havana on his way back home of Moscow's Number Two man would be fruitful—all the more so since Brezhnev had "expressed his disappointment at Castro's failure to give the Soviet Union advance notice concerning the dispatch of Guevara, and in strong terms criticized the decision of Castro to undertake guerrilla activities in Bolivia. . . . He inquired what right Castro had to foment revolution in Latin America without appropriate coordination with other socialist countries."[97]

Further, Kosygin learned that Lyndon Johnson was closely monitoring Che's movements in Bolivia. Although the summit was mainly devoted to the Middle East, Vietnam, and disarmament, the U.S. President registered a firm protest over Cuba's interventionism:

> Finally, I pressed Kosyguin [sic] hard to use Soviet influence in Havana to deflect Castro from his direct and active encouragement of guerrilla operations. I told him that we had evidence that the Cubans were operating in seven Latin American countries. I cited in particular the case of Venezuela and told him that it was most dangerous to the peace of the Hemisphere and the world for Castro to conduct this illegal activity.[98]

The U.S.S.R. therefore felt obliged to pressure Castro, once again, to renounce his continental aspirations, even as it sought a reconciliation.[99] Kosygin was given an icy reception; Castro did not meet him at the airport, and refused to see him initially, relenting only after enormous pressure from the Soviet Embassy. They met on three occasions: on July 26 in the company of the entire Cuban Politburo and Osmany Cienfuegos, and on July 27

---

*At the August Conference of the Organization of Latin Americas Solidarity in Havana, the Cubans tabled a resolution restating Castro's speech condemning aid and trade policies of the socialist countries vis-à-vis Latin America. Despite Soviet threats and intense lobbying, the resolution was passed, 15 to 3 with 12 abstentions, though the text was never made public. See Central Intelligence Agency, Directorate of Intelligence, The Latin American Solidarity Organization Conference and Its Aftermath, Intelligence Memorandum, September 20, 1967 (Secret), *Declassified Documents Catalog,* Research Publications (Woodbridge, Conn.), file series no. 0649, vol. 21, March–April 1995.

and 28 with President Dorticós and Raúl Castro. During the July 27 conversation, in response to the Soviet Premier's none-too-delicate complaint
that Cuba's shenanigans in the region were "playing into the hands of the
imperialists and weakening and diverting the efforts of the socialist world to
liberate Latin America,"[100] Fidel brought up the painful issue of Che.
According to the notes taken by Oleg Daroussenkov, the only translator
present at the meeting, Castro stated:

> I wish to emphasize that the revolution is an objective factor, that it cannot
> be stopped. Comrade Guevara is in Bolivia now. But we did not participate
> directly in this struggle, simply we do not have the means to do so; we are
> supporting the local party, through public statements.[101]

Kosygin retorted that he harbored serious doubts as to whether Guevara's actions in Bolivia were correct. In the first place: "One cannot pre-
tend that the sending of a dozen men to a country will lead to a revolution.
One cannot act as if the Communist Party did not exist until Comrade Guevara landed there and started the struggle."[102] He criticized the very notion
of the export of revolution, and protested the terms used by Castro to
denounce the Latin American Communist Parties.[103] On the other hand, the
Soviet did try to persuade Castro that the report remitted by his ambassador in Moscow of an imminent U.S. attack on Cuba was false, and that in
any case the U.S.S.R. was certainly not washing its hands of the Cuban
affair. Still, the meeting was tense and unpleasant; the reconciliation failed;
relations between the two countries remained extremely fractious for over a
year, reaching their lowest point in early 1968.

    In the meantime, however, an operation to boost the Bolivian *foco*
became unthinkable. The only option left was to rescue Guevara, or to
abandon him to his fate—with enormous grief, but also resignation. But
even the rescue had to be discarded as a result of Kosygin's trip to Havana.
Almost ten years later, Juan Carretero, Ariel, then Cuba's ambassador to
Iraq, revealed to Benigno the details of one of the most dramatic moments
of the Cuban Revolution. After a few drinks, overwhelmed by resentment
against Manuel Piñeiro and guilt toward the only survivor of Bolivia, Ariel
narrated the following account. When Kosygin visited Havana in July, Carretero participated in the first meeting with the Soviet delegation. Carretero
was invited because Piñeiro was away; normally Barbaroja would have
attended without any deputies. According to Carretero, the Soviets tacitly
delivered a virtual ultimatum: either Havana stopped helping the guerrillas
in Latin America or else Moscow would cease aiding the Cubans. At that
point, Carretero was asked to leave and locate Piñeiro wherever he was; he
was not summoned again.

As already noted, Carretero and Armando Campos had previously formed a group of Cubans to assist or save Guevara if it ever became necessary. They had done so on their own, without orders from Castro, but suspecting that Fidel might one day instruct them to do so, they wanted to be ready. A couple of days after the Kosygin meeting, though, Piñeiro gave Carretero the following instructions: "Hey, those people we've prepared—take whatever measures are necessary and send them home."[104]

In 1987, during an interview with a journalist who was sympathetic to his cause, Fidel Castro disdainfully discarded the possibility of a rescue. The chances of sending a group into Bolivia were nil, said Castro. Che's isolation, the military encirclement, and the lack of communications rendered any commando operation virtually impossible. As always with Fidel, this apparent truism is relative: it all depends. Several persons have expressed contrary views as to the possibility of a rescue, and even about Cuban preparations for such a contingency. When Benigno, one of three survivors, returned from Bolivia in 1968, he had the following dialogue in Havana with Campos and Carretero:

> "You knew that the only means of communication were yourselves. What did you do?" Carretero and Armando Campos, as if trying to justify themselves, said, "We are not responsible in any way because as soon as we found out about Tania and heard about the deserters talking, we immediately began to prepare a group here in Cuba, in case the high leadership ordered an operation to get you out. We prepared the group, we informed Piñeiro, and Piñeiro says he informed Fidel, but we never received any order to carry out the operation." And they said to me, "That was as far as our responsibility went. We did what we had to do, but we never received any orders."*

The fact is that three survivors were able to escape the Bolivian mouse trap by crossing the Andes into Chile, partly thanks to the remnants of the urban network. The problem, then, lay not in the abstract chances for success, but in the timing, the placement and organization of resources, and the willingness to proceed. By sending several autonomous special forces teams to Bolivia and using the knowledge of Montero (now back in Cuba), Rodolfo Saldaña (still in La Paz), and other Bolivians familiar with the area, it might have been possible to rescue Guevara. One-way communications, such as they were, would have sufficed to tell him that help was on the

---

*Benigno, interview with the author, Paris, November 18, 1996. The Cubans tapped for the mission included several veterans of the 1958 "inyasion," who had not been accepted for the Bolivia expedition. A few of their names are known: Enrique Acevedo (a brother of Rogelio, one of the heroes of Santa Clara), the Tamayito brothers (from Vaquerito's suicide battalion), and Harold Ferrer.

way; he could have been sent instructions for meeting points. If necessary, the expedition could have been initially disguised as a reinforcement effort, instead of a rescue mission. The worst that could have happened was failure, and there was no lack of Cuban commandos who would gladly have given their lives to save Comandante Guevara.

In fact, beyond his conflicts with the Soviets, Fidel had several other reasons to discard the rescue operation. The problem was not so much failure, as success: what would he do with Che once he had saved him? It would be the third time in as many years that the question had arisen. First there had been Salta, a fiasco which Che had avoided only because he waited too long and the *foco* was eliminated too quickly; then the Congo, and now Bolivia. Fidel would be faced anew with a lacerating dilemma. Once again, he would have to find an alternative function for Che, other than death or a bitterly resigned residence in Cuba. The perpetual guerrilla fighter would have to be persuaded that his latest venture had come to an end. And once convinced, what would happen after Che had returned to Cuba?*

If Fidel Castro did at some point contemplate a rescue operation, he might well have decided that a Che martyred in Bolivia would better serve the Revolution than a Che living frustrated and discouraged in Havana. The former would become a myth, a bulwark for the hard decisions ahead; he would be the emblematic martyr required by the Revolution in its pantheon of heroes, along with Camilo Cienfuegos and Frank País. Guevara alive and disgruntled in Cuba would be a source of ongoing problems, tension, and dissent—all incapable of solution; and, at the end of the road, a similar, if not identical, destination. To imagine Fidel Castro incapable of such cold-blooded cynicism is to ignore the methods which have kept him in power for almost forty years, and to disregard his conduct in other crises, albeit none as emotionally or mythically charged as that of Che Guevara. Fidel did not send Che to his death in Bolivia; nor did he betray or sacrifice him. He simply allowed history to run its course, fully aware of its inevitable outcome. Fidel did not shape the event; he let it happen.

Aside from the evidence supporting this hypothesis, two additional events merit mention. The first took place after Che's death. In 1968, the Cubans attempted a similar rescue mission in Venezuela; they were able to save twenty-four surrounded guerrillas (including Arnaldo Ochoa, whose

---

*In the last chapter of a fictionalized and unfinished account of Che's life, his childhood friend Pepe Aguilar stated that Fidel Castro asked Che to leave Bolivia when it became clear that the struggle was in vain. Aguilar repeats a conversation he held with Castro during the first days after Che's death was announced: "Ernesto's mistake was not to have come back when you asked him to." If true, this version would confirm that Fidel Castro was fully aware of how desperate Che's situation in Bolivia was. José Aguilar, unpublished manuscript, "The Final Chapter," p. 11, obtained by the author.

execution would be ordered by Fidel Castro twenty-one years later). They escaped via Brazil, thanks in part to that country's Communist Party. The second event is the peculiar experience of François Maspéro. The French publisher had close ties to the Cubans, and traveled to Bolivia to try and visit Debray in the Camiri jail and report back to Havana. He returned from La Paz just in time to attend an important cultural congress and the 26th of July celebrations in the Sierra Maestra. When Fidel Castro, who knew him and was aware of his trip to Bolivia, greeted him and asked how things were in that country, Maspéro replied, "Terrible."[105] But Fidel never requested any details; he never sought out the Frenchman for a conversation. One may conclude that Castro did not need to know more than he already knew. This may also explain why the Cubans forestalled Mario Monje's visit during this period; they preferred to leave him waiting in Chile, rather than deal with him in Cuba.

This attitude is corroborated by the impressions obtained by two witnesses who were with Fidel Castro immediately after the news of Che's death reached Cuba. Pepe Aguilar depicts a man obsessed with convincing Guevara's family in Argentina that Che had died, and much more involved in politically managing the situation than in mourning his friend. Castro was whipsawed by the dilemma of, on the one hand, possessing direct information from Bolivia, thanks to the presence of several virtual Cuban agents—Antonio Arguedas, Gustavo Sánchez, Carlos Vargas Velarde—who all confirmed Che's death, and, on the other, the impossibility of using that information to convince Ernesto Guevara Lynch of his son's execution. Carlos Franqui, called in by Castro to confirm that the handwriting from the photographed pages of Che's diary was truly his, remembers finding Fidel "frankly euphoric." Both portraits show a man who, though undoubtedly saddened by the loss of his companion of a thousand battles, had resigned himself a long time earlier to the inevitable outcome of the Bolivian adventure.*

However, the other explanation of Che's death, based upon an impressive series of errors and misunderstandings in Cuba and Bolivia, is equally plausible. The ineptitude of Havana's apparatus and Guevara's support team, Che's theoretical misconceptions, Fidel's tactlessness toward the Bolivian Communists, the irresponsibility of recruits and recruiters in Bolivia, all these factors exposed the mission's essential weakness: the overwhelming disproportion between ends and means. Three examples suffice to illustrate this point.

---

*José Aguilar, unpublished manuscript, "The Final Chapter," pp. 10–11, obtained by the author; and Carlos Franqui, interview with the author, San Juan, August 24, 1996.

First, Che never doubted that the conflict he hoped to trigger would become internationalized very quickly. Once the Bolivian army found itself overwhelmed by events, he surmised, it would seek help from its friends—especially Argentina and the United States. This would confer upon the war a nationalist dimension, creating Che's famous "two, three, several Vietnams." The revolutionary group would soon receive support from hitherto undecided or reluctant political factions alienated by Yankee interventionism.

Nothing could have been further from the truth: foreign involvement was limited in both time and scope. The Bolivian army obtained scant assistance from abroad, aside from small amounts of weapons, food, and supplies, the handful of CIA agents previously mentioned, and about twenty Green Berets led by Pappy Shelton, who trained the Second Rangers Battalion of the Eighth Division. Granted, Gary Prado and the Bolivian military underestimated the importance of U.S. backing at the margins; the latter would surely have been stepped up, had it been necessary. And, as Larry Sternfield has suggested, it is true that the Bolivians' initial reluctance to confront the guerrillas was reversed largely at U.S. urging; the Americans firmed up Barrientos's backbone.[106] Still, Che was defeated by the Bolivian armed forces, with help from an imperial power that achieved its ends without overcommitting itself. If Guevara thought the U.S. would be drawn into a Vietnam-type quagmire, he was wrong; if he supposed it would stand idly by, he was equally mistaken.

A second example was the recruitment process, riddled with disasters, desertions, incompetence, and broken promises. Papi (Martínez Tamayo), Tania, Renán Montero, Ariel (Juan Carretero), Marcos (Pinares Antonio Sánchez Díaz), Joaquín (Juan Vitalio Acuña), Arturo Martínez Tamayo (Papi's brother, in charge of radio equipment which he was never able to operate), and others, carefully picked by Che and the Havana team, proved useless for the mission at hand. Poorly selected, badly trained, and undermotivated, they were not up to a revolutionary project of continental scale. Their undeniable courage and dedication could not possibly make up for their inadequacy. They were completely unsuited for the chore; and if nobody else was available, the mission should have been aborted.

A third example was the Cubans' improvised relationship with the Bolivian Communist Party, full of deceptions and misunderstandings. In the final analysis, the only thing Havana could hold against the Party was that it had opposed the creation of a guerrilla *foco* led by Che Guevara in its own country. This was perfectly understandable, given its history and ideological position. But it was a delusion to believe that Monje supported the armed struggle and would join the *foco* against his own Party leadership, or that the Party's pro-Cuba faction would prevail against the rest of the organization. Such fantasies were typical of Manuel Piñeiro's team, but were entirely unrealistic. It was foolhardy to expect four semimilitary cadres from the Communist Party, together with a few young men trained in Cuba and youth leaders like Loyola Guzmán, to drag the rest of the Party—particularly its small miners' base—into a guerrilla war. Unfortunately, this sort of miscalculation has proved recurrent in the history of the Left in Latin America.

Given the astounding degrees of incompetence and improvisation involved, one can hardly be surprised at the expedition's failure. As is emphasized by Gustavo Villoldo, the CIA's chief field officer in Bolivia during those months:

> Everything happened very quickly. In Havana, Fidel had no idea how many assets we had within the country, and he was afraid to start something which our group would pick up on. That kept him from taking steps to help Che. Not because there was a break, or a division, or problems between Che and Havana. Simply, their system failed; and when it failed, they didn't know what to do. In these cases, either you are very aggressive or you do nothing at all; and he decided to do nothing. The aggressive thing to do, for instance, would have been to parachute people into the area of operations, or have an alternative plan for communications. This proves that the operation was not mounted in a truly professional way.[107]

The expedition's cadres, its apparatus, and the Cuban leadership were all ill prepared for the task imposed on them by Che Guevara. François Maspéro remembers the day it was reported that Joaquín's group had been annihilated at Vado del Yeso. Piñeiro, Ariel, Lino, and Armando Campos asked him over to view a newsreel that showed the guerrillas' bodies. Afterward, he was invited to stay in the screening room and watch a film starring Ronald Reagan. Such was the indifference of Che's support team.

Just as he had at the Ministry of Industries, Guevara asked too much— of the Revolution, the Cuban population, the island's economy, the U.S.S.R. In Bolivia, his demands became increasingly exorbitant. His companions sought to humor him, attend to his needs, and fulfill his aspirations, out of altruism, devotion, recklessness, and irresponsibility. They were overwhelmed by the magnitude of the mission, especially when they were tacitly asked to share in the Christlike destiny which Che had pursued since his early youth. As in any tragedy, the last act of Che Guevara's history is to be found in both its origins and its gradual unfolding; it was both heart-wrenching and unavoidable. Che's fatal destiny was already written; only death could save him, offering him the respite and the place in history which he had always pursued. His fate caught up with him at La Higuera, in the wilds of the Bolivian southeast, on a morning in October. Thus ended the calvary of Che Guevara; and there, with his peaceful face photographed on the cement slab in Vallegrande, began the resurrection and the myth.

Chapter 11

Death and Resurrection

C he Guevara's death gave meaning to his life. Without his execution at the hands of Lieutenant Mario Terán in the dark, damp, and dilapidated schoolroom at La Higuera, he would still have achieved epic feats and lived a glorious life, but his face would not appear on millions of T-shirts decades later. He doubtless would have rendered far greater service to the causes he espoused had he been spared by the Bolivian government, or saved by the CIA, but the saga of revolution and self-sacrifice he came to symbolize would never have swelled as it did. Death for Che was not only an expected, and perhaps welcome, event; it also marked an inevitable, predictable beginning of a new road to travel, not the end of a career, of a path, of a life. Every feature of that death contributed to its transcending the tragic but after all common occurrence that befalls everyone; it gave birth to a myth that would endure through the end of the century. It was, as Che had always imagined, quite a death: in cold blood, heroic and stoical, beautiful and tranquil—as his face showed in the posthumous photographs this story began with—in a word, emblematic.

But just as the specific circumstances of Che's passing are inseparable from the legend they begot, the timing is also uniquely relevant to the aura of fame that levitated from the clear- and open-eyed corpse of Vallegrande. Had Guevara perished in the Congo two years earlier, or in Argentina sometime later, the singular harmony between the man and the epoch might not have come about. Che died on the eve of a crucial year in the second half of

the twentieth century, 1968, when for the last time everything seemed possible, and for the first time the youth of a large slice of the world engaged in
short-lived but far-reaching revolts that Che, more than anyone else, would
come to personify. Weeks after his death, North Vietnamese troops and
the Vietcong unleashed the Tet offensive that inspired rebellion across the
United States, Western Europe, and Latin America. Even before then, the
first effigies of Alberto Korda's portrait appeared in the angry autumn of
Turin; then, students led the irreverent sit-ins at Columbia University in New
York and the mass demonstrations in the Latin Quarter in Paris; less than a
year after Che's capture at the Yuro Ravine, the ubiquitous blood-red posters
would vainly attempt to exorcise Soviet tanks rumbling through the streets
of Prague. Almost a year later to the day, hundreds marching beneath his
banner would be shot by the Mexican army in the colonial and pre-
Columbian square of Tlatelolco. The synchronicity is striking, and beguiling: it was Che's death at that particular time that allowed him to voice the
desires and dreams of the millions who bore his image, but it was his life that
created the bond between his fallen figure and the dreams of a generation
born out of the havoc and grief of World War II.

The affinities are countless. They include the ideological consonance
within families belonging to the "movement," as described by alternative
sociologists in the United States.[1] Guevara shared his mother's political
views until her death. But the analogies also comprise his very life story.
Prominent figures of the so-called "new left" in Europe and the United
States were almost all a product of the white, educated middle classes that
emerged from the postwar baby boom. Such was the family formed in Córdoba by Ernesto Guevara Lynch and Celia de la Serna during the Argentine
demographic bubble before the Depression. Even in death there were similarities: millions of teenagers in the fifties and students in the sixties would
experience intellectual or political epiphanies over the early, tragic death of
their precocious heroes. The death that cancels a life's promise before its
time would become a leitmotif of that era, and no one symbolized it as vigorously as Che Guevara. All of these parallels helped create that crucial
identification between myth and context. Another life would never have
captured the spirit of its time; another historical moment would never have
found itself reflected as it did in him.

More than impatience or arrogance, the youth of that time found its distinctive mark in a blend of idealism and felt omnipotence which only turned
to action in 1968, but had been building for years. The slogans "La plage
sous les pavés," "We want the world and we want it now," "We must be realistic and demand the impossible"; the exuberance, the narcissistic determination to have and achieve everything hic et nunc announced the advent of

the empire of the will, where Che lived and died. The objects of desire were also changing drastically: instead of money, freedom; instead of power, revolution; instead of comfort, generosity; instead of profit and ambition, the rhythms of rock. To stop violence and war, distribute wealth, preach the liberation of passion and desire, live strong and unexplored sensations without risk or cost: these were the values of the generation Guevara came to represent, especially after his death.

The kinship between Ernesto Guevara and the youth of his time has elicited many metaphors, but Julio Cortázar's is perhaps the most eloquent: "The Argentine students who took over their dormitory in the University City of Paris called it Che Guevara, for the same simple reason that leads thirst to water and man to woman."[2] Che was no longer young when he became the symbol of youthful insurrection atop the Paris barricades, but something in his premature death rejuvenated him, completing his assimilation by the generation that followed his own. A young man on the verge of middle age is executed in Bolivia; not just a revolutionary, but a martyr: one who was "pure." Or perhaps the murder victim becomes a mirror-like object of recognition for youth precisely because of the way he died.

A 1968 survey of American university students found that the historical figure they most identified with was Che, more than any of the U.S. presidential candidates that year, and more than any of the other personalities proposed by the study.[3] Moreover, 80 percent of American college students in 1969 identified with "my generation": a sense of belonging and self-definition that would not repeat itself soon.[4] The outstanding features of that generation would not last forever, of course; the aging process would finally bring back to the fold the majority of demonstrators, militants, and heroes of that rebellious era. In the meantime, though, the need to establish links between the "here" and "there," present and future, political position and lifestyle, would permeate the thinking of the generation of 1968, and of Che Guevara.

The young people of Paris and Berkeley wanted both revolution in their own countries and neighborhoods, and solidarity with Vietnam and Cuba. Che proposed to forge a new man in Cuba, while also fighting for the liberation of the former Belgian Congo. The students sought to change life itself—not just the political sphere: to overthrow customs, manners, tastes, and taboos—without waiting for the glorious new dawn or the "building of socialism." Guevara, through his volunteer work, personal asceticism, and international solidarity, tried to link the individual efforts of today with the social and political utopia he envisaged for the future. And his strangely apolitical stance as a university student would extend into his stature as a nonpolitical politician. If a generation that was both highly politicized and disgusted with its parents' politics came to see itself in him, it was because of that paradox. Che was never, strictly speaking, a politician.

Similarly, the other guiding principle in Che's life—his eternal avoidance of ambivalence, which would pursue him like a shadow from his childhood asthma to Ñancahuazú—coincided with the attitudes of an era. The sixties rejected life's contradictions: theirs was a perpetual *fuite en avant* of much of that first postwar generation, that repeatedly fled contradictory feelings, desires, or political goals. The attitudes and sentiments of the protesters of the sixties could hardly tolerate shades of gray, nuances, realism, and coexisting opposites; the times and the nature of the struggles—against segregation in the American South, against the Vietnam war or barracks-style mass education in France and Italy, against Soviet-style socialism in Czechoslovakia, and benign or not-so-nice dictatorships in Latin America—that gave birth to their protests were largely incompatible with moderate, reasonable, "on the one hand this, but on the other hand that" views of the world. Yet Che, like the young of the sixties, possessed a hidden reservoir of tolerance flowing from another well: a fascination with things and people different, that would translate into acceptance and respect for otherness.

Doubtless, within some dark conceptual corner there lurked a monumental tangle of contradictions between Guevara's authentic self and the persona crafted by his standard-bearers. The exorbitant demands he exacted upon himself could not be transferred onto others without a brutal imposition of authority. The new man embodied by him had no place in the world of that time, nor perhaps in any world conceivable to his contemporaries. But during the sixties, that contradiction was not perceived by the demonstrators who bore his likeness along streets throughout the world. He was seen only as a symbol of subversion, in a decade that sanctified and cultivated it.

As several Cuban authors have noted,* the lasting impact of Che Guevara derives also from his identification with the subversive significance of the time. In that era of revolt, he became the emblem of three different types of subversion. The first, and most evident, was directly linked to the Cuban Revolution: it sought to overthrow the global hierarchy which would later be couched in North-South terms. It encompassed an effort, ultimately unsuccessful but plausible at the time, to invert the relationship between rich, powerful, dominant countries and small, poor, dominated ones like the Caribbean island. For the young protesting against French colonialism

---

*Two stand out: Juan Antonio Blanco, who generously shared his thoughts with the author during a conversation in Havana in January 1996, and Fernando Martínez, who among other texts on the same subject has published one with similar ideas in *Actual* (Havana), January 1996, pp. 5–10.

in Algeria in the early sixties or the U.S. bombing of Vietnam in the middle or end of the decade, the task of transforming an unjust and evil geopolitical status quo was no minor matter.

The second subversion was rooted in the middle-class youth of the United States and then Western Europe in 1967–68: its target was nothing less than the existing *domestic* order. As Todd Gitlin[5] and the authors of *Génération*[6] have so aptly written, the rebellious youth of industrialized countries, in their desperate and fruitless search for positive values and models, finally found them in the opposite of their own realities. Their personal idols and political archetypes were drawn among the enemies of their enemies: first Patrice Lumumba, the Algerian FLN, and its guerrillas from the Kasbah and the desert; then Ho Chi Minh and the FLN in Vietnam; and, always, the Cuban Revolution and Che himself. Later, as the movement waned, a further retreat toward faraway figures and struggles took place. The fewer Americans, French, or Dutch Provos in the demonstrations, the more portraits of Che and proclamations of solidarity with "the people's struggle." The more remote revolution became at home, the more attractive the foreign *ersatz*—whether Algerian, Vietnamese, or Cuban.

The third target was existing socialism, the prison gray of Stalinism associated with the crushed Prague spring, but also with the French Communist Party's betrayal in Paris, and that of the Italian Party in Milan. Granted, Che's affinity with this struggle was less evident, as Régis Debray has suggested: the students bearing Che posters throughout the parks and avenues of Western or Czech cities and university campuses did not know that their hero had been deeply pro-Soviet in his early revolutionary years. They neglected to see that his libertarian spirit stopped short of challenging the values of military hierarchy and leadership, denoted by his beret and star and olive-green army fatigues. Yet their perception of him was not entirely inaccurate: Che's spirit, theses, and behavior toward the end of his life constituted a ferocious and well-directed critique of Soviet-bloc socialism and its implantation in Cuba.

But it was his death itself that counted most in the creation of the myth, and in the construction of the consonance between the man and the time. From early October 1967, when the first news stories of his capture and execution began to filter out of Bolivia, through the summer of 1968, when his campaign diary was surreptitiously removed from that country and subsequently published in *Ramparts* magazine in the United States, by François Maspéro in France and Feltrinelli in Italy, and by Arnaldo Orfila and Siglo XXI in Mexico, every detail, every last minute of Guevara's life fit into the mold of the myth. It is a death worth reliving.

Initially, Che did not believe the reports regarding the annihilation of
Joaquín's rearguard patrol at Vado del Yeso. In his journal he noted that the
reports could well stem from government propaganda or disinformation,
although as more specifics surfaced he gradually seemed to resign himself
to the group's loss. Pombo, one of the three survivors of the Bolivian
escapade, has stated on various occasions that Che finally did accept the
truth of the elimination of Tania and the rest*; Benigno, another survivor,
is less categorical.† What seems indisputable is that Che did not consider the
loss of his rearguard as an event that wrought irreparable damage to his
campaign. Nor did it induce him to find a way out of Bolivia or the region,
rather than persevering in his endeavor. At no point in his diary or in the
testimony of the three survivors (Urbano, or Leonel Tamayo, is the third
living Cuban member of the group; Inti Peredo also survived, but died two
years later in La Paz) does Guevara indicate a desire to wrap matters up and
escape from the deathtrap closing around him.

Through the month of September the small group of guerrillas—now
numbering between twenty and twenty-five, depending on the day—beset
by illness, fatigue, malnutrition, and dissension, wandered northwest from
the Rio Grande toward the villages of Pucará and La Higuera, not far from
the larger town of Vallegrande. There the Eighth Division of the Bolivian
army had established its headquarters, bent on sealing off any escape route
to the southeast, across the river. Together with the Fourth Division from
Camiri, they had boxed Che in: the Rio Grande to the southeast, canyons
and gorges to the east and west, and Vallegrande and thousands of troops
to the north. From Vallegrande also, the Second Ranger Battalion, whipped
into shape by Pappy Shelton and the couple of CIA Cuban operatives dispatched from the United States, would soon undertake the pursuit and
extermination of the rebel band. The Bolivian Rangers were not quite ready
in early September; not till midmonth were they truly able to participate in

---

*"After we crossed the Rio Grande, Che really convinced himself the news of Joaquín's
death was true." Harry Villegas, "Pombo," interview with British journalists, Havana, October, 1995. Transcript made available to author.

† Felix Rodríguez, the CIA radio man sent to Bolivia to defeat Che, also recalls that during his couple of hours of conversation with Che after he was captured, Guevara said in
relation to the destruction of the rearguard: "Since you are telling me this I believe it, but
until now I thought it was a lie. I suspected maybe some of them had died, but that it was
government propaganda that all of them had been eliminated." Felix Rodríguez, interview
with the author, Miami, April 24, 1995. It is worth noting that there are some doubts about
the accuracy of Rodríguez's assertions. Gustavo Villoldo, his superior in Bolivia, states for
example that "Che was in the little room in the schoolhouse, and Felix was outside pho-
tographing the captured materiel. Felix did not talk with Che, and was not there when he
was killed." Gustavo Villoldo, interview with the author, Miami, November 27, 1995.

the hunt, and even then they were probably thrown in prematurely. Fully trained or not, by the end of September more than 1,500 troops were completely devoted to catching Che and his companions; it was just a matter of time.

The beginning of the end came on September 26. After entering the tiny hamlet of Alto Seco, just south of La Higuera, Che himself addressed the minuscule crowd, pulled some teeth, and chatted with the inhabitants, realizing, as he had already ruefully jotted down in his diary, that the faces of the Bolivian peasants were impenetrable; he was simply not communicating. His health, according to the impressions registered by the townspeople with the Bolivian press, had deteriorated terribly: "Guevara appeared sick and exhausted; he rode a mule and appeared unable to walk without support."* Worse still, at the first opportunity, the natives dashed off to inform the army of the revolutionaries' presence. A vanguard of three rebels was assigned to explore the path north to Jaguey; from the heights above the road, an army patrol spotted them and opened fire. Miguel and Julio were gunned down instantly; Coco Peredo was fatally wounded. Benigno managed to carry him off, but could not escape with the Bolivian on his shoulders. Peredo was either killed by a new round of gunfire or else shot himself, hoping at least to save his comrades and knowing that he had but hours to live. With the death of one of the two leading Bolivian combatants, morale plummeted; there was nowhere left to go. In the confusion, two Bolivians deserted: Camba, or Orlando Jiménez Bazán, one of the older, original cadres from the Communist Party, and León, or Antonio Rodríguez Flores.

On September 30, Rodríguez Flores was questioned by the Eighth Division. His interrogators extracted precious information about Che's plans, strength, and disposition. The Bolivian military quickly concluded that Guevara hoped to push toward Vallegrande through the ravines just outside La Higuera, leading toward the larger town of Pucará. They immediately deployed their men along the ranges looking down upon the ravines, seeking either to force Che's men to higher ground, where the vegetation was sparse and visibility in daylight was virtually total, or to pin them down in the gorges. Conversely, Che's intentions during those last few days remained mysterious and confused. Pombo has recalled that the idea of entering and "taking" Vallegrande, as harebrained as it might seem, made some sense. The group would attempt this desperate act in order to leave its wounded—

*Edwin Chacón, "Reportaje de Alto Seco," *Presencia* (La Paz), October 4, 1967, quoted in AmEmbassy La Paz to Department of State, October 4, 1967 (Unclassified), p. 3. Actually, his physical state had improved over the previous days; according to Benigno, he had been getting better for nearly a fortnight. Benigno, interview with the author, Paris, November 3, 1995.

Chino, the Peruvian, as well as the doctor, Morogoro, both in awful shape—
with some putative sympathizers, obtain the medication Che required,
make known their existence to the outside world, and break through the
army encirclement to the northeast, in the direction of Cochabamba and
the Chapare region.[7]

Benigno has stressed the more irrational aspects of the stratagem. In his
view, Che simply wanted to engage in one last, glorious firefight in which he
and his men would perish in flames and embrace immortality. If all he
wished was to requisition medicines, Benigno today wonders why he did not
just send him and one of the other strong Cubans into Vallegrande to hold
up a pharmacy. Or even if Che hoped to strike a spectacular blow by taking
Vallegrande, it made little sense to have all his men carrying seventy-pound
knapsacks and dragging the wounded around with them.[8]

In the next-to-last entry in his diary, on October 6, Che wrote that the
rebels came upon an old woman with a dwarf daughter; the guerrillas
bribed her to remain quiet about their presence, without great expectations
regarding her silence. They speculated that by marching at night and hiding
and resting in the depth of the ravines during the day, perhaps they would
eventually be able to penetrate the noose the army was fastening around
them. The old woman acted as anticipated; she promptly notified the closest military outpost of the guerrillas' whereabouts. The circle tightened.
After a day of "bucolic rest," as Che put it in the final note in his journal,
on the night of October 7 the seventeen men broke out along the bottom of
the Yuro or Churo gorge, in the thicker and tougher, but still unprotecting,
vegetation. A potato farmer across the stream distinguished their figures in
the moonlight: a band of bearded, emaciated ghosts carrying guns and
rucksacks and doubled over under their weight. He had no doubt; it had to
be the guerrillas. He quickly dispatched his son to the military command
post of Captain Gary Prado Salmón, just a few miles away. This soldier's
soldier needed no further notice; he immediately set up a textbook ambush,
with men stationed at the entrance and exit of the ravine, and his command
post on the high ground.* Che's last battle was about to begin.

Guevara had also issued his combat instructions, though he was not
absolutely certain that the army had discovered the presence of his group.†

---

*For some strange reason, the official Cuban version of events rejects the idea that the
army ambushed Che's group; the Cubans insist that what took place was a firefight between
two forces. In a sense they are right; the skirmish was not totally unexpected by Che and his
men. See Fidel Castro, televised speech to the nation, Havana, October 15, 1967, and
Pombo, Benigno, and Urbano, "La Quebrada del Yuro," Recuerdos de un combate, *Tricontinental* (Havana), July–October, 1969, p. 113.

† The account is based on the Bolivian military's reports, mainly Gary Prado's, quoted
above; on those of the three surviving guerrillas, referred to in the previous note; and on
Fidel Castro's speech to the nation in Cuba, also referred to in the previous note.

He split up his platoon into several small squads, each ordered to explore the narrow creeks ahead of them, to determine if there was a way out of the ravine. As the sun rose, Benigno and Pacho realized that there were already dozens of soldiers on the high ground above them. Che had two choices: withdraw toward the back of the ravine and hope the soldiers had not bottled it up, or remain quiet until nightfall, trusting that the army would not detect his detachment. He chose the latter option and placed his men in a defensive perimeter, in case the troops did discover them. Around 1:30 on October 8, the vanguard position, at the mouth of the ravine, was hit by army fire; the different rebel positions were isolated from each other. Soon, two jets and a helicopter overflew the area, but did not bomb or strafe the hills. Che's squad, made up of seven guerrillas, attempted to withdraw into the ravine; it would not be able to sustain the army's fire for long. Guevara divided his group in two: first the wounded and weak, then he himself with two men remaining behind to cover them.

Minutes later, his M-1 jammed or was hit by gunfire; either way, it was rendered useless; soon he was hit in the calf, a flesh wound that nonetheless made it difficult for him to walk. Willi, or Simón Cuba, one of Moisés Guevara's mine-union activists, dragged him along a small ridge, his machine gun in one hand, the other propping up his *comandante* as best he could; Aniceto Reynaga, another Bolivian, was right behind. Three soldiers from Prado's platoon saw them approaching, waited for them to climb a tiny cliff, and when they showed themselves, shouted out: "Drop your weapons and raise your hands." Che could not shoot back; his pistol had no clip and his carbine was disabled; Willi held his fire, either because he could not shoot with one hand or because prudence indicated that as the wisest course. According to some accounts, Che then spoke up: "Don't shoot, I am Che Guevara and I am worth more to you alive than dead"; other versions, tainted by Bolivian military spin, attribute a different statement to the defeated Argentine: "I am Che Guevara and I have failed."* Another, more plausible story is that it was Willi who threw down his rifle and raised his voice when the two soldiers, nervous and exhausted, took aim and seemed indecisive about what to do: "Shit, this is Commander Guevara and he deserves respect."†

Captain Gary Prado was immediately advised of Che's capture and

---

*This version was propagated by General Alfredo Ovando, in his initial statements after the battle, whereby he claimed that Che had died in combat. See Carlos Soria Galvarro, ed., *El Che en Bolivia, Documentos y Testimonios,* vol. 2 (La Paz: Cedoin, 1993), p. 91.

† This account was supplied by Antonio Arguedas, Bolivia's minister of the interior, who would subsequently flee Bolivia and deliver Che's diary to Fidel Castro in 1968. Arguedas was originally a CIA asset, as confirmed to the author by a source in the CIA at the time, but also close to the Cubans, to whom he went over definitively after Che's death. See Soria Galvarro, *El Che en Bolivia,* vol. 2, p. 111.

scrambled down the ravine as the shooting continued below. He made two or three quick checks of Guevara's identity, requisitioned his knapsack, and promptly and excitedly radioed Eighth Division headquarters: Che had been taken. A long procession formed, as Prado marched him off to La Higuera, two kilometers away. Behind them followed the other prisoners, mules carrying the bodies of the fallen rebels, the wounded soldiers, and soon, hundreds of onlookers. Guevara was thrown into a mud-floored room in the local schoolhouse; Willi was locked up next door.

Through the night the troops celebrated their success, while the Bolivian High Command in La Paz deliberated about what to do with its legendary and intensely discomfiting captive. Che was in minor pain, and obviously depressed, but from available accounts, did not seem ready to die, though he must have contemplated this prospect. If he did exclaim, "I am worth more to you alive than dead," in the ravine or somewhat later, he probably thought so. He may have concluded that the Bolivian government would prefer to try him and brandish his capture as a symbol of victory against foreign aggression, rather than execute him. But things did not turn out that way.

At night and in the early dawn, Gary Prado and Andres Selich, the first with politeness and dignity, the second arrogantly, attempted fruitlessly to interrogate Guevara and establish some form of communication with him. Next morning, around 6:30, a helicopter flew in from Vallegrande with three passengers: Major Niño de Guzmán, the pilot; Colonel Joaquín Zenteno, the head of the Eighth Division; and Felix Rodríguez, the CIA's Cuban-American radio man, sent along both out of deference for U.S. support—as Rodríguez explains it—and to ensure proper identification of Che. Rodríguez also was instructed to question Che and photograph his notebooks and the other seized documents.

The army had a monumental problem on its hands. There was no death penalty in Bolivia, and virtually no high-security prison where Guevara could serve a long sentence. The very thought of a trial sent shudders down the spines of President Barrientos, General Ovando, and the Armed Forces Chief of Staff, Juan José Torres. If the country and the government had been subjected to unending international pressure and condemnation for judging Régis Debray, what kind of outcry and campaign would not erupt in favor of Che Guevara, the famous and heroic guerrilla commander? Che in jail, anywhere in Bolivia, would represent an enormous temptation for commandos from Cuba either to seek to free him or to force an exchange for hostages taken elsewhere. It was a nightmare scenario for the three military men who held his fate in their hands. Similarly, handing Che over to the Americans, and having them fly him out to Panama for debriefing, was equally unacceptable—the nationalist tradition of the military would not allow it; moreover, the government would thereby confirm everything the Cubans and others had been claiming: the counterinsurgency effort was nothing more than a disguised form of Yankee interventionism. Every available testimony and account suggests that deliberately, consciously, and unanimously, the Bolivian authorities decided that Che Guevara should be put to death as soon as possible, before pressure from abroad and/or from the Americans became intolerable.

The order went out from La Paz at midmorning; it was received in La Higuera, where Felix Rodríguez relayed it to Zenteno, who commissioned a squad of soldiers to carry it out.[9] After a picture-taking session, where far more photographs were snapped than have been made public until today, the soldiers drew lots and it fell to Lieutenant Mario Terán to finish off the disheveled, limp, depressed, but still defiant man lying on the floor of the school at La Higuera. The designated executioner hesitated; after several false starts, a few hard swigs of scotch, and Che's invocation to carry on, Terán fired half a dozen shots into Guevara's torso; one of them pierced his heart and killed him instantly. His last words, according to Colonel Arnaldo Saucedo Parada, head of intelligence of the Eighth Division and the man responsible for delivering the official report on Che's final moments, were: "I knew you were going to shoot me; I should never have been taken alive. Tell Fidel that this failure does not mean the end of the revolution, that it will triumph elsewhere. Tell Aleida to forget this, remarry and be happy, and keep the children studying. Ask the soldiers to aim well."[10] His body was lashed onto the landing skids of Zenteno's helicopter and flown off to Vallegrande; there, after being washed and cleaned, it was put on display in the laundry room of the hospital of Our Lady of Malta, where this story began.

Although the Bolivians attempted to obscure the cold-blooded assassination of the revolutionary by saying he died in combat, their story quickly crumbled. The doctors who performed the postmortem medical examination hurriedly declared that Guevara had been dead less than five hours when they inspected his corpse that afternoon in Vallegrande. But if Che was alive on October 9 at midday, and the skirmish during which he was captured had taken place on October 8, how could he have died in combat? Hundreds had witnessed the dismal cortege trudging from the Yuro Gorge to La Higuera. It soon became evident to all the journalists clustered around the hospital in Vallegrande that Ernesto Guevara de la Serna had been executed. The next day, Che's body disappeared. Although General Ovando initially ordered his hands and head severed for identification purposes, and the rest of his body cremated to discourage the eventual construction of a shrine, history took another course. Various Bolivian officers and Gustavo Villoldo, the senior Cuban CIA man, opposed the decapitation; only his hands were

amputated. They were conserved in formaldehyde for more than a year in
Bolivia, until they were surreptitiously removed from the country, only to
surface later in Cuba. Legend has it that Fidel Castro wished to place them
in a sort of mausoleum in Havana, but that Che's family objected; they are
stored somewhere in the Palace of the Revolution, where various visiting
dignitaries say they have been allowed to see them.

The three remaining enigmas of Che's life and death do not concern the
details and circumstances of his murder. They involve different issues: What
role did the United States play in his execution? Did Che expect, wish, or just
courageously and resignedly accept his unavoidable end? Was his body incin-
erated, the ashes spread out in the hills around Vallegrande, as was always
claimed by the Bolivian authorities, or was he buried somewhere in the town?

The semiofficial Cuban version of Che's death claims that President Barrientos, when informed of Guevara's apprehension, promptly visited the
U.S. ambassador at his residence that evening and was ordered to eliminate
the guerrilla warrior.[11] Ambassador Douglas Henderson, both in his oral-
history accounts at the JFK and LBJ presidential libraries[12] and in two written communications to the author, vehemently denies the Cuban story.*
According to Henderson, he not only did not receive a visit from Barrientos
at his residence that night, but was not even consulted by the Bolivians as to
how they should proceed. He argues that there was good reason for them
not to solicit his advice: he had strongly opposed the execution of Régis
Debray months before, and the Bolivians could guess that he would be as
adamantly opposed to Guevara's slaying.[†]

Other surviving witnesses all tend to confirm this interpretation, though
they possess an undeniable vested interest in this version of the story. Felix
Rodríguez, in his memoirs, asserts categorically that he received the order
from the Bolivian authorities in La Paz to have Che shot. He considered
complying, instead, with his own instructions from Langley:

*"I have to rely on memory, but I do not remember any contact with Barrientos (or for
that matter any Bolivian—Armed Forces or civilian) on October 8, 1967, nor on any of the
succeeding days. My recollection is that no member of the Bolivian Government gave me
information about Guevara's capture and execution. I have ascribed this silence to my
strong opposition to the proposed execution of Debray." Douglas Henderson, letter to the
author, December 1, 1995.

† Although history and politics are plethoric with acts destined to cover one's backside
for posterity, there is a memo from Walt Rostow to Lyndon Johnson, dated October 11, at
10:30 a.m., that apparently corroborates U.S. innocence: "The latest information is that
Guevara was taken alive. After a short interrogation to establish his identity, General
Ovando—Chief of the Bolivian Armed Forces—ordered him shot. I regard this as stupid,
but it is understandable from a Bolivian standpoint." Walt Rostow, Memorandum to the
President, October 11, 1967 (Secret).

The first thing they told us in Washington was that the Bolivians had a tendency to finish off their prisoners and were Guevara to be taken alive we should use all means to keep him alive and have him taken to Panama.*

In the opinion of other CIA people on the ground or who knew him subsequently, Rodríguez probably exaggerated his own role in the entire affair—he was just a radio man, at the time—but essentially told the truth. John Tilton, the CIA station chief in La Paz, absent from the country during those days, has confirmed this version to the author in a series of phone conversations; but, again, he would hardly say the contrary.[13] Gustavo Villoldo, the head of the CIA country team, was a bit more forthright about his own sentiments. He has narrated how upon his arrival in Bolivia, he was driven to Barrientos's home to meet him. In no uncertain terms he told Barrientos: if Che were captured, he personally would do everything in his power to have him executed. Then he asked, If we take Che alive, what will you do with him? The president replied: "If he is alive, he will be summarily judged and condemned to death. You have the word of the President of the Republic."[14]

Gary Prado, the only surviving Bolivian army officer directly involved in Che's capture and in the deliberations over his execution—the others have all died in the following years, through a sort of Che hex that seems to have pursued them all over the world—stressed that the choice to kill Che was strictly a Bolivian one. Though he regretted it, since he admired Che's valor and commitment to his convictions, Prado nonetheless today considers the decision a wise one from the point of view of the Bolivian military and state interests.

Prado has provided perhaps the most reliable testimony of Che's state of mind and reflections in the last few hours of his life. He took notes of his conversation with the prisoner, and published them as an appendix to his book in 1987. Guevara acknowledged that the selection of Bolivia may not have been a judicious one, but that on the other hand it was not exclusively his; the most enthusiastic advocates of the Andean nation were the Boli-

---

*Felix Rodríguez and John Weisman, *Shadow Warrior* (New York: Simon and Schuster, 1989), pp. 160, 164–165. According to Rodríguez's sworn, secret statement to the CIA Inspector General on June 3, 1975, released in the course of the agency's historical review program: "Rodríguez prepared a 100-word message . . . in code reporting Guevara's capture and asking that an Embassy representative be sent to the area to prevail upon the Bolivians to spare Guevara's life, since he did not believe that he could succeed in doing so. This message was prepared for the scheduled 10 a.m. transmission of 9 October, and was not transmitted to the relay point in Asunción, Paraguay, until about 10:30 a.m., after Rodríguez arrived in Higueras [*sic*] and set up his radio transmitter, an RS-48." According to Rodríguez, the message took a long time to reach the U.S. because the relay operator in Paraguay refused to keep the transmission frequency open. By the time it got to the U.S., Che was dead. Felix Rodríguez, interview.

vians themselves. He also revealed his expectations regarding his own destiny; when he inquired of Prado what would happen to him, he noted that on the radio he had heard that if captured by the Eighth Division, he would be tried in Santa Cruz, instead of in Camiri, where he would have been sent had he been taken prisoner by the Fourth Division. Moreover, Prado emphasizes that the way in which Che was captured—that is, moving up the hill and out of the ravine—shows that he wanted to live, not die:

> If he had wanted to die he could have stayed further down and kept fighting. But no, he was trying to get out. Once captured, after the initial depression, when he saw we were treating him correctly and speaking with him, he began to feel better, his mood improved.*

Rodríguez also recalled how Che seemed to think he would be tried and sentenced, but not shot; he remembered how the prisoner blanched when he received the news that his fate was sealed.[15]

Lastly, there is the testimony of the townspeople of La Higuera who had access to him for one reason or another (to feed him, for example) and spoke with him during that night and the next morning; they also suggested a man who retained his will to live, and who did not seem at all persuaded that he had only a few hours left before dying. Julia Cortés, a schoolteacher, recalled how after thanking her for some food she brought him and chatting about education and La Higuera, Che asked her to find out what his captors were up to: " 'I don't know, maybe they will shoot me or take me out alive, but I think it is more in their interest to keep me alive, because I am worth a great deal.' He seemed to think he would make it alive; he told me he would not forget me."[16] The other Bolivian officers who exchanged bits of conversation with Che that night—mainly Zenteno and Selich—died before age and wisdom could ensure the accuracy and sincerity of their testimony. Most likely, Ernesto Guevara faced death with the enormous courage that his entire life had cultivated, but also with the fear and despair that anyone who loved life as much as he did must feel when he is about to lose it.

In November 1995, the *New York Times* ran a page-long article based on the statements of a retired Bolivian army general, Mario Vargas Salinas. Vargas, the architect of the ambush at Vado del Yeso, reiterated to the *Times* what he had stated previously, and what other Bolivian officers—such as Luis Reque Terán of the Fourth Division, in his memoirs—had

---

*Gary Prado Salmón, interview with the author, Santa Cruz de la Sierra, October 26, 1994. This is also Benigno's view: "I do not think he wanted to die." Benigno, interview.

been repeating for some time: contrary to the generally held belief that Che's body had been cremated by the military, it had in fact been buried beneath the airstrip at Vallegrande. But because on this occasion it was the *New York Times* that published the story, it became hard news and the Bolivian government was forced to launch a search for the remains. Argentine forensic experts were flown in; later, Cuban experts descended upon the old town in the hills of southeast Bolivia. Some twenty months later, in July 1997, several bodies were discovered near the airfield at Vallegrande; one of them was officially proclaimed to be Che's by the Cuban government, with the acquiescence of the Argentine experts, though some actors in the original drama, like Felix Rodríguez, remained skeptical.

Although it took three decades to dispel the myth that Guevara had been cremated,* there were always sound reasons for suspecting that he had actually been buried.† There is no tradition of cremation in a highly Catholic country like Bolivia; it would not have been a simple matter to carry the procedure out secretly. The funeral pyre necessary to incinerate a corpse completely is not small; in a town like Vallegrande, it would have been sighted for miles around that night of October 9, when, after having been viewed by countless correspondents, curious locals, and other spectators, Che's body vanished. Secondly, while burial would require only a couple of strong men, lighting, fanning, and sustaining the fire necessary for cremation would have involved many more participants, one or more of whom would inevitably have come forward in the course of thirty years. No one has.

Gustavo Villoldo was absent from La Higuera on the day of Che's execution. On the other hand, he was the leading U.S. official in Vallegrande during the two days when these events took place, and was, he firmly avers, directly responsible for the interment of the body:

> I buried Che Guevara. He was never cremated; I didn't allow it, in the same manner I strongly opposed the mutilation of his body. At dawn the following morning I hauled his body away, together with the corpses of the two other guerrillas, in a pickup truck. A Bolivian driver and a Lieutenant Barrientos, if I am not mistaken, accompanied me. We drove to the airstrip and

*In the files at the LBJ Library concerning Che's capture and death, there is a two-line unclassified note from Walt Rostow to Lyndon Johnson saying: "I am told you asked Covey Oliver [a Latin America staffer at the State Department at the time] if it were true that the Bolivians had cremated the body of Che Guevara. CIA has told State that is the case." Rostow, Memorandum, The White House, October 13, 1967, 6:15 p.m.

† Felix Rodríguez has also stated "categorically" that the body was buried. Felix Rodríguez, interview, op. cit. Benigno also is absolutely certain that Che's body was buried, and believes Lino, or Angel Braguer, as well as a priest in Vallegrande, know where. Benigno, interview with the author, Paris, March 7, 1996.

buried the bodies there. I would recognize the site immediately. They will
find his body if they keep looking. They will recognize it because of the sur-
gically removed hands; he was not mutilated.

There is still no electricity in La Higuera; the small town is as miserable and
lost in the wilderness as when Che Guevara died there thirty years ago. In
this sense, his sacrifice was in vain; his impact on the lives of the forsaken
and destitute peasants of southeastern Bolivia was slight and ephemeral.
For its part, the Cuban Revolution, despite a brief fling with his ideas soon
after his death and through the summer of 1968, quickly left Che behind;
Havana's alignment with the Soviet Union came full circle as the Prague
spring came to an end. By 1970, when Fidel Castro transformed the foolhardy goal of harvesting ten million tons of sugar into a national crusade,
the economic and social ideals that Che fought for were relegated to Stalinist oblivion. Finally, although Cuba's internationalist adventures lasted
through the nineties, and met with far greater success later in the century
than during Che's time, they all ended indifferently or ignominiously. So
where is Che's legacy, and what difference did he make?

While the distinctive qualities of the sixties generation endured, their link
with Che Guevara enclosed an almost magical symbiosis of symbol and
zeitgeist, based upon a real affinity. That unique combination of determination and change, omnipotence and altruism, arrogance and detachment,
reflected the stance of broad sectors in various rejuvenated societies and of
an individual. If the masses and the movements were all so similar, then
their symbols had to be too. The clue to Che's ubiquity lies perhaps in the
virtually universal nature of the protests and protesters of 1968; he came
to embody the aspirations and beliefs of '68ers in Berkeley and Prague,
Mexico City and Paris, Córdoba and Berlin. There were differences, to
be sure, within the varying dimensions of that homogeneity. The French
students were a vanguard sector which also represented a vast, bored, and
discontented middle class. In contrast, the massacred Mexican youths
belonged to an exceptional, enlightened minority which was irreparably
elitist and out of place in a deeply divided society. Nonetheless, it was Guevara's *idée-mère* of change and the omnipotence of desire, together with
the spectacular growth of public-university enrollment across the world
that generated a new universality: the many in rich nations and the few in
poor ones.

The figures are worth recalling. An expansion of the generations actually did take place. In 1960, there were only 16 million individuals between
the ages of eighteen and twenty-four in the United States; by 1970, the
number had reached 25 million, a 50 percent increase in ten years.[17] In
France, university rolls jumped from 201,000 in 1961 to 514,000 in 1968.[18]

In Japan the number of universities soared from only 47 just after the war to 236 by 1960.[19] The growth rate was just as high in the United States. In 1960, there were 3 million students enrolled in higher education. By August 1964 that figure had reached 4 million; it passed 5 million in 1965, and was twice that many by 1973.[20] Before World War II, only 14 percent of U.S. high-school graduates attended college; by 1961 the rate grew to 38 percent and by 1971, to over 50 percent.[21] In Chile, Brazil, and Mexico, three Latin American countries which saw large student uprisings during the sixties, student body expansion rates reached figures of 200 to 400 percent for the decade.[22]

To paraphrase the Beatles, the road was indeed a long and winding one from the early sixties, before Che's death, to the final dismemberment of all of the movements and their drift into nostalgia and a deeper impact, long after his passing. It began with baby-boom demographics in the West and led to the explosion of public higher education around the world. It proceeded from the massing of education, demonstrations, and rebellion against *in loco parentis* regulations at Berkeley, Columbia, and Nanterre, to marches for civil rights in Mississippi, against the war in Vietnam, and against authoritarian rule in Mexico and Eastern Europe. It then moved on to shrill student politicization on the Boul' Mich, proletarian general strikes in Billancourt and Milan, radical stridency on the campus, and existential revolt and "cultural" rejection of the status quo in the communes. It finally ranged from the endless debates at the Odéon in 1968 in Paris to rock, drugs, and sex at Woodstock. The passage from the political to the cultural stranded many and disappointed others, but transformed societies which otherwise might well have remained stagnant and closed.

But before leaving their more lasting cultural imprint on the world, the sixties also traced a political trail, though not necessarily the one most of the actors expected. The hubris of those deluded, exuberant young people manning the barricades was built upon an essential foundation that even today gives meaning and relevance to the era. In a sense, those arrogant partisans of a willed, radical transformation of the world were almost right. For the last occasion this century—and doubtless for a long time to come—it seemed reasonable to seek to change the order of things according to a pre-established plan, different from anything already in existence. That occasion would be followed by more successful attempts at other types of transformation: the destruction of the socialist world and the establishment of a capitalist order or the overthrow of the welfare state and the Keynesian economy. But never again would broad sectors from different societies propose to change the world starting not from a status quo ante or even other existing realities, but from a utopian ideal: to build a world that had simply never existed before, anywhere.

In Czechoslovakia, 1968 truly did represent a last chance to change the course—and the soul—of barracks socialism. The Soviet invasion in August canceled any possibility of reform in the Eastern bloc, in a foreclosure whose cost would become apparent twenty years later. Perhaps the Stalinist regimes were not reformable; but at that time the reformers' hopes seemed both plausible and heroic. Similarly, the vast student and labor movements of those years in France and Italy signaled the last time that a profound transmutation of industrial society seemed at all feasible. And the fleeting hope combining optimism, joy, and social solidarity which culminated in Robert Kennedy's presidential bid in the spring of 1968 reflected a final effort to build a more equitable and noble America. Along with Martin Luther King's attempt to unite the civil rights movement with economic and social justice and opposition to the Vietnam war, it was perhaps the last chance for social-democracy in the United States.

The revolution imagined by the militants of the Latin Quarter did not take place, nor could it have. But the opportunities for profound change were genuine, even if they were ultimately unrealized. In the perceptive words of Eric Hobsbawm:

> And if there was a single moment in the golden years after 1945 which corresponds to the simultaneous upheaval of which the revolutionaries had dreamed after 1917, it was surely 1968, when students rebelled from the USA and Mexico in the West to socialist Poland, Czechoslovakia and Yugoslavia, largely stimulated by the extraordinary outbreak of May 1968 in Paris, epicentre of a Continent-wide student uprising.[23]

But since it did not happen, the thrust of the sixties was defeated, as Che was in the barren hills of Bolivia. And so it was nearly unavoidable that if those years and their icon were to leave lasting footprints for the future, they would have to be of another nature: not political or ideological. For Che and his protesting pallbearers to have constructed a political legacy, they would have had to win, somewhere, sometime, somehow. They did not—as unfair as this judgment may seem, or however uneven the playing field may have been. Even in 1968, victory was dragged out of their reach: in Bolivia and throughout Latin America, by coups and counterinsurgency strategies; in France and Italy, by significant social reform and conservative backlash; in Czechoslovakia by Brezhnev's bayonets and doctrines; and in the United States by assassinations, excesses, and the ultimate pragmatism of an American establishment that preferred to cut its losses and acknowledge defeat in Vietnam.

So Che Guevara did not end up in a mausoleum or pharaonic square but on T-shirts, Swatches, and beer mugs. The sixties, of which he was so emblematic, did not alter the fundamental economic and political structures of the societies the young revolted against, but had their impact relegated to the more intangible confines of power and society. Given their druthers, Che and the movements he came to symbolize would have undoubtedly preferred the former course: to achieve the political revolution they fought for, one way or the other. But in the end, perhaps the true and lasting relevance of the epoch Che personified lies precisely in the other sphere: less spectacular, less immediate, less romantic; more profound and broader, just as meaningful, if not more so. Che Guevara is a cultural icon today largely because the era he typified left cultural tracks much more than political ones.

In the sixties, politics and culture converged, but culture lasted, and politics did not—which is why a European definition, after Michel Foucault, is probably more precise. The sixties mainly affected the sphere of power and powers: those infinite, meandering channels of power beyond the state that circumscribe, order, classify, and delineate human lives in modern societies. What the sixties wrought everywhere was, first, an acknowledgment of the existence of power in society outside politics, economics, and the state; and second, the need to resist these latter powers, erode their prerogatives, question their legitimacy, deny their permanence. This is the lasting legacy of that decade, and what bestows on it the singular importance it still bears and the surprising nostalgia it evokes. It is also what made Che the perfect fit, the supreme emblem of that cultural revolt—a man whose politics were conventional but whose attitude toward power and politics attained epic and unique dimensions.

The sixties are still with us today for the same reason that Che Guevara's likeness remains visible across the world: because they brought about an irreversible cultural insurrection in the "modern" part of the globe. Something changed in 1968, and the world would never again be quite the same. The upheaval affected relations between young and old, men and women, between sanity and madness, health and illness; between subjects and objects of power, between teachers and the taught, between black and white, even between rich and poor. Liberation of sexual mores, dress habits, musical and visual tastes; irreverence in the face of authority and, beyond, the recognition of otherness of all persuasions remain today the most outstanding bequests of the sixties. Granted, the extension to all corners of the earth of middle-class propensities in their archetypal American manifestations—jeans and rock 'n' roll, homogeneity and equality among those hitherto unequal—is not everyone's utopia. But it was better than the status quo ante, and a huge step forward for those banned from the previous tidy and exclusionary arrangements that "modern" societies worshipped.

Che can be found just where he belongs: in the niches reserved for cultural icons, for symbols of social uprisings that filter down deep into the soil of society, that sediment in its most intimate nooks and crannies. Many of us today owe the few attractive and redeeming features of our daily existence to the sixties, and Che Guevara personifies the era, if not the traits, better than anyone. Celia de la Serna's son might not necessarily have recognized these traits as those he fought and perished for, but then even Comandante Ernesto Guevara was not allowed to write the epitaph he desired. He was only destined, like so few others in his time, to die the death he wished, and to live the life he dreamed.

Notes

Prologue

1. Gary Prado Salmon, interview with the author, Santa Cruz de la Sierra, October 26, 1994.

2. Ernesto Che Guevara, *Escritos y discursos,* vol. 9 (Havana: Editorial de Ciencias Sociales, 1977), p. 391.

Chapter 1:
Childhood, Youth, and Asthma in Argentina

1. Carmen Córdova Itúrburu, interview with the author, Buenos Aires, August 21, 1996.

2. Ibid.

3. Ernesto Guevara Lynch, *Mi hijo el Che* (Barcelona: Editorial Planeta, 1981), p. 112.

4. Victor Bulmer-Thomas, *Economic History of Latin America* (New York: Cambridge University Press, 1994), pp. 104, 107.

5. Ercilia Guevara Lynch, quoted in Adys Cupull and Froilán González, *Ernestito: Vivo y presente: Iconografía testimoniada de la infancia y la juventud de Ernesto Che Guevara, 1928–1953* (Havana: Editora Política, 1989), p. 9.

6. Roberto Guevara, quoted in Claudia Korol, *El Che y los argentinos* (Buenos Aires: Editorial Dialéctica, 1988), p. 32.

7. Dolores Moyano Martín, interview with the author, Washington, D.C., February 26, 1996.

8. Celia de la Serna, interview in *Granma* (Havana), October 16, 1967, p. 8.

9. Guevara Lynch, *Mi hijo,* p. 148.

10. Rosendo Zacarías, interview with the author, Alta Gracia, February 17, 1995.

11. Elba Rossi Oviedo Zelaya, interview with the author, Alta Gracia, February 17, 1995.

12. Guevara Lynch, *Mi hijo,* p. 186.

13. Ibid., p. 201.

14. Ahmed Ben Bella, interview with the author, Geneva, November 4, 1995.

15. Tomás Granado, interview with the author, Caracas, March 13, 1995.

16. Colegio Nacional Deán Funes y Liceo de Señoritas, Ernesto Guevara, report card, 1945, reproduced in Cupull and González, *Ernestito,* p. 100.

17. Alberto Granado, interview in *Página 12* (Buenos Aires), July 3, 1994, p. 28.

18. Cupull and González, *Ernestito,* p. 100.

19. Tomás Granado, interview.

20. Guevara Lynch, *Mi hijo,* p. 217.

21. Carmen Córdova Itúrburu, interview.

22. Katherine Maldonado, interview with the author, New York, February 29, 1996.

23. Ibid.

24. Carmen Córdova Itúrburu, interview.

25. Juan Martín Guevara de la Serna, quoted in Cupull and González, *Ernestito,* p. 97.

26. Fernando Córdova Itúrburu, interview with the author, Buenos Aires. August 22, 1996.

27. This version of the anecdote is quoted directly from Alberto Granado, "Mis encuentros con el Che," unpublished manuscript made available to the author, undated, p. 4.

28. Roberto Guevara de la Serna, quoted in Cupull and González, *Ernestito,* p. 111.

29. Fernando Córdova Itúrburu, interview.

Chapter 2:
Years of Love and Indifference in Buenos Aires:
Medical School, Perón, and Chichina

1. Ernesto Guevara de la Serna, "Inaugural Address at the Indoctrination Course Given at the Ministry of Public Health," August 19, 1960, in Ernesto Che Guevara, *Escritos y discursos,* vol. 4 (Havana: Editorial de Ciencias Sociales, 1977), p. 175.

2. Alberto Granado, quoted in Claudia Korol, *El Che y los argentinos* (Buenos Aires: Ediciones Dialéctica, 1988), p. 60.

3. Ernesto Guevara Lynch, *Mi hijo el Che* (Madrid: Editorial Planeta, 1981), p. 339.

4. Ernesto Guevara de la Serna, letter to Chichina Ferreyra, December 5, 1951.

5. Alberto Granado, *Con el Che Guevara de Córdoba a la Habana* (Córdoba: Op Oloop Ediciones, 1995), p. 42.

6. Alberto Granado, "Mis encuentros con el Che," unpublished manuscript lent to the author, undated, p. 18.

7. Ernesto Guevara de la Serna, letter to Chichina Ferreyra, February 1, 1951.

8. Horacio Daniel Rodríguez, *Che Guevara: ¿Aventura o revolución?* (Barcelona: Plaza y Janés, 1968), p. 39.

9. Relevant sources include: Ernesto Guevara Lynch, *Mi hijo el Che* and *Aquí va un soldado de América* (Buenos Aires: Editorial Sudamericana/Planeta, 1987); Adys Cupull and Froilán González, *Cálida presencia: Cartas de Ernesto Guevara de la Serna a Tita Infante* (Santiago de Cuba: Editorial Oriente, 1995) and *Un hombre bravo* (Havana: Editorial Capitán San Luis, 1994); and Adys Cupull and Froilán González, *Ernestito: Vivo y presente* (Havana: Editora Política, 1989).

10. Ernesto Guevara de la Serna, letter to Celia de la Serna de Guevara, quoted in Ernesto Guevara Lynch, *Aquí va,* p. 86

11. Ana María Guevara de la Serna, quoted in Korol, *El Che,* p. 67.

12. Korol, *El Che,* p. 70; and Carlos Ferrer, telephone interview with the author, Buenos Aires, August 23, 1996.

13. Chichina Ferreyra, interview with the author, Malagueño, February 18, 1995.

14. Ernesto Guevara Lynch, interview given to Esteban Morales and Fabián Ríos, in *Comandante Che Guevara* (Buenos Aires: Cuadernos de América Latina, 1968), p. 5.

15. Cupull and González, *Cálida presencia,* p. 77.

16. Ernesto Guevara de la Serna, letter to Celia de la Serna de Guevara, September 24, 1955, in Guevara Lynch, *Aquí va,* p. 109.

17. Ibid., p. 110.

18. Ibid.

19. Ernesto Guevara de la Serna, letter to Beatriz Guevara Lynch, quoted in Korol, *El Che,* p. 70.

20. Ernesto Guevara de la Serna, letter to Celia de la Serna de Guevara, in Guevara Lynch, *Aquí va,* p. 110.

21. Tulio Halperín Donghi, *La larga agonía de la Argentina peronista* (Buenos Aires: Ariel, 1994), p. 26.

22. Ibid.

23. Ernesto Che Guevara, "Angustia (eso es cierto)," *Primer Plano* (Buenos Aires), August 2, 1992. The text was released for publication by Ana María Erra, Che's father's widow.

24. Berta Gilda Infante, quoted in Cupull and González, *Ernestito,* p. 117.

25. Ferreyra, interview.

26. Roberto Guevara de la Serna, quoted in Korol, *El Che*, p. 76.

27. Fernando Córdova Itúrburu, interview with the author, Buenos Aires, August 23, 1996.

28. Carlos Figueroa, quoted in Cupull and González, *Ernestito*, p. 76.

29. Cupull and González, *Cálida presencia*, p. 9.

30. Ibid., p. 15.

31. Chichina Ferreyra, letter to Dolores Moyano Martín, Malagueño, January 4, 1968.

32. Ibid.

33. Ferreyra, interview.

34. Ernesto Guevara de la Serna, letter to Chichina Ferreyra, February 1, 1951.

35. Chichina Ferreyra, letter to Dolores Moyano Martín, January 4, 1968.

36. Ernesto Guevara de la Serna, letter to Chichina Ferreyra, February 1, 1951.

37. Ernesto Guevara de la Serna, letter to Chichina Ferreyra, December 5, 1951.

38. Ibid.

39. Ibid.

40. Ferreyra, interview.

41. José Aguilar, quoted in Cupull and González, *Ernestito*, p. 135.

42. Ernesto Guevara de la Serna, letter to Ernesto Guevara Lynch, quoted in Guevara Lynch, *Mi hijo*, p. 334.

43. Ernesto Che Guevara, quoted in Korol, *El Che*, p. 81.

44. Ernesto Guevara de la Serna, letter to Beatriz Guevara Lynch, quoted in Cupull and González, *Un hombre bravo*, p. 22.

45. Chichina Ferreyra, letter to Dolores Moyano Martín, January 4, 1968.

46. Ibid.

47. Ernesto Che Guevara, *Mi primer gran viaje: de la Argentina a Venezuela en motocicleta* (Buenos Aires: Seix Barral, 1994), pp. 50–51.

48. Chichina Ferreyra, letter to the author, August 22, 1996.

49. Ernesto Guevara de la Serna, letter to Chichina Ferreyra, March 1952.

Chapter 3:
First Blood: Navigating Is Necessary, Living Is Not

1. This idea derives from conversations and letters, always valuable, with Enrique Hett at Dartmouth College and in Paris, March and November 1996.

2. Ernesto Che Guevara, *Mi primer gran viaje: de la Argentina a Venezuela en motocicleta* (Buenos Aires: Seix Barral, 1994), p. 100.

3. Ibid., p. 76.

4. Ibid., pp. 86–87.

5. Ibid., pp. 91–92.

6. Ibid., p. 100.

7. Ibid., p. 101.

8. Ibid., p. 103.

9. Ibid., p. 109.

10. Ibid., p. 143.

11. An episode masterfully described by Alberto Granado, *Con el Che por Sudamérica* (Havana: Editorial Letras Cubanas), p. 103.

12. Guevara, *Viaje,* p. 115.

13. Ibid., p. 174.

14. Ernesto Che Guevara, "Machu Picchu: Enigma de piedra en América," *Revista de Casa de las Américas* (Havana), vol. 28, no. 163, July–August 1987, p. 51.

15. Ibid., p. 53.

16. Ibid.

17. Ibid., p. 51.

18. Jean Cormier, *Che Guevara* (Paris: Editions du Rocher, 1995), p. 53.

19. Quoted in Alberto Granado, "Mis encuentros con el Che," unpublished manuscript lent to the author, p. 88.

20. Guevara, *Viaje,* p. 171.

21. Granado, *Con el Che,* pp. 131, 133, 134, 135.

22. Ibid., p. 199. The passages reproduced at the end of the book seem to have been taken directly from Ernesto's unrevised diary.

23. This passage comes from a letter to Che's mother but is not included in his journal. Ernesto Guevara de la Serna, letter to Celia de la Serna de Guevara, July 6, 1952, quoted in Ernesto Che Guevara, *Viaje,* p. 208.

24. Guevara, *Viaje,* p. 212.

25. Ibid., p. 182.

26. Granado, *Con el Che,* p. 235.

27. Jimmy Roca, quoted in *Primera Plana* (Buenos Aires), October 17, 1967, p. 29.

28. Tita Infante, "Testimonio argentino," reprinted in Ernesto Guevara Lynch, *Aquí va un soldado de América* (Buenos Aires: Editorial Sudamericana/ Planeta, 1987), p. 168.

29. Guevara, *Viaje,* p. 20.

30. This omission was noted by Lawrence Whitehead in his review of the English version of Che's travel journal. Lawrence Whitehead, "Furibundo de la Serna," *London Review of Books,* November 2, 1995, p. 20.

31. Guevara, *Viaje,* p. 187. Several people who have reviewed these passages from the diary and who knew Che from those years have expressed doubts as to

their authenticity. The person they knew simply does not jibe with the writing. This is Chichina Ferreyra's opinion, for example, as suggested to the author in a letter dated August 22, 1996.

32. Ibid.

33. Alberto Granado, quoted by I. Lavretsky (Josef Grigulevich), *Ernesto Che Guevara* (Moscow: Progress Publishers), p. 38.

34. Celia de la Serna Guevara, interview with Julia Constenla, *Bohemia* (Havana), August 27, 1971, p. 33.

35. Chichina Ferreyra, letter to the author, March 7, 1996.

36. Chichina Ferreyra, letter to Dolores Moyano Martín, January 4, 1968.

37. Ibid.

38. Domingo Granata, quoted in Adys Cupull and Froilán González, *Ernestito, Vivo y presente* (Havana: Editora Política, 1989), p. 167.

39. Ibid.

40. José Aguilar, quoted in *Granma* (Havana), October 16, 1967.

41. Ernesto Guevara de la Serna, letter to Tita Infante, November 29, 1954, quoted in Guevara Lynch, *Aquí va*, p. 80.

42. Jorge Ferrer, letter to the author, Philadelphia, March 15, 1996.

43. Matilde Lezica, quoted in Cupull and González, *Ernestito*, p. 172.

44. Isaías Nougués, letter to the author, Buenos Aires, March 29, 1996.

45. Carlos Ferrer, telephone interview with the author, Buenos Aires/ Gualaguaches, August 25, 1996.

46. Mario Monje, interview with the author, Moscow, November 1, 1995.

47. Ernesto Guevara de la Serna, letter to Ernesto Guevara Lynch, July 24, 1953, quoted in Guevara Lynch, *Aquí va*, p. 15.

48. Ernesto Guevara de la Serna, letter to Tita Infante, September 3, 1953, quoted in Guevara Lynch, *Aquí va*, pp. 21–22.

49. Ernesto Guevara de la Serna, letter to Celia de la Serna de Guevara, undated, quoted in Jean Cormier, *Che Guevara* (Paris: Editions du Rocher, 1995), p. 71.

50. Carlos Ferrer, letter to Ernesto Guevara Lynch, quoted in Guevara Lynch, *Aquí va*, p. 13.

51. Ricardo Rojo, *Mi amigo el Che* (Buenos Aires: Editorial Legasa, 1985; first edition, 1968), p. 33.

52. Ernesto Guevara de la Serna, "Notas de su segundo diario de viaje," quoted in María del Carmen Ariet, *Che: Pensamiento político* (Havana: Editora Política, 1988), p. 41. Ariet worked as a sort of secretary to Che's widow, Aleida March, and had access to several texts by Che unpublished at the time, and others which remain so. The unpublished works she refers to all seem authentic.

53. Ibid., p. 40.

54. Ernesto Guevara de la Serna, letter to Beatriz Guevara Lynch, December 10, 1953, quoted in Guevara Lynch, *Aquí va*, p. 29.

55. Ernesto Guevara de la Serna, "Notas," in Claudia Korol, *El Che y los argentinos* (Buenos Aires: Ediciones Dialéctica, 1988), p. 96.

56. Hilda Gadea, *Che Guevara: Años decisivos* (Mexico City: Aguilar, 1972), p. 22.

57. Rojo, *Mi amigo,* p. 60.

58. Victor Bulmer-Thomas, *The Economic History of Latin America Since Independence* (New York: Cambridge University Press, 1994), p. 312.

59. François Chevalier, *L'Amérique Latine de l'indépendance à nos jours* (Paris: Presses Universitaires de France, 1977), p. 218.

60. Ernesto Guevara de la Serna, letter to Ana María de la Serna, January 15, 1954, quoted in Guevara Lynch, *Aquí va,* p. 34.

61. Ernesto Guevara de la Serna, letter to Celia de la Serna de Guevara, quoted in Guevara Lynch, *Aquí va,* p. 50.

62. Hilda Guevara Gadea, interview with the author, Havana, February 15, 1995.

63. Ernesto Guevara de la Serna, letter to Celia de la Serna de Guevara, April 1954, quoted in Guevara Lynch, *Aquí va,* p. 53.

64. Gadea, *Años decisivos,* p. 58.

65. Ibid., p. 116.

66. Ibid., p. 119.

67. Hugo Gambini, *El Che Guevara* (Buenos Aires: Editorial Paidós, 1968), p. 99.

68. Oleg Daroussenkov, interview with the author, San Diego, January 16, 1996.

69. Ernesto Guevara de la Serna, letter to Ana María Guevara de la Serna, quoted in Guevara Lynch, *Aquí va,* p. 36.

70. Adys Cupull and Froilán González, *Calida presencia: Cartas de Ernesto Guevara de la Serna a Tita Infante* (Santiago de Cuba: Editorial Oriente, 1995), p. 53.

71. Ernesto Guevara de la Serna, letter to Celia de la Serna de Guevara, May 1954, quoted in Guevara Lynch, *Aquí va,* p. 49.

72. Ibid., p. 56.

73. Ibid.

74. Ernesto Guevara de la Serna, letter to Celia de la Serna de Guevara, July 4, 1954, quoted in Guevara Lynch, *Aquí va,* p. 57.

75. Ernesto Guevara de la Serna, letter to Tita Infante, quoted in Cupull and González, *Cálida presencia,* p. 60.

76. Rojo, *Mi amigo,* pp. 68, 72.

77. Gadea, *Años decisivos,* pp. 71–73.

78. Ernesto Guevara de la Serna, letter to Celia de la Serna de Guevara, December 28, 1953, quoted in Guevara Lynch, *Aquí va,* p. 31.

79. Ernesto Guevara de la Serna, letter to Celia de la Serna de Guevara, July 4, 1954, quoted in Guevara Lynch, *Aquí va,* p. 58, and Ernesto Guevara de la Serna, letter to Beatriz Guevara Lynch, July 22, 1954, quoted in Guevara Lynch, *Aquí va,* p. 59.

80. Celia de la Serna de Guevara, interview with Julia Constenla, *Bohemia* (Havana), August 27, 1961, p. 33.

81. Ernesto Guevara de la Serna, letter to Beatriz Guevara Lynch, October 7, 1955, quoted in Guevara Lynch, *Aquí va,* p. 114.

82. Gadea, *Años decisivos,* p. 29.

83. Rolando Morán, unpublished interview with Francis Pisani, provided to the author by Pisani, Mexico, November 18, 1985.

84. Hilda Gadea, interview with Cuba's Office of Historical Affairs, published in *Granma* (Havana), October 16, 1967.

85. Ernesto Guevara de la Serna, interview with Jorge Ricardo Masetti, reprinted in *Granma* (Havana), October 16, 1967.

86. Adys Cupull and Froilán González, *Un hombre bravo* (Havana: Editorial Capitán San Luis, 1994), p. 58.

87. Ernesto Guevara de la Serna, letter to Celia de la Serna de Guevara, June 20, 1954, quoted in Guevara Lynch, *Aquí va,* p. 56.

88. Ernesto Guevara de la Serna, "Notas," in Ariet, p. 47.

89. Mario Dalmau and Darío López, interviews published in *Granma* (Havana), October 16, 1967.

90. Ernesto Guevara de la Serna, letter to Beatriz Guevara Lynch, September 1954, quoted in Guevara Lynch, *Aquí va,* p. 76.

91. Ernesto Guevara de la Serna, letter to Ernesto Guevara Lynch, February 10, 1955, quoted in Guevara Lynch, *Aquí va,* pp. 88–89.

92. Ernesto Che Guevara, letter to Celia de la Serna de Guevara, July 20, 1955, quoted in Guevara Lynch, *Aquí va,* p. 106.

93. Paco Ignacio Taibo II, "Estaciones de paso: El Che Guevara en México," *El Universal* (Mexico City), February 1996.

Chapter 4:
Under Fire with Fidel

1. Marifeli Pérez-Stable, *The Cuban Revolution: Origins, Course and Legacy* (New York: Oxford University Press, 1993), p. 16.

2. Victor Bulmer-Thomas, *The Economic History of Latin America Since Independence* (New York: Cambridge University Press, 1994), p. 309.

3. François Chevalier, *L'Amérique Latine de l'indépendance à nos jours* (Paris: Presses Universitaires de France, 1977), p. 218.

4. Ibid., p. 122.

5. Ibid., p. 314.

6. Ernesto Che Guevara, "Pasajes de la guerra revolucionaria," *Escritos y discursos,* vol. 2 (Havana: Editorial de Ciencias Sociales, 1977), p. 5.

7. Hilda Gadea, *Che Guevara: Años decisivos* (Mexico City: Aguilar, 1972), p. 124.

8. Speech by Fidel Castro during the solemn vigil in Havana in memory of Ernesto Che Guevara, October 18, 1967, in Fidel Castro, *Che: A Memoir* (Melbourne: Ocean Press, 1994), p. 68.

9. Speech by Fidel Castro in Santiago de Chile, in Fidel Castro, *Che: A Memoir,* p. 99.

10. Gadea, p. 125.

11. Centro para el estudio de la historia militar, *De Tuxpan a La Plata* (Havana: Editorial Orbe, 1981), p. 9. Hugh Thomas also speculates that the meeting took place "soon afterward." Hugh Thomas, *Cuba: la lucha por la libertad, 1909–1958,* vol. 2 (Mexico City: Grijalbo, 1974), p. 1132.

12. Robert Quirk, *Fidel Castro* (New York: Norton, 1993), p. 97. The most recent Cuban chronology also mentions July, the celebration of July 26, and a dinner at which Fidel cooked spaghetti. See also Tad Szulc, *Fidel: A Critical Portrait* (New York: Avon, 1987; first edition, 1986), p. 360; Jean-Pierre Clerc, *Fidel de Cuba* (Paris: Ramsay, 1988), p. 115; Georgie Anne Geyer, *Guerrilla Prince* (Boston: Little, Brown, 1991), p. 143.

13. Ernesto Guevara de la Serna, interview with Jorge Ricardo Masetti, "Che en Guatemala," *Granma* (Havana), October 16, 1967.

14. Ernesto Che Guevara, "Notas de su segundo diario de viaje," quoted in María del Carmen Ariet, *Che: Pensamiento político* (Havana: Editorial Política, 1988), p. 148.

15. Speech by Fidel Castro in Santiago de Chile, in Fidel Castro, *Che: A Memoir,* p. 100.

16. Fidel Castro, quoted in Lee Lockwood, *Castro's Cuba, Cuba's Fidel* (New York: Macmillan, 1967), pp. 143, 144.

17. Lucila Velázquez, in *El Nacional* (Caracas), October 1967, quoted in Geyer, *Guerilla Prince,* p. 144.

18. Ernesto Guevara de la Serna, letter to Celia de la Serna de Guevara, October 1956, quoted in Ernesto Guevara Lynch, *Aquí va un soldado de América* (Buenos Aires: Sudamericana/Planeta, 1987), p. 150.

19. Ernesto Guevara de la Serna, letter to Celia de la Serna de Guevara, December 5, 1955, quoted in Guevara Lynch, *Aquí va,* p. 121.

20. Ernesto Che Guevara, "Palenque," quoted in Gadea, *Años decisivos,* pp. 235–236.

21. Ernesto Guevara de la Serna, letter to Celia de la Serna de Guevara, September 24, 1955, quoted in Guevara Lynch, *Aquí va,* p. 111.

22. Ernesto Guevara de la Serna, letter to Tita Infante, quoted in Guevara Lynch, *Aquí va,* p. 130.

23. Ernesto Che Guevara, "Pasajes de la guerra revolucionaria," *Encritos y discursos,* vol. 2 (Havana: Editorial de Ciencias Sociales, 1977), p. 5.

24. Thomas, *Cuba,* p. 1132.

25. Fernando Gutiérrez Barrios, interview with the author, Mexico City, July 28, 1995.

26. Nikolai Leonov, interview with the author, Moscow, October 29, 1995.

27. Ibid.

28. Gutiérrez Barrios, interview.

29. Alberto Bayo, photocopy of original notes, quoted in Adys Cupull and

Froilán González, *Un hombre bravo* (Havana: Editorial Capitán San Luis, 1994), p. 78.

30. Alberto Bayo, *Mi aporte a la revolución cubana* (Havana: Imprenta Ejército Rebelde, 1960), p. 76.

31. "Che was convinced that he had found a mission and a way of leaving his wife." Quirk, *Fidel,* p. 98.

32. Ernesto Guevara de la Serna, letter to Tita Infante, October 1956, quoted in Adys Cupull and Froilán González, *Cálida presencia: Cartas de Ernesto Guevara de la Serna a Tita Infante* (Santiago de Cuba: Editorial Oriente, 1995), p. 87.

33. Juan Ortega Arenas, interview with the author, Mexico City, May 23, 1996.

34. Theodore Draper, *Castroism: Theory and Practice* (New York: Praeger, 1965), p. 165.

35. Thomas, *Cuba,* pp. 1074–1076.

36. Pérez-Stable, *Cuban Revolution,* p. 59.

37. Fidel Castro, quoted in Ernesto Che Guevara, "Pasajes," p. 22.

38. Che Guevara and Raúl Castro, *La conquista de la esperanza* (Mexico City: Ediciones Joaquín Mortíz, 1995), p. 141.

39. Harry "Pombo" Villegas, interview with British journalists, Havana, September 1995. Transcript made available to the author.

40. Guevara, "Pasajes," pp. 57–58.

41. Ibid., p. 63.

42. Ibid., p. 65.

43. Ibid., pp. 88–89.

44. Villegas, interview.

45. Castro, quoted in Cupull and González, *Un hombre bravo,* p. 107.

46. Guevara, "Pasajes," p. 123.

47. Ernesto Che Guevara, letter to Fidel Castro, July 31, 1957, Carlos Franqui Archives, box 3, file 2, Firestone Library, Princeton University.

48. Guevara, "Pasajes," p. 161.

49. Ibid.

50. Ibid., p. 165.

51. Ibid., p. 119.

52. Ibid., p. 120.

53. See René Ramos Latour, letter to Ernesto Guevara, October 4, 1957, quoted in Carlos Franqui, *Diario de la revolución cubana* (Barcelona: R. Torres, 1976), p. 318.

54. Carlos Franqui, interview with the author, San Juan, August 20, 1996.

55. Guevara, "Pasajes," p. 222.

56. Ernesto Guevara, letter to René Ramos Latour, December 14, 1957, quoted in Franqui, *Diario,* p. 362.

57. Ibid.

58. Ernesto Guevara, letter to Fidel Castro, December 15, 1957, quoted in Quirk, *Fidel,* p. 154.

59. Ernesto Guevara, letter to Fidel Castro, January 6, 1958, quoted in Ernesto Che Guevara, *Escritos y discursos,* vol 2. (Havana: Editorial de Ciencias Sociales, 1977), p. 300.

60. Franqui, *Diario,* p. 367.

61. Ibid., p. 368.

62. This anecdote appears in Joel Iglesias, "Mis vivencias con el Che," *Verde Olivo* (Havana), October 13, 1974, p. 7.

63. Carlos María Gutiérrez, "Conversación en la Sierra Maestra," *Brecha* (Montevideo), October 9, 1987.

64. The content of Bigart's report appears in a cable from the U.S. Embassy in Cuba to the State Department dated March 3, 1958, published in *Foreign Relations of the United States, 1958–1969,* Department of State Central File, vol. 6, p. 46.

65. Carlos Franqui, "List of Books Requested for the Sierra," November 1957, in the Carlos Franqui Archives, Princeton University, box 19, file 4.

66. Joel Iglesias, quoted in Adys Cupull and Froilán González, *Entre nosotros* (Havana: Ediciones Abril, 1992), p. 9.

67. Zoila Rodríguez García, quoted in Cupull and González, *Entre nosotros,* pp. 12–13.

68. Carlos Franqui, handwritten note, "La huelga de abril," Carlos Franqui Archives, box 19, file 6.

69. Ibid.

70. Ernesto Che Guevara, "Una reunión decisiva," in "Pasajes," p. 250.

71. Pablo Ribalta, interview with Juan Carrasco, *Verde Olivo* (Havana), August 1988, p. 21.

72. Ibid.

Chapter 5:
Our Man in Havana

1. Fidel Castro, letter to Ernesto Guevara, "Marching Orders," quoted in *Che Sierra Adentro* (Havana, 1970), p. 141.

2. Ernesto Che Guevara, "Pasajes de la guerra revolucionaria," *Escritos y discursos,* vol. 2 (Havana: Editorial de Ciencias Sociales, 1977), p. 258.

3. Joel Iglesias, quoted in Adys Cupull and Froilán González, *Entre nosotros* (Havana: Ediciones Abril, 1992), p. 10.

4. Ernesto Che Guevara, "Proyecciones sociales del Ejército Rebelde," January 27, 1959, Ernesto Che Guevara, *Escritos y discursos,* vol. 4 (Havana: Editorial de Ciencias Sociales, 1977), p. 11.

5. Ibid., pp. 11, 15.

6. Ibid., p. 17.

7. José Pardo Llada, *Fidel y el "Che"* (Barcelona: Plaza y Janés, 1989), p. 132.

8. Guevara, "Proyecciones," p. 16.

9. Pardo Llada, p. 131.

10. Sergio Rodríguez, quoted in *Che Sierra Adentro,* p. 113.

11. Enrique Oltuski, interview with Paco Ignacio Taibo II, granted to Taibo and the author, Havana, February 1995.

12. Ovidio Díaz Rodríguez, quoted in Cupull and Gonzáles, *Entre nosotros,* p. 71.

13. Ernesto Che Guevara, letter to Faure Chomón, November 7, 1958, quoted in "Pasajes," p. 306.

14. Ibid., p. 200.

15. Ibid.

16. Oniria Gutiérrez, quoted in *Che Sierra Adentro,* p. 25.

17. Ibid., p. 19.

18. Enrique Oltuski, "Gente del llano," *Revista Casa de las Américas* (Havana), vol. 7, no. 40, January–February 1967, p. 53.

19. Ibid.

20. Roy Rubottom to the Secretary of State, "Arms Policy with Respect to Cuba," August 11, 1958 (Secret), National Archives, lot 61D274, box 2, College Park, Maryland.

21. Oltuski, "Gente," p. 54.

22. These three passages are from Ernesto Guevara, letter to Enrique Oltuski, November 3, 1958, quoted in Guevara, "Pasajes," pp. 309–310.

23. Eloy Gutiérrez Menoyo, interview with the author, Miami, August 3, 1995.

24. Carlos Franqui, *Vida, aventuras y desastres de un hombre llamado Castro* (Mexico City: Planeta, 1989), p. 126.

25. Fidel Castro, letter to Ernesto Che Guevara, December 26, 1958, quoted in Carlos Franqui, *Diario de la revolución cubana* (Barcelona: R. Torres, 1976), p. 667.

26. Franqui, *Diario,* p. 725.

27. Gutiérrez Menoyo, interview.

28. Guevara, "Pasajes," p. 260.

29. Franco Pierini, "As duas mulheres de Che Guevara," *Manchete* (Rio de Janeiro), April 20, 1968.

30. José Aguilar, "The Final Chapter," unpublished ms., p. 8, made available to the author.

31. Oscar Fernández Mell, "La Batalla de Santa Clara," quoted in Migdalia Cabrera Cuello, *Batalla de Santa Clara,* leaflet, p. 32.

32. Ibid., p. 35.

33. Gutiérrez Menoyo, interview.

34. Antonio Nuñez Jiménez, interview with the author, Havana, August 24, 1995.

35. Batista cites an interview given by Francisco Rodríguez Tamayo ("el Mexicano") to Stanley Ross of the *Diario de Nueva York.* See Fulgencio Batista, *Respuesta* (Mexico City: private edition, 1960), p. 106.

36. Ramón Barquin and Ismael Suárez de la Paz, interviews with the author, San Juan, August 19, 1996.

37. Antonio Nuñez Jiménez, *El Che en combate, La Campaña Guerrillera en Cuba Central* (Havana: Fundación de la Naturaleza y del Hombre, Instituto del Libro, 1995), p. 192.

38. Paco Ignacio Taibo II, *La batalla del Che, Santa Clara* (Mexico City: Planeta, 1988), p. 96.

39. Ibid., p. 98.

40. Rogelio Acevedo González, *Audacia,* quoted in *Batalla de Santa Clara,* p. 42.

41. Antonio Nuñez Jiménez, *La rendición del regimiento Leoncio Vidal* (Archivo de la Sección de Investigaciones Históricas), quoted in *Batalla de Santa Clara,* p. 115.

42. Director of Central Intelligence, Special National Intelligence Estimate, nos. 85–58, "The Situation in Cuba," November 24, 1958, quoted in Georgie Anne Geyer, *Guerrilla Prince* (Boston: Little, Brown, 1991), p. 190.

43. Fidel Castro, letter to Ernesto Che Guevara, December 26, 1958, quoted in Franqui, *Diario,* p. 667.

44. Guevara, "Pasajes," p. 263.

45. Franqui, *Diario,* p. 713.

46. Carlos Franqui, interview with the author, San Juan, August 20, 1996.

47. Ernesto Che Guevara, letter to Ernesto Sabato, April 12, 1960, quoted in Claudia Korol, *El Che y los argentinos* (Buenos Aires: Editorial Diógenes, 1988), p. 113.

48. Guevara, "Proyecciones," p. 20.

49. Carlos Franqui, *Retrato de familia con Fidel* (Barcelona: Seix Barral, 1981), p. 458.

50. Ernesto Guevara Lynch, *Mi hijo el Che* (Barcelona: Planeta, 1981), p. 70.

51. Nuñez Jiménez, interview.

52. Hugh Thomas, *Cuba: la lucha por la libertad, 1958–1970,* vol. 3 (Mexico City: Grijalbo, 1974), p. 1533.

53. Ernesto Che Guevara, letter to *Revolución* (Havana), March 10, 1959, quoted in Ernesto Che Guevara, *Cartas inéditas* (Montevideo: Editorial Sandino, 1968), p. 8.

54. Adys Cupull and Froilán González, *Un hombre bravo* (Havana: Editorial Capitán San Luis, 1994), p. 143.

55. Ibid.

56. See Richard Gott, *Las guerrillas en América Latina* (Santiago: Editorial Sudamericana, 1971), p. 21.

57. Antonio Nuñez Jiménez, *En marcha con Fidel* (Havana: Editorial Letras Cubanas, 1982), p. 147.

58. See especially Theodore Draper, *Castroism: Theory and Practice* (New York: Praeger, 1965), pp. 60–61.

59. Quoted in Tad Szulc, *Fidel: A Critical Portrait* (New York: Avon, 1987; first edition, 1986), p. 525.

60. Ernesto Che Guevara, interview with Kung Mai and Ping An, quoted in

William Ratcliff, "A New Old Che Guevara Interview," *Hispanic-American Historical Review,* August 1966, pp. 296–300.

61. Ibid., p. 296.

62. Ibid., p. 294.

63. Quoted in Marifeli Pérez-Stable, *The Cuban Revolution: Origins, Course and Legacy* (New York: Oxford University Press, 1993), p. 69.

64. Guevara, "Proyecciones," p. 19.

65. William Bowdler/AmEmbassy Havana to Dept. of State, March 20, 1959, "Communist Penetration at La Cabaña Fortress" (Confidential), U.S. Department of State Files, vol. 10, dispatch 1053.

66. Department of Defense, "Working Paper for Castro Visit," Survey of the Present Status of Cuban Armed Forces, April 15, 1959 (Secret), National Security Files, box 8, LBJ Library.

67. Quoted in Szulc, *Fidel,* p. 521.

68. Franqui, interview.

69. Arnoldo Martínez Verdugo, interview with the author, Mexico City, September 10, 1996.

70. Bowdler/AmEmbassy Havana to Dept. of State, April 21, 1959, "Political Orientation of Ernesto Che Guevara" (Confidential), U.S. Department of State Files, vol. 7, dispatch 1194.

71. Topping/AmEmbassy Havana to Dept. of State, May 4, 1959, "Allegations that Ernesto Che Guevara Is Communist" (Confidential), U.S. Department of State Files, vol. 8, dispatch 1242.

72. Quoted in Geyer, *Guerrilla Prince,* p. 201. Geyer states that another person present at the dinner corroborated Ascencio's account.

73. Hugo Gambini, *El Che Guevara* (Buenos Aires: Paidós, 1968), p. 207.

74. Memorandum of Conversation, John O'Rourke, Jules Dubois, and William Weiland, June 10, 1959, "Dubois Expects Castro Crackdown on Communists in Cuban Army" (Confidential), *Foreign Relations of the United States, 1958–1960,* Department of State Central File, vol. 6.

75. Franqui, interview.

76. Ibid.

77. Hilda Gadea, quoted in Pierini, "As duas mulheres."

78. Hilda Guevara Gadea, interview with the author, Havana, January 26, 1995.

79. José Pardo Llada, interview with Georgie Anne Geyer, quoted in Geyer, *Guerrilla Prince,* p. 222.

Chapter 6:
The "Brain of the Revolution"; the Scion of the Soviet Union

1. Ernesto Che Guevara, "La República Arabe Unida," *Verde Olivo* (Havana), October 12, 1959, in *Che periodista* (Havana: Editorial Pablo de la Torrente, 1988), p. 28.

2. Salvador Vilaseca, interview with the author, Havana, January 23, 1996.

3. Mohammed Hassanen Heikal, *The Cairo Documents* (New York: Double-day, 1973), p. 344.

4. José Pardo Llada, *Fidel y el Che* (Barcelona: Plaza y Janés, 1989), p. 143.

5. Memorandum from the Deputy Director of Intelligence and Research to the Secretary of State, "Che Guevara's Mission to Afro-Asian Countries," August 19, 1959, quoted in *Foreign Relations of the United States (FRUS), 1958–1960,* vol. 6, p. 589.

6. Ernesto Che Guevara, "La India, país de grandes contrastes," *Verde Olivo* (Havana), October 12, 1959, in *Che periodista,* p. 39.

7. Memorandum from the Deputy Director, *FRUS, 1958–1960.*

8. Ernesto Che Guevara, "Japón," *Verde Olivo* (Havana), October 19, 1959, in *Che periodista,* pp. 43–44.

9. Ernesto Che Guevara, "Indonesia," *Verde Olivo* (Havana), October 26, 1959, in *Che periodista,* p. 49.

10. Ibid., p. 54.

11. Ernesto Che Guevara, "América desde el Balcón Afroasiático, septiembre–octubre, 1959," in *Escritos y discursos,* vol. 9 (Havana: Editorial de Ciencias Sociales, 1977), p. 2.

12. Ernesto Che Guevara, "Pasajes de la guerra revolucionaria (el Congo)," unpublished manuscript, Havana, p. 86. See footnote about this text in Chapter 1, p. 5.

13. Ibid., p. 4.

14. Ernesto Che Guevara, "Yugoslavia," *Verde Olivo* (Havana), November 26, 1959, in *Che periodista,* p. 65.

15. Ibid., p. 66.

16. Ibid., pp. 69, 71.

17. Ibid., p. 69.

18. Omar Fernández, quoted in Jean Cormier, *Che Guevara* (Paris: Editions du Rocher, 1995), p. 270.

19. Philip Bonsal to Roy Rubottom, November 6, 1959 (Secret), in *FRUS, 1958–1960,* p. 659.

20. Ernesto Che Guevara, letter to Lorenzo Alujas Piñeiro, August 9, 1959, quoted in *Bohemia* (Havana), October 16, 1970, p. 28.

21. Ernesto Betancourt, interview with the author, Washington, D.C., July 12, 1995.

22. Ibid.

23. Ibid.

24. Raúl Maldonado, interview with Paco Ignacio Taibo II, made available to the author by Taibo, Mexico City, March 16, 1996.

25. Ernesto Che Guevara, quoted in Jean Cormier, *Che Guevara* (Paris: Editions du Rocher, 1995), p. 279.

26. Director of Central Intelligence, Special National Intelligence Estimate, "Communist Influence in Cuba," no. 85-60, March 22, 1960 (Secret), *Declassified*

Documents Catalog, Research Publication (Woodbridge, Conn.) vol. 18, no. 1, Jan/Feb. 1992, file series no. 0003, pp. 1–2.

27. Aleksandr Alexeiev, interview with the author, Moscow, October 28, 1995.

28. Aleksandr Alexeiev, "Che," *Novoe Vremia* (Moscow), no. 24, June 10, 1988, p. 16.

29. Aleksandr Alexeiev, "Cuba después del triunfo de la revolución," *Revista de América Latina* (Moscow), no. 10, October 1984, p. 57.

30. Nikolai Leonov, interview with the author, Moscow, October 28, 1995.

31. Ibid.

32. Ibid.

33. Alexeiev, "Che," p. 17.

34. Alexeiev, interview.

35. Telegram no. 205, Fordham to Foreign Office, June 21, 1960 (Confidential), Foreign Office Archive FO371/148295, Public Record Office, London.

36. Alexeiev, interview.

37. André Fontaine, *Histoire de la guerre froide,* vol. 2 (Paris: Fayard, 1967), p. 388.

38. K. S. Karol, *Les guérilleros au pouvoir* (Paris: Robert Laffont, 1970), pp. 206–207.

39. Ernesto Che Guevara, "Discurso a estudiantes y profesores de la Escuela Técnica Industrial," July 1, 1960, in Guevara, *Escritos y discursos,* vol. 4, p. 171.

40. Che Guevara, quoted in "Memorandum of Discussion at the 451st Meeting of the National Security Council," July 15, 1960 (Top Secret), *FRUS, 1958–1960,* p. 1014.

41. Carlos Franqui, interview with the author, San Juan, August 20, 1996.

42. Philip Bonsal to Roy Rubottom, July 13, 1960 (Secret, Eyes Only), *FRUS, 1958–1960.*

43. *Time* magazine, August 8, 1960, p. 36. Laura Berquist used the same idea in *Look* four months later, entitling her piece "The Brain of the Regime." *Look* magazine, November 8, 1960, p. 38.

44. *Time.*

45. MID-12051-28-X-60, Sergei Kudriavtsev, "Memorandum of Conversation of the Ambassador of the USSR with the Director of the National Bank of Cuba, Ernesto Che Guevara," Havana, September 1, 1960 (Secret), Archives of the Foreign Ministry, Moscow.

46. MID-11113-27-IX-60, Sergei Kudriavtsev, "Memorandum of Conversation of the Ambassador of the USSR and the Director of the National Bank of Cuba, Ernesto Che Guevara," Havana, September 27, 1960 (Secret), Archives of the Foreign Ministry, Moscow.

47. MID-12999-29-XI-60, Sergei Kudriavtsev. The agenda and discussion of topics appears in "Memorandum of a Conversation of Kudriavtsev with Ernesto Che Guevara of September 30, 1960, sent to Anatoly Dobrynin, Undersecretary of Foreign Affairs" (Top Secret), Archives of the Foreign Ministry, Moscow.

48. MID-4719-21-XI-60. See "Program for the Stay in the Soviet Union of the State Economic Mission from the Republic of Cuba," Draft for Undersecretary Dobrynin (no classification), Archives of the Foreign Ministry, Moscow.

49. Leonov, interview.

50. Ibid.

51. MID-4607-10XI-60, Ernesto Guevara to Faure Chomón, October 26, 1960 (no classification), Archives of the Foreign Ministry, Moscow.

52. MID-1648, Anatoly Dobrynin to Pushkin, October 29, 1960 (no classification), Archives of the Foreign Ministry, Moscow.

53. Leonov, interview.

54. Statements quoted in Department of State, "The Castro Regime in Cuba," August 1961, p. 4.

55. Karol, *Les guérilleros*, p. 209.

56. Cormier, *Che*, p. 296.

57. Department of State, Bureau of Intelligence and Research, Intelligence Report no. 8430, "Cuban Economic Mission to the Sino-Soviet Bloc" (Secret), March 23, 1961, pp. 2, 3.

58. Memorandum of Discussion at the 472nd Meeting of the National Security Council (Top Secret), December 29, 1960, quoted in *FRUS, 1958–1960*, p. 1187.

59. Sir F. Roberts (Moscow) to Foreign Office, Soviet-Cuba Relations, November 28, 1960 (Confidential), Foreign Office Archive FO371/48211, Public Record Office, London.

60. Leonov, interview.

61. Ernesto Che Guevara, "Comparencia televisada de la firma de acuerdos con los países socialistas," in Guevara, *Escritos y discursos*, vol. 5, p. 17.

62. Ernesto Che Guevara, "Iniciando el trabajo voluntario," *Bohemia* (Havana), October 18, 1985, p. 76.

63. Ernesto Che Guevara, "Una actitud nueva frente al trabajo," speech delivered on August 15, 1964, *Casa de las Américas*, vol. 2, p. 165, quoted in Michael Lowy, *El pensamiento del Che Guevara* (Mexico City: Siglo XXI, 1971), p. 79.

64. Ernesto Che Guevara, "Discurso pronunciado en la entrega de Certificados de Trabajo Comunista," quoted in Carlos Tablada Pérez, *El pensamiento económico de Ernesto Che Guevara* (Havana: Casa de las Américas, 1987), p. 125.

65. Ernesto Che Guevara, "Sobre el trabajo voluntario," quoted in Ernesto Che Guevara, *El libro verde olivo* (Mexico City: Editorial Diógenes, 1970), p. 102.

66. MID-11113-27-IX-60, Sergei Kudriavtsev.

67. MID-12051-28-X-60, Sergei Kudriavtsev.

68. Franqui, interview.

69. Ernesto Che Guevara, *La guerra de guerrillas*, in Guevara, *Escritos y discursos*, vol. 1, p. 33.

70. Ibid., pp. 34, 35.

71. Ibid., p. 85.

72. Ibid., p. 64.

73. Ibid., p. 113.

74. Alberto Korda, interview with the author, Havana, August 23, 1995.

Chapter 7:
"Socialism Must Live, It Isn't Worth Dying Beautifully."

1. Manuel Manresa, conversation with Paco Ignacio Taibo II, provided to the author by Taibo, Havana, February 1995.

2. Ernesto Che Guevara, "Discurso a las Milicias en Pinar del Río," April 15, 1961, quoted in Ernesto Che Guevara, *Escritos y discursos,* vol. 5 (Havana: Editorial de Ciencias Sociales, 1977), p. 73.

3. Quoted in Hugh Thomas, *Cuba: La lucha por la libertad, 1959–1970,* vol. 3 (Mexico City: Grijalbo, 1974), pp. 1661–1662.

4. See Peter Wyeth, *Bay of Pigs: The Untold Story* (New York: Simon and Schuster, 1979), p. 101.

5. Ibid., p. 102.

6. Ibid., p. 179. Tad Szulc corroborates this in *Fidel: A Critical Portrait* (New York: Avon, 1987; first edition, 1986), p. 601.

7. Richard Goodwin, "Annals of Politics, A Footnote," *The New Yorker,* May 25, 1968, p. 98.

8. British Embassy, Havana, to the Earl of Home (Foreign Office), January 11, 1962 (Confidential), Foreign Office Archive FO371/62308, Ref. 9843, p. 5, Public Record Office, London.

9. MID-2089-24-VI-61, Sergei Kudriavtsev, "Memorandum of Conversation of June 3, 1961, with the Minister of Industry Ernesto Guevara," July 12, 1961 (Secret), Archives of the Foreign Ministry, Moscow.

10. British Embassy to Earl of Home, January 11, 1962, p. 4.

11. MID-2526-9-IX-61, Sergei Kudriavtsev, "Memorandum of Conversation of July 26, 1961, with the Minister of Industry Ernesto Guevara," August 15, 1961 (Secret), Archives of the Foreign Ministry, Moscow.

12. MID-11113-27-IX-60, Sergei Kudriavtsev.

13. "Summary Guidelines Paper, United States Policy Toward Latin America," July 3, 1961 (Secret), quoted in *Foreign Relations of the United States (FRUS), 1961–1963,* Department of State Central File, vol. 12, 1996, p. 35.

14. Miriam Urrutía, interview with the author, Buenos Aires, February 15, 1995.

15. Richard Goodwin, Memorandum for the President, August 22, 1961 (Secret), JFK Library, Cambridge, Mass.

16. Ernesto Che Guevara, "Discurso en Punta del Este del 8 de agosto de 1961," in Ernesto Che Guevara, *Obra revolucionaria* (Mexico City: Ediciones ERA, 1969), p. 415.

17. Ibid.

18. "Douglas Dillon to John F. Kennedy," Montevideo, August 9, 1961 (Secret), quoted in *FRUS 1961–1963,* p. 50.

19. Guevara, "Discurso en Punta del Este."

20. Ibid.

21. Douglas Dillon to John F. Kennedy, Montevideo, August 16, 1961 (Secret, Eyes Only), quoted in *FRUS 1961–1963,* p. 60.

22. This account springs from the most recent reminiscence of Richard Goodwin, published in *Cigar Aficionado* (New York), October 1996, p. 86.

23. Goodwin, "Memorandum." Unless otherwise indicated, all the quotations from and paraphrases of what was said at this encounter in the text are from this memorandum.

24. Goodwin, "Annals," p. 104.

25. Richard Goodwin, interview with the author, Concord, Mass., May 5, 1995.

26. In the initial declassified version of the memorandum, these paragraphs were "sanitized"; the version made public in 1995 includes them verbatim.

27. Goodwin, "Annals," p. 110.

28. Adys Cupull and Froilán González, *Che: Entre la multitud* (Havana, Editorial Capitán San Luis, 1995), pp. 69–70.

29. Central Intelligence Agency, "Current Intelligence Weekly Summary," August 24, 1961 (Secret), p. 12, *Weekly Review.*

30. Department of State, Cuban Economic Mission to the Sino-Soviet Bloc, Intelligence Report No. 8430, March 23, 1961 (Secret), p. 3.

31. Arturo Frondizi, interview in *Página 12* (Buenos Aires), October 8, 1992, p. 11.

32. Carlos Castello Branco, *A renúncia de Janio* (Rio de Janeiro: Editora Revan, 1996), p. 61.

33. Luis Bruschtein and Carlos María Gutiérrez, "Che Guevara, Los Hombres de la historia," *Página 12* (Buenos Aires), p. 5.

34. Ernesto Che Guevara, interview in *Al-Tal-'ah* (Cairo), April 1965, published in Rolando E. Bonachea and Nelson P. Valdés, eds., *Che: Selected Works of Ernesto Guevara* (Cambridge: MIT Press, 1969), p. 408.

35. Régis Debray, *Loués soient nos seigneurs* (Paris: Gallimard, 1996), p. 179.

36. Ernesto Che Guevara, interview by Juan Carlos Portantiero, in *Che* (Argentina), July 27, 1961, quoted in Hugo Gambini, *El Che Guevara* (Buenos Aires: Paidós, 1968), pp. 342–343.

37. Executive Committee of the Central Planning Board, Decision No. 11, April 1961, quoted in Ernesto Che Guevara, *Ministry of Industries Minutes,* p. 731. Originally the final volume in Guevara's *Obras Completas,* the *Minutes* had a limited special distribution and is (as stated previously) not available to the general public.

38. Leo Huberman and Paul Sweezy, *Socialism in Cuba* (New York: Monthly Review Press, 1969), p. 24.

39. Ibid., p. 49.

40. British Embassy to Earl of Home, January 11, 1962, p. 8.

41. MID-1265-16-IV-61, Sergei Kudriavtsev, "Memorandum of Conversation

of April 14, 1961, with the Minister of Industry Ernesto Guevara," April 26, 1961 (Secret), Archives of the Foreign Ministry, Moscow.

42. Dudley Seers, Richard Jolly, Andrés Bianchi, and Max Nolff, *Cuba: The Economic and Social Revolution* (Raleigh: University of North Carolina Press, 1963), quoted in Gambini, *El Che*, p. 381.

43. Theodore Draper, *Castroism, Theory and Practice* (New York: Praeger, 1965), p. 152.

44. "Ernesto Guevara to Anastas Mikoyan," June 30, 1961 (no classification), Archives of the Foreign Ministry, Moscow.

45. Thomas, *Cuba*, p. 1706.

46. "Ernesto Che Guevara, intervención televisada," March 1962, quoted in Robert E. Quirk, *Fidel Castro* (New York: Norton, 1993), p. 402.

47. MID-366, Sergei Kudriavtsev, "Notes on Conversation of December 8, 1961, with the Minister of Industry Ernesto Guevara," December 18, 1961 (Secret), Archives of the Foreign Ministry, Moscow.

48. Thomas, *Cuba*, p. 1705.

49. Gustavo Arcos-Bergnés, interview with the author, Havana, August 25, 1995.

50. Alfredo Guevara, conversation with the author, Havana, January 23, 1996.

51. Ibid.

52. Executive Committee of the Central Planning Board, Decision No. 11.

53. Ernesto Che Guevara, "Contra el burocratismo," in Guevara, *Obra revolucionaria*, p. 545.

54. Ernesto Che Guevara, "Sobre el sistema presupuestario de financiamiento," in Guevara, *Obra revolucionaria*, p. 599.

55. Ernesto Che Guevara, "Discurso en la primera reunión nacional de producción," August 27, 1961, in Guevara, *Escritos y discursos*, vol. 5, pp. 211, 212, 213, 221.

56. Charles Bettelheim, interview with the author, Paris, February 5, 1996.

57. Guevara, *Minutes*, p. 177.

58. Ibid., p. 216.

59. MID-010171-20-VI-62, Ernesto Che Guevara, quoted in Sergei Kudriavtsev, "Memorandum of Conversation of May 8, 1962, with the Minister of Industries Ernesto Guevara," May 21, 1962 (Top Secret), Archives of the Foreign Ministry, Moscow.

60. Ernesto Che Guevara, "Discurso en el seminario sobre planificación en Argelia," in Ernesto Che Guevara, *Temas económicos* (Havana: Editorial de Ciencias Sociales, 1988), p. 210.

61. Ibid., p. 211.

62. Ibid., p. 213.

63. Ibid.

64. Cf., for example, "Memorandum of Conversation Between President Kennedy and President López Mateos," Mexico City, June 29, 1962 (Secret), *FRUS 1961–1963*, p. 312.

65. Sergo Mikoyan, quoted in James G. Blight and David A. Welch, *On the Brink: Americans and Soviets Reexamine the Cuban Missile Crisis* (New York: Farrar, Straus and Giroux, 1991), p. 249.

66. Aleksandr Alexeiev, interview with the author, Moscow, October 28, 1995.

67. Ibid.

68. Fidel Castro, "Transcripción de sus palabras en la conferencia sobre la Crisis del Caribe," Foreign Broadcast Information Service, Havana, January 11, 1992, quoted in The National Security Archive, Lawrence Chang and Peter Kornbluh, eds., *The Cuban Missile Crisis* (New York: The New Press, 1992), p. 332.

69. Theodore Sorensen, quoted in Blight and Welch, *On the Brink,* p. 28.

70. McGeorge Bundy, quoted in Blight and Welch, *On the Brink,* p. 249.

71. Robert McNamara, quoted in Blight and Welch, *On the Brink,* p. 249.

72. Sergo Mikoyan, quoted in Blight and Welch, *On the Brink,* p. 239.

73. Robert McNamara, Foreword, in Chang and Kornbluh, eds., *Missile Crisis,* p. xii.

74. Sergo Mikoyan, quoted in Blight and Welch, *On the Brink,* p. 239.

75. Oleg Daroussenkov, interview with the author, San Diego, Calif., February 8, 1996.

76. Castro, "Transcripción de sus palabras," p. 333.

77. Emilio Aragonés, interview with the author, Havana, January 23, 1996.

78. Ibid.

79. Alexeiev, interview.

80. Ibid.

81. Fidel Castro, quoted in Blight and Welch, *On the Brink,* p. 85.

82. Aragonés, interview.

83. Emilio Aragonés, quoted in Blight and Welch, *On the Brink,* p. 351.

84. Castro, "Transcripción de sus palabras," p. 337.

85. McNamara, Foreword, pp. xii–xiii.

86. Arthur Schlesinger, Jr., "Four Days with Castro, A Havana Diary," in the *New York Review of Books,* March 16, 1992.

87. U.S. estimates are quoted in Blight and Welch, *On the Brink,* p. 382, note 26. McNamara gives the same figure, in Foreword, pp. xii, xiii.

88. W. W. Rostow to the President, September 3, 1962 (Top Secret and Sensitive), quoted in Chang and Kornbluh, eds., *Missile Crisis,* p. 67.

89. Fidel Castro, quoted in Chang and Kornbluh, eds., *Missile Crisis,* p. 380.

90. Ibid.

91. Quoted in K. S. Karol, *Les Guérilleros au Pouvoir* (Paris: Robert Laffont, 1970), p. 260.

92. Nikita Khrushchev, letter to Fidel Castro, January 31, 1963, published in Chang and Kornbluh, eds., *Missile Crisis,* pp. 319–329.

93. Rafael del Pino, interview with the author, Washington, D.C., September 30, 1995.

94. Ibid.

95. Ibid.

96. Ricardo Rojo, *Mi amigo el Che* (Buenos Aires: Editorial Legasa, 1985; first edition, 1968), p. 150.

97. Daroussenkov, interview.

98. Ernesto Che Guevara, "Táctica y estrategia de la revolución latinoamericana," *Verde Olivo* (Havana), October 6, 1968, p. 16.

99. Aleksandr Alexeiev, interview.

Chapter 8:
With Fidel, Neither Marriage Nor Divorce

1. Canek Sánchez Guevara, interview with the author, Havana, January 26, 1996.

2. Ricardo Rojo, *Mi amigo el Che* (Buenos Aires: Editorial Legasa, pp. 160–161.

3. Ernesto Che Guevara, "Cuba ¿Excepción histórica o vanguardia en la lucha anticolonialista?", in Ernesto Che Guevara, *Obra revolucionaria* (Mexico City: Ediciones ERA, 1969), p. 525. All the quotes from this essay are taken from this edition.

4. Ernesto Goldar, "John William Cooke: de Perón al Che Guevara," in *Todo es historia* (Buenos Aires), vol. 25, no. 288, p. 26.

5. Adys Cupull and Froilán González, *Un hombre bravo* (Havana: Editorial San Luis, 1994), p. 219.

6. Amalio Rey, interview with the author, Cordoba, November 25, 1994.

7. Letter from some Argentine friends to Alcira de la Peña, Center for the Storage of Contemporary Documents, Central Committee of the Communist Party of the Soviet Union, file 89, list 28, document 16, Moscow.

8. This was recounted by a leader of Cuban women, Carolina Aguilar, quoted in Marta Rojas and Mirta Rodríguez, *Tania: La guerrillera inolvidable* (Havana: Instituto Cubano del Libro, 1970), p. 110.

9. Amalio Rey, interview.

10. K. S. Karol, *Les Guérilleros au Pouvoir* (Paris: Robert Laffont, 1970), p. 323.

11. Dolores Moyano Martín, "From El Cid to El Che: The Hero and the Mystique of Liberation in Latin America, *The World and I,* February 1998, p. 571.

12. Ahmed Ben Bella, interview with the author, Geneva, November 4, 1995.

13. Piero Gleijeses, "Cuba's First Venture in Africa: Algeria, 1961–1965," *Journal of Latin American Studies* (London University), no. 28, Spring 1996.

14. Jorge Serguera, interview with the author, Havana, January 23, 1996.

15. Juan E. Benemelis, *Castro subversión y terrorismo en Africa* (Madrid: San Martín, 1988), p. 46.

16. Gleijeses, "Cuba's First Venture," pp. 187–188.

17. Alberto Castellanos, interview with the author, Havana, January 23, 1996.

18. Ibid.

19. Ibid.

20. Ibid.

21. Ibid.

22. Carlos Franqui, *Retrato de familia con Fidel* (Barcelona: Seix Barral, 1981), p. 449.

23. Carlos Franqui, interview with the author, San Juan, August 2, 1996.

24. Ibid.

25. Ciro Bustos, telephone conversation with the author, September 7, 1996.

26. Mikhail Suslov, quoted in Thomas Hughes/INR-DOS, Cuba 1964, Bureau of Intelligence and Research, Research Memorandum, Department of State, April 17, 1964 (Secret), p. 10, NSF, Country File, Cuba, vol. 1, LBJ Library.

27. MID-9-V-63, Aleksandr Alexeiev, "Memorandum of Conversation of February 25, 1963, with Minister of Industries Ernesto Guevara," May 9, 1963 (Secret), Archives of the Foreign Ministry, Moscow.

28. Ibid.

29. Department of Defense Intelligence Information Report (Col. J. E. Boyt), "Disarming of Cuban Military Personnel and Transfer of Military Bases to Soviet Control," July 12, 1963 (Confidential), Miami, Report No. 2201094463.

30. Ernesto Che Guevara, Ministry of Industries Meeting of December 5, 1964, *Minutes,* p. 568.

31. MID-374-4.IX.63, Oleg Daroussenkov, "Memorandum of Conversation of August 27 with Minister of Industries Ernesto Guevara," September 4, 1963 (Top Secret), Archives of the Foreign Ministry, Moscow.

32. Ibid.

33. Oleg Daroussenkov, "Memorandum of Conversation of October 16, 1964, with Minister of Industries Ernesto Guevara," October 27, 1964, Russian National Archive, File no. 5, List no. 49, no. 758, Moscow.

34. George Ball to All American Diplomatic Posts, "Significance of Castro's Second Visit to the USSR," Department of State, January 28, 1964 (Confidential). See also a report by the State Department's Bureau of Intelligence and Research, "Castro's Second Visit to Moscow: History Repeats Itself," INR to Acting Secretary, INR Research Memorandum, Department of State, January 24, 1964 (Secret), p. 6, NSF, Country File, Cuba Cables, vol. 1, LBJ Library.

35. Report delivered by the Brazilian ambassador in Washington to Secretary Rusk, forwarded to McGeorge Bundy, National Security Adviser, undated, no classification. The report is quoted in a secret intelligence note from Thomas Hughes to Secretary Rusk, dated July 22, 1964, NSF, Country File, Cuba, INR Reports, Vol. I, no. 16 memo, LBJ Library.

36. Ernesto Che Guevara, Bi-Monthly Meeting, October 12, 1963, *Minutes,* pp. 387–390.

37. Victor Bogorod, interview with the author, Paris, February 11, 1995.

38. Ernesto Che Guevara, *Minutes,* pp. 387–388. This text appears word for word in the Carlos Franqui archive, Princeton University, Collection CO644, box 22, folder 7, October 12, 1963.

39. Bogorod, interview, and Charles Bettelheim, interview with the author, Paris, March 5, 1996.

40. Alban Lataste, "El próximo quinquenio económico 1966–1970," *Comercio Exterior* (Havana), July–September 1963, p. 44.

41. Ibid.

42. Carlos Rafael Rodríguez, "Sobre la contribución del Che al desarrollo de la economía cubana," *Cuba Socialista* (Havana), No. 33, May–July 1988, p. 11.

43. Ernesto Che Guevara, "Discurso en el seminario sobre planificación en Argelia," July 13, 1963, quoted in Ernesto Che Guevara, *Temas Económicos* (Havana: Editorial de Ciencias Sociales, 1988), pp. 215–216.

44. George Kidd, Canadian Embassy, Havana, to Under-Secretary of State for External Affairs, Ottawa, "Industrialisation in Cuba," September 4, 1963 (Confidential), Foreign Office Archive FO371/168174, Public Record Office, London.

45. René Dumont, *Cuba Est-Il Socialiste?* (Paris: Seuil, 1970), p. 42.

46. "Cuba: Changing Policy for Industrial Development," *Intelligence Digest* (Secret), quoted in Haselden to Eccles, British Embassy, Havana, December 13, 1963 (Confidential), Foreign Office Archive FO371/168174, Public Record Office, London.

47. MID-374-4.IX.63, Oleg Daroussenkov.

48. Ernesto Che Guevara, *Minutes,* p. 447.

49. Ernesto Che Guevara, *Minutes,* 1964, p. 577.

50. Marifeli Pérez-Stable, *The Cuban Revolution: Origins, Course and Legacy* (New York: Oxford University Press, 1993), p. 96.

51. Bettelheim, interview.

52. Ernesto Che Guevara, "La planificación socialista," p. 346.

53. Carlos Rafael Rodríguez, "Sobre la contribución del Che," p. 20.

54. Victor Bondarchuk, interview with the author, Moscow, October 31, 1995.

55. Ernesto Che Guevara, *Minutes,* p. 508.

56. Richard Helms, Deputy Director for Planning to Director of Central Intelligence, "Plans of Cuban Exiles to Assassinate Selected Cuban Government Leaders," June 10, 1964 (Secret), Gerald L. Ford Presidential Library.

57. Ernesto Che Guevara, letter to Aleida Coto Martínez, May 23, 1964, quoted in Cupull and González, *Un hombre bravo,* p. 258.

58. Marta Rojas and Mirta Rodríguez, *Tania: La guerrillera inolvidable* (Havana: Instituto Cubano del Libro, 1970), p. 210.

59. Canek Sánchez Guevara, interviews with the author, Havana, January 26, 1996, and Mexico City, August 15, 1996.

60. Ernesto Che Guevara, Meeting of July 11, 1964, *Minutes,* pp. 527–528.

61. The memories of Sergo Mikoyan are categorical in this regard. Sergo Mikoyan, "Encuentros con Che Guevara," *Revista América Latina,* Academia de Ciencias de la URSS, Instituto de América Latina, no. 1, 1974, p. 192.

62. Ernesto Che Guevara, "Discurso en la Conferencia de Naciones Unidas sobre Comercio y Desarrollo," Geneva, March 25, 1964, quoted in Ernesto Che Guevara, *Temas Económicos,* p. 416.

63. Ibid., p. 424.

64. Oleg Daroussenkov, "Memorandum of Conversation of April 29, 1964, with Ernesto Guevara," May 18, 1964 (Secret), Russian National Archive, File No. 5, List No. 49, Document 760.

65. Gustavo Petriciolli, interview with the author, Cuernavaca, Mexico, September 18, 1996.

66. Central Intelligence Agency, "Special Report, Cuban Training and Support for African Nationalists," January 31, 1964.

67. Oleg Daroussenkov, interview with the author, San Diego, January 10, 1996.

68. Arnoldo Martínez Verdugo, interview with the author, Mexico City, September 11, 1996. The statement was also quoted by Cayetano Carpio in his book, *La lucha de clases, motor del desarrollo de la Guerra Popular de Liberación* (San Salvador: Ediciones enero 32), p. 138.

69. Ernesto Che Guevara, Meeting of December 5, 1964, *Minutes,* pp. 565–569.

70. Martínez Verdugo, interview.

71. G. Michael Schatzberg, *Mobutu or Chaos? The United States and Zaire, 1960–1990* (New York and Philadelphia: University Press of America/Foreign Policy Research Institute, 1991), p. 28. See also G. Madeleine Kalb, *The Congo Cables* (New York: Macmillan, 1982), pp. 378–379.

72. Havana Telegram No. 50 to Foreign Office, Cuban Political Situation (Confidential), December 12, 1964, Foreign Office Archive FO317/174007, Public Record Office, London.

73. Ernesto Che Guevara, "Discurso en la Asamblea General de las Naciones Unidas," in Ernesto Che Guevara, *Escritos y discursos,* vol. 9 (Havana: Editorial de Ciencias Sociales, 1977), p. 288.

74. Ibid., pp. 291–292.

75. Tad Szulc, *Fidel: A Critical Portrait* (New York: Avon, 1987; first edition 1986), p. 665.

76. Gordon Chase to McGeorge Bundy, Che Guevara, Washington (Top Secret, Eyes Only), December 15, 1964 (copy, LBJ Library).

77. The memorandum in which McCarthy's name first appears unexpurgated is one from Gordon Chase to McGeorge Bundy, dated December 18, 1964 (Secret). The sanitized sections were reinstated on December 7, 1994, The White House, Washington.

78. Department of State, Memorandum of Conversation, Under Secretary George Ball, Senator Eugene McCarthy to Assistant Secretary Thomas Mann, December 17, 1964 (Secret), *Declassified Documents Catalog,* Research Publications (Woodbridge, Conn.).

79. Ernesto Che Guevara, "Discurso en el Conglomerado Industrial 30 de noviembre," Santiago, Cuba, November 30, 1964, quoted in Zarco Bozik, "Cuban Panorama: To Overcome Monoculture by Developing Monoculture," *Borba* (Belgrade), December 28, 1964.

80. Thompson (Havana) to Brown (American Department), Internal Situation, September 1, 1964 (Confidential), Foreign Office Archive FO371/74006, Public Record Office, London.

81. Quoted in Clissold/Havana to Foreign Office, Internal Situation, May 29, 1964 (no classification), Foreign Office Archive FO371/174005, Public Record Office, London.

Chapter 9:
Che Guevara's Heart of Darkness

1. Ahmed Ben Bella, interview with the author, Geneva, November 4, 1995.

2. Catherine Coquery-Vidrovitch, Alain Forest, and Herbert Weiss, *Rébel-lions-Révolution au Zaïre, 1963–1965* (Paris: Editions L'Harmattan, 1987), vol. 1, p. 164.

3. Ludo Martens, *Pierre Mulele, ou la Seconde Vie de Patrice Lumumba* (Antwerp: Editions EPO, 1985), p. 12.

4. See Madeleine G. Kalb, *The Congo Cables: The Cold War in Africa—From Eisenhower to Kennedy* (New York: Macmillan, 1982), p. 378.

5. Ibid., p. 220.

6. David Gibbs, *The Political Economy of Third World Intervention: Mines, Money and U.S. Policy in the Congo Crisis* (Chicago: University of Chicago Press, 1991), p. 157.

7. Coquery-Vidrovitch et al., *Rébellions*, pp. 158–159.

8. According to a cable from the U.S. Embassy in The Hague, Dutch sources in Havana reported this information. Department of State, Airgram AmEmbassy The Hague to DOS, African Travels of Che Guevara, February 16, 1965 (Confidential), NSF, Country File, Box 17, Vol. 4, #71 airgram, LBJ Library.

9. Ben Bella, interview.

10. INR/Thomas Hughes to the Secretary, Che Guevara's African Venture, RAR-13, April 19, 1965 (Secret), NSF, Country File, Cuba, Activities of Leading Personalities, no. 18 memo, LBJ Library.

11. Ben Bella, interview.

12. Jorge Serguera, interview with the author, Havana, January 23, 1996.

13. Piero Gleijeses, "Cuba's First Venture in Africa: Algeria, 1961–1965," *Journal of Latin American Studies* (London University), no. 28, Spring 1996, p. 175.

14. Ibid.

15. Ben Bella, interview.

16. Pablo Ribalta, interview with the author, Havana, August 26, 1996.

17. Serguera, interview.

18. Dariel Alarcón Ramírez, "Benigno," *Vie et Mort de la Revolution Cubaine* (Paris: Fayard, 1996), p. 102.

19. Dariel Alarcón Ramírez, "Benigno," interview with the author, Paris, November 3, 1995. Benigno "was appointed chief of Che's personal security detail when he was President of the National Bank of Cuba." *Revista Habanera* (Havana), January 1995, p. 16.

20. Director of Intelligence and Research, U.S. Department of State, Intelligence Note, January 22, 1965 (copy LBJ Library).

21. Thomas Hughes to the Secretary INR/DOS, Latin American Communists Hold Strategy Conference (Secret). See also George Denney to Acting Secretary, INR/DOS, Guerrilla and Terrorist Activity in Latin America Over the Past Four Months, April 8, 1965 (Secret), *Declassified Documents Catalog,* Research Publications (Woodbridge, Conn.), file series no. 3354, vol. 18, no. 6, Nov.–Dec. 1992.

22. Mario Monje, interview with the author, Moscow, October 28, 1995.

23. Ibid.

24. Ibid.

25. Emilio Aragonés, interview with the author, Havana, January 23, 1996.

26. Ibid.

27. Ibid.

28. AmEmbassy Dar-es-Salaam to SecState, February 16, 1965 (Confidential), NSF, Country File, Cuba, Activities of Leading Personalities, Box 20, #32 cable, LBJ Library, based upon a report from the Nigerian Chargé d'Affaires.

29. Ernesto Che Guevara, "Pasajes de la guerra revolucionaria (el Congo), Unpublished manuscript, 1966, p. 4.

30. Ibid., pp. 3–4.

31. Central Intelligence Agency, Intelligence Information Cable, Presence of Cuban Technical Advisers at Secret Training Camp for Algerian Militia, January 26, 1965 (Secret).

32. Rafael del Pino, interview with the author, Washington, D.C., September 30, 1995.

33. Guevara, "Pasajes . . . (el Congo)," p. 6.

34. Ernesto Che Guevara, "Discurso en el Segundo Seminario Económico de Solidaridad Afroasiática," Algiers, February 24, 1965, quoted in Ernesto Che Guevara, *Temas Económicos* (Havana: Editorial de Ciencias Sociales, 1988), pp. 434–435.

35. Ibid., pp. 439–440.

36. See especially Thomas Hughes to the Secretary, INR Research Memorandum 21, The Cuban Revolution: Phase Two, August 10, 1965 (Confidential), p. 3, NSF, Country File, Cuba. W. G. Bowdler File, vol. 1, no. 46 memo, LBJ Library. Also see an analysis of Cuba's response to the U.S. invasion of the Dominican Republic. Thomas Hughes to the Secretary, Cuba: Resurgent Faith in the Latin American Revolution, INR-DOS, May 20, 1965, NSF, Country File, Cuba, INR Reports, vol. 1, no. 4 memo, LBJ Library.

37. ARA/CCA: WWSmith:vc, British Embassy in Havana, Memorandum for the Files, "Whereabouts of Che Guevara" (Secret), undated, Foreign Office Archive FO/371/AK1015/46, Public Record Office, London.

38. Mohammed Heikal, *The Cairo Documents* (Garden City, N.Y.: Doubleday, 1973), p. 353.

39. Carlos Franqui, *Vida, aventuras y desastres de un hombre llamado Castro* (Mexico City: Planeta, 1988), p. 330.

40. Serguera, interview.

41. Dariel Alarcón Ramírez, "Benigno," interview with the author, Paris, November 3, 1995.

42. Guevara, "Pasajes . . . (el Congo)," pp. 25, 148.

43. Fidel Castro, in Gianni Miná, *Un encuentro con Fidel,* Office of Publications of the State Council, Havana, 1988, p. 324.

44. Carlos Franqui, interview with the author, San Juan, August 20, 1996.

45. Ibid.

46. Víctor Dreke, interview with the authors, quoted in Félix Guerra, Froilán Escobar, and Paco Ignacio Taibo II, *El año que estuvimos en ninguna parte* (Mexico City: Planeta, 1994), p. 35.

47. See the authors' interviews with several members of the expeditionary force, especially Kumi, in Taibo et al., *El año,* p. 37.

48. Aleksandr Alexeiev, interview with the author, Moscow, October 28, 1995.

49. Roberto Guevara, interview with the author, Buenos Aires, August 23, 1996.

50. Central Intelligence Agency, Intelligence Memorandum No. 2333/65, The Fall of Che Guevara and the Changing Face of the Cuban Revolution, October 18, 1965 (Limited Official Use), NSF, Country File, Cuba, Bowdler File, vol. 1, LBJ Library.

51. Fidel Castro, speech of July 26, 1965, quoted in *Bohemia* (Havana), July 30, 1965, p. 35.

52. Central Intelligence Agency, Intelligence Memorandum No. 2333/65, p. 8.

53. Ernesto Che Guevara, interview in *Al-Tali-'ah,* published in Rolando E. Bonachea and Nelson P. Valdés, eds., *Che: Selected Works of Ernesto Guevara* (Cambridge: MIT Press, 1969), p. 413.

54. Ibid., p. 411.

55. Ernesto Che Guevara, "El socialismo y el hombre en Cuba," *Marcha* (Montevideo), March 12, 1965, quoted in Guevara, *Escritos y discursos,* vol. 8 (Havana: Editorial de Ciencias Sociales, 1977), p. 259.

56. Ibid., pp. 256–257.

57. Ibid., pp. 261, 270.

58. Pablo Ribalta, interview.

59. Guevara, "Pasajes . . . (el Congo)," p. 7.

60. Ibid., p. 14.

61. Oscar Fernández Mell, interview with the author, Havana, August 24, 1995.

62. Guevara, "Pasajes . . . (el Congo)," pp. 18, 19.

63. Ibid., p. 34.

64. Guevara, *Journal,* p. 39.

65. Ibid., pp. 41, 44.

66. Guevara, "Pasajes . . . (el Congo)," p. 60.

67. Ibid., p. 63.

68. Aragonés, interview, August 24, 1995.

69. Fernández Mell, interview.

70. Aragonés, interview.

71. Ibid.

72. Bem Hardenne, "Les Opérations Anti-Guerillas dans l'Est du Congo en 1965–1966," report February 1969, mimeograph, p. 22.

73. Lawrence Devlin, telephone conversation with the author, Princeton, N.J., November 1995.

74. Ibid.

75. Guevara, "Pasajes . . . (el Congo)," pp. 81–82.

76. Fernández Mell, interview.

77. Gustavo Villoldo, interview, Miami, November 21, 1995.

78. Devlin, telephone conversation with author.

79. Guevara, "Pasajes . . . (el Congo)," p. 85.

80. Benigno, interview.

81. Guevara, "Pasajes . . . (el Congo)," p. 85.

82. Ernesto Che Guevara, letter to Fidel Castro, October 5, 1966, quoted in Guevara, "Pasajes . . . (el Congo)," pp. 86–87.

83. Benigno, interview.

84. Aragonés and Fernández Mell, interviews with the author, Havana, August 24, 1995.

85. Guevara, "Pasajes . . . (el Congo)," p. 151.

86. Benigno, interview.

87. Guevara, "Pasajes . . . (el Congo)," p. 99.

88. Robert W. Kormer to McGeorge Bundy, The White House, October 29, 1965 (Secret), NSF, Country File, Congo, vol. 12, October 1965–66, memo, LBJ Library.

89. Aragonés, interview.

90. Guevara, "Pasajes . . . (el Congo)," p. 99.

91. Benigno, interview.

92. Fidel Castro, letter to Ernesto Che Guevara, November 4, 1965, quoted in Guevara, "Pasajes . . . (el Congo)," pp. 118–119.

93. Ibid.

94. Aragonés, interview.

95. Ibid.

96. Ibid.

97. Benigno, interview, and Guevara, "Pasajes . . . (el Congo)," p. 138.

98. Guevara, "Pasajes . . . (el Congo)," p. 1.

99. Lawrence Devlin, telephone conversation.

100. Major Bem Hardenne, "Les Opérations Anti-Guerillas," pp. 19–20.

101. These comments and those in the two paragraphs that follow were shared with the author by Jules Gérard-Libois in the course of several telephone conversations, especially on November 18, 1995, and in December 1995, and in an exchange of letters in early 1996.

102. Devlin, telephone conversation; Villoldo, interview; William Bowdler, telephone conversation with author, November 8, 1996.

103. Guevara, "Pasajes . . . (el Congo)," pp. 150, 151, 152.

Chapter 10:
Betrayed by Whom in Bolivia?

1. Colman Ferrer, interview with the author, Havana, August 25, 1995.

2. Dariel Alarcón Ramírez, "Benigno," interview with the author, Paris, November 3, 1995.

3. Pablo Ribalta, quoted in Froilán Escobar, Félix Guerra, and Paco Ignacio Taibo II, *El año que estuvimos en ninguna parte* (Mexico City: Joaquín Mortiz/Planeta, 1994), pp. 242–243.

4. Angel Braguer, "Lino," interview with the author, Havana, January 24, 1996.

5. Benigno, *Vie et mort de la Révolution Cubaine* (Paris: Fayard, 1995), p. 107.

6. Oscar Fernández Mell, interview with the author, Havana, August 25, 1995.

7. Ferrer, interview.

8. Ribalta, in Taibo et al., *El año,* p. 239.

9. Dariel Alarcón Ramírez, "Benigno," telephone conversation with the author, May 15, 1996.

10. Ulises Estrada, interview with the author, August 23, 1995.

11. Carlos Franqui, *Vida aventuras y desastres de un hombre llamado Castro* (Mexico City: Planeta, 1988), p. 331.

12. Teodoro Petkoff, telephone conversation with the author, October 1996.

13. Mario Monje, interview with the author, Moscow, October 25, 1995.

14. Ibid.

15. Ibid.

16. Ibid.

17. Ibid.

18. Ibid.

19. Protocol number 8 of the Politburo meeting of the Central Committee, June 24, 1966 (Top Secret), Resolution of the International Section of the Central Committee of the Soviet Communist Party, Central Archive for the Conservation of Contemporary Documents, Moscow.

20. Monje, interview.

21. Ibid.

22. Jorge Kolle, interview with the author, Cochabamba, October 29, 1994.

23. Harry Villegas, "El verdadero diario de Pombo," *La Razón* (La Paz), October 9, 1996), p. 15.

24. Ibid., p. 18.

25. Jorge Kolle, quoted in Carlos Soria Galvarro, interview with the author, La Paz, November 5, 1994.

26. Eliseo Reyes Rodríguez ("Capitán San Luis"), "Diario de Bolivia," quoted in Carlos Soria Galvarro, ed., *El Che en Bolivia, Documentos y Testimonios,* vol. 4 (La Paz: Cedoin, 1994), p. 101.

27. All the quotations in this passage are from Villegas, "El verdadero diario," p. 21.

28. Ibid., p. 19.

29. Kolle, interview.

30. Ibid.

31. Monje, interview.

32. Benigno, *Vie et mort,* pp. 126–127.

33. Ibid.

34. Aleksandr Alexeiev, interview with the author, Moscow, October 28, 1995. See also Central Intelligence Agency, Intelligence Information Cable, October 17, 1967, National Security File, Memos to the President, vol. 46, Oct. 16–20, 1967, Doc. no. 68a (Secret), LBJ Library.

35. Humberto Vázquez Viaña and Ramiro Aliaga Saravia, *Bolivia: Ensayo de revolución continental,* provisional edition, restricted circulation, July 1970, pp. 18–19.

36. Ibid.

37. Villegas, "El verdadero diario," p. 23.

38. Benigno, *Vie et mort.*

39. Luis J. González and Gustavo A. Sánchez Salazar, *The Great Rebel: Che Guevara in Bolivia* (New York: Grove Press, 1969), p. 48.

40. Daniel James, *Che Guevara: Una biografía* (Mexico City: Editorial Diana, 1971), pp. 250–251.

41. Benigno, *Vie et mort,* p. 137.

42. Humberto Vázquez Viaña, "Antecedentes de la guerrilla del Che en Bolivia," Institute of Latin American Studies, University of Stockholm, research paper, Series no. 46, September 1987, p. 13.

43. Ibid., p. 19.

44. Régis Debray, *La guerrilla del Che* (Mexico City: Siglo XXI, 1975), p. 44.

45. Central Intelligence Agency, Directorate of Intelligence, Instability in the Western Hemisphere, Memorandum, December 9, 1966 (Secret), *Declassified Documents Catalog* (Woodbridge, Conn.: Research Publications), vol. 21, no. 2, March/April 1995.

46. Mario Monje, "Carta al Comité Central del Partido Comunista de Bolivia," La Paz, July 15, 1968, quoted in Soria Galvarro, ed., *El Che,* vol. 1, p. 117.

47. Reyes Rodríguez, *Diario,* p. 103.

48. Ernesto Che Guevara, "Diario de Bolivia," new annotated edition, published in Carlos Soria Galvarro, ed., *El Che,* vol. 5, p. 71.

49. Villegas, "El verdadero diario," p. 25.

50. Benigno, interview.

51. Quoted in Inti Peredo, *Mi campaña con el Che* (Mexico City: Editorial Diógenes, 1971), p. 27.

52. Benigno, interview.

53. Gary Prado Salmón, *La guerrilla inmolade* (Santa Cruz: Grupo Editorial Punto y Coma, 1987), p. 232.

54. Guevara, *Diario,* p. 88.

55. Régis Debray, *Les Masques* (Paris: Gallimard, 1987), p. 71.

56. Vázquez Viaña and Aliaga Saravia, *Bolivia,* p. 84.

57. Prado Salmón, *La guerrilla,* p. 84.

58. Régis Debray, interview with the author, Paris, November 3, 1995.

59. Debray, *Masques,* p. 73.

60. "Tamara Bunke, Drei Leben in einer Haut," *Der Spiegel,* no. 39, September 23, 1996.

61. Gunther Mannel, interviewed in "Tania beschattete 'Che' Guevara," *Welt am Sonntag* (Berlin), May 26, 1968.

62. Ibid.

63. Wolfe reiterated this view in the long article about Tania in *Der Spiegel,* no. 39, September 23, 1996, previously cited.

64. Benigno, telephone conversation with the author, May 15, 1996.

65. Debray, interview.

66. Lino, interview.

67. Benigno, telephone conversation.

68. Lino, interview.

69. Prado Salmón, *La guerrilla,* p. 95.

70. Gustavo Villoldo, interview with the author, Miami, November 21, 1995.

71. Larry Sternfield, telephone conversation with the author, November 4, 1996.

72. John Tilton, unpublished memoirs, graciously lent to the author by John Tilton.

73. This account also appears in Debray, *Masques,* and in Adys Cupull and Froilán González, *La CIA contra el Che* (Havana: Editora Política, 1992), p. 35.

74. Benigno, telephone conversation.

75. Prado Salmón, *La guerrilla,* p. 100.

76. Ernesto Che Guevara, "Mensaje a la *Tricontinental,*" quoted in *Obra revolucionaria* (Mexico, D.F.: Ediciones ERA, 1969), p. 648.

77. General William Tope to General Porter USCINCSO, Department of State Incoming Telegram, April 22, 1967 (Confidential), NSF, Country File, Bolivia, vol. 4, box 8, cable, LBJ Library.

78. Walt Rostow to the President, June 23, 1967 (Secret-Sensitive), copy LBJ Library.

79. Benigno, interview.

80. Estrada, interview.

81. Soria Galvarro, *El Che,* vol. 4, p. 304.

82. Renán Montero, interview with the author, Havana, August 25, 1995.

83. Ibid.

84. Ibid.

85. Guevara, *Diario,* p. 158.

86. Ibid., pp. 146, 168.

87. Ibid., p. 188.

88. Mario Monje, interview.

89. Guevara, *Diario,* pp. 207–208.

90. Ibid., pp. 210–211.

91. Debray, interview.

92. Benigno, interview.

93. Villoldo, interview.

94. Ibid.

95. Walt Rostow to the President, September 5, 1967 (Secret), NSF, Country File, Bolivia, vol. 4, box 8, Memo, LBJ Library.

96. Walt Rostow to the President, October 18, 1967 (Secret).

97. Central Intelligence Agency, Intelligence Information Cable, October 17, 1967 (Secret), National Security File, Memos to the President, vol. 46, Oct. 16–20, 1967, Doc. no. 68a, LBJ Library.

98. National Security Council, Draft Talking Points for the President's Meeting with Chairman Kosyguin [sic], June 26, 1967 (no classification), National Security File, Country File, USSR, Container 230, Doc. no. 7, LBJ Library.

99. See Jacques Lévesque, *L'USSR et la Révolution Cubaine* (Paris: Presses de la Fondation Nationale des Sciences Politiques, 1976), p. 157; and Jorge Domínguez, *To Make a World Safe for Revolution* (Cambridge: Harvard University Press, 1989), p. 71.

100. Central Intelligence Agency, Intelligence Information Cable, October 17, 1967 (Secret).

101. Oleg Daroussenkov, written communication to the author, Mexico City, December 19, 1996.

102. Ibid.

103. Ibid.

104. Benigno, interview with the author, Paris, November 18, 1996.

105. François Maspéro, conversation with the author, Paris, November 9, 1996.

106. Sternfield, telephone conversation.

107. Villoldo, interview.

Chapter 11:
Death and Resurrection

1. See Todd Gitlin, *The Sixties: Years of Hope, Days of Rage* (New York: Bantam Books, 1993), p. 19.

444

Notes for Chapter 11

2. Julio Cortázar, *Ultimo Round* (Mexico City: Siglo XXI, 1969), p. 94.

3. "A Special Kind of Rebellion," *Fortune,* January 1969, pp. 70–71.

4. Terry H. Anderson, *The Movement and the Sixties* (New York: Oxford University Press, 1994), p. viii.

5. Gitlin, *The Sixties,* pp. 262–263.

6. Hervé Hamon and Patrick Rothman, *Génération* (Paris: Editions du Seuil, 1987), p. 125.

7. Pombo, Benigno, and Urbano, "La Quebrada del Yuro," Recuerdos de un combate, *Tricontinental* (Havana), July–October 1969, p. 108.

8. Dariel Alarcón Ramírez, "Benigno," interview with the author, Paris, November 3, 1995.

9. Felix Rodríguez and John Weisman, *Shadow Warrior* (New York: Simon and Schuster, 1989), p. 163.

10. Arnaldo Saucedo Parada, *"No disparen, soy el Che,"* private edition, La Paz, 1987.

11. Adys Cupull and Froilán González, *La CIA contra el Che* (Havana: Editora Política, 1992), pp. 136–137.

12. Oral History Interview with Douglas Henderson, by Sheldon Stern, for the JFK Library, Weston, Mass., August 30, 1978.

13. John Tilton, phone conversation with the author, Princeton, N.J., November 1995.

14. Gustavo Villoldo, interview with the author, Miami, November 27, 1995.

15. Rodríguez and Weisman, *Shadow Warrior,* p. 169.

16. Julia Cortés, interview with the author, Vallegrande, October 26, 1994.

17. Anderson, *The Movement,* p. 89.

18. Hamon and Rothman, *Génération,* p. 171.

19. George Katsiaficas, *The Imagination of the New Left* (Boston: South End Press, 1987), p. 57.

20. Anderson, *The Movement,* p. 95.

21. David Burner, *Making Peace with the Sixties* (Princeton, N.J.: Princeton University Press, 1996), p. 136.

22. UNESCO Statistical Yearbooks, Paris, 1970, 1982.

23. Eric Hobsbawm, *Age of Extremes: The Short Twentieth Century* (London: Michael Joseph Ltd., 1994), p. 298.

Index

456 *Index*

ALSO BY JORGE G. CASTAÑEDA

UTOPIA UNARMED

The Latin American Left After the Cold War

Castro's Cuba is isolated; the guerrillas who once spread havoc through Uruguay and Argentina are dead, dispersed, or running for office as moderates. And in 1990, Nicaragua's Sandinistas were rejected at the polls by their own constituents. Are these symptoms of the fall of the Latin American left? Or are they merely temporary lulls in an ongoing revolution that may yet transform our hemisphere?

This perceptive and richly eventful study by one of Mexico's most distinguished political scientists tells the story behind the failed movements of the past thirty years while suggesting that the left has a continuing relevance in a continent that suffers from destitution and social inequality.

Latin American Studies/Current Affairs/
0-679-75141-6

Available in Spanish from Vintage Español:

COMPAÑERO,
0-679-78161-7

VINTAGE BOOKS
Available at your local bookstore, or call toll-free to order:
1-800-793-2665 (credit cards only).